HEALTH AND HUMAN RIGHTS

HEALTH AND HUMAN RIGHTS

Global and European Perspectives

Brigit TOEBES
Mette HARTLEV
Aart HENDRIKS
Katharina Ó CATHAOIR
Janne ROTHMAR HERRMANN
Henriette SINDING AASEN

2nd edition

INTERSENTIA

Cambridge – Antwerp – Chicago

Intersentia Ltd
8 Wellington Mews
Wellington Street | Cambridge
CB1 1HW | United Kingdom
Tel: +44 1223 736 170
Email: mail@intersentia.co.uk
www.intersentia.com | www.intersentia.co.uk

Distribution for the UK and
Rest of the World (incl. Eastern Europe)
NBN International
1 Deltic Avenue, Rooksley
Milton Keynes MK13 8LD
United Kingdom
Tel: +44 1752 202 301 | Fax: +44 1752 202 331
Email: orders@nbninternational.com

Distribution for Europe
Lefebvre Sarrut Belgium NV
Hoogstraat 139/6
1000 Brussels
Belgium
Tel: +32 (0)800 39 067
Email: mail@intersentia.be

Distribution for the USA and Canada
Independent Publishers Group
Order Department
814 North Franklin Street
Chicago, IL 60610
USA
Tel: +1 800 888 4741 (toll free) | Fax: +1 312 337 5985
Email: orders@ipgbook.com

Health and Human Rights. Global and European Perspectives. 2nd edition
© Brigit Toebes, Mette Hartlev, Aart Hendriks, Katharina Ó Cathaoir,
Janne Rothmar Herrmann, Henriette Sinding Aasen 2022

Artwork on cover: Edvard Munch, Bathing Men on Rocks (1915). Photo © Munchmuseet

ISBN 978-1-83970-057-6
D/2022/7849/16
NUR 828

British Library Cataloguing in Publication Data. A catalogue record for this book is available from the British Library.

PREFACE AND ACKNOWLEDGEMENTS TO THE SECOND EDITION

Dear reader,

It is with great pleasure that we present to you the second edition of our handbook on health and human rights, in which we systematically disentangle a range of themes and dimensions of this burgeoning branch of human rights law. There are some changes to the previous edition, which we believe have considerably enriched this new publication.

While the 2012 edition had its focus on Europe, this edition has a broader scope, also taking into account global perspectives, including a chapter on the UN health and human rights framework. We have kept themes which we consider important, including the valuable chapters on the Council of Europe's and EU's approaches to health and human rights, as well as the worthwhile chapters on reproductive health, death and dying. Added to the new edition are chapters on relevant principles, access to health, health technologies and public health. Instead of focusing on a few selected vulnerable groups, the focus is now, more holistically, on the concept of vulnerability. As such, the book takes into account new developments and trends in the field.

As with any book, its composition came with some inconvenience and frustration, including a struggle to find the time to work on the book. However, looking back, the overall process and collaboration have been very pleasant and enriching, notwithstanding the fact that we were in the midst of a pandemic. It has been a pleasure to welcome Katharina Ó Cathaoir to the team as a new author. I wish to thank all the authors for their worthwhile contributions, and for their support and dedication to this project.

We are grateful for the opportunity to publish a book in such an important and continuously evolving field, reflecting dimensions of human rights law that will demand our attention over the years to come. We thank Intersentia Publishing, in particular Rebecca Moffat and Alan O'Dowd, for their efficient support and excellent editorial work. We also thank Markus Frischhut, Jacob Wested, Catherine Jacqueson and Sophie van den Nieuwenhuijsen for their support with the EU chapter, Meaghan Beyer for support with the chapter on the UN, and Maxine van Ekelenburg for support with the list of cases. We wish scholars, students and practitioners inspiration and success with their important work in the field of health and human rights. We hope – and expect – that this book will be a useful resource guide.

With best wishes on behalf of all the authors,
Brigit Toebes

CONTENTS

Preface and Acknowledgements to the Second Edition v

List of Cases xv

List of Abbreviations xxxiii

About the Authors xxxv

PART I. INTRODUCTION

**Chapter 1. Introducing Health and Human Rights: Global and European
Perspectives**

Brigit TOEBES 3

1. Rationale and aim of this book 3
2. Historical introduction to 'health and human rights' 5
   2.1. Introduction 5
   2.2. The human rights movement 6
   2.3. Medical law, health law, medical ethics and bioethics,
        and patients' rights 8
   2.4. The public health movement 10
3. Theoretical approach 13
   3.1. Main theoretical questions underpinning this research 13
   3.2. Conceptual grounding of human rights law 14
   3.3. Conceptual grounding and analysis of economic, social
        and cultural rights 16
   3.4. Identification of main concepts and principles underpinning
        this study 17
4. Method and chapter outline 20

Chapter 2. The Right to Health: Central Concepts

Brigit TOEBES and Katharina Ó CATHAOIR 23

1. Introduction 23
2. Introducing the right to health 24
3. Elements of the right to health 30
   3.1. Intersection with the right to life 32
   3.2. Guiding principles of the right to health 33

3.3. Legal obligations 36
    3.3.1. Respect, protect, fulfil 36
    3.3.2. Progressive realisation 40
    3.3.3. Core obligations 42
    3.3.4. Determinants of health 44
3.4. UN Sustainable Development Goals 45
4. Controversies and confusions surrounding the right to health 46
4.1. Justiciability of the right to health 46
4.2. Responsibilities of non-state actors 48
4.3. Lingering ambiguities 49
5. Conclusions 50

Chapter 3. Human Rights Principles and Patient Rights
Henriette SINDING AASEN and Mette HARTLEV 53

1. Introduction 53
2. Human dignity – the core of human rights 53
3. Autonomy and integrity 57
4. Non-discrimination 60
5. Patients' rights as human rights in relation to healthcare 65
5.1. Introduction 65
5.2. Development of patients' rights 67
5.3. Right to self-determination – informed consent 70
5.4. Limits to the right to self-determination 75
6. Privacy and confidentiality 80
6.1. Confidential relationships and informational self-determination 80
6.2. Processing of health data in connection with medical
    treatment 82
6.3. Use of health data for purposes other than medical care 84
7. Concluding reflections 86

PART II. LEGAL FRAMEWORK

Chapter 4. UN Institutions and Health and Human Rights
Katharina Ó CATHAOIR 91

1. Introduction 91
2. International human rights institutions 92
2.1. The Human Rights Council 93
2.2. Treaty-based bodies 95
    2.2.1. General comments 97
    2.2.2. Concluding observations 100
    2.2.3. Complaints under optional protocols 102
2.3. Conclusions on UN human rights bodies 106

3. International health law governance 107
   3.1. The World Health Organization. 107
   3.2. Other UN health-related agencies 111
   3.3. UN organisations with implications for health 113
4. Conclusions 116

Chapter 5. The Council of Europe
   Aart HENDRIKS. 119

1. Introduction 119
2. European Convention on Human Rights 120
   2.1. General introduction. 120
   2.2. Rights and case law 123
         2.2.1. General 124
               2.2.1.1. Positive obligations 125
               2.2.1.2. Margin of appreciation 127
               2.2.1.3. Availability of healthcare 128
               2.2.1.4. Protection and prevention 128
         2.2.2. Health and human rights topics 130
               2.2.2.1. Right to health 130
               2.2.2.2. Right to life (Article 2) 133
               2.2.2.3. Right to care (Article 3) 137
               2.2.2.4. Right to liberty and security (Article 5) 140
               2.2.2.5. Patients' rights (Article 8). 144
                     2.2.2.5.1. Right to information 144
                     2.2.2.5.2. Right to consent. 147
                     2.2.2.5.3. Storage and use of personal data 149
   2.3. Conclusions 152
3. European Social Charter. 153
4. European Convention for the Prevention of Torture. 157
5. Convention on Human Rights and Biomedicine 159
6. Conclusions 161

Chapter 6. The European Union: A Health and Human Rights Perspective
   Janne ROTHMAR HERRMANN, Katharina Ó CATHAOIR
   and Brigit TOEBES 163

1. Introduction 163
2. EU, health and human rights 165
   2.1. The European Charter of Fundamental Rights. 165
   2.2. The interpretation of rights through the case law of the CJEU 170
   2.3. Non-discrimination. 172
3. Specific responsibilities for health in the EU 174

3.1. Focus on human health in the TFEU 174
3.2. EU engagement with public health 177
 3.2.1. Clinical research.................................. 177
 3.2.2. Infectious disease control 178
 3.2.3. Regulation of behavioural risk factors of noncommunicable
 diseases (NCDs)................................. 180
 3.2.4. Workplace protection of health 183
4. Free movement and health 184
4.1. Introduction... 184
4.2. Free movement of services: cross-border healthcare services........ 184
 4.2.1. The legal framework 184
 4.2.2. Cross-border healthcare and issues of morality 189
 4.2.3. Evaluation..................................... 190
4.3. Free movement of goods: pharmaceuticals.................... 192
4.4. Free movement of goods: blood (safety)..................... 196
4.5. Free movement of goods: cells and tissues (safety, standards
 and quality) 197
4.6. Free movement of data 198
5. Conclusions 199

PART III. SELECTED TOPICS

Chapter 7. Access to Health
Mette HARTLEV 203

1. Introduction... 203
2. Health inequalities.. 204
3. Equal access 207
4. Limitations on access to health 212
4.1. Limitations justified by resource restraints.................. 213
4.2. Limitations justified by cultural, ethical or religious
 traditions or societal concerns.......................... 217
5. Conclusion 219

Chapter 8. Vulnerability and Autonomy: Competing Ideas in Human Rights
Henriette SINDING AASEN...................................... 221

1. Introduction.. 221
2. The vulnerable human being 222
3. Vulnerable groups and non-discrimination 224
4. Protection of autonomy...................................... 227
5. The potential conflict between health protection and autonomy...... 229
6. Vulnerability – concept and discourse 231

6.1.   Origins and legal developments. 231
6.2.   Vulnerability in the European Court of Human Rights 234
        6.2.1.   The concept of 'group vulnerability'. 234
        6.2.2.   Group vulnerability – expanding the understanding. 237
        6.2.3.   Vulnerability and the dangers of generalisation
                 and stigmatisation 238
7.   The capability approach 241
8.   Refugees, asylum seekers and undocumented migrants 243
      8.1.   Introduction. 243
      8.2.   Refugees and asylum seekers 245
      8.3.   Unauthorised or undocumented migrants 246
              8.3.1.   Overview. 246
              8.3.2.   The legal situation in Norway. 249
9.   Concluding remarks on vulnerability and state obligations 252

Chapter 9. Disability
Aart HENDRIKS. 255

1.   Introduction. 255
2.   Disability. 255
3.   Global Disability Rights Convention on the Rights of Persons
      with Disabilities 257
      3.1.   Legal documents – the rights of persons with disabilities 257
      3.2.   The Committee on the Rights of Persons with Disabilities. 259
4.   Disability rights in Europe 263
      4.1.   Legal documents 263
              4.1.1.   Council of Europe 263
              4.1.2.   European Union. 264
      4.2.   Definitions 265
              4.2.1.   Council of Europe 265
              4.2.2.   European Union. 265
      4.3.   European case law 266
              4.3.1.   Council of Europe 266
              4.3.2.   European Union. 270
5.   Conclusions 272

Chapter 10. Reproductive Health
Janne ROTHMAR HERRMANN 275

1.   Introduction. 275
2.   Women's reproductive health and human rights 276
      2.1.   Maternal health 278
      2.2.   Reproductive autonomy 280

2.3. Right to respect for privacy and family life. 281
2.4. The prohibition of discrimination 282
3. Family planning. 283
3.1. Contraception and sex education 284
3.2. Abortion 286
3.2.1. The UN conventions 286
3.2.2. The European Convention on Human Rights. 290
3.2.2.1. The balancing of interests between woman
and foetus. 290
3.2.2.2. The balancing of interests between woman
and state 294
3.2.2.3. The balancing of interests between woman
and man 298
4. Procreative healthcare services. 299
4.1. Fertility treatment 301
4.1.1. A private life issue 301
4.1.2. Access to treatment 303
4.2. Embryo and foetus selection 306
5. Pregnancy, health and autonomy. 309
5.1. Maternal and foetal health 309
5.2. Forced treatment of pregnant women. 311
6. Concluding remarks 312

Chapter 11. Death and Dying
Aart HENDRIKS. 315

1. Introduction. 315
2. Environmental and industrial questions. 317
3. Persons under the care of the state 318
4. Healthcare settings. 319
5. End-of-life issues 320
5.1. Withholding or withdrawing medical treatment. 321
5.2. Physician-assisted dying and euthanasia 323
6. Conclusions 325

Chapter 12. Digital Healthcare Technologies and Human Rights
Katharina Ó CATHAOIR. 327

1. Introduction. 327
2. Promises and pitfalls of digital technologies 330
3. A right to access new healthcare technologies? 334
4. Which human rights are at risk? 338
4.1. The right to privacy. 338
4.2. The right to data protection 344

4.3. The right to an explanation. 346
4.4. Non-discrimination. 349
4.5. Accountability 354
5. Conclusion 357

Chapter 13. Public Health and Human Rights
Brigit TOEBES and Katharina Ó CATHAOIR. 359

1. Introduction 359
2. Origins and scope of public health 360
3. Balancing public health and individual rights 362
   3.1. Public health and the right to health. 362
   3.2. Tensions between public health and competing rights
        and interests 363
        3.2.1. Derogations and limitations on civil and political rights 364
        3.2.2. Tensions between the right to health and other societal
               interests and rights. 367
        3.2.3. Restricting the right to health. 367
   3.3. Procedural questions when exercising a collective right
        to health 369
4. Infectious disease prevention and control 370
   4.1. Introduction. 370
   4.2. International Health Regulations. 371
   4.3. A health and human rights approach to infectious disease 374
   4.4. Vaccination. 377
5. NCDs and risk factor reduction. 380
   5.1. The global and European NCD pandemic 380
   5.2. A rights approach to NCDs 381
6. Social determinants of health. 384
   6.1. Introduction. 384
   6.2. The link with human rights 386
7. Conclusions 388

PART IV. CONCLUSIONS, CHALLENGES AND RECOMMENDATIONS

Chapter 14. Conclusions
Aart HENDRIKS. 393

1. Summary of conclusions of various chapters 394
2. Final observations 403

Annex: Rights and Principles Relevant to the Protection and Promotion
of Health. 405

LIST OF CASES

COMMITTEE ON ECONOMIC, SOCIAL AND CULTURAL RIGHTS

CESCR, *Views adopted by the Committee under the Optional Protocol to the International Covenant on Economic, Social and Cultural Rights with regard to communication No. 5/2015*, E/C.12/61/D/5/2015, 2017 40

CESCR, *Views adopted by the Committee under the Optional Protocol to the International Covenant on Economic, Social and Cultural Rights, concerning communication No. 22/2017, S.C. and G.P. v. Italy*, E/C.12/65/D/22/2017, 2019 . . . . . 39, 104

COMMITTEE ON THE ELIMINATION OF ALL FORMS OF DISCRIMINATION AGAINST WOMEN

Committee on the Elimination of Discrimination against Women, 29 August 2006, *A.S v. Hungary*, CEDAW/C/36/D/4/2004 104

Committee on the Elimination of Discrimination against Women, 10 August 2011, *Maria de Lourdes da Silva Pimentel v. Brazil*, Views Communication no. 17/2008, CEDAW/C/49/D/17/2008 104

Committee on the Elimination of Discrimination against Women, 4 November 2011, *L.C. v. Peru*, no. 22/2009, CEDAW/C/50/D/22/2009 105

Committee on the Elimination of Discrimination against Women, 28 February 2020, *S.F.M. v. Spain*, CEDAW/C/75/D/138/2018 104

Committee on the Elimination of Discrimination against Women, 26 August 2020, *Decision adopted by the Committee under article 4 (2) (c) of the Optional Protocol concerning communication*, CEDAW/C/76/D/124/2018 104

COMMITTEE ON THE RIGHTS OF PERSONS WITH DISABILITIES

CRPD Committee, 19 April 2012, *H.M. v. Sweden*, communication no. 3/2011 261

CRPD Committee, 17 May 2017, *L.M.L. v. the United Kingdom*, communication no. 27/2015 260

CRPD Committee, 15 September 2017, *O.O.J. v. Sweden*, communication no. 28/2015 260

CRPD Committee, 24 October 2018, *Munir al-Adam v. Saudi Arabia*, communication no. 38/2016 261

CRPD Committee, 2 April 2019, *T.M. v. Greece*, communication no. 42/2017 260

COURT OF JUSTICE OF THE EUROPEAN UNION

Graziana Luisi and Giuseppe Carbone v. Ministero del Tesoro, 286/82 and 26/83,
    ECLI:EU:C:1984:35 189
Dekker v. Stichting Vormingscentrum voor Jonge Volwassenen Plus, C-177/88,
    ECLI:EU:C:1990:383 172
*The Society for the Protection of Unborn Children Ireland Ltd v. Stephen Grogan
    and others*, C-159/90, ECLI:EU:C:1991:378. 189
Raymond Kohll v. Union des caisses de maladie, C-158/96, ECLI:EU:C:1998:171. 185
*United Kingdom of Great Britain and Northern Ireland v. Commission
    of the European Communities*, C-180/96, ECLI:EU:C:1998:192 178
*Federal Republic of Germany v. European Parliament and Council of the
    European Union*, C-376/98, ECLI:EU:C:2000:544. . . . . .175, 182
*V.G. Müller-Fauré v. Onderlinge Waarborgmaatschappij OZ Zorgverzekeringen UA
    and E.E.M van Riet v. Onderlinge Waarborgmaatschappij ZAO Zorgverzekeringen*,
    C-385/99, ECLI:EU:C:2003:270. 185
María Victoria González Sánchez v. Medicina Asturiana SA, C-183/00,
    ECLI:EU:C:2002:255 196
*Rechnungshof (C-465/00) v. Österreichischer Rundfunk and Others and Christa
    Neukomm (C-138/01) and Joseph Lauermann (C-139/01) v. Österreichischer
    Rundfunk*, C-465/00, C-138/01 and C-139/01, ECLI:EU:C:2003:294 198
Criminal proceedings against Bodil Lindqvist, C-101/01, ECLI:EU:C:2003:596. . . . . 171, 198
British American Tobacco, C-491/01, ECLI:EU:C:2002:741 383
*Federal Republic of Germany v. European Parliament and Council of the
    European Union*, C-380/03, ECLI:EU:C:2006:772. . . . . .176, 182
Chacón Navas, C-13/05, ECLI:EU:C:2006:45. 265
Coleman, C-303/06, ECLI:EU:C:2008:415 270
*José Manuel Blanco Pérez and María del Pilar Chao Gómez v. Consejería de
    Salud y Servicios Sanitarios (C-570/07) and Principado de Asturias (C-571/07)*,
    C-570/07 and C-571/07, ECLI:EU:C:2010:300 170
*Volker und Markus Schecke GbR (C-92/09) and Hartmut Eifert (C-93/09) v.
    Land Hessen*, C-92/09 and C-93/09, ECLI:EU:C:2010:662 198
Dita Danosa v. LKB Līzings SIA, C-232/09, ECLI:EU:C:2010:674. 173
Oliver Brüstle v. Greenpeace eV, C-34/10, ECLI:EU:C:2011:669 171
Deutsches Weintor eG v. Land Rheinland-Pfalz, C-544/10, ECLI:EU:C:2012:526 170–171
Marja-Liisa Susisalo and Others, C-84/11, ECLI:EU:C:2012:374 170
HK Danmark, C-335/11 and 337/11, ECLI:EU:C:2013:222. .266, 272
*Google Spain SL and Google Inc. v. Agencia Española de Protección de Datos
    (AEPD) and Mario Costeja González*, C-131/12, ECLI:EU:C:2014:317 167
*Association de médiation sociale v. Union locale des syndicats CGT
    and Others Case*, C-176/12, ECLI:EU:C:2014:2. 183
Glatzel, C-358/12, ECLI:EU:C:2014:350 271
*Z. v. A Government department and The Board of management of a community
    school*, C-363/12, ECLI:EU:C:2014:159 . . . . .183, 271
*Elena Petru v. Casa Județeană de Asigurări de Sănătate Sibiu and Casa Națională
    de Asigurări de Sănătate*, C-268/13, ECLI:EU:C:2014:2271. 186
Fag og Arbejde (FOA) v. Kommunernes Landsforening (KL), C-354/13,
    ECLI:EU:C:2014:2463 . . . . .173, 266
*International Stem Cell Corporation v. Comptroller General of Patents, Designs
    and Trade Marks*, C-364/13, ECLI:EU:C:2014:2451 171

Opinion pursuant to Article 218(11) TFEU, Case Opinion 2/13,
   ECLI:EU:C:2014:2454 166
Maximillian Schrems v. Data Protection Commissioner, C-362/14,
   ECLI:EU:C:2015:650 167
Philip Morris Brands SARL and Others v. Secretary of State for Health,
   C-547/14, ECLI:EU:C:2016:325 171
Swedish Match AB v. Secretary of State for Health, C-151/17,
   ECLI:EU:C:2018:938 170
Bedi, C-312/17, ECLI:EU:C:2018:734 271
PI v. Landespolizeidirektion Tirol, C-230/18, ECLI:EU:C:2019:383 170
Data Protection Commissioner v. Facebook Ireland Limited and Maximillian Schrems,
   C-311/18, ECLI:EU:C:2020:559 167
A v. Veselības ministrija, Case C-243/19, ECLI:EU:C:2020:872 . . . . 187, 188
VL, C-16/19, ECLI:EU:C:2021:64 272

EUROPEAN COMMISSION OF HUMAN RIGHTS

EComHR 12 July 1977, *Rose Marie Brüggemann & Adelheid Scheuten v.
   the Federal Republic of Germany*, no. 6959/75 . . . . 291, 294
EComHR 13 May 1980, *Paton v. the United Kingdom*, no. 8416/78,
   ECLI:CE:ECHR:1980:0513DEC000841678 136
EComHR 13 May 1980, *X v. the United Kingdom* (also known as *Paton v. UK*),
   no. 8416/79, ECLI:CE:ECHR:1980:0513DEC000841678 . . . . 217, 290
EComHR 9 May 1984, *X v. Germany*, no. 10565/83, ECLI:CE:ECHR:1984:0509D
   EC001056583 135
EComHR 10 December 1984, *Acmanne et al. v. Belgium*, no. 10435/83,
   ECLI:CE:ECHR:1984:1210DEC001043583 129
EComHR 19 May 1992, *Hercz v. Norway*, no. 17004/90,
   ECLI:CE:ECHR:1992:0519DEC001700490 . . . . 136, 298
EComHR 7 December 1992, *Lupker et al. v. the Netherlands*, no. 18395/91,
   ECLI:CE:ECHR:1992:1207DEC001839591 149
EComHR 28 February 1996, *Martin v. the United Kingdom* (dec.), no. 27533/95,
   ECLI:CE:ECHR:1996:0228DEC002753395 152
EComHR 16 October 1996, *Wackenheim v. France* (dec.), no. 29961/96,
   ECLI:CE:ECHR:1996:1016DEC002996196 . . . . 80, 147
EComHR 26 February 1997, *Buckley v. the United Kingdom*, no. 28323/95,
   ECLI:CE:ECHR:1997:0226DEC002832395 . . . . 135, 148
EComHR 15 January 1998, *Boffa et al. v. San Marino*, no. 26536/95,
   ECLI:CE:ECHR:1998:0115DEC002653695 . . . . 129, 378

EUROPEAN COMMITTEE OF SOCIAL RIGHTS

ECSR 3 November 2004, *International Federation for Human Rights Leagues
   (FIDH) v. France*, no. 14/2003 . . . . 153, 155
ECSR 5 December 2007, *ATD Fourth World v. France*, no. 33/2006 369
ECSR 6 February 2007, *Marangopoulos Foundation for Human Rights
   (MFHR) v. Greece*, no. 30/2005 155

ECSR 16 December 2008, *European Roma Rights Centre (ERRC) v. Bulgaria*,
no. 46/2007 . . . . .369–370, 155
ECSR 9 April 2009, *Interights v. Croatia*, no. 45/2007 . . . . .156, 369
ECSR 27 October 2009, *DCI v. the Netherlands*, no. 47/2008 . . . . .153, 369
ECSR 4 February 2013, *International Federation for Human Rights
(FIDH) v. Greece*, no. 72/2011 . . . . .155, 369
ECSR 27 July 2013, *International Federation for Human Rights (FIDH) v. Belgium*,
no. 75/2011 269
ECSR 11 September 2013, *European Action of the Disabled (AEH) v. France*,
no. 81/2012 269
ECSR 7 November 2013, *International Planned Parenthood Federation –
European Network (IPPF EN) v. Italy*, no. 87/2012 156
ECSR 29 March 2018, *Mental Disability Advocacy Center (MDAC) v. Belgium*,
no. 109/2014 269
ECSR 31 May 2018, *Transgender Europe and ILGA-Europe v. the Czech Republic*,
no. 117/2015 156
ECSR 16 October 2018, *European Disability Forum (EDF) and Inclusion
Europe v. France (dec.)*, no. 168/2018 269
ECSR 18 December 2019, *European Roma Rights Centre (ERRC) v. Bulgaria*,
no. 151/2017 156
ECSR 20 November 2020, *European Roma Rights Centre (ERRC) and Mental
Disability Advocacy Centre (MDAC) v. Czech Republic*, no. 157/2017 269
ECSR 3 February 2021, *International Federation for Human Rights (FIDH)
and Inclusion Europe v. Belgium*, no. 141/2017 269

EUROPEAN COURT OF HUMAN RIGHTS

ECtHR 23 July 1968, *Belgian Linguistic Case*, no. 1474/62, ECLI:CE:ECHR:
1967:0209JUD000147462 126
ECtHR 7 December 1976, *Kjeldsen, Busk Madsen & Pedersen v. Denmark*,
nos. 5095/71; 5920/72; 5926/72, ECLI:CE:ECHR:1976:1207JUD000509571 285
ECtHR 25 April 1978, *Tyrer v. the United Kingdom*, no. 5856/72,
ECLI:CE:ECHR:1978:0425JUD000585672 . . . . .56, 124
ECtHR 13 June 1979, *Marckx v. Belgium*, no. 6833/74, ECLI:CE:ECHR:1979:
0613JUD000683374. 277
ECtHR 9 October 1979, *Airey v. Ireland*, no. 6289/73, ECLI:CE:ECHR:
1979:1009JUD000628973 . . . . .124, 229
ECtHR 24 October 1979, *Winterwerp v. the Netherlands*, no. 6301/73,
ECLI:CE:ECHR:1979:1024JUD000630173 142
ECtHR 27 February 1980, *Deweer v. Belgium*, no. 6903/75, ECLI:CE:ECHR:
1980:0227JUD000690375. 147
ECtHR 6 November 1980, *Guzzardi v. Italy*, no. 7367/76, ECLI:CE:ECHR:
1980:1106JUD000736776 141
ECtHR 26 March 1985, *X and Y v. the Netherlands*, no. 8978/80,
ECLI:CE:ECHR:1985:0326JUD000897880 . . . . 126, 132,
138, 147
ECtHR 28 May 1985, *Ashingdane v. the United Kingdom*, no. 8225/78,
ECLI:CE:ECHR:1985:0528JUD0008225783 143

ECtHR 26 March 1987, *Leander v. Sweden*, no. 9248/81, ECLI:CE:ECHR:
1987:0326JUD000924881 149

ECtHR 21 June 1988, *Plattform 'Ärzte für das Leben' v. Austria*, no. 10126/82,
ECLI:CE:ECHR:1988:0621JUD001012682 126

ECtHR 7 July 1989, *Gaskin v. the United Kingdom* (GC), no. 10454/83,
ECLI:CE:ECHR:1989:0707JUD001045483 . . . . 146, 152

ECtHR 25 February 1992, *Pfeifer and Plankl v. Austria*, no. 10802/84,
ECLI:CE:ECHR:1992:0225JUD001080284 147

ECtHR 24 September 1992, *Herczegfalvy v. Austria*, no. 10533/83,
ECLI:CE:ECHR:1992:0924JUD001053383 . . . . 125, 129, 135, 139, 148

ECtHR 29 October 1992, *Open Door and Dublin Well Woman v. Ireland*,
no. 14234/88 and 14235/88, ECLI:CE:ECHR:1992:1029JUD001423488. . . . . 75, 144, 295

ECtHR 28 January 1994, *Hurtado v. Switzerland*, no. 17549/90,
ECLI:CE:ECHR:1994:0128JUD001754990 . . . . 131, 318

ECtHR 23 September 1994, *Hokkanen v. Finland*, no. 19823/92,
ECLI:CE:ECHR:1994:0923JUD001982392 145

ECtHR 9 December 1994, *López Ostra v. Spain*, no. 16798/90, ECLI:CE:ECHR:
1994:1209JUD001679890 317

ECtHR 31 January 1995, *Friedl v. Austria*, no. 15225/89, ECLI:CE:ECHR:1995:
0131JUD001522589. 149

ECtHR 27 September 1995, *McCann et al. v. the* United *Kingdom*, no. 18984/91,
ECLI:CE:ECHR:1995:0927JUD001898491 . . . . 133, 136, 315

ECtHR 19 February 1997, *Laskey, Jaggard and Brown v. the United Kingdom*,
no. 21627/93; 21826/93 and 21974/93, ECLI:CE:ECHR:1997:
0219JUD002162793. . . . . 80, 147

ECtHR 25 February 1997, *Z. v. Finland*, no. 22009/93, ECLI:CE:ECHR:
1997:0225JUD002200993 . . . . 60, 81, 85,
151, 248

ECtHR 2 May 1997, *D. v. the United Kingdom*, no. 30240/96, ECLI:CE:ECHR:
1997:0502JUD003024096 138

ECtHR 27 August 1997, *M.S. v. Sweden*, no. 20837/92, ECLI:CE:ECHR:
1997:0827JUD002083792 . . . . 81, 85, 151, 366

ECtHR 19 February 1998, *Guerra et al. v. Italy*, no. 14967/89,
ECLI:CE:ECHR:1998:0219JUD001496789 . . . . 75, 144, 317

ECtHR 19 February 1998, *Kaya v. Turkey*, no. 22729/93, ECLI:CE:ECHR:
1998:0219JUD002272993 136

ECtHR 9 June 1998, *L.C.B. v. the United Kingdom*, no. 23413/94,
ECLI:CE:ECHR:1998:0609JUD002341394 133

ECtHR 30 July 1998, *Aerts v. Belgium*, no. 25357/94, ECLI:CE:ECHR:1998:
0730JUD002535794. 139

ECtHR 2 September 1998, *Yaşa v. Turkey*, no. 22495/93, ECLI:CE:ECHR:1998:
0902JUD002249593. 316

ECtHR 28 October 1998, *Osman v. the United Kingdom* (GC), no. 23452/94,
ECLI:CE:ECHR:1998:1028JUD002345294 . . . . 133, 147

ECtHR 26 October 1999, *Erikson v. Italy* (dec.), no. 37900/97, ECLI:CE:ECHR:
1999:1026DEC003790097. . . . . 133, 140

ECtHR 21 March 2000, *Younger v. the United Kingdom* (dec.), no. 57420/00,
ECLI:CE:ECHR:2003:0107DEC005742000 316

ECtHR 6 April 2000, *Thlimmenos v. Greece* (GC), no. 34369/97,
ECLI:CE:ECHR:2000:0406JUD003436997 63

ECtHR 4 May 2000, *Powell v. the United Kingdom* (dec.), no. 45305/99,
ECLI:CE:ECHR:2000:0504DEC004530599 . . . . .140, 150
ECtHR 4 May 2000, *Rotaru v. Romania* (GC), no. 28341/95, ECLI:CE:ECHR:
2000:0504JUD002834195 . . . . .149, 152
ECtHR 31 July 2000, *A.D.T. v. the United Kingdom*, no. 35765/97,
ECLI:CE:ECHR:2000:0731JUD003576597 149
ECtHR 5 October 2000, *Varbanov v. Bulgaria*, no. 31365/96,
ECLI:CE:ECHR:2000:1005JUD003136596 143
ECtHR 10 October 2000, *Akkoç v. Turkey*, no. 22947/93 and 22948/93,
ECLI:CE:ECHR:2000:1010JUD002294793 . . . . .32, 123
ECtHR 26 October 2000, *Sanles v. Spain* (dec.), no. 48335/99,
ECLI:CE:ECHR:2000:1026DEC004833599 323
ECtHR 28 November 2000, *Fiorenza v. Italy* (dec.), no. 44393/98,
ECLI:CE:ECHR:2001:1206JUD004439398 130
ECtHR 3 April 2001, *Keenan v. the United Kingdom*, no. 27229/95,
ECLI:CE:ECHR:2001:0403JUD002722995 . . . . 134, 139, 150, 267, 316
ECtHR 19 April 2001, *Peers v. Greece*, no. 28524/95, ECLI:CE:ECHR:
2001:0419JUD002852495 123
ECtHR 4 May 2001, *Kelly et al. v. the United Kingdom*, no. 30054/96,
ECLI:CE:ECHR:2001:0504JUD003005496 136
ECtHR 10 May 2001, *Cyprus v. Turkey* (GC), no. 25781/94,
ECLI:CE:ECHR:2014:0512JUD002578194 . . . . .32, 123, 137, 157
ECtHR 2 June 2001, *Pichon and Sajous v. France* (dec.), no. 49853/99,
ECLI:CE:ECHR:2001:1002DEC004985399 324
ECtHR 10 July 2001, *Price v. the United Kingdom*, no. 33394/96,
ECLI:CE:ECHR:2001:0710JUD003339496 . . . . .63, 266, 319
ECtHR 21 November 2001, *Al-Adsani v. the United Kingdom* (GC),
no. 35763/97, ECLI:CE:ECHR:2001:1121JUD003576397 122
ECtHR 17 January 2002, *Calvelli and Ciglio v. Italy* (GC), no. 32967/96,
ECLI:CE:ECHR:2002:0117JUD003296796 . . . . 131, 134, 140, 319
ECtHR 7 February 2002, *Mikulic v. Croatia*, no. 53176/99, ECLI:CE:ECHR:
2002:0207JUD005317699 . . . . .146, 152
ECtHR 14 March 2002, *Paul and Audrey Edwards v. the United Kingdom*,
no. 46477/99, ECLI:CE:ECHR:2002:0314JUD004647799 318
ECtHR 21 March 2002, *Nitecki v. Poland* (dec.), no. 65653/01, ECLI:CE:ECHR:
2002:0321DEC006565301. 320
ECtHR 29 April 2002, *Pretty v. the United Kingdom*, no. 2346/02,
ECLI:CE:ECHR:2002:0429JUD000234602 . . . . 56, 58–59, 72,
138, 217–218,
316, 320, 324
ECtHR 2 July 2002, *Wilson et al. v. the United Kingdom*, no. 30668/96,
30671/96 and 30678/96, ECLI:CE:ECHR:2002:0702JUD003066896. 122
ECtHR 11 July 2002, *Christine Goodwin v. the United Kingdom* (GC),
no. 28957/95, ECLI:CE:ECHR:2002:0711JUD002895795 . . . . .56, 124, 285
ECtHR 5 September 2002, *Boso v. Italy* (dec.), no. 50490/99, ECLI:CE:ECHR:
2002:0905DEC005049099. . . . . .136, 299
ECtHR 14 November 2002, *Mouisel v. France*, no. 67263/01, ECLI:CE:ECHR:
2002:1114JUD006726301 138
ECtHR 17 December 2002, *Venema v. the Netherlands*, no. 35731/97,
ECLI:CE:ECHR:2002:1217JUD003573197 145

ECtHR 28 January 2003, *Peck v. the United Kingdom*, no. 44647/98,
ECLI:CE:ECHR:2003:0128JUD004464798 149

ECtHR 13 February 2003, *Odièvre v. France* (GC), no. 42326/98,
ECLI:CE:ECHR:2003:0213JUD004232698 146–147

ECtHR 6 March 2003, *Sijakova and others v. the former Yugoslav Republic
of Macedonia*, no. 67914/01, ECLI:CE:ECHR:2003:0306DEC006791401 .... 285, 303

ECtHR 28 October 2003, *Rakevich v. Russia*, no. 58973/00, ECLI:CE:ECHR:
2003:1028JUD005897300 142

ECtHR 4 December 2003, *M.C. v. Bulgaria*, no. 39272/98, ECLI:CE:ECHR:
2003:1204JUD003927298 147

ECtHR 10 February 2004, *Gennadi Naoumenko v. Ukraine*, no. 42023/98,
ECLI:CE:ECHR:2004:0210JUD004202398 135

ECtHR 9 March 2004, *Glass v. the United Kingdom*, no. 61827/00,
ECLI:CE:ECHR:2004:0309JUD006182700 .... 58, 72, 123, 129,
138, 147, 157

ECtHR 18 May 2004, *Plon (Société) v. France*, no. 58148/00, ECLI:CE:ECHR:
2004:0518JUD005814800 ....86, 151

ECtHR 8 July 2004, *Vo v. France* (GC), no. 53924/00, ECLI:CE:ECHR:
2004:0708JUD005392400 .... 123, 125,
127, 157, 293

ECtHR 5 October 2004, *H.L. v. the United Kingdom*, no. 45508/99,
ECLI:CE:ECHR:2004:1005JUD004550899 149

ECtHR 30 November 2004, *Öneryıldız v. Turkey* (GC), no. 48939/99,
ECLI:CE:ECHR:2004:1130JUD004893999 ....33, 317, 318

ECtHR 4 January 2005, *Pentiacova et al. v. Moldova* (dec.), no. 14462/03,
ECLI:CE:ECHR:2005:0104DEC001446203 320

ECtHR 25 January 2005, *Enhorn v. Sweden*, no. 56529/00, ECLI:CE:ECHR:
2005:0125JUD005652900 .... 77, 142,
143, 366

ECtHR 5 April 2005, *Nevmerzhitsky v. Ukraine*, no. 54825/00,
ECLI:CE:ECHR:2005:0405JUD005482500 ....134, 135

ECtHR 12 May 2005, *Öcalan v. Turkey* (GC), no. 46221/99, ECLI:CE:ECHR:
2005:0512JUD004622199; 315

ECtHR 7 June 2005, *Kılınç et al. v. Turkey*, no. 40145/98, ECLI:CE:ECHR:
2005:0607JUD004014598 134

ECtHR 16 June 2005, *Storck v. Germany*, no. 61603/00, ECLI:CE:ECHR:
2005:0616JUD006160300 ....58, 132, 148

ECtHR 5 July 2005, *Trubnikov v. Russia*, no. 49790/99, ECLI:CE:ECHR:
2005:0705JUD004979099 318

ECtHR 11 October 2005, *Tarariyeva v. Russia* (dec.), no. 4353/03,
ECLI:CE:ECHR:2006:1214JUD000435303 ....150, 318

ECtHR 13 October 2005, *Mogoş v. Romania*, no. 20420/02,
ECLI:CE:ECHR:2005:1013JUD002042002 150

ECtHR 8 November 2005, *Gongadze v. Ukraine*, no. 34056/02,
ECLI:CE:ECHR:2005:1108JUD003405602 136

ECtHR 5 January 2006, *K.T. v. Norway* (dec.), no. 26664/03,
ECLI:CE:ECHR:2008:0925JUD002666403 .... 85–86, 130, 151, 366

ECtHR 7 February 2006, *Scavuzzo-Hager et al. v. Switzerland*,
no. 41773/98, ECLI:CE:ECHR:2006:0207JUD004177398 136

ECtHR 28 February 2006, *Wilkinson v. the United Kingdom* (dec.),
no. 14659/02, ECLI:CE:ECHR:2006:0228DEC001465902........... 125, 129, 135, 148

ECtHR 23 May 2006, *Taïs v. France* (GC), no. 39922/03, ECLI:CE:ECHR:
2006:0601JUD003992203 . . . . 134, 150

ECtHR 27 June 2006, *Byrzykowski v. Poland*, no. 11562/05, ECLI:CE:ECHR:
2006:0627JUD001156205 140

ECtHR 4 July 2006, *Ramirez Sanchez v. France* (GC), no. 59450/00,
ECLI:CE:ECHR:2006:0704JUD005945000 139

ECtHR 11 July 2006, *Jalloh v. Germany* (GC), no. 54810/00,
ECLI:CE:ECHR:2006:0711JUD005481000 . . . . 78, 129, 131,
135, 148

ECtHR 11 July 2006, *Rivière v. France*, no. 33834/03, ECLI:CE:ECHR:2006:
0711JUD003383403 138

ECtHR 13 July 2006, *Jäggi v. Switzerland*, no. 58757/00, ECLI:CE:ECHR:2006:
0713JUD005875700 146

ECtHR 5 October 2006, *Trocellier v. France* (dec.), no. 75725/01,
ECLI:CE:ECHR:2006:1005DEC007572501 . . . . 72, 145

ECtHR 10 October 2006, *L.L. v. France*, no. 7508/02, ECLI:CE:ECHR:2006:
1010JUD000750802 . . . . .85–86, 151

ECtHR 18 October 2006, *Hermi v. Italy* (GC), no. 18114/02, ECLI:CE:ECHR:
2006:1018JUD001811402 147

ECtHR 24 October 2006, *Vincent v. France*, no. 6253/03, ECLI:CE:ECHR:2006:
1024JUD000625303 267

ECtHR 4 January 2007, *Smith v. the United Kingdom* (dec.), no. 39658/05,
ECLI:CE:ECHR:2007:0104DEC003965805 152

ECtHR 7 February 2007, *Köhler and Köhler v. Germany* (dec.), no. 1628/03,
ECLI:CE:ECHR:2007:0205DEC000162803 145

ECtHR 20 March 2007, *Tysiąc v. Poland*, no. 5410/03, ECLI:CE:ECHR:2007:
0320JUD000541003 . . . . .137, 291, 294

ECtHR 5 April 2007, *Todor Todorov v. Bulgaria*, no. 50765/99,
ECLI:CE:ECHR:2007:0405JUD005076599 123

ECtHR 10 April 2007, *Evans v. the United Kingdom* (GC), no. 6339/05,
ECLI:CE:ECHR:2007:0410JUD000633905 . . . . 72, 78, 282, 123,
157, 218, 301–302

ECtHR 3 May 2007, *Hüseyin Yıldırım v. Turkey*, no. 2778/02,
ECLI:CE:ECHR:2007:0503JUD000277802 267

ECtHR 15 May 2007, *Ramsahai et al. v. the Netherlands* (GC), no. 52391/02,
ECLI:CE:ECHR:2007:0515JUD005239199 136

ECtHR 24 May 2007, *Gorodnichev v. Russia*, no. 52058/99, ECLI:CE:ECHR:
2007:0524JUD005205899 . . . . .138, 150

ECtHR 19 June 2007, *Ciorap v. Moldova*, no. 12066/02, ECLI:CE:ECHR:
2007:0619JUD001206602 135

ECtHR 12 July 2007, *Testa v. Croatia*, no. 20877/04, ECLI:CE:ECHR:2007:
0712JUD002087704 . . . . 72, 145

ECtHR 17 July 2007, *Jevremović v. Serbia*, no. 3150/05, ECLI:CE:ECHR:2007:
0717JUD000315005 146

ECtHR 6 September 2007, *Kucheruk v. Ukraine*, no. 2570/04,
ECLI:CE:ECHR:2007:0906JUD000257004 139

ECtHR 11 September 2007, *L. v. Lithuania*, no. 27527/03,
ECLI:CE:ECHR:2007:0911JUD002752703 124

ECtHR 9 October 2007, *K.H. et al. v. Slovakia* (dec.), no. 32881/04,
ECLI:CE:ECHR:2009:0428JUD003288104 137

ECtHR 13 November 2007, *D.H. and Others v. the Czech Republic* (GC),
    no. 57325/00, ECLI:CE:ECHR:2007:1113JUD005732500 ....235, 240
ECtHR 4 December 2007, *Dickson v. the United Kingdom* (GC), no. 44362/04,
    ECLI:CE:ECHR:2007:1204JUD004436204 ....139, 303
ECtHR 18 December 2007, *Dybeku v. Albania*, no. 41153/06, ECLI:CE:ECHR:
    2007:1218JUD004115306 ....125, 129, 150
ECtHR 20 December 2007, *Phinikaridou v. Cyprus*, no. 23890/02,
    ECLI:CE:ECHR:2007:1220JUD002389002 145
ECtHR 29 January 2008, *Villnow v. Belgium* (dec.), no. 16938/05,
    ECLI:CE:ECHR:2008:0129DEC001693805 125
ECtHR 31 January 2008, *Dönmüs and Kaplan v. Turkey*, no. 9908/03,
    ECLI:CE:ECHR:2008:0131JUD000990803 318
ECtHR 7 February 2008, *Mechenkov v. Russia*, no. 35421/05,
    ECLI:CE:ECHR:2008:0207JUD003542105 150
ECtHR 28 February 2008, *Saadi v. Italy* (GC), no. 37201//06,
    ECLI:CE:ECHR:2008:0228JUD003720106 122
ECtHR 20 March 2008, *Budayeva et al. v. Russia*, no. 15339/02,
    ECLI:CE:ECHR:2008:0320JUD00153390 317
ECtHR 27 March 2008, *Shtukaturov v. Russia*, no. 44009/05,
    ECLI:CE:ECHR:2008:0327JUD004400905 268
ECtHR 29 April 2008, *Petrea v. Romania*, no. 4792/03, ECLI:CE:ECHR:2008:
    0429JUD000479203...139
ECtHR 6 May 2008, *Juhnke v. Turkey*, no. 20817/04, ECLI:CE:ECHR:2008:
    0513JUD005251599...148
ECtHR 27 May 2008, *N. v. the United Kingdom* (GC), no. 26565/05,
    ECLI:CE:ECHR:2008:0527JUD002656505 132
ECtHR 12 June 2008, *Bevacqua and S. v. Bulgaria*, no. 71127/01,
    ECLI:CE:ECHR:2008:0612JUD007112701 132
ECtHR 12 June 2008, *Kotsaftis v. Greece*, no. 39780/06 and ECtHR
    22 December 2008, *Aleksanyan v. Russia*, no. 46468/06, ECLI:CE:ECHR:
    2008:1222JUD004646806 138
ECtHR 8 July 2008, *Tokić et al. v. Bosnia and Herzegovina*, nos. 12455/04,
    14140/05, 12906/06 and 26028/06, ECLI:CE:ECHR:2008:0708JUD001245504......267
ECtHR 17 July 2008, *I. v. Finland*, no. 20511/03, ECLI:CE:ECHR:2008:
    0717JUD002051103...84, 151–152
ECtHR 17 July 2008, *X. v. Croatia*, no. 11223/04, ECLI:CE:ECHR:2008:
    0717JUD001122304...145
ECtHR 5 September 2008, *Sampanis and others v. Greece*, no. 32526/05,
    ECLI:CE:ECHR:2008:0605JUD003252605 235
ECtHR 7 October 2008, *Bogumil v. Portugal*, no. 35228/03,
    ECLI:CE:ECHR:2008:1007JUD003522803 ....78–79, 123, 129,
                                                            140, 148, 157
ECtHR 16 October 2008, *Renolde v. France*, no. 5608/05, ECLI:CE:ECHR:
    2008:1016JUD000560805 316
ECtHR 6 November 2008, *Gulub Atanasov v. Bulgaria*, no. 73281/01,
    ECLI:CE:ECHR:2008:1106JUD007328101 148
ECtHR 12 November 2008, *Demir and Baykara v. Turkey* (GC), no. 34503/97,
    ECLI:CE:ECHR:2008:1112JUD003450397 123
ECtHR 13 November 2008, *Khaylo v. Ukraine*, no. 39964/02,
    ECLI:CE:ECHR:2008:1113JUD003996402 136

ECtHR 25 November 2008, *Armoniené v. Lithuania*, no. 36919/02,
ECLI:CE:ECHR:2008:1125JUD003691902 151
ECtHR 4 December 2008, *S. and Marper v. the United Kingdom* (GC),
no. 30562/04 and 30566/04, ECLI:CE:ECHR:2008:1204JUD003056204 . . . . . 85, 149, 341
ECtHR 16 December 2008, *Frankowicz v. Poland*, no. 53025/99, ECLI:CE:ECHR:
2008:1216JUD005302599 125
ECtHR 16 December 2008, *Rupa v. Romania*, no. 58478/00, ECLI:CE:ECHR:
2008:1216JUD005847800 150
ECtHR 18 December 2008, *Kats et al. v. Ukraine*, no. 29971/04, ECLI:CE:ECHR:
2008:1218JUD002997104 136
ECtHR 13 January 2009, *Todorova v. Italy*, no. 33932/06, ECLI:CE:ECHR:2009:
0113JUD003393206 148
ECtHR 15 January 2009, *Reklos and Davourlis v. Greece*, no. 1234/05,
ECLI:CE:ECHR:2009:0115JUD000123405 . . . . 147, 149
ECtHR 20 January 2009, *Slawomir Musial v. Poland*, no. 28300/06,
ECLI:CE:ECHR:1999:0325JUD002455794 138–139
ECtHR 20 January 2009, *Uslu v. Turkey (no. 2)*, no. 23815/04, ECLI:CE:ECHR:
2009:0120JUD002381504 152
ECtHR 27 January 2009, *Tatar v. Romania*, no. 67021/01, ECLI:CE:ECHR:
2009:0127JUD006702101 . . . . 317, 318
ECtHR 24 February 2009, *Poghossian v. Georgia*, no. 9870/07 335
ECtHR 10 March 2009, *Paladi v. Moldova* (GC), no. 39806/05, ECLI:CE:ECHR:
2009:0310JUD003980605 140
ECtHR 28 April 2009, *K.H. et al. v. Slovakia*, no. 32881/04, ECLI:CE:ECHR:
2009:0428JUD003288104 . . . . 74, 137, 152
ECtHR 30 April 2009, *Glor v. Switzerland*, no. 13444/04, ECLI:CE:ECHR:
2009:0430JUD001344404 . . . . 63, 264, 268
ECtHR 28 July 2009, *Dvořáček and Dvořáčková v. Slovakia*, no. 30754/04,
ECLI:CE:ECHR:2009:0728JUD003075404 130
ECtHR 30 July 2009, *Pitalev v. Russia*, no. 34393/03, ECLI:CE:ECHR:2009:
0730JUD003439303. 319
ECtHR 15 October 2009, *Tsourlakis v. Greece*, no. 50796/07, ECLI:CE:ECHR:
2009:1015JUD005079607 152
ECtHR 14 January 2010, *Moskalyuk v. Russia*, no. 3267/03, ECLI:CE:ECHR:
2010:0114JUD000326703 319
ECtHR 2 March 2010, *Al-Saadoon and Mufdhi v. the United Kingdom* (dec.),
no. 61498/08, ECLI:CE:ECHR:2010:0302JUD006149808 . . . . 126, 133, 315
ECtHR 2 March 2010, *Lütfi Demirci et al. v. Turkey*, no. 28809/05,
ECLI:CE:ECHR:2010:0302JUD002880905 134
ECtHR 16 March 2010, *Oršuš and others v. Croatia*, no. 15766/03,
ECLI:CE:ECHR:2010:0316JUD001576603 235
ECtHR 23 March 2010, *Oyal v. Turkey*, no. 4864/05, ECLI:CE:ECHR:2010:
0323JUD000486405. 130
ECtHR 1 April 2010, *S.H. et al. v. Austria*, no. 57813/00, ECLI:CE:ECHR:
2011:1103JUD005781300 . . . . 63, 125, 139, 157,
285, 303, 305
ECtHR 20 April 2010, *C.B. v. Romania*, no. 21207/03, ECLI:CE:ECHR:
2010:0420JUD002120703 142
ECtHR 20 May 2010, *Alajos Kiss v. Hungary*, no. 38832/06, ECLI:CE:ECHR:
2010:0520JUD003883206 268

ECtHR 10 June 2010, *Jehovah's Witnessess of Moscow v. Russia*, no. 302/02,
    ECLI:CE:ECHR:2010:0610JUD000030202 .... 58–59, 79,
                                                                    130, 324
ECtHR 15 June 2010, *Ashot Harutyunyan v. Armenia*, no. 34334/04,
    ECLI:CE:ECHR:2010:0615JUD003433404 150
ECtHR 6 July 2010, *Neulinger and Shuruk v. Switzerland* (GC), no. 41615/07,
    ECLI:CE:ECHR:2010:0706JUD004161507 .... 122, 145
ECtHR 11 July 2010, *Dossi et al. v. Italy* (dec.), no. 26053/07, ECLI:CE:ECHR:
    2010:1012DEC002605307.. 130
ECtHR 2 September 2010, *Uzun v. Germany*, no. 35623/05, ECLI:CE:ECHR:
    2010:0902JUD003562305 127
ECtHR 16 December 2010, *A., B. and C. v. Ireland* (GC), no. 25579/05,
    ECLI:CE:ECHR:2010:1216JUD002557905 .... 127, 136, 292
ECtHR 21 December 2010, *Chavdarov v. Bulgaria*, no. 3465/03,
    ECLI:CE:ECHR:2010:1221JUD000346503 145
ECtHR 21 December 2010, *Jasinskis v. Latvia*, no. 45744/08, ECLI:CE:ECHR:
    2010:1221JUD004574408 266
ECtHR 11 January 2011, *Servet Gündüz et al. v. Turkey*, no. 4611/05,
    ECLI:CE:ECHR:2011:0111JUD000461105 318
ECtHR 20 January 2011, *Haas v. Switzerland*, no. 31322/07, ECLI:CE:ECHR:
    2011:0120JUD003132207 .... 125, 218, 324
ECtHR 21 January 2011, *M.S.S. v. Belgium and Greece*, no. 30696/09,
    ECLI:CE:ECHR:2011:0121JUD003069609 236
ECtHR 10 March 2011, *Kiyutin v. Russia*, no. 2700/10, ECLI:CE:ECHR:2011:
    0310JUD000270010... 236, 239,
                                                                    264, 267
ECtHR 24 March 2011, *Giuliani and Gaggio v. Italy* (GC), no. 23458/02,
    ECLI:CE:ECHR:2011:0324JUD002345802 137
ECtHR 17 May 2011, *Izevbekhai et al. v. Ireland* (dec.), no. 43408/08,
    ECLI:CE:ECHR:2011:0517DEC004340808 133
ECtHR 26 May 2011, *R.R. v. Poland*, no. 27617/04, ECLI:CE:ECHR:2011:
    0526JUD002761704... 125, 292, 297, 307
ECtHR 7 July 2011, *Al-Skeini v. the United Kingdom* (GC), no. 55721/07,
    ECLI:CE:ECHR:2011:0707JUD005572107 126
ECtHR 12 July 2011, *Šneersone and Kampanella v. Italy*, no. 14737/09,
    ECLI:CE:ECHR:2011:0712JUD001473709 122
ECtHR 26 July 2011, *George and Georgeta Stoicescu v. Romania*, no. 9718/03,
    ECLI:CE:ECHR:2011:0726JUD000971803 129
ECtHR 18 October 2011, *Acet et al. v. Turkey*, no. 22427/06, ECLI:CE:ECHR:
    2011:1018JUD002242706... 318
ECtHR 3 November 2011, *S.H. & Others v. Austria* (GC), no. 57813/00,
    ECLI:CE:ECHR:2011:1103JUD005781300 217–218
ECtHR 8 November 2011, *V.C. v. Slovakia*, no. 18968/07, ECLI:CE:ECHR:2011:
    1108JUD001896807.. 235
ECtHR 10 January 2012, *Arutyunyan v. Russia*, no. 48977/09, ECLI:CE:ECHR:
    2012:0110JUD004897709 267
ECtHR 17 January 2012, *Varapnickaité-Mazyliené v. Lithuania*, no. 20376/05,
    ECLI:CE:ECHR:2012:0117JUD002037605 151
ECtHR 14 February 2012, *D.D. v. Lithuania*, no. 13469/06, ECLI:CE:ECHR:
    2012:0214JUD001346906 .... 141, 267

ECtHR 23 February 2012, *Creangă v. Romania* (GC), no. 29226/03,
ECLI:CE:ECHR:2012:0223JUD002922603 141
ECtHR 28 February 2012, *Kolyadenko et al. v. Russia*, no. 17423/05,
ECLI:CE:ECHR:2012:0228JUD001742305 317
ECtHR 13 March 2012, *Reynolds v. the United Kingdom*, no. 2694/08,
ECLI:CE:ECHR:2012:0313JUD000269408 319
ECtHR 15 March 2012, *Solomakhin v. Ukraine*, no. 24429/03, ECLI:CE:ECHR:
2012:0315JUD002442903 ....129–130, 379
ECtHR 20 March 2012, *C.A.S. and C.S. v. Romania*, no. 26692/05,
ECLI:CE:ECHR:2012:0320JUD002669205 145
ECtHR 10 April 2012, *Panaitescu v. Romania*, no. 30909/06,
ECLI:CE:ECHR:2012:0410JUD003090906 320
ECtHR 12 June 2012, *N.B. v. Slovakia*, no. 29518/10, ECLI:CE:ECHR:2012:
0612JUD002951810...137
ECtHR 24 July 2012, *Fülöp v. Romania*, no. 18999/04, ECLI:CE:ECHR:2012:
0724JUD001899904..77, 144
ECtHR 28 August 2012, *Costa and Pavan v. Italy*, no. 54270/10,
ECLI:CE:ECHR:2012:0828JU005427010 ....139, 218, 307
ECtHR 18 September 2012, *S.R. v. the Netherlands* (dec.), no. 13837/07,
ECLI:CE:ECHR:2012:0918DEC001383707 142
ECtHR 2 October 2012, *L.B. v. Belgium*, no. 22831/08, ECLI:CE:ECHR:
2012:1002JUD002228310 143
ECtHR 16 October 2012, *Stanisław Kędzior v. Poland*, no. 45026/07,
ECLI:CE:ECHR:2012:1016JUD004502607 141
ECtHR 30 October 2012, *P. and S. v. Poland*, no. 57375/08, ECLI:CE:ECHR:
2012:1030JUD005737508 293
ECtHR 13 November 2012, *Bajić v. Croatia*, no. 41108/10, ECLI:CE:ECHR:
2012:1113JUD004110810 136
ECtHR 13 November 2012, *I.G. et al. v. Slovakia* (dec.), no. 15966/04,
ECLI:CE:ECHR:2012:1113JUD001596604 137
ECtHR 13 November 2012, *Z v. Poland*, no. 46132/08, ECLI:CE:ECHR:
2012:1113JUD004613208 136
ECtHR 18 December 2012, *Jeladze v. Georgia*, no. 1871/08, ECLI:CE:ECHR:
2012:1218JUD000187108 318
ECtHR 18 December 2012, *Kudra v. Croatia*, no. 13904/07, ECLI:CE:ECHR:
2012:1218JUD001390407 126
ECtHR 15 January 2013, *Csoma v. Romania*, no. 8759/05, ECLI:CE:ECHR:
2013:0115JUD000875905 ....129, 145
ECtHR 29 January 2013, *Horváth and Kiss v. Hungary*, no. 11146/11,
ECLI:CE:ECHR:2013:0129JUD001114611 268
ECtHR 18 February 2013, *A.L. v. Poland*, no. 28609/08, ECLI:CE:ECHR:
2014:0218JUD002860908 145
ECtHR 18 February 2013, *Ruiz Rivera v. Switzerland*, no. 8300/06,
ECLI:CE:ECHR:2014:0218JUD000830006 142
ECtHR 26 March 2013, *Rappaz v. Switzerland* (dec.), no. 73175/10,
ECLI:CE:ECHR:2013:0326DEC007317510 135
ECtHR 2 April 2013, *Tarantino et al. v. Italy*, no. 25851/09, ECLI:CE:ECHR:
2013:0402JUD002585109 128
ECtHR 9 April 2013, *Mehmet Şentürk and Bekir Şentürk v. Turkey*,
no. 13423/09, ECLI:CE:ECHR:2013:0409JUD001342309 ....134, 278

ECtHR 16 April 2013, *Dimitar Shopov v. Bulgaria*, no. 17253/07,
ECLI:CE:ECHR:2012:0223JUD002776509 58

ECtHR 25 April 2013, *M.S. v. Croatia*, no. 36337/10, ECLI:CE:ECHR:2013:
0425JUD003633710 268

ECtHR 25 April 2013, *Petukhova v. Russia*, no. 28796/07, ECLI:CE:ECHR:
2013:0502JUD002879607 148

ECtHR 14 May 2013, *Gross v. Switzerland*, no. 67810/10, ECLI:CE:ECHR:
2013:0514JUD006781010 324

ECtHR 23 May 2013, *E.A. v. Russia*, no. 44187/04, ECLI:CE:ECHR:2013:
0523JUD004418704 319

ECtHR 6 June 2013, *Avilkina et al. v. Russia*, no. 1585/09, ECLI:CE:ECHR:
2013:0606JUD000158509 149

ECtHR 18 June 2013, *Nencheva et al. v. Bulgaria*, no. 48609/06,
ECLI:CE:ECHR:2013:0618JUD00486090 ....134, 319

ECtHR 25 June 2013, *Grimailovs v. Latvia*, no. 6087/03, ECLI:CE:ECHR:
2013:0625JUD000608703 267

ECtHR 17 October 2013, *Keller v. Russia*, 26824/04, ECLI:CE:ECHR:
2013:1017JUD002682404 318

ECtHR 14 November 2013, *Blokhin v. Russia*, no. 47152/06,
ECLI:CE:ECHR:2016:0323JUD004715206 138

ECtHR 28 November 2013, *Glien v. Germany*, no. 7345/12,
ECLI:CE:ECHR:2013:1128JUD000734512 142

ECtHR 5 December 2013, *Arskaya v. Ukraine*, no. 45076/05,
ECLI:CE:ECHR:2013:1205JUD004507605 134

ECtHR 5 December 2013, *Vilnes et al. v. Norway*, no. 52806/09
and no. 22703/10, ECLI:CE:ECHR:2013:1205JUD005280609 ....75, 129, 144, 318

ECtHR 28 January 2014, *T.M. and C.M. v. Moldova*, no. 26608/11,
ECLI:CE:ECHR:2014:0128JUD002660811 132

ECtHR 25 March 2014, *Biao v. Denmark*, no. 38590/10, ECLI:CE:ECHR:2014:
0325JUD003859010 351

ECtHR 15 April 2014, *Radu v. Moldova*, no. 50073/07, ECLI:CE:ECHR:2014:
0415JUD005007307 151

ECtHR 17 April 2014, *G.C. v. Italy*, no. 73869/10, ECLI:CE:ECHR:2014:
0422JUD007386910 139

ECtHR 29 April 2014, *L.H. v. Latvia*, no. 52019/07, ECLI:CE:ECHR:
2014:0429JUD005201907 ....85, 137, 145, 149

ECtHR 12 June 2014, *Marić v. Croatia*, no. 50132/12, ECLI:CE:ECHR:2014:
0612JUD005013212 145

ECtHR 26 June 2014, *Mennesson v. France*, no. 65192/11, ECLI:CE:ECHR:
2014:0626JUD006519211 ....139, 277

ECtHR 17 July 2014, *Valentin Câmpeanu v. Romania* (GC), no. 47848/08,
ECLI:CE:ECHR:2014:0717JUD004784808 .... 131, 138, 266, 319

ECtHR 24 July 2014, *Brincat et al. v. Malta*, no. 60908/11, 62110/11, 62129/11,
62312/11 and 62338/11, ECLI:CE:ECHR:2014:0724JUD006090811...........131, 318

ECtHR 16 September 2014, *Atudorei v. Romania*, no. 50131/08,
ECLI:CE:ECHR:2014:0916JUD005013108 145

ECtHR 30 September 2014, *Gross v. Switzerland* (GC), no. 67810/10,
ECLI:CE:ECHR:2014:0930JUD006781010 324

ECtHR 9 December 2014, *McDonnell v. the United Kingdom*, no. 19563/11,
ECLI:CE:ECHR:2014:1209JUD001956311 136

ECtHR 15 January 2015, *Nogin v. Russia*, no. 58530/08, ECLI:CE:ECHR:
2015:0115JUD005853008 319
ECtHR 27 January 2015, *Asiye Genç v. Turkey*, no. 24109/07, ECLI:CE:ECHR:
2015:0127JUD002410907 . . . . 131, 134
ECtHR 3 March 2015, *Sandu Voicu v. Romania*, no. 45720/11, ECLI:CE:ECHR:
2015:0303JUD004572011 267
ECtHR 10 March 2015, *Y.Y. v. Turkey*, no. 14793/08, ECLI:CE:ECHR:2015:
0310JUD001479308 146
ECtHR 12 March 2015, *Muršić v. Croatia*, no. 7334/13, ECLI:CE:ECHR:2016:
1020JUD000733413 123
ECtHR 5 June 2015, *Lambert et al. v. France* (GC), no. 46043/14,
ECLI:CE:ECHR:2015:0605JUD004604314 . . . . 125, 217, 322
ECtHR 18 June 2015, *Yaikov v. Russia*, no. 39317/05, ECLI:CE:ECHR:
2015:0618JUD0039317059 142
ECtHR 30 June 2015, *Altuğ et al. v. Turkey*, no. 32086/07, ECLI:CE:ECHR:
2015:0630JUD003208607 131
ECtHR 27 August 2015, *Parrillo v. Italy* (GC), no. 46470/11, ECLI:CE:ECHR:
2015:0827JUD004647011 123
ECtHR 28 September 2015, *Bouyid v. Belgium* (GC), no. 23380/09,
ECLI:CE:ECHR:2015:0928JUD002338009 137–138
ECtHR 8 October 2015, *Sellal v. France*, no. 32432/13, ECLI:CE:ECHR:
2015:1008JUD003243213 . . . . 134, 150
ECtHR 13 October 2015, *Akkoyunlu v. Turkey*, no. 7505/06, ECLI:CE:ECHR:
2015:1013JUD000750506 318
ECtHR 26 November 2015, *Annen v. Germany*, no. 3690/10, ECLI:CE:ECHR:
2015:1126JUD000369010 137
ECtHR 12 January 2016, *Bilbija and Blažević v. Croatia*, no. 62870/13,
ECLI:CE:ECHR:2016:0112JUD006287013 136
ECtHR 4 February 2016, *Isenc v. France*, no. 58828/13, ECLI:CE:ECHR:
2016:0204JUD005882813 . . . . 135, 316
ECtHR 16 February 2016, *Soares de Melo v. Portugal*, no. 72850/14,
ECLI:CE:ECHR:2016:0216JUD007285014 137
ECtHR 23 February 2016, *Çam v. Turkey*, no. 51500/08, ECLI:CE:ECHR:2016:
0223JUD005150008 268
ECtHR 23 February 2016, *Y.Y. v. Russia*, no. 40378/06, ECLI:CE:ECHR:2016:
0223JUD004037806 149
ECtHR 1 March 2016, *Mihu v. Roemenië*, no. 36903/13, ECLI:CE:ECHR:2016:
0301JUD003690313 136
ECtHR 15 March 2016, *Novruk et al. v. Russia*, no. 31039/11 et al.,
ECLI:CE:ECHR:2016:0315JUD003103911 128
ECtHR 17 March 2016, *Vasileva v. Bulgaria*, no. 23796/10, ECLI:CE:ECHR:
2016:0317JUD002379610 130
ECtHR 26 April 2016, *Murray v. the Netherlands* (GC), no. 10511/10,
ECLI:CE:ECHR:2016:0426JUD001051110 123
ECtHR 31 May 2016, *A.N. v. Lithuania*, no. 17280/08, ECLI:CE:ECHR:2016:
0531JUD001728008 267–268
ECtHR 7 June 2016, *R.B.A.B. et al. v. the Netherlands*, no. 7211/06,
ECLI:CE:ECHR:2016:0607JUD000721106 133
ECtHR 21 June 2016, *Al-Dulimi and Montana Management Inc. v. Switzerland*,
no. 5809/08, ECLI:CE:ECHR:2016:0621JUD000580908 123

ECtHR 28 June 2016, *Halime Kılıç v. Turkey*, no. 63034/11, ECLI:CE:ECHR:
2016:0628JUD006303411 132

ECtHR 30 August 2016, *Aydoğdu v. Turkey*, no. 40448/06, ECLI:CE:ECHR:
2016:0830JUD004044806 . . . . .33, 131, 134, 319

ECtHR 25 October 2016, *Otgon v. Moldova*, no. 22743/07, ECLI:CE:ECHR:
2016:1025JUD002274307 . . . . 132, 317

ECtHR 8 November 2016, *Magyar Helsinki Bizottság v. Hungary* (GC),
no. 18030/11, ECLI:CE:ECHR:2016:1108JUD001803011 144

ECtHR 15 November 2016, *Dubská and Krejzová v. the Czech Republic* (GC),
no. 28859/11 and 28473/12, ECLI:CE:ECHR:2016:1115JUD002885911 123,
125–126, 157

ECtHR 17 November 2016, *V.M. and Others v. Belgium* (GC), no. 60125/11,
ECLI:CE:ECHR:2016:1117JUD006012511 238

ECtHR 22 November 2016, *Hiller v. Austria*, no. 1967/14, ECLI:CE:ECHR:
2016:1122JUD000196714 . . . . 134, 319

ECtHR 6 December 2016, *Trutko v. Russia*, no. 40979/04, ECLI:CE:ECHR:
2016:1206JUD004097904 141

ECtHR 13 December 2016, *Bélány Nagy v. Hungary* (GC), no. 53080/13,
ECLI:CE:ECHR:2016:1213JUD005308013 123

ECtHR 15 December 2016, *Khlaifia et al. v. Italy* (GC), no. 16483/12,
ECLI:CE:ECHR:2016:1215JUD001648312 138

ECtHR 10 January 2017, *Ioniță v. Romania*, no. 81270/12, ECLI:CE:ECHR:
2017:0110JUD008127012 130

ECtHR 2 February 2017, *Ilnseher v. Germany*, no. 27505/14, ECLI:CE:ECHR:
2017:0202JUD001021112 142

ECtHR 14 February 2017, *Karakhanyan v. Russia*, no. 24421/11,
ECLI:CE:ECHR:2017:0214JUD002442111 150

ECtHR 23 February 2017, *Tommaso v. Italy* (GC), no. 43395/09,
ECLI:CE:ECHR:2017:0223JUD004339509 141

ECtHR 23 March 2017, *A.-M.V. v. Finland*, no. 53251/13, ECLI:CE:ECHR:
2017:0323JUD005325113 268

ECtHR 6 April 2017, *A.P., Garçon and Nicot v. France*, no. 79885/12, 52471/13
and 52596/13, ECLI:CE:ECHR:2017:0406JUD007988512 . . . . .124, 133, 157

ECtHR 2 May 2017, *Jurica v. Croatia*, no. 30376/13, ECLI:CE:ECHR:
2017:0502JUD003037613 130

ECtHR 12 May 2017, *Simeonovi v. Bulgaria* (GC), no. 21980/04,
ECLI:CE:ECHR:2017:0512JUD002198004 123

ECtHR 23 May 2017, *Bălşan v. Romania*, no. 49645/09, ECLI:CE:ECHR:2017:
0523JUD004964509 132

ECtHR 22 June 2017, *Aycaguer v. France*, no. 8806/12, ECLI:CE:ECHR:2017:
0622JUD000880612 346

ECtHR 28 June 2017, *Gard et al. v. the United Kingdom* (dec.), no. 39793/17,
ECLI:CE:ECHR:2017:0627DEC003979317 322

ECtHR 25 July 2017, *Carvalho Pinto de Sousa Morais v. Portugal*, no. 17484/15,
ECLI:CE:ECHR:2017:0725JUD001748415 132

ECtHR 7 December 2017, *Yonchev v. Bulgaria*, no. 12504/09, ECLI:CE:ECHR:
2017:1207JUD001250409 152

ECtHR 19 December 2017, *Lopes de Sousa Fernandes v. Portugal* (GC),
no. 56080/13, ECLI:CE:ECHR:2017:1219JUD005608013 . . . . .130, 133–134, 137,
140, 157, 315, 319–320

ECtHR 9 January 2018, *Kadusic v. Switzerland*, no. 43977/13,
   ECLI:CE:ECHR:2018:0109JUD004397713 ....135, 141–142
ECtHR 23 January 2018, *Afiri and Biddarri v. France* (dec.), no. 1828/18,
   ECLI:CE:ECHR:2018:0123DEC000182818 322
ECtHR 20 February 2018, *Mehmet Günay and Güllü Günay v. Turkey*,
   no. 52797/08, ECLI:CE:ECHR:2018:0220JUD005279708 136
ECtHR 26 April 2018, *Khaksar v. the United Kingdom* (dec.), no. 2654/18,
   ECLI:CE:ECHR:2018:0403DEC000265418 138
ECtHR 26 June 2018, *D.R. v. Lithuania*, no. 691/15, ECLI:CE:ECHR:2018:
   0626JUD000069115... 141
ECtHR 11 September 2018, *Kasat v. Turkey*, no. 61541/09, ECLI:CE:ECHR:
   2018:0911JUD00615410 318
ECtHR 20 September 2018, *Annen v. Germany* (no. 2–5), 3682/10, 3687/10,
   9765/10 and 70693/11, ECLI:CE:ECHR:2018:0920JUD000368210 137
ECtHR 4 October 2018, *Pojatina v. Croatia*, no. 18568/12, ECLI:CE:ECHR:
   2018:1004JUD001856812 125
ECtHR 11 October 2018, *S.V. v. Italy*, no. 55216/08, ECLI:CE:ECHR:2018:
   1011JUD005521608... 146
ECtHR 22 October 2018, *S., V. and A. v. Denmark* (GC), 35553/12, 36678/12
   and 36711/12, ECLI:CE:ECHR:2018:1022JUD003555312 141
ECtHR 29 January 2019, *Mifsud v. Malta*, no. 62257/15, ECLI:CE:ECHR:2019:
   0129JUD006225715... 146
ECtHR 31 January 2019, *Fernandes de Oliveira v. Portugal* (GC), no. 78103/14,
   ECLI:CE:ECHR:2019:0131JUD007810314 .... 123, 125, 134, 319
ECtHR 31 January 2019, *Rooman v. Belgium* (GC), no. 18052/11,
   ECLI:CE:ECHR:2019:0131JUD001805211 .... 125, 139, 143, 157
ECtHR 4 June 2019, *Kosaitė-Čypienė et al. v. Lithuania*, no. 69489/12,
   ECLI:CE:ECHR:2019:0604JUD006948912 125
ECtHR 11 June 2019, *Prizreni v. Albania*, no. 29309/16, ECLI:CE:ECHR:2019:
   0611JUD002930916...136, 150
ECtHR 25 June 2019, *Ulusoy v. Turkey*, no. 54969/09, ECLI:CE:ECHR:2019:
   0625JUD005496909... 150
ECtHR 2 July 2019, *R.S. v. Hungary*, no. 65290/14, ECLI:CE:ECHR:2019:
   0702JUD006529014... 148
ECtHR 3 October 2019, *Nikolyan v. Armenia*, no. 74438/14, ECLI:CE:ECHR:
   2019:1003JUD007443814 268
ECtHR 8 October 2019, *Fedulov v. Russia*, no. 53068/08, ECLI:CE:ECHR:
   2019:1008JUD005306808 ....267, 320
ECtHR 17 October 2019, *López Ribalda et al. v. Spain* (GC), no. 1874/13
   and 8567/13, ECLI:CE:ECHR:2019:1017JUD000187413 149
ECtHR 5 December 2019, *Petithory Lanzmann v. France* (dec.), no. 23038/19,
   ECLI:CE:ECHR:2019:1112DEC002303819 139
ECtHR 21 January 2020, *Strazimiri v. Albania*, 34602/16, ECLI:CE:ECHR:
   2020:0121JUD003460216 123
ECtHR 23 January 2020, *L.R. v. North Macedonia*, 38067/15, ECLI:CE:ECHR:
   2020:0123JUD003806715 ....122, 138, 157
ECtHR 28 January 2020, *Nicolaou v. Cyprus*, no. 29068/10, ECLI:CE:ECHR:
   2020:0128JUD002906810 136
ECtHR 29 January 2020, *Stankūnaitė v. Lithuania*, no. 67068/11,
   ECLI:CE:ECHR:2019:1029JUD006706811 130

ECtHR 30 January 2020, *Studio Monitori et al. v. Georgia*, no. 44920/09
and 8942/10, ECLI:CE:ECHR:2020:0130JUD004492009 144

ECtHR 13 February 2020, *Gaughran v. the United Kingdom*, no. 45245/15,
ECLI:CE:ECHR:2020:0213JUD004524515 149

ECtHR 18 February 2020, *Cinţa v. Romania*, no. 3891/19, ECLI:CE:ECHR:
2020:0218JUD000389119 . . . . 145, 268

ECtHR 25 February 2020, *Y.I. v. Russia*, no. 68868/14, ECLI:CE:ECHR:
2020:0225JUD006886814 130

ECtHR 10 March 2020, *Hudorovič et al. v. Slovenia*, no. 24816/14 and 25140/14,
ECLI:CE:ECHR:2020:0310JUD002481614 131

ECtHR 12 March 2020, *Grimmark v. Sweden* (dec.), no. 43726/17,
ECLI:CE:ECHR:2020:0211DEC004372617 . . . . 137, 324

ECtHR 12 March 2020, *Steen v. Sweden* (dec.), no. 62309/17,
ECLI:CE:ECHR:2020:0211DEC006230917 . . . . 137, 325

ECtHR 31 March 2020, *Jeanty v. Belgium*, no. 82284/17, ECLI:CE:ECHR:
2020:0331JUD008228417 . . . . 133, 142

ECtHR 7 May 2020, *Vardosanidze v. Georgia*, no. 43881/10, ECLI:CE:ECHR:
2020:0507JUD004388110 134

ECtHR 14 May 2020, *Astruc v. France* (dec.), no. 5499/15, ECLI:CE:ECHR:
2020:0415DEC000549915 139

ECtHR 26 May 2020, *Aftanache v. Romania*, no. 999/19, ECLI:CE:ECHR:
2020:0526JUD000099919 141

ECtHR 26 May 2020, *P.T. v. Moldova*, no. 1122/12, ECLI:CE:ECHR:2020:
0526JUD000112212 . . . . .81, 149–150

ECtHR 16 June 2020, *Boljević v. Serbia*, no. 47443/14, ECLI:CE:ECHR:
2020:0616JUD004744314 146

ECtHR 30 June 2020, *Frick v. Switzerland*, no. 23405/16, ECLI:CE:ECHR:
2020:0630JUD002340516 316

ECtHR 30 June 2020, *S.F. v. Switzerland*, no. 23405/16, ECLI:CE:ECHR:
2020:0630JUD002340516 318

ECtHR 9 July 2020, *Y.T. v. Bulgaria*, no. 41701/16, ECLI:CE:ECHR:2020:
0709JUD004170116 124

ECtHR 16 July 2020, *Rana v. Hungary*, no. 40888/17, ECLI:CE:ECHR:2020:
0716JUD004088817 124

ECtHR 4 August 2020, *Tërshana v. Albania*, no. 48756/14, ECLI:CE:ECHR:
2020:0804JUD004875614 132

ECtHR 10 September 2020, *G.L. v. Italy*, no. 59751/15, ECLI:CE:ECHR:
2020:0910JUD005975115 64

ECtHR 15 September 2020, *Aggerholm v. Denmark*, no. 45439/18,
ECLI:CE:ECHR:2020:0915JUD004543918 59

ECtHR 18 October 2020, *Annen v. Germany*, no. 3779/11, no. 6,
ECLI:CE:ECHR:2018:1018JUD000377911 137

ECtHR 3 December 2020, *Le Mailloux v. France* (dec.), no. 18108/20,
ECLI:CE:ECHR:2020:1105DEC001810820 128

ECtHR 2 February 2021, *Strøbye and Rosenlind v. Denmark*, nos. 25802/18
and 27338/18, ECLI:CE:ECHR:2021:0202JUD002580 218

ECtHR 16 February 2021, *Gawlik v. Liechtenstein*, no. 23922/19,
ECLI:CE:ECHR:2021:0216JUD002392219 321

ECtHR 23 February 2021, *Hirsi Jamaa and Others v. Italy*, (GC) no. 27765/09,
ECLI:CE:ECHR:2012:0223JUD002776509 244

ECtHR 23 March 2021, *Fenech v. Malta* (dec.), no. 19090/20, ECLI:CE:ECHR:
2021:0323DEC001909020. 128
ECtHR 8 April 2021, *Vavřička et al. v. the Czech Republic* (GC), no. 47621/13,
ECLI:CE:ECHR:2021:0408JUD004762113 . . . . .129–130, 379
ECtHR 21 April 2021, *Parfitt v. the United Kingdom* (dec.), no. 18533/21,
ECLI:CE:ECHR:2021:0420DEC001853321 322
ECtHR 11 May 2021, *Caamaño Valle v. Spain*, no. 43564/17, ECLI:CE:ECHR:
2021:0511JUD004356417 268
ECtHR 25 May 2021, *Big Brother Watch and Others v. The United Kingdom* (GC),
nos. 58170/13, 62322/14 and 24960/15, ECLI:CE:ECHR:2021:
0525JUD005817013. 338
ECtHR 2 September 2021, *Ražnatović v. Montenegro*, no. 14742/18,
ECLI:CE:ECHR:2021:0902JUD001474218 134
ECtHR 7 October 2021, *Zambrano v. France* (dec.), no. 41994/21,
ECLI:CE:ECHR:2021:1007DEC004199421 128

HUMAN RIGHTS COMMITTEE

Human Rights Committee, *Karen Noelia Llantoy Huamán v. Peru*,
Communication no. 1153/2003, CCPR/C/85/D/1153/2003, 2005. . . . . .104, 288
Human Rights Committee, 17 November 2016, *Views adopted by the Committee
under article 5 (4) of the Optional Protocol, concerning communication
No. 2324/2013, Mellet v. Ireland*, CCPR/C/116/D/2324/2013 105
Human Rights Committee, 11 July 2017, *Views adopted by the Committee
under article 5 (4) of the Optional Protocol, concerning communication
No. 2425/2014, Whelan v. Ireland*, CCPR/C/119/D/2425/2014. 105

LIST OF ABBREVIATIONS

Biomedicine Convention	Convention on Human Rights and Biomedicine (CoE)
CAT	Convention against Torture and Other Cruel, Inhuman or Degrading Treatment or Punishment (UN, 1984)
CEDAW	Convention on the Elimination of All Forms of Discrimination Against Women (UN, 1979)
CEDAW (Committee)	Committee on the Elimination of All Forms of Discrimination Against Women
CFREU	Charter of Fundamental Rights of the European Union (EU, 2000)
CIE	Committee of Independent Experts (ESC, CoE)
CJEU	Court of Justice of the European Union
CoE	Council of Europe
CPT	European Convention for the Prevention of Torture (CoE, 1987)
CRC	Convention on the Rights of the Child (UN, 1989)
CRC (Committee)	Committee on the Rights of the Child
CRPD	Convention on the Rights of Persons with Disabilities (UN, 2006)
CRPD (Committee)	Committee on the Rights of Persons with Disabilities
CSDH	Committee on the Social Determinants of Health (WHO)
EC Treaty	Treaty establishing the European Community (EU, 1993)
ECHR	Convention for the Protection of Human Rights and Fundamental Freedoms (European Convention on Human Rights, CoE, 1950)
ECJ	European Court of Justice
EComHR	European Commission of Human Rights (EU)
ECSR	European Committee of Social Rights (ESC, CoE)
ECtHR	European Court of Human Rights (CoE)

ESC	European Social Charter (CoE, 1961)
EU	European Union
GC	Grand Chamber (of the ECtHR)
GC	UN General Comment
HIV	human immunodeficiency virus
ICCPR	International Convention on Civil and Political Rights (UN, 1966)
ICERD	International Convention on the Elimination of All Forms of Racial Discrimination (UN, 1965)
ICESCR	International Covenant on Economic, Social and Cultural Rights (UN, 1966)
ICESCR Committee	International Committee on Economic, Social and Cultural Rights (UN)
ICF	International Classification of Functioning, Disability and Health
IHR	International Health Regulations (WHO, 2005)
ILO	International Labour Organization
MIPAA	Madrid Political Declaration and International Plan of Action on Ageing (UN)
MWC	International Convention on the Protection of the Rights of All Migrant Workers and Members of their Families (UN, 1990)
OECD	Organisation for Economic Co-operation and Development
Oviedo Convention	Convention on Human Rights and Biomedicine (CoE)
PAS	physician-assisted suicide
(Revised) ESC	(Revised) European Social Charter (CoE, 1996)
TEU	Treaty on European Union (EU, 1992)
TFEU	Treaty on the Functioning of the European Union (EU, 2007)
UDHR	Universal Declaration of Human Rights (UN, 1948)
UN	United Nations
UNECE	UN Economic Commission of Europe
UNESCO	UN Educational, Scientific and Cultural Organization
WHO	World Health Organization
WMA	World Medical Association

ABOUT THE AUTHORS

Mette Hartlev (PhD and LL.D) is Professor of Health Law at the University of Copenhagen, Denmark. Her main research interests are patients' rights, health and human rights, health technologies, law, science and technology studies, data protection law and poverty and vulnerability law. She has also researched and published in the field of biolaw and bioethics. She has participated in a vast number of EU-funded cross-disciplinary research projects, and is a co-editor of the *European Journal of Health Law*. She also holds the position as chair of the Danish National Committee of Research Ethics in Health Sciences.

Aart Hendriks (PhD) is Professor of Health Law at Leiden University/Leiden University Medical Centre (LUMC), the Netherlands; a health law advisor to the Royal Dutch Medical Association (KNMG); a substitute judge at the District Court of Rotterdam; a member of the Regional Disciplinary Court Group of specialists on predictivity, genetic testing and insurance of the Council of Europe; a member of the Board of Supervisors of the Erasmus University Medical Hospital; a board member of various national and international non-governmental organisations (NGOs) working in the field of health, disability and human rights law; and an editor of several academic journals. He obtained his PhD from the University of Amsterdam (UvA) on a dissertation concerning the right of persons with disabilities to equal access in the employment market, and has written extensively on such issues as human rights, health law, minority rights and patients' rights.

Katharina Ó Cathaoir (PhD) is Associate Professor of Law at the Faculty of Law at the University of Copenhagen, Denmark and Pro Futura Scientia Fellow at the Swedish Collegium for Advanced Studies. Katharina researches and lectures in the field of health and human rights, focusing on big data, personalised medicine, COVID-19 and childhood obesity. She is particularly interested in the rights of children, older persons and women. She is a board member of Nordic PerMed Law and sits on the international expert panel of the Genetic Discrimination Observatory (GDO).

Janne Rothmar Herrmann (PhD) is Professor with special responsibilities in health law and technology at the Faculty of Law at the University of Copenhagen, Denmark. Her main research interests include reproductive rights, conscientious objections, abortion, end of life decisions, and privacy. She is Governor of the World Association for Medical Law, a member of the Nordic Committee on Bioethics, appointed member of the Danish Dataethics Council and The Danish Committee on Research Misconduct. She is Principal Investigator of the research project Reconceptualising Reproductive Rights funded by Independent Research Fund Denmark and partner in several cross-disciplinary research projects. She is co-editor-in-chief of the *Nordic Journal of Feminist and Gender Studies*.

Henriette Sinding Aasen (dr. juris) is Professor at the Faculty of Law at the University of Bergen, Norway. She is the head of the research group on welfare state law at the faculty, a member of the University of Bergen's strategic group for global challenges (health, migration, social inequality), and a member of the strategic working group of University of Bergen's interdisciplinary Pandemic Centre. Her research interests are in the multiple connections between health- and welfare regulations and human rights, including autonomy, privacy and non-discrimination. Recent publications cover constitutional protection of welfare rights; the right to adequate healthcare for undocumented migrants and the elderly; balancing of rights in conflict; reproductive rights; protection against harmful practices; rape and consent; and rights of the elderly during the COVID-19 pandemic. She has led and participated in several interdisciplinary research projects in the areas of health, juridification and social equality, and has served in a number of national law commissions, the latest being on drug policy reform in Norway.

Brigit Toebes (PhD) is Professor of Health Law in a Global Context at the Faculty of Law at the University of Groningen, the Netherlands. Her main research interests are in the interface between health and human rights, the identification of 'global health law' as a branch of international law, and the regulation of risk factors for noncommunicable diseases (including tobacco, unhealthy diets, and oral health). Toebes has published widely in legal, public health and multidisciplinary journals, including *Human Rights Quarterly*, *Harvard Health and Human Rights*, the *BMJ*, and *Tobacco Control*. She is the academic leader of the Groningen Centre for Health Law at the Faculty of Law, and fellow at the Aletta Jacobs School of Public Health. She is co-chair of the Global Health Law Committee of the International Law Association and chair of the board of the Dutch Association of Health Law. Funded by the Dutch Cancer Society/ Lung Foundation, Toebes has researched tobacco control since 2016, specifically tobacco regulation through a human rights lens. Toebes is a consultant to various international bodies, including the World Health Organization and the UN Special Rapporteur on the Right to Health.

PART I
INTRODUCTION

CHAPTER 1

INTRODUCING HEALTH
AND HUMAN RIGHTS

Global and European Perspectives

Brigit Toebes[*]

1. RATIONALE AND AIM OF THIS BOOK

'Health and human rights' is an important dimension of international and European human rights and health law. It is multi-disciplinary, engaging scholars and practitioners of public health and medicine, as well as legal scholars and human rights lawyers. Taking a 'health and human rights approach' means applying international, regional and domestic human rights law to a wide range of health-related issues, including access to medical services, medicines and medical aids, infectious disease control, the social determinants of health, health data protection, reproductive health, as well as embryo selection, abortion and environmental health.[1] Human rights law informs other areas of law that engage with health issues, including international and domestic health law, biolaw and bioethics, patients' rights and environmental law. It brings a new, and often more international, as well as moral, dimension, to existing legal analyses of health issues. This is essential in an increasingly interconnected and internationalised world, where health concerns are omnipresent and can no longer be addressed solely at a domestic level.

This book focuses on the legal interfaces between 'health' and 'human rights', taking both a global and a European approach. Globally speaking, there

---

[*]   The author thanks the co-authors of this volume for their useful feedback.

[1]   On the discourse of health and human rights see also, inter alia, Thérèse Murphy, *Health and Human Rights*, London: Bloomsbury Publishing (Hart), 2013; Michael A. Grodin, Daniel Tarantola, George J. Annas and Sofia Gruskin (eds.), *Health and Human Rights in a Changing World*, New York and London: Routledge, Taylor and Francis Group, 2013; and, more recently, Benjamin Mason Meier and Lawrence O. Gostin (eds.), *Foundations of Global Health & Human Rights*, Oxford: Oxford University Press, 2020.

are tremendous challenges when it comes to the protection of collective and individual health. Such challenges include weak (primary) healthcare systems, the spread of infectious diseases and the increase of noncommunicable diseases (NCDs), as well as the health effects of air pollution and climate change.[2] At the time of writing, the COVID-19 pandemic remains ongoing, leading to direct loss of life and lasting health impacts ('long COVID') from the disease, but also indirect health impacts, like loneliness and cancelled healthcare appointments.

While most of these issues also exist outside Europe, the European context raises certain specific concerns, in terms of health issues and outcomes. Many parts of Europe face ageing populations and – to some extent related to this – rising healthcare costs.[3] Certain groups are particularly vulnerable to exclusion from healthcare services, including (undocumented) migrants and people with a low socio-economic status (see Chapters 7, 8 and 13). Important public health concerns include air pollution and other risk factors to health, in particular smoking and obesity. Smoking remains the most important cause of death across the EU (see Chapters 6 and 13). New and emerging technologies have been proposed as a means of meeting these challenges, but these carry their own risks, which need further analysis (see Chapter 12).

In such settings, human rights can, potentially, play a powerful and crucial role in protecting the rights of vulnerable individuals. Human rights law is a compelling framework for assessing these and other questions in the health field, as it couples such health problems with a legal and moral dimension. From a global perspective, there are a range of international human rights and health treaties that are important for the protection of such health and health-related concerns. The international recognition and definition of the 'right to health' is at the centre of this (see Chapters 2, 4 and 7), but there are many other relevant human rights standards, too, including the right to life, the right to respect for privacy and family life, and the right of access to information. International case law in the health field has made its mark when it comes to matters like access to health services, abortion, and inhuman and degrading treatment in health settings (see Chapters 4 and 10). Increasingly, links are being identified between human rights and other international standards protecting health, in particular the standards adopted by the World Health Organization (WHO).

As mentioned, the European context is, to some extent, a region *sui generis*, not only in terms of health issues and outcomes, but also from a political and

---

[2]   See also World Health Organization (WHO), Ten threats to global health in 2019. Available at https://www.who.int/news-room/spotlight/ten-threats-to-global-health-in-2019.

[3]   European Commission, The 2021 Ageing Report: Economic and Budgetary Projections for the EU Member States (2019–2070), available at https://ec.europa.eu/info/publications/2021-ageing-report-economic-and-budgetary-projections-eu-member-states-2019-2070_en. See also Katharina Ó Cathaoir et al, 'Older Persons and the Right to Health in the Nordics under Covid-19', *European Journal of Health Law*, 28(5) (2021), 417–44.

legal perspective. In response to a legacy of wars and massive human rights violations, European states have established two exceptionally strong regional organisations, the Council of Europe and the European Union, both of which aim to promote human rights and well-being. While it is important to study the implications of this framework for European countries, this discourse also has merit and potential implications beyond the regional scope of Europe. The authoritative case law of the European Court of Human Rights (ECtHR) of the Council of Europe has increasingly touched upon health-related issues (see Chapter 5). Furthermore, as a result of the (Revised) European Social Charter (ESC), the mandate of the Council of Europe has increased significantly with regard to health rights. In addition, within the context of the Council of Europe, the Convention on Human Rights and Biomedicine ('Biomedicine Convention') has been adopted, and this has been complemented by various protocols (see Chapters 2 and 4). And while the European Union was originally established as a regional organisation to promote the economic integration of its Member States, it has become increasingly clear that its treaties and case law also impact upon issues falling within the realm of health and human rights.

2. HISTORICAL INTRODUCTION TO 'HEALTH AND HUMAN RIGHTS'

2.1. INTRODUCTION

Several key historical moments and trends have been important for the development of 'health and human rights'. While the term 'health and human rights' has, increasingly, been used since the 1980s, the underlying fields of human rights, bioethics and patients' rights date back further, having gradually developed, in particular, since the Second World War.

During the aftermath of the Second World War, there was a general sense of awareness that the atrocities committed during the war should not be repeated, and that mechanisms should be established to offer protection against such human rights abuses. Initiatives were taken, both in the field of human rights law and in the field of bioethics. While the Universal Declaration of Human Rights (UDHR 1948) marked the beginning of a phase of standard setting in the area of human rights law, the Nuremberg Code was a milestone in the area of health law, as well as bioethics and medical ethics. As such, both the Universal Declaration and the Nuremberg Code have been called 'post-Holocaust documents'.[4]

---

[4]   Robert Baker, 'Bioethics and Human Rights: A Historical Perspective' *Cambridge Quarterly of Healthcare Ethics* 10 (2001), 241–52, 243.

The decades after the Second World War were marked by a phase of standard setting in both the areas of human rights and bioethics. While the two fields developed separately, they influenced each other. As part of these developments, the cross-cutting area of 'health and human rights' gradually emerged. These subsequent developments will be discussed below.

2.2. THE HUMAN RIGHTS MOVEMENT

Since the Second World War, a large number of human rights treaties and other documents have gradually been adopted. Many of these documents are relevant to the area of health (see, for more detail, Chapters 2 to 6). The first important international landmark for the area of health and human rights was the recognition of the enjoyment of the 'highest attainable standard of health' as a 'fundamental right of every human being'. This appeared in the Preamble to the Constitution of the WHO, adopted in 1946.[5] After that, a set of general human rights documents, containing many references to health, were gradually adopted: the so-called 'International Bill of Human Rights', which embraces the Universal Declaration of Human Rights (UDHR 1948); the International Covenant on Civil and Political Rights (ICCPR 1966); and the International Covenant on Economic, Social and Cultural Rights (ICESCR 1966).[6] The UDHR, which contains both civil and political rights and economic, social and cultural rights, recognises a right to an adequate standard of living (Article 25), including a right to 'medical care and necessary social services'. While the ICCPR contains a number of health-related civil and political human rights, including the right to life and the prohibition of torture, the ICESCR recognises, in Article 12, the 'right to the highest attainable standard of health'. Subsequently, a number of UN human rights treaties that integrate civil and political rights, and economic, social and cultural rights were gradually adopted, the most important being the Convention on the Elimination of All Forms of Discrimination Against Women (CEDAW 1979), the Convention on the Rights of the Child (CRC 1989), the International Convention on the Protection of the Rights of All Migrant Workers and Members of Their Families (MWC 1990) and the Convention on the Rights

---

[5] The Constitution of the WHO was formally adopted by the International Health Conference held in New York from 19 June to 22 July 1946, and was signed on 22 July 1946 by the representatives of 61 states, entering into force on 7 April 1948.

[6] Universal Declaration of Human Rights (UDHR), G.A. Res. 217A (III), UN Doc. A/810 at 71 (1948), 8 December 1948; International Covenant on Civil and Political Rights (ICCPR), 999 U.N.T.S. 171; S. Exec. Doc. E, 95-2 (1978); S. Treaty Doc. 95-20; 6 I.L.M. 368 (1967), 16 December 1966; and the International Covenant on Economic, Social and Cultural Rights (ICESCR), 993 U.N.T.S. 3; S. Exec. Doc. D, 95-2 (1978); S. Treaty Doc. No. 95-19; 6 I.L.M. 360 (1967), 16 December 1966.

of Persons with Disabilities (CRPD 2006).[7] Each of these instruments, as well as the drafts of the proposed Convention on the Rights of Older Persons, contain specific provisions on the 'right to health' and several other health-related rights (see also Chapters 2 and 4).[8]

A similar trend took place at a European level: within the framework of the Council of Europe a number of regional human rights treaties were gradually adopted, which reflected a similar split between civil and political rights, and economic, social and cultural rights. While the rights in the European Convention on Human Rights and Fundamental Freedoms (ECHR 1950) and the European Convention for the Prevention of Torture and Inhuman or Degrading Treatment or Punishment (1987) have, in many ways, a relevance to health, the (Revised) European Social Charter (ESC 1961/1996) recognises a 'right to protection of health' in Article 11, and a 'right to social and medical assistance' in Article 13 (see also Chapters 2 and 5).[9]

From the 1980s onwards, human rights scholars began to analyse the meanings and implications of economic, social and cultural rights, which had remained undeveloped and undefined in comparison with civil and political rights. Courts and policymakers had, until then, been very reluctant to apply economic, social and cultural rights, as they feared the financial consequences for governments once socio-economic rights had been granted.[10] Scholars attempted to prove and underline that economic and social rights were more equal to civil and political rights than had previously been assumed. The so-called 'interdependence' of all human rights was confirmed by the Vienna Declaration and Programme of Action, which affirmed that all human rights were 'universal, indivisible and interdependent and interrelated'.[11] Scholars also started to explore the specific meaning of economic, social and cultural rights, including the right to health. A range of general comments were gradually adopted by the Committee on

---

[7] Convention on the Elimination of All Forms of Discrimination Against Women (CEDAW), 1249 U.N.T.S. 13; 19 I.L.M. 33 (1980), 18 December 1979; Convention on the Rights of the Child (CRC), 1577 U.N.T.S. 3; 28 I.L.M. 1456 (1989), 20 November 1989; International Convention on the Protection of the Rights of All Migrant Workers and Members of Their Families (MWC), 2220 U.N.T.S. 93; 30 I.L.M. 1517 (1991), 18 December 1990; and the Convention on the Rights of Persons with Disabilities (CRPD), UN Doc. A/RES/61/106, Annex I, 3 May 2008.

[8] Arts. 12 CEDAW, 24 CRC, 28 Migrant Workers' Convention, and 25 of the Disability Convention. See also, e.g. Art. 25 of ILO Convention 169 on Indigenous Peoples, and Rules 22 to 26 of the Standard Minimum Rules for the Treatment of Prisoners.

[9] Convention for the Protection of Human Rights and Fundamental Freedoms (ECHR), Europ.T.S. No. 5; 213 U.N.T.S. 221, adopted 4 November 1950; European Social Charter (ESC), 529 U.N.T.S. 89; Europ. T.S. No. 35, adopted 18 October 1961, revised in 1996 (3 May 1996); European Convention for the Prevention of Torture and Inhuman and Degrading Treatment or Punishment, Europ.T.S. No. 126, adopted 26 November 1987.

[10] Brigit C.A. Toebes, *The Right to Health as a Human Right in International Law*, Antwerp/ Oxford: Intersentia/Hart, 1999, 169.

[11] Art. 5 Vienna Declaration and Programme of Action (UN Doc. A/Conf.157/23), 12 July 1993 (World Conference on Human Rights, Vienna, 14–25 June 1993).

Economic, Social and Cultural Rights (ICESCR Committee), which, inter alia, addressed the meanings and implications of the substantive economic, social and cultural rights. The General Comment on the Right to the Highest Attainable Standard of Health (contained in Article 12 ICESCR) was adopted in 2000.[12] From then onwards, the 'right to health' has been addressed by many forums, and from many angles, not least by successive Special Rapporteurs on the right to physical and mental health.[13]

In 2013, the Optional Protocol to the ICESCR entered into force, followed, in 2014, by the Third Optional Protocol to the CRC. Although not yet widely ratified, these optional protocols, alongside the optional protocols to CEDAW, the CRPD and CERD, give individuals and groups new avenues to complain about violations of their rights to health. For example, in 2019, sixteen children brought a claim against five states, arguing that the failure to address climate change violated, inter alia, their rights to health. While the CRC Committee declared the complaints inadmissible for failure to exhaust domestic remedies, it made several important observations, such as, that a state can be held responsible for failure to regulate carbon emissions that have extra territorial health impacts.[14] The Human Rights Committee has found that states should not deport individuals who face climate-induced conditions that violate their rights to life.[15] All decisions are available online, as well as the Committees' concluding observations to individual states.[16]

As will be explored in more detail in Chapter 5, the right to protection of health is, increasingly, being addressed by the European Committee of Social Rights of the Council of Europe. In addition, the ECtHR has ruled on a wide variety of health issues, on numerous occasions.

2.3. MEDICAL LAW, HEALTH LAW, MEDICAL ETHICS AND BIOETHICS, AND PATIENTS' RIGHTS

For the purposes of this study, it is worth briefly identifying the scope of the terms 'medical law', 'health law', 'medical ethics' and 'bioethics', and 'patients' rights'.

---

[12] UN Committee on Economic, Social and Cultural Rights (ICESCR Committee), General Comment No. 14 on the Right to the Highest Attainable Standard of Health, UN Doc. E/C.12/2000/4, 11 August 2000.

[13] Since July 2020, Ms. Tlaleng Mofokeng from South Africa has been the Special Rapporteur on the right to physical and mental health. Her focus is on non-discrimination in sexual and reproductive rights. See UN Doc. A/HRC/47/28, 7 April 2021, and https://www.ohchr.org/EN/Issues/Health/Pages/SRRightHealthIndex.aspx.

[14] Committee on the Rights of the Child, CRC/C/88/D/104/2019, CRC/C/88/D/105/2019, CRC/C/88/D/106/2019, CRC/C/88/D/107/2019, CRC/C/88/D/1058/2019, 8 October 2021.

[15] Human Rights Committee, Views adopted by the Committee under Art. 5(4) of the Optional Protocol, concerning communication no. 2728/2016, 23 September 2020.

[16] See https://juris.ohchr.org/ and https://uhri.ohchr.org/en/.

While 'medicine' is focused mainly on the individual, and often aimed at secondary and tertiary care, 'public health' is population-based, and largely preventive in its orientation (see Chapter 13). Related to this, some see 'medical law' and 'health law' as two distinct disciplines, whereby medical law is associated with issues such as medical doctors' duties, professional standards and autonomy, and medical negligence, while health law places more emphasis on prevention, the provision of healthcare (including healthcare insurance) and the rights of the patient. Others use the terms interchangeably, or use one of the two terms to refer to the field as a whole. Sometimes – and this is the approach taken in this book – 'medical law' is seen as a narrower dimension of 'health law', primarily focused on the legal and professional standards applying to healthcare practitioners and patients.[17] Furthermore, it is important to note that there is an increasing emphasis on the so-called underlying or social determinants of health: conditions that are decisive for people's health (see Chapters 7 and 13). Such conditions are considered to be essential components of the 'right to health', and they blur the line between medical law, health law and other forms of law, since they are intersectoral.

Medical ethics and bioethics serve as important sources of inspiration for health law. In medical ethics, reference is made to a system of moral principles that apply to the practice of medicine, and the term tends to be understood as being concerned with professional ethics. Bioethics, which is closely connected to medical ethics, is, generally, more concerned with ethical questions brought about by advances in biology and medicine. As such, bioethics can be broader than medical ethics, addressing the philosophy of science and issues of biotechnology, with a focus on the consequences for human beings. Given the substantive overlap between the two fields, the terms medical ethics and bioethics are used interchangeably in this study. For the purposes of this study, it is important to note that medical ethics and bioethics have, increasingly, come to incorporate rights-based approaches (see also Chapter 3).

Patients' rights are often considered to be an elaboration of human rights law in the field of healthcare (see Chapter 3). They are rooted in health law, and have been influenced by medical ethics, bioethics and human rights law.

---

[17] In the UK, the term 'medical law' is often still used, while it seems that, on the European Continent, there has been a shift towards the use of the term 'health law'. For the UK perspective, see J.K. Mason (ed.), *Mason and McCall Smith's Law and Medical Ethics*, 11th edition, Oxford: Oxford University Press, 2019 (which also focuses on 'health law'), and Shaun D. Pattinson, *Medical Law and Medical Ethics*, 5th edition, London: Sweet & Maxwell, 2017. For more on these distinctions, see, inter alia, Margaret Brazier and Nicola Glover, 'Does Medical Law Have a Future?' in David Hayton (ed.), *Law's Future*, Oxford: Hart, 2000, 371–88; see also Tamara K. Hervey and Jean V. McHale, *Health Law and the European Union*, Cambridge: Cambridge University Press, 2015, 13–17 and, e.g. the approach taken in the *European Journal of Health Law*, inter alia Sjef Gevers, 'Health Law in Europe: From the Present to the Future', *European Journal of Health Law* 15 (2008), 261–72.

Developments towards the creation of patients' rights started many centuries ago. An important landmark was the above-mentioned Nuremberg Code, which constitutes a set of ethical principles for human experimentation, formulated as a result of the subsequent Nuremberg Trials at the end of the Second World War. This document was followed by two documents adopted by the World Medical Association (WMA),[18] which focused on the role of the physician: a short 'Physician's Oath' in the Declaration of Geneva (1948), and a more elaborate document on the duties of doctors, in general, in the International Code of Medical Ethics (1949).[19] This short-lived phase of 'post-war idealism' was replaced by a phase of 'realism', during the Cold War era. During this era, politicians treated human rights as barriers to foreign policy, while research policy also shifted towards 'realism', for example with the introduction of a restricted informed consent in relation to experiments involving therapeutic benefit.[20]

Patients' rights were really placed on the agenda in the 1970s.[21] Gradually, a body of (bio)medical law came into existence, which further extended the focus on the individual, and on individual rights that had begun to be recognised in the aftermath of the Second World War. An important landmark in Europe was the adoption of the Convention on Human Rights and Biomedicine (Biomedicine Convention 1997), which addresses a wide range of biomedical issues, but also contains patients' rights and a general right to healthcare (see Chapter 3). Also worth mentioning is the EU Directive on patients' rights (2009), which is, to some extent, based on the Biomedicine Convention (see Chapter 6).

As will become clear in this book, 'human rights' and 'patients' rights' both play important roles in the area of 'health and human rights'. Patients' rights and human rights overlap to a considerable extent, and there is an increasing congruence between the two. However, although human rights have been a powerful source of inspiration for the development of patients' rights, it is important to recall that patients' rights have various roots, and, as such, they are not a mere branch of human rights law.

2.4. THE PUBLIC HEALTH MOVEMENT

In the 1980s, the public health movement started to pay attention to the specific links between health and human rights. The main impetus for this attention

---

[18] The WMA is an international non-governmental organisation representing physicians, founded in 1947.

[19] See http://ethics.iit.edu/ecodes/node/4676. WMA standards are accessible through www.wma.net.

[20] Robert Baker, 'Bioethics and Human Rights: A Historical Perspective' *Cambridge Quarterly of Healthcare Ethics* 10 (2001), 241–52, 245.

[21] Ibid.

came from the HIV/AIDS pandemic and the associated reproductive and sexual health concerns. According to Gruskin, these developments have been instrumental in clarifying the ways in which the concepts of health and rights connect with one another (see below in this section).[22]

The first global health and human rights strategy was launched in the late 1980s, addressing HIV/AIDS: the 'Global Programme on AIDS', directed by the late Jonathan Mann at the WHO.[23] The main motivation for taking a human rights approach to HIV/AIDS was because there was evidence that discrimination was undermining people's access to prevention and care programmes.[24] Gradually, a human rights approach to public health emerged, led by a number of influential scholars in this area, including Jonathan Mann, Lawrence Gostin, Sofia Gruskin and Daniel Tarantola.[25] By taking a human rights approach, the focus, in the public health movement, shifted from focusing merely on the health of society as a whole to a more integrated approach, where the health and human rights of individuals were balanced against the interests of society at large.[26]

By the end of 1994, the first issue of the *Health and Human Rights Journal*, in which the links between health and human rights were discussed, had been published by Harvard University Press. In one of the contributions to this issue, a three-part framework was proposed for considering linkages between health and human rights: (1) the notion that health policies, programmes and practices impact on human rights; (2) the understanding that human rights violations have health impacts; and (3) the notion that the protection of human rights and the protection of health are fundamentally linked.[27] This approach has been instrumental for the further development of this field, while the *Health and Human Rights Journal* continues to play an influential role in defining this field.[28]

---

[22]   Sofia Gruskin, Edward J. Mills and Daniel Tarantola, 'History, principles and practice of health and human rights', *The Lancet*, Vol. 370, 4 August 2007, pp. 449–55, 449. See also Sofia Gruskin, Edward J. Mills and Daniel Tarantola, 'History, Principles and Practice of Health and Human Rights', in Michael A. Grodin, Daniel Tarantola, George J. Annas and Sofia Gruskin (eds.), *Health and Human Rights in a Changing World*, New York and London: Routledge, Taylor and Francis Group, 2013, 32–39.

[23]   WHO, Global Strategy for the prevention and control of HIV/AIDS, Res. WHA40.26, World Health Assembly, 40th Sess., 1987.

[24]   Jonathan M. Mann and Daniel Tarantola, 'Responding to HIV/Aids: a historical perspective', *Health and Human Rights* 2 (1998), 5–8, at 5.

[25]   Sofia Gruskin, Edward J. Mills and Daniel Tarantola, 'History, principles and practice of health and human rights', *The Lancet*, Vol. 370, 4 August 2007, pp. 449–55, at 449.

[26]   For 'public health' developments in Europe, see the website of the European Public Health Organisation at www.eupha.org, which pays attention to issues like health disparities, but not from a human rights perspective. Furthermore, the European Public Health Alliance pays attention to the intersection between health and human rights: see www.epha.org.

[27]   Jonathan M. Mann, Lawrence Gostin, Sofia Gruskin, Troyen Brennan, Zita Lazzarini, and Harvey Fineberg, 'Health and Human Rights', *Health and Human Rights* 1(1) (1994) 6–23, at 12.

[28]   See https://www.hhrjournal.org/. Another journal that played an influential role was *BMC International Health and Human Rights* (which ceased publication in 2020).

In a related development, governmental and non-governmental organisations increasingly started to embed 'health and human rights' approaches in their strategies and policies. Such activities were undertaken by, inter alia, the WHO and civil society organisations, as well as by academic institutions.[29]

In recent years, new scholarly works have followed, including a recent book by Gostin and Meier, reflecting on the foundations of global health and human rights from various dimensions.[30] Extensive research has been conducted on the right to health[31] and the institutions underpinning it.[32] Meanwhile, a health and human rights approach has been applied to both long-established and emerging health concerns alike, such as mental health,[33] reproductive health,[34] infectious diseases[35] and noncommunicable diseases.[36]

---

[29] See, inter alia, the WHO's Health and Human Rights page, available at https://www.who.int/news-room/fact-sheets/detail/human-rights-and-health. Also worth consulting is the Global Health and Human Rights Database of the O'Neill Institute, available at https://oneill.law.georgetown.edu/projects/ghhr/. Relevant NGOs include Physicians for Human Rights, available at https://phr.org/, the International Federation of Health and Human Rights Organisations (IFHHRO), available at www.ifhhro.org, and, e.g. the 'Law and Health Initiative' of the Open Society Institute (OSI), available at https://www.opensocietyfoundations.org/publications/global-strategy-law-and-health-initiative.

[30] Benjamin Mason Meier and Lawrence O. Gostin (eds.), *Foundations of Global Health & Human Rights*, Oxford: Oxford University Press, 2020.

[31] John Tobin, *The Right to Health in International Law*, Oxford: Oxford University Press, 2012; Thérèse Murphy, 'Hardwired human rights: a health and human rights perspective on global health law' in Gian Luca Burci and Brigit Toebes (eds.), *Research Handbook on Global Health Law*, Cheltenham: Edward Elgar Publishing, 2018, 82–103.

[32] Benjamin Mason Meier and Lawrence O. Gostin, *Human Rights in Global Health: Rights-Based Governance for a Globalizing World*, Oxford: Oxford University Press, 2018; Benjamin Mason Meier and Lawrence O. Gostin (eds.), *Foundations of Global Health & Human Rights*, Oxford: Oxford University Press, 2020.

[33] Yana Litins'ka, *Assessing capacity to decide on medical treatment: On human rights and the use of medical knowledge in the laws of England, Russia and Sweden* (PhD thesis, 2018).

[34] E.g. Alicia Ely Yamin, 'The Politics of Knowledge Claims: Sexual and Reproductive Rights in the SDG Era', *Global Policy* 9 (2019), 52–60; Terry McGovern and Aziz Ahmed, 'Equity in Health: Sexual and Reproductive Health and Rights' in Benjamin Mason Meier and Lawrence O. Gostin (eds.), *Foundations of Global Health & Human Rights*, Oxford: Oxford University Press, 2020, 307–28; Lucia Berro Pizzarossa, *Abortion, health and gender stereotypes: a critical analysis of the Uruguayan and South African abortion laws through the lens of human rights*, Groningen: University of Groningen, 2019, available at https://pure.rug.nl/ws/portalfiles/portal/81811638/Complete_thesis.pdf; Janne Rothmar Herrmann, 'Applying the Right to Health to Reproductive Rights – The Case of Elective Egg Freezing', *European Human Rights Law Review* 2 (2021), 172–80; Cynthia L. Tach, Brigit Toebes and Juliana M.F. Feriato, 'Obstetric violence: a women's human and personality rights violation', *Revista Jurídica*, 1(58) (2020), 187–206.

[35] Benjamin Mason Meier, Dabney P. Evans and Alexandra Phelan, 'Rights-Based Approaches to Preventing, Detecting, and Responding to Infectious Disease' in Mark Eccleston-Turner and Iain Brassington (eds.), *Infectious Diseases in the New Millennium*, Springer, 2020.

[36] Céline E.J.L. Brassart Olsen, *The Intersection between International Public Health and Human Rights Law for Obesity Prevention: Synergies, Conflicts, or Parallelism* (PhD thesis, 2017); Amandine Garde, Joshua Curtis and Olivier De Schutter, *Ending Childhood Obesity – A Challenge*

All of these developments form an important basis for our analysis of the legal perspectives on 'health and human rights'. There is a growing understanding of the various and multiple legal interfaces between 'health' and 'human rights', and of the implications of this approach for legal research and practice. Notwithstanding these developments, many aspects remain under-studied, and could benefit from greater clarity. It remains important to clarify what we mean by 'health and human rights', from a legal perspective: how have international and national judicial bodies dealt with these interfaces? which human rights are relevant, and in what way? how do international human rights laws affect domestic (health) law?[37] how are patient rights and human rights intertwined? and what are the core topics in this field?[38] In short, what does the legal health and human rights discourse look like? In this work, we attempt to offer a systematic analysis of these questions.

3. THEORETICAL APPROACH

3.1. MAIN THEORETICAL QUESTIONS UNDERPINNING THIS RESEARCH

The starting point for health and human rights discourse is a set of health-related human rights that are recognised in various international and European human rights treaties. At the core of these health-related rights lies the 'right to health', which functions as a key right that connects to a set of other rights relevant to the protection and promotion of human health. These other rights include both civil and political rights, as well as economic, social and cultural rights, including the rights to life, privacy and family life, information, food, education, housing and the prohibition of torture. Hence, an important point of departure for this study is that all human rights are indivisible, interdependent and interrelated, as

---

at the Crossroads of International Economic and Human Rights Law, Edward Elgar, 2020; Marie E. Gispen and Brigit Toebes (eds.), Human Rights and Tobacco Control, Edward Elgar Publishing, 2020; Mette Hartlev, 'Stigmatisation as a public health tool against obesity – a health and human rights perspective', European Journal of Health Law 21(4) (2014) 365–86; Katharina Ó Cathaoir, A Children's Rights Perspective on Obesogenic Food Marketing (PhD thesis, Copenhagen: University of Copenhagen, 2017).

[37] E.g. Gillian McNaughton and Angela Duger, 'Translating International Law into Domestic Law, Policy, and Practice' in Benjamin Mason Meier and Lawrence O. Gostin (eds.), Foundations of Global Health & Human Rights, Oxford: Oxford University Press, 2020, 113–30.

[38] Regarding the intersections between human rights and bioethics/patients' rights, see Richard E. Ashcroft, 'Could Human Rights Supersede Bioethics?' Human Rights Law Review, 10(4) (2010), 639–60; and T.A. Faunce, 'Will international human rights subsume medical ethics? Intersections in the UNESCO Universal Bioethics Declaration', Journal of Medical Ethics 31 (2004) 173.

has been confirmed in various human rights forums.[39] Taking such an approach raises a number of intricate theoretical questions, as outlined below:

- What is the conceptual grounding of human rights law, and what is the rationale for using it, in a global and European context?
- What, more specifically, is the conceptual grounding of economic, social and cultural, or 'welfare' rights?
- What are the main principles or concepts underlying the area of 'health and human rights'?

3.2. CONCEPTUAL GROUNDING OF HUMAN RIGHTS LAW

As mentioned above, human rights have been laid down in a set of international treaties that were gradually adopted after the Second World War. Through these treaties, rights are guaranteed to individuals, and correlative duties fall upon states to guarantee those rights. Critics of human rights law have pointed at the lack of a conceptual grounding of human rights, in the way that they have been adopted since. They have questioned the origins and soundness of rights, in particular the economic and social or 'welfare' rights', and the collective rights.[40] This criticism allows us to critically assess our approach of taking human rights law as a starting point for assessing health issues in global, European and domestic legal settings.

At a fundamental level, such criticism goes against the idea that people can have rights unconditionally, simply by virtue of their humanity.[41] It is, in essence, a rebuttal of the idea that human rights derive from natural law.[42] Over the course of the past few decades, legal scholars have moved away from the idea that human rights should have a basis in natural law, and have sought out more practical bases.[43] Our study chooses to rely on such more practical theories of

---

[39] Art. 5 Vienna Declaration and Programme of Action (UN Doc. A/Conf.157/23), 12 July 1993 (World Conference on Human Rights, Vienna, 14–25 June 1993). For a critical analysis, see Ida Elisabeth Koch, *Human Rights as Indivisible Rights*, Leiden: Martinus Nijhoff Publishers, 2009, inter alia 2–3.

[40] One of the first critics of human rights was Jeremy Bentham, who argued that natural rights were 'nonsense upon stilts': Jeremy Bentham, *Anarchical Fallacies: Being an Examination of the Declaration of Rights Issued during the French Revolution* (1792); republished in *The Works of Jeremy Bentham* (1792), Vol. II, John Bowring (ed.), Edinburgh: William Tait, 1843, 501. His theory on 'legal positivism' was later refined by other scholars, including H.L.A. Hart.

[41] Amartya Sen, 'Elements of a Theory of Human Rights', *Philosophy & Public Affairs* 32(4) (2004), 315–56.

[42] Natural law: 'the law of nature; law as the emanation of the Divine providence and rooted in the nature and reason of man' (*Osborn's Concise Law Dictionary*, London: Sweet & Maxwell, 2005).

[43] See Ronald Dworkin's study, *Taking Rights Seriously*, Bath: Duckworth, 1977. See also Charles R. Beitz, *The Idea of Human Rights*, Oxford: Oxford University Press, 2009; and Amartya Sen, 'Elements of a Theory of Human Rights', *Philosophy & Public Affairs* 32(4) (2004), 315–56.

human rights. It will not look for a basis for human rights law in natural law or naturalist theories. Nor will it look for a basis for human rights in 'agreement theories', which conceptualise human rights as standards over which people from dissimilar cultures agree, and which argue that human rights express a 'common core' or an 'intercultural agreement'.[44] Rather, in line with the approach of the scholar Beitz,[45] it will look for the sources of human rights law in an *emergent practice* whereby human rights are increasingly being applied. In line with Beitz's approach, it will take, as a starting point, that a human rights practice is emerging globally and in Europe, reflecting, to some extent, a 'common global and European standard'.[46] We do observe that it is probably more feasible to expect a common standard in Europe, as a smaller and, therefore, more coherent 'jurisdiction'. We also assert that, while there are different ethical standpoints, rights can still be rights, as they have been recognised as legally binding entitlements.

In this work, we study human rights practices by conducting a thorough study of global and European human rights law in relation to health, at an institutional and at a state level. As such, to quote Beitz, we will attempt to 'grasp the concept of a human right as it occurs within an existing practice'.[47] Beitz defines human rights as:

> an emergent discursive practice consisting of a set of norms for the regulation of the conduct of governments and a range of actions open to various agents for which a government's failure to abide by these norms supplies reasons.[48]

As such, Beitz develops a model in which he distinguishes between two levels:

- governments as primary duty-holders under human rights law; and
- other 'agents' or institutions that address failures to comply with human rights by states.

As such, while states are the primary duty-holders under international human rights law, they are not the only entities that carry out this responsibility.[49] There are 'agents' outside the state that may take action when states fail to realise human rights. This justifies this book's emphasis on the UN human rights bodies,

---

44 Charles R. Beitz, *The Idea of Human Rights*, Oxford: Oxford University Press, 2009, 73–74. The study builds upon a study by John Rawls: *The Law of Peoples*, Cambridge, MA: Harvard University Press, 1999. In Beitz, ibid., 96–98.

45 Charles R. Beitz, *The Idea of Human Rights*, Oxford: Oxford University Press, 2009.

46 For a similar approach see Jack Donnelly, *Universal Human Rights in Theory and Practice*, 3rd edition, Ithaca, NY: Cornell University Press, 2013.

47 Charles R. Beitz, *The Idea of Human Rights*, Oxford: Oxford University Press, 2009, 102.

48 Ibid., 44.

49 Ibid., 114.

Council of Europe and the EU, as important 'agents' outside the state. The health and human rights practices of these institutions will be the starting point of our study (see Chapters 2 to 6). Where relevant, subsequent state practice will be discussed throughout the book (for example, in relation to euthanasia: see Chapter 11).

3.3. CONCEPTUAL GROUNDING AND ANALYSIS OF ECONOMIC, SOCIAL AND CULTURAL RIGHTS

A more specific criticism of human rights concerns the character of the so-called 'economic, social and cultural rights', also called 'second-generation rights' or 'welfare rights'. Critics have maintained that, given their presumed 'positive' or programmatic nature, these rights are 'costly' for governments, and interfere with a margin of appreciation that governments have, in relation to their social policies. Some authors have gone so far as to argue that they are not enforceable before a court of law.[50]

Under human rights law, governments are distinguished as the primary duty-holders for the achievement of human rights. As the entities that have ratified and become parties to the treaties, they have legal responsibilities to recognise and realise the rights of individuals. To clarify the character of the state duties, scholars have tried to specify the human rights obligations of state actors (and, increasingly, also of other duty-holders, including multinational corporations). In the 1980s, human rights scholar Asbjørn Eide presented a tripartite typology of state obligations, which is now well-established, and frequently used, in human rights law and practice. This approach takes, as a starting point, that inherent in *all* human rights are state obligations to:

- 'respect' the underlying interests;
- 'protect' the underlying interests against threats from non-state agents; and
- 'aid' or 'assist' those who are, non-voluntarily, victims of deprivation.[51]

This approach makes it clear that both positive and negative state undertakings may result from all human rights – economic, social and cultural, as well as civil and political – as both 'positive' and 'negative' obligations are inherent in all human rights ('respect' being a 'negative' obligation to refrain from action,

---

[50] Inter alia, E.W. Vierdag, 'The Legal Nature of the Rights Granted by the International Covenant on Economic, Social and Cultural Rights', *Netherlands Yearbook of International Law* 9 (1978), 69–105.

[51] Asbjørn Eide, UN Doc. E/CN.4/Sub.2/1987. For a similar analysis, see Henry Shue, *Basic Rights, Subsistence, Affluence and U.S. Foreign Policy*, New Jersey: Princeton, 1980.

with 'protect and fulfil' implying positive actions). For example, while a right to a fair trial may have positive or 'costly' implications for states (for example, the need to establish a legal system), so may a right to health imply negative duties (for example, not to harm individual health, and to ask for informed consent prior to treatment). As such, this approach argues in defence of the moral weight and legal grounding of economic, social and cultural rights. It rebuts the above-mentioned assertion that civil and political rights carry more weight, and are more readily enforceable before a court of law, than economic, social and cultural rights. This underlines the notion that all human rights are 'indivisible, interdependent and interrelated', as proclaimed by the Vienna Declaration and Programme of Action in 1993.[52]

However, the approach of the tripartite typology has also been criticised. Koch has argued that the approach is too rigid, as states' duties cannot always be easily classified into obligations to respect, protect or fulfil.[53] Given that the ECtHR is not concerned with fitting a certain obligation into a certain category, Koch suggests speaking, instead, of 'waves of duties' rather than specific obligations to respect, protect and fulfil (see Chapter 2).[54] This study will take a flexible approach towards the identification of states' duties, and will use the tripartite typology where it is considered useful to do so.

3.4. IDENTIFICATION OF MAIN CONCEPTS AND PRINCIPLES UNDERPINNING THIS STUDY

In Beitz's model, human rights are described as 'urgent individual interests', as opposed to 'universal' human interests that are necessarily shared by all human beings '[as] such'.[55] In relation to his identification of 'urgent interests', Beitz develops a scheme for identifying the strength of a human rights claim. He states that the interests protected must be *sufficiently important*, when reasonably regarded from the perspective of those protected; that it would be *advantageous*

---

[52] Vienna Declaration and Programme of Action, UN Doc. A/Conf. 157/23, 12 July 1993 (World Conference on Human Rights, Vienna, 14–25 June 1993).

[53] Ida Elisabeth Koch, *Human Rights as Indivisible Rights*, Leiden: Martinus Nijhoff Publishers, 2009, 14–28.

[54] Ibid.

[55] Charles R. Beitz, *The Idea of Human Rights*, Oxford: Oxford University Press, 2009, 73–74, 109. There is some similarity with Dworkin's study *Taking Rights Seriously*, which argued that rights have a dimension that rules do not: the dimension of 'weight and importance'. See Ronald Dworkin, *Taking Rights Seriously*, Bath: Duckworth, 1977. For a critical approach toward Beitz's model, see also John Tobin, *The Right to Health in International Law*, Oxford, 2012; Thérèse Murphy, 'Hardwired human rights: a health and human rights perspective on global health law' in Gian Luca Burci and Brigit Toebes (eds.), *Research Handbook on Global Health Law*, Cheltenham: Edward Elgar Publishing, 2018, 54–60.

to protect the underlying interest by means of legal policy instruments available to the state; and that a failure to protect this interest would be a *matter of international concern.*

Several such important interests or principles, which derive from human rights law, as well as from the area of patients' rights, play a role in this study. Important principles include (human) dignity, health, autonomy, integrity, privacy, confidentiality and non-discrimination (see also Chapter 3). In addition, the so-called 'AAAQ' – the notion that all necessary health services and determinants have to be available, accessible, acceptable and of good quality – plays an important role in this study (see Chapter 2). Lastly, in relation to human rights, the notions of 'participation' in the human rights and healthcare decision-making processes, and 'accountability' for human rights violations, are increasingly being mentioned.[56] This study identifies these principles as important interests that merit protection under health and human rights law.

The principle of *'(human) dignity'* is often referred to as the core principle underlying human rights law, and plays an important role in the area of patients' rights (see also Chapter 3).[57] The concept of human dignity has deep roots in theology, philosophy and anthropology.[58] Such analyses often go back to the philosophy of Immanuel Kant, who saw human dignity as being inviolable and unconditional. Kant's approach is often discussed when it comes to the distinction between human dignity and autonomy, and, as such, the question of whether persons unable to take autonomous actions possess dignity.[59] While, in Kant's view, dignity and autonomy were interrelated, others argue that dignity can be a broader concept, encompassing all human beings, including those who do not have the capacity for autonomous actions.[60] Based on this broader approach, Hartlev identifies three dimensions of dignity: (1) dignity in the way it relates

---

56   See various entries in Marlies Hesselman, Antenor Hallo de Wolf and Brigit Toebes (eds.), *Socio-Economic Human Rights for Essential Public Services Provision*, London/New York: Routledge (Taylor and Francis Group) – Human Rights Law Series, 2016.

57   Human dignity is mentioned in the Preamble to, and in Article 1 of, the Universal Declaration of Human Rights (UDHR), in the Preambles to the UN Covenants on Civil and Political Rights and Economic, Social and Cultural Rights (ICCPR and ICESCR), as well as in the Preamble to, and Article 1 of, the Charter of Fundamental Rights of the European Union (ECFR 2000). See also Articles 10 ICCPR and 13 ICESCR.

58   'Foreword' in Eckart Klein and David Kretzmer (eds.), *The Concept of Human Dignity in Human Rights Discourse*, The Hague/London/New York: Kluwer Law International, 2002, v–vii, vi.

59   See also António Barbosa da Silva, 'Autonomy, Dignity and Integrity in Health Care Ethics – A Moral Philosophical Perspective' in Henriette Sinding Aasen, Rune Halvorsen and António Barbosa da Silva (eds.), *Human Rights, Dignity and Autonomy in Health Care and Social Services: Nordic Perspectives*, Antwerp: Intersentia, 2009, 13–52.

60   See, in more detail, Mette Hartlev, 'Coercive Treatment and Human Dignity' in Henriette Sinding Aasen, Rune Halvorsen and António Barbosa da Silva (eds.), *Human Rights, Dignity and Autonomy in Health Care and Social Services: Nordic Perspectives*, Antwerp: Intersentia, 2009, 129–44, at 130. Hartlev refers to Ronald Dworkin's study *Life's Dominion*, London: Harper/Collins, 1993, 236.

to *human freedom and personal autonomy*; (2) dignity relating to the *intrinsic worth of every human being*; and (3) dignity associated with *conditions essential to living a life with dignity*.[61] The first two dimensions will be touched upon in Chapter 3. The third dimension refers to the conditions that are provided for, or accepted by, individuals. For example, this dimension is relevant with regard to cases where prisoners in need of medical care are not provided with access to healthcare services, or where psychiatric patients are kept in poor conditions, in institutions or hospitals. This notion will come to the fore in Chapter 11, which is concerned with death and dying, as this touches upon the notion of 'dying with dignity'. It also plays a role in Chapters 8 and 9, in which the concept of vulnerability is discussed, with a focus on migrants (Chapter 8), and the rights of disabled persons, in the field of health (Chapter 9).

The concept of *'health'* is, evidently, a key concept underpinning health and human rights. Sigerist, in his 1941 study, explained that the understanding of health had changed through the ages, varying from being seen as a merely physical concept, to a broader concept including mental or spiritual health.[62] Over the course of the twentieth century, the concept gradually developed into an even broader notion, including not only physical and mental health, but also social well-being.[63] Inspired by this broader understanding of health, the WHO Constitution (1946) defines health as 'a state of complete physical, mental and social well-being and not merely the absence of disease or infirmity'.[64] This definition reflects a great deal of post-war idealism, and great expectations for the role of medicine and public health, on the international plane. It has, therefore, often been criticised for being too broad, too absolute, difficult to apply, and for equating health with well-being.[65] Despite its shortcomings, the definition has merit for its recognition of the importance of mental and social well-being. This 'broad well-being definition'[66] provides an effective illustration that health is not

---

[61] Mette Hartlev, 'Coercive Treatment and Human Dignity' in Henriette Sinding Aasen, Rune Halvorsen and António Barbosa da Silva (eds.), *Human Rights, Dignity and Autonomy in Health Care and Social Services: Nordic Perspectives*, Antwerp: Intersentia, 2009, 129–44.

[62] Henry E. Sigerist, *Medicine and Human Welfare*, New Haven/London: Yale University Press/ Oxford University Press, 1941, 53–104. For example, during the Roman period the concept was extended to also include mental health and well-being: *'mens sana in corpore sano'*. Brigit C.A. Toebes, *The Right to Health as a Human Right in International Law*, Antwerp/Oxford: Intersentia/Hart, 1999, 21–23; Brigit Toebes, 'Health and Human Rights: in Search of the Legal Dimension', *Human Rights & International Legal Discourse*, 2(9) (2015), 212–41.

[63] Henry E. Sigerist, *Medicine and Human Welfare*, New Haven/London: Yale University Press/ Oxford University Press, 1941, 53–104, 100.

[64] Preamble to the Constitution of the World Health Organization (14 UNTS, pp. 186, Basic Documents WHO, 32nd ed., Geneva 1981), 22 July 1946, entry into force: 7 April 1948.

[65] See also Iris Bakx, *eHealth and Patients' Rights*, Rotterdam: Erasmus University, 2021, 33–43; Sridhar Venkatapuram, *Health Justice: An Argument from the Capabilities Approach*, Cambridge/Malden: Polity Press, 2011.

[66] Term used by Iris Bakx, *eHealth and Patients' Rights*, Rotterdam: Erasmus University, 2021, 33. Available at hdl.handle.net/1765/135629.

only about the absence of disease, and that our socio-economic circumstances are pivotal to our health.

More recently, there has been a gradual acceptance of a definition of health that is less absolute, and which focuses on the individual's capacity to function properly in society, and to pursue their life plans. Such attempts can be associated with the so-called 'capability approach', as developed by Amartya Sen, Martha Nussbaum and, specifically for health, by Sridhar Venkatapuram.[67] This approach harks back to the 'interests theory' identified above. Amartya Sen, in his above-referenced work on human capabilities, has asserted that the interests which ground human rights are those that enhance the capabilities of an individual.[68] The 'capability to be healthy' approach, which Venkatapuram proposes, recognises every human being's moral entitlement to a capability to be healthy.[69]

In line with these positions, Huber et al argue that the WHO's definition of health is increasingly problematic, inter alia because it would contribute to the medicalisation of society, and because the definition would be counterproductive by declaring the rising number of people with chronic diseases to be ill.[70] They propose a dynamic definition, based more on the resilience or capacity to cope and maintain one's integrity, equilibrium and sense of well-being. According to Huber et al, the definition should be 'the ability to adapt and self-manage'.[71] This approach emphasises the importance of focusing on what the individual requires for his or her participation in society. Yet the flip side of this approach is that much responsibility is placed on the individual for maintaining his or her health. Clearly, the debate about the definition of 'health' continues. As illustrated above, this is an important discussion, as the choice of a definition has implications for how we perceive health, and for how society seeks to protect it.

4. METHOD AND CHAPTER OUTLINE

This work consists of four parts. Part I analyses the foundations of health and human rights by offering a theoretical foundation (Chapter 1), and central concepts falling under the right to health (Chapter 2), and discussing relevant human rights and patients' rights principles (Chapter 3). Based on these chapters,

---

[67] Sridhar Venkatapuram, *Health Justice: An Argument from the Capabilities Approach*, Cambridge/Malden: Polity Press, 2011.

[68] Inter alia, Amartya Sen, *The Idea of Justice*, London: Penguin Books, 2009. See also Internet Encyclopaedia of Philosophy, Sen's capability approach, available at www.iep.utm.edu/sen-cap/.

[69] Sridhar Venkatapuram, *Health Justice: An Argument from the Capabilities Approach*, Cambridge/Malden: Polity Press, 2011, 113–15.

[70] Machteld Huber et al, 'How should we define health?', *BMJ* (2011) 343:d4163.

[71] Ibid., 2.

the reader will obtain an insight into the key notions and concepts underpinning this field, including the right to health as a central right in this discourse, and important principles, including, for example, non-discrimination.

Building on these chapters, Part II analyses the emerging health and human rights practice of the UN and European institutions. It takes an integrated approach to human rights, based on the notion that human rights are interdependent and interrelated. Chapter 4 offers a thorough analysis of the international human rights institutions that are addressing health and human rights, including the Human Rights Council and, in particular, the treaty-based bodies: the World Health Organization (WHO) and World Trade Organization (WTO).

Chapters 5 and 6 focus on the two main European institutions: the Council of Europe and the European Union (EU). Chapter 5 addresses the protection of human rights within the Council of Europe. With its 47 Member States, the Council of Europe has a broader regional scope of application than the EU, which has 27 Member States. States enjoy a certain liberty to opt in and out of the obligations derived from the human rights conventions. The Council of Europe can only 'shape' laws by means of treaties and legal decision-making, and states are free to ratify these (or not). Chapter 6 discusses the way in which the EU influences the area of health and human rights. The EU is a legal order *sui generis* that prevails over national law. And while the EU is not, primarily, a human rights organisation, it may still have implications, in a human rights and health context. For example, the possibility of seeking cross-border health services under EU law may have an impact on the right of access to healthcare services.

Subsequently, in Part III, the study focuses on a number of selected topics in the area of health and human rights. Over seven chapters, a range of key dimensions of the area of health and human rights are discussed. Chapter 7 covers access to health, and focuses, broadly, on how the principle of non-discrimination applies, in the context of accessing health-related services. Chapter 8 is related to this, as it discusses the principle of vulnerability, in the context of health and human rights. Rather than discussing a range of specific vulnerable groups, the chapter approaches the topic more holistically, looking at vulnerability as a whole, and using the position of migrants as a case study. Chapter 9 discusses the rights of persons with disabilities in the context of healthcare. The Convention on the Rights of Persons with Disabilities (CRPD) plays an important role in this chapter, demonstrating that both UN and European human rights laws are important for this vulnerable group in Europe, even though the global and European interpretations of the CRPD do not overlap completely. Chapter 10 focuses on the protection of reproductive rights, both globally and in a European setting. Attention is paid to a number of important underlying principles, as well as a number of important reproductive health issues, including family planning and abortion. Chapter 11 offers a broad and comprehensive analysis of a range of human rights questions related to death and dying, including end-of-life issues such as physician-assisted suicide and euthanasia. Chapter 12 is a new addition to our book, introducing digital healthcare technologies, and discussing their potential to contribute to the attainment of the right to health, while also reflecting on the risks that new technologies may pose to human rights. Chapter 13, lastly, is also a new chapter, identifying a range of human rights dimensions to public health. It discusses how public health and human rights can be balanced, and addresses infectious disease control and the reduction of noncommunicable diseases and health inequalities.

Part IV of this book consists of Chapter 14, which draws overall concluding observations on the scope and implications of the area of 'health and human rights', at a global and a European level.

CHAPTER 2

THE RIGHT TO HEALTH

Central Concepts

Brigit TOEBES and Katharina Ó CATHAOIR

1. INTRODUCTION

This chapter introduces the central concepts underpinning the right to health. Firstly, it describes the genesis of the international right to health, starting with the Constitution of the World Health Organization (WHO). Secondly, it introduces key elements of states' legal obligations for the right to health, as developed by the UN Committee on Economic, Social and Cultural Rights. Thirdly, it discusses how the right to health embraces a broad range of issues, including the determinants of health, and the Sustainable Development Goals. Fourthly, it introduces controversies associated with the right to health, including matters such as interpretation, justiciability and responsibility for the realisation of the right.

While the right to health is the focus of this chapter, it should be emphasised that it is not an umbrella right. Such an approach would make the right too broad and intangible, and would also deny the specific meanings of the other rights that have importance for health. The Committee on Economic, Social and Cultural Rights (ICESCR Committee) affirms that:

> the right to health is closely related to and dependent upon the realisation of other human rights, as contained in the International Bill of Rights, including the rights to food, housing, work, education, human dignity, life, non-discrimination, equality, the prohibition against torture, privacy, access to information, and the freedoms of association, assembly and movement.[1]

---

[1] UN Committee on Economic, Social and Cultural Rights (ICESCR Committee), General Comment No. 14: The Right to the Highest Attainable Standard of Health (Art. 12), E/C.12/2000/4, 2000, para. 3.

The right to health, therefore, does not stand alone, but is reinforced and supported by other rights; a wide range of human rights are connected to health. The Annex of this book gives an overview of the most important health-related rights.

The second section of this chapter introduces the right to health, outlining its genesis, legal sources and framing, at international and European levels. It then explores the central elements of the right to health, such as its definition, the AAAQ principles, the tripartite typology, progressive realisation, core obligations, the determinants of health, and the SDGs. Finally, it outlines some central controversies, such as justiciability of the right, obligations of non-state actors, and the ambiguities that remain. The concepts introduced in this chapter will be further analysed and applied to specific health challenges and topics throughout this book.

2. INTRODUCING THE RIGHT TO HEALTH

A right to health, or to healthcare, suggests that states bear responsibility for the health of their inhabitants. A sense of state responsibility, or at least community responsibility, for the health of the public has existed since the time of ancient civilisations. Public health concerns during earlier centuries were, however, mainly utilitarian in character. It was recognised that, without government intervention, serious public health problems, including the spread of infectious diseases, were likely to arise. Gradually, the concerns became geared more towards individual well-being, which eventually led to the recognition of health as a right in the various human rights instruments adopted after the Second World War.[2]

Currently, it is generally recognised that government intervention in the maintenance and promotion of public health is required to prevent health disparities and other threats to people's health. There is a general acceptance that the provision of healthcare cannot be left solely to private parties. Although private healthcare providers may provide good quality health-related services, they do not have an intrinsic interest in improving the health of the population as a whole, or of certain 'unprofitable' marginalised groups. It is, therefore, accepted that government intervention is required to prevent the selection of customers on the basis of, for example, health criteria, income, or geographic conditions.[3] Even countries where an individualist culture prevails, like the United States of America, recognise the unique role

---

[2]   B. Toebes, 'Right to Health and Health Care' in D.P. Forsythe (ed.), *Encyclopaedia of Human Rights*, Vol. I, Oxford: Oxford University Press, 2009, 365–76, 365.

[3]   Ibid., 365–66.

of the state in coordinating public health, regulating harmful products and governing health research.[4]

Government intervention is also often necessary because individuals are not always capable of fully safeguarding their own health, due to factors such as a shortage of financial resources, a lack of information, or impaired decision-making capacities. They may carry a certain personal responsibility for their own health, but governments have to provide a health infrastructure, and create conditions under which the availability, accessibility, and quality of health services are guaranteed.[5]

While health may be an important social good, the full realisation of the right to health remains an unfulfilled promise. Health as a human right raises concerns regarding the distribution of health services and personal responsibility. As such, the 'right to health' is a controversial right that has led to debate. It can be difficult to agree on a definition of 'health', and it is challenging to indicate the boundaries of entitlements to health-related services.[6] Since the 1980s, however, much progress has been made regarding the scope of the right to health, with a growing body of case law supporting an individual right to health (see Chapters 4 and 5). At the same time, the appropriate role of the state in furthering the public's health, as well as the scope of legitimate limitations on the right, remain contentious issues. Since the 2008 financial crisis, governments around the world have, often through austerity measures, limited public benefits and services, in some cases with devastating health impacts.[7] In response to the COVID-19 pandemic, governments prioritised human health to an unprecedented degree, without clarifying when limitations, for example, on routine treatments violate the right to health.[8]

The Constitution of the WHO, adopted in 1946, was the first legal instrument to lay down a right to health.[9] The Preamble to the Constitution, which defines

---

[4]   L.O. Gostin and L.F. Wiley, *Public Health Law: Power, Duty, Restraint*, 3rd ed., Oakland: University of California Press, 2016.

[5]   B. Toebes, 'Right to Health and Health Care' in D.P. Forsythe (ed.), *Encyclopaedia of Human Rights*, Vol. I, Oxford: Oxford University Press, 2009, 365–76, 366.

[6]   Ibid.

[7]   Amnesty International, *Wrong Prescription: The Impact of Austerity Measures On The Right To Health In Spain*, 2018, available at www.amnesty.org/en/documents/eur41/8136/2018/en/; Trade Union Advisory Committee (TUAC), *OECD brief on COVID-19 health policy responses and a dire reminder of the need for well-funded universal healthcare*, 2020, available at https://tuac.org/news/oecd-brief-on-covid-19-health-policy-responses-and-a-dire-reminder-of-the-need-for-well-funded-universal-healthcare/.

[8]   K. Ó Cathaoir, 'Human rights in times of pandemics: Necessity and proportionality' in M. Kjaerum, M.F. Davis and A. Lyons (eds.), *COVID-19 and Human Rights*, Oxon: Routledge, 2021.

[9]   World Health Organization (WHO), Constitution of the World Health Organization, New York, 22 July 1946, entry into force: 7 April 1948. See Chapter 4 of this book, for an introduction to the WHO.

'health' and recognises health as a right, was a breakthrough in the field of international health and human rights law. It created an important point of departure for the further elaboration of a right to health in human rights documents. It is also interesting that this text defines both 'health' and 'health as a right' (for a definition of the term 'health', see Chapter 1). The text of the preamble defines 'health' as 'a state of complete physical, mental and social well-being and not merely the absence of disease'. It is striking that this provision contains an absolute and broad definition of health, which not only embraces physical, but also mental and social, well-being. Furthermore, as mentioned, the preamble recognises health as an individual human right. In this connection, the text refers to the relationship between health problems and the gaps in development between different countries, to the importance of the healthy development of the child, and to the importance of the informed opinion and active cooperation of the public. This approach was not met with universal approval: for example, the American Medical Association stressed that the provision of healthcare services should be considered a concern of the individual nation, rather than of an international health organisation.[10]

In spite of such objections, the text was adopted, and has clearly inspired right to health provisions that were drafted at a later stage, in particular Article 12 of the UN International Covenant on Economic, Social and Cultural Rights (ICESCR) (see Chapter 4 for an analysis of the ICESCR Committee). Article 12 ICESCR contains a provision along the lines of the WHO Constitution. This provision is broader than the previously adopted Article 25 of the Universal Declaration of Human Rights (UDHR 1948), which embeds a right to health into a provision on a right to an adequate standard of living.[11]

An issue that was heavily debated during the drafting process of Article 12 ICESCR was the question of whether the provision should contain a definition of health. Several drafters objected to the insertion of such a definition on the basis of the argument that such a definition is not appropriate in a legal instrument. The final text of Article 12 ICESCR, therefore, does not contain a definition of health.[12] What has not been deserted is the broad approach to health: the notion that health is not merely the 'absence of disease'. Although the concept of 'social well-being' was deleted from the text of Article 12 ICESCR during the drafting process, the steps mentioned in the Article reflect the interpretation of

---

[10] B. Toebes, *The Right to Health as a Human Right in International Law*, Antwerp/Oxford: Intersentia/Hart, 1999, 32.

[11] Ibid., 43.

[12] Art. 10 of the 'Protocol of San Salvador (Additional Protocol to the American Convention on Human Rights 1999)', on the right to health, was the first human rights provision to explicitly use the terms 'right to health' and 'physical, mental and social well-being', as per the WHO Constitution.

health as a broad concept, in referring also to environmental hygiene, preventive healthcare and occupational diseases.[13]

Subsequently, the right to health was enshrined in Article 12 of the Convention on the Elimination of All Forms of Discrimination Against Women (CEDAW 1979) and Article 24 of the Convention of the Rights of the Child (CRC 1989). Article 12 CEDAW focuses, primarily, on access to healthcare for women, and on providing women with additional protection to eliminate discrimination. Article 24 CRC covers the right to health of children, referring not only to healthcare facilities, but also to adequate food, drinking water, and the prohibition of harmful traditional practices. Article 24 and its ensuing general comment purport to restate the principles of the WHO Constitution, and of Article 12 ICESCR, with respect to children.[14]

In addition to the above-mentioned provisions, a number of other UN Treaties and Declarations refer to a right to health. Some of these provisions focus on equal access to medical services. For example, the Convention on the Protection of the Rights of All Migrant Workers and Members of their Families (MWC 1990) emphasises equal access to medical care for migrant workers.[15] Article 5(e)(iv) of the Convention on the Elimination of All Forms of Racial Discrimination (CERD 1965) is slightly more elaborate, in that it provides, in general terms, that States Parties are to prohibit and eliminate racial discrimination in the enjoyment of public health, medical care, social security and social services. Also worth mentioning are the Standard Minimum Rules for the Treatment of Prisoners (1957), revised in 2015, and named 'the Mandela Rules', which lay down a number of principles for the treatment of sick prisoners.[16] Finally, the Conventions of the ILO contain numerous references to specific areas of health: specifically, occupational health. Different in character is Article 25 of ILO Convention No. 169 (1989), which explicitly recognises a right to health of indigenous and tribal peoples. Lastly, the Convention on the Rights of Persons with Disabilities (CRPD 2006), contains several important provisions empowering the health of disabled persons, including Article 25 (see also Chapter 9).

---

[13]   B. Toebes, *The Right to Health as a Human Right in International Law*, Antwerp/Oxford: Intersentia/Hart, 1999, 40–52.

[14]   In its General Comment on the Right to Health, the CRC Committee acknowledged that the WHO's definition underpins its approach to public health: CRC Committee, General Comment No. 15: The Right of the Child to the Enjoyment of the Highest Attainable Standard of Health (CRC/C/GC/15) (2013), para. 4.

[15]   It should be noted that the Migrant Workers Convention only grants an equal right to healthcare services to *documented* migrant workers, while *all* migrant workers have a right to emergency medical care.

[16]   UN General Assembly, Resolution adopted by the General Assembly on 17 December 2015, A/RES/70/175.

In addition to such global provisions, the right to health is set out in a number of regional human rights instruments. Given the scope of this book, we will focus on the relevant European provisions.[17] The European Social Charter (ESC), adopted in 1951 and revised in 1996, contains a 'right to protection of health', in Article 11. An initial draft, which was similar in several ways to Article 12 ICESCR, was eventually narrowed, after several states objected to such a far-reaching text. The provision tries to bring the role of governments into perspective by referring to individual responsibility in matters of health, and to cooperation with public and private organisations. The text does not refer to child health and environmental health, yet these matters are raised within the framework of the reporting procedure.[18] The 1996 amendment of this Article, within the context of the revision of the European Social Charter (revised ESH), added the prevention of accidents to the state undertaking to prevent, as far as possible, epidemic, endemic and other diseases.

The Charter of Fundamental Rights of the European Union (ECFR 2000) contains, in Article 35, a provision on healthcare. The first sentence of this provision recognises an individual *right* to preventive as well as curative healthcare, albeit under the conditions established by national laws and practices. The second sentence expresses a 'mainstreaming' state obligation of health protection, by providing that a high level of human health protection has to be ensured in the definition and implementation of all Union policies and activities (see also Chapters 4 and 6).

The right to health is also firmly embedded in constitutional law. At least 60 per cent of the world's constitutions contain provisions protecting a right to health.[19] A distinction can be made between common law and civil law countries. Constitutions of common law countries, generally, do not have an

---

[17] Other regional right to health provisions: the American Declaration of the Rights and Duties of Man (ADHR 1948) contains a general provision in Art. XI that has similarities with Art. 25 of the UDHR; the Protocol of San Salvador (1988), which forms an Additional Protocol to the American Convention on Human Rights (ACHR), contains a right to health in Art. 10, and a right to a healthy environment in Art. 11; the African Charter on Human and Peoples' Rights (1981) contains a right to health in Art. 16; the Universal Islamic Declaration of Human Rights (adopted by the Islamic Council in 1981) mentions the right to medical care as part of the right to social security (Art. XVIII). The Arab Charter on Human Rights (which entered into force in 2008 after several members of the League of Arab States ratified it) contains a right to health in Art. 39, as well as several other references to health.

[18] B. Toebes, *The Right to Health as a Human Right in International Law*, Antwerp/Oxford: Intersentia/Hart, 1999, 63–69.

[19] J. Heymann, A. Sprague and A. Raub, *Advancing Equality: How Constitutional Rights Can Make a Difference Worldwide*, Oakland: University of California Press, 2020, 232.

explicit right to health.[20] Many civil law countries, on the other hand, have either an explicit or implicit right to health in their constitutions. The wording, and level of action required from states, in these provisions varies.[21] The Constitution of the Netherlands, for example, does not contain an individual right to health, but is mostly 'programmatic' in nature, defining the duty of the Dutch government to take steps to promote the health of the population.[22] More explicit recognitions of a right to health can be found in the constitutions of the former socialist countries of Central and Eastern Europe. The Charter of Fundamental Rights and Basic Freedoms of the Czech Republic, for example, contains the following provision in Article 31:

> Everyone has the right to the protection of his health. Citizens shall have the right, on the basis of public insurance, to free medical care and to medical aids under conditions provided for by law.[23]

This provision contains an explicit right to protection of health, which is made subject to public insurance and national legal conditions.

The inclusion of the right to health in national constitutions copper-fastens states' legal duties to use law and policy to pursue good health.[24] However, as will be explored below, constitutional protection of the right to health does not guarantee that states will fully respect their obligations. These provisions are sometimes framed as aspirations, and too vague to use as a basis for successful constitutional claims. Even where the right to health has been litigated, questions have been raised as to whether structural change has been achieved.[25] Still, we consider constitutional protection to be a significant legal step in the protection of the right to health that can be used to focus government attention.

---

[20]   Yet, a reference to health is sometimes made in the preamble to the constitution, or couched in terms of a state policy. An example is India, where a state duty to improve health is stipulated as one of the 'Directive Principles of State Policy'. Interestingly, this provision has been used by the Indian Supreme Court to broaden the scope of the right to life in the Indian Constitution, so as to give it a health dimension. See also B. Toebes, *The Right to Health as a Human Right in International Law*, Antwerp/Oxford: Intersentia/Hart, 1999, 79–84.

[21]   For a comprehensive overview, see D. Sześcilow, 'Is the Equity of Access to Healthcare a European Constitutional Standard? A Comparative Review', *European Journal of Health Law* 24 (2017), 445–62.

[22]   The Constitution of the Kingdom of the Netherlands, 2008, Art. 22-1.

[23]   Charter of Fundamental Rights and Basic Freedoms, 1993, which forms an integral part of the Constitution of the Czech Republic. See, inter alia, www.wipo.int/wipolex/en/details.jsp?id=7330.

[24]   D. Sześcilow, 'Is the Equity of Access to Healthcare a European Constitutional Standard? A Comparative Review', *European Journal of Health Law* 24 (2017), 445–62.

[25]   For a summary of these issues, see A.E. Yamin, 'Editorial: Special Issue on Health Rights Litigation Promoting Equity in Health: What Role for Courts?', *Health and Human Rights Journal* 16(2) (2014), 1–9.

3. ELEMENTS OF THE RIGHT TO HEALTH

An important landmark with respect to clarifying the meaning of the right to health concerned the adoption of General Comment No. 14 on the right to the highest attainable standard of health in Article 12 ICESCR (General Comment No. 14).[26] This document was adopted in 2000 by the ICESCR Committee, after consultation with non-governmental organisations (NGOs) and the WHO. A general comment is a document drawn up by a UN treaty monitoring body that explains the meaning and implications of a certain aspect of the treaty concerned, and that seeks to assist States Parties to fulfil their reporting obligations. While general comments are not, strictly speaking, legally binding (they are 'soft law instruments'), general comments are increasingly referred to in legal scholarship and practice (see, further, Chapter 4).[27] As such, they can be considered as influential and authoritative documents that can surpass the status of mere soft law (see, further Chapter 4).

General Comment No. 14 reflects the debate about the right to health that took place in the years leading up to its adoption. It is an influential document that gives an authoritative explanation of the meaning and implications of the right to health. The general comment tempers the somewhat absolute wording of the term 'right to health' by stating that the right to health is not a right to be healthy.[28] As such, it confirms the notion expressed by Leary: that the right to health is to be used as a 'shorthand expression' that refers to the more elaborate treaty texts.[29] At the international level, therefore, the term 'right to health' is used instead of the narrower term 'right to healthcare'. The term 'right to healthcare' is, however, suitable, and more specific, where it concerns discussions regarding access to health*care* services.[30]

Furthermore, it is important to note that General Comment No. 14 takes a broad approach to the definition of health as a human right. It recognises that the right to health in Article 12 ICESCR is not confined to the right to health*care*, but extends to the underlying or social determinants of health, such as food and nutrition, housing, access to safe and potable water and adequate sanitation, safe

---

[26]   UN Committee on Economic, Social and Cultural Rights (ICESCR Committee), General Comment No. 14: The Right to the Highest Attainable Standard of Health (Art. 12), E/C.12/2000/4, 2000 (hereinafter referred to, in this chapter, as General Comment No. 14).

[27]   See, e.g. *Laxmi Mandal v. Deen Dayal Harinagar Hospital & Ors*, WP(C) Nos. 8853 of 2008, and 10700 of 2009 (2010) (India, High Court of Delhi, Judgment 4 June 2010), para. 23; Australian Government, Attorney-General's Department, *Right to health – Public sector guidance sheet*, available at www.ag.gov.au/rights-and-protections/human-rights-and-anti-discrimination/human-rights-scrutiny/public-sector-guidance-sheets/right-health.

[28]   General Comment No. 14, para. 8.

[29]   V.A. Leary, 'Implications of a Right to Health' in K.E. Mahoney and P. Mahoney (eds.), *Human Rights in the Twenty-First Century: A Global Challenge*, Kluwer, 1993, 481–93.

[30]   E.g. Y. Zhang, *Advancing the Right to Health Care in China*, Cambridge: Intersentia, 2019.

and healthy working conditions, and a healthy environment.[31] This reinforces the notion that underlying (or social) determinants of health are at least as important for people's health as access to healthcare services. Research demonstrates that the circumstances under which people live and work are decisive for their health and well-being.[32] It is increasingly argued that the growing health inequalities (that also exist in Europe) should be addressed by trying to improve people's living conditions and their lifestyles (see also Chapter 13 of this book).[33]

As was mentioned, the right to health covers access to healthcare services, as well as a number of determinants of health. Access to such services is formulated in the form of state duties or undertakings. The second paragraph of Article 12 ICESCR mentions the following, broadly formulated, state undertakings:

- the provision for the reduction of the stillbirth rate, and of infant mortality, and for the healthy development of the child;
- the improvement of all aspects of environmental and industrial hygiene;
- the prevention, treatment and control of epidemic, endemic, occupational and other diseases;
- the creation of conditions which would assure, to all, medical service and medical attention, in the event of sickness.

While the wording of this text may be somewhat outdated, the list of undertakings, as a whole, is forward-looking and comprehensive. Along similar lines, Article 11 (Revised) ESC contains the following state undertakings:

- to remove, as far as possible, the causes of ill health;
- to provide advisory and educational facilities for the promotion of health and the encouragement of individual responsibility in matters of health;
- to prevent, as far as possible, epidemic, endemic and other diseases, as well as accidents.

Although both provisions focus on different health-related issues, it is clear that the range of state undertakings goes further than providing mere healthcare services. As will be discussed further in Chapter 5, the practice of the European Committee of Social Rights (ECSR) confirms this broad approach, focusing on a wide range of health-related issues that go beyond the mere 'provision of

---

[31] General Comment No. 14, para. 4.
[32] J.P. Mackenbach et al., 'Socioeconomic Inequalities in Health in 22 European Countries', *The New England Journal of Medicine* 385 (2008), 2468–481. See also Chapter 13 of this volume.
[33] E.g. World Health Organization (WHO), Commission on Social Determinants of Health (2008), *Closing the gap in a generation: health equity through action on the social determinants of health – Final report of the commission on social determinants of health*, available at https://apps.who.int/iris/handle/10665/43943.

healthcare services'. Attention is paid, inter alia, to the reduction of environmental risks, food safety, health education in schools, measures to combat smoking, tobacco control, and accidents.[34]

3.1. INTERSECTION WITH THE RIGHT TO LIFE

The right to health is intrinsically intertwined with the right to life. While a core aspect of the right to life is the *deprivation* of life,[35] the scope of the right to life has gradually expanded, and courts now embrace a broader set of issues, several of which have clear connections to health and the sphere of medical care.

The right to life embraces positive obligations to take measures to *protect* life, not confined to patients receiving healthcare in hospitals or other health institutions. This means, inter alia, that states must adopt criminal legislation to punish individuals who deprive others of their right to life, and must establish a police force and take other measures to maintain law and order.[36] But it may also embrace positive measures to offer protection against serious health and environmental problems, and to offer essential health services. The UN Human Rights Committee (HRC) offers a broad interpretation, in its most recent General Comment on the right to life (2019), by claiming that 'the duty to protect life also implies that States parties should take appropriate measures to address the general conditions in society that may give rise to direct threats to life or prevent individuals from enjoying their right to life with dignity'.[37] Measures called for include access to essential goods, services and amenities such as food, water, shelter, healthcare, electricity and sanitation, as well as the 'bolstering of effective emergency health services', and 'improving access to medical examinations and treatments designed to reduce maternal and infant mortality'.[38]

As will also be illustrated in Chapter 5, the ECtHR takes an approach comparable to the HRC. In *Cyprus v. Turkey*, the ECtHR recognised that 'an issue may arise under Article 2 of the Convention where it is shown that the authorities put an individual's life at risk through the denial of healthcare which they have made available to the population generally'.[39] In *Aydoğdu v. Turkey*, the Court found that structural deficiencies in the Turkish health system, which

---

[34]   See, further, C. Lougarre, 'What Does the Right to Health Mean?: The Interpretation of Art. 11 of the European Social Charter by the European Committee of Social Rights', *Netherlands Quarterly of Human Rights* 33 (2015), 326–54.

[35]   See Art. 2 ECHR, Art. 6 ICCPR.

[36]   ECtHR 10 October 2000, *Akkoc v. Turkey*, nos. 22947/93 and 22948/93 (in which the Court held that the right to life had been violated by the respondent state, as it had not taken sufficient steps to protect the applicant's (Kurdish) husband from being murdered).

[37]   UN Human Rights Committee, General Comment No. 36, Art. 6: right to life, CCPR/C/GC/36, adopted 3 September 2019, para. 2.

[38]   Ibid.

[39]   ECtHR 10 May 2001, *Cyprus v. Turkey*, no. 25781/94, para. 219.

led to the death of a newborn, violated the right to life.[40] The 'protection of life' also embraces questions surrounding hunger strikes, and refusal of life-saving treatment. Furthermore, the protection of life may entail protection against environmental health threats, such as in the case of *Öneryildiz v. Turkey*, where a methane explosion at a rubbish tip caused the death of 39 slum dwellers.[41]

Altogether, when it comes to the duty to protect life, the right to life clearly has a health-related dimension, and, in this regard, it connects and overlaps with aspects of the right to health. Furthermore, the right to life is recognised in the ECHR and, thereby, subject to the Court's jurisdiction. As we will see below, the right to health offers more comprehensive standards and commitments, however.

3.2. GUIDING PRINCIPLES OF THE RIGHT TO HEALTH

General Comment No. 14 draws on the 'AAAQ' principles, as part of its general framework for the right to health (paragraph 12), as well as in its general comments on the right to food, housing, and education. The principles relate not only to healthcare services, but to the broad range of 'functioning public health and healthcare facilities, goods and services'.[42]

They can be useful for assessing health-related rights in a policy framework, for example, or for analysing the impact of planned healthcare commercialisation trends. Countries could use this framework for so-called 'human rights impact assessments' of planned healthcare reforms.[43] The Scottish public health agency lists the principles on its website, for example, as important aspects of the right to health.[44] The WHO, as well as civil society and academics, also draw on the AAAQ principles as a human rights standard.[45]

---

[40]   ECtHR 30 August 2016, *Aydoğdu v. Turkey*, no. 40448/06.

[41]   ECtHR 30 November 2004, *Öneryildiz v. Turkey* (GC), no. 48939/99.

[42]   General Comment No. 14, para. 12. See also UN Committee on Economic, Social and Cultural Rights (ICESCR Committee), General Comment No. 22 on the right to sexual and reproductive health, UN Doc. E/C12/GC/22, 2 May 2016, which analyses the AAAQ in relation to sexual and reproductive health (paras. 11–21).

[43]   In this regard, see, e.g. B. Toebes, 'Taking a human rights approach to health care commercialization' in P.A. Cholewka and M.M. Motlagh (eds.), *Health Capital and Sustainable Socioeconomic Development*, New York: Taylor & Francis, 2008, 441–59.

[44]   Public Health Scotland, Improving health, *The right to health*, 2021, available at www.healthscotland.scot/health-inequalities/the-right-to-health/overview-of-the-right-to-health.

[45]   World Health Organization (WHO), *Sexual health, human rights and the law* (2015), available at https://apps.who.int/iris/bitstream/handle/10665/175556/9789241564984_eng.pdf?sequence=1; The Danish Institute for Human Rights (2014), *The AAAQ Framework and the Right to Water – international indicators*, available at https://www.humanrights.dk/publications/aaaq-framework-right-water-international-indicators; J. Shrestha-Ranjit, D. Payne, J. Koziol-McLain, I. Crezee and E. Manias, 'Availability, Accessibility, Acceptability, and Quality of Interpreting Services to Refugee Women in New Zealand', *Qualitative Health Research* 30 (2020), 1697–709.

The AAAQ principles, as they apply to health, are as follows:

- *Availability* of health-related services requires that 'functioning public health and healthcare facilities, goods and services, as well as programmes, are available in sufficient quantity within the State party'.
- *Accessibility* implies that 'health facilities, goods and services have to be accessible to everyone without discrimination, within the jurisdiction of the State party'. According to the general comment, accessibility has four overlapping dimensions:
  (1) *non-discrimination*: 'health facilities, goods and services must be accessible to all, especially the most vulnerable or marginalized sections of the population, in law and in fact, without discrimination on any of the prohibited grounds';
  (2) *physical accessibility*: 'health facilities, goods and services must be within safe physical reach for all sections of the population, especially vulnerable or marginalized groups, such as ethnic minorities and indigenous populations, women, children, adolescents, older persons, persons with disabilities and persons with HIV/AIDS';
  (3) *economic accessibility*: 'health facilities, goods and services must be affordable for all. Payment for healthcare services, as well as services related to the underlying determinants of health, has to be based on the principle of equity, ensuring that these services, whether privately or publicly provided, are affordable for all, including socially disadvantaged groups'; and
  (4) *information accessibility*: 'the right to seek, receive and impart information and ideas concerning health issues'. This undertaking embraces the duty to provide information about community health problems (for example, epidemics).
- *Acceptability* requires that 'all health facilities, goods and services are respectful of medical ethics and culturally appropriate, i.e. respectful of the culture of individuals, minorities, peoples and communities, sensitive to gender and life-cycle requirements, as well as being designed to respect confidentiality and improve the health status of those concerned'.
- *Quality* implies that 'health facilities, goods and services are scientifically and medically appropriate and of good quality'. This requires, inter alia, 'skilled medical personnel, scientifically approved and unexpired drugs and hospital equipment, safe and potable water, and adequate sanitation'.

The principles of 'information accessibility' and 'acceptability' are specifically relevant to the patient–doctor relationship, and are also addressed (albeit in a slightly different context) in Chapter 3. Two further principles are also accepted as part of the right to health: accountability and participation (and, as such, one could refer to a broader set of principles which could be abbreviated to 'AAAQ-AP'):

- *Accountability*[46] has been described by Potts as a broad process that requires governments to show, explain and justify how they have discharged their obligations regarding the right to health. An effective accountability process comprises the following essential elements, according to Potts: monitoring, accountability mechanisms, remedies and participation.[47] Monitoring is aimed at providing governments with the information that they need to create transparent health policies, as well as providing rights-holders with essential health-related information.[48] 'Accountability mechanisms' can be judicial or quasi-judicial (for example, a health ombudsman or other independent complaint mechanism), as well as administrative, political or social in character.[49] States should establish supervisory bodies that monitor the actions and decisions of all actors in the health sector, be they public or private actors, ranging from hospitals to health equipment providers, and, where necessary, impose sanctions upon them.
- *Participation* requires that the public has a say in important decisions concerning the health sector, for example the decision to privatise or decentralise (parts of) the health sector. States should ensure political participation in decision-making regarding the organisation of the health sector.[50] Political participation is not only realised through a democratic system of elections, but also by providing for public consultation on planned health sector reform.[51] The public and/or civil society can also be actively included in all stages of the budget cycle for the health sector. Public budget hearings can be held at the local level, to involve citizens in the way that public services are delivered.[52]

---

[46]   H. Potts, *Accountability and the Right to the Highest Attainable Standard of Health*, Human Rights Centre, University of Essex, available at http://repository.essex.ac.uk/9717/1/ accountability-right-highest-attainable-standard-health.pdf. See also M. Hesselman, A. Hallo de Wolf and B. Toebes, 'Introduction and Conclusions' in M. Hesselman, A. Hallo de Wolf and B. Toebes, *Socio-Economic Human Rights for Essential Public Services Provision*, London/New York: Routledge (Taylor and Francis Group), 2016, 1–20 and 299–327; and Y. Zhang, *Advancing the Right to Health Care in China*, Cambridge: Intersentia, 2019.

[47]   H. Potts, *Accountability and the Right to the Highest Attainable Standard of Health*, Human Rights Centre, University of Essex, available at http://repository.essex.ac.uk/9717/1/accountability-right-highest-attainable-standard-health.pdf, 13–17.

[48]   Ibid.

[49]   Ibid., 17–27.

[50]   H. Potts and P. Hunt, *Participation and the Right to the Highest Attainable Standard of Health*, Colchester: Human Rights Centre, University of Essex, 2008, available at http://repository. essex.ac.uk/9714/.

[51]   UN High Commissioner for Human Rights, *Report on universal health coverage and human rights*, E/2019/52, 2019, paras. 43–44, available at www.ohchr.org/EN/Issues/ESCR/Pages/ UniversalHealthCoverage.aspx.

[52]   Office of the High Commissioner and International Budget Partnership, *Realizing human rights through government budgets*, UN Human Rights, HR/PUB/17/3, 2017, available at www.ohchr.org/Documents/Publications/RealizingHRThroughGovernmentBudgets.pdf.

That is not to imply that participation equates with consensus. As discussed in section 2.1 above, individuals often disagree as to the precise role that the state should play in health, i.e. whether the state should regulate, or allow market forces to make determinations. Furthermore, health raises moral issues: for example, abortion and assisted suicide may prompt opposition. Participation, therefore, promotes inclusion and discussion, particularly among affected groups, but does not mean that health rights or obligations may be violated because of the will of the majority.

Finally, the Convention on Human Rights and Biomedicine (Biomedicine Convention – see, further, Chapter 3) also formulates a duty on the part of Member States to provide 'equitable access to health care of appropriate quality'.[53] The terms 'equitable access' and 'appropriate quality' are comparable to the principles formulated under the 'AAAQ' in General Comment No. 14, as discussed further, below.

3.3. LEGAL OBLIGATIONS

3.3.1. Respect, protect, fulfil

As a legal human right, the right to health imposes binding obligations on states (every state has ratified at least one treaty that recognises the right to health). General Comment No. 14 explains that the right to health, like all human rights, imposes three types or levels of obligations on States Parties: the obligations 'to respect', 'to protect' and 'to fulfil'. The typology seeks to transcend the entrenched distinction between negative and positive rights and, instead, proposes a common approach to human rights duties.

This so-called 'tripartite typology of state obligations' was first introduced into the human rights debate by Asbjørn Eide in 1981, later refined by several other scholars, and, subsequently, introduced into the UN human rights regime.[54] It is, generally, considered to be a useful tool for analysing the positive as well as negative obligations inherent in all rights, and, as such, for underlining

---

53   Adopted by the Council of Ministers of the Council of Europe in 1996, opened for signature and ratification in 1997, entered into force on 1 December 1999.

54   A. Eide, 'Economic, Social and Cultural Rights as Human Rights' in A. Eide, C. Krause and A. Rosas (eds.), Economic, Social and Cultural Rights: A Textbook, Dordrecht/Boston/London: Martinus Nijhoff Publishers, 2001, 21–41; G.J.H. van Hoof, 'The Legal Nature of Economic, Social and Cultural Rights: a Rebuttal of Some Traditional Views' in P. Alston and K. Tomaševski (eds.), The Right to Food, Utrecht: SIM, 1984, 97–110. See also Shue's comparable categorisation in H. Shue, Basic Rights, Subsistence, Affluence and U.S. Foreign Policy, New Jersey: Princeton, 1980. The typology was first applied by the ICESCR Committee in General Comment No. 12 (1999), The Right to Adequate Food (Art. 11) E/C.12/1999/5, para. 15.

the equality and interdependence of all human rights. The South African Constitution, for example, expressly imposes obligations on the state to respect, protect, promote and fulfil rights, including a number of socio-economic rights, such as, rights to housing and health.[55]

What are the implications of the obligations to respect, protect and fulfil, respectively? The obligation to *respect* is a negative state obligation, and requires states to refrain from interfering, directly or indirectly, with the enjoyment of the right to health. Examples of violations of these obligations are, according to General Comment No. 14, denying or limiting equal access to health services; enforcing discriminatory practices as a state policy; unlawfully polluting air, water and soil, for example through industrial waste from state-owned facilities, or through using or testing nuclear, biological or chemical weapons, if such testing results in the release of substances harmful to human health.[56]

The obligations to *protect* and to *fulfil* are positive state obligations, requiring states to take measures to prevent third parties from interfering with Article 12 guarantees ('protect'), and to adopt appropriate legislative, administrative, budgetary, judicial, promotional and other measures with a view to the full realisation of the right to health ('fulfil'). Violations of the obligation to protect may occur, for example, when states decline to adopt legislation, or to take other measures, to ensure equal access to healthcare and health-related services provided by third parties, or fail to ensure that harmful social or traditional practices do not interfere with access to pre- and post-natal care and family planning.[57]

With regard to the obligation to fulfil, General Comment No. 14 distinguishes between obligations to facilitate (to take positive measures to enable and assist individuals and communities to enjoy the right to health), to provide (when individuals or a group are unable, for reasons beyond their control, to realise that right themselves, by the means at their disposal), and to promote (to undertake actions that create, maintain and restore the health of the population).[58] Violations of the obligation to fulfil may, according to General Comment No. 14, occur when insufficient recognition is given to the right to health, in the national political and legal systems; when states decline to adopt a national health policy with a detailed plan for realising the right to health; or when they decline to ensure provision of healthcare, including immunisation programmes against the major infectious diseases, and to ensure equal access for all to the underlying

---

[55]   The Constitution of The Republic of South Africa, 1996, s. 7(2).
[56]   General Comment No. 14, para. 34.
[57]   Ibid., para. 35.
[58]   Ibid., para. 37.

determinants of health, such as nutritious and safe food and potable drinking water, basic sanitation, and adequate housing and living conditions.[59]

However, the usefulness of this typology has also been questioned. Koch, for example, argues that the distinction between the three categories is blurred, and that it is very difficult to fit certain obligatory measures into the tripartite typology. She argues that, 'confronted with the complexities of real life the various obligations are hard to distinguish from one another'.[60] Instead 'the adequate metaphor would rather be a slope, not divided into levels.'[61] Elsewhere, Koch also notes that the case law of the ECtHR does not apply the tripartite typology: 'The Court is not preoccupied with the issue of fitting a certain obligation into a certain category'.[62] In a similar vein, San Giorgi criticises the ICESCR Committee for rarely using the typology in its Concluding Observations.[63] The rarity of its use in this setting may also suggest that its application has been overemphasised.

Furthermore, the typology was not included in the text of the Optional Protocol to the ICESCR. Instead, reasonableness is enshrined as the legal standard for assessing violations. Under Article 8.4:

> When examining communications under the present Protocol, the Committee shall consider the reasonableness of the steps taken by the State Party in accordance with part II of the Covenant. In doing so, the Committee shall bear in mind that the State Party may adopt a range of possible policy measures for the implementation of the rights set forth in the Covenant.

The inclusion of reasonableness echoes the standard imposed by the South African Constitutional Court when assessing socio-economic rights. Porter views reasonableness as a 'double-edged sword':

> For sceptical States, reasonableness review was seen as a way of preventing inappropriate or unnecessary incursions into policy choices or resource allocation decisions. For States supportive of a comprehensive and effective Optional Protocol, a reference to reasonableness was seen as affirming a standard of review that had been proven effective at the domestic level.[64]

---

59   Ibid., para. 36.
60   I.E. Koch, 'Dichotomies, Trichotomies or Waves of Duties?', *Human Rights Law Review* 5 (2005), 81–103, 92.
61   Ibid., 93.
62   I.E. Koch, *Human Rights as Indivisible Rights: The Protection of Socio-Economic Demands under the European Convention on Human Rights*, Martinus Nijhoff Publishers, Leiden/ Boston, 2009, 21.
63   Maite M. San Giorgi, *The Human Right to Equal Access to Health Care*, Intersentia, 2012, 50.
64   B. Porter, 'The Reasonableness of Art. 8(4) – Adjudicating Claims from the Margins' *Nordic Journal of Human Rights* 27 (2009), 39–53, 47.

In 2007, the ICESCR Committee issued guidance on the way it planned to assess states' compliance under the Optional Protocol, drawing attention to the following factors:

(a) The extent to which the measures taken were deliberate, concrete and targeted towards the fulfilment of economic, social and cultural rights;

(b) Whether the State party exercised its discretion in a non-discriminatory and non-arbitrary manner;

(c) Whether the State party's decision (not) to allocate available resources is in accordance with international human rights standards;

(d) Where several policy options are available, whether the State party adopts the option that least restricts Covenant rights;

(e) The time frame in which the steps were taken;

(f) Whether the steps had taken into account the precarious situation of disadvantaged and marginalised individuals or groups and, whether they were non-discriminatory, and whether they prioritised grave situations or situations of risk.[65]

These standards, although not binding, offer states a potential checklist from which they can determine the reasonableness of their actions. In its only decision, as of October 2021, on the right to health, the ICESCR Committee found a violation of the right to health, but did not engage with the typology or the concept of reasonableness, as the case centred on informed consent (see Chapter 4).[66] Furthermore, while the ICESCR Committee has, in other decisions, mentioned both reasonableness and proportionality, it seems, in its limited jurisprudence to date, to be more comfortable with assessing proportionality under Article 4 ICESCR than exploring the requirements of reasonableness.[67] In one decision, it explored reasonableness in more detail, stating that social service conditions must be communicated in a 'transparent, timely and complete manner', and should not stigmatise

---

[65] Economic and Social Council, ICESCR, *An Evaluation of the Obligation to Take Steps to the 'Maximum of Available Resources' under an Optional Protocol to the Covenant Statement*, E/C.12/2007/1, 2007, available at www2.ohchr.org/english/bodies/cescr/docs/statements/Obligationtotakesteps-2007.pdf.

[66] ICESCR Committee, *Views adopted by the Committee under the Optional Protocol to the International Covenant on Economic, Social and Cultural Rights, concerning communication no. 22/2017, S.C. and G.P. v. Italy*, E/C.12/65/D/22/2017, 2019.

[67] ICESCR Committee, *Views adopted by the Committee under the Optional Protocol to the International Covenant on Economic, Social and Cultural Rights, concerning communication No. 37/2018, Maribel Viviana López Albán v. Spain*, E/C.12/66/D/37/2018, 2019. CESCR, *Views adopted by the Committee under the Optional Protocol to the Covenant concerning communication No. 10/2015*, E/C.12/63/D/10/2015, 2018.

applicants, before determining that the state had not put forward 'reasonable arguments'.[68]

3.3.2. Progressive realisation

Furthermore, socio-economic rights, including the right to health, are subject to 'progressive realisation', meaning that governments are required to work progressively towards their full realisation. Following Article 2 ICESCR, the state is under an obligation to take steps 'to the maximum of its available resources, with a view to achieving progressively the full realization of the rights'. The ICESCR Committee has specified that the obligation to take steps requires that these are 'deliberate, concrete and targeted as clearly as possible towards meeting the obligations recognized in the Covenant'.[69] Furthermore, states should move as 'expeditiously and effectively' as possible toward full realisation of the rights.[70] This includes, but is not limited to, 'all appropriate means', such as 'judicial or other remedies' and 'administrative, financial, educational, and social measures'.[71] While legislation is not essential, it is particularly emphasised in the text.[72]

Therefore, States Parties to the ICESCR must take steps, acting in good faith and subject to resources, to ensure individuals' full enjoyment of the rights under the Covenant. While taking steps is less onerous than *guaranteeing* rights, states should approach these obligations with commitment.[73] Tarantola considers that progressive realisation requires 're-examination of governmental obligations as they are fulfilled and as health needs and technologies evolve'.[74] Progressive realisation can be considered an immediate obligation, although full implementation will be progressive.[75]

While states have wide discretion in their use of resources, this cannot be completely open without rendering the Covenant impotent.[76] Resources are

---

[68] ICESCR Committee, *Views adopted by the Committee under the Optional Protocol to the International Covenant on Economic, Social and Cultural Rights with regard to communication No. 5/2015*, E/C.12/61/D/5/2015, 2017, paras. 17.2 and 17.8.

[69] ICESCR Committee, General Comment No. 3, The Nature of States Parties' Obligations (Art. 2, para. 1), E/1991/23, 1990, para. 2.

[70] Ibid., para. 9.

[71] Ibid., para. 7.

[72] P. Alston and G. Quinn, 'The Nature and Scope of States Parties' Obligations under the International Covenant on Economic, Social and Cultural Rights', *Human Rights Quarterly* 9 (1987), 156–229, 167.

[73] Ibid., 165.

[74] D. Tarantola, 'Global Justice and Human Rights: Health and Human Rights in Practice', *Global Justice: Theory, Practice, Rhetoric* 1 (2014), 11–26, 20.

[75] P. Alston and G. Quinn, 'The Nature and Scope of States Parties' Obligations under the International Covenant on Economic, Social and Cultural Rights', *Human Rights Quarterly* 9 (1987), 156–229, 166.

[76] Ibid., 177.

considered to go beyond simple budgetary calculations and include human, technical and scientific resources.[77] Compliance could be monitored through examining the extent to which states meet indicators in relation to different types of resources: human, technological, informational, natural and financial.[78] Hunt and Backman suggest that the state must adopt the most effective measures, in light of resources and other rights demands.[79]

The ICESCR Committee has stated that 'deliberate' retrogressive measures must be justified, without addressing what such justification requires.[80] Nolan, Lusiani and Courtis distinguish between 'normative' and 'empirical' regression: the former means steps backward in terms of legal, *de jure* guarantees, the latter relates to de facto regression.[81] Warwick builds on this approach, and criticises the doctrine as 'understudied and uncertain'.[82]

Progressive realisation explicitly recognises that states will need time to fulfil socio-economic rights, in light of resource constraints. However, the concept should not be used to deny the legal character of rights. In all cases, a distinction should be made between 'inability' to realise rights, for example due to a natural disaster or financial constraints, and 'unwillingness'.

Finally, the obligations owed, in relation to health, by wealthy states to states with fewer resources, remain controversial. Should these form part of states' obligations to progressively realise socioeconomic rights? General Comment No. 14 mentions the international obligations of states with regard to the right to health, which are also stipulated in Article 2(1) of the ICESCR. States are to respect the right to health in other countries, and to prevent third parties from violating the right in other countries. For example, this obligation is of importance with regard to the tension between patent protection and the accessibility of drugs in developing countries. In addition, this international

[77]   S. Skogly, 'The Requirement of Using the "Maximum of Available Resources" for Human Rights Realisation: A Question of Quality as Well as Quantity?', *Human Rights Law Review* 12 (2012), 393–420, 404.

[78]   R.E. Robertson, 'Measuring State Compliance with the Obligation to Devote the "Maximum Available Resources" to Realizing Economic, Social, and Cultural Rights' *Human Rights Quarterly* 16 (1994), 693–714.

[79]   P. Hunt and G. Backman and, 'Health systems and the right to the highest attainable standard of health', *Health and Human Rights* 10 (2008), 81–84, 92.

[80]   A. Nolan, 'Budget Analysis and Social and Economic Rights' in E. Riedel, G. Giacca, and C. Golay (eds.), *Economic, Social and Cultural Rights in International Law: Contemporary Issues and Challenges*, Oxford Scholarship Online, 2014, 376. DOI:10.1093/acprof: oso/9780199685974.001.0001.

[81]   A. Nolan, N.J. Lusiani and C. Courtis, 'Two Steps Forward, No Steps Back? Evolving Criteria on the Prohibition of Retrogression in Economic, Social and Cultural Rights' in A. Nolan (ed.), *Economic and Social Rights after the Global Financial Crisis*, Cambridge: Cambridge University Press, 2014.

[82]   B.T.C. Warwick, 'Unwinding Retrogression: Examining the Practice of the Committee on Economic, Social and Cultural Rights', *Human Rights Law Review* 19 (2019), 467–90, 467.

obligation contains a reference to providing development aid, where necessary. The general comment refers to the obligation to facilitate access to essential health facilities, goods and services in other countries, wherever possible, and to provide the necessary aid, when required.[83]

3.3.3. Core obligations

Although socio-economic rights are subject to progressive realisation, the ICESCR Committee also introduced the concept of core obligations.[84] Following this approach, the ICESCR Committee holds that all rights impose 'a minimum core obligation to ensure the satisfaction of, at the very least, minimum essential levels of each of the rights'. This has been described as 'the nature or essence of a right, that is, the essential element or elements without which it loses its substantive significance as a human right and in the absence of which a State Party should be considered to be in violation of its international obligations'.[85]

General Comment No. 14 refers, in paragraphs 43 to 44, to core obligations, i.e. that States Parties have certain minimum obligations to ensure, under all circumstances, the delivery of minimum basic levels of, in this case, essential health services. The general comment draws from the Programme of Action of the International Conference on Population and Development (UNDP, Cairo 1994), and the Primary Health Care Strategy, as set out in the Alma-Ata Declaration (WHO, 1978). As such, the core obligations include, among other things, the obligation to provide access to health facilities on a non-discriminatory basis, in particular reproductive, maternal and child healthcare; immunisation against the major infectious diseases; prevention, treatment and control of epidemic and endemic diseases; education and access to information concerning the main health problems in the community; and appropriate training for health personnel, including education on health and human rights.

In the general comment, the Committee specifies that core obligations are non-derogable.[86] This suggests that core obligations hold an elevated status. However, the meaning of this wording is unclear, given that the ICESCR does not include a derogation clause, only permitting limitations 'determined by law', and 'compatible with the nature of these rights'.

---

[83] General Comment No. 14, para. 39.
[84] UN Committee on Economic, Social and Cultural Rights (ICESCR Committee), General Comment No. 3: The Nature of States Parties' Obligations (E/1991/23) (1990).
[85] S. Russell and A. Chapman, 'Introduction' in S. Russell and A. Chapman (eds.), *Core Obligations: Building a Framework for Economic, Social and Cultural Rights*, Antwerp: Intersentia, 2002, 9.
[86] General Comment No. 14, para. 47.

The CRC Committee has followed the ICESCR Committee approach, and has identified further core obligations:

(1) Reviewing the national and subnational legal and policy environment and, where necessary, amending laws and policies;

(2) Ensuring universal coverage of quality primary health services, including prevention, health promotion, care and treatment services, and essential drugs;

(3) Providing an adequate response to the underlying determinants of children's health; and

(4) Developing, implementing, monitoring and evaluating policies and budgeted plans of actions that constitute a human rights-based approach to fulfilling children's right to health.[87]

These core obligations are less directive and precise than those of the ICESCR Committee, which may be a result of the criticism of the ICESCR Committee's general comment. The CRC Committee's approach is also more flexible in that, although it highlights political and legal accountability as well as remedies,[88] it does not focus on violations to the same extent as the ICESCR Committee.

The minimum core has proven controversial. On the one hand, this method highlights the legal quality of socioeconomic rights by relying on a violations approach that considers failure to meet minimum standards as a breach of the Covenant. Although the minimum core was rejected in the oft-cited South African judgments on socio-economic rights, it has been embraced by the Colombian Constitutional Court and the Costa Rican Supreme Court.[89] On the other hand, core obligations can be arbitrary, contradictory,[90] impractical,[91] and focus too much on the obligations of developing states.[92] They suggest that certain urgent priorities can trump others when implementing rights.[93] Furthermore,

---

[87] CRC Committee, General Comment No. 15: The Right of the Child to the Enjoyment of the Highest Attainable Standard of Health (CRC/C/GC/15) (2013), para. 73.

[88] Ibid., para. 59.

[89] L. Forman et al., 'What could a strengthened right to health bring to the post-2015 health development agenda?: interrogating the role of the minimum core concept in advancing essential global health needs', *BMC International Health and Human Rights* 13 (48) (2013).

[90] E.W. Vierdag, 'The Legal Nature of the Rights Granted by the International Covenant on Economic, Social and Cultural Rights', *Netherlands Yearbook of International Law* 9 (1978), 69–105, 143.

[91] M. Wesson, '*Grootboom* and Beyond: Reassessing the Socioeconomic Jurisprudence of the South African Constitutional Court', *South African Journal of Human Rights* 20 (2004), 284–308.

[92] E.W. Vierdag, 'The Legal Nature of the Rights Granted by the International Covenant on Economic, Social and Cultural Rights', *Netherlands Yearbook of International Law* 9 (1978), 69–105, 143.

[93] M. Wesson, '*Grootboom* and Beyond: Reassessing the Socioeconomic Jurisprudence of the South African Constitutional Court', *South African Journal of Human Rights* 20 (2004), 284–308, 298.

focusing on a minimum core does not tackle structural inequalities, such as the underlying reasons for poverty and marginalisation. Smith describes core obligations as 'impressive', but 'more aspirational than determinative'.[94]

Despite seeking to add clarity to state obligations, the minimum core leaves many unanswered questions. Bódig questions whether the minimum core is 'state specific or universal'.[95] In other words, do the rights contain a minimum core that applies across the board, or is the minimum core for Canada different from the minimum core for Kenya?

Furthermore, one can question whether core obligations are useful in a European context, where generally accessible healthcare packages go beyond the scope of the core obligations mentioned above. The notion of a 'core' could possibly be of some use, however, in the debate on the issue of what healthcare services should be available to deprived or uninsured persons or population groups, including undocumented migrants. Moreover, core obligations have been significant during the COVID-19 pandemic, where governments have reduced 'non-essential' care to be able to manage an influx of COVID patients.

3.3.4. Determinants of health

The right to health recognises, in line with research, that socio-economic conditions, and not merely access to healthcare, are often decisive for people's health. States not only have obligations to ensure equitable access to healthcare, but also to create conditions that allow individuals to lead healthy lives. As per General Comment No. 14, states should ensure health promotion ('promote conditions in which people can lead a healthy life'), and take preventative measures to avoid disease.

From the perspective of the obligation to *respect* rights, this implies a duty on the part of governments to refrain from denying or limiting equal access to all health-related services, as well as abstaining from enforcing discriminatory practices as state policy in this regard (General Comment No. 14, paragraph 34). The obligations to protect and to fulfil rights require states to take actions to promote good health and prevent disease. This includes measures that prevent third parties from interfering with Article 12 ICESCR guarantees ('protect'), and to adopt appropriate legislative, administrative, budgetary, judicial, promotional and other measures with a view to the full realisation of the right to health ('fulfil').

---

[94] G.P. Smith, 'Human Rights and Bioethics: Formulating a Universal Right to Health, Health Care, or Health Protection?', *Vanderbilt Journal of Transnational Law* 38 (2005), 1295–325, 1296.

[95] M. Bódig, 'Doctrinal Innovation and State Obligations: The Patterns of Doctrinal Development in the Jurisprudence of the UN Committee on Economic, Social and Cultural Rights', in Kurt Mills and David D. Jason Karp (eds.), *Human Rights Protection in Global Politics: Responsibilities of States and Non-State Actors*, UK: Palgrave MacMillan, 2015, 56.

The obligation to protect is important when tackling the role of industry in relation to the social determinants: there is a clear role for governments to regulate private companies so as to ensure that they do not market unhealthy products, for example. In turn, the obligation to fulfil is about ensuring access, not only to health services, but also to the underlying determinants of health. Reading the right to health in conjunction with the other economic and social rights, it means an obligation to ensure access to early childhood services, and amenities including education, housing, employment and a clean environment.

While Chapman has argued that the human rights approach insufficiently considers social determinants as factors determining the health status and outcomes of individuals and communities,[96] this premise has also been subject to critique. Tobin warns against colonising the 'discrete normative territory' of other economic and social rights.[97] Lougarre agrees, adding that the social determinants should generally not be monitored within the right to health.[98]

Chapter 13, which addresses the interface between public health and human rights, will elaborate further on the relationship between human rights and the determinants of health.

3.4.   UN SUSTAINABLE DEVELOPMENT GOALS

The UN Sustainable Development Goals (SDGs) include goals, targets and indicators that are of importance to the right to health. In this manner, the SDGs can be used to contribute to setting indicators and benchmarks to monitor the determinants of health: indicators provide a reference point for the situation at a particular point in time, while benchmarks are self-set goals or targets to be achieved at some future date. In order to give full expression to the human rights perspective in such an assessment, it is important that these indicators be disaggregated by reference to any category that may reveal meaningful inequalities, such as the sex of the persons concerned, whether they live in an urban or rural area, or the socio-economic or ethnic group to which they belong.

While all of the goals have importance for realising the right to health, the goal of ensuring healthy lives and promoting well-being for all, at all ages (Goal 3), is particularly pertinent. This includes targets such as reducing

---

[96]   A.R. Chapman, 'The social determinants of health, health equity, and human rights', *Health and Human Rights Journal* 12 (2010), 4, available at https://www.hhrjournal.org/2013/08/the-social-determinants-of-health-health-equity-and-human-rights/.

[97]   J. Tobin, 'Still getting to know you: global health law and the right to health' in G.L. Burci and B. Toebes (eds.), *Research Handbook on Global Health Law*, Cheltenham: Edward Elgar Publishing, 2018, 69.

[98]   C. Lougarre, 'Clarifying the Right to Health through Supranational Monitoring: The Highest Standard of Health Attainable', *Public Health Ethics* 11 (2014).

maternal mortality, ending epidemics, prevention and treatment of substance abuse, and strengthening implementation of the WHO Framework Convention on Tobacco Control.

The SDGs are political commitments grounded in human rights. Although not legally binding, they can be seen as complementary to states' binding obligations, and as reinforcing these obligations. The SDGs can also be used to concretise states' existing obligations, and to press for their implementation. On the other hand, the goals can be criticised for their broad formulation, which might potentially limit their impact on European states, which already meet some of the basic targets, and are sometimes considered to hold more weighty obligations than those with less developed economies.[99]

4. CONTROVERSIES AND CONFUSIONS SURROUNDING THE RIGHT TO HEALTH

As this book will illustrate, the legal understanding of the right to health has developed over the last thirty years through general comments, reports of the Special Rapporteur on the Right to Health, court judgments in select jurisdictions, and research by a growing number of academics who seek to strengthen the content of the right to health. Yet, confusions and controversies remain, some of which are summarised here.

4.1. JUSTICIABILITY OF THE RIGHT TO HEALTH

The justiciability or legal enforceability of the right to health, and of other economic, social and cultural rights has been the subject of much debate.[100] There is, generally, reluctance on the part of the judiciary (particularly in Europe and North America) to assess cases on the basis of economic, social and cultural rights, not only because the wording of these rights is often general and open-ended, but also because the judiciary does not want to interfere with the margin of appreciation of the executive and legislative bodies. At the same time, in some jurisdictions, international and domestic courts are increasingly willing to enforce access to health-related services.

Most of the examples of enforceability of the right to health have materialised in lower and middle-income countries, where more dramatic cases have been

---

[99] A. Eide, C. Krause and A. Rosas, *Economic, Social and Cultural Rights*, 2nd ed., Martinus Nijhoff Publishers, 2001, 27.

[100] See, generally, F. Coomans (ed.), *Justiciability of Economic, Social and Cultural Rights*, Antwerp: Intersentia, 2006.

heard in the courts.[101] Due to the absence of the minimum social security in many countries, violations of the rights there are clear and persistent. Furthermore, the burden for bringing a constitutional claim is often lower.

The most significant jurisprudence on the right to health has, therefore, come from courts in the Global South. Some of earliest seminal cases were brought under the post-apartheid South African Constitution, which enshrines socio-economic rights. In *Treatment Action Campaign*, the South African Constitutional Court found that the applicants' rights to healthcare had been violated by governmental restrictions on access to antiretroviral drugs.[102] In recent years, South American courts have taken centre stage in litigation on the right to health, as many South American countries enshrine this right in their constitutions.[103] For example, in the seminal judgment T-760/08, the Colombian Constitutional Court found the government had violated the right to health, and the court set broad structural changes that the government should undertake to comply.[104]

The recognition of the right to health by courts is met with enthusiasm by some, given that courts can provide remedies for litigants, and order governments to address structural violations.[105] At the same time, litigation can place financial burdens on low-income countries, and divert funds away from public health programmes of collective benefit, into the hands of victims of violations.[106] Focusing on individual access to treatments can obscure the need to address the causes of disease.[107]

In the developed world, where the debate is much more about the sufficiency of benefits, there is more resistance to the enforceability, or so-called 'justiciability', of economic and social rights, including the rights to health, education and employment. In Europe, some of the most illustrative decisions have been produced by the European Committee of Social Rights, and these are discussed in Chapter 5. While such cases address a wide range of health-related

---

[101] A well-known example concerns the decision of the South African Constitutional Court in *Minister of Health and Others v. Treatment Action Campaign and Others* (No 2) (CCT8/02) [2002] ZACC 15, on the general availability of the drug nevirapine, which is used to prevent the spread of HIV from mother to child.

[102] *Minister of Health v. Treatment Action Campaign* (TAC) (2002) 5 SA 721 (CC).

[103] A.E. Yamin, 'The Right to Health in Latin America: The Challenges Of Constructing Fair Limits', *Pennsylvania Journal of International Law* 40 (2019), 698–734, 719.

[104] Judgment T-760/08, 31 July 2008. English summary available at www.escr-net.org/sites/default/files/English_summary_T-760.pdf.

[105] A.I. Arrieta-Gómez, 'Realizing the Fundamental Right to Health through Litigation: The Colombian Case', *Health and Human Rights Journal* 20(1) (2018), 133–45.

[106] E. Lamprea, 'Colombia's Right-to-Health Litigation in a Context of Health Care Reform' in C.M. Flood and A. Gross (eds.), *The Right to Health at the Public/Private Divide: A Global Comparative Study*, Cambridge: Cambridge University Press, 2014, 131–58.

[107] J. Biehl, J.J. Amon, M.P. Socal and A. Petryna, 'Between the court and the clinic: lawsuits for medicines and the right to health in Brazil', *Health and Human Rights Journal* 14(1) (2012).

topics, a recurrent theme is the socio-economic protection of vulnerable groups, including the Roma and undocumented migrants. It seems that, in situations where generally available services are not available, or are denied to a certain population group, the Committee is willing to assess compliance with the rights set out in the (revised) ESC.

The debate about the justiciability or legal enforceability of economic and social rights is increasingly linked to a broader debate about creating accountability for these rights. Legal accountability, identified above as one of the dimensions of accountability, is thus perceived as an avenue through which the justiciability of rights can be enhanced.

4.2. RESPONSIBILITIES OF NON-STATE ACTORS

Given that the resources of certain companies dwarf those of many states, it can be argued that the full realisation of the right to health is beyond the scope of states alone. One of the major issues in modern human rights law is the definition of the human rights responsibilities of all actors in the health sector, which vary from health ministries, social security organisations, public and private insurers, hospitals, doctors and pharmacists, to pharmaceutical companies, producers of medical equipment and patients. For example, the perceived responsibility of the pharmaceutical industry for producing and providing affordable and good quality drugs geared towards the health needs of the population at large has been the subject of intense debate.

It is, increasingly, argued that non-state actors also have obligations under human rights law. International human rights law provides several bases for this line of argumentation.[108] For example, the preamble to the UDHR recognises the human rights responsibilities of 'all organs of society';[109] and, important for our purposes, Article 11 (Revised) ESC refers to the collaboration between the state and public and private organisations in the realisation of the right to protection of health. Even at the time of the drafting of this provision, there was awareness of the role that private organisations played in the provision of medical care.[110]

As health service provision is increasingly privatised, it is important to consider the human rights responsibilities of all actors in the health sector.

---

[108]   In this regard, reference is often made to the body of international humanitarian law, and to the Genocide Convention, which both contain references to the human rights responsibilities of non-state actors. For this debate, see, inter alia, N. Jägers, *Corporate Responsibility for Human Rights Violations*, Antwerp/Oxford: Intersentia/Hart, 2000.

[109]   For a similar statement, see General Comment No. 14, para. 42.

[110]   Draft report examined by the Committee on General Affairs relating to a preliminary draft recommendation, submitted by Mr. Toncic (6 August 1956) – AS/AG (8) 16, *Collected 'Travaux Préparatoires'*, Vol. III, 1956, p. 507, in B. Toebes, *The Right to Health as a Human Right in International Law*, Antwerp/Oxford: Intersentia/Hart, 1999, 65.

While governments remain ultimately responsible for human rights violations, it is important to develop the tools to address the responsibilities of private actors directly. Furthermore, health sectors are very complex in character, due to the fact that many actors engage with each other in multiple relationships. This makes health sectors extremely vulnerable to abuse and corruption, hence the importance of addressing abuse and corruption by all actors.[111]

At present, however, it is generally accepted that companies do not have binding human rights obligations. In 2011, the UN Human Rights Council endorsed the Guiding Principles on Business and Human Rights, which called on companies to respect human rights, and to provide remedies where they have caused or contributed to adverse impacts.[112] For pharmaceutical companies this could include relatively soft obligations, like adopting human rights policy statements, or refraining from conduct that undermines human rights, such as discriminatory clinical trials.[113] However, these principles are not binding law. Suerie Moon reflects, therefore, that companies are unlikely to invest in, for example, neglected diseases without state action, as this does not benefit their 'bottom lines'. In summary, until a new international treaty is adopted, companies do not, currently, have human rights *obligations*, but have non-binding *responsibilities*. Since 2015, a Human Rights Council working group has released several drafts of a binding treaty on transnational business and human rights.[114]

4.3. LINGERING AMBIGUITIES

Finally, and fundamentally, it remains unclear exactly what services need to be granted on the basis of the right to health. Yet, as Therese Murphy and others have pondered, the wording of all types of rights (including civil and political rights) are imprecise, and subject to resources.[115]

---

[111] B. Toebes, 'Human Rights and Health Sector Corruption' in J. Harrington and M. Stuttaford (eds.), *Global Health and Human Rights: Legal and Philosophical Perspectives*, Oxon/ New York: Routledge, 2010, 102–34.

[112] UN Human Rights Council, Human rights and transnational corporations and other business enterprises, A/HRC/RES/17/4.

[113] S. Moon, 'Respecting the right to access to medicines: Implications of the UN Guiding Principles on Business and Human Rights for the pharmaceutical industry', *Health and Human Rights Journal* 15(1) (2013), 32–43.

[114] Open-ended intergovernmental working group, 'Legally Binding Instrument to Regulate, in International Human Rights Law, the Activities of Transnational Corporations and other Business Enterprises, Zero Draft', 16 July 2018; Revised Draft (2019); Second Revised Draft (2020), Third Revised Draft (2021).

[115] T. Murphy, 'Hardwired human rights: a health and human rights perspective on global health law' in G.L. Burci and B. Toebes (eds.), *Research Handbook on Global Health Law*, Cheltenham: Edward Elgar Publishing, 2018, 96.

In his work on the right to health, Tobin, therefore, calls for a 'persuasive' account of the right, given its ambiguity, and the absence of 'an authoritative adjudicative body'. He posits that interpretation of the right to health should be: (a) principled (in line with general principles of international law); (b) clear and practical; (c) coherent (in its own reasoning, and with other systems of international law); and (d) context-sensitive (both locally and globally).[116] This approach recognises the political realities of the international human rights system, and the weakness of enforcement measures.

Tobin's methodology has, however, been critiqued: in particular, part (d), which calls for consensus within the interpretive community. Former Special Rapporteur on the Right to Health, Paul Hunt, for example, has weighed in, criticising the method for failing to include those living in poverty within the scope of the interpretive community. Hunt, instead, argues that the special character of human rights treaties allows for a distinctive method of interpretation, which focuses on the object and purpose of the ICESCR as being to reduce and eliminate poverty.[117]

Lougarre is also critical of Tobin's approach, although, ultimately, she draws heavily on it, while calling for more emphasis on human dignity and non-discrimination. Too much focus on consensus among key actors, she warns, can allow those actors to shape the right to health, contrary to its ethos.[118]

5. CONCLUSIONS

Based on the internationally guaranteed right to health, there is a legally binding right to healthcare services, and a right to the necessary conditions for health, including access to health-related information, access to safe drinking water, occupational health, and the protection of environmental health. However, the right to health should not become a panacea: the state cannot guarantee good health.

This chapter has traced the central elements of the right to health, predominantly with reference to General Comment No. 14. The Committee on Economic, Social and Cultural Rights has contributed significantly to understanding the entitlements and obligations imposed by the right to health.

---

[116]   J. Tobin, 'A Methodology to Produce a Meaning for the Right to Health' in J. Tobin (ed.), *The Right to Health in International Law*, Oxford: Oxford University Press, 2012.

[117]   P. Hunt, 'Interpreting the International Right to Health in a Human Rights-Based Approach to Health', *Health and Human Rights Journal* 18(2) (2016) 109–30. See also C. Lougarre, 'Review of *The Right to Health in International Law* by John Tobin', *The Modern Law Review* 77(2) (2014), 336–42.

[118]   C. Lougarre, 'Review of *The Right to Health in International Law* by John Tobin', *The Modern Law Review* 77(2) (2014), 336–42.

As we will see in the coming chapters, the right to health is an expansive right that goes beyond access to healthcare services, and includes collective public health measures.

In combination with the principle of non-discrimination, the right to health proves an effective tool for protecting the health needs of vulnerable population groups, including women, children and (undocumented) migrants (see Chapter 8). Other health-related human rights reinforce the right to health, for example when it comes to the principle of non-discrimination, and in situations in which the right to life protects health. On other occasions, such rights have a distinct meaning for the protection of health, for example where the right to privacy gives women the freedom to choose to have an abortion. Lastly, some rights have a specific meaning in healthcare settings, for example the right to liberty and security, which sets limits to the involuntary placement in institutions of persons with mental disabilities.

CHAPTER 3

HUMAN RIGHTS PRINCIPLES AND PATIENT RIGHTS

Henriette Sɪɴᴅɪɴɢ Aᴀsᴇɴ and Mette Hᴀʀᴛʟᴇᴠ

1. INTRODUCTION

This chapter starts out by exploring human dignity as a core concept and value in human rights law, generally, and in health-related human rights, in particular (section 2). The notion of human dignity is rooted in enlightenment philosophy and ethics, and forms a central aspect of the modern human rights doctrine. Other central concepts are autonomy and integrity, which are introduced briefly (section 3), and placed in relation to the concept of dignity. The principle of non-discrimination cuts across all human rights, and is of crucial importance regarding health protection. This principle is presented (section 4), before we turn to the section on patient rights (section 5). Patient rights are human rights, in the context of health protection, i.e. when people have become patients through their interaction with the healthcare system. Section 5 starts out with an overview of the development of patient rights, before exploring, in more detail, respect for patient autonomy and informed consent, followed by the right to privacy and confidentiality (section 6).[1]

2. HUMAN DIGNITY – THE CORE OF HUMAN RIGHTS

All human rights, including the right to health (see Chapter 2), share one essential aspect: they protect human dignity. The Universal Declaration of Human Rights (UDHR)[2] proclaims, in the first sentence of its preamble, that 'recognition of the inherent dignity and of the equal and inalienable rights of all members of the human family is the foundation of freedom, justice and peace

---

[1]   The right to access healthcare is also a patient right, which is discussed separately in Chapter 7 of this volume.
[2]   United Nations, 1948.

in the world'. The preambles of both the International Covenant on Civil and Political Rights (ICCPR)[3] and the International Covenant on Economic, Social and Cultural Rights (ICESCR)[4] emphasise that the Convention rights 'derive from the inherent dignity of the human person'. The formulation 'derive from' indicates that respect for, and protection of, human dignity is the core and purpose of all the Convention rights, civil as well as social. It is safe to say that human dignity is one of the most essential concepts in human rights law.[5]

The wording of the two UN instruments also indicates that human rights are means or tools for realising the necessary protection of human dignity. In other words, human dignity is to be preserved through a spectrum of human rights. In the health field, the following rights or requirements are essential: availability and accessibility of quality healthcare and underlying conditions for health (such as water, food, sanitation, shelter and education), privacy and autonomy. All rights include both negative and positive state obligations to respect, protect and fulfil them.[6]

In Europe, several regional human rights instruments are relevant for the purposes of this volume: the European Convention on Human Rights, the revised European Social Charter (called the Social Constitution of Europe), the Biomedicine Convention, and the European Union Charter of Fundamental Rights are of particular interest. Together, they form essential aspects of the European human rights architecture.

The concept of human dignity, and what it entails in different contexts, is not, however, clear and uncontested. Rather, as the concept of dignity is essential in moral philosophy, religion, ethics and law, in all parts of the world, the understanding varies significantly, depending on culture, religion, discipline, personal belief, conviction, background, profession and other factors.[7] This volume refers to human dignity based particularly on the thinking of the German philosopher Immanuel Kant (1724–1804), one of the most influential thinkers of modern Europe. Kant places the human being in the centre of the modern society's social and political organisation.[8] The humanistic ideas developed by

---

3   United Nations, 1966.
4   Ibid.
5   M. Hartlev, 'Coercive Treatment and Human Dignity' in H.S. Aasen, R Halvorsen and A.B. da Silva (eds.), *Human Rights, Dignity and Autonomy in Health Care and Social Services: Nordic Perspectives*, Intersentia, 2009, 129–45, 131. Hartlev points out that human dignity is mentioned before rights in Article 1 of the UDHR: Art. 1 proclaims that all human beings 'are born free and equal in dignity and rights'.
6   See, particularly, A. Hendriks in Chapter 5, and in other chapters, analysing the content of rights and state obligations.
7   E. Klein and D. Kretsmer, 'Foreword' in E. Klein and D. Kretsmer (eds.), *The Concept of Human Dignity in Human Rights Discourse*, Kluwer Law International, 2002, v–vii, vi.
8   M. Düwell et al., 'Why a handbook on human dignity?', in M. Düwell et al. (eds.), *The Cambridge Handbook of Human Dignity: Interdisciplinary Perspectives*, Cambridge University Press, 2014, xvii–xxiii, xviii.

Kant are essential for the understanding of modern human rights principles. Of particular importance is the distinction between *objects*, which have a price, and are replaceable by an equivalent, and *persons*, who have dignity (intrinsic worth), and are irreplaceable.[9] On the basis of this distinction, Kant argued that human beings should always be treated as ends/aims in themselves, with inviolable and unconditional worth.[10]

The Kantian understanding of human dignity rejects the instrumentalisation of human beings, and is firmly established in human rights instruments, such as the Convention on Human Rights and Biomedicine (hereafter 'Biomedicine Convention'),[11] adopted by the Council of Europe. Article 2 (Primacy of the human being) of the Biomedicine Convention states that, '[t]he interests and welfare of the human being shall prevail over the sole interest of society or science'. The provision assumes an overall priority of the interests and welfare of the human being, when it comes to health decisions, including individuals not able to give valid consent on their own, but also decisions of moral concern to the public, where the concept of human dignity is at stake. For example, in Article 14, the Biomedicine Convention prohibits the use of techniques of medically assisted procreation for the purpose of choosing a future child's sex, except where serious hereditary disease associated with one particular sex is to be avoided. Several other limits and protective measures are put forward, in relation to research, organ and tissue removal, genetic testing, etc. Article 21 states that, '[t]he human body and its parts shall not, as such, give rise to financial gain'. Thus, the Biomedicine Convention provides clear expressions of Kantian humanism, seeing human beings as 'priceless' beings with inherent dignity, as opposed to objects with an economic or scientific value.[12] The Explanatory Report to the Convention emphasises that the 'concept of human dignity ... constitutes the essential value to be upheld. It is the basis of most of the values emphasised in the Convention'.[13]

Article 1 of the European Union Charter of Fundamental Rights (hereafter 'EU Charter')[14] states that 'Human dignity is inviolable. It must be respected

---

9   I. Kant, *Foundations of the Metaphysics of Morals*, Hutchinson University Library, 1966, 96–97.
10   M. Hartlev, 'Patients' Rights', *Health and Human Rights in Europe*, Intersentia, 2012, 119.
11   The full title is 'Convention for the protection of Human Rights and Dignity of the Human Being with regard to the Application of Biology and Medicine' (Council of Europe, Oviedo, opened for signatures 4 April 1997), ETS No. 164.
12   H.S. Aasen, 'Dignity and Human Rights in the Modern Welfare State' in H.S. Aasen, R. Halvorsen and A.B. da Silva (eds.), *Human Rights, Dignity and Autonomy in Health Care and Social Services: Nordic Perspectives*, Intersentia, 2009, 53–69, 60.
13   Council of Europe, 'Explanatory Report to the Convention on Human Rights and Biomedicine', Strasbourg, May 1997, para. 9.
14   Charter of Fundamental Rights of the European Union (2012/C 326/02).

and protected.' Article 3 of the EU Charter,[15] on the right to integrity of the person, is placed under the broader umbrella of 'Dignity', in the first section of the Charter, prohibiting eugenic practices in the fields of medicine and biology, in particular those aimed at the selection of persons (2 b). Furthermore, Article 3 prohibits making the human body and its parts, as such, a source of financial gain, as well as the reproductive cloning of human beings (2 c and d).

Interestingly, the main human rights instrument in Europe, the European Convention of Human Rights (ECHR),[16] does not mention human dignity explicitly, but emphasises civil rights and fundamental freedoms. However, in the case law of the European Court of Human Rights (ECtHR), we find many references to human dignity.[17] In both *Goodwin v. UK* (para. 65) and *Pretty v. UK* (para. 90), the Court states that 'the very essence of the Convention is respect for human dignity and human freedom'. Human dignity and human freedom are reflected as twin values, interrelated and with equal emphasis, although separate. This volume engages with the notion of human dignity and its relation to different, but intertwined, human rights in the field of healthcare and health protection, including public health measures.

Hartlev has identified three separate but interrelated conceptions of human dignity:

(1) dignity related to human freedom and individual autonomy;
(2) dignity seen as an intrinsic worth of every human being; and
(3) dignity associated with conditions essential for a dignified life.[18]

This volume considers all of these conceptions of dignity, seeing them as concrete articulations of how to understand the meaning of human dignity in various situations and contexts. Furthermore, we consider two other situations in which human dignity serves as a core consideration:

(1) human dignity as a balancing value in situations of conflict between human rights, e.g when a choice must be made between saving the life or health of a patient or respecting his/her refusal of treatment;[19] and

---

15   2012/C 326/02.
16   The Convention for the Protection of Human Rights and Fundamental Freedoms (Council of Europe, 1950).
17   The first reference by the Court was in *Tyrer v. the UK*, 25 April 1978, no. 5856/72, ECLI:CE: ECHR:1978:0425JUD000585672.
18   M. Hartlev, 'Coercive Treatment and Human Dignity' in H.S. Aasen, R Halvorsen and A.B. da Silva (eds.), *Human Rights, Dignity and Autonomy in Health Care and Social Services: Nordic Perspectives*, Intersentia, 2009, 132–36.
19   H.S. Aasen, 'Dignity and Human Rights in the Modern Welfare State' in H.S. Aasen, R. Halvorsen and A.B. da Silva (eds.), *Human Rights, Dignity and Autonomy in Health Care and Social Services: Nordic Perspectives*, Intersentia, 2009, 53–69, 54 and 57.

(2) human dignity as part of moral concerns at the societal or public level, e.g related to decisions on contested issues like abortion, reproductive and genetic technologies, foetus selection, euthanasia, etc., where public concerns about the value of human life is especially pressing.

3. AUTONOMY AND INTEGRITY

An important aspect of Kant's humanism that is reflected in law, ethics and philosophy is the emphasis on human beings' capacity for independent reasoning, indicating a close relationship between human dignity and individual autonomy.[20] The understanding of individual autonomy as closely related to and/or constituting an important aspect of human dignity is also visible in modern human rights law. The rights of liberty, privacy, and freedom from torture, slavery and forced labour, as well as freedom of thought and religion, all protect individual autonomy and integrity,[21] and the right of everyone to live as an independent and autonomous being, according to personal values, beliefs and choices. The ideas of freedom of will, respect for individual freedom, and the right of self-determination are key components of the modern autonomy principle.[22]

However, as with the notion of human dignity, there is no universal consensus about the precise content, boundaries, premises and implications of the autonomy principle. In the health field, however, the concept and doctrine of informed consent provides a common reference for the historical, bioethical and legal perspectives on individual autonomy, as an ethical and legal concept and requirement.[23]

Article 7 of the ICCPR provides that, 'no one shall be subjected without his free consent to medical or scientific experimentation' (second sentence). This provision is situated together with the prohibition of torture, cruel, inhuman or degrading treatment or punishment,[24] arising out of the horrific experiments

---

[20] A.B. da Silva, 'Autonomy, Dignity, and Integrity in Health Care Ethics – A Moral Philosophical Perspective' in H.S. Aasen, R Halvorsen and A.B. da Silva (eds.), *Human Rights, Dignity and Autonomy in Health Care and Social Services: Nordic Perspectives*, Intersentia, 2009, 13–53, 15–21. See also M. Hartlev, 'Coercive Treatment and Human Dignity' in H.S. Aasen, R Halvorsen and A.B. da Silva (eds.), *Human Rights, Dignity and Autonomy in Health Care and Social Services: Nordic Perspectives*, Intersentia, 2009, 129–45, 137.

[21] 'Integrity' understood in terms of untouchability, both mentally and physically, as an intrinsic and unchangeable aspect of the human being (Hartlev, 'Patients' Rights', 120).

[22] E.D. Pellegrino, 'Patient and Physician Autonomy: Conflicting Rights and Obligations in the Physician–Patient Relationship', *The Journal of Contemporary Health Law and Policy* 10 (1994), 47–69; A.B. da Silva, 'Autonomy, Dignity, and Integrity in Health Care Ethics – A Moral Philosophical Perspective' in H.S. Aasen, R Halvorsen and A.B. da Silva (eds.), *Human Rights, Dignity and Autonomy in Health Care and Social Services: Nordic Perspectives*, Intersentia, 2009, 13–53, 15–21.

[23] T.L. Beauchamp and J.F. Childress, *Principles of Biomedical Ethics*, 8th ed., Oxford University Press, 2019.

[24] See the first sentence of Article 7.

performed on Jews, disabled persons and other inmates of the Nazi concentration camps during the Second World War. The voluntary informed consent of the human subject was one of ten standards laid out by the Nuremberg Military Tribunal in the Nuremberg Code.[25]

Article 5 of the Biomedicine Convention specifies the principle of autonomy in the health setting, including both treatment and research, stating that:

> [a]n intervention in the health field may only be carried out after the person concerned has given free and informed consent to it. This person shall beforehand be given appropriate information as to the purpose and nature of the intervention as well as on its consequences and risks.

This provision carries both negative and positive obligations. Negative obligations require health personnel and researchers to refrain from interventions to which the person concerned has not consented. Positive obligations refer to the duty to provide sufficient, appropriate and understandable information on which the person may (preferably after having been given sufficient time to reflect) base his or her decision. Likewise, Article 3(2)(a) of the EU Charter specifically requires free and informed consent to medical interventions.

In contrast, the ECHR has no explicit requirement of informed consent from the individual for interventions in the health field. However, the ECtHR has, in several cases, found that the right to privacy and family life in Article 8 of the ECHR includes the requirement of a voluntary informed consent to healthcare. Article 8 reads as follows:

1. Everyone has the right to respect for his private and family life, his home and his correspondence.
2. There shall be no interference by a public authority with the exercise of this right except such as is in accordance with the law and is necessary in a democratic society in the interests of national security, public safety or the economic well-being of the country, for the prevention of disorder or crime, for the protection of health or morals, or for the protection of the rights and freedoms of others.

Article 8(1) includes the right of competent adults to refuse proposed treatment, even if the life of the person concerned is seriously threatened.[26] This was

---

[25] B.M. Meier, T. Murphy and L.O. Gostin, 'The Birth and Development of Human Rights for Health' in L.O. Gostin and B.M. Meier (eds.), *Foundations of Global Health & Human Rights*, Oxford University Press, 2020, 23–45, 31–33.

[26] ECtHR 29 April 2002, *Pretty v. the United Kingdom*, no. 2346/02; ECtHR 9 March 2004, *Glass v. the United Kingdom*, no. 61827/00; ECtHR 16 June 2005, *Storck v. Germany*, no. 61603/00; ECtHR *Shopov v. Bulgaria*, no. 17253/07; ECtHR 10 June 2010, *Jehovah's Witnesses of Moscow v. Russia*, no. 302/02.

confirmed in the case *Jehovah's Witnesses of Moscow and Others v. Russia*,[27] in which the Court addressed the issue of refusal of life-saving treatment (blood transfusion), using the same line of reasoning as in the *Pretty* case.[28] The ECtHR asserted that

> *the very essence of the Convention is respect for human dignity and human freedom and the notions of self-determination and personal autonomy are important principles underlying the interpretation of its guarantees* (see *Pretty* …). The ability to conduct one's life in a manner of one's own choosing includes the opportunity to pursue activities perceived to be of a physically harmful or dangerous nature for the individual concerned. In the sphere of medical assistance, even where the refusal to accept a particular treatment might lead to a fatal outcome, *the imposition of medical treatment without the consent of a mentally competent adult patient would interfere with his or her right to physical integrity and impinge on the rights protected under Article 8 of the Convention* (para. 135, emphasis added).

In *Pretty*, the Court pointed to the existence of rapid medical development:

> In an era of growing medical sophistication combined with longer life expectancies, many people are concerned that they should not be forced to linger on in old age or in states of advanced physical or mental decrepitude which conflict with strongly held ideas of self and personal identity (para. 65).

Unjustified coercive admittance to institutional care and coercive treatment are considered as violations of the rights to liberty and privacy. In order for coercive care or treatment to be acceptable, it must – according to ECHR Articles 5(2) and 8(2) – serve a legitimate purpose, have a solid legal basis in domestic law, be necessary and proportionate, and based on an adequate assessment by an independent medical expert.[29] Consequently, the principle of proportionality is a key principle when considering human rights interventions. Coercive treatment in psychiatric care that goes beyond what is necessary and proportional, and which creates a high degree of suffering or humiliation, may also be regarded as a violation of the ECHR Article 3 prohibiting torture and inhumane or degrading treatment or punishment.[30] An important aspect of the right to integrity and privacy is the right to data protection, for example regulation of the handling of

---

[27]   Application No. 302/02, Judgment (final) of 22 November 2010.
[28]   Chamber Judgment of 29 April 2002.
[29]   For more details, see section 5 below.
[30]   M. Hartlev, 'Coercive Treatment and Human Dignity' in H.S. Aasen, R Halvorsen and A.B. da Silva (eds.), *Human Rights, Dignity and Autonomy in Health Care and Social Services: Nordic Perspectives*, Intersentia, 2009, 129–45, 139; ECtHR 15 September 2020, *Aggerholm v. Denmark*, no. 45439/18, ECLI:CE:ECHR:2020:0915JUD004543918.

patient information. This is essential in all healthcare, securing necessary trust in the healthcare system,[31] and will be further explored in section 5 below.

4. NON-DISCRIMINATION

The right to be free from discrimination is a cross-cutting human rights principle and requirement, applicable to all human rights, including rights of particular relevance in the health field: the rights to adequate health services and health determinants, and the cluster of rights protecting liberty, autonomy and privacy.[32] These rights are to be enjoyed, on an equal basis, for all members of society. The ICESCR Committee emphasises non-discrimination as a key element of the right to health: 'Health facilities, goods and services have to be accessible to everyone without discrimination, within the jurisdiction of the State party ... especially the most vulnerable or marginalised sections of the population.'[33] The non-discrimination requirement is of special relevance to vulnerable groups, because these groups are the most likely to be victims of discrimination.[34]

Discrimination is about denial of equality, which contravenes the basic idea of human rights. The Preamble to the Universal Declaration of Human Rights (UDHR) recognises 'the inherent dignity and ... the equal and inalienable rights of all members of the human family'. Human dignity and equality are closely related to each other. Article 2 states that, '[e]veryone is entitled to all the rights and freedoms set forth in this Declaration, without distinction of any kind, such as race, colour, sex [etc.]'.

All later human rights instruments prohibit discrimination, using similar formulations as the UDHR, but with some differences. Article 14 of the ECHR is formulated in the following way:

> The enjoyment of the rights and freedoms set forth *in this Convention* shall be secured without discrimination on any ground such as sex, race, colour, language, religion, political or other opinion, national or social origin, association with a national minority, property, birth or other status (emphasis added).

Discriminatory treatment due to sex, race, language, or the like, with regard to the rights protected by the Convention (civil and political rights) is prohibited.

---

[31] See statements by the ECtHR in *Z v. Finland*.
[32] See Chapter 2 of this volume, on the right to health and non-discrimination, and Chapter 7, on access to health.
[33] ICESCR Committee, General Comment No. 14 (2000), para. 12(b).
[34] On vulnerability, see, especially, Aasen in Chapter 8 of this book.

Discrimination in other fields, for example in relation to access to health services (unless this is perceived as an infringement on the rights to life or privacy (see below)) is not covered, as such, by Article 14 of the ECHR, in contrast to Article 26 of the ICCPR, which has the following wording:

> All persons are equal before the law and are entitled without any discrimination to the equal protection of the law. In this respect, *the law shall prohibit any discrimination and guarantee to all persons equal and effective protection against discrimination* on any ground such as race, colour, sex, language, religion, political or other opinion, national or social origin, property, birth or other status (emphasis added).

This provision supplements Article 2(1) in the ICCPR,[35] which is formulated in line with Article 14 of the ECHR. As can be seen, Article 26 of the ICCPR provides protection against discrimination in *all* areas of society, not only in relation to the rights protected by the Covenant. The law shall prohibit 'any discrimination', and all persons shall be guaranteed 'equal and effective protection' against discrimination. While Article 14 of the ECHR provides so-called accessorial protection against discrimination, Article 26 of the ICCPR is a general non-discrimination provision, also applicable to rights covered by other instruments, for example the ICESCR. Article 2(2) of the ICESCR is formulated in the following way:

> The States Parties to the present Covenant undertake to guarantee that the rights enunciated in the present Covenant will be exercised without discrimination of any kind as to race, colour, sex, language, religion, political or other opinion, national or social origin, property, birth *or other status* (emphasis added).

The reference to 'other status', and its relation to the non-discrimination duty, is not clear. A pressing issue is the rights of refugees and migrants without legal residence in their receiving countries. To what extent are States Parties allowed to deny persons within their jurisdictions access to healthcare services? Is this discriminatory, or are such policies and regulations justified by the fact that the persons concerned are not legally entitled to stay in the country, according to the immigration regulations? This and other questions will be addressed further in Chapter 8, on vulnerability, which includes a section on domestic regulations and practices excluding migrants without legal residence from healthcare services.

---

[35] 'Each State Party to the present Covenant undertakes to respect and to ensure to all individuals within its territory and subject to its jurisdiction the rights recognized in the present Covenant, without distinction of any kind, such as race, colour, sex, language, religion, political or other opinion, national or social origin, property, birth or other status.'

Article 4 of the ICESCR is also relevant, in the context of discrimination, as it emphasises that restrictive social policies and regulations towards certain groups may violate the Convention:

> The States Parties to the present Covenant recognize that, in the enjoyment of those rights provided by the State in conformity with the present Covenant, *the State may subject such rights only to such limitations as are determined by law only in so far as this may be compatible with the nature of these rights and solely for the purpose of promoting the general welfare in a democratic society* (emphasis added).

This is a strict provision that may only be used in circumstances where it is clearly justified to restrict the enjoyment of socio-economic rights, in general or for certain groups. Article 4 cannot be used to discriminate against persons, as seen in Article 2(2). The ICESCR Committee has emphasised that the limitation clause in Article 4 'is primarily intended to protect the rights of individuals rather than to permit the imposition of limitations by States'.[36] For example, limitations on the grounds of national security or public order will be met by suspicion, and will, usually, be seen as attempts to restrict rights in a manner that violates the covenant: States parties have 'the burden of justifying such serious measures in relation to each of the elements identified in Article 4'.[37] During the COVID-19 pandemic, most countries have had to restrict access to certain health services, in order to secure sufficient availability of life-saving COVID-19 treatments and preventive measures. This is an example of a situation in which reduced access to healthcare for some patient groups may be legitimate and justified, as long as the restrictions are based on law and are necessary, proportionate and not discriminatory.[38]

Prohibition against discrimination is a key element of human rights protection. The ECtHR has the following approach to discrimination: first, it establishes whether the applicant has been treated differently compared to a similar case handled by the same state; second, if this is the case, it inquires whether the state has put forward objective and reasonable grounds for the different treatment. If there is no different treatment, or the different treatment is justified in a convincing manner acceptable to the Court, the discrimination claim is rejected. See, for example, the reasoning in the case *SH and others v. Austria*:

> The Court has established in its case-law that, in order for an issue to arise under Article 14, there must be a difference in the treatment of persons in relevantly similar

---

[36] ICESCR Committee, General Comment No. 14 (2000), para. 28.
[37] Ibid.
[38] See K. Ó Cathaoir et al., 'Older Persons and the Right to Health in the Nordics during COVID-19' *European Journal of Health Law* 28(5) (2021), 417–44.

situations … Such a difference in treatment is discriminatory if it has no objective and reasonable justification; in other words, if it does not pursue a legitimate aim or if there is not a reasonable relationship of proportionality between the means employed and the aim sought to be realised.

The Contracting State enjoys a margin of appreciation in assessing whether and to what extent differences in otherwise similar situations justify a different treatment.[39]

As can be seen, States parties enjoy a certain margin of appreciation. However, the margin only allows reasoning that is deemed compatible with the basic ideas, principles and values of the Convention. While it is not too difficult to determine when unequal treatment has occurred, it is often a challenge to determine whether the unequal treatment is properly justified or not. Several cases handled by the ECtHR demonstrate the often-difficult task of balancing conflicting needs and interests. Certain grounds for differentiated treatment will almost always be rejected: ethnic origin or race, sex, nationality, religion, gender, sexual orientation, disability, health status and the like, see ICESCR Article 2(2) and General Comment No. 14, para. 18.

In 2009, the ECtHR added disability to the list of 'suspect' grounds, saying that the state's margin of appreciation is 'greatly reduced' in cases involving discrimination on the grounds of disability (*Glor v. Switzerland*[40]). It seems that the Convention on the Rights of Persons with Disabilities (CRPD 2006) has had an impact on interpretations and decisions based on other human rights instruments prohibiting discrimination, similar to other developments involving the mutual impact of human rights instruments.[41]

The right to non-discrimination has evolved from a right not to be treated differently, into a right to reasonable accommodation for differences. The ECtHR has stated that the non-discrimination clause is also violated 'when states without an objective and reasonable justification fail to treat differently persons whose situations are significantly different' (*Thlimmenos v. Greece*[42]). Positive obligations stemming from the duty of non-discrimination form an important aspect of human rights protection. In *Price v. UK*,[43] the Court found that the treatment of Price, a severely disabled woman who was not able to move on her own, amounted to degrading treatment under Article 3 of the ECHR, due to failure to provide the necessary accommodation of her

---

[39] *SH and others v. Austria* (Application No. 57813/00), para. 71.
[40] ECtHR 30 April 2009, *Glor v. Switzerland*, no. 13444/04.
[41] On the impact of the Convention on the Elimination of All Forms of Discrimination Against Women (CEDAW) on other human rights instruments and bodies, see 'Conclusions' in A. Hellum and H.S Aasen (eds.), *Women's Human Rights – CEDAW in International, Regional and National Law*, Cambridge University Press, 2013, 625–56, 634–41.
[42] ECtHR 6 April 2000, *Thlimmenos v. Greece* (GC), no. 34369/97.
[43] ECtHR 10 July 2001, *Price v. the United Kingdom*, no. 33394/96.

basic needs. Judge Greve noted, in her separate opinion in *Price* (with reference to *Thlimmenos*), that the applicant's treatment was also discriminatory due to the lack of compensatory measures, which 'come to form part of the disabled person's physical integrity'.[44]

The CRPD's definition of discrimination on the basis of disability (in Article 2) is:

> any distinction, exclusion or restriction on the basis of disability which has the purpose or effect of impairing or nullifying the recognition, enjoyment or exercise, on an equal basis with others, of all human rights and fundamental freedoms in the political, economic, social, cultural, civil or any other field. *It includes all forms of discrimination, including denial of reasonable accommodation*;

> 'Reasonable accommodation' means *necessary and appropriate modification and adjustments not imposing a disproportionate or undue burden*, where needed in a particular case, to ensure to persons with disabilities the enjoyment or exercise on an equal basis with others of all human rights and fundamental freedoms (emphasis added).

Article 5(3) of the CRPD requires that:

> In order to promote equality and eliminate discrimination, States Parties shall take all appropriate steps to ensure that reasonable accommodation is provided.

The EU Charter establishes a general non-discrimination requirement, in Article 21(1):

> *Any discrimination based on any ground* such as sex, race, colour, ethnic or social origin, genetic features, language, religion or belief, political or any other opinion, membership of a national minority, property, birth, disability, age or sexual orientation shall be prohibited (emphasis added).

As can be seen, disability, age and sexual orientation have been included in the list of potential forms of discriminatory treatment in the EU Charter. Age is another area where the application of the non-discrimination principle is important in the health field, applying to both elderly and young persons, for example in situations where age should not be a basis for differing treatment. Sex and genetic features are other potential grounds for discrimination, for example through differing treatment in relation to reproductive health services.[45]

---

[44]   On reasonable accommodation, see also ECtHR 10 September 2020, *G.L. v. Italy*, no. 59751/15, ECLI:CE:ECHR:2020:0910JUD005975115.

[45]   See J.R. Herrmann, in Chapter 10.

5. PATIENTS' RIGHTS AS HUMAN RIGHTS IN RELATION TO HEALTHCARE

5.1. INTRODUCTION

The general human rights principles explored above are of significant importance to the individual, in the context of healthcare, and they are reflected both in international and national *patients' rights and health law*.[46]

As individuals, we will all experience contact with healthcare services – for many of us, from the moment we are born (or sometimes even before birth), to the moment we die. We are all, potentially, in a position to become patients, and, as patients, we have rights.

Since the 1970s, patients' rights have attracted increasing political and legal attention. Before then, it was not common for patients' relationships with healthcare services to be conceptualised in *'rights terms'*. Rather, such relationships were governed by the duties and discretion of healthcare professionals, and patients were supposed to 'follow doctors' orders'. Nowadays, patients' rights are commonly recognised, both nationally and internationally.

Despite the widespread recognition of patients' rights, there is no specific definition of what is meant by them. It is, however, possible to get some idea about the delimitation of patients' rights from international patients' rights legislation, and from textbooks and other academic writings in this particular field of law.[47] The WHO's regional European office was the first to initiate a more systematic approach to patients' rights. It instigated two separate studies on health law and patients' rights in Europe, in the early 1980s,[48] which were instrumental for the discussions at a consultation meeting in Amsterdam, in 1994, hosted by the Dutch government, under the auspices of the aforementioned regional office. The outcome of this meeting was 'A Declaration of the Promotion of Rights of Patients in Europe' (hereafter, 'the WHO Declaration'),[49] the first comprehensive international legal instrument dealing with patients' rights. The Declaration

---

[46] J. Dute, 'The Leading Principles of the Convention of Human Rights and Biomedicine' in J.K.M. Gevers, E.H. Hondius and J.H. Hubben (eds.), *Health Law, Human Rights and the Biomedicine Convention: Essays in Honour of Henriette Roscam Abbing*, Koninklijke Brill NV, 2005, 3–12; Mette Hartlev, 'Diversity and Harmonisation: Trends and Challenges in European Health Law', *European Journal for Health Law* 17 (2010), 37–50.

[47] L. Fallberg, 'Patients' Rights in the Nordic Countries', *European Journal of Health Law,* 7(2) (2000), 123–43.

[48] H.J.J. Leenen, G. Pinet and A.V. Prims, *Trends in Health Legislation in Europe*, Masson, 1986; H.J.J. Leenen, J.K.M Gevers and G. Pinet, *Patients' Rights in Europe*, Kluwer, 1993. See also H.J.J. Leenen, 'Patients' Rights', *European Journal of Health Law* (1) (1994), 5–13.

[49] WHO, 'A declaration on the promotion of patients' rights in Europe', World Health Organization Office for Europe, 1994.

provides a picture of the different rights attributed to patients, namely the rights to: (1) information; (2) consent; (3) confidentiality and privacy; (4) care and treatment; and (5) justice and compensation. Consequently, patients' rights can be understood as a cluster of rights that include the right to become a patient, rights while receiving treatment, and rights after treatment.[50] The *right to become a patient* includes the right to have access to care, and also rights with regard to the quality of such care, waiting times, and other availability and accessibility issues (see Chapter 2). The *rights patients have while receiving treatment* include the right to self-determination, the right to information, and the right to privacy and confidentiality. Finally, there are *the rights patients have after treatment*, which include the right to post-treatment information (including access to medical files), access to justice (the right to complain), and the availability of compensation for harm caused by the treatment.[51]

The basic rights stipulated in the WHO Declaration have received general recognition in both international and national patients' rights legislation, and they have also served as a source of inspiration for academic lawyers in the field of health law. This chapter will focus mostly on the right to information and self-determination (section 5.3), and the right to privacy and confidentiality (section 5.4).

When discussing patients' rights, it is necessary to consider what we understand as a 'patient'. Together with other concepts such as 'sickness' and 'health' (see Chapter 2), it is not easy to agree on a single definition of what constitutes 'a patient'. However, the World Health Organization (WHO) works with a definition of patients as 'user(s) of healthcare systems whether healthy or sick' – a definition that will also be used in this chapter.[52] As with the WHO definition of health, the characterisation of patients is very broad, as it includes all persons – sick and healthy – who use healthcare services, whether on their own initiative or not. Because of the breadth of the 'patient' concept, it is important to be aware of the actual diversity among patients of different genders, ages, social and cultural backgrounds, levels of education, beliefs, needs and resources – differences that may call for special concern with regard to both the individual patient and special groups of patients.

In discussing patients' rights, it is also common to make a distinction between *positive* and *negative* rights.[53] Whereas a positive right is a 'right to' something,

---

[50] See, e.g. A. Kjønstad, 'Twelve main principles in Norwegian health law', *Retfærd* 33(3) (2010), 60–78.

[51] Ibid.

[52] WHO, 'A Declaration of the Promotions of Rights of Patients in Europe', Copenhagen, 1994, part 7.

[53] See, e.g. L. Fallberg, 'Patients' Rights in the Nordic Countries', *European Journal of Health Law,* 7(2) (2000), 123–43, and H.J.J. Leenen, 'Patients' Rights', *European Journal of Health Law* (1) (1994), 5–13. See also section 2 of this chapter, and Chapter 2.

a negative right is defined as a 'right to be free from' something. Positive rights oblige somebody (for example a government) to fulfil the right, for example, to ensure sufficient and equal distribution of resources, such as access to healthcare. Negative rights impose a duty on governments to ensure that individuals are not subjected to unjustified infringement of their freedoms and other fundamental individual rights, for example treatment that is against the patients' will.

5.2. DEVELOPMENT OF PATIENTS' RIGHTS

A closer look at the list of patients' rights reveals both some very old rights and some quite new ones. The right to *confidentiality* is probably the oldest patient right. It dates back to the writings of Hippocrates on medical ethics, in which it is stipulated that, 'Whatever, in connection with my professional practice or not, in connection with it, I see or hear, in the life of men, which ought not to be spoken of abroad, I will not divulge, as reckoning that all such should be kept secret.'[54] The Hippocratic oath is framed as a *duty* that doctors must comply with, and this duty-oriented approach dominated the relationship between patients and healthcare professionals until recently.

Respect for patients' *autonomy and right to self-determination* is often associated with the Nuremberg code, and the requirement of informed *consent* laid down in this text (see section 3 above). However, patients' right to self-determination was acknowledged long before the Second World War. Plato discusses the importance of obtaining consent from 'free men' (in contrast to slaves) in the *Laws*,[55] and the Enlightenment brought the idea of personal freedom to the fore, thereby supporting the requirement to obtain consent for medical treatment. Even though it was recognised, both in medical ethics and the history of ideas, that it was normally not legitimate to expose patients to compulsory treatment, there was, until recently, the perception that a patient's voluntary contact with a doctor or other healthcare services, in itself, implied sufficient consent to necessary treatment. To understand the full scope of the right to self-determination, it is, thus, necessary to look not only at the patient's right to consent, but also to include the right to information and the right to privacy.

The idea that patients are entitled to *information* is – in contrast to the right to consent – quite new, and was developed in close collaboration with

---

[54] Cited here from the *Encyclopaedia Britannica*. Hippocrates is supposed to have lived from around 460 to 370 BC. Britannica, The Editors of Encyclopaedia. 'Hippocratic oath'. *Encyclopedia Britannica*, 4 Dec. 2019, https://www.britannica.com/topic/Hippocratic-oath.

[55] P. Dalla-Vorgia, J. Lascaratos, P. Skiadas and T. Garanis-Parpadatos, 'Is consent in medicine a concept only of modern times?', *Journal of Medical Ethics* 27 (2001), 59–61.

the increasing importance attached to the right to self-determination under the Nuremberg Code, which stressed the importance of obtaining *voluntary, informed consent* from the research subject.

Even though the Code reflected the general principles of medical ethics, the requirement to inform a patient about their diagnosis and risks associated with treatment was, historically, not considered good medical practice. Previously, professional medical ethics required doctors to remain silent on the diagnosis – especially if the patient was suffering from a serious condition – and not to reveal the risks and side effects associated with the treatment to the patient. Consequently, it was considered not to be in the patient's best interests to receive complicated and sometimes disappointing information about their health and treatment options, and it was the 'doctor's privilege' to assess whether patients should be informed or not.[56] However, gradually, this attitude changed. The Nuremberg Code paved the way for this change, but it did not represent a genuine breakthrough for the principle of informed consent, given that the code focuses on regulating medical experiments, and not medical treatment in general. After the war crimes trials in Nuremberg, the informed consent requirement was largely ignored, but in the 1950s and 1960s a number of US court cases revitalised the discussion about patients' rights to information, and it is now generally acknowledged that, in giving valid and proper consent to treatment, patients are entitled to information about their health condition, treatment opportunities, and the possible advantages and side-effects of specific kinds of treatment.[57] Another dimension of the right to information is the patient's right to have access to their medical file. This right is also more recent, and has been influenced by the development of data protection law.

Compared to the right to information, the rights of *complaint* and to be *compensated* for medical malpractice are of longer standing. However, in practice, patients often face difficulties in getting their complaints and compensation claims through the normal judicial system (health authorities and/or courts). Hence, this is an area in which many countries have taken initiatives to strengthen patients' rights by introducing patient ombudsmen or other specific complaints mechanisms, and some countries have also established special no-fault compensation schemes that provide patients with easier access to compensation, in cases of medical malpractice.[58]

All in all, the development of patients' rights has been the product of a long journey from the ancient writings in medical ethics of 400–300 BC, through the

---

56   J. Katz, *The Silent World of Doctor and Patient*, Johns Hopkins University Press, 2001.
57   For more details, see R. Faden and T.L. Beauchamp, *A History and Theory of Informed Consent*, Oxford University Press, 1986.
58   This is the case in, e.g. the Nordic countries and New Zealand.

recognition of individual liberty advanced during the Enlightenment, passing through the post-war reaction to the medical atrocities of the Second World War – especially the recognition of the dignity and equal worth of all human beings – and, finally, to today, where the development of welfare societies and digital and gene technologies have added new dimensions to the concept of patients' rights. New rights have been recognised during the journey, most notably the right to information, and more specific rights with regard to access to healthcare and new health technologies, and the old rights have all been revised and supplemented over time to adapt them to developments in society. Along this journey, patients' rights have also changed in character, from being reflections of duties imposed on doctors, to being stipulated as the individual rights of patients. This transformation to a rights-based approach has been supported by the general recognition of human rights in most of the world, especially since the end of the 1980s.

Human rights have been a faithful travel partner in the last part of this journey, and, since the Nuremberg Code, health law and human rights law have developed in close collaboration, as an interaction between national experts and scholars, and initiatives taken by international organisations.[59] Legal developments at national levels have influenced the initiatives taken by the international community, which, in turn, have been a source of inspiration for further national developments.[60] The WHO was very instrumental in the development of the first comprehensive patients' rights instrument, and both the Council of Europe and UNESCO have been very active in this field of law during the last 20 years. The Council of Europe adopted the Convention on Human Rights and Biomedicine in 1997,[61] and UNESCO has also adopted a number of declarations, especially in the area of new technologies.[62] These new patient-oriented human rights instruments have supplemented the general human rights instruments, which have also proved to be of importance for patients' rights (for more details, see Chapters 4 and 5). The EU is also playing

---

[59]   J. Dute, 'The Leading Principles of the Convention of Human Rights and Biomedicine' in J.K.M. Gevers, E.H. Hondius and J.H. Hubben (eds.), *Health Law, Human Rights and the Biomedicine Convention: Essays in Honour of Henriette Roscam Abbing*, Koninklijke Brill NV, 2005, 3–12; Mette Hartlev, 'Diversity and Harmonisation: Trends and Challenges in European Health Law', *European Journal for Health Law* 17 (2010), 37–50.

[60]   H.J.J. Leenen, 'Patients' Rights', *European Journal of Health Law* (1) (1994), 5–13.

[61]   Council of Europe, 'Convention for the protection of Human Rights and Dignity of the Human Being with regard to the Application of Biology and Medicine', Oviedo, opened for signatures 4 April 1997, ETS No. 164. The convention is often called the 'Biomedicine Convention' or the 'Oviedo Convention', and is supplemented by a number of additional protocols. See, further, Chapter 5, section 5.

[62]   UNESCO, 'Universal Declaration on the Human Genome and Human Rights' (1997), 'the International Declaration on Human Genetic Data' (2003), 'The Universal Declaration on Bioethics and Human Rights' (2005).

an increasingly important role in this area: a role that has been strengthened by the Lisbon Treaty and the formal role of the EU Charter of Fundamental Rights (for more detail, see Chapter 6). Consequently, it is not possible to understand patients' rights properly without including a human rights perspective.

5.3. RIGHT TO SELF-DETERMINATION – INFORMED CONSENT

As mentioned in section 3 above, the general idea of autonomy is that individuals are entitled to live their lives in accordance with their own preferences. In other words, it is the individual him- or herself, and not other persons, who is in a position to make decisions regarding important personal matters, and these decisions must be respected, including in situations in which other persons would have chosen differently.[63] Health-related decisions touching upon issues of life and death are definitely issues that belong to the individual's personal sphere. It is, therefore, not surprising that autonomy plays an important role in patients' rights law. Respect for patient autonomy and the right to self-determination is often expressed in terms of *informed consent requirements*, and, thus, as recognition of a 'negative right' to self-determination.

To be able to exercise autonomy and give valid informed consent presupposes, first of all, that the individual has *decision-making capacity*, legally, as well as factually. Legal capacity presupposes the personal capacity to make a rational decision, and requires a certain age of capacity to be laid down in national legal orders. Children below the stipulated age do not have decision-making capacity, in a legal sense, and normally their parents are entitled to make decisions on their behalf. The UN Convention on the Rights of the Child provides a framework for such decisions, including the obligation to pursue the best interests of the child, and the child's right to be heard. In national law, it is often presumed that adults, in some situations, may also lack legal capacity, due to psychosocial and/or intellectual disabilities. In this context, it should, however, be noted that, according to human rights law, a person can only be deprived of his/her legal capacity in exceptional cases.[64] If an individual is assessed as lacking the

---

[63]   A.B. da Silva, 'Autonomy, Dignity, and Integrity in Health Care Ethics – A Moral Philosophical Perspective' in H.S. Aasen, R Halvorsen and A.B. da Silva (eds.), *Human Rights, Dignity and Autonomy in Health Care and Social Services: Nordic Perspectives*, Intersentia, 2009, 13–53; M. Hartlev, 'Coercive Treatment and Human Dignity' in H.S. Aasen, R Halvorsen and A.B. da Silva (eds.), *Human Rights, Dignity and Autonomy in Health Care and Social Services: Nordic Perspectives*, Intersentia, 2009, 129–45.

[64]   See Art. 12 of UN Convention on Rights of Persons with Disabilities, and the CRPD Committee's General Comment No. 1 (2014) on equal recognition before the law. The ECtHR has also been critical towards deprivation of a person's legal capacity in a number of cases. See, further, Chapter 9.

ability (temporarily or permanently) to make a rational decision (temporarily or permanently), it is not possible to rely on consent as a legal basis for treatment, and another legal basis for medical intervention must be considered, for example substitute decision-making regimes. The Convention on Human Rights and Biomedicine stipulates, in Article 6, certain criteria that must be in place in order to rely on such regimes.

Another precondition for the exercise of self-determination is the ability to act *voluntarily*. Persons who are subjected to pressure or influence from other persons or institutions, or who are in a position where they have difficulties in making decisions in accordance with their own preferences, cannot give valid consent to treatment. Hence, the prisoners in the German concentration camps who were commanded to participate in a number of cruel and horrendous medical experiments were not in a position to make a voluntary decision, and the same goes for patients who are in detention.[65] There are also other situations which call for protective measures, for example where it may be suspected that patients are under a certain pressure and not able to act voluntarily. With regard to organ donation, for example, in the Council of Europe's Additional Protocol on Organ Donation it is stipulated that donors are not allowed to put their own health at serious risk.[66] Even though some donors may be prepared to take a considerable risk to save the life of a family member, this is not permitted.[67] The same reasoning is reflected in the rules regarding acceptable risks in the Additional Protocol on Biomedical Research.[68]

Finally, it is also required that the patient be properly *informed*. If information is concealed from the patient, it is impossible for them to exercise self-determination, and to give a *valid, informed consent* to medical intervention. However, patients may also have an interest in being given access to health information in situations other than those relating to specific medical decisions. *Access to medical files* may be important for various reasons, and it is also vital that patients have *access to general information* regarding how to protect their health, and about the rights to care and to treatment possibilities.

The obligation to obtain the patient's *informed consent* to medical interventions is regulated in a number of international and regional human rights instruments. Although the ECHR does not specifically mention a right to

---

[65]   E.g. prisoners and involuntarily institutionalised psychiatric patients.

[66]   Council of Europe, 'Additional Protocol to the Convention on Human Rights and Biomedicine on Transplantation of Organs and Tissues of Human Origin', CETS 186, Strasbourg, 2002, Art. 11.

[67]   See para. 69 in Council of Europe, 'Explanatory Report to Additional Protocol to the Convention on Human Rights and Biomedicine on Transplantation of Organs and Tissues of Human Origin', CETS 186, Strasbourg, 2002.

[68]   Council of Europe, 'Additional Protocol to Convention on Human Rights and Biomedicine concerning Biomedical Research', CETS 195, Strasbourg, 2005, Art. 6.

autonomy and self-determination (see, further, section 3 above, and Chapter 5) or an obligation to obtain consent to treatment, the ECtHR has stressed that respect for autonomy and a right to self-determination is protected by Article 8 ECHR (the right to private and family life),[69] and, in a number of cases, the Court has also ruled that there has been a violation of Article 8(1) where the individual concerned has been subjected to a medical intervention *without sufficient prior information* about the treatment, or even *against his or her will*.[70] The importance of obtaining express *consent* was also addressed by the Court in *Glass v. UK*, in which it held that the British government had not succeeded in establishing that free, expressed and informed consent had been given.[71] The Court has also established a right to be informed when consenting to medical interventions, to ensure a sufficient basis for exercising the right to self-determination. Hence, in *Trocellier v. France*, the Court stated that the Contracting States are bound to 'adopt the necessary regulatory measures to ensure that doctors consider the foreseeable consequences of the planned medical procedure on their patients' physical integrity and to inform patients of these beforehand in such a way that they are able to give informed consent'.[72] Similarly, in *Testa v. Croatia*, it was stressed that the applicant (a prisoner) had not been provided with appropriate diagnostic treatment, and had been left without relevant information in respect of her illness, 'thus keeping her in dark about her health condition and depriving her of any control over it'.[73]

In contrast to the ECHR, the EU Charter specifically requires informed consent to medical interventions, and consent requirements are also very visible in international patients' rights law. The visibility of consent requirements in more recent human rights and patients' rights instruments illustrates the growing recognition of autonomy that developed in international law during the second part of the twentieth century.

Article 5 of the Biomedicine Convention stipulates that, 'An intervention in the health field may only be carried out after the person concerned has given free and informed consent to it'. The 'person shall beforehand be given appropriate information as to the purpose and nature of the intervention as well as on its consequences and risks', and consent may be withdrawn freely at any time. Similar expressions are found in other patients' rights instruments,[74]

---

69 ECtHR 29 April 2002, *Pretty v. the UK*, no. 2346/02; ECtHR 10 April 2007, *Evans v. UK*, no. 6339/05, para. 71.
70 See references to the ECtHR case law regarding right to information and right to consent in Chapter 5, section 2.2.2.5.2.
71 ECtHR 9 March 2004, *Glass v. the UK*, no. 61827/00, para. 82.
72 ECtHR 5 October 2006, *Trocellier v. France*, no. 75725/01.
73 ECtHR 12 July 2007, *Testa v. Croatia*, no. 20877/04, para. 52.
74 See, e.g. Art. 6 of UNESCO Declaration on Bioethics and Human Rights, and Art. 3 of the EU Charter on Fundamental Rights.

and these express the 'negative variant' of the right to self-determination: the right not to be subjected to an intervention.[75] The Explanatory Report to the Convention explains that intervention should be understood in a broad sense,[76] and it is, furthermore, laid out that consent may take various forms: implied or express, and oral or written, depending on the nature of the intervention. Routine interventions will normally only require implied consent, whereas other more invasive interventions call for expressly articulated consent.[77] The Biomedicine Convention lays down more specific consent requirements with regard to medical research and organ transplantation (Articles 16 and 19), and the additional protocols to the Convention on Organ Transplantation, Research and Genetic Testing also contain more specific rules regarding the quality of the patient's consent.[78] Furthermore, special issues regarding consent may occur in other areas, such as reproduction and end-of-life decisions (for more detail, see Chapters 10 and 11).

As the right to information is a component of patients' rights to self-determination, it follows automatically that a patient's *wish not to be informed* should also be respected. Both the WHO Declaration and the Biomedicine Convention recognise patients' *right 'not to know'*.[79] The right not to know is of special importance with regard to genetic testing and genetic information, where it is recognised that the tested person may have good reasons for wishing not to know, for example, about the presence of a gene causing a serious disease for which there is currently no effective treatment.[80]

It is important to note that the right not to know typically applies to the conventional treatment setting, in which the treatment is deemed to have a

---

[75] Positive and negative rights are introduced above, in sections 2 and 5.1 of this chapter. See also Chapter 2.

[76] See Council of Europe, 'Explanatory Report to the Convention for the Protection of Human Rights and Dignity of the Human Being with regard to the Application of Biology and Medicine: Convention on Human Rights and Biomedicine', CETS 164, Oviedo, 1997, para. 34, where it is stipulated that interventions cover 'all medical acts, in particular interventions performed for the purpose of preventive care, diagnosis, treatment or rehabilitation or in a research context'.

[77] Ibid., para. 37.

[78] Arts. 12–13 of Council of Europe, 'Additional Protocol to the Convention on Human Rights and Biomedicine on Transplantation of Organs and Tissues of Human Origin', CETS 186, Strasbourg, 2002; Council of Europe, 'Additional Protocol to the Convention on Human Rights and Biomedicine concerning Biomedical Research', CETS 195, Strasbourg, 2005, Art. 14; Council of Europe, 'Additional Protocol to the Convention on Human Rights and Biomedicine on Genetic Testing for Health Purposes', CETS 203, Strasbourg, 2008, Arts. 8–9.

[79] Council of Europe, 'Convention for the protection of Human Rights and Dignity of the Human Being with regard to the Application of Biology and Medicine', Oviedo, opened for signatures 4 April 1997, ETS No. 164, Art. 10.2; para. 2.5 of WHO Declaration.

[80] Para. 134 of Council of Europe, 'Explanatory Report to the Additional Protocol to the Convention on Human Rights and Biomedicine on Genetic Testing for Health Purposes', CETS 203, Strasbourg, 2008.

therapeutic effect, or to serve diagnostic purposes. It is generally considered inappropriate to apply the right to situations in which the patient cannot expect a positive effect from the treatment, such as in the case of biomedical research or organ donation. Here, provision of information is considered indispensable to obtaining the consent of the patient.

Apart from the right to obtain information when being treated, patients also have a right to *access their medical files*. Individuals may have an interest in gaining access to their medical files either in connection with current or planned medical treatments, or simply to obtain knowledge of past or existing medical conditions, medical treatment and the like. Medical files may also contain information regarding birth, family relations, and other issues that are of importance to the individual's family life and possibilities of establishing an identity. These interests are recognised in human rights law, where access to personal information is considered part of the right to private and family life, and, as such, is protected by ECHR Article 8 and Article 8(2) of the EU Charter on Fundamental Rights.[81] Also included in the right to gain access is a right to make photocopies of the files.[82]

International patients' rights law is also concerned with access to medical files, and the right to retrieve information is stipulated in both the Biomedicine Convention and the WHO Declaration.[83] However, it is also accepted in human rights and international patients' rights law that the right to information may be restricted, with reference to the patient's best interests, to protect the rights and interests of others, or in the interests of public health, public safety or the prevention of crime (see below, in section 5.4).

In contrast to the right to information in a clinical situation, the right to access personal and medical files does not impose a positive obligation on the Contracting States that obliges them, on their own initiative, to provide comprehensive information to patients about the content of personal files. However, the EU General Data Protection Regulation (GDPR) requires, in a number of situations, that data subjects are informed about the processing of personal data, and this could impose a duty on healthcare providers to inform patients about the collection of medical data.[84]

Finally, *general public health-related information* is also of significant importance. General health information about access to care and treatment possibilities, as well as about health prevention and health risks, provides the

---

[81] For further details and references to relevant case law, see Chapter 5, section 2.2.2.5.

[82] ECtHR 28 April 2009, *K.H. and others v. Slovakia*, no. 32881/04, paras. 47–48.

[83] See Art. 10 of the Biomedicine Convention and para. 4.4 of the WHO Declaration.

[84] European Union Regulation 2016/679 of the European Parliament and of the Council of 27 April 2016 on the protection of natural persons with regard to the processing of personal data and on the free movement of such data and repealing Directive 95/46/EC (hereinafter 'General Data Protection Regulation'), 2016 OJ (L119) 1, Arts. 13–14.

individual with opportunities to navigate the healthcare system, and to take care of their own health. The right to health laid down in Article 12 of the ICESCR is interpreted as also including certain rights to information about health-related matters and treatment possibilities. Hence, General Comment No. 14 notes that a state is required to meet 'its obligations in the dissemination of appropriate information relating to healthy lifestyles and nutrition, harmful traditional practices and the availability of services', and 'to provide education and access to information concerning the main health problems in the community, including methods of preventing and controlling them'.[85] Similarly, the WHO Declaration (in paragraph 2.1) stipulates that information about health services and how best to use them should be made available to the public, so that everybody can benefit from them. Within the EU, the Directive on Cross-border Healthcare is also concerned with the provision of adequate information to patients, and it prescribes (in Articles 4(2) and 6(3)) that it is the responsibility of the Member States to provide patients with information about treatment possibilities in cross-border care.[86] The ECHR does not oblige its Contracting States to issue general information about healthcare services, but Article 10 protects the rights of healthcare providers or others to inform the public about treatment options.[87]

Turning to information about general health risks, case law from the ECtHR supports the existence of a general obligation to provide information to citizens in situations in which health hazards and risks have occurred, such as in cases of environmental disaster.[88] A similar obligation follows from Article 12 of ICESCR, which addresses the duty to provide information in cases of community health problems in general (for example, epidemics).[89]

5.4.   LIMITS TO THE RIGHT TO SELF-DETERMINATION

Despite the importance of respect for the patient's right to self-determination, situations may occur in which medical treatment is justified without the patient's consent, either to prevent harm to others (for example, to prevent the spread of epidemic diseases), or to protect the life and health of the patient. Situations

---

[85]   UN, ICESCR Committee, General Comment No. 14 (2000), *The right to the highest attainable standard of health (Article 12 of the International Covenant on Economic, Social and Cultural Rights)*, paras. 37 and 43(d).

[86]   European Union, 'Directive 2011/24/EU on the application of patients' rights in cross-border healthcare'.

[87]   ECtHR 29 October 1992, *Open Door & Dublin Well Woman v. Ireland*, nos. 14234/88 and 14235/88, para. 63. See also Chapter 5, on reproductive health.

[88]   See, e.g. ECtHR 19 February 1998, *Guerra and others v. Italy*, no. 14967/89, para. 60 and ECtHR 5 December 2013, *Vilnes and Others v Norway*, nos. 52806/09 and 22793/10. See, further, Chapter 5, section 2.2.2.5.

[89]   UN, ICESCR Committee, General Comment No. 14 (2000), para. 44.

may also occur where medical treatment is unjustified, despite the consent of the patient.

In general, most of the provisions in the ECHR permit derogations from individual rights, in certain situations, based on a proportionality assessment (see also section 3 above). Furthermore, Article 15 of the ECHR is concerned with derogation in times of emergency. With regard to the right to self-determination, it is stipulated in Article 8(2) of the ECHR that the rights of the individual may be limited according to law, provided that the intervention is necessary for the protection of certain vital private and public interests, including health and moral interests. Similarly, Article 26 of the Biomedicine Convention acknowledges the necessity of balancing opposing interests, and provides that restrictions on the rights and protective provisions in the Convention are acceptable if they are 'prescribed by law and are necessary in a democratic society in the interest of public safety, for the prevention of crime, for the protection of public health or for the protection of the rights and freedoms of others'.[90]

These exemptions are relevant to patients' rights to self-determination in a number of different, but partially overlapping, areas. First of all, there are situations in which the interests of public health and safety may necessitate a restriction of the patient's right to self-determination. Secondly, there are situations where, in exercising autonomy, the patient violates the rights of other persons. Thirdly, there are situations in which patients are acting contrary to what is considered to be in their own best interests. Finally, there are situations where the patient is exercising autonomy in a manner that violates fundamental human rights values, such as dignity.

It is generally recognised in both human rights and patients' rights law that the interests of *public health and safety* may justify restrictions to a patient's right to self-determination (see, further, Chapter 13). This is especially relevant in situations in which patients are suffering from infectious diseases that, if left untreated, could cause serious epidemics. In such situations, the first step will normally be the voluntary quarantine and treatment (if possible) of the patient, and detention and coercive treatment will only be justified in situations where voluntary measures are not sufficient to avoid the danger.[91] In any case, infringement of the individual's personal liberty and integrity must be prescribed by law, and deemed to be necessary for the protection of other persons, or of

---

[90] According to Article 26(2), restrictions may not, however, affect the rights stipulated in Articles 11, 13–14, 16–17, and 19–21.

[91] For a discussion regarding legal obligations to self-isolate, see Y. Litins'ka and O. Karpenko, 'Does Self-isolation violate the right to liberty? An Analysis of the European Court of Human Rights' Practice in Light of the Ukrainian Experience', *European Journal of Health Law* 27(4) (2020), 368–85.

public health and safety.[92] The ECtHR has laid down the basic criteria for the justification of detention in cases of infectious diseases in *Enhorn v. Sweden*, which was concerned with the compulsory detention of a Mr. Enhorn, who had been infected by HIV.[93] As to the general criteria, the Court noted that:

> the essential criteria when assessing the 'lawfulness' of the detention of a person 'for the prevention of the spreading of infectious diseases' are whether the spreading of the infectious disease is dangerous to public health or safety, and whether detention of the person infected is the last resort in order to prevent the spreading of the disease, because less severe measures have been considered and found to be insufficient to safeguard the public interest.[94]

Having assessed the case, the Court reached the conclusion that HIV was an infectious disease threatening public health, but it was not convinced that the detention of Mr. Enhorn was a last resort, because 'less severe measures had not been considered and found to be insufficient to safeguard the public interest'. Furthermore, it noted that the Swedish authorities had failed to strike a fair balance between competing interests, because the detention amounted to one and a half years in total, which, in the Court's opinion, was not sufficiently balanced to the needs of society in preventing the spread of HIV.[95]

In a number of cases, the ECtHR has addressed the infringement of personal liberty (ECHR, Article 5) and the right to self-determination (ECHR, Article 8) with regard to the detention and coercive treatment of *psychiatric patients* (see, further, Chapters 5 and 9). In general, it is required that the mental disorder be of a character and degree that makes compulsory confinement absolutely necessary, and the continuation of this confinement must be justified by the persistence of the disorder.

In addition to the treatment of psychiatric patients and epidemic diseases, the ECtHR has also addressed the justiciability of medical interventions with a purpose other than medical treatment, such as forensic investigations (blood or saliva samples), injections, and medical examinations such as virginity tests. As discussed, in more detail, in Chapter 5, such interventions are accepted by the Court, provided that there is compliance with the proportionality principle: they

---

[92] For justification of derogation from the CCPR in UN Commission on Human Rights, see UN Commission of Human Rights, 'Siracusa Principles on the Limitation and Derogation Provisions in the international Covenant on Civil and Political Rights', 28 September 1984, E/CN.4/1985/4, www.unhcr.org/refworld/docid/4672bc122.html.

[93] ECtHR 25 January 2005, *Enhorn v. Sweden*, no. 56529/00.

[94] Ibid., para. 41. See also ECtHR 24 July 2012, *Fülöp v. Romania*, no. 18999/04, which was concerned with the protection of prisoners against exposure to infectious diseases (in this case, tuberculosis).

[95] ECtHR 25 January 2005, *Enhorn v. Sweden*, no. 56529/00, para. 55.

must be convincingly justified on the facts of the particular case, and alternative, less intrusive methods of recovering evidence must have been considered. In forensic investigations, the seriousness of the offence must be taken into consideration when assessing the legitimacy of the intervention, and, if particularly intrusive procedures are to be used, strict scrutiny is required. Furthermore, the procedure must not entail any risk of lasting detriment to the person's health, and account must be taken of whether the person concerned has experienced, or would experience, serious physical pain or suffering as a result of the forcible medical intervention. Finally, it must also be determined whether the forcible medical procedure was ordered and administered by medical doctors, and whether the person concerned was placed under constant medical supervision.[96]

The second situation in which restrictions to a patient's right to self-determination may be justified is where the patient's decision regarding treatment *violates other persons' rights*. Some of these situations overlap with cases of public health and safety. Hence, patients who refuse to be treated for infectious diseases may be a threat to another person's right to health, as well as to public health in general. However, special situations may occur where there is, exclusively, a conflict between two persons' rights. This is especially relevant in cases concerning reproductive issues. In *Evans v. UK*, the ECtHR reached the conclusion that an applicant's right to retain frozen embryos in order to become a parent should be balanced against her former partner's decision not to have a genetically related child with her, and the Court found that her right to self-determination could not be accorded greater weight than the partner's right to self-determination.[97]

In some situations, it may also be considered to *be in the patient's best interests* not to respect his or her decisions. This is a sensitive reason for derogating from the right to self-determination, because a person's right to live a life in accordance with his or her own preferences, irrespective of what others believe, is an important justification for the principle of autonomy and respect for dignity. Consequently, interventions in the right to self-determination based on paternalistic considerations are de facto in conflict with the essence of the autonomy principle. This was also recognised by the ECtHR in *Jehovah's Witnesses of Moscow v. Russia*, in which the Court clearly stated that:

> The ability to conduct one's life in a manner of one's own choosing includes the opportunity to pursue activities perceived to be of a physically harmful or dangerous nature for the individual concerned. In the sphere of medical assistance, even

---

[96] ECtHR 11 July 2006, *Jalloh v. Germany*, no. 54810/00, para. 69–74. See also ECtHR 7 October 2008, *Bogumil v. Portugal*, no. 35228/03, para. 77–79.

[97] ECtHR 10 April 2007, *Evans v. UK*, no. 6339/05. There is a more detailed discussion of the case in Chapter 10.

where the refusal to accept a particular treatment might lead to a fatal outcome, the imposition of medical treatment without the consent of a mentally competent adult patient would interfere with his or her right to physical integrity and impinge on the rights protected under Article 8 of the Convention.[98]

The Court further noted that:

> The freedom to accept or refuse specific medical treatment, or to select an alternative form of treatment, is vital to the principles of self-determination and personal autonomy. A competent adult patient is free to decide, for instance, whether or not to undergo surgery or treatment or, by the same token, to have a blood transfusion. However, for this freedom to be meaningful, patients must have the right to make choices that accord with their own views and values, regardless of how irrational, unwise or imprudent such choices may appear to others.[99]

Considering Article 8(2) of the ECHR, it is interesting to observe that the interests of the individual concerned are not listed as legitimate reasons for an infringement of the right to private life and self-determination. Article 8(2) only covers the interests of other persons, and of society. Article 26 of the Biomedicine Convention takes exactly the same line as Article 8(2) of the ECHR.

In addition to these examples, the ECtHR has also accepted medical interventions against a patient's will in other situations of medical necessity. In *Bogumil v. Portugal*, the applicant had swallowed a packet of cocaine and tried to smuggle it into Portugal. He claimed not to have consented to a medical intervention to which he was subjected, to remove the packet from his stomach. This was initiated due to a risk of fatal intoxication, and the Court reached the conclusion that, irrespective of the lack of consent, the intervention was justified due to therapeutic necessity.[100]

The last examples of justified restrictions to patients' rights to self-determination refer to cases in which patients wish to exercise autonomy in a manner that is contradictory to basic human rights. This could be the case in a variety of situations where patients wish to embark on treatment that, from a human rights perspective, is considered problematic.[101] The Explanatory Report to the Biomedicine Convention draws attention to the risk associated

---

[98]   ECtHR 10 June 2010, *Jehovah's Witnesses of Moscow v. Russia*, no. 302/02, para. 135.

[99]   Ibid., para. 136.

[100] ECtHR 7 October 2008, *Bogumil v. Portugal*, no. 35228/03, paras. 89–90. See, for a critical discussion of an obligation for, e.g. elderly persons to self-isolate during the COVID-19 pandemic to protect their own health, Y. Litins'ka and O. Karpenko, 'Does Self-isolation violate the right to liberty? An Analysis of the European Court of Human Rights' Practice in Light of the Ukrainian Experience', *European Journal of Health Law* 27(4) (2020), 368–85.

[101] It is a general rule in European human rights law that individuals cannot consent to treatment that is contrary to basic human rights, notably the right to dignity (see section 2 above). The ECtHR has addressed this issue in a few cases, which were not concerned with patients' rights,

with technological progress in the biomedical field, and stresses that, 'It is no longer the individual or society that may be at risk but the human species itself.'[102] The Biomedicine Convention deals with the risk to the human species, as such, in a few provisions, for example in Article 14 (non-selection of sex), and in Article 21 (prohibition of commercialisation of the human body). The Additional Protocol to the Convention, on cloning, also exemplifies the concern in this area, stressing in the preamble that, 'the instrumentalisation of human beings through the deliberate creation of genetically identical human beings is contrary to human dignity'.[103] Other problematic interventions discussed in medical ethics include situations where patients ask for the amputation of a well-functioning arm or leg. The question of limiting the individual's right to self-determination in these situations is concerned with the risk that a more general lack of respect for human integrity and dignity may occur, if individuals are allowed to compromise their own dignity.

6.   PRIVACY AND CONFIDENTIALITY

6.1.   CONFIDENTIAL RELATIONSHIPS AND INFORMATIONAL SELF-DETERMINATION

Patients' contact with healthcare services will necessarily affect their private lives, as they will have to reveal information about their health status, and expose their bodies and thoughts, to healthcare professionals, to obtain diagnoses and receive proper treatment. Information about an individual's health condition is very sensitive and belongs, clearly, to the private sphere. Medical ethics have, for many years, imposed a duty of confidentiality on doctors and other healthcare professionals, and the need to protect patients' rights to privacy is recognised in human rights law, as well as in international patients' rights law.[104]

---

but which may, nevertheless, give the impression of a balancing of interests in such cases. See ECtHR 19 February 1997, *Laskey, Jaggard and Brown v. UK*, nos. 21627/93, 21826/93 and 21974/93 (sadomasochistic activities); Eur. Commiss. HR 16 October 1996, *Wackenheim v. France*, no. 29961/96 (dwarf-throwing). The latter case was also addressed by the UN Human Rights Committee in *Manuel Wackenheim v. France*, Communication 854/1999, UN Doc. CCPR/C/75/D/854/1999 (2002). See also D. Beyleveld and R. Brownsword, *Human Dignity in Bioethics and Biolaw*, Oxford/New York: Oxford University Press, 2001, in which the authors argue that the concept of dignity encompasses a right to respect for one's own dignity, as well as an obligation not to compromise one's dignity.

[102]   See Council of Europe, 'Explanatory Report to the Convention for the Protection of Human Rights and Dignity of the Human Being with regard to the Application of Biology and Medicine: Convention on Human Rights and Biomedicine', CETS 164, Oviedo, 1997, para. 14.

[103]   Council of Europe, 'Additional Protocol to the Convention on Human Rights and Biomedicine on the Prohibition of Cloning Human Beings', CETS 168, Paris, 1998.

[104]   See section 6.2 of this chapter.

Article 8 of the ECHR protects medical privacy, and the ECtHR has also, in several cases, emphasised that health information is very sensitive, and at the heart of the protection offered by Article 8. In *Z. v. Finland*, the Court stressed that, 'the protection of personal data, particularly medical data, is of fundamental importance to a person's enjoyment of his or her right to respect for private and family life as guaranteed by Article 8 of the Convention'.[105] The importance is attached not only to the privacy of the individual, but also to the protection of the confidential relationship between the patient and the healthcare provider. This is acknowledged by the Court, which has also stressed that:

> It is crucial not only to respect the sense of privacy of a patient but also to preserve his or her confidence in the medical profession and in the health services in general. Without such protection, those in need of medical assistance may be deterred from revealing such information of a personal and intimate nature as may be necessary in order to receive appropriate treatment and, even, from seeking such assistance, thereby endangering their own health and, in the case of transmissible diseases, that of the community.[106]

The relational character of confidentiality is also stressed by Beauchamp and Childress when explaining the difference between privacy and confidentiality. They argue that:

> An infringement of a person's right to confidentiality occurs only if the person (or institution) to whom the information was disclosed in confidence fails to protect the information or deliberately discloses it to someone without first-party consent. By contrast, a person who without authorization enters a hospital record room or computer databank violates rights of privacy rather than rights of confidentiality. Only the person (or institution) who receives information in a confidential relationship can be charged with violating rights of confidentiality.[107]

Article 10 of the Biomedicine Convention is concerned with the protection of patients' rights to privacy. However, neither this provision nor the Explanatory

---

[105] ECtHR 25 February 1997, *Z v. Finland*, no. 22009/93, para. 95. See also ECtHR 27 August 1997, *M.S. v. Sweden*, no. 20837/92, para. 41; ECtHR 26 May 2020, *P.T. v. Moldova*, no. 1122/12, para. 31.

[106] ECtHR 25 February 1997, *Z v. Finland*, no. 22009/93, para. 95. The case concerned an individual affected by HIV, and the Court referred to Council of Europe Recommendation no. R (89) 14 on 'the ethical issues of HIV infection in the health care and social settings', adopted by the Committee of Ministers of the Council of Europe on 24 October 1989, in particular the general observations on confidentiality of medical data in para. 165 of the explanatory memorandum. See also ECtHR 26 May 2020, *P.T. v. Moldova*, no. 1122/12, para. 31.

[107] T.L. Beauchamp and J.F. Childress, *Principles of Biomedical Ethics*, 8th ed., Oxford University Press, 2019, 342–43. See also M. Hartlev, 'Striking the right balance: patient's rights and opposing interests with regard to health information', *European Journal of Health Law* 14(2) (2007), 165–76.

Report to the Convention provide more detailed guidance regarding the numerous situations in which a patient's right to privacy is at stake in concurrence with other interests. In this area, data protection law and general human rights law seem to be more helpful.

Patients' rights to privacy are also at issue with regard to the collection, storage, disclosure, alteration and erasure of health data. The case law of the ECtHR has, primarily, been concerned with the disclosure of medical data. However, it must be emphasised that other forms of data processing, and especially the collection and storage of health data, are also important from a privacy perspective and, thus, need justification.[108]

Historically, data protection law has put emphasis on the right to informational self-determination, and this has often been reflected in obligations to obtain informed consent from the person to whom the personal data relates. However, although the GDPR includes consent as a legal basis for the processing of personal data,[109] it is not the first choice when looking for a legal basis to process data. A number of other legal grounds can justify processing of data, including situations where processing is prescribed by law and deemed to be necessary in a democratic society to protect interests such as, for example, public safety, the prevention of disorder or crime, the economic well-being of society, the protection of health or morals, or the protection of the rights and freedoms of others.

Third parties may wish to access medical data for different purposes, and it may be expedient to distinguish between situations where medical data are needed for the purpose of *medical treatment*, and situations where the processing of medical data serves *purposes that are not directly linked to the provision of medical care*.[110]

6.2. PROCESSING OF HEALTH DATA IN CONNECTION WITH MEDICAL TREATMENT

The collection and sharing of health data, stored in medical files, is mandatory to ensure the quality and continuity of medical treatment. Healthcare professionals need to have access to their patients' medical histories, as well as to exchange information with other healthcare professionals involved in their patients' treatment, to be able to make proper diagnoses and provide good-quality care.[111]

---

[108] All sorts of processing are covered by the EU General Data Protection Regulation.

[109] Consent requirements are stipulated in Articles 6(1)(a) and 9(2)(a) of EU General Data Protection Regulation.

[110] M. Hartlev, 'Striking the Right Balance: Patients Rights and Opposing Interests with regard to Health Information', *European Journal of Health Law* 14(2) (2007), 165–176.

[111] M.E. Sokalska, 'Medical Confidentiality: Quo Vadis?', *European Journal of Health Law* 11(1) (2004), 35–43.

Normally, this will be in accordance with the patient's own will and interest, and it could be argued that, when a patient gives informed consent to the proposed medical treatment, this also *implies consent* to the communication of information that is necessary to provide the patient with the proper treatment and care. This line of reasoning is reflected in the WHO Declaration, which requires consent, as a point of departure (paragraph 4.1), but accepts (in paragraph 4.2) that, 'Consent may be presumed where disclosure is to other healthcare providers involved in that patient's treatment.' If we follow this line of reasoning, this form of communication does not violate any right to privacy and confidentiality, because the patient has given consent.

As already mentioned, data protection law also provides other legal grounds for processing personal data, other than obtaining explicit consent. Articles 9(2)(h)–(i) and 9(3) of the GDPR stipulates that the prohibition of the processing of sensitive data does not apply where personal data are required for medical diagnosis and the provision of care and treatment, provided that these data are processed '[by] or under responsibility of a professional subject to the obligation of professional secrecy under Union or Member State law or rules established by national competent bodies.'[112] Accordingly, as long as health data are communicated to other healthcare professionals who are under a confidentiality obligation, the information stays within a *'circle of confidentiality'*, and no infringement of privacy rights has occurred. This is in line with Council of Europe Recommendation R (97) 5 on the Protection of Medical Data, which, in principles 4.4 and 7.3, stipulates that data may be processed without explicit consent, if permitted by law, and provided that it is necessary for preventive medical purposes, or for diagnostic or therapeutic purposes, with regard to the patient.[113] This indicates that, in principle, the disclosure of information to other healthcare professionals may be a violation of the patient's right to a private life, as protected by Article 8 of the ECHR, but that this right may be restricted in accordance with the conditions set out in Article 8(2).

In other words, the legal basis of communication among healthcare professionals may either be the presumed or implied consent of the patient, or a sufficiently clear legal basis. In the latter case, the other conditions laid down in Article 8(2) must also be fulfilled, which means that it must be necessary, in a democratic society, to ensure free communication among healthcare professionals in order to protect, for example, public security or public health, and that it is, consequently, not sufficient that data be communicated to other healthcare professionals under a duty of confidentiality. This was stressed by the

---

[112]   See also recital 53 to the EU General Data Protection Regulation, which stresses that derogation from the prohibition to process sensitive data can be justified, particularly where the processing of data is being carried out for certain health related purposes, and by persons subject to a legal obligation of professional secrecy.

[113]   Council of Europe, Recommendation R (97) 5 on the protection of medical data.

ECtHR in *I v. Finland*, in which the Court concluded that the patient's medical file had not been sufficiently protected against unauthorised disclosure to healthcare professionals who were not involved in their treatment. In this case, colleagues of an HIV-infected nurse had accessed her medical file to acquire information about her health condition.[114]

6.3. USE OF HEALTH DATA FOR PURPOSES OTHER THAN MEDICAL CARE

Data about an individual patient's health may also be important in *settings other than healthcare settings*. For example, the social services may require health information when assessing applications for sickness benefits or social pensions, insurance companies may have an interest in having access to health information in cases of insurance claims, the police may require medical information for forensic purposes, and others, such as employers and relatives, may also be interested in information about the health conditions of employees or family members. Furthermore, health data may also be of interest for scientific, quality assurance, and educational purposes.

In contrast to the situation described in the previous paragraph, there is no presumption in these situations that communication to third parties is in accordance with the patient's will and best interests, and it is not, consequently, possible to rely on the implied consent of the patient. The legal bases for the processing of health information in these situations must, therefore, be considered separately.

Article 9(1) of the GDPR prohibits, as a point of departure, the processing of sensitive data, but, according to Article 9(2), such information may be processed with the individual's explicit consent, or if it is necessary for the establishment, exercise or defence of legal claims. The latter ground includes the processing of data for various legal purposes, including: (1) the settlement of insurance claims and claims relating to employment relations; (2) forensic investigations; and (3) administrative purposes in general.[115] According to Article 9(2), sensitive data may also be processed if it is necessary to protect the vital interests of a person who is physically or legally incapable of giving her consent. This is relevant in cases of patients without decision-making capacities. All in all, it appears that the GDPR ascribes equal importance to the patient's consent as it does to other legitimate reasons.

In this respect, human rights law seems to attach more importance to the right to informational self-determination, requiring that processing without the

---

[114] ECtHR 17 July 2008, *I v. Finland*, no. 20511/03, paras. 38–49.
[115] See also Council of Europe, 'Recommendation R (2002) 9 on the protection of personal data collected and processed for insurance purposes' (18 September 2002) and 'Recommendation R (89) 2 on the protection of personal data used for employment purposes' (18 January 1989).

patient's consent needs special justification under Article 8(2) of the ECHR.[116] The balancing of competing interests may be illustrated by the ECtHR's ruling in *M.S. v. Sweden*.[117]

The case is concerned with a woman who had applied for compensation at the Social Insurance Office (SIO) due to a back injury she had experienced at work. The SIO had demanded, and had been provided with, information about her medical condition from the hospital clinic where she had received treatment for her back condition, as well as for other health problems. Her application was not successful, as the SIO found that her back condition was caused by a chronic disorder and not by the work injury. The woman claimed a violation of her right to private life under ECHR Article 8 because the clinic had provided more extensive information about her medical condition to the SIO than was justified by her application. The disclosed medical data included, for example, information about an abortion she had requested because of severe back pain. She also claimed that she should have been consulted prior to the disclosure of her medical data to the SIO. However, the Court found that the disclosure was justified under Article 8(2), as the purpose was to enable the SIO to determine whether the conditions for granting compensation had been met, and this could be regarded as having pursued the aim of protecting the economic well-being of the country. Furthermore, the SIO also had a legitimate need to check information received from the patient herself, to determine whether her claim was well founded. In addition, the Court found that the contested measure was 'subject to important limitations and was accompanied by effective and adequate safeguards against abuse'.[118]

Other ECtHR cases have concerned the collection and retention of health data for forensic purposes,[119] or for the settlement of other legal claims.[120] Consequently, irrespective of the emphasis put on privacy rights, both EU law

---

[116]   See, for a more detailed analysis of the case law, Chapter 5, section 2.2.2.5.3. (Storage and use of personal data).

[117]   ECtHR 27 August 1997, *M.S. v. Sweden*, no. 20837/92. The Council of Europe has addressed the processing of personal data for social security purposes in 'Recommendation R (86) 1 on the protection of personal data for social security purposes' (23 January 1986). It follows from principle 3.3 thereof that sensitive information may only be obtained from others with the informed and express consent of the individual, or in accordance with other safeguards laid down by law. See also ECtHR 29 April 2014, *L.H. v. Latvia*, no. 52019/07, where the court found that the legal basis for a public authority to have access to medical information for quality assessment purposes was not sufficiently clear to ensure sufficient protection of the applicant's right to private life. For a general discussion of use of data for quality assurance purposes, see T. Mattson, 'Quality Registries in Sweden, Healthcare Improvements and Elderly Persons with Cognitive Impairments', *European Journal of Health Law* 23(5) (2016), 453–69.

[118]   ECtHR 27 August 1997, *M.S. v. Sweden*, no. 20837/92.

[119]   See, e.g. ECtHR 25 February 1997, *Z v. Finland*, no. 22009/93; ECtHR 4 December 2008, *S and Marper v. UK*, no. 30562/04 and 30566/04 (retention of DNA samples).

[120]   See, e.g. ECtHR 5 January 2006, *K.T. v. Norway*, no. 26664/03 (child custody); ECtHR 10 October 2006, *L.L. v. France*, no. 7508/02 (divorce).

and human rights law are sensitive to administrative interests in having access to health data to ensure law enforcement, to make proper administrative decisions, and to pursue legal claims.

The rights of other persons could also justify the dissemination of medical data, and this is especially relevant with regard to the patient's family members or partner. In cases of infectious diseases, informing other persons about the risk of having contracted a disease that may be fatal may be justified. The Explanatory Report to the Biomedicine Convention stipulates that, in the case of conditions transmissible to others, the prevention of the risk to the third party warrants his or her right to be informed of the condition taking precedence over the patient's right to privacy, in accordance with Article 26 of the Biomedicine Convention.[121] The interests of family members, with regard to genetic information, may also justify restrictions to the right to privacy. The Additional Protocol on Genetic Testing does not provide clear guidance on the balancing of interests in situations where family members could benefit from obtaining knowledge of the risk of having a genetic disorder, but, instead, leaves it to the states to issue rules and regulations.[122] In some cases, the ECtHR has ruled that the interests of other persons could justify the disclosure of medical information,[123] but the assessments of the Court have been thorough, and in other cases it has reached the opposite conclusion.[124]

All in all, patients' rights to privacy and confidentiality appear to be an area where the balancing of interests needs special consideration. With new digital technologies, genetic sequencing, big data' and artificial intelligence increasingly being integrated into healthcare services, finding a human rights-compliant balance is of utmost importance (see, further, Chapter 12).

7. CONCLUDING REFLECTIONS

This chapter has introduced basic principles of human rights law as they apply to health, especially in relation to the provision of healthcare services.

---

[121] Council of Europe, 'Explanatory Report to the Convention for the Protection of Human Rights and Dignity of the Human Being with regard to the Application of Biology and Medicine: Convention on Human Rights and Biomedicine', CETS 164, Oviedo, 1997, para. 70.

[122] Explanatory Report to the Additional Protocol to the Convention on Human Rights and Biomedicine concerning Genetic Testing for Health Purposes, CETS 203, Strasbourg 2008, para. 140.

[123] ECtHR 5 January 2006, *K.T. v. Norway*, no. 26664/03. In ECtHR 18 May 2004, *Plon (Société) v. France*, no. 58148/00, the Court's conclusion was based on a balancing of the freedom of expression (ECHR Article 10) with the interests of protecting the privacy of the deceased French president François Mitterrand. In reaching a conclusion in favour of freedom of expression, the Court emphasised both the fact that President Mitterrand's medical condition had already been revealed, and the passage of time since his death (para. 53).

[124] ECtHR 10 October 2006, *L.L. v. France*, no. 7508/02, para. 23.

Human dignity is at the core of all human rights, when protecting autonomy, integrity and confidentiality, and when securing human life and health at the expense of individual autonomy and liberty. In the healthcare sector, the rights of individual autonomy and liberty may conflict with a right to health protection, or public health goals, in a number of situations where people, for various reasons, reject proposed treatment or health-related measures. The rights to privacy and liberty protect individual choice and freedom, but the provisions also give public authorities, on strict conditions, the right to restrict individual rights when other rights and concerns justify intervention. This volume contains a rich range of material illustrating the difficulty of such balancing, in a range of health-related cases where important concerns are at stake. In particular, this and other chapters highlight the protection of human dignity through human rights: human dignity is both a key aspect of each individual person and an aspect of individuals as members of a human collective. The individual cannot be 'sacrificed' for collective purposes, but the individual has certain basic obligations to other members of society, who are also human beings with basic rights that the state must protect. Acknowledging certain obligations of the individual is also a way of recognising the dignity of the person. Thus, although human rights are often – including in this volume – emphasised as basic individual entitlements, owed to individuals by a powerful state, this book also highlights the important balancing aspects inherent in the human rights system. Without the possibility of securing essential public interests on behalf of human societies, such as public health interests, the human rights system would fail its important mission in society.

PART II
LEGAL FRAMEWORK

CHAPTER 4

UN INSTITUTIONS AND HEALTH AND HUMAN RIGHTS

Katharina Ó Cathaoir

1. INTRODUCTION

The aim of this chapter is to introduce the central international legal organisations with standard-setting competencies in health and human rights. It focuses on UN institutions that contribute to the development, framing and monitoring of legal obligations for health and human rights through treaties, declarations, recommendations and dispute mechanisms.

Health and human rights is an emerging field. Traditionally, specific UN organisations – primarily the World Health Organization (WHO) – have held health competencies, while the Committee on Economic, Social and Cultural Rights (ICESCR Committee) has primarily monitored the human right to health. However, through human rights mainstreaming (integrating human rights into actions, policies and standards),[1] the mandates of UN health-related organisations have become increasingly infused with human rights. Similarly, through reforms at the UN level, charter-based bodies now also play a role in monitoring the right to health. This chapter introduces the central UN organisations that govern and influence international health, as well as UN human rights bodies with a health-related mandate.

In the chapter's second section, the powers and functions of international human rights bodies with competencies within health are introduced, namely bodies created pursuant to an authority conferred by the UN Charter[2] (charter-based bodies), such as the Human Rights Council, and bodies created by UN treaties (treaty-based bodies), focusing on the ICESCR Committee. These entities

---

[1]   E.g., C. McCrudden, 'Mainstreaming Human Rights' in C. Harvey (ed.), *Human Rights in the Community: Rights as Agents for Change*, London: Hart, 2004, 9–28.

[2]   UN, *Charter of the United Nations*, Adopted 24 October 1945, 1 UNTS XVI.

perform multiple functions which inform the legal content of the human right to health, and provide assessments on disputes between states and individuals.

The third section, on international health organisations, focuses on the WHO as the specialist health agency at UN level. Other UN agencies with complementary aims to, and importance for, health and bioethics are also introduced, namely the International Children's Emergency Fund (UNICEF), the Food and Agriculture Association (FAO), and the United Nations Educational, Scientific and Cultural Organization (UNESCO). This section also shows that UN agencies are, increasingly, committing to incorporating human rights in their mandates, creating a growing interconnection between once-isolated fields. It notes, furthermore, that the global health landscape is changing, and that non-state actors are playing a burgeoning role, but does not explore them in any detail, due to the institutional focus of this chapter.[3] Finally, the chapter recognises that institutions with legal mandates within trade and intellectual property have implications for states' abilities to meet their health obligations, and, therefore, introduces the World Trade Organization (WTO).

2. INTERNATIONAL HUMAN RIGHTS INSTITUTIONS

The origins of modern international law and human rights are found in the 1945 Charter of the United Nations. The Charter establishes the UN and its organs, such as the General Assembly, the Economic and Social Council and the Security Council.

The Charter includes 'promoting and encouraging respect for human rights' and fundamental freedoms 'without distinction as to race, sex, language, or religion', in Article 1 on the purposes of the UN. Furthermore, according to Article 55(c) of the Charter, the UN is to promote 'universal respect for, and observance of, human rights'. In line with these obligations, in 1948 the UN General Assembly adopted the Universal Declaration on Human Rights (UDHR). It has, to date, adopted nine binding human rights treaties (see below).

At the same time, tension between respect for human rights and state sovereignty is embedded in the Charter. International human rights law, unlike classic international law, is fundamentally concerned with activities that take place within the state, yet Article 2(7) of the Charter warns that nothing in the Charter 'shall authorise the United Nations to intervene in matters which are essentially within the domestic jurisdiction of any State'. UN organs (with the

---

[3] For an in-depth analysis of the many organisations involved in global health, see C. Clinton and D. Sridhar, *Governing Global Health: Who Runs the World and Why?*, New York: Oxford University Press, 2017; B.M. Meier and L.O. Gostin, *Human Rights in Global Health: Rights-Based Governance for a Globalizing World*, New York: Oxford University Press, 2018.

exception of the UN Security Council) are, thereby, reliant on consensus and support to build compliance with human rights and global health norms.

The UN has, in recent years, sought to operationalise the post-war commitment to human rights through a process of mainstreaming.[4] Since 1997, the UN General Assembly has called upon all of its agencies and programmes to mainstream human rights into their programmes and activities.[5] A common understanding of a human rights-based approach was developed in 2003, which outlined three elements of a human rights-based approach to development.[6] First, all policies, programmes and actions should *further the realisation of human rights*. Secondly, *human rights standards and principles should guide* all actions, cooperation and programming in all sectors, and in all phases of the process.[7] Finally, all policies, programmes and actions should *contribute to the development of the capacities* of duty-bearers to meet their obligations, and/or rights-holders to claim their rights. While the extent to which UN agencies have successfully implemented rights-based approaches can be questioned, such approaches have become common parlance among UN agencies' mandates.[8]

There is no international human rights court: instead, several human rights organs (both charter-based and treaty-based bodies) play important roles in standard setting, recommendations and deciding human rights complaints. These are introduced in the next sections.

2.1. THE HUMAN RIGHTS COUNCIL

The Human Rights Council is an intergovernmental body responsible for the promotion and protection of human rights.[9] It replaced the Commission on Human Rights, which was a subsidiary body of the Economic and Social Council. Every three years, 47 states are elected, by secret ballot, to the Council, by the

---

[4]   C. McCrudden, 'Mainstreaming Human Rights' in C. Harvey (ed.), *Human Rights in the Community: Rights as Agents for Change*, London: Hart, 2004, 9–28.

[5]   UN General Assembly, *Renewing the United Nations: A Programme for Reform*, UN Doc A/51/950, 17 July 1997.

[6]   UNSDG Human Rights Working Group, *The Human Rights-Based Approach to Development Cooperation – Towards a Common Understanding among the United Nations Agencies*, May 2003.

[7]   UNSDG Human Rights Working Group, *The Human Rights-Based Approach to Development Cooperation – Towards a Common Understanding among the United Nations Agencies*, May 2003, lists human rights *standards* and *principles*, including universality and inalienability; indivisibility; inter-dependence and inter-relatedness; non-discrimination and equality; participation and inclusion; accountability and the rule of law.

[8]   See further, B.M. Meier and W. Onzivu, 'The Evolution of Human Rights in World Health Organization Policy and the Future of Human Rights Through Global Health Governance', *Public Health* 128(2) (2014), 179–87, 179.

[9]   UN General Assembly, Human Rights Council, Resolution 60/251, 2006.

Members of the General Assembly. The Council's functions include human rights education, technical guidance to states, making recommendations, and conducting universal periodic review (UPR). The mandate of the Council spans all human rights, thereby encompassing the right to health.

Key Human Rights Council resolutions related to health are as follows:

- Human Rights Council Resolution on mental health and human rights, 2016 (A/HRC/RES/32/18),
- Human Rights Council Resolution on preventable mortality and morbidity of children under 5 years of age as a human rights concern, 2016 (A/HRC/RES/33/11),
- Human Rights Council Resolution on preventable maternal mortality and morbidity and human rights, 2016 (A/HRC/RES/33/18).

The Council is, furthermore, responsible for the Special Procedures mandates, which are held by unpaid experts, and focused on individual countries or themes.[10] A Special Rapporteur on the right of everyone to the enjoyment of the highest attainable standard of physical and mental health has been in place since 2002, and the mandate has been extended by the Human Rights Council.[11] The Special Rapporteur reports to the Human Rights Council each year on the right to health, monitors the right to health, and communicates with states (where violations are alleged) through an individual complaints mechanism. The Special Rapporteurs have been important in raising the profile of the right to health, and developing the legal understanding of the content of states' obligations.[12]

States' compliance with the right to health can also be assessed through the UPR (established in 2008).[13] The Human Rights Council 'undertake[s] a universal periodic review, based on objective and reliable information, of the fulfilment by each State of its human rights obligations and commitments in a manner which ensures universality of coverage and equal treatment with respect

---

[10]   UN Human Rights, Office of the High Commissioner, *Special Procedures of the Human Rights Council*, available at www.ohchr.org/EN/HRBodies/SP/Pages/Welcomepage.aspx.

[11]   UN Human Rights, Office of the High Commissioner, *Special Rapporteur on the Right to Physical and Mental Health*, available at www.ohchr.org/EN/Issues/Health/Pages/SRRightHealthIndex.aspx.

[12]   E.g. UN General Assembly, *Report of the Special Rapporteur on the right of everyone to the enjoyment of the highest attainable standard of physical and mental health*, A/61/338, 2006; UN General Assembly, *Report of the Special Rapporteur on the right of everyone to the enjoyment of the highest attainable standard of physical and mental health, Unhealthy foods, non-communicable diseases and the right to health*, A/HRC/26/31, 2014; General Assembly, Human Rights Council, Resolution A/RES/60/251, 2006; General Assembly, *Report of the Special Rapporteur on the right of everyone to the enjoyment of the highest attainable standard of physical and mental health*, A/HRC/38/36, 2018.

[13]   UN General Assembly, Human Rights Council, Resolution 60/251, 2006.

to all States'. Through this process, states report on their compliance with human rights (the UDHR, and other treaties that they have ratified), while 'shadow' information on the state's actions is supplied by stakeholders, like civil society organisations, national human rights agencies, and international agencies and human rights bodies. An interactive discussion then takes place between the state under review, the UPR working group, and other states. Following the review, an outcome report is prepared, with comments and recommendations. States must respond to the recommendations received, but are not obligated to implement them. Unlike other mechanisms examined below, the UPR is state-driven, not expert-led.

In a review on the right to health in the UPR process, the WHO found that states frequently issued health-related recommendations.[14] In the first cycle, 22 per cent of recommendations were related to health.[15] However, the effectiveness of such recommendations was undermined by their generality, and their focus on certain health issues, such as domestic violence, to the neglect of targeted health recommendations. Noncommunicable and communicable diseases were, for example, rarely addressed.[16] The authors recommended greater input from civil society and the WHO, as means of increasing the specificity of the UPR recommendations.[17]

The Human Rights Council was founded with a view to depoliticising human rights, and contributing to better compliance with all human rights treaties. However, the Council remains deeply politicised, which impacts on its legitimacy.[18] This politicisation trickles down to the right to health, meaning, for example, that recommendations on abortion are rare.[19]

2.2. TREATY-BASED BODIES

State compliance with the core international human rights treaties is monitored by committees ('treaty-based bodies'). Unlike the Human Rights Council, which is composed of states, committees are composed of independent experts

---

[14] World Health Organization, Human Rights Centre Clinic, *Advancing the right to health through the universal periodic review* (2019), available at https://apps.who.int/iris/bitstream/handle/10665/277114/9789241513883-eng.pdf.

[15] J.B. De Mesquita, 'The Universal Periodic Review: A Valuable New Procedure for the Right to Health?', *Health and Human Rights Journal*, 21(2) (2019), 263–77.

[16] Ibid.

[17] Ibid.

[18] R. Freedman and R. Houghton, 'Two Steps Forward, One Step Back: Politicisation of the Human Rights Council', *Human Rights Law Review* 17(4) (2017), 753–69.

[19] J.B. De Mesquita, 'The Universal Periodic Review: A Valuable New Procedure for the Right to Health?', *Health and Human Rights Journal*, 21(2) (2019), 263–77.

'of high moral character and recognized competence in the field of human rights'.[20] Committees are made up of independent experts who, though nominated and elected by states, do not represent them. UN Committees meet two or three times a year, in Geneva.

Table 1. UN Human Rights Treaties and Committees

Treaty	Committee
International Covenant on Civil and Political Rights 1966	Human Rights Committee (HRC)
International Covenant on Economic Social and Cultural Rights 1966	Committee on Economic, Social and Cultural Rights (ICESCR)
International Convention on the Elimination of All Forms of Racial Discrimination (ICERD) 1965	Committee on the Elimination of Racial Discrimination (CERD)
Convention on the Elimination of All Forms of Discrimination against Women (CEDAW) 1979	Committee on the Elimination of Discrimination Against Women (CEDAW Committee)
Convention against Torture and Other Cruel, Inhuman or Degrading Treatment or Punishment (CAT) 1984	Committee Against Torture (CAT Committee)
Convention on the Rights of the Child (CRC) 1989	Committee on the Rights of the Child (CRC Committee)
International Convention on Protection of the Rights of All Migrant Workers and Members of Their Families (ICMRW) 1990	Committee on Migrant Workers (CMW)
International Convention for the Protection of All Persons from Enforced Disappearance (CPED) 2006	Committee on Enforced Disappearances (CED)
CRPD Convention on the Rights of Persons with Disabilities 2006	Committee on the Rights of Persons with Disabilities (CRPD Committee)

Source: Compiled by the author.

It should be noted that the status of the Committee on Economic, Social and Cultural Rights (ICESCR Committee) is unique. Unlike the other UN committees, it is not established by the relevant Convention but, instead, by the UN Economic and Social Council (ECOSOC), under ECOSOC Resolution 1985/17 of 28 May 1985.[21] The Council elects new members after four years (members can be re-elected), while members of the other committees are elected by States Parties to the relevant treaties.

---

[20] E.g., UN General Assembly, *International Covenant on Civil and Political Rights*, 1966, Article 28(2).

[21] ECOSOC is one of the six organs of the UN, alongside the General Assembly, Security Council, Trusteeship Council, International Court of Justice and Secretariat, that were established by Article 7 of the UN Charter.

Treaty bodies hold important normative functions, notably issuing concluding observations based on their assessment of states' compliance with treaties, adopting general comments that outline the content of rights and treaties, and (where an optional protocol has been ratified) adopting views on complaints submitted through the communications procedures. None of these functions are binding, but they do carry legal and political weight.[22]

The primary role of UN Committees is not to pronounce on violations of the Conventions, but to assist states in understanding, and complying with, their obligations.[23] Thus, the committees approach state reporting through 'constructive dialogue' with the state, for the purpose of improving human rights in the country.[24] This concept has been implicit since the drafting of the Covenants, whereby 'the idea is to help governments to fulfil their obligations rather than to penalize them for violations'.[25] The constructive dialogue approach, thus, seeks to reduce the politicisation of the UN Committees' work through dealing with issues constructively, rather than in an adversarial manner.[26] Reporting should work as a catalyst for increased engagement and fulfilment of rights,[27] including through changing attitudes towards rights.[28] At the same time, this can also render Committees 'weak', as compared to courts' adversarial approaches; there is a risk that an overly conciliatory approach does not improve human rights compliance or protect the rights of those affected.

2.2.1. General comments

General comments are analyses of individual rights and related state obligations under the relevant convention.[29] The ICESCR Committee uses general

---

[22] UN Human Rights, Office of The High Commissioner, *Human Rights Bodies*, available at www.ohchr.org/en/hrbodies/Pages/HumanRightsBodies.aspx.

[23] However, CESCR has been known, on occasion, to accuse a state of violating the Covenant: P. Alston, 'Out of the Abyss: The Challenges Confronting the New U.N. Committee on Economic, Social and Cultural Rights', *Human Rights Quarterly* 9(3) (1987), 332–81.

[24] UN Human Rights, Office of The High Commissioner, *Guidance note for States parties on the constructive dialogue with the human rights treaty bodies*, A/69/285, Annex 1, available at http://tbinternet.ohchr.org/Treaties/CMW/Shared%20Documents/1_Global/INT_CMW_ INF_7956_E.pdf. UN General Assembly, *Report of the Committee on the Rights of the Child, Forty-seventh Session*, Supplement no. 41, A/47/41, 2002.

[25] D. Whelan, 'Including Economic, Social, and Cultural Rights' in D.J. Whelan, *Indivisible Human Rights: A History*, University of Pennsylvania Press, 2010, 87–111.

[26] W.F. Felice, 'The UN Committee on the Elimination of All Forms of Racial Discrimination: Race, and Economic and Social Human Rights', *Human Rights Quarterly* 24(1) (2002), 205–36, 217.

[27] P. Alston and B. Simma, 'Second Session of the UN Committee on Economic, Social and Cultural Rights', *The American Journal of International Law* 82(3) (1988), 603–15, 610.

[28] S. Leckie, 'The UN Committee on Economic, Social and Cultural Rights and the Right to Adequate Housing: Towards an Appropriate Approach', *Human Rights Quarterly* 11(4) (1989), 522–60, 544.

[29] UN, *Convention on the Rights of the Child*, 1989, Treaty Series, vol. 1577, p. 3, Art. 45(d).

comments, inter alia, 'to make the experience gained through the examination of States' reports available for the benefit of all States parties in order to assist and promote their further implementation of the Covenant'.[30] According to the CRC Rules of Procedure, the aim of general comments is to 'promot[e] [the Convention's] further implementation and assist ... States parties in fulfilling their reporting obligations'.[31] General comments outline the normative content of rights, and recommend a wide spectrum of state action, from enshrining concepts in legislation to state-led action plans. Recommendations in general comments range from 'obvious and generic' to 'more practical and precise'.[32]

Three human rights committees have issued General Comments on the right to health: CEDAW General Comment No. 24 (1999), on Article 12 of the Convention (women and health); ICESCR General Comment No. 14 (2000), on the highest attainable standard of health; and CRC General Comment No. 15 (2013), on the right of the child to the highest attainable standard of health. Also relevant are ICESCR General Comment No. 22 (2016), on the right to sexual and reproductive health; General Comment No. 4 (2003), on adolescent health and development in the context of the Convention on the Rights of the Child; and General Comment No. 3 (2003), on HIV/AIDS and the rights of the child. There are also several interconnected general comments on the right to water, the right to housing and the nature of states' obligations.

General comments are widely viewed as an authoritative interpretation of state obligations under a treaty.[33] As this book makes clear, CESCR General Comment No. 14 has had a profound impact on the legal interpretation of the right to health. Although not legally binding, general comments influence central legal actors' interpretations of states' obligations.[34] For example, the International Court of Justice has referred to general comments in two advisory opinions and one judgment.[35] Furthermore, there are several examples of

---

[30] UN, *Working Methods: Excerpt from the Report on the Forty-Fourth and Forty-Fifth Sessions*, E/2011/22 – E/C.12/2010/3, paras. 19–59, available at www.ohchr.org/EN/HRBodies/ CESCR/Pages/WorkingMethods.aspx.

[31] UN, *Committee on the Rights of the Child: Rules of Procedure*, CRC/C/4/Rev.4, 2015, rule 77, available at http://tbinternet.ohchr.org/_layouts/treatybodyexternal/Download.aspx?symbolno= CRC/C/4/Rev.4&Lang=en.

[32] B. Saul, D. Kinley and J. Mowbray, *The International Covenant on Economic, Social and Cultural Rights: Cases, Materials, and Commentary*, Oxford: Oxford University Press, 2014, 169.

[33] UN, *Working Methods: Excerpt from the Report on the Forty-Fourth and Forty-Fifth Sessions*, E/2011/22 – E/C.12/2010/3, para. 58, available at: www.ohchr.org/EN/HRBodies/CESCR/ Pages/WorkingMethods.aspx.

[34] For an explanation of the concepts in General Comment No. 14, see Chapter 2 of this book.

[35] UN, *ICJ Advisory opinion on the Legal Consequences of the Construction of a Wall in the Occupied Palestinian Territory*, ICJ Reports 2004, 193; *Judgment No. 2867 of the Administrative Tribunal of the International Labour Organization upon a Complaint Filed against the International Fund for Agricultural Development*, Advisory Opinion, ICJ Reports 2012, 10, para. 39; *Ahmadou Sadio Diallo (Republic of Guinea v. Democratic Republic of the Congo)*, Merits, Judgment, ICJ Reports 2010, 639, see paras. 66–67.

domestic courts referring to general comments when interpreting national and international law:[36] for example, the UK Supreme Court has referred to the CRC Committee's General Comments.[37]

However, general comments are limited by the working methods and status of the UN Committees. In contrast to the European Court of Human Rights (ECtHR), introduced in the next chapter, Committees are not made up of full-time judges, but part-time experts, who have other full-time jobs. Also, UN Committees operate by consensus, which may result in their final documents representing the lowest standard of protection. At the same time, UN Committees have been criticised for going beyond their legal mandate.[38] For example, states objected to the Human Rights Committee's general comment on reservations, while the ICESCR Committee was criticised for its general comment on the right to water.[39]

UN Committees must strike a balance between persuasion of states and progressive interpretation. If they are too creative or expansive, states may withdraw engagement, whereas if they are overly cautious, civil society may disengage in disappointment. Riedel et al. noted that the UN Committees must 'steer a careful course in [their] interpretation' in their general comments.[40] Similarly, Bhattacharya concludes that it is 'problematic to create obligations that are not reasonably foreseeable', as this may lead to states withdrawing from the treaty, or those states that have not ratified it deciding against ratification.[41]

Therefore, while general comments are an important source of states' obligations, they should be clear and feasible. Otherwise, it is unlikely that states will attribute weight to them. Further, civil society may consider weak interpretations unhelpful when pressing for rights fulfilment.

---

[36]   See, generally, M. Kanetake, 'UN Human Rights Treaty Monitoring Bodies before Domestic Courts', *International and Comparative Law Quarterly* 67(1) (2018), 201–32.

[37]   *In re JR* 1 July 2015 [2015] UKSC 42 [2016] AC 1131; Supreme Court, 1 February 2011, *ZH (Tanzania) v. Secretary of State for the Home Department*, UKSC 4 [2011] 2 AC 16; see also, Irish Supreme Court, 30 May 2017, *NHV v. Minister for Justice & Equality and ors*, IESC 35, para. 16.

[38]   P. Alston and R. Goodman, *International Human Rights*, Oxford: Oxford University Press, 2nd ed., 2012, 289 and 803.

[39]   The US Congress threatened to remove funding if the Committee did not revoke the General Comment on Reservations: see E.A. Baylis, 'General Comment 24: Confronting the Problem of Reservations to Human Rights Treaties', *Berkeley Journal of International Law* 17(2) (1999), 319–22; S. Tully, 'A Human Right to Access Water? A Critique of General Comment No. 15', *Netherlands Quarterly of Human Rights* 23(1) (2005), 35–63, 44.

[40]   E. Riedel, G. Giacca and C. Golay, 'The Development of Economic, Social, and Cultural Rights in International Law' in E. Riedel, G. Giacca and C. Golay (eds.), *Economic, Social, and Cultural Rights in International Law: Contemporary Issues and Challenges*, Oxford: Oxford University Press, 2014, 22.

[41]   D. Bhattacharya, *Global Health Disputes and Disparities: A Critical Appraisal of International Law and Population Health*, Oxon/New York: Routledge Studies in Public Health, 2013, 50.

2.2.2. Concluding observations

UN Committees also issue concluding observations, advising states on actions to improve compliance with human rights, including the right to health. Concluding observations are state-specific recommendations issued subsequent to the Committee's examination of the state's report, and data from civil society and UN agencies.[42]

All UN human rights treaties require that states periodically report to the treaty body on the measures they have adopted, and the progress they have made in achieving compliance with the treaty.[43] Several reforms have been adopted with a view to simplifying the reporting procedure, due in part to states' failure to report on time.[44] Treaty bodies have adopted harmonised reporting guidelines, which require states to submit a common core document and a treaty-specific document. The common core document should provide information, inter alia, on the situation in the country with regard to the implementation of the treaties, such as the status of human rights treaties in national law, as well as how legal instruments are reflected in the local realities, and the general conditions in the country. The Committees also expect disaggregated statistical data, to allow comparisons over time. States should also provide information on measures taken to address previous concluding observations.[45]

The treaty-specific report should contain information on the specific actions taken to meet the obligations under the Convention, including previous concluding observations. Treaty body guidelines provide specific questions that states should answer in their reports. In relation to Article 12, these include information on universal access to primary healthcare, training of health personnel, measures taken to improve child and maternal health, measures to prevent the abuse of alcohol and tobacco, to prevent HIV/AIDS, to ensure affordable access to essential drugs, and to ensure adequate mental health care.[46]

The Committees have also adopted working methods to improve the efficacy of reporting. Firstly, a pre-sessional working group meets to identify a list

---

42   See UN Committee on the Rights of the Child, *Working Methods*, Part II.C., available at www. ohchr.org/EN/HRBodies/CRC/Pages/WorkingMethods.aspx.

43   ICESCR, Art. 16(1).

44   UN Human Rights, Office of the High Commissioner, *List of States Parties without overdue reports*, available at https://tbinternet.ohchr.org/_layouts/15/TreatyBodyExternal/ LateReporting.aspx. Despite several reforms, detailed above, a mere 22 states do not currently have any overdue reports.

45   UN Secretary General, *Compilation of Guidelines on the Form and Content of Reports to be Submitted by States Parties to the International Human Rights Treaties*, HRI/GEN/2/Rev.63, June 2009.

46   UN Economic and Social Council, *Guidelines on treaty-specific documents to be submitted by States parties under articles 16 and 17 of the International Covenant on Economic, Social and Cultural Rights*, E/C.12/2008/224, March 2009.

of questions. The list is non-exhaustive, but aims to improve the dialogue with the state by giving them an opportunity to prepare in advance. The state submits written responses to the list of issues. Civil society is also permitted to furnish information in writing prior to the consideration of the state's report.[47]

For the review, representatives of the state are invited to attend a meeting with the Committee. States are given the opportunity to introduce the new report, followed by a consideration of the report and the list of issues. Committee members may then ask the representatives specific questions, which can either be answered immediately or subsequently in writing.[48] After the dialogue, an assigned country rapporteur from the Committee drafts a list of concluding observations, including positive aspects, principal subjects of concern, and suggestions and recommendations. The final concluding observations are agreed, through consensus, by the Committee.[49] Finally, Article 22 ICESCR states that the Economic and Social Council may:

> bring to the attention of other organs of the United Nations, their subsidiary organs and specialized agencies concerned with furnishing technical assistance any matters arising out of the reports referred to in this part of the present Covenant which may assist such bodies in deciding, each within its field of competence, on the advisability of international measures likely to contribute to the effective progressive implementation of the present Covenant.

In their analysis on concluding observations on the right to health, Meier et al find that critical observations far outweigh positive ones.[50] Their analysis highlights how certain health topics, such as mental health, are frequently targeted, while others, such as pandemic preparedness, are neglected. In line with other research, they note that noncommunicable diseases are also given inadequate weight, despite their disease burden.[51] The authors call for better technical engagement from the WHO, and clearer indicators.

Concluding observations can be influential 'in shaping discussion at the national level as to how such recommendations and suggestions can be

---

47 ICESCR Committee, *Working Methods: Excerpt from the Report on the Forty-Fourth and Forty-Fifth Sessions (E/2011/22 – E/C.12/2010/3)*, paras. 19–59.
48 Ibid.
49 Ibid. Prior to 1990, members issued recommendations in their personal capacities.
50 B.M. Meier, M. De Milliano, A. Chakrabarti and Y. Kim, 'Accountability for the human right to health through treaty monitoring: Human rights treaty bodies and the influence of concluding observations', *International Journal for Research, Policy and Practice* 13(11) (2018), 1558–576.
51 K. Ó Cathaoir, M. Hartlev and C. Brassart Olsen, 'Global health law and obesity: towards a complementary approach of public health and human rights law' in G.L. Burci and B. Toebes (eds.), *Research Handbook on Global Health Law*, Cheltenham: Edward Elgar Publishing, 2018.

implemented in domestic law'.[52] Although non-binding, the CRC Committee has described its recommendations to States Parties as 'an authoritative statement'.[53] Accordingly, their authority is strongest where a violation is pronounced.[54] In order to harness their impact, O'Flaherty calls for UN Committee recommendations to be 'SMART': 'specific, measurable, attainable, realistic and time-bound'.[55] Although non-binding, the author considers that states should give serious consideration to the recommendations, in light of the obligation to fulfil international treaties in good faith, following Article 26 of the Vienna Convention on the Laws of Treaties, as well as the Committees' status as overseers of the treaty.[56]

2.2.3. Complaints under optional protocols

Issuing views in response to individual (or group) complaints made under an optional protocol is the closest UN Committees come to resembling a court. Committee views have had a limited impact on the right to health, given that the Optional Protocol to the ICESCR (OP ICESCR) was not adopted until 2008 (entering into force in 2013). In contrast, the Human Rights Committee has been able to pronounce views since its inception. As of October 2021, the OP ICESCR has a mere 26 ratifications, meaning that general comments and concluding observations are currently likely to have a broader impact on the development of the right to health than complaints under this optional protocol.

Communications are subject to the admissibility criteria set out in Articles 3 and 4 of the OP ICESCR:

(a) All domestic remedies must have been exhausted;
(b) Communications must be submitted within one year after the exhaustion of domestic remedies, except in cases where the author can demonstrate that it had not been possible to submit the communication within that time limit;
(c) The facts that are the subject of the communication cannot have occurred prior to the entry into force of the present Protocol for the State Party concerned, unless those facts continued after that date;

---

52   E. Riedel, G. Giacca and C. Golay, 'The Development of Economic, Social, and Cultural Rights in International Law' in E. Riedel, G. Giacca and C. Golay (eds.), *Economic, Social, and Cultural Rights in International Law: Contemporary Issues and Challenges*, Oxford: Oxford University Press, 2014, 11.
53   UN Committee on the Rights of the Child, *Report adopted by the Committee at its 46th Meeting, on 9 October 1992*, CRC/C/10, Geneva; UN General Assembly, *Report on the second session*, CRC/C/10, para. 42.
54   M. O'Flaherty, 'The Concluding Observations of United Nations Human Rights Treaty Bodies', *Human Rights Law Review* 6(1) (2006), 27–52.
55   Ibid.
56   UN, Vienna Convention on the Laws of Treaties, 1969, 8 ILM 679.

(d) The same matter cannot have been examined by the Committee already, and cannot have been (or be in the process of being) examined under another procedure of international investigation or settlement;

(e) The communication must not be incompatible with the provisions of the Covenant;

(f) The communication cannot be manifestly ill-founded, insufficiently substantiated or exclusively based on reports disseminated by mass media;

(g) The communication must not be an abuse of the right to submit a communication;

(h) The complaint cannot be anonymous, nor can it be in writing;

(i) The Committee may, if necessary, decline to consider a communication where it does not reveal that the author has suffered a clear disadvantage, unless the Committee considers that the communication raises a serious issue of general importance.[57]

Where states have ratified the optional protocol, individuals and groups are afforded an important means by which to complain that their rights (to health) have been violated. Should the Committee find that the state has violated the treaty, it will recommend specific measures that the state should take to remedy the violation caused to the individual, and general steps to bring its law and/or practices into compliance with the treaty. States are not obligated to enact the views of Committees, but must give 'due consideration' to the recommendations. This is in contrast to the ECtHR, which restrains itself to ordering financial compensation, and whose decisions are binding on the state in question.

For example, in the one view adopted where the ICESCR Committee found a violation of the right to health, two years later the government in question appears yet to have implemented the Committee's recommendations.[58] The individuals had undergone *in vitro* fertilisation, but the embryos created had a low chance of successfully implanting. One of the individuals was prohibited from stopping the transfer of the embryos to her uterus, and from donating them to scientific research. The Committee determined that the transfer violated the principle of informed consent and, thereby, also the right to health. It issued specific recommendations to the state to establish 'the appropriate conditions to enable the authors' right to access *in vitro* fertilization treatments with trust that their right to withdraw their consent to medical treatments will be respected', to protect the applicant's bodily integrity, award compensation for damages,

---

[57] Author's summary of Article 3, OP ICESCR. For a detailed analysis, see, e.g. O. De Schutter, *International Human Rights Law*, 2nd ed., Cambridge: Cambridge University Press, 2014.

[58] UN Committee on Economic, Social and Cultural Rights, *Follow-up progress report on individual communications*, E/C.12/68/3, 3 November 2020.

and reimburse legal costs. General recommendations included the adoption of appropriate legislative and administrative measures to guarantee informed consent, withdrawal of consent, and to guarantee access to generally available reproductive treatments.[59]

Prior to and since the adoption of the OP ICESCR, the Human Rights Committee and CEDAW Committee have adopted several views on complaints brought in relation to women's health. For example, the ICESCR Committee view echoes a 2006 decision by the CEDAW Committee which held that Hungary had violated a Roma woman's right to health by failing to obtain her informed consent to sterilisation.[60] The CEDAW Committee has also found Brazil to have been in violation of CEDAW, for a private health institution's failure to provide appropriate medical treatment in connection with pregnancy, and timely obstetric care.[61] The Committee recommended that the state provide adequate reparation, including financial compensation. It also issued general recommendations, in line with its 1999 General Recommendation on the Right to Health, advising the state to ensure women's reproductive health rights, adequate professional training, sanctions and remedies where rights are violated, and that private facilities comply with standards on reproductive health rights, as well as reduce maternal deaths, in line with previous concluding observations. More recently, the CEDAW Committee found that a complainant's right to health had been violated, based on 'obstetric violence' she experienced when giving birth, and due to the national court's application of 'stereotypical and thus discriminatory notions' by assuming that it was for the doctor to decide the course of treatment during childbirth.[62]

In fact, both the CEDAW and Human Rights Committees have issued legally ground-breaking views on women's reproductive rights. In *K.L. v. Peru*, the Human Rights Committee found that the rights of the author of the complaint (a minor) had been violated, as she had been denied an abortion, even though the pregnancy was unviable, thereby causing mental and emotional distress.[63] In *L.C. v. Peru*, the CEDAW Committee found that the complainant's right to

---

59   UN Economic and Social Council, Committee on Economic, Social and Cultural Rights, 28 March 2019, *S.C. and G.P. v. Italy*, E/C.12/65/D/22/2017.

60   UN Committee on the Elimination of Discrimination Against Women, 29 August 2006, *A.S. v. Hungary*, CEDAW/C/36/D/4/2004.

61   UN Committee on the Elimination of Discrimination against Women, 10 August 2011, *Maria de Lourdes da Silva Pimentel v. Brazil*, Views Communication No. 17/2008, CEDAW/C/49/D/17/2008.

62   UN Committee on the Elimination of Discrimination against Women, 26 August 2020, *Decision adopted by the Committee under article 4(2)(c) of the Optional Protocol concerning communication*, CEDAW/C/76/D/124/2018; UN Committee on the Elimination of Discrimination against Women, 28 February 2020, *S.F.M. v. Spain*, CEDAW/C/75/D/138/2018.

63   UN Human Rights Committee, *Karen Noelia Llantoy Huamán v. Peru*, Communication no. 1153/2003, CCPR/C/85/D/1153/2003, 2005.

health had been violated, as she did not have access to an 'effective and accessible procedure' to establish whether she was legally entitled to an abortion.[64] The Committees recommended that the authors of the complaints be provided with reparations. Furthermore, the Committee advised Peru to review its laws, to establish effective access to abortion under conditions that protect women's health, and to consider decriminalising abortion when pregnancy results from rape or sexual abuse.

Dunn, Lesyna and Zaret analysed these landmark decisions and their domestic impact. They found that the relevant governments were slow to pay reparations, eventually doing so three years later in the case of Pimental, and ten years later in the case of K.L., and formally apologising to L.C. only five years after the decision. Eventually, Peru adopted new guidelines in response to the complaints. The authors concluded that the decisions galvanised civil society and brought attention to the states' obligations, but that the recommendations still needed to be implemented: in Peru, access to abortion remains restricted.[65]

The Human Rights Committee's findings that Ireland's abortion laws and practice violated the ICCPR have had a more significant impact. In *Mellet*, the Committee noted that the state party's criminalisation of abortion, in cases of fatal foetal abnormality, caused the complainant 'intense physical and mental suffering'. Coupled with the lack of available information, and the need to travel to Britain to access abortion, the Committee found that Ireland had violated Article 7 (which prohibits cruel, inhumane and degrading treatment). The Committee, furthermore, held that Ireland had violated the women's rights to privacy by arbitrarily interfering with access to abortion.[66] Furthermore, the criminalisation of abortion in cases of fatal foetal impairment violated their rights to equality and non-discrimination, by forcing the women to travel abroad to access medical care.[67] The Irish government paid each woman 30,000 euro in compensation.[68] Ultimately, the decisions contributed to the government

---

[64]   UN Committee on the Elimination of Discrimination against Women, 4 November 2011, *L.C. v. Peru*, no. 22/2009, CEDAW/C/50/D/22/2009.

[65]   J.T. Dunn, K. Lesyna and A. Zaret, 'The role of human rights litigation in improving access to reproductive health care and achieving reductions in maternal mortality', *BMC Pregnancy & Childbirth* 17 (2018), 367.

[66]   UN Human Rights Committee, 17 November 2016, *Views adopted by the Committee under article 5(4) of the Optional Protocol, concerning communication No. 2324/2013, Mellet v. Ireland*, CCPR/C/116/D/2324/2013; Human Rights Committee, 11 July 2017, *Views adopted by the Committee under article 5(4) of the Optional Protocol, concerning communication No. 2425/2014, Whelan v. Ireland*, CCPR/C/119/D/2425/2014.

[67]   Human Rights Committee, 11 July 2017, *Views adopted by the Committee under article 5(4) of the Optional Protocol, concerning communication No. 2425/2014, Whelan v. Ireland*, CCPR/C/119/D/2425/2014.

[68]   M. Houston, 'Woman denied abortion in Ireland is offered €30 000 compensation', *The BMJ* (2016), 355.

proposing a referendum to amend the Irish Constitution to allow for abortion, which was successfully passed in 2018. These decisions can be compared with the tempered approach of the ECtHR, explored in Chapter 10.

Given that Committees' views are not legally binding, i.e. under the OP ICESCR, the state 'shall give due consideration' to, but is not bound to follow, the Committees' recommendations, it is again important that committees' views are persuasive. As of 2020, the ICESCR Committee had adopted just seven views in response to individual complaints under the OP ICESCR, and it is, therefore, too early for conclusions to be drawn.[69] In a review of the Committee's early substantive decisions and decisions on admissibility, Liebenberg suggests that the Committee has pursued a 'cautious but steady course in constructing its normative legitimacy'. She judges that the Committee has recognised that states can exercise a range of budgetary and social policy choices, and has avoided absolutist interpretations.[70]

2.3. CONCLUSIONS ON UN HUMAN RIGHTS BODIES

Several UN bodies now have the mandate to contribute to the realisation of the human right to health, including the state-led Human Rights Council. This chapter has identified the Special Rapporteur as an important actor in developing the normative content of the right to health. The role of UPR in promoting the right to health has potential, but seems to require greater engagement and coherence with other health-focused bodies, like the WHO.

Furthermore, the chapter has explored the crucial role of UN Committees in developing the right to health. However, as the UN Committees have no powers to impose sanctions on states, they must rely, primarily, on their persuasive ability to induce states to comply with their obligations, an ability significantly strengthened when complemented by external pressure from domestic and regional courts, national human rights bodies, civil society and other UN mechanisms, including the UPR. The concern with this approach is that it stands in stark contrast to the binding force that can be invoked by other normative actors, such as the EU.

Beyond the reforms on reporting requirements, other experts have proposed larger-scale reforms of the UN Committee system, such as a unified treaty body

---

[69]   V. Shikhelman, 'Implementing Decisions of International Human Rights Institutions – Evidence from the United Nations Human Rights Committee', *European Journal of International Law* 30(3) (2019), 753–77.

[70]   S. Liebenberg, 'Between Sovereignty and Accountability: The Emerging Jurisprudence of the United Nations Committee on Economic, Social and Cultural Rights Under the Optional Protocol', *Human Rights Quarterly* 42(1) (2020), 48–84.

or a world court on human rights.[71] A single international body could promote coherence among the currently fragmented system. On the other hand, it could result in the neglect of socio-economic rights, and reduce the specificity achieved by the current approach. Politically, given the controversies surrounding the International Criminal Court, the prospects of states agreeing to, and ratifying, a new treaty establishing an international human rights court are low.

3. INTERNATIONAL HEALTH LAW GOVERNANCE

Modern international (or global) health law spans a vast network of agencies, organisations, entities and task forces.[72] It is beyond the scope of this book to comprehensively account for the mandates of each organ. Here we focus on the WHO, while noting the specialised agencies with hard- and soft-law power within international health governance.[73]

3.1. THE WORLD HEALTH ORGANIZATION

The WHO is an intergovernmental organisation,[74] focused primarily on international health,[75] with the bold objective of 'the attainment by all peoples of the highest possible level of health'.[76] The preamble of the WHO Constitution, notoriously, defines health as 'a state of complete physical, mental and social well-being and not merely the absence of diseases or infirmity'. This bold vision can be praised for viewing health in a holistic fashion, encompassing a wide range of determinants, instead of a purely medical model. Although the definition has been subject to critique, it illustrates the scope of both the mission of the WHO, and the obstacles facing its attainment (see Chapter 2 of this book).

The Organization has existed almost as long as the UN, having been established on 8 April 1948, when its Constitution came into force. Indeed, the

---

[71]   UN General Assembly, *Plan of action submitted by the United Nations High Commissioner for Human Rights*, A/59/2005/Add.3, 2005; M. Nowak, 'A World Court of Human Rights' in G. Oberleitner (ed.), *International Human Rights Institutions, Tribunals, and Courts*, Singapore: Springer, 2018, 271–90.

[72]   S. Moon, 'Global health law and governance: concepts, tools, actors and power' in G.L. Burci and B. Toebes (eds.), *Research Handbook on Global Health Law*, Cheltenham: Edward Elgar Publishing, 2018, 24–56.

[73]   G.L. Burci, 'Global Health Law: present and future', in G.L. Burci and B. Toebes (eds.), *Research Handbook on Global Health Law*, Cheltenham: Edward Elgar Publishing, 2018, 486–528 and 489–93.

[74]   WHO, *Constitution of the World Health Organization*, 2006, Art. 3.

[75]   Ibid., Art. 2(a).

[76]   Ibid., Art. 1.

establishment of a specialised agency for health is noted in Article 57 of the UN Charter, and the WHO's roots can be traced to the first International Sanitary Conference in 1851.[77] Although regional organisations preceded the WHO, it is the first global health organisation, currently consisting of 194 Member States. Furthermore, it remains the only health organisation where each state has an equal vote,[78] through the World Health Assembly (WHA), which sets the policies of the WHO.[79]

The WHO Constitution outlines the functions of the organisation: these are, inter alia, 'to act as the directing and coordinating authority on international health work',[80] working collaboratively with UN organs, specialised agencies and governments. The WHO must, furthermore, 'furnish appropriate technical assistance and, in emergencies, necessary aid',[81] and promote cooperation. The Organization holds a much broader mandate than previous health bodies, which spans 'all necessary action' to meet the aim of disease prevention.

From the perspective of international law, the WHO has, furthermore, important normative powers: on the basis of Article 19 of the Constitution, it can adopt (by a two-thirds vote) legally binding conventions relating to its objectives. However, its resolve to do so has, thus far, been limited to adopting the Framework Convention on Tobacco Control (FCTC).[82] Furthermore, the WHO can also introduce binding regulations in relation to the objectives of Article 21, for example the International Health Regulations (see Chapter 13 of this book).[83] Article 23 allows the WHA to make recommendations, by a simple majority, on any matter,[84] for example the International Code of Marketing of Breast-milk Substitutes.[85] Finally, the WHA can adopt non-binding resolutions, which it has done in a wide range of fields, spanning nutrition, emergency care, e-health, COVID-19 and HIV/AIDS.

Despite these functions, the WHO does not have the power to compel interventions in states, and all technical assistance is subject to state consent. Furthermore, its Constitution provides no means of sanction, although voting

---

[77] M. McCarthy, 'A brief history of the World Health Organization', *The Lancet* 360(9340) (2002), 1111–113.

[78] WHO, *Constitution of the World Health Organization*, 2006, Art. 10.

[79] Ibid, Art. 18(a).

[80] Ibid, Art. 2.

[81] Ibid, Art. 2.

[82] WHO, *WHO Framework Convention on Tobacco Control*, Geneva, 2003. See also Chapter 13 of this book.

[83] WHO, *Constitution of the World Health Organization*, 2006, Arts. 21 and 22; WHO, *International Health Regulations*, Geneva, 2005.

[84] WHO, *Constitution of the World Health Organization*, 2006, Art. 23.

[85] WHO, *International Code of Marketing of Breast-milk Substitutes*, Geneva, 1981 [The text recommended by the Executive Board was adopted by the Thirty-fourth World Health Assembly, on 21 May 1981, as resolution WHA34.22].

rights may be suspended.[86] Even its aforementioned FCTC relies on state reporting and state implementation, not international enforcement backed by sanctions.[87] Therefore, in important aspects, the WHO, as an organ of international health, resembles the international human rights system's modest enforcement mechanisms.

Furthermore, the record of the WHO has been mixed. In 1980, it succeeded in eradicating smallpox.[88] Yet, other eradication campaigns, such as malaria, have been unsuccessful, thus far. The response of the WHO to the West African Ebola outbreak also received criticism, as has the response to COVID-19.[89] Meanwhile, Cockerham and Cockerham attribute the WHO's weak response in relation to 'unhealthy' diets to insufficient political will, lack of recognition of the causal connection between diet and chronic disease, and the influence of the food (and particularly the sugar) industry (see Chapter 13).[90] For example, in 1981, the WHA approved the International Code on Marketing of Breast-milk Substitutes, but it never became binding law due to powerful opposition.[91] These criticisms have materialised into numerous reviews and programmes for reform. Yet, the WHO's capacity to reform is severely limited, due to states' unwillingness to adequately fund the Organisation. 75 per cent of its budget is currently funded by 'voluntary' contributions.[92] During the COVID-19 pandemic, the US – previously the WHO's biggest funder – withdrew economic and political support. Some experts even called for the WHO to be retired.[93]

Furthermore, while the WHO was founded as *the* global organisation for health, it now competes with a range of public and private health organisations. Donors, therefore, can (and do) fund competing, targeted organisations, such as the Joint United Nations Programme on HIV/AIDS (UNAIDS); the Global Fund to Fight AIDS, Tuberculosis and Malaria; and the Global Alliance on Vaccines

---

86 WHO, *Constitution of the World Health Organization*, 2006, Art. 7.

87 WHO, *WHO Framework Convention on Tobacco Control*, Geneva, 2003, Art. 23.

88 See WHO, *Thirty-third World Health Assembly – Declaration of Eradication of Smallpox*, WHA33.3, 1980.

89 L.O. Gostin and E.A. Friedman, 'Ebola: a crisis in global health leadership', *The Lancet* 384(9951) (2014), 1323–325; A. Maxmen, 'Why did the world's pandemic warning system fail when COVID hit?' *Nature* 589 (2021), 499–500.

90 G.B. Cockerham and W.C. Cockerham, 'International Law and Global Health' in M. Freeman, S. Hawkes and B. Bennett (eds.), *Law and Global Health*, Oxford: Oxford University Press, 2014, 504.

91 G.L. Burci and C. Vignes, *World Health Organization*, Kluwer Law International, 2004, 144.

92 K. Lee and J. Piper, 'The WHO and the COVID-19 Pandemic', *Global Governance: A Review of Multilateralism and International Organizations* 26(4) (2020), 523–33.

93 UN, Constitution of the World Health Organization, New York, 22 July 1946, C.N.302.2020. TREATIES-IX.1 (Depositary Notification), United States of America: Notification of Withdrawal, July 14, 2020; Foreign Affairs, 'Does the World Need a New Global Health Organization? Foreign Affairs Asks the Experts', 8 December 2020, available at www. foreignaffairs.com/ask-the-experts/2020-12-08/does-world-need-new-global-health-organization.

and Immunization (GAVI).[94] One of the biggest funders of global health, the Gates Foundation, has been described as a 'disruptor of global health', given its huge financial means (far beyond that of the WHO) and ability, thereby, to set the agenda in global health.[95]

While the criticisms of WHO must be acknowledged, its mandate and law-making powers are currently unparalleled. As a result, in those respects, it remains unrivalled, and fulfils an important function. In Chapter 13, its treaties and recommendations are analysed in more detail.

The WHO and human rights

The WHO has, classically, been 'relatively isolated' from, and ambivalent about, human rights.[96] This has been attributed to 'conservatism of the public health tradition, the suspicion that most health care workers have of lawyers, and a degree of caution and scepticism'.[97] In tracing the history of the WHO and human rights, Meier argues that the WHO avoided human rights to maintain its status as a technical organisation, and avoid the 'politicisation' associated with human rights.[98] The WHO, therefore, had little engagement with human rights organisations, preferring to keep the closest ties with public health organisations.[99]

At the same time, there has been a certain amount of collaboration between the WHO and human rights treaty bodies. For example, the WHO participated in the general discussion on Article 12 ICESCR in 1992, which eventually led to a general comment on the right to health.[100] The World Health Assembly (WHA) has also, repeatedly, recognised health as a human right.[101]

Based on the UN common understanding, the WHO has developed its own understanding of a rights-based approach:

> A human rights-based approach to health specifically aims at realizing the right to health and other health-related human rights. Health policy making and programming

---

[94] K. Lee and J. Piper, 'The WHO and the COVID-19 Pandemic', *Global Governance: A Review of Multilateralism and International Organizations* 26(4) (2020), 523–33.

[95] M. Tichenor and D. Sridhar, 'Global health disruptors: The Bill and Melinda Gates Foundation', *The BMJ Opinion*, 28 November 2018, available at https://blogs.bmj.com/bmj/2018/11/28/global-health-disruptors-the-bill-and-melinda-gates-foundation/.

[96] M. Kirby, 'The Right to Health Fifty Years On: Still Skeptical?', *Health & Human Rights* 4(1) (1999), 14.

[97] Ibid., 21.

[98] B.M. Meier, 'Global Health Governance and the Contentious Politics of Human Rights: Mainstreaming the Right to Health for Public Health Advancement', *Stanford Journal of International Law* 46(1) (2010).

[99] G.L. Burci and C. Vignes, *World Health Organization*, The Hague/New York: Kluwer Law International, 2004, 91.

[100] H.K. Nielsen, *The World Health Organization*, Europublishers, 2001, 58.

[101] WHO, Twenty-Third World Health Assembly, Resolution No. 184, 1970, WHA 23.41; WHO, Thirtieth World Health Assembly, Resolution No. 240, 1977, WHA 30.43, 1977.

are to be guided by human rights standards and principles and aim at developing the capacity of duty bearers to meet their obligations and empowering rights-holders to effectively claim their health rights.[102]

In recent years, the WHO has begun to more actively mainstream human rights into its policies.[103] While this began with HIV/AIDS treatment and prevention, it has since expanded to other policy areas.[104] Thomas and Magar note its commitment to a right to primary healthcare, and the findings of the Commission on the Social Determinants of Health as significant milestones in the WHO's approach.[105] Bustreo et al. commend the WHO's increased mainstreaming of human rights, while calling for a firmer institutional commitment thereto.[106] As will be discussed in later chapters, WHO treaties recognise human rights, although they are not strictly human rights treaties.

3.2. OTHER UN HEALTH-RELATED AGENCIES

The United Nations International Children's Emergency Fund (UNICEF) (established in 1964) has a mandate within international child health. The Fund works alongside the WHO in communicable disease prevention, and the development of the Marketing Code. The Convention on the Rights of the Child is embedded in UNICEF's work on child health, and it pursues a close relationship with the Committee on the Rights of the Child.

Meanwhile, the International Labour Organization (ILO) is a specialised UN agency that predates the UN system, having been established in 1919. The ILO is committed to improving work conditions, such as protection against sickness, disease and injury. The ILO develops international labour standards through legally binding conventions and non-binding recommendations. While human rights have not played a central role in the ILO's mandate, it has adopted a formal commitment to human rights, through the Declaration of Fundamental Principles and Rights at Work.

---

[102] WHO, *A Human Rights-Based Approach to Health*, available at www.who.int/hhr/news/hrba_ to_health2.pdf.

[103] WHO, *Factsheet – Human rights and health*, 29 December 2017, available at www.who.int/ mediacentre/factsheets/fs323/en/.

[104] B.M. Meier and W. Onzivu, 'The Evolution of Human Rights in World Health Organization Policy and the Future of Human Rights Through Global Health Governance', *Public Health* 128(2) (2014), 179–87, 179.

[105] R. Thomas and V. Magar, 'Mainstreaming Human Rights across WHO' in B.M. Meier and L.O. Gostin (eds.), *Human Rights in Global Health: Rights-Based Governance for a Globalizing World*, Oxford: Oxford University Press, 2018.

[106] F. Bustreo, V. Magar, R. Khosla, M. Stahlhofer and R. Thomas, 'The Future of Human Rights in WHO' in B.M. Meier and L.O. Gostin (eds.), *Human Rights in Global Health: Rights-Based Governance for a Globalizing World*, Oxford; Oxford University Press, 2018.

The Food and Agricultural Organization (FAO) has a focus on the eradication of hunger, food insecurity and malnutrition. Like the WHO, the FAO has a technical mandate, although it does not have international lawmaking powers. However, the FAO is involved in standard setting, establishing the Codex Alimentarius with the WHO. The Codex aims to establish international food standards to ensure safety, quality and fairness in international food trade.

The FAO has been an important force in developing the right to adequate food. In 1996, heads of state and government reaffirmed the 'right of everyone to have access to safe and nutritious food, consistent with the right to adequate food and the fundamental right of everyone to be free from hunger'.[107] In 1999, in response to a request at the 1996 World Food Summit, ICESCR Committee drafted General Comment No. 12 on the Right to Adequate Food.[108] In 2004, an intergovernmental working group under the FAO drafted Voluntary Guidelines on the right to adequate food.[109] Although the Guidelines are non-binding, the fact that they were drafted by states is important in terms of their legal significance. Further, the Human Rights Council developed a mandate for a Special Rapporteur on the right to adequate food, who visits countries and successively issues reports that help to shape the content of the right to adequate food.[110] Moreover, the FAO has been active in advising states on implementing the Voluntary Guidelines.[111] While these interpretations are soft law, they are significant, as there is limited jurisprudence on the right to adequate food.[112]

Finally, the United Nations Educational, Scientific and Cultural Organization (UNESCO), established in 1945, is focused on education, science and culture. Its purpose is human rights-based: to contribute to peace and security by promoting collaboration among the nations through education, science and culture, in order to further universal respect for justice, for the rule of law, and for the human rights and fundamental freedoms which are affirmed for the peoples of

---

[107]   Food and Agriculture Organization of the United Nations (FAO), Rome Declaration on World Food Security and World Food Summit Plan of Action, 1996, Rome.

[108]   UN Committee on Economic Social and Cultural Rights, General Comment No. 12: The Right to Adequate Food (Art. 11 of the Covenant), E/C.12/1999/5, 1999.

[109]   Food and Agriculture Organization of the United Nations (FAO), Voluntary Guidelines to Support the Progressive Realization of the Right to Adequate Food in the Context of National Food Security, 2004, Rome.

[110]   UN Commission on Human Rights, The right to food, Resolution No. 2000/10, 2000.

[111]   See, further, Food and Agriculture Organization of the United Nations (FAO), *Right to Food Methodological Toolbox*, available at www.fao.org/righttofood/knowledge-centre/rtf-methodological-toolbox/en/.

[112]   For a detailed analysis of the drafting history of the guidelines, see A. Oshaug, 'Developing Voluntary Guidelines for Implementing the Right to Adequate Food: Anatomy of an Intergovernmental Process' in U. Kracht and W.B. Eide (eds.), *Food and Human Rights in Development: Legal and Institutional Dimensions and Selected Topics*, Antwerp/Cambridge: Intersentia, 2005.

the world, without distinction of race, sex, language or religion, by the Charter of the United Nations.

UNESCO's importance in the field of health and human rights is clearest through its bioethics declarations: the Universal Declaration on the Human Genome and Human Rights (1997), the International Declaration on Human Genetic Data (2003), and The Universal Declaration on Bioethics and Human Rights (2005). The Venice Statement on the Right to Enjoy the Benefits of Scientific Progress (2009) should also be noted.

3.3. UN ORGANISATIONS WITH IMPLICATIONS FOR HEALTH

Finally, beyond these health-related institutions, other UN organisations hold mandates that can conflict with international health. The World Trade Organization (WTO), for example, is an international forum for negotiating international trade agreements that can have important implications for health.[113] Conflicts can arise from misinterpretations of existing WTO rules, as well as through dispute settlement and discussions in committees, where states can informally challenge and discuss domestic public health measures' compliance with WTO obligations. The Agreement establishing the WTO spans trade in goods and services, as well as intellectual property.[114] Unlike the WHO, the WTO has a forum for disputes and sanctions, through the WTO dispute settlement mechanism and appellate body.[115]

International trade law is based on the premise that trade liberalisation will improve individual welfare. However, free trade of goods and services may have unintended consequences, such as increased availability of processed food.[116] Furthermore, states' right to regulate on the basis of the right to health, such as introducing nutritional labelling and taxation, or pausing imports due to the spread of disease, are limited by certain trade agreements. While it is possible to restrict trade, based on public health grounds, this usually requires scientific evidence, which can be challenging when emerging public health threats are involved.

---

[113] For a detailed look at states' regulatory autonomy in light of international trade law, see B. McGrady, *Trade and Public Health: The WTO, Tobacco, Alcohol, and Diet*, Cambridge: Cambridge University Press, 2011.

[114] See, e.g. WTO, General Agreement on Tariffs and Trade, 1994; WTO, Marrakesh Agreement Establishing the World Trade Organization, 1994, Annex 1A, 1867 UNTS 187 preamble.

[115] WTO, Final Act Embodying the Results of The Uruguay Round of Multilateral Trade Negotiations, 1999, No. 4, 1867 UNTS 154.

[116] A.M. Thow and C. Hawkes, 'The implications of trade liberalization for diet and health: a case study from Central America', *Globalization and Health* 5(5)(2009).

Exceptions are permitted under the various treaties. For example, the General Agreement on Tariffs and Trade (GATT) Article XX lays out general exemptions from GATT rules:

> Subject to the requirement that such measures are not applied in a manner which would constitute a means of arbitrary or unjustifiable discrimination between countries where the same conditions prevail, or a disguised restriction on international trade, nothing in this Agreement shall be construed to prevent the adoption or enforcement by any contracting party of measures …
>
> (b) necessary to protect human, animal or plant life or health …[117]

There have been a number of disputes before the WTO related to health.[118] In the *Asbestos* case, the WTO appellate body confirmed that a French ban on imports of asbestos fell within the scope of Article XX (b), as it was designed to protect health (inhaling asbestos can, for example, cause cancer). Canada's argument that controlled use of asbestos was an equally effective measure that was less restrictive to trade was not accepted as offering adequate health protection.[119] In the *Clove Cigarettes* case, the WTO appellate body upheld the first instance Panel's decision that a US ban on clove cigarettes discriminated against cigarettes imported from Indonesia, while favouring menthol cigarettes (manufactured in the US).[120] Still, the US and Indonesia eventually settled the case, and the US retained its law prohibiting clove cigarettes; the US Congress continues to discuss banning menthol cigarettes.[121]

Recently, several cases were brought by Philip Morris, at domestic level, regarding Australia's plain packaging tobacco legislation,[122] and under a bilateral investment treaty,[123] and by Honduras and the Dominican Republic in an

---

[117]   GATT 1994, General Agreement on Tariffs and Trade 1994, 15 April 1994, Marrakesh Agreement Establishing the World Trade Organization, Annex 1A, 1867 UNTS 187, 33 ILM 1153 (1994) [hereinafter GATT 1994].

[118]   For a broader overview, see B. McGrady, 'Health and International Trade Law', in G.L. Burci and B. Toebes (eds.), *Research Handbook on Global Health Law*, Cheltenham: Edward Elgar Publishing Limited, 2018.

[119]   WTO, *European Communities – Measures Affecting Asbestos and Products Containing Asbestos*, Report of the Appellate Body, WT/DS135/AB/R, 2001.

[120]   WTO, *United States – Measures Affecting the Production and Sale of Clove Cigarettes*, AB-2012-1, Report of the Appellate Body, WT/DS406/AB/R, 2012.

[121]   A. Behsudi, 'U.S., Indonesia end clove dispute – Brussels official WTO bound – Obama boots Russia from GSP – Froman's busy week', *Politico – Weekly Trade*, 10 June 2014, available at www.politico.com/tipsheets/morning-trade/2014/10/us-indonesia-end-clove-dispute-brussels-official-wto-bound-obama-boots-russia-from-gsp-fromans-busy-week-212543.

[122]   High Court of Australia, 5 October 2012, *JT International SA v. Commonwealth of Australia*, Nos. S409/2011 and S389/2011.

[123]   Allens Arthur Robinson, *Notice of Arbitration – Australia/Hong Kong Agreement for Promotion and Protection of Investments*, 2011, available at https://www.italaw.com/sites/default/files/case-documents/ita0665.pdf.

eight-year-long dispute at the WTO. In its mammoth decision, the WTO's Dispute Settlement Body found in favour of Australia, noting, inter alia, that the measure was not more trade-restrictive than necessary.[124] This decision suggests that a non-discriminatory and far-reaching public health measure can be designed in a manner that is compliant with trade rules and, simultaneously, can provide a high level of protection for public health.

Furthermore, under the Agreement on Trade-Related Aspects of Intellectual Property Rights (TRIPS), states are obligated to establish patent rules, which can restrict access to medicines.[125] However, in the 2001 Doha Declaration, WTO members recognised that TRIPS should not prevent members from taking measures to protect public health.[126] In 2003, this was followed up by a declaration that poorer countries who do not have the capacity to manufacture drugs may import cheaper generic drugs from countries where the drugs are patented.[127] In response to the unequal distribution of COVID-19 vaccines, developing countries proposed a new TRIPS waiver, which was initially rejected by developed countries, who stated that manufacturing capacity, and not intellectual property, was the main barrier to COVID-19 vaccines. At the time of writing, the US administration has expressed support for a waiver, but the EU continues to oppose one.[128]

International economic law has a profound impact on states' abilities to adopt law and policies with public health aims. However, the WTO regime has matured to recognise exceptions to trade and patent rules.[129] At the

---

[124] WTO, *Australia – Certain Measures concerning Trademarks, Geographical Indications and other Plain Packaging Requirements applicable to Tobacco Products and Packaging*, WT/DS435/R, Add.1 and Suppl.1, and WT/DS441/R, Add.1 and Suppl.1, 2020, as upheld by Appellate Body Reports WT/DS435/AB/R and WT/DS441/AB/R.

[125] WTO, Agreement on Trade-Related Aspects of Intellectual Property Rights, ANNEX 1C, 1994, Arts. 7 and 8; WTO, Marrakesh Agreement Establishing the World Trade Organization, 1994, Annex 1C, 1869 UNTS. 299, 33 ILM 1197.

[126] WTO, Declaration on the TRIPS Agreement and Public Health – Ministerial Declaration of 14 November 2001, Doc. WT/MIN(01)DEC/2, 41. ILM 755, 2002.

[127] WTO, Implementation of Paragraph 6 of the Doha Declaration on the TRIPS Agreement and Public Health – Decision of 30 August 2003, WTO Doc. WT/L/540, 2003; WTO, Implementation of Paragraph 6 of the Doha Declaration on the TRIPS Agreement and Public Health – Decision of 30 August 2003, Corrigendum, WTO Doc. WT/L/540/Corr.1, 2005. WTO, Agreement on Trade-Related Aspects of Intellectual Property Rights, ANNEX 1C, 2017.

[128] WTO – Council for Trade-Related Aspects of Intellectual Property Rights, *Waiver from Certain Provisions of the TRIPS Agreement for the Prevention, Containment and Treatment of COVID-19 – Communication from India and South Africa*, IP/C/W/669, 2020; see also A.D. Usher, 'South Africa and India Push for COVID-19 Patents Ban', *The Lancet* 396(10265) (2020), 1790–791.

[129] See, further, T. Voon and A. Mitchell, 'Community Interests and the Right to Health in Trade and Investment Law' in E. Benvenisti and G. Nolte (eds.), *Community Interests Across International Law*, Oxford: Oxford University Press, 2018.

same time, as with the WHO, the WTO is under pressure: years of trade negotiations have failed to end in new agreements, and states are, increasingly, stepping outside of the WTO system to negotiate bilateral and multilateral trade and investment agreements.[130] This undermines not only the WTO, but potentially public health, as arbitration often takes place behind closed doors.

Finally, a word should be offered on the role of the UN Security Council in international health. This powerful organ has neither a health nor human rights focus and, instead, centres, as its name would suggest, on international peace and security. The Security Council has, however, adopted resolutions on Ebola[131] and COVID-19,[132] considering that these viruses are 'likely to endanger the maintenance of international peace and security'.[133] In February 2021, it called for the strengthening of cooperation, including through COVAX, to ensure access to COVID-19 vaccines in situations of armed conflict, and humanitarian emergencies.[134] While the Security Council emphasised 'the urgent need for solidarity, equity and efficacy [of vaccines]', it suggested that this should be achieved through donations and preserving 'innovation', thereby rejecting the solutions proposed by developing countries.[135]

4. CONCLUSIONS

This chapter has given insights into the systems monitoring health and human rights at a UN level. It has highlighted that this landscape is changing, with the WHO's normative authority within international health law, arguably, increasingly under threat from powerful non-state actors. Will these actors commit to honouring the right to the highest attainable standard of health? The chapter also underscores that health and human rights are subject to modest means of enforcement when compared to economic normative systems like the WTO. The approaches available to enforce state obligations are, primarily, based

---

[130] See C. Giorgetti, 'Health and International Investment Law' in G.L. Burci and B. Toebes (eds.), *Research Handbook on Global Health Law*, Cheltenham: Edward Elgar Publishing, 2018, 164.

[131] UN Security Council, Resolution 2439 (2018) – Adopted by the Security Council at its 8385th meeting, on 30 October 2018.

[132] UN Security Council, Resolution 2565 (2021) – Adopted by the Security Council on 26 February 2021.

[133] UN Security Council, Resolution 2532 (2020) – Adopted by the Security Council on 1 July 2020; UN Security Council, Resolution 2177 (2014) – Adopted by the Security Council at its 7268th meeting, on 18 September 2014.

[134] COVAX is a partnership between UNICEF, WHO, GAVI and CEPI, whereby well-supplied countries donate COVID-19 vaccine doses to countries with low supply.

[135] UN Security Council, Resolution 2565 (2021).

on state consent, which can allow states to neglect their obligations, such as reporting to treaty bodies. Therefore, external pressure exerted by, for example, NGOs, as well as state commitment, are important factors in realising the right to health. In later chapters, the treaties, interpretations and mechanisms introduced in this chapter will be analysed with specific focus on the right to health, and health challenges.

CHAPTER 5

THE COUNCIL OF EUROPE

Aart Hendriks

1. INTRODUCTION

The Council of Europe, founded in the aftermath of the Second World War, is an intergovernmental organisation seeking to create a common democratic and legal area throughout the whole of the European region, ensuring respect for human rights, democracy and the rule of law. Or, according to Article 1(a) of the Statute of the Council of Europe (1949): 'The aim of the Council of Europe is to achieve a greater unity between its members for the purpose of safeguarding and realising the ideals and principles which are their common heritage and facilitating their economic and social progress.' The membership of the organisation has gradually grown from 10 (1949) to 47 (since 2007) states. In addition, there are five states formally affiliated to the Council with the status of observer (Canada, the Holy See, Japan, Mexico and the United States). Furthermore, Israel is merely an observer to the Parliamentary Assembly, while Belarus is the only European state that is not a member of the Council of Europe. With respect to the latter country, actions have been taken to integrate it into the Council of Europe, notably by way of the (second) Action Plan for Belarus 2019–2021, but the outcome of the 2020 Belarus elections have negatively affected these efforts. It can, all in all, be concluded that the organisation covers almost all states of the entire European continent, even though some are not yet full members.

The Council of Europe is particularly well known for its standard-setting activities in the field of human rights.[1] The most famous achievement in this respect is the adoption, in 1950, of the Convention for the Protection of Human Rights and Fundamental Freedoms, better known as the European Convention on Human Rights (ECHR). This treaty entails various rights, and corresponding obligations for contracting states, on the interface of health and human rights.

---

[1]   All treaties, including those referred to in this chapter, can be downloaded by going to www.coe.int/en/web/conventions/full-list.

In this chapter, the most relevant articles of the Convention, and related case law of the European Court of Human Rights (ECtHR), an inexhaustible source of information and inspiration for all interested in health and human rights law, will be examined (section 2). This analysis will be followed by an examination of the health and human rights standards protected by three other monumental treaties adopted within the context of the Council of Europe, being the European Social Charter (section 3), the European Convention for the Prevention of Torture (section 4) and the Convention on Human Rights and Biomedicine (section 5).

2. EUROPEAN CONVENTION ON HUMAN RIGHTS

2.1. GENERAL INTRODUCTION

The European Convention on Human Rights (ECHR) sets forth a number of rights and freedoms pertaining to the domain of civil and political rights (life, liberty, privacy, freedom of speech etc.). The Convention was adopted in 1950, and entered into force in 1953. Additional Protocols, adopted as from 1952, grant more rights, or contain changes with respect to the ECHR's enforcement mechanism.[2] In addition, Protocol No. 15, amending the ECHR, emphasises the principle of subsidiarity, as well as the doctrine of the margin of appreciation and reduces, from six to four months, the time limit within which an application may be made to the Strasbourg-based European Court of Human Rights (ECtHR or Court). This protocol entered into force on 1 August 2021.

The ECHR is considered the Council of Europe's crown jewel. Having such a powerful human rights instrument distinguishes the Council from the European Union, which remains, above all, an economic and political authority, despite its expanding competences in the fields of health and human rights. Nevertheless, there are strong links between the Council of Europe and the European Union, in the field of human rights. Nowadays a state cannot become a member of the Council of Europe, or accede to the European Union, without signing and ratifying the ECHR. Ratification of the ECHR means not only that the state is bound to observe its provisions, and is required to secure that everyone within its jurisdiction can enjoy the rights and freedoms laid down in the Convention, but also implies that the state is subject to the ECHR's exceptionally powerful enforcement mechanism. This basically means that a contracting state accepts that individuals whose rights, as protected by the ECHR, have allegedly been violated by, or on account of, this state, within its jurisdiction, can petition a body established under the Convention. Non-governmental organisations and groups

---

[2] At present, the ECHR has been supplemented/amended by 16 Protocols.

of individuals claiming to be victims of human rights violations (Article 34) can also petition such bodies, as can states that feel that another contracting state has breached its ECHR obligations. Different from non-governmental organisations and groups of individuals, states can file a so-called inter-state complaint against another contracting state (Article 33 ECHR).[3]

The investigation of such complaints is performed by the ECtHR. This is an independent body composed of full-time judges, instituted for a period of nine years (Article 23, para. 1). The number of judges is equal to the number of contracting states, thus, at the moment there are 47 judges. All judges are elected with respect to a contracting state, by the Council of Europe's Parliamentary Assembly. They do not necessarily have to share the nationality of the contracting state by which they have been nominated; knowledge and impartiality are the most important requirements for judges.

In 1998, the currently operating Court replaced the former, non-permanent European Commission of Human Rights (Commission or EComHR), established in 1954, and the (old) European Court of Human Rights, created in 1959. Until 1994, individuals could only petition the Court indirectly. It was for the European Commission to decide on the admissibility of complaints ('applications'), and, therefore, whether cases were forwarded to the Court or not. The abolition of the Commission not only implies that individuals can invoke the Court directly, but also that there is no longer a separate body determining the admissibility of the complaints. The filtering – as it is often perceived – of admissible complaints now has to be performed by the Court itself (more than 90 per cent of the petitions are declared inadmissible, or are struck out of the list by the Court), which lays a considerable burden on the Court.

Much has changed since the entering into force of Protocol No. 14 (2004), on 1 June 2010. This Protocol amended the ECHR, thus allowing the ECtHR to sit in a single-judge formation, and in committees of three judges, besides in chambers of seven judges and a Grand Chamber of seventeen judges. Single judges, and committees of three judges, are entitled to declare complaints inadmissible, or strike them out of the Court's list of cases, thus allowing the Court to perform its tasks more efficiently. The flip side, however, is that complaints are not always reviewed by seven or more judges, and that plaintiffs do not have the right to appeal against a decision of a single judge, or a committee of three judges.

The jurisprudence of the Court is not confined to the interpretation of the Convention: the Court is also authorised to decide upon matters of application (Article 32 ECHR). The jurisdiction of the Court, therefore, goes even further than that of the Court of Justice of the European Union which, under the Treaty

---

[3]   In recent years, there have been various inter-state complaints against Russia, e.g. from Ukraine, Georgia and the Netherlands. See www.echr.coe.int/Documents/InterState_applications_ENG.pdf.

on the Functioning of the European Union (TFEU), has the power to interpret the EU treaties, to measure the interpretation of these treaties by EU bodies and institutions, and to judge a limited number of conflicts within the realm of EU law.[4]

Judgments of the Court are legally binding (Article 46, para. 2 ECHR), thus attaching additional importance to them. The judgments adopted by a chamber of the Court become final and binding three months after the date of the judgment, unless the judgment was referred to the aforementioned Grand Chamber (GC). Judgments of the Grand Chamber are final and binding once they have been published (Article 44 ECHR). The execution of the Court's judgments is monitored by the Committee of Ministers of the Council of Europe (Article 46, para. 2 ECHR).

Whereas the judgments of the Court are, officially, only binding on the respective contracting states, their relevance reaches much further. In fact, due to the authority that the Court has gained throughout the years, its case law is closely followed by courts, governments, non-governmental organisations and legal scholars both within and outside the Council of Europe. References to the ECtHR's jurisprudence can be found in the opinions of other human rights bodies, including the UN Human Rights Committee, and in the judgments of the highest judicial bodies of various countries, including Canada, Germany, South Africa and the United States.[5]

Through its case law, the Court has articulated the meaning of the various ECHR rights, which has turned out to be of particular relevance, from a health and human rights perspective. But before looking at these judgments in greater detail, it should be emphasised that the Court does not operate in a normative vacuum. In fact, the Court seeks to interpret the ECHR 'in harmony with the general principles of international law',[6] and emphasises that contracting states also have an international law responsibility.[7] In doing so, the Court takes into account the rules of international law, (emerging) European standards and practices, and the opinions of other judicial and human rights bodies.[8]

---

[4]   Arts. 267–79 Treaty of the Functioning on the European Union.
[5]   E. Voeten, 'Borrowing and Nonborrowing among International Courts', *The Journal of Legal Studies* 39(2) (2010), 547–76.
[6]   ECtHR 6 July 2010, *Neulinger and Shuruk v. Switzerland* (GC), no. 41615/07, ECLI:CE:ECHR: 2010:0706JUD004161507, §131 and ECtHR 12 July 2011, *Šneersone and Kampanella v. Italy*, no. 14737/09, ECLI:CE:ECHR:2011:0712JUD001473709, §85.
[7]   ECtHR 23 January 2020, *L.R. v. North Macedonia*, no. 38067/15, ECLI:CE:ECHR:2020:0123 JUD003806715, §92.
[8]   ECtHR 21 November 2001, *Al-Adsani v. the United Kingdom* (GC), no. 35763/97, ECLI: CE:ECHR:2001:1121JUD003576397 and ECtHR 28 February 2008, *Saadi v. Italy* (GC), no. 37201//06, ECLI:CE:ECHR:2008:0228JUD003720106, §62.

When it comes to the interpretation of health-related rights protected by the ECHR, the Court regularly refers to the European Social Charter,[9] the European Convention for the Prevention of Torture,[10] the Convention on Human Rights and Biomedicine, and the work of the bodies authorised to monitor compliance with these treaties.[11] To a lesser extent, the Court also refers to the work and standards of United Nations human rights bodies (see Chapter 4 of this book). This is another reason why separate attention will be paid to the other Council of Europe human rights conventions below.

2.2. RIGHTS AND CASE LAW

As mentioned above, the ECHR contains various rights that are highly relevant from a health and human rights perspective. This may come as a surprise, considering that the ECHR and its Additional Protocols, almost exclusively, contain civil and political rights that seem to allow for the restriction of the right to health. This holds particularly true for Article 5 (right to liberty and security), which allows the detention of persons of unsound mind (Article 5, para. 1(e)). According to the case law of the ECtHR, the rights protected by the ECHR and its Additional Protocols, including the right to life (Article 2), the prohibition of torture (Article 3), and the right to private and family life (Article 8),

---

[9] See, e.g. ECtHR 2 July 2002, *Wilson et al. v. the United Kingdom*, no. 30668/96, 30671/96 and 30678/96, ECLI:CE:ECHR:2002:0702JUD003066896; ECtHR 12 November 2008, *Demir and Baykara v. Turkey* (GC), no. 34503/97, ECLI:CE:ECHR:2008:1112JUD003450397, §103; ECtHR 21 June 2016, *Al-Dulimi and Montana Management Inc. v. Switzerland*, no. 5809/08, ECLI:CE:ECHR:2016:0621JUD000580908 and ECtHR 13 December 2016, *Bélány Nagy v. Hungary* (GC), no. 53080/13, ECLI:CE:ECHR:2016:1213JUD005308013.

[10] See, e.g. ECtHR 10 October 2000, *Akkoç v. Turkey*, no. 22947/93 and 22948/93, ECLI:CE:ECHR:2000:1010JUD002294793; ECtHR 19 April 2001, *Peers v. Greece*, no. 28524/95, ECLI:CE:ECHR:2001:0419JUD002852495; ECtHR 5 April 2007, *Todor Todorov v. Bulgaria*, no. 50765/99, ECLI:CE:ECHR:2007:0405JUD005076599; ECtHR 12 March 2015, *Muršić v. Croatia*, no. 7334/13, ECLI:CE:ECHR:2016:1020JUD000733413; ECtHR 26 April 2016, *Murray v. the Netherlands* (GC), no. 10511/10, ECLI:CE:ECHR:2016:0426JUD001051110; ECtHR 12 May 2017, *Simeonovi v. Bulgaria* (GC), no. 21980/04, ECLI:CE:ECHR:2017:0512JUD002198004; ECtHR 31 January 2019, *Fernandes de Oliveira v. Portugal* (GC), no. 78103/14, ECLI:CE:ECHR:2019:0131JUD007810314 and ECtHR 21 January 2020, *Strazimiri v. Albania*, 34602/16, ECLI:CE:ECHR:2020:0121JUD003460216.

[11] See, e.g. ECtHR 10 May 2001, *Cyprus v. Turkey* (GC), no. 25781/94, ECLI:CE:ECHR:2014:0512JUD002578194; ECtHR 9 March 2004, *Glass v. the United Kingdom*, no. 61827/00, ECLI:CE:ECHR:2004:0309JUD006182700; ECtHR 8 July 2004, *Vo v. France* (GC), no. 53924/00, ECLI:CE:ECHR:2004:0708JUD005392400; ECtHR 10 April 2007, *Evans v. the United Kingdom* (GC), no. 6339/05, ECLI:CE:ECHR:2007:0410JUD000633905; ECtHR 7 October 2008, *Bogumil v. Portugal*, no. 35228/03, ECLI:CE:ECHR:2008:1007JUD003522803; ECtHR 27 August 2015, *Parrillo v. Italy* (GC), no. 46470/11, ECLI:CE:ECHR:2015:0827JUD004647011 and ECtHR 15 November 2016, *Dubská and Krejzová v. the Czech Republic* (GC), no. 28859/11 and 28473/12, ECLI:CE:ECHR:2016:1115JUD002885911.

not only impose 'negative' obligations on contracting States, but also 'positive obligations'.[12] This means that the obligations enshrined in these rights require contracting states both to refrain from taking measures that interfere with the rights and freedoms, and to take measures to ensure that these rights can be enjoyed by individuals. Consequently, the precise meaning of the human rights protected by the ECHR, which, due to the adoption of the positive obligations, sometimes also resemble social and economic rights, cannot be understood correctly without taking into account the case law of the ECtHR. Therefore, before turning to some of the most relevant provisions of the ECHR, and the way that the Court has elaborated on their meaning, in the field of health and human rights law, a few features of the interpretation methods of the ECtHR will, first, be described.

2.2.1. General

In the first decades after its creation, the ECtHR (as well as the EComHR) relied heavily upon *travaux préparatoires* when interpreting the various treaty provisions.[13] As of 1978, the Court started to take a slightly different approach. When confronted with a question as to how to read a right in a concrete situation, it started by underlining that the ECHR is a living instrument that 'must be interpreted in the light of present-day conditions'.[14] As a result, the case law of the Court evolved, for example with respect to transsexuality and home births. The Court emphasised, with respect to transsexuality, that it would keep a close eye on 'medical and scientific considerations'.[15] In 2020, the Court imposed upon the national authorities the duty that they could only refuse a person's request for a change of gender recorded in a civil status register, following a gender-reassignment operation, on the basis of relevant and sufficient reasons.[16] The fact that an applicant was born in a country other than that of their residence is not a valid reason to refuse to change the gender recorded on their birth certificate.[17] When it comes to the regulation of home births, the Court affords – in the absence of a European consensus on this issue – contracting states a wide

---

[12]   The first reference to positive obligations in ECtHR was on 9 October 1979, *Airey v. Ireland*, no. 6289/73, ECLI:CE:ECHR:1979:1009JUD000628973, §32. See, e.g. D. Xenos, *The Positive Obligations of the State under the European Convention of Human Rights*, Abington on Thames: Routledge, 2012.

[13]   The official records of the negotiations preceding the adoption of the ECHR.

[14]   ECtHR 25 April 1978, *Tyrer v. the United Kingdom*, no. 5856/72, ECLI:CE:ECHR:1978:0425 JUD000585672, §31.

[15]   ECtHR 11 July 2002, *Christine Goodwin v. the United Kingdom* (GC), no. 28957/95, ECLI: CE:ECHR:2002:0711JUD002895795. See also ECtHR 11 September 2007, *L. v. Lithuania*, no. 27527/03, ECLI:CE:ECHR:2007:0911JUD002752703 and ECtHR 6 April 2017, *A.P., Garçon and Nicot v. France*, no. 79885/12, 52471/13 and 52596/13, ECLI:CE:ECHR:2017:0406 JUD007988512.

[16]   ECtHR 9 July 2020, *Y.T. v. Bulgaria*, no. 41701/16, ECLI:CE:ECHR:2020:0709JUD004170116.

[17]   ECtHR 16 July 2020, *Rana v. Hungary*, no. 40888/17, ECLI:CE:ECHR:2020:0716JUD004088817.

margin of appreciation, when assessing whether the national authorities have struck a fair balance between the competing interests at stake.[18]

In general, the Court recognises that the treatment an individual should receive has to be based on a decision by the medical authorities, on the basis of their professional standards.[19] Health professionals should also comply with these standards,[20] while the Court has consistently emphasised that contracting states should secure high professional standards among health professionals.[21] Given the importance of these professional norms, the Court is reluctant to impose its own views, particularly with regard to sensitive moral and ethical issues.[22] In this respect, it is significant that the Court has reiterated that healthcare represents an important value in a democratic society.[23] According to the Court, 'the very purpose of the medical profession' is 'to protect the health and life of patients'.[24] These principles serve as a yardstick against which both acts of commission and omission by a state can be measured, with due respect for the patient's personal autonomy.[25]

2.2.1.1. Positive obligations

As mentioned above, according to the case law of the ECtHR, the rights and freedoms guaranteed by the ECHR do not merely impose, on contracting states, duties to respect, and refrain from interfering with, the rights and freedoms of

---

[18]   ECtHR 15 November 2016, *Dubská and Krejzová v. the Czech Republic* (GC), no. 28859/11 and 28473/12, ECLI:CE:ECHR:2016:1115JUD002885911, §189. See also ECtHR 4 October 2018, *Pojatina v. Croatia*, no. 18568/12, ECLI:CE:ECHR:2018:1004JUD001856812 and ECtHR 4 June 2019, *Kosaitė-Čypienė et al. v. Lithuania*, no. 69489/12, ECLI:CE:ECHR:2019: 0604JUD006948912.

[19]   ECtHR 24 September 1992, *Herczegfalvy v. Austria*, no. 10533/83, ECLI:CE:ECHR:1992:0924 JUD001053383, §82; ECtHR 18 December 2007, *Dybeku v. Albania*, no. 41153/06, ECLI:CE: ECHR:2007:1218JUD004115306, §47; ECtHR 28 February 2006, *Wilkinson v. the United Kingdom* (dec.), no. 14659/02, ECLI:CE:ECHR:2006:0228DEC001465902. See also Art. 4 of the Biomedicine Convention.

[20]   ECtHR 26 May 2011, *R.R. v. Poland*, no. 27617/04, ECLI:CE:ECHR:2011:0526JUD002761704.

[21]   ECtHR 31 January 2019, *Fernandes de Oliveira v. Portugal* (GC), no. 78103/14, ECLI:CE: ECHR:2019:0131JUD007810314, §168.

[22]   cf. ECtHR 8 July 2004, *Vo v. France* (GC), no. 53924/00, ECLI:CE:ECHR:2004:0708 JUD005392400; ECtHR 1 April 2010, *S.H. et al. v. Austria*, no. 57813/00, ECLI:CE:ECHR: 2011:1103JUD005781300; ECtHR 20 January 2011, *Haas v. Switzerland*, no. 31322/07, ECLI:CE:ECHR:2011:0120JUD003132207; ECtHR 5 June 2015, *Lambert et al. v. France* (GC), no. 46043/14, ECLI:CE:ECHR:2015:0605JUD004604314; ECtHR 31 January 2019, *Rooman v. Belgium* (GC), no. 18052/11, ECLI:CE:ECHR:2019:0131JUD001805211 and ECtHR 31 January 2019, *Fernandes de Oliveira v. Portugal* (GC), no. 78103/14, ECLI:CE:ECHR:2019: 0131JUD007810314.

[23]   ECtHR 29 January 2008, *Villnow v. Belgium* (dec.), no. 16938/05, ECLI:CE:ECHR:2008:0129 DEC001693805.

[24]   ECtHR 16 December 2008, *Frankowicz v. Poland*, no. 53025/99, ECLI:CE:ECHR:2008:1216 JUD005302599.

[25]   ECtHR 26 May 2011, *R.R. v. Poland*, no. 27617/04, ECLI:CE:ECHR:2011:0526JUD002761704.

---

individuals ('negative obligations'), but also duties to take adequate measures to actively protect and ensure the full enjoyment of the rights concerned ('positive obligations'). This follows from Article 1 of the ECHR: 'The High Contracting Parties shall *secure* to everyone within their jurisdiction the rights and freedoms …'. This duty to ensure the enjoyment of rights enshrined in the ECHR holds true with respect to everyone who finds themselves within the jurisdiction of a contracting state, even if this is not their home country.[26]

The Court's doctrine on positive obligations has strengthened the bonds between health and human rights, providing guidance for the interpretation of health-related human rights. The doctrine of positive obligations is essential for health law, because it is on this basis that the Court imposes various duties of care on the state. The doctrine of positive obligations, as developed by the ECtHR, is characterised by a contextual approach,[27] in which the distinction between negative and positive obligations is not always clear-cut. Or, as the Court observed in the *Kudra* case, 'In the context of health care, the acts and omissions of the authorities may in certain circumstances engage their responsibility under the positive limb of Article 2 of the Convention.'[28] This explains why the Court sometimes has to decide '[w]hether the case should be examined from the standpoint of the State's negative or positive obligations'.[29] Also, the difference between civil and political rights, on the one hand, and economic and social rights, on the other, becomes blurred as a result of this doctrine. Irrespective of this, the Court has stated that it does not seek to become a court of fourth instance, or to otherwise try to substitute the role of national authorities: 'In so doing [the Court] cannot assume the role of the competent national authorities, for it would thereby lose sight of the subsidiary nature of the international machinery of collective enforcement established by the Convention.'[30] This was confirmed by Protocol No. 15 (2013), which added the following to the Preamble to the ECHR: 'Affirming that the High Contracting Parties, in accordance with the principle of *subsidiarity*, have the *primary responsibility* to secure the rights and freedoms defined in this Convention and the Protocols thereto'. As mentioned above, Italy was, in 2021, the last contracting State to ratify this Protocol, as a result of which it entered into force on 1 August 2021.

---

[26] ECtHR 2 March 2010, *Al-Saadoon and Mufdhi v. the United Kingdom* (dec.), no. 61498/08, ECLI:CE:ECHR:2010:0302JUD006149808, and ECtHR 7 July 2011, *Al-Skeini v. the United Kingdom* (GC), no. 55721/07, ECLI:CE:ECHR:2011:0707JUD005572107.

[27] E.g. ECtHR 26 March 1985, *X and Y v. the Netherlands*, no. 8978/80, ECLI:CE:ECHR:1985: 0326JUD000897880, §23 and ECtHR 21 June 1988, *Plattform 'Ärzte für das Leben' v. Austria*, no. 10126/82, ECLI:CE:ECHR:1988:0621JUD001012682, §32.

[28] ECtHR 18 December 2012, *Kudra v. Croatia*, no. 13904/07, ECLI:CE:ECHR:2012:1218 JUD001390407, §102.

[29] ECtHR 15 November 2016, *Dubská and Krejzová v. the Czech Republic* (GC), nos. 28859/11 and 28473/12, ECLI:CE:ECHR:2016:1115JUD002885911, §164.

[30] ECtHR 23 July 1968, *Belgian Linguistic Case*, no. 1474/62, ECLI:CE:ECHR:1967:0209 JUD000147462, §10.

2.2.1.2.   Margin of appreciation

It naturally follows from the above that the Court affords the national authorities a margin to make their own assessments on how human rights can best be protected, given the particular context. This so-called *margin of appreciation* corresponds with the strictness of the test applied by the Court to determine whether one of the ECHR's rights has been violated. In the absence of common standards within Europe with respect to an issue at stake, as is the case with the legal status of a foetus, the Court leaves a wide margin of appreciation for the national authorities to regulate such an issue as they are so inclined:

> the issue of when the right to life begins comes within the margin of appreciation which the Court generally considers that States should enjoy in this sphere ... The reasons for that conclusion are, firstly, that the issue of such protection has not been resolved within the majority of the Contracting States themselves, in France in particular, where it is the subject of debate ... and, secondly, that there is no European consensus on the scientific and legal definition of the beginning of life.[31]

The breadth of the margin of appreciation with respect to Article 8 of the Convention (the right to private and family life) is, however, also dependent on other factors:[32]

> Where a particularly important facet of an individual's existence or identity is at stake, the margin allowed to the State will normally be restricted (see *Evans v. the United Kingdom* [GC], cited above, §77). Where, however, there is no consensus within the Member States of the Council of Europe, either as to the relative importance of the interest at stake or as to the best means of protecting it, particularly where the case raises sensitive moral or ethical issues, the margin will be wider (*Evans v. the United Kingdom* [GC], cited above, §77; *X, Y and Z v. the United Kingdom*, judgment of 22 April 1997, *Reports of Judgments and Decisions* 1997-II, §44; *Frette v. France*, no. 36515/97, §41, ECHR 2002-I; *Christine Goodwin*, cited above, §85).[33]

For the Court, it is also important to what extent an impugned measure interferes with a person's rights and freedoms: the more intrusive a measure, the stricter the safeguards applied by the Court against its abuse.[34]

---

[31]   ECtHR 8 July 2004, *Vo v. France* (GC), no. 53924/00, ECLI:CE:ECHR:2004:0708 JUD005392400, §82.

[32]   The way the Court applies the margin is sometimes subject to criticism. See, e.g. ECtHR 16 December 2010, *A., B. and C. v. Ireland* (GC), no. 25579/05, ECLI:CE:ECHR:2010:1216 JUD002557905.

[33]   ECtHR 16 December 2010, *A., B. and C. v. Ireland* (GC), no. 25579/05, ECLI:CE:ECHR:2010: 1216JUD002557905, §232.

[34]   ECtHR 2 September 2010, *Uzun v. Germany*, no. 35623/05, ECLI:CE:ECHR:2010:0902 JUD003562305.

2.2.1.3. Availability of healthcare

Another aspect of access to healthcare concerns the availability and training of physicians, dentists, nurses and other health professionals. The Court has acknowledged the importance of availability and training, but has granted states a wide margin of appreciation with respect to the way they organise their education systems.[35]

Before turning to the rights and freedoms guaranteed by the ECHR that are of particular relevance from a health and human rights perspective, it should be mentioned that only a few of these rights are absolute, that is to say not allowing any exceptions, justifications or limitations, irrespective of the circumstances of the case, or the conduct of the person concerned. This holds true, for example, with respect to the right to life (Article 2), the prohibition of torture (Article 3) and the prohibition of slavery and forced labour (Article 4). Most of the other rights and freedoms allow, however, for a balancing of interests that may result in a restriction of the right concerned. As regards the rights protected by Articles 8 to 11 ECHR, the conditions under which such a restriction can be deemed justified are exhaustively listed in the second paragraphs of these Articles. Basically, these clauses stipulate that the restriction should be: (a) prescribed by law; (b) necessary in a democratic society; and (c) aimed at achieving one of the listed general interests.

2.2.1.4. Protection and prevention

The protection of health is one of the grounds on the basis of which most rights and freedoms guaranteed by the ECHR can be restricted. What is meant by protection of health? And does this criterion also include prevention? (for more on the latter question, see also Chapter 13). This is a particularly topical question since, during the COVID-19 pandemic, states throughout Europe imposed rigorous measures restricting rights and freedoms of individuals, in an effort to prevent the further spread of COVID-19 – measures that the Court condoned.[36] This, incidentally, was not new: states have imposed similar measures to contain the spread of other epidemic diseases, like SARS, or diseases like HIV/AIDS.[37]

From the Court's case law, it can be learned that the Court, first of all, imposes a duty on states to provide essential health information to individuals

---

[35] ECtHR 2 April 2013, *Tarantino et al. v. Italy*, no. 25851/09, ECLI:CE:ECHR:2013:0402 JUD002585109.

[36] ECtHR 3 December 2020, *Le Mailloux v. France* (dec.), no. 18108/20, ECLI:CE:ECHR:2020: 1105DEC001810820; ECtHR 23 March 2021, *Fenech v. Malta* (dec.), no. 19090/20, ECLI:CE: ECHR:2021:0323DEC001909020 and ECtHR 7 October 2021, *Zambrano v. France* (dec.), no. 41994/21, ECLI:CE:ECHR:2021:1007DEC004199421.

[37] ECtHR 15 March 2016, *Novruk et al. v. Russia*, no. 31039/11 et al., ECLI:CE:ECHR:2016:0315 JUD003103911.

so that they can, for themselves, assess the health risks of certain forms of behaviour.[38] Besides this positive obligation, the Court largely leaves it to the national health authorities to determine whether there is an individual or public health justification to interfere with the rights and freedoms set forth by the ECHR: 'It is not the Court's task to substitute itself for the competent domestic authorities in determining the best policy to adopt in dealing with problems of public health and safety.'[39] Instead, 'it is for the medical authorities to decide, on the basis of the recognised rules of medical science, on the therapeutic methods to be used.'[40] Compliance with this standard implies that a contested measure 'cannot in principle be regarded as inhuman and degrading.'[41] While the Court initially considered complaints about compulsory vaccination programmes to be inadmissible,[42] this approach changed after 2010. In a case against Ukraine, the Court decided that the forced vaccination of the son of the plaintiff was justified, and did not violate his right to private life.[43] Subsequently, in 2021, the Grand Chamber of the Court decided that a statutory child vaccination duty did not violate the rights of the child or its parents.[44]

The Court also attaches great weight to the therapeutic necessity of a form of treatment.[45] This does not mean that patients should always accept interference with their personal integrity in order to avoid (further) damage to their health. As a rule, a medical intervention is only permitted on the basis of 'free, express and informed' consent (hereinafter 'informed consent').[46] In the event that the individual concerned cannot consent, for example due to his or her young age or intellectual incapacity, then the individual's representative can provide

---

[38]   ECtHR 5 December 2013, *Vilnes et al. v. Norway*, no. 52806/09 and no. 22703/10, ECLI:CE: ECHR:2013:1205JUD005280609.

[39]   ECtHR 26 July 2011, *George and Georgeta Stoicescu v. Romania*, no. 9718/03, ECLI:CE:ECHR: 2011:0726JUD000971803, §59.

[40]   ECtHR 24 September 1992, *Herczegfalvy v. Austria*, no. 10533/83, ECLI:CE:ECHR:1992:0924 JUD001053383, §82; ECtHR 18 December 2007, *Dybeku v. Albania*, no. 41153/06, ECLI:CE: ECHR:2007:1218JUD004115306, §47, and ECtHR 28 February 2006, *Wilkinson v. the United Kingdom* (dec.), no. 14659/02, ECLI:CE:ECHR:2006:0228DEC001465902.

[41]   ECtHR 11 July 2006, *Jalloh v. Germany* (GC), no. 54810/00, ECLI:CE:ECHR:2006:0711 JUD005481000, §69.

[42]   EComHR 10 December 1984, *Acmanne et al. v. Belgium*, no. 10435/83, ECLI:CE:ECHR:1984: 1210DEC001043583 and EComHR 15 January 1998, *Boffa et al. v. San Marino*, no. 26536/95, ECLI:CE:ECHR:1998:0115DEC002653695.

[43]   ECtHR 15 March 2012, *Solomakhin v. Ukraine*, no. 24429/03, ECLI:CE:ECHR:2012:0315 JUD002442903, §36–38.

[44]   ECtHR 8 April 2021, *Vavřička et al. v. the Czech Republic* (GC), no. 47621/13, ECLI:CE:ECHR: 2021:0408JUD004762113.

[45]   ECtHR 7 October 2008, *Bogumil v. Portugal*, no. 35228/03, ECLI:CE:ECHR:2008:1007 JUD003522803, §89–90.

[46]   ECtHR 9 March 2004, *Glass v. the United Kingdom*, no. 61827/00, ECLI:CE:ECHR:2004:0309 JUD006182700, §82 and ECtHR 15 January 2013, *Csoma v. Romania*, no. 8759/05, ECLI:CE: ECHR:2013:0115JUD000875905, §42.

such informed consent.[47] However, the Court fully acknowledges the right to refuse medical treatment, even if such a refusal may have a fatal outcome for the individual concerned: 'the imposition of medical treatment without the consent of a mentally competent adult patient would interfere with his or her right to physical integrity and impinge on the rights protected under Article 8 of the Convention'.[48]

Intervening in the rights and freedoms guaranteed by the ECHR and its Protocols can also be justified in view of the health interests of others, notably children. A father who may pose a health risk to his children cannot object to child protection measures that interfere with his private life, including necessary and proportionate assessments of his medication consumption.[49]

From these and other judgments, it follows that the Court is inclined to accept, quite readily, that a measure restricting the rights and freedoms of individuals, and thereby interfering with one of the rights or freedoms guaranteed by the ECHR, is justified, if this is considered necessary for the protection of the health of others, provided that there is a fair balance of interests and that procedural rules have been followed.[50]

2.2.2. Health and human rights topics

2.2.2.1. Right to health

The Court has repeatedly stated that the ECHR cannot be read as guaranteeing the right to health.[51] This may also explain why the Court was hesitant to judge that the absence of access to clean drinking water constituted a violation

---

[47] ECtHR 28 July 2009, *Dvořáček and Dvořáčková v. Slovakia*, no. 30754/04, ECLI:CE:ECHR: 2009:0728JUD003075404; ECtHR 23 March 2010, *Oyal v. Turkey*, no. 4864/05, ECLI:CE: ECHR:2010:0323JUD000486405 and ECtHR 10 January 2017, *Ioniță v. Romania*, no. 81270/12, ECLI:CE:ECHR:2017:0110JUD008127012.

[48] ECtHR 10 June 2010, *Jehovah's Witnesses of Moscow v. Russia*, no. 302/02, ECLI:CE:ECHR: 2010:0610JUD000030202, §135.

[49] ECtHR 5 January 2006, *K.T. v. Norway*, no. 26664/03/03, ECLI:CE:ECHR:2008:0925 JUD002666403. See also ECtHR 29 January 2020, *Stankūnaitė v. Lithuania*, no. 67068/11, ECLI:CE:ECHR:2019:1029JUD006706811 and ECtHR 25 February 2020, *Y.I. v. Russia*, no. 68868/14, ECLI:CE:ECHR:2020:0225JUD006886814.

[50] ECtHR 15 March 2012, *Solomakhin v. Ukraine*, no. 24429/03, ECLI:CE:ECHR:2012: 0315JUD002442903, §36–38 and ECtHR 8 April 2021, *Vavřička et al. v. the Czech Republic* (GC), no. 47621/13, ECLI:CE:ECHR:2021:0408JUD004762113.

[51] ECtHR 28 November 2000, *Fiorenza v. Italy* (dec.), no. 44393/98, ECLI:CE:ECHR:2001:1206 JUD004439398; ECtHR 11 July 2010, *Dossi et al. v. Italy* (dec.), no. 26053/07, ECLI:CE:ECHR: 2010:1012DEC002605307; ECtHR 2 May 2017, *Jurica v. Croatia*, no. 30376/13, ECLI:CE: ECHR:2017:0502JUD003037613; ECtHR 17 March 2016, *Vasileva v. Bulgaria*, no. 23796/10, ECLI:CE:ECHR:2016:0317JUD002379610, §63 and ECtHR 19 December 2017, *Lopes de Sousa Fernandes v. Portugal* (GC), no. 56080/13, ECLI:CE:ECHR:2017:1219JUD005608013, §165.

---

of the ECHR.[52] At the same time, the Court has emphasised that the contracting states have a number of positive obligations with respect to health and the provision of healthcare. In this respect, the Grand Chamber mentioned, in its judgment in *Calvelli and Ciglio*, that states are required, under the ECHR, to make regulations compelling hospitals to adopt appropriate measures for the protection of their patients' lives, and to ensure an effective independent judicial system, so that the causes of death of patients in the care of the medical profession, whether in the public or the private sector, can be determined, and any persons responsible held accountable.[53] In more recent judgments, the Court has found that failure to ensure the appropriate implementation of the relevant legislative and statutory framework geared to protecting patients' rights to life can result in a violation of Article 2 (the right to life).[54] The same Article of the ECHR may also be violated if a state fails to provide adequate care to patients in medical institutions,[55] does not ensure that individuals are adequately protected and informed of the risks that being exposed to asbestos pose to their health and lives,[56] fails to sufficiently ensure the proper organisation and functioning of the public hospital service, or its protection of health,[57] or fails to act, in the event of a lack of coordination between healthcare professionals, coupled with structural deficiencies in its hospital system.[58]

Besides Article 2, other rights protected by the ECHR require states to undertake action with respect to health and the provision of healthcare. Not providing adequate care to persons deprived of their liberty may result in a violation of Article 3 (prohibition of inhuman and degrading treatment),[59] as may forcibly administering treatment to detained persons.[60] According to the Court, under Article 8 (the right to private and family life), states must have in place regulations compelling both public and private hospitals to adopt

---

[52]   ECtHR 10 March 2020, *Hudorovič et al. v. Slovenia*, no. 24816/14 and 25140/14, ECLI:CE: ECHR:2020:0310JUD002481614.

[53]   ECtHR 17 January 2002, *Calvelli and Ciglio v. Italy* (GC), no. 32967/96, ECLI:CE:ECHR:2002: 0117JUD003296796, §49.

[54]   ECtHR 30 June 2015, *Altuğ et al. v. Turkey*, no. 32086/07, ECLI:CE:ECHR:2015:0630 JUD003208607.

[55]   ECtHR 17 July 2014, *Valentin Câmpeanu v. Romania* (GC), no. 47848/08, ECLI:CE:ECHR: 2014:0717JUD004784808.

[56]   ECtHR 24 July 2014, *Brincat et al. v. Malta*, no. 60908/11, 62110/11, 62129/11, 62312/11 and 62338/11, ECLI:CE:ECHR:2014:0724JUD006090811.

[57]   ECtHR 27 January 2015, *Asiye Genç v. Turkey*, no. 24109/07, ECLI:CE:ECHR:2015:0127 JUD002410907.

[58]   ECtHR 30 August 2016, *Aydoğdu v. Turkey*, no. 40448/06, ECLI:CE:ECHR:2016:0830 JUD004044806.

[59]   ECtHR 28 January 1994, *Hurtado v. Switzerland*, no. 17549/90, ECLI:CE:ECHR:1994:0128 JUD001754990.

[60]   ECtHR 11 July 2006, *Jalloh v. Germany* (GC), no. 54810/00, ECLI:CE:ECHR:2006:0711 JUD005481000.

appropriate measures for the protection of their patients' physical integrity, and provide victims of medical negligence with access to proceedings in which they can, in appropriate cases, obtain compensation for damage. The amount of damages provided to victims should be proportionate.[61]

The responsibility of states to protect the health of individuals is not confined to vertical relations. States are, for example, obliged to formulate adequate legislation to protect the life and physical, mental and sexual integrity of individuals against threats from others.[62] The Court interprets the right to integrity broadly:

> even a minor interference with the physical integrity of an individual must be regarded as an interference with the right to respect for private life under Article 8 if it is carried out against the individual's will.[63]

The Court is fully aware of the threats to the health of individuals stemming from sexual or domestic violence,[64] as well as other forms of gender discrimination[65] or sexual orientation-related violence.[66] This also holds true with respect to gender discrimination within the healthcare system.[67] To the extent possible, states are obliged to prevent and combat sexual and other forms of violence detrimental to human health. However, the states' responsibilities for the prevention and protection of the health of individuals is not endless. In a case concerning the forced return of a woman with AIDS to Uganda, the Court considered as follows:

> Article 3 does not place an obligation on the Contracting State to alleviate such disparities [between the level of treatment available in the Contracting State and the country of origin] through the provision of free and unlimited health care to all aliens without a right to stay within its jurisdiction.[68]

---

[61] ECtHR 25 October 2016, *Otgon v. Moldova*, no. 22743/07, ECLI:CE:ECHR:2016:1025 JUD002274307.

[62] ECtHR 26 March 1985, *X and Y v. the Netherlands*, no. 8978/80, ECLI:CE:ECHR:1985:0326 JUD000897880, §23.

[63] ECtHR 16 June 2005, *Storck v. Germany*, no. 61603/00, ECLI:CE:ECHR:2005:0616 JUD006160300, §143.

[64] ECtHR 26 March 1985, *X and Y v. the Netherlands*, no. 8978/80, ECLI:CE:ECHR:1985:0326 JUD000897880, §23 and ECtHR 4 August 2020, *Tërshana v. Albania*, no. 48756/14, ECLI:CE:ECHR:2020:0804JUD004875614.

[65] ECtHR 12 June 2008, *Bevacqua and S. v. Bulgaria*, no. 71127/01, ECLI:CE:ECHR:2008:0612 JUD007112701, §65; ECtHR 28 June 2016, *Halime Kılıç v. Turkey*, no. 63034/11, ECLI:CE:ECHR:2016:0628JUD006303411 and ECtHR 23 May 2017, *Bălşan v. Romania*, no. 49645/09, ECLI:CE:ECHR:2017:0523JUD004964509.

[66] ECtHR 28 January 2014, *T.M. and C.M. v. Moldova*, no. 26608/11, ECLI:CE:ECHR:2014:0128 JUD002660811.

[67] ECtHR 25 July 2017, *Carvalho Pinto de Sousa Morais v. Portugal*, no. 17484/15, ECLI:CE:ECHR:2017:0725JUD001748415.

[68] ECtHR 27 May 2008, *N. v. the United Kingdom* (GC), no. 26565/05, ECLI:CE:ECHR:2008:0527JUD002656505, §44.

A considerable burden of proof lies on the applicant to show that his or her health is at risk – for example, as a result of female genital mutilation practices[69] – if they are to be returned to their country of origin.

The subsections below will take a closer look at the case law of the Court on the rights that are probably most relevant for the right to health dimensions that the Court recognises, namely Articles, 2, 3, 5 and 8.

2.2.2.2. Right to life (Article 2)

Article 2 of the ECHR stipulates that 'everyone's right to life shall be protected by law'. The right to life is one of 'the most fundamental provisions in the Convention'.[70] For national authorities, this implies a prohibition (negative obligation) on deliberately taking people's lives, and a (positive) obligation to protect the lives of all human beings within their national jurisdiction.[71] Initially, the ECHR left a margin of appreciation for states to make use of force, with the risk of death, in the contexts of policing societies, and imposing the death penalty. Throughout the years, this margin has been narrowed, while the original exception laid down in Article 2 to permit the death penalty has been set aside.[72]

With respect to health, the Court has decided, in several cases, that the right to life also imposes positive obligations on the authorities to protect the lives of persons receiving care. For example, the authorities have to make sure that healthcare institutions have effective systems, both for establishing the causes of death of patients, and for examining the possible liability of the carers concerned.[73] Further, Article 2 of the ECHR not only guarantees rights in relation to persons who have died, but also of individuals who could have died due to an alleged failure to protect their lives.[74] Chapter 11 will explore how the right to life relates to issues such as euthanasia and physician-assisted suicide.

---

[69]   ECtHR 17 May 2011, *Izevbekhai et al. v. Ireland* (dec.), no. 43408/08, ECLI:CE:ECHR:2011: 0517DEC004340808 and ECtHR 7 June 2016, *R.B.A.B. et al. v. the Netherlands*, no. 7211/06, ECLI:CE:ECHR:2016:0607JUD000721106.

[70]   ECtHR 27 September 1995, *McCann et al. v. the United Kingdom*, no. 18984/91, ECLI:CE: ECHR:1995:0927JUD001898491, §147 and ECtHR 19 December 2017, *Lopes de Sousa Fernandes v. Portugal* (GC), no. 56080/13, ECLI:CE:ECHR:2017:1219JUD005608013, §164.

[71]   ECtHR 9 June 1998, *L.C.B. v. the United Kingdom*, no. 23413/94, ECLI:CE:ECHR:1998:06 09JUD002341394, §36 and ECtHR 28 October 1998, *Osman v. the United Kingdom* (GC), no. 23452/94, ECLI:CE:ECHR:1998:1028JUD002345294, §115.

[72]   ECtHR 2 March 2010, *Al-Saadoon and Mufdhi v. the United Kingdom*, no. 61498/08, ECLI: CE:ECHR:2010:0302JUD006149808, §120. See also Additional Protocol No. 13 (2002).

[73]   Since ECtHR 26 October 1999, *Erikson v. Italy* (dec.), no. 37900/97, ECLI:CE:ECHR:1999: 1026DEC003790097.

[74]   ECtHR 31 March 2020, *Jeanty v. Belgium*, no. 82284/17, ECLI:CE:ECHR:2020:0331 JUD008228417.

Depriving persons in need of necessary healthcare of such care is, according to the Court, with reference to Article 2 of the ECHR,[75] to be distinguished from medical negligence.[76] An error of judgment with respect to healthcare provided does not necessarily lead to a violation of Article 2. The positive obligations enshrined in Article 2 require states, above all, to make regulations compelling hospitals, whether public or private, to adopt appropriate measures for the protection of their patients' lives. As mentioned above, they also require states to set up effective independent judicial systems, so that the causes of death of patients in the care of the medical profession, whether in the public or the private sector, can be determined, and those responsible held accountable.[77] Moreover, under Article 2, states are responsible for the proper functioning of their public health systems,[78] if necessary by adopting laws.[79]

On the basis of Article 2, states are required, pursuant to the case law of the ECtHR, to take the necessary measures to prevent individuals from committing suicide,[80] from endangering their lives by going on hunger strike,[81] or from dying prematurely in any other way,[82] for reasons of illness or under pressure from others. The Court has, however, considered that the duty of the state to protect life does not extend to situations in which the efforts of an individual to commit suicide were completely unpredictable.[83] One cannot expect the impossible from the state, and impose an excessive burden on it.[84] However, in an effort to prevent individuals from committing suicide when under the control of the

---

[75]   ECtHR 9 April 2013, *Mehmet Şentürk and Bekir Şentürk v. Turkey*, no. 13423/09, ECLI: CE:ECHR:2013:0409JUD001342309 and ECtHR 18 June 2013, *Nencheva et al. v. Bulgaria*, no. 48609/06, ECLI:CE:ECHR:2013:0618JUD00486090.

[76]   ECtHR 19 December 2017, *Lopes de Sousa Fernandes v. Portugal* (GC), no. 56080/13, ECLI: CE:ECHR:2017:1219JUD005608013.

[77]   ECtHR 17 January 2002, *Calvelli and Ciglio v. Italy* (GC), no. 32967/96, ECLI:CE:ECHR:2002: 0117JUD003296796, §49.

[78]   ECtHR 27 January 2015, *Asiye Genç v. Turkey*, no. 24109/07, ECLI:CE:ECHR:2015:0127 JUD002410907, §72–76.

[79]   ECtHR 30 August 2016, *Aydoğdu v. Turkey*, no. 40448/06, ECLI:CE:ECHR:2016:0830 JUD004044806, §99.

[80]   ECtHR 3 April 2001, *Keenan v. the United Kingdom*, no. 27229/95, ECLI:CE:ECHR:2001:0403 JUD002722995; ECtHR 7 June 2005, *Kılınç et al. v. Turkey*, no. 40145/98, ECLI:CE:ECHR: 2005:0607JUD004014598; ECtHR 2 March 2010, *Lütfi Demirci et al. v. Turkey*, no. 28809/05, ECLI:CE:ECHR:2010:0302JUD002880905 and ECtHR 5 December 2013, *Arskaya v. Ukraine*, no. 45076/05, ECLI:CE:ECHR:2013:1205JUD004507605.

[81]   ECtHR 5 April 2005, *Nevmerzhitsky v. Ukraine*, no. 54825/00, ECLI:CE:ECHR:2005:0405 JUD005482500.

[82]   ECtHR 23 May 2006, *Taïs v. France* (GC), no. 39922/03, ECLI:CE:ECHR:2006:0601 JUD003992203.

[83]   ECtHR 8 October 2015, *Sellal v. France*, no. 32432/13, ECLI:CE:ECHR:2015:1008 JUD003243213; ECtHR 22 November 2016, *Hiller v. Austria*, no. 1967/14, ECLI:CE:ECHR: 2016:1122JUD000196714; ECtHR 31 January 2019, *Fernandes de Oliveira v. Portugal* (GC), no. 78103/14, ECLI:CE:ECHR:2019:0131JUD007810314 and ECtHR 2 September 2021, *Ražnatović v. Montenegro*, no. 14742/18, ECLI:CE:ECHR:2021:0902JUD001474218.

[84]   ECtHR 7 May 2020, *Vardosanidze v. Georgia*, no. 43881/10, ECLI:CE:ECHR:2020:0507 JUD004388110, §55 and §61.

authorities, for example in a prison, during military service, or in a psychiatric institution, medical assessment may be carried out before the person is placed in such situations.[85]

As regards force-feeding hunger strikers, the Court recognised, from the start, that force-feeding without medical necessity contains elements that suggest degrading treatment and, in certain circumstances, could result in a violation of Article 3 ECHR (the prohibition of inhuman and degrading treatment).[86] The European Commission of Human Rights had already acknowledged that, in the event that a detained person persists in a hunger strike, a tension emerges between the (negative) obligation to respect a person's integrity, covered by Article 8, and the (positive) obligation to protect the person's life, covered by Article 2, for which the ECHR does not provide a clear-cut solution.[87] In this respect, the Court proceeds on the basis that, 'as a general rule, a measure which is of therapeutic necessity cannot be regarded as inhuman or degrading',[88] and that '[t]his can be said, for instance, about force-feeding that is aimed at saving the life of a particular detainee who consciously refuses to take food'.[89] Nevertheless, measures that are therapeutic necessities also have to be given in appropriate institutional environments.[90]

The Court interprets the requirement of 'therapeutic necessity' considerably more broadly than the concept of 'life-saving' treatment.[91] Similarly, the Court has repeatedly ruled that a therapeutically necessary (forced) treatment – whether or not in the case of a hunger strike – does not constitute a violation of Article 3 ECHR.[92] In the case of *Nevmerzhitsky*, the Court formulated additional requirements to justify force-feeding, in the event of a hunger strike.[93]

---

[85] ECtHR 4 February 2016, *Isenc v. France*, no. 58828/13, ECLI:CE:ECHR:2016:0204 JUD005882813.

[86] ECtHR 5 April 2005, *Nevmerzhitsky v. Ukraine*, no. 54825/00, ECLI:CE:ECHR:2005:0405 JUD005482500.

[87] EComHR 9 May 1984, *X v. Germany*, no. 10565/83, ECLI:CE:ECHR:1984:0509 DEC001056583.

[88] ECtHR 24 September 1992, *Herczegfalvy v. Austria*, no. 10533/83, ECLI:CE:ECHR:1992:0924 JUD001053383, §82 and ECtHR 19 June 2007, *Ciorap v. Moldova*, no. 12066/02, ECLI:CE: ECHR:2007:0619JUD001206602, §77.

[89] ECtHR 11 July 2006, *Jalloh v. Germany* (GC), no. 54810/00, §69.

[90] ECtHR 9 January 2018, *Kadusic v. Switzerland*, no. 43977/13, ECLI:CE:ECHR:2018:0109 JUD004397713.

[91] EComHR 26 February 1997, *Buckley v. the United Kingdom*, no. 28323/95, ECLI:CE:ECHR: 1997:0226DEC002832395 and ECtHR 28 February 2006, *Wilkinson v. the United Kingdom* (dec.), no. 14659/02, ECLI:CE:ECHR:2006:0228DEC001465902.

[92] ECtHR 24 September 1992, *Herczegfalvy v. Austria*, no. 10533/83, ECLI:CE:ECHR:1992: 0924JUD001053383, §82 and ECtHR 10 February 2004, *Gennadi Naoumenko v. Ukraine*, no. 42023/98, ECLI:CE:ECHR:2004:0210JUD004202398, §112.

[93] ECtHR 5 April 2005, *Nevmerzhitsky v. Ukraine*, no. 54825/00, ECLI:CE:ECHR:2005:0405 JUD005482500, §94. See also ECtHR 19 June 2007, *Ciorap v. Moldova*, no. 12066/02, ECLI: CE:ECHR:2007:0619JUD001206602 and ECtHR 26 March 2013, *Rappaz v. Switzerland* (dec.), no. 73175/10, ECLI:CE:ECHR:2013:0326DEC007317510.

The right to life also imposes procedural obligations on the authorities, including the obligation to conduct a diligent investigation of any deaths:[94] '[t]he essential purpose of such an investigation is to secure the effective implementation of the domestic laws which protect the right to life and, in those cases involving State agents or bodies, to ensure their accountability for deaths occurring under their responsibility.'[95] From the case law of the Court, it emerges that an investigation into the cause of death is often too slow to be effective.[96]

The duty to investigate the cause of death also applies to situations in which it is highly unlikely that the death is attributable to unlawful violence on the part of the authorities. Furthermore, this duty also holds true, irrespective of whether or not next of kin have requested an investigation.[97] However, the duty applies *a fortiori* in cases of suspected unnatural death.[98]

The Court has repeatedly been asked to rule on whether the right to life interferes with providing pregnant women with the possibility of having an abortion. The Court is of the opinion that it is for the contracting state to find a balance between the necessity of protecting the foetus, and the woman's interests.[99] In this respect, the Court allows the contracting states a wide margin of appreciation.[100] Therefore, the sole fact that abortion is legal in a country does not, in itself, constitute a violation of Article 2 ECHR.[101]

---

[94]   ECtHR 27 September 1995, *McCann et al. v. the United Kingdom*, no. 18984/91, ECLI:CE:
ECHR:1995:0927JUD001898491; ECtHR 19 February 1998, *Kaya v. Turkey*, no. 22729/93, ECLI:
CE:ECHR:1998:0219JUD002272993; ECtHR 15 May 2007, *Ramsahai et al. v. the Netherlands*
(GC), no. 52391/02, ECLI:CE:ECHR:2007:0515JUD005239199; ECtHR 13 November 2012,
Z v. Poland, no. 46132/08, ECLI:CE:ECHR:2012:1113JUD004613208 and ECtHR 11 June
2019, *Prizreni v. Albania*, no. 29309/16, ECLI:CE:ECHR:2019:0611JUD002930916.

[95]   ECtHR 4 May 2001, *Kelly et al. v. the United Kingdom*, no. 30054/96, ECLI:CE:ECHR:2001:
0504JUD003005496, §94.

[96]   ECtHR 13 November 2012, *Bajić v. Croatia*, no. 41108/10, ECLI:CE:ECHR:2012:1113
JUD004110810; ECtHR 9 December 2014, *McDonnell v. the United Kingdom*, no. 19563/11,
ECLI:CE:ECHR:2014:1209JUD001956311; ECtHR 12 January 2016, *Bilbija and Blažević v.
Croatia*, no. 62870/13, ECLI:CE:ECHR:2016:0112JUD006287013; ECtHR 1 March 2016,
Mihu v. Roemenië, no. 36903/13, ECLI:CE:ECHR:2016:0301JUD003690313 and ECtHR
20 February 2018, *Mehmet Günay and Güllü Günay v. Turkey*, no. 52797/08, ECLI:CE:ECHR:
2018:0220JUD005279708.

[97]   ECtHR 8 November 2005, *Gongadze v. Ukraine*, no. 34056/02, ECLI:CE:ECHR:2005:1108
JUD003405602, §175 and ECtHR 7 February 2006, *Scavuzzo-Hager et al. v. Switzerland*,
no. 41773/98, ECLI:CE:ECHR:2006:0207JUD004177398, §75.

[98]   ECtHR 13 November 2008, *Khaylo v. Ukraine*, no. 39964/02, ECLI:CE:ECHR:2008:1113
JUD003996402, §62; ECtHR 18 December 2008, *Kats et al. v. Ukraine*, no. 29971/04, ECLI:CE:
ECHR:2008:1218JUD002997104, §115–16 and ECtHR 28 January 2020, *Nicolaou v. Cyprus*,
no. 29068/10, ECLI:CE:ECHR:2020:0128JUD002906810, §149.

[99]   ECtHR 16 December 2010, *A., B. and C. v. Ireland* (GC), no. 25579/05, ECLI:CE:ECHR:2010:
1216JUD002557905, §26.

[100]   EComHR 13 May 1980, *Paton v. the United Kingdom*, no. 8416/78, ECLI:CE:ECHR:1980:0513
DEC000841678 and EComHR 19 May 1992, *Hercz v. Norway*, no. 17004/90, ECLI:CE:ECHR:
1992:0519DEC001700490.

[101]   ECtHR 5 September 2002, *Boso v. Italy* (dec.), no. 50490/99, ECLI:CE:ECHR:2002:0905
DEC005049099.

In 2021, abortion is, with the exception of Malta, permitted in all contracting states, under certain (divergent) conditions. Moreover, in *Tysiąc* the Court decided that, if national legislation provides for the right of women to have an abortion, they should also be able to exercise this right.[102] While it is, under Article 10 of the ECHR, allowed to the express concern about the (non) existence of abortion laws, this does not mean that all kind of criticism is allowed, particularly if this violates the rights of healthcare providers.[103] Along similar lines, the fact that abortion is allowed does not mean that healthcare providers can refuse to participate in providing abortion,[104] or that women can be sterilised against their will.[105]

2.2.2.3. Right to care (Article 3)

Article 3 ECHR prohibits torture, as well as other forms of inhuman or degrading treatment or punishment. Article 3, thus, enshrines, according to the Court, one of the most fundamental values of democratic society.[106] The Court has repeatedly found that depriving a person of necessary care may constitute a violation of Article 3 and/or Article 2, both fundamental provisions that complement each other.[107] Indeed, given that failing to render the necessary care to a person could lead to death and/or severe suffering, this may also breach an authority's duty of care – to be distinguished from the duty to regulate in order to prevent medical negligence.[108]

---

[102] ECtHR 20 March 2007, *Tysiąc v. Poland*, no. 5410/03, ECLI:CE:ECHR:2007:0320 JUD000541003, §124.

[103] ECtHR 26 November 2015, *Annen v. Germany*, no. 3690/10, ECLI:CE:ECHR:2015:1126 JUD000369010; ECtHR 20 September 2018, *Annen v. Germany* (no. 2–5), 3682/10, 3687/10, 9765/10 and 70693/11, ECLI:CE:ECHR:2018:0920JUD000368210 and ECtHR 18 October 2020, *Annen v. Germany*, no. 3779/11, no. 6, ECLI:CE:ECHR:2018:1018JUD000377911.

[104] ECtHR 12 March 2020, *Grimmark v. Sweden* (dec.), no. 43726/17, ECLI:CE:ECHR:2020:0211 DEC004372617 and ECtHR 12 March 2020, *Steen v. Sweden* (dec.), no. 62309/17, ECLI:CE:ECHR:2020:0211DEC006230917.

[105] ECtHR 9 October 2007, *K.H. et al. v. Slovakia* (dec.), no. 32881/04, ECLI:CE:ECHR:2009:0428JUD003288104; ECtHR 28 April 2009, *K.H. et al. v. Slovakia*, no. 32881/04, ECLI:CE:ECHR:2009:0428JUD003288104; ECtHR 12 June 2012, *N.B. v. Slovakia*, no. 29518/10, ECLI:CE:ECHR:2012:0612JUD002951810; ECtHR 13 November 2012, *I.G. et al. v. Slovakia* (dec.), no. 15966/04, ECLI:CE:ECHR:2012:1113JUD001596604; ECtHR 29 April 2014, *L.H. v. Latvia*, no. 52019/07, ECLI:CE:ECHR:2014:0429JUD005201907 and ECtHR 16 February 2016, *Soares de Melo v. Portugal*, no. 72850/14, ECLI:CE:ECHR:2016:0216JUD007285014.

[106] ECtHR 28 September 2015, *Bouyid v. Belgium* (GC), no. 23380/09, ECLI:CE:ECHR:2015:0928 JUD002338009, §81.

[107] ECtHR 10 May 2001, *Cyprus v. Turkey* (GC), no. 25781/94, ECLI:CE:ECHR:2014:0512 JUD002578194, §219 and ECtHR 24 March 2011, *Giuliani and Gaggio v. Italy* (GC), no. 23458/02, ECLI:CE:ECHR:2011:0324JUD002345802, §174.

[108] ECtHR 19 December 2017, *Lopes de Sousa Fernandes v. Portugal* (GC), no. 56080/13, ECLI:CE:ECHR:2017:1219JUD005608013, §182.

For the same reason, Article 3 precludes, in 'exceptional circumstances', the extradition of an individual with a life-threatening disease to a country lacking the necessary care facilities.[109] Withholding adequate care can also violate a person's dignity in other ways and, thus, be in contravention of Article 3.[110] According to the Court, such a situation could occur where the authorities fail to transfer a detainee with complex care needs to a specialised hospital.[111]

The manner and circumstances in which care is given can also be in contravention of the right to a private life, as protected by Article 8 ECHR. Indeed, according to settled case law, this right includes the right to physical and moral integrity.[112]

The duty of care holds particularly true vis-à-vis individuals who have been deprived of their liberty, or individuals who are particularly vulnerable (see Chapters 8 and 9 of this book).[113] According to the Court, potential immigrants are also considered as vulnerable persons.[114] The Court, further, has held that the prison authorities have to ensure that due account is taken of a detainee's health and well-being, more specifically by providing medical care.[115] Furthermore, this care must be tailored to the medical needs of the individual: giving equal care to all could constitute a violation of Article 3.[116]

Governments' responsibilities for people's health also calls for the protection of detainees with mental health problems, including psychiatric patients:

> the assessment of whether the treatment or punishment concerned is incompatible with the standards of Article 3 has, in the case of mentally ill persons, to take into

---

[109] ECtHR 2 May 1997, *D. v. the United Kingdom*, no. 30240/96, ECLI:CE:ECHR:1997:0502 JUD003024096, §53. See also ECtHR 26 April 2018, *Khaksar v. the United Kingdom* (dec.), no. 2654/18, ECLI:CE:ECHR:2018:0403DEC000265418.

[110] ECtHR 24 May 2007, *Gorodnichev v. Russia*, no. 52058/99, ECLI:CE:ECHR:2007:0524 JUD005205899, §83; ECtHR 28 September 2015, *Bouyid v. Belgium* (GC), no. 23380/09, ECLI: CE:ECHR:2015:0928JUD002338009, §100 and ECtHR 23 January 2020, *L.R. v. North Macedonia*, 38067/15, ECLI:CE:ECHR:2020:0123JUD003806715.

[111] ECtHR 11 July 2006, *Rivière v. France*, no. 33834/03, ECLI:CE:ECHR:2006:0711 JUD003383403; ECtHR 12 June 2008, *Kotsaftis v. Greece*, no. 39780/06 and ECtHR 22 December 2008, *Aleksanyan v. Russia*, no. 46468/06, ECLI:CE:ECHR:2008:1222JUD004646806.

[112] ECtHR 26 March 1985, *X and Y v. the Netherlands*, no. 8978/80, §22; ECtHR 29 April 2002, *Pretty v. the United Kingdom*, no. 2346/02, ECLI:CE:ECHR:2002:0429JUD000234602, §61–63 and ECtHR 9 March 2004, *Glass v. the United Kingdom*, no. 61827/00, ECLI:CE:ECHR:2004: 0309JUD006182700, §70.

[113] ECtHR 17 July 2014, *Valentin Câmpeanu v. Roemenië* (GC), no. 47848/08, ECLI:CE:ECHR: 2014:0717JUD00478480814, §143–44.

[114] ECtHR 15 December 2016, *Khlaifia et al. v. Italy* (GC), no. 16483/12, ECLI:CE:ECHR:2016: 1215JUD001648312, §161.

[115] ECtHR 14 November 2002, *Mouisel v. France*, no. 67263/01, ECLI:CE:ECHR:2002:1114 JUD006726301, §40 and ECtHR 14 November 2013, *Blokhin v. Russia*, no. 47152/06, ECLI: CE:ECHR:2016:0323JUD004715206, §136.

[116] ECtHR 20 January 2009, *Slawomir Musial v. Poland*, no. 28300/06, ECLI:CE:ECHR:1999:0325 JUD002455794.

---

consideration their vulnerability and their inability, in some cases, to complain coherently or at all about how they are being affected by any particular treatment.[117]

The authorities' duty of care vis-à-vis these persons includes the guarantee of continued psychiatric care.[118] The authorities also have a responsibility with regard to the suitability of the establishment where mentally-ill people are being accommodated: 'having the applicant detained in establishments not suitable for incarceration of the mentally-ill, raises a serious issue under the Convention'.[119] Solitary confinement of detainees is particularly problematic, from a human rights perspective.[120]

In several cases, the Court has been called on to consider the access to artificial procreation techniques (see also Chapter 10 of this book).[121] The ECtHR allows the authorities a wide margin of appreciation in determining the eligibility and treatment criteria. The Court has acknowledged the wide margin of appreciation that national authorities enjoy, for example in cases due to the lack of common ground between the approaches adopted by the various contracting states. In relevant cases, such as *S.H. et al. v. Austria*, the Court has added, however, that these differences 'do not, as such, make any solution reached by a legislature acceptable. [They do] not absolve the Court from carefully examining the arguments discussed in the legislative process and from examining whether the arguments advanced by the Government for justifying the difference of treatment in issue are relevant and sufficient'.[122] On the basis of a rather strict assessment of all the arguments put forward, the Court concluded that the prohibition of heterologous artificial procreation techniques for *in vitro* fertilisation, as laid down in the Austrian Artificial Procreation Act, violated the ECHR.

---

[117] ECtHR 24 September 1992, *Herczegfalvy v. Austria*, no. 10533/83, ECLI:CE:ECHR:1992: 0924JUD001053383, §82; ECtHR 30 July 1998, *Aerts v. Belgium*, no. 25357/94, ECLI:CE: ECHR:1998:0730JUD002535794, §66; ECtHR 3 April 2001, *Keenan v. the United Kingdom*, no. 27229/95, ECLI:CE:ECHR:2001:0403JUD002722995, §111.

[118] ECtHR 29 April 2008, *Petrea v. Romania*, no. 4792/03, ECLI:CE:ECHR:2008:0429 JUD000479203.

[119] ECtHR 20 January 2009, *Slawomir Musial v. Poland*, no. 28300/06, ECLI:CE:ECHR:2009: 0120JUD002830006, §94 and ECtHR 31 January 2019, *Rooman v. Belgium* (GC), no. 18052/11, ECLI:CE:ECHR:2019:0131JUD001805211.

[120] ECtHR 4 July 2006, *Ramirez Sanchez v. France* (GC), no. 59450/00, ECLI:CE:ECHR:2006: 0704JUD005945000; ECtHR 6 September 2007, *Kucheruk v. Ukraine*, no. 2570/04, ECLI: CE:ECHR:2007:0906JUD000257004; ECtHR 17 April 2014, *G.C. v. Italy*, no. 73869/10, ECLI: CE:ECHR:2014:0422JUD007386910 and ECtHR 14 May 2020, *Astruc v. France* (dec.), no. 5499/15, ECLI:CE:ECHR:2020:0415DEC000549915.

[121] ECtHR 4 December 2007, *Dickson v. the United Kingdom* (GC), no. 44362/04, ECLI:CE: ECHR:2007:1204JUD004436204; ECtHR 26 June 2014, *Mennesson v. France*, no. 65192/11, ECLI:CE:ECHR:2014:0626JUD006519211 and ECtHR 5 December 2019, *Petithory Lanzmann v. France* (dec.), no. 23038/19, ECLI:CE:ECHR:2019:1112DEC002303819.

[122] ECtHR 1 April 2010, *S.H. et al. v. Austria*, no. 57813/00, ECLI:CE:ECHR:2011:1103 JUD005781300, §69. See also ECtHR 28 August 2012, *Costa and Pavan v. Italy*, no. 54270/10, ECLI:CE:ECHR:2012:0828JU005427010.

Through its case law, the Court has made it clear that care not only has to meet quality requirements, but must also be provided *on time*, and *safely*. If the necessary care fails to be provided, this could, according to the Court, be regarded as a violation of the ECHR.[123] The requirement of safe care follows from the authorities' positive obligations, under Article 2 ECHR. On the basis thereof, the authorities must take the proper measures to protect life: '[t]he aforementioned positive obligations therefore require States to make regulations compelling hospitals, whether public or private, to adopt appropriate measures for the protection of their patients' lives.'[124] However, if a patient dies as a consequence of a medical error,[125] this does not necessarily mean that Article 2 ECHR has been violated, as long as an effective and independent investigation of the cause of death is provided for.[126]

Consequently, on the basis of Articles 2, 3 and 8 ECHR, the authorities have a duty of care, subject to provisos. This duty of care also includes elements of quality (adequacy, safety and speed), and care has to be provided in a manner appropriate to the rights and dignity of individuals. Detainees cannot invoke the principle of equivalence. If care is medically necessary – even if the intervention is extremely radical and no *informed consent* has been obtained – there is no violation of Article 3 or 8 ECHR, provided that it has been shown convincingly that treatment was necessary, proportionate and performed adequately.[127]

2.2.2.4. Right to liberty and security (Article 5)

According to Article 5 of the ECHR, no one shall be deprived of his or her liberty, except in a number of specified situations and, in those cases, subject to procedural regulations being guaranteed. This provision is particularly relevant in the field of health and healthcare, now that numerous physical and mental conditions can be reasons to detain a person, in a healthcare setting or elsewhere, where that individual's health condition may require them to receive healthcare. In this respect, it is significant that, according to the Court, a deprivation of liberty is not confined to detention following arrest or conviction, but may take

---

[123] ECtHR 10 March 2009, *Paladi v. Moldova* (GC), no. 39806/05, ECLI:CE:ECHR:2009:0310 JUD003980605.

[124] ECtHR 17 January 2002, *Calvelli and Ciglio v. Italy* (GC), no. 32967/96, ECLI:CE:ECHR:2002:0117JUD003296796, §49.

[125] ECtHR 27 June 2006, *Byrzykowski v. Poland*, no. 11562/05, ECLI:CE:ECHR:2006:0627 JUD001156205, §104.

[126] ECtHR 26 October 1999, *Erikson v. Italy* (dec.), no. 37900/97, ECLI:CE:ECHR:1999:1026 DEC003790097; ECtHR 4 May 2000, *Powell v. the United Kingdom* (dec.), no. 45305/99, ECLI:CE:ECHR:2000:0504DEC004530599 and ECtHR 19 December 2017, *Lopes de Sousa Fernandes v. Portugal* (GC), no. 56080/13, ECLI:CE:ECHR:2017:1219JUD005608013.

[127] ECtHR 7 October 2008, *Bogumil v. Portugal*, no. 35228/03, ECLI:CE:ECHR:2008:1007 JUD003522803.

numerous other forms (see also Chapter 13 of this book).[128] Above all, the aim of Article 5 ECtHR is to ensure that no one will be deprived of his or her liberty in an arbitrary fashion.[129]

But what meaning does the Court attach to the term 'detention'? According to the Court, not every restriction on movement is considered a deprivation of liberty, as understood under Article 5, para. 1 of the ECHR. The Court has also noted that '[t]he difference between deprivation of and restriction upon liberty is … merely one of degree or intensity, and not one of nature or substance.'[130] On this very basis, a person with schizophrenia who stayed in a social care home for persons with learning difficulties was, according to the Court, not 'detained', but, since the management of the home 'exercised complete and effective control by medication and supervision over her assessment, treatment, care, residence and movement', her stay could be assessed under Article 5, para. 1(e) ECHR.[131] A person with diabetes who was forced to go into a psychiatric hospital to be examined for drug use also fell under the realm of Article 5(1)(e).[132] Equally dependent on the context is whether the forced hospitalisation of a person, merely to conduct research, is a form of detention within the scope of Article 5(1)(e).[133] Moreover, some restrictions on movement fall under Article 2 of Protocol No. 4 (1963), which guarantees the freedom to move from one part of a country to another.[134] Restrictions on this freedom were one of the measures that various states imposed when seeking to reduce the spread of COVID-19.

Article 5(1)(e) of the ECHR provides that 'the lawful detention of persons for the prevention of the spreading of infectious diseases, of persons of unsound mind, alcoholics or drug addicts or vagrants' is, under certain circumstances, permitted. This subparagraph refers to several categories of individuals who may be deprived of their liberty, either in order to be given medical treatment, or because of considerations dictated by social policy, or on a combination of

---

[128]   ECtHR 6 November 1980, *Guzzardi v. Italy*, no. 7367/76, ECLI:CE:ECHR:1980:1106 JUD000736776, §95.

[129]   Ibid., §92 and ECtHR 22 October 2018, *S., V. and A. v. Denmark* (GC), 35553/12, 36678/12 and 36711/12, ECLI:CE:ECHR:2018:1022JUD003555312, §74.

[130]   ECtHR 6 November 1980, *Guzzardi v. Italy*, no. 7367/76, ECLI:CE:ECHR:1980:1106 JUD000736776, §93.

[131]   ECtHR 14 February 2012, *D.D. v. Lithuania*, no. 13469/06, ECLI:CE:ECHR:2012:0214 JUD001346906, §146. See also ECtHR 16 October 2012, *Stanisław Kędzior v. Poland*, no. 45026/07, ECLI:CE:ECHR:2012:1016JUD004502607; ECtHR 6 December 2016, *Trutko v. Russia*, no. 40979/04, ECLI:CE:ECHR:2016:1206JUD004097904 and ECtHR 9 January 2018, *Kadusic v. Switzerland*, no. 43977/13, ECLI:CE:ECHR:2018:0109JUD004397713.

[132]   ECtHR 26 May 2020, *Aftanache v. Romania*, no. 999/19, ECLI:CE:ECHR:2020:0526 JUD000099919.

[133]   ECtHR 26 June 2018, *D.R. v. Lithuania*, no. 691/15, ECLI:CE:ECHR:2018:0626JUD000069115.

[134]   ECtHR 23 February 2012, *Creangă v. Romania* (GC), no. 29226/03, ECLI:CE:ECHR:2012: 0223JUD002922603, §92 and ECtHR 23 February 2017, *Tommaso v. Italy* (GC), no. 43395/09, ECLI:CE:ECHR:2017:0223JUD004339509, §80.

both grounds.[135] Deprivation of the liberty of individuals falling within these groups may, thus, be justified to prevent a danger to public safety, as well as to protect the individuals' own interests. This is not to suggest that anyone with the conditions mentioned in this subparagraph may be detained: whether or not a detention is justified depends on its 'lawfulness'.

Most cases presented to the Court on the basis of this provision concern the detention of persons of 'unsound mind', mostly persons with psychiatric disorders.[136] The term 'unsound mind' – that is to say, a true mental disorder – has an autonomous meaning under the ECHR.[137] It is not possible to give a precise definition of this term, since its meaning is continually evolving, as research in psychiatry progresses. In all cases, its meaning under this subparagraph has to be determined by an objective medical expert,[138] sometimes an expert with a special qualification, if not a psychiatric expert.[139] The report of this expert has to be sufficiently recent.[140] The mental disorder must be of a kind or degree warranting compulsory confinement. The validity of continued confinement depends upon the persistence of such a disorder.[141] This is not to suggest that persons who hold views that are different from the dominant norms in society are necessarily of unsound mind.[142] At the same time, individuals who, due to their psychiatric disorders, have also committed criminal offences, can also been seen as persons of unsound mind if it is necessary for them to receive comprehensive therapy.[143] In other words, it is not a requirement that the persons concerned suffer from conditions that exclude or diminish their criminal responsibility under domestic law.[144]

---

[135] ECtHR 25 January 2005, *Enhorn v. Sweden*, no. 56529/00, ECLI:CE:ECHR:2005:0125 JUD005652900, §43.

[136] ECtHR 31 March 2020, *Jeanty v. Belgium*, no. 82284/17, ECLI:CE:ECHR:2020:0331 JUD008228417.

[137] ECtHR 24 October 1979, *Winterwerp v. the Netherlands*, no. 6301/73, ECLI:CE:ECHR:1979: 1024JUD000630173, §39.

[138] ECtHR 18 February 2013, *Ruiz Rivera v. Switzerland*, no. 8300/06, ECLI:CE:ECHR:2014: 0218JUD000830006, §59 and ECtHR 18 September 2012, *S.R. v. the Netherlands* (dec.), no. 13837/07, ECLI:CE:ECHR:2012:0918DEC001383707, §31.

[139] ECtHR 20 April 2010, *C.B. v. Romania*, no. 21207/03, ECLI:CE:ECHR:2010:0420 JUD002120703, §56.

[140] ECtHR 18 June 2015, *Yaikov v. Russia*, no. 39317/05, ECLI:CE:ECHR:2015:0618 JUD0039317059 and ECtHR January 2018, *Kadusic v. Switzerland*, no. 43977/13, ECLI:CE: ECHR:2018:0109JUD004397713, §44 and §55.

[141] ECtHR 28 November 2013, *Glien v. Germany*, no. 7345/12, ECLI:CE:ECHR:2013:1128 JUD000734512, §78.

[142] ECtHR 28 October 2003, *Rakevich v. Russia*, no. 58973/00, ECLI:CE:ECHR:2003:1028 JUD005897300, §39.

[143] ECtHR 2 February 2017, *Ilnseher v. Germany*, no. 27505/14, ECLI:CE:ECHR:2017:0202 JUD001021112, §151.

[144] Ibid., §149.

In the case of *Varbanov*, the Court held that the person concerned had not reliably been shown to be of unsound mind. The authorities should have tried to obtain an expert medical opinion establishing the mental disorder prior to the deprivation of liberty of the individual concerned.[145] Furthermore, the Court later emphasised that there must be some relationship between the ground of permitted deprivation of liberty relied on, and the place and conditions of detention. In principle, the 'detention' of a person as a mental health patient is only considered 'lawful', for the purposes of Article 5(1)(e), if effected in a hospital, clinic or other appropriate institution.[146] This does not necessarily mean, however, that a person being detained in another institution automatically constitutes a violation of the provision.[147]

The administration of suitable therapy for persons with a psychiatric disorder has become a requirement of the wider concept of the lawfulness of the deprivation of liberty. First of all, the detention of a person with a psychiatric disorder must have a therapeutic purpose. This means that the aim of the therapy is to cure or alleviate the mental health condition of the person concerned, including, where appropriate, to bring about a reduction in, or control over, their dangerousness.[148] In other words, the deprivation of liberty for persons with a psychiatric disorder, under Article 5 (1)(e), thus, has a dual function. On the one hand, there is the social function of protection, and, on the other hand, there is a therapeutic function, related to the interests of the person of unsound mind in receiving an appropriate and individualised form of therapy, or course of treatment.[149]

So far, the Court has only dealt with a few cases concerning the spread of infectious diseases. Under the ambit of this ground, the lawfulness of the detention of a person suspected of spreading an infectious disease depends on the degree of danger to public health or safety, as well as the extent to which detention is the last resort (*ultimum remedium*) in preventing the spreading of the disease. In the event that these criteria are not, or are no longer, met, the basis for a deprivation of liberty ceases to exist.[150]

---

[145] ECtHR 5 October 2000, *Varbanov v. Bulgaria*, no. 31365/96, ECLI:CE:ECHR:2000:1005 JUD003136596.

[146] ECtHR 28 May 1985, *Ashingdane v. the United Kingdom*, no. 8225/78, ECLI:CE:ECHR:1985: 0528JUD0008225783, §46.

[147] ECtHR 2 October 2012, *L.B. v. Belgium*, no. 22831/08, ECLI:CE:ECHR:2012:1002 JUD002283108, §94.

[148] ECtHR 31 January 2019, *Rooman v. Belgium* (GC), no. 18052/11, ECLI:CE:ECHR:2019:0131 JUD001805211, §208.

[149] Ibid., §210.

[150] ECtHR 25 January 2005, *Enhorn v. Sweden*, no. 56529/00, ECLI:CE:ECHR:2005:0125 JUD005652900, §44.

With respect to infected persons in prison, the Court has held that the prison authorities have the duty to identify, isolate and treat prisoners with infectious diseases.[151] This duty exists to prevent health dangers to others, and to allow the prison authorities to act in the best interests of the persons concerned.

2.2.2.5. Patients' rights (Article 8)

As mentioned above, Article 8 of the ECHR guarantees the right to respect for private and family life (see also Chapter 3 of this book). This right forms the basis of various patients' rights, including the right to informed consent, even though patients' rights are also grounded in other rights protected by the ECHR.

2.2.2.5.1. RIGHT TO INFORMATION

With respect to the right to informed consent, the ECHR contains a separate provision with regard to the right to freedom of expression (Article 10). This right includes the freedom to receive or disseminate information, including on health issues. In a case against Ireland, the Court held that the ban on the dissemination of information regarding the possibilities of having an abortion in another country could be justified, in view of the protection of public morals, namely 'profound moral values concerning the nature of life'.[152] Nonetheless, eventually, the Court decided that Article 10 ECHR had been violated. In the situation at hand, the ban constituted a disproportionate breach of the right to freedom of expression, as protected by Article 10.[153] Therefore, this violation can be characterised as an impermissible interference with freedom of expression, on the part of the authorities.

The right of freedom to information cannot, however, be 'construed as imposing on a State ... positive obligations to collect and disseminate information of its own motion'.[154] Over the years, the Court has accepted that this denial of a positive obligation should be nuanced.[155] Equally, with respect to health and healthcare, the Court has acknowledged that the State should provide essential information to allow individuals to protect their own health.[156] It follows that

---

[151] ECtHR 24 July 2012, *Fülöp v. Romania*, no. 18999/04, ECLI:CE:ECHR:2012:0724 JUD001899904, §38.

[152] ECtHR 29 October 1992, *Open Door and Dublin Well Woman v. Ireland*, no. 14234/88 and 14235/88, ECLI:CE:ECHR:1992:1029JUD001423488, §63.

[153] Ibid., §80.

[154] ECtHR 19 February 1998, *Guerra et al. v. Italy*, no. 14967/89, ECLI:CE:ECHR:1998:0219 JUD001496789, §53.

[155] ECtHR 8 November 2016, *Magyar Helsinki Bizottság v. Hungary* (GC), no. 18030/11, ECLI: CE:ECHR:2016:1108JUD001803011 and ECtHR 30 January 2020, *Studio Monitori et al. v. Georgia*, no. 44920/09 and 8942/10, ECLI:CE:ECHR:2020:0130JUD004492009.

[156] ECtHR 5 December 2013, *Vilnes et al. v. Norway*, no. 52806/09 and no. 22703/10, ECLI:CE: ECHR:2013:1205JUD005280609.

the State is not required, on the basis of Article 10, to provide all kinds of information, but that essential health information should be made accessible, on the basis of Article 8.

In line with this interpretation of Article 8, the Court has underlined the importance of adequate information as a prerequisite for authorising a violation of an individual's physical integrity.[157] According to settled case law, the contracting states have a positive obligation to make certain that physicians discuss the possible effects of a treatment with patients, in such a way that the requirement of *informed consent* is complied with.[158] In the Court's opinion, failing to provide patients with adequate information harms the self-determination of the person concerned, and could constitute a violation of Article 8.[159]

According to the Court's case law, the medical professionals' duty to provide information also applies with regard to the parents and carers of minors. On the basis of the right to family life, also protected by Article 8, parents are, in principle, entitled to be informed on, and involved in, the treatment of their children.[160] However, an exception to this rule is possible, notably when this is deemed necessary with a view to the child's best interests.[161] The authorities are allowed a wide margin of appreciation in determining this necessity.[162]

Many people have applied to the Court because, at least in their view, the authorities had not been sufficiently cooperative in helping them to obtain information about their (biological) parents.[163] In these cases, applicants have regularly invoked the right to a private life, as protected by Article 8. This raises the question of whether a person has the right to know their origins or genetic

---

[157] ECtHR 5 October 2006, *Trocellier v. France* (dec.), no. 75725/01, ECLI:CE:ECHR:2006:1005 DEC007572501 and ECtHR 29 April 2014, *L.H. v. Latvia*, no. 52019/07, ECLI:CE:ECHR:2014: 0429JUD005201907.

[158] ECtHR 15 January 2013, *Csoma v. Romania*, no. 8759/05, ECLI:CE:ECHR:2013:0115 JUD000875905; ECtHR 29 April 2014, *L.H. v. Latvia*, no. 52019/07, ECLI:CE:ECHR:2014:0429 JUD005201907 and ECtHR 16 September 2014, *Atudorei v. Romania*, no. 50131/08, ECLI: CE:ECHR:2014:0916JUD005013108.

[159] ECtHR 12 July 2007, *Testa v. Croatia*, no. 20877/04, ECLI:CE:ECHR:2007:0712JUD002087704, §52.

[160] ECtHR 17 December 2002, *Venema v. the Netherlands*, no. 35731/97, ECLI:CE:ECHR:2002: 1217JUD003573197; ECtHR 17 July 2008, *X. v. Croatia*, no. 11223/04 and ECtHR 12 June 2014, *Marić v. Croatia*, no. 50132/12, ECLI:CE:ECHR:2014:0612JUD005013212.

[161] ECtHR 23 September 1994, *Hokkanen v. Finland*, no. 19823/92, ECLI:CE:ECHR:1994:0923 JUD001982392; ECtHR 6 July 2010, *Neulinger and Shuruk v. Switzerland* (GC), no. 41615/07, ECLI:CE:ECHR:2010:0706JUD004161507 and ECtHR 18 February 2020, *Cînța v. Romania*, no. 3891/19, ECLI:CE:ECHR:2020:0218JUD000389119.

[162] ECtHR 7 February 2007, *Köhler and Köhler v. Germany* (dec.), no. 1628/03, ECLI:CE: ECHR:2007:0205DEC000162803 and ECtHR 20 March 2012, *C.A.S. and C.S. v. Romania*, no. 26692/05, ECLI:CE:ECHR:2012:0320JUD002669205.

[163] ECtHR 20 December 2007, *Phinikaridou v. Cyprus*, no. 23890/02, ECLI:CE:ECHR:2007:1220 JUD002389002; ECtHR 21 December 2010, *Chavdarov v. Bulgaria*, no. 3465/03, ECLI:CE: ECHR:2010:1221JUD000346503 and ECtHR 18 February 2013, *A.L. v. Poland*, no. 28609/08, ECLI:CE:ECHR:2014:0218JUD002860908.

descent, as well as the related question of whether a person has the right to contest a genetic bond with a child.

In the case of *Gaskin*, the Court approvingly quoted the EComHR, which had held that 'respect for private life requires that everyone should be able to establish details of their identity as individual human beings and that in principle they should not be obstructed by the authorities from obtaining such very basic information without specific justification'.[164] Building on this line of thought, the Court decided, in a case against Croatia, that the right to a private life refers to 'a person's physical and psychological integrity and can sometimes embrace aspects of an individual's physical and social identity'.[165] This reasoning may also hold true with respect to parentage,[166] and one's gender identity.[167] In applying the importance of identity in this way, the Court acknowledged that, in principle, knowledge of one's origins is protected by the ECHR, in the sense that the person concerned must be able to gain access to the relevant information: '[i]n the Court's opinion, persons in the applicant's situation have a vital interest, protected by the Convention, in receiving the information necessary to uncover the truth about an important aspect of their personal identity'.[168] This may include information about biological parentage.[169] The right to receive information about biological parentage requires a balancing of all the interests at stake.[170] At the same time, the importance of one's own identity may impede states from requiring transsexuals to become permanently sterile before getting access to gender reassignment surgery.[171]

The Court acknowledges that providing information about biological parentage also affects the private life of the biological parents. This issue came up in the case of *Odièvre*, where the Grand Chamber held that 'the two private

---

[164]   ECtHR 7 July 1989, *Gaskin v. the United Kingdom* (GC), no. 10454/83, ECLI:CE:ECHR: 1989:0707JUD001045483, §39.

[165]   ECtHR 7 February 2002, *Mikulic v. Croatia*, no. 53176/99, ECLI:CE:ECHR:2002:0207 JUD005317699, §53.

[166]   ECtHR 29 January 2019, *Mifsud v. Malta*, no. 62257/15, ECLI:CE:ECHR:2019:0129 JUD006225715.

[167]   ECtHR 11 October 2018, *S.V. v. Italy*, no. 55216/08, ECLI:CE:ECHR:2018:1011JUD005521608.

[168]   ECtHR 7 February 2002, *Mikulic v. Croatia*, no. 53176/99, ECLI:CE:ECHR:2002:0207 JUD005317699, §64. See also ECtHR 13 February 2003, *Odièvre v. France* (GC), no. 42326/98, ECLI:CE:ECHR:2003:0213JUD004232698, §29.

[169]   ECtHR 13 February 2003, *Odièvre v. France* (GC), no. 42326/98, ECLI:CE:ECHR:2003:0213 JUD004232698, §29 and ECtHR 13 July 2006, *Jäggi v. Switzerland*, no. 58757/00, ECLI: CE:ECHR:2006:0713JUD005875700, §25 and ECtHR 17 July 2007, *Jevremović v. Serbia*, no. 3150/05, ECLI:CE:ECHR:2007:0717JUD000315005, §106.

[170]   ECtHR 16 June 2020, *Boljević v. Serbia*, no. 47443/14, ECLI:CE:ECHR:2020:0616 JUD004744314.

[171]   ECtHR 10 March 2015, *Y.Y. v. Turkey*, no. 14793/08, ECLI:CE:ECHR:2015:0310 JUD001479308, §119 and ECtHR 6 April 2017, *A.P., Garçon and Nicot v. France*, no. 79885/12, 52471/13 and 52596/13, ECLI:CE:ECHR:2017:0406JUD007988512, §133.

interests with which the Court is confronted in the present case are not easily reconciled'.[172]

2.2.2.5.2. Right to consent

The ECHR does not contain any provisions on the basis of which obtaining consent is required to be able to treat a person, or to place him or her in a care institution. Also, in respect of other acts possible within the framework of healthcare, such as taking photographs or conducting medical research, the ECHR does not explicitly stipulate that these are only allowed where there is voluntary consent.[173] However, from the ECHR system, it follows that, in principle, an individual can only give up the enjoyment of an ECHR right after he or she has voluntarily and unambiguously consented to this, and this consent is not contrary to an important public interest.[174] The Court has extended this principle to the right to private life (Article 8) and the right to liberty and security (Article 5). However, regarding the enjoyment of these rights, the rule remains that a person cannot lawfully consent to treatment which is at odds with the norms and values of the ECHR, such as in the case of dwarf-tossing,[175] or otherwise subjecting oneself to treatment considered to be incompatible with human dignity.[176]

Violating a person's private life, including his or her physical, mental or sexual integrity,[177] in the context of healthcare is, in principle, only permitted after obtaining the voluntary, explicit and informed consent of the person concerned, or his or her representative.[178] To answer the question of whether there has, indeed, been *voluntary* consent, the Court engages in a critical appraisal of the situation in which the person concerned has found themselves. In the case of detention, or if the person concerned is suspected of having committed a serious offence, it is not

---

[172] ECtHR 13 February 2003, *Odièvre v. France* (GC), no. 42326/98, ECLI:CE:ECHR:2003:0213 JUD004232698, §44.

[173] ECtHR 15 January 2009, *Reklos and Davourlis v. Greece*, no. 1234/05, ECLI:CE:ECHR:2009: 0115JUD000123405.

[174] ECtHR 27 February 1980, *Deweer v. Belgium*, no. 6903/75, ECLI:CE:ECHR:1980:0227 JUD000690375, §51; ECtHR 25 February 1992, *Pfeifer and Plankl v. Austria*, no. 10802/84, ECLI:CE:ECHR:1992:0225JUD001080284, §37 and ECtHR 18 October 2006, *Hermi v. Italy* (GC), no. 18114/02, ECLI:CE:ECHR:2006:1018JUD001811402, §73.

[175] EComHR 16 October 1996, *Wackenheim v. France* (dec.), no. 29961/96, ECLI:CE:ECHR:1996: 1016DEC002996196.

[176] ECtHR 19 February 1997, *Laskey, Jaggard and Brown v. the United Kingdom*, no. 21627/93; 21826/93 and 21974/93, ECLI:CE:ECHR:1997:0219JUD002162793.

[177] ECtHR 26 March 1985, *X and Y v. the Netherlands*, no. 8978/80, ECLI:CE:ECHR:1985:0326 JUD000897880, §23 and ECtHR 28 October 1998, *Osman v. the United Kingdom* (GC), no. 23452/94, ECLI:CE:ECHR:1998:1028JUD002345294, §128–30 and ECtHR 4 December 2003, *M.C. v. Bulgaria*, no. 39272/98, ECLI:CE:ECHR:2003:1204JUD003927298, §152.

[178] ECtHR 9 March 2004, *Glass v. the United Kingdom*, no. 61827/00, ECLI:CE:ECHR:2004:0309 JUD006182700, §82.

possible to assume, without question, that the consent to an invasive examination was genuinely voluntary.[179] Similar problems with regard to free decision-making may occur when a person is confined to a psychiatric institution,[180] and when decisions are taken in the interests of that person's psychological need that could have a major impact on their private and family life.[181]

However, it does not follow from the above that voluntary and informed consent on the part of the person in question, or his or her representative, is required in order to proceed with treatment. Indeed, enjoyment of the right to private life, as protected by Article 8, can be limited in view of health, national security, public safety, or the protection of the rights and freedoms of others.

The Court is inclined to regard the failure to comply with the requirement of consent as justified when this involves a 'therapeutic necessity' for treatment,[182] a criterion which the Court interprets broadly.[183] Furthermore, the Court's case law shows that forced treatment – and, thus, an interference with Article 8 rights – can also be justified without this being in the interests of the health of the person concerned.[184] A forced urine test by the police, without a medical reason, to investigate whether a person was under the influence of alcohol may amount to inhuman and degrading treatment.[185]

Just like forced treatment, involuntary confinement in a care institution constitutes a far-reaching infringement of a person's personal freedom. Therefore, the rule is that, in principle, such admission is only lawful if the person concerned consents to it. Indeed, consenting to treatment does not mean consenting to the deprivation of liberty.[186] Consent for institutionalisation should be given voluntarily, explicitly and on the basis of prior information. If the person concerned is deemed not to be capable of giving consent, it would be appropriate to examine whether his or her ECHR rights can be guaranteed

---

[179] ECtHR 6 May 2008, *Juhnke v. Turkey*, no. 20817/04, ECLI:CE:ECHR:2008:0513 JUD005251599, §77; ECtHR 7 October 2008, *Bogumil v. Portugal*, no. 35228/03, ECLI:CE: ECHR:2008:1007JUD003522803, §58–71 and ECtHR 25 April 2013, *Petukhova v. Russia*, no. 28796/07, ECLI:CE:ECHR:2013:0502JUD002879607, §52.

[180] ECtHR 16 June 2005, *Storck v. Germany*, no. 61603/00, ECLI:CE:ECHR:2005:0616 JUD006160300, §103.

[181] ECtHR 13 January 2009, *Todorova v. Italy*, no. 33932/06, ECLI:CE:ECHR:2009:0113 JUD003393206, §75.

[182] ECtHR 24 September 1992, *Herczegfalvy v. Austria*, no. 10533/83, ECLI:CE:ECHR:1992:0924 JUD001053383; ECtHR 7 October 2008, *Bogumil v. Portugal*, no. 35228/03 and ECtHR 11 October 2011, *Gorobet v. Moldova*, no. 30951/10, ECLI:CE:ECHR:2011:1011JUD003095110.

[183] EComHR 26 February 1997, *Buckley v. the United Kingdom*, no. 28323/95, ECLI:CE:ECHR: 1997:0226DEC002832395 and ECtHR 28 February 2006, *Wilkinson v. the United Kingdom* (dec.), no. 14659/02, ECLI:CE:ECHR:2006:0228DEC001465902.

[184] ECtHR 11 July 2006, *Jalloh v. Germany* (GC), no. 54810/00, ECLI:CE:ECHR:2006:0711 JUD005481000, §70.

[185] ECtHR 2 July 2019, *R.S. v. Hungary*, no. 65290/14, ECLI:CE:ECHR:2019:0702JUD006529014.

[186] ECtHR 6 November 2008, *Gulub Atanasov v. Bulgaria*, no. 73281/01, ECLI:CE:ECHR:2008: 1106JUD007328101, §65.

in another way.[187] In determining whether these conditions have been fulfilled, the Court will have a critical look at the situation in which the person concerned has found themselves.[188]

2.2.2.5.3. STORAGE AND USE OF PERSONAL DATA

In the healthcare system, patient information is stored and used with a view to guaranteeing continuity and quality of care. These forms of utilisation of personal data affect the patient's private life, as protected by Article 8 ECHR, particularly if this information is used for other ends.[189] The Court has repeatedly pointed out that data storage and use that is concerned with the private life of a person falls within the scope of Article 8.[190] This particularly holds true with respect to health-related personal data.[191]

The Court has interpreted the concept of 'private life' and related information broadly. According to the Court, this concept refers to both videos[192] and photographs.[193] It also follows from the Court's case law that there are certain requirements with regard to the collection, recording, storage and dissemination of personal data: in short, the processing of data.

With respect to healthcare, the Court has never explicitly considered that Article 8 entails a (positive) obligation to store a patient's health data and other personal data in a medical file, whether in electronic or paper format. Nonetheless, some judgments do tend in that direction. In the case of *Powell*, the parents of the deceased child declared, inter alia, that the medical file was incomplete, and had been tampered with. The Court's decision of admissibility is no reason to conclude that the authorities are compelled to guarantee

---

[187]   ECtHR 5 October 2004, *H.L. v. the United Kingdom*, no. 45508/99, ECLI:CE:ECHR:2004:1005 JUD004550899, §90.

[188]   Ibid., §91.

[189]   ECtHR 6 June 2013, *Avilkina et al. v. Russia*, no. 1585/09, ECLI:CE:ECHR:2013:0606 JUD000158509; ECtHR 23 February 2016, *Y.Y. v. Russia*, no. 40378/06, ECLI:CE:ECHR:2016: 0223JUD004037806 and ECtHR 26 May 2020, *P.T. v. Moldova*, no. 1122/12, ECLI:CE:ECHR: 2020:0526JUD000112212.

[190]   ECtHR 26 March 1987, *Leander v. Sweden*, no. 9248/81, ECLI:CE:ECHR:1987:0326 JUD000924881, §48; ECtHR 4 May 2000, *Rotaru v. Romania* (GC), no. 28341/95, ECLI:CE: ECHR:2000:0504JUD002834195, §43; ECtHR 4 December 2008, *S. and Marper v. the United Kingdom* (GC), no. 30562/04 and 30566/04, ECLI:CE:ECHR:2008:1204JUD003056204, §43.

[191]   ECtHR 29 April 2014, *L.H. v. Latvia*, no. 52019/07, ECLI:CE:ECHR:2014:0429JUD005201907.

[192]   ECtHR 31 July 2000, *A.D.T. v. the United Kingdom*, no. 35765/97, ECLI:CE:ECHR:2000:0731 JUD003576597; ECtHR 28 January 2003, *Peck v. the United Kingdom*, no. 44647/98, ECLI: CE:ECHR:2003:0128JUD004464798, §57 and ECtHR 17 October 2019, *López Ribalda et al. v. Spain* (GC), no. 1874/13 and 8567/13, ECLI:CE:ECHR:2019:1017JUD000187413.

[193]   EComHR 7 December 1992, *Lupker et al. v. the Netherlands*, no. 18395/91, ECLI:CE:ECHR: 1992:1207DEC001839591; ECtHR 31 January 1995, *Friedl v. Austria*, no. 15225/89, ECLI: CE:ECHR:1995:0131JUD001522589; ECtHR 15 January 2009, *Reklos and Davourlis v. Greece*, no. 1234/05, ECLI:CE:ECHR:2009:0115JUD000123405 and ECtHR 13 February 2020, *Gaughran v. the United Kingdom*, no. 45245/15, ECLI:CE:ECHR:2020:0213JUD004524515.

completeness and accuracy of medical files.[194] Yet, the Court does attach great value to the good documentation of health-related personal information in certain contexts, and this is also illustrated by the significance attributed, in numerous other judgments, to data recorded in medical files,.[195] The absence of full and detailed records of the health status of a patient can, according to the Court, undermine the effectiveness of any monitoring or supervision process.[196] Moreover, judging by the critical remarks made by the Court in various cases, the file has to comply with certain quality requirements:

> According to a one-page document that presumably forms part of a medical record, on 11 February 2005 the applicant visited a doctor and complained that he had been infected with hepatitis C. The applicant, who had refused to take anti-tuberculosis treatment, was prescribed with essenciale, vitamin B6 and two more medicines, the names of which are illegible …

> The case file contains a barely legible one-page document from which it transpires that the applicant spent some time in an unspecified medical institution with a diagnosis of recurrence of tuberculosis concurrent with viral hepatitis C with zero activity. The document contains no information concerning the treatment prescribed to the applicant.[197]

The Court has also repeatedly attached great weight to the confidentiality of medical data, in its statements:[198]

> The protection of personal data, in particular medical data, is of fundamental importance to a person's enjoyment of his or her right to respect for private and family

---

[194] ECtHR 4 May 2000, *Powell v. the United Kingdom* (dec.), no. 45305/99, ECLI:CE:ECHR:2000: 0504DEC004530599.

[195] See, e.g. ECtHR 13 October 2005, *Mogoş v. Romania*, no. 20420/02, ECLI:CE:ECHR:2005:1013 JUD002042002; ECtHR 23 May 2006, *Taïs v. France* (GC), no. 39922/03, ECLI:CE:ECHR: 2006:0601JUD003992203; ECtHR 18 December 2007, *Dybeku v. Albania*, no. 41153/06, ECLI: CE:ECHR:2007:1218JUD004115306; ECtHR 15 June 2010, *Ashot Harutyunyan v. Armenia*, no. 34334/04, ECLI:CE:ECHR:2010:0615JUD003433404; ECtHR 8 October 2015, *Sellal v. France*, no. 32432/13, ECLI:CE:ECHR:2015:1008JUD003243213 and ECtHR 11 June 2019, *Prizreni v. Albania*, no. 29309/16, ECLI:CE:ECHR:2019:0611JUD002930916.

[196] ECtHR 3 April 2001, *Keenan v. the United Kingdom*, no. 27229/95, ECLI:CE:ECHR:2001:0403 JUD002722995, §114. See also ECtHR 16 December 2008, *Rupa v. Romania*, no. 58478/00, ECLI:CE:ECHR:2008:1216JUD005847800; ECtHR 14 February 2017, *Karakhanyan v. Russia*, no. 24421/11, ECLI:CE:ECHR:2017:0214JUD002442111 and ECtHR 25 June 2019, *Ulusoy v. Turkey*, no. 54969/09, ECLI:CE:ECHR:2019:0625JUD005496909.

[197] ECtHR 7 February 2008, *Mechenkov v. Russia*, no. 35421/05, ECLI:CE:ECHR:2008:0207 JUD003542105, §69. See also ECtHR 24 May 2007, *Gorodnichev v. Russia*, no. 52058/99, ECLI: CE:ECHR:2007:0524JUD005205899, §87; ECtHR 11 October 2005, *Tarariyeva v. Russia* (dec.), no. 4353/03, ECLI:CE:ECHR:2006:1214JUD000435303 and ECtHR 15 June 2010, *Ashot Harutyunyan v. Armenia*, no. 34334/04, ECLI:CE:ECHR:2010:0615JUD003433404

[198] ECtHR 26 May 2020, *P.T. v. Moldova*, no. 1122/12, ECLI:CE:ECHR:2020:0526JUD000112212.

life as guaranteed by Article 8 of the Convention. Respecting the confidentiality of health data is a vital principle in the legal systems of all the Contracting Parties to the Convention. It is crucial not only to respect the sense of privacy of a patient but also to preserve his or her confidence in the medical profession and in the health services in general.[199]

Along the same lines, the Court places weight on the physician's duty to respect the confidentiality of medical data.[200] In the event of a breach of the secrecy of medical data, it will be necessary to examine, on a case-by-case basis, whether, and for how long, further infringements on the private life of the person concerned will have to be prevented. In a French case where the authorities had prohibited a publishing company from publishing a book written by former president Mitterand's personal physician, for an indefinite period, the Court found that this was a disproportionate violation of the freedom of expression.[201]

The physician's duty not to disclose medical data does not imply an absolute ban on handing over details from a patient's file. In the social security case *M.S.*, where details from the applicant's medical file had been released following her application for incapacity benefits, the Court's conclusion was that all conditions justifying an infringement on the right to private life had been satisfied. The circumstance that 'the medical records in question contained highly personal and sensitive data about the applicant, including information relating to an abortion' did not alter this.[202] As long as there are enough guarantees, handing over information from a father's medical records to the child protection authorities can also be justified.[203]

---

[199] ECtHR 25 February 1997, Z. v. Finland, no. 22009/93, ECLI:CE:ECHR:1997:0225 JUD002200993, §95; ECtHR 10 October 2006, L.L. v. France, no. 7508/02, ECLI:CE:ECHR: 2006:1010JUD000750802, §44; ECtHR 17 July 2008, I. v. Finland, no. 20511/03, ECLI:CE: ECHR:2008:0717JUD002051103, §38; ECtHR 25 November 2008, Armoniene v. Lithuania, no. 36919/02, ECLI:CE:ECHR:2008:1125JUD003691902, §40 and ECtHR 17 January 2012, Varapnickaité-Mazliené v. Lithuania, no. 20376/05, ECLI:CE:ECHR:2012:0117JUD002037605, §44.

[200] ECtHR 10 October 2006, L.L. v. France, no. 7508/02, ECLI:CE:ECHR:2006:1010 JUD000750802, §23; ECtHR 25 November 2008, Armoniené v. Lithuania, no. 36919/02, ECLI:CE:ECHR:2008:1125JUD003691902 and ECtHR 15 April 2014, Radu v. Moldova, no. 50073/07, ECLI:CE:ECHR:2014:0415JUD005007307.

[201] ECtHR 18 May 2004, Plon (Société) v. France, no. 58148/00, ECLI:CE:ECHR:2004:0518 JUD005814800.

[202] ECtHR 27 August 1997, M.S. v. Sweden, no. 20837/92, ECLI:CE:ECHR:1997:0827 JUD002083792, §35.

[203] ECtHR 5 January 2006, K.T. v. Norway (dec.), no. 26664/03, ECLI:CE:ECHR:2008:0925 JUD002666403.

On the presumption that information kept in a medical file lies at the core of Article 8,[204] it is obvious that the person concerned is also entitled to have access to the file.[205] Access can only be refused in exceptional circumstances.[206]

According to the Court's settled case law, access should also be possible with a view to correcting mistakes or preventing abuse of information relating to the person concerned,[207] or with a view to obtaining information on the individual's origins and identity.[208] Individuals whose personal data have been processed should not be obliged to specifically justify a request for a copy of their personal data files. It is, according to the Court, for the authorities, instead, to show that there are compelling reasons for refusing this facility.[209]

Even though the Court considers that people should be able to access such stored information, the ECHR does not extend to accessing files that contain only professional information unrelated to the identities or personal histories of individuals.[210]

2.3. CONCLUSIONS

Despite the fact that the ECHR does not set forth a right to health or healthcare, it can be learned from an analysis of the Court's case law that the Convention imposes various obligations on contracting states (including, notably, positive ones) to provide adequate healthcare, and protect the rights of patients, as well as obligations that are relevant to the promotion of health and prevention of disease. These obligations do not confine themselves to vertical relations, but also entail duties for individuals towards each other ('horizontal relations').

---

[204] ECtHR 17 July 2008, *I. v. Finland*, no. 20511/03, ECLI:CE:ECHR:2008:0717JUD002051103, §35.

[205] ECtHR 28 April 2009, *K.H. et al. v. Slovakia*, no. 32881/04, ECLI:CE:ECHR:2009:0428 JUD003288104 and ECtHR 7 December 2017, *Yonchev v. Bulgaria*, no. 12504/09, ECLI:CE: ECHR:2017:1207JUD001250409.

[206] EComHR 28 February 1996, *Martin v. the United Kingdom* (dec.), no. 27533/95, ECLI: CE:ECHR:1996:0228DEC002753395 and ECtHR 20 January 2009, *Uslu v. Turkey (no. 2)*, no. 23815/04, ECLI:CE:ECHR:2009:0120JUD002381504.

[207] ECtHR 4 May 2000, *Rotaru v. Romania* (GC), no. 28341/95, ECLI:CE:ECHR:2000:0504 JUD002834195.

[208] ECtHR 7 July 1989, *Gaskin v. the United Kingdom*, no. 10454/83, ECLI:CE:ECHR:1989:0707 JUD001045483, §39 and ECtHR 7 February 2002, *Mikulic v. Croatia*, no. 53176/99, ECLI:CE: ECHR:2002:0207JUD005317699, §54.

[209] ECtHR 28 April 2009, *K.H. et al. v. Slovakia*, no. 32881/04, ECLI:CE:ECHR:2009:0428 JUD003288104, §48. See also ECtHR 15 October 2009, *Tsourlakis v. Greece*, no. 50796/07, ECLI:CE:ECHR:2009:1015JUD005079607.

[210] ECtHR 4 January 2007, *Smith v. the United Kingdom* (dec.), no. 39658/05, ECLI:CE:ECHR: 2007:0104DEC003965805.

3. EUROPEAN SOCIAL CHARTER

The European Social Charter (hereinafter 'Charter' or 'ESC') was adopted in 1961, and entered into force in 1965. It is the counterpart of the ECHR, that is to say 'a human rights instrument envisaged to complement the European Convention on Human Rights'.[211] Since the ECHR, almost exclusively, protects civil and political rights, the need was felt to also introduce legal guarantees for the enjoyment of social and economic rights. At the same time, the supervision mechanism established under the ECHR, notably the possibility for individuals and states to file complaints with the Court, was deemed less appropriate when it came to promoting compliance with social and economic rights. In the 1960s, social and economic rights were generally considered to lack justiciability.[212] It was claimed that these rights, including the right to health, above all reflected vague political intentions that could not be enforced by courts.[213] It was exclusively for governments to decide how they wanted to progressively realise the aspirations enshrined in these rights, particularly given the large sums of money involved.

The ESC 1961[214] entails various rights of imminent importance, from a health and human rights perspective. First of all, Article 11 explicitly recognises the right to protection of health.[215] According to this provision, contracting states are, among other things, required to take appropriate measures to remove the causes of ill health, to provide facilities for the promotion of health, and to prevent epidemic, endemic and other diseases. The ESC 1961 also recognises the right to safe and healthy working conditions (Article 3), the right of children and young persons to protection (Article 7), and the right to social and medical assistance (Article 13).

Since it was, nevertheless, thought that states should, somehow, be held accountable for their policies and laws for achieving these aspirations, the ESC includes periodic reporting procedures. When it comes to monitoring compliance, the European Committee of Social Rights (hereinafter 'Committee'

---

[211] ECSR 3 November 2004, *FIDH v. France*, no. 14/2003, §27; Ibid; ECSR 27 October 2009, *DCI v. the Netherlands*, no. 47/2008, §34.

[212] C. Courtis, 'Standards to Make ESC Rights Justiciable: A Summary Exploration', *Erasmus Law Review* (4) (2009), 379–95.

[213] B.C.E. Toebes, *The Right to Health as a Human Right in International Human Rights Law*, Antwerp/Oxford: Intersentia/Hart, 1999.

[214] The text of the ESC, as well as the Additional Protocols, can be found at www.coe.int/en/web/european-social-charter/charter-texts.

[215] European Committee of Social Rights, *Digest of the case law of the European Committee of Social Rights*, Council of Europe, Strasbourg, December 2018, 128–36. See also European Committee of Social Rights, *Statement of interpretation on the right to protection of health in times of pandemic*, Council of Europe, Strasbourg, April 2020.

or 'ECSR') plays a key role. The ECSR, previously known as the Committee of Independent Experts (CIE), is composed of 15 experts, appointed by the Council of Europe's Committee of Ministers (Article 25 ESC). The members are appointed for a period of six years, after which time they can be reappointed for one more term of six years. Contracting states are required to report to this committee every two years on their implementation of the ESC, and any problems they may have encountered. After an examination of these reports by the ECSR, the reports, together with the ECSR's views on them ('conclusions'), are considered by the Governmental Committee (a body of national senior civil servants) and the Committee of Ministers. The latter may make recommendations to contracting states that have not fully complied with the rights specified in the ESC. The ECSR's conclusions and the Committee of Ministers' recommendations provide useful insights as to the interpretation and correct application of the ESC.

In the 1990s, the need was felt to revitalise the ESC.[216] This led to a revision of the ESC in 1996 (revised ESC), and the adoption of two Additional Protocols. The revised ESC, which entered into force in 1999, did not substantially change the rights most relevant from a health and human rights perspective. The numbering of the Articles also remained the same. However, new provisions were added, too, like the right of children and young persons to social, legal and economic protection (Article 17), and a general provision prohibiting discrimination in the enjoyment of the rights set forth by the ESC, including discrimination on grounds of 'health' (Article E).

The overwhelming majority of the Member States of the Council of Europe have signed and ratified the revised ESC, if not the 1961 ESC. Only a few states have failed to ratify either treaty.

Of great importance for health and human rights in Europe was the introduction of the Additional Protocol, which provided a system of collective complaints. This protocol was adopted in 1995. On the basis of this protocol, which came into force in 1998, a number of national and international non-governmental organisations can now lodge complaints with the ECSR. In the event that the ECSR finds a complaint admissible, it will submit a report with its findings and conclusions on the merits of the case.[217] These mostly well-substantiated and well-reasoned reports, which are followed by a resolution adopted by the Committee of Ministers deciding on whether the complaint is upheld, are authoritative even though they do not have the same status as legally binding decisions such as the judgments of the European Court of Human Rights. Nevertheless, the ECSR has made it very clear that 'The right to protection of health guaranteed in Article 11 of the Charter complements Articles 2 and 3 of

---

[216] R.R. Churchill and U. Khaliq, 'The Collective Complaints System of the European Social Charter: An Effective Mechanism for Ensuring Compliance with Social and Economic Rights?', *European Journal of International Law* 15(3) (2004), 417–56.

[217] All reports can be found at www.coe.int/en/web/european-social-charter/case-law.

the European Convention on Human Rights – as interpreted by the European Court of Human Rights – by imposing a range of positive obligations designed to secure its effective exercise.'[218]

In 2004, the ECSR found that the reforms, in France, of 'L'Aide médicale de l'Etat' (state medical assistance) and the 'couverture maladie universelle' (universal sickness coverage), which deprived a large number of adults and children with insufficient resources of medical assistance, resulted in a violation of Article 17 of the revised ESC (the right of children and young persons to social, legal and economic protection). A (narrow) majority of the ECSR ruled that Article 17 protected, in a general manner, the rights of children and young persons, including unaccompanied minors, to care and assistance, and that the French law reforms undermined this entitlement.[219]

In 2006, the ECSR found that Greece had violated the ESC by not responding adequately to the health hazards caused by lignite, which was being mined in certain areas of Greece. The main provision that Greece failed to adhere to was Article 11 ESC, the provision on the right to health. According to the ECSR, 'Under Article 11 of the Charter, everyone has the right to benefit from any measures enabling him to enjoy the highest possible standard of health attainable. The Committee sees a clear complementarity between Article 11 of the Charter and Article 2 (right to life) of the European Convention on Human Rights, as interpreted by the European Court of Human Rights ... Measures required under Article 11 should be designed, in the light of current knowledge, to remove the causes of ill-health resulting from environmental threats such as pollution.'[220]

In 2008, the ECSR found that the Bulgarian health insurance legislation discriminated against particular groups, notably Roma. The ECSR concluded that the way this body of legislation was framed constituted a violation of Article 11 (right to health), in conjunction with Article E (non-discrimination).[221]

In 2009, the ECSR issued a report on sexual and reproductive health information, as delivered in Croatian schools. In its report, the ECSR formulated the following criteria for this type of health information.

States must ensure:

(a) that sexual and reproductive health education forms part of the ordinary school curriculum;

---

[218] ECSR 4 February 2013, *International Federation for Human Rights (FIDH) v. Greece*, no. 72/2011.

[219] ECSR 3 November 2004, *International Federation for Human Rights Leagues (FIDH) v. France*, no. 14/2003.

[220] ECSR 6 February 2007, *Marangopoulos Foundation for Human Rights (MFHR) v. Greece*, no. 30/2005. See also ECSR 4 February 2013, *International Federation for Human Rights (FIDH) v. Greece*, no. 72/2011.

[221] ECSR 16 December 2008, *European Roma Rights Centre (ERRC) v. Bulgaria*, no. 46/2007.

(b) that the education provided is adequate in quantitative terms, i.e. in respect of the time and other resources devoted to it (teachers, teacher training, teaching materials, etc.);

(c) that the form and substance of the education, including curricula and teaching methods, are relevant, culturally appropriate and of sufficient quality, in particular that education is objective, based on contemporary scientific evidence and does not involve censoring, withholding or intentionally misrepresenting information, for example as regards contraception and different means of maintaining sexual and reproductive health; and

(d) that a procedure is in place for monitoring and evaluating the education with a view to effectively meeting the above requirements.

The ESCR unanimously found that the health information provided in Croatian schools did not meet these criteria, and that the information conveyed was discriminatory towards homosexuals, thus finding a violation of Article 11, in conjunction with Article E of the revised ESC.[222]

By the end of 2013, the ESCR had concluded vis-à-vis Italy that the failure to provide women with the opportunity to terminate their pregnancies constituted a violation of their rights. Instead of having a safe abortion, many women were exposed to causes of ill health, something the state should have been aware of. Thus, the practice of many Italian physicians, in requesting recognition as being conscious objectors, thus relieving them of the obligation to perform a legally recognised form of healthcare, resulted in a violation of Article 11 ESC.[223]

The ECSR also received a complaint from Transgender Europe and ILGA-Europe on the requirement for forced sterilisation of transsexuals in the Czech Republic, before they would be permitted access to a form of gender-reassignment surgery. Like the Court under the ECHR,[224] the ECSR considered, though on different grounds, that this requirement was not necessary to protect the health of the persons concerned.[225]

In 2019, the ECSR found that the unequal access of pregnant Roma women to birth care in Bulgaria constituted a form of unequal treatment towards, and segregation of, these women.[226]

It can, therefore, be seen that the ESC and the work of the ECSR are of major importance when it comes to interpreting and strengthening the

---

[222] ECSR 9 April 2009, *Interights v. Croatia*, no. 45/2007.

[223] ECSR 7 November 2013, *International Planned Parenthood Federation – European Network (IPPF EN) v. Italy*, no. 87/2012.

[224] ECtHR 6 April 2017, *A.P., Garçon and Nicot v. France*, no. 79885/12, 52471/13 and 52596/13, ECLI:CE:ECHR:2017:0406JUD007988512, §133.

[225] ECSR 31 May 2018, *Transgender Europe and ILGA-Europe v. the Czech Republic*, no. 117/2015.

[226] ECSR 18 December 2019, *European Roma Rights Centre (ERRC) v. Bulgaria*, no. 151/2017.

interrelationships between health and human rights law in Europe. Yet, the work is still at its beginning. It is to be hoped that the ECSR and its opinions in the field of health and human rights can become as authoritative as the judgments of the ECtHR.[227]

4. EUROPEAN CONVENTION FOR THE PREVENTION OF TORTURE

Another Council of Europe treaty that merits mentioning when it comes to analysing the bonds between health and human rights law is the European Convention for the Prevention of Torture and Inhuman or Degrading Treatment or Punishment (hereinafter the 'European Convention for the Prevention of Torture' or 'CPT'). This treaty was adopted in 1987, and entered into force in 1989. In 1993, two Protocols amending the CPT were adopted, and these became effective as of 2002. The CPT has been ratified by all Member States of the Council of Europe, and its ratification is now a precondition for joining the Council of Europe.

The CPT, which does not have any material provisions, seeks to reinforce the right not to be subjected to torture, or to inhuman or degrading treatment or punishment, as laid down in Article 3 of the ECHR. It was assumed that the – above all, retrospective – protection offered by Article 3 of the ECHR would benefit from proactive measures aimed at 'strengthening, if necessary, the protection of ... persons [deprived of their liberty] from torture and from inhuman or degrading treatment or punishment' (Article 1 of the CPT). The CPT provides for the fulfilment of these aims by establishing an independent committee, the European Committee for the Prevention of Torture and Inhuman or Degrading Treatment or Punishment, composed of members with different professional backgrounds. Their number is equal to that of the States Parties to the CPT. The members of this committee, nominated by the contracting states, are required to be independent and impartial. They are elected by the Council of Europe's Council of Ministers.

The Committee is permitted to visit and inspect all 'places of detention' of the Council of Europe's Member States without prior announcement or approval by the authorities. Places of detention, as defined by the CPT, are all places in which people are deprived of their liberty by a public authority. This broad term,

---

[227] C. Lougarre, 'What Does the Right to Health Mean? The Interpretation of Article 11 of the European Social Charter by the European Committee of Social Rights', *Netherlands Quarterly of Human Rights* 33(3) (2015), 326–54.

therefore, includes psychiatric institutions and (other) care institutions where people are held without their consent.

After a visit, the Committee prepares a report with its findings and recommendations, and sends this to the government of the relevant state. Officially, these reports are only made public with the consent of the government concerned, but, in practice, all reports are accompanied by the government's response when published.[228]

The reports of the Committee contain useful information on the detention situations in Member States, and provide insights into how the Committee defines torture, inhuman or degrading treatment or punishment, with respect to persons deprived of their liberty. These reports, and the standards applied by the Committee, are frequently used by the ECtHR in cases where applicants claim that Article 3 of the ECHR has been violated. Examples of two reports are given below.

In 2009, the Committee's delegation published its report following a visit to the Czech Republic in 2008. In this report, the Committee made a number of critical remarks on the treatment of sentenced sex offenders. After examining the situation, the Committee recommended that the Czech authorities review the treatment offered to such offenders, and revise their legislation to ensure their compatibility with the CPT.[229]

That same year, the Committee published a report following a country visit to Spain. In this report, the Committee addressed – amongst other things – the issue of force-feeding. According to the Committee, a decision to force-feed a prisoner should be based upon medical necessity, and should be carried out under suitable conditions, reflecting the medical nature of the measure. Moreover, the Committee considered that the methods used to execute force-feeding should not be unnecessarily painful, and should be applied with skill and minimum force. It can, therefore, be concluded that, in principle, the Committee does not reject force-feeding, but considers that it is only acceptable when strict requirements are met.[230]

After a country visit to Italy in 2019, the Committee noticed the prolonged accommodation of mentally ill persons in a prison setting, due to the absence of places in appropriate facilities, such as the so-called Residences for the Execution of Security Measures, and the specialised psychiatric sections in prisons. Measures should be taken, according to the Committee, to ensure that mentally ill prisoners are transferred to a healthcare facility without delay. From the official statistics on suicide provided to the Committee, and from the findings of its delegation, it appeared that persons who were placed in de facto

---

[228]   See www.cpt.coe.int/en/.
[229]   CPT 5 February 2009, Report on Czech Republic, CPT/Inf (2009) 8.
[230]   CPT 2 March 2009, Report on Italy, CPT/Inf (2020) 2.

solitary confinement were at much greater risk of committing suicide. Even persons who were assessed as being suicidal were often isolated from other prisoners, rather than being placed under direct staff supervision and being offered both meaningful contact with other staff members and prisoners, and access to activities, as appropriate.[231]

Following a visit to Ukraine, the Committee's delegation noted that the three 'internats' (psychoneurological institutions) visited were grossly understaffed with doctors, nurses and orderlies. Furthermore, there were, according to the Committee, hardly any other staff qualified to provide psychosocial therapy and other activities. The Committee recommended that efforts be made to improve the healthcare staffing situation in various internats, by substantially increasing the numbers of ward-based staff (nurses and orderlies), filling all vacant doctors' posts and recruiting other qualified staff (psychologists, occupational therapists, physiotherapists, social workers, etc.).[232]

In 2019, the Committee published its report following its visit to the United Kingdom. Amongst other things, the Committee's delegation found that some aspects of the healthcare provision in the prisons visited needed to be strengthened, including the provision of additional general practitioners. Also, the documentation of injuries needed to be improved, as well as the guarantees of medical confidentiality. The delegation also noted that a high number of prisoners suffered from mental health disorders, and a considerable number of prisoners had self-harmed, some severely, in the past year.[233]

It follows that the mechanism of the CPT is quite effective at highlighting various issues that are, from a health and human rights perspective, problematic, since these (potentially) reflect violations of the duty not to subject detained persons to inhuman and degrading treatment. The CPT commonly also indicates what measures should be taken to change such shortfalls in human rights.

5. CONVENTION ON HUMAN RIGHTS AND BIOMEDICINE

In 1996, the Council of Ministers of the Council of Europe adopted a framework convention laying down the main human rights principles, and some general standards, for the protection of human rights and human dignity in areas concerning the application of biology and medicine. This treaty, the Convention for the Protection of Human Rights and Dignity of the Human Being with regard to the Application of Biology and Medicine (hereinafter, the 'Convention

---

231   CPT 2 August 2019, Report on Spain, CPT/Inf (2020) 10.
232   CPT 29 November 2019, Report on Ukraine, CPT/Inf (2020) 1.
233   CPT 3 December 2019, Report on United Kingdom (England), CPT/Inf (2020) 18.

on Human Rights and Biomedicine' or 'Biomedicine Convention', also called the 'Oviedo Convention'), elaborates some of the principles and rights enshrined in the European Convention on Human Rights. In fact, the Biomedicine Convention can be considered as an addition to – or a *lex specialis* vis-à-vis – the ECHR, with a view to the rapid developments in biology and medicine.

The Biomedicine Convention was opened for signature and ratification in Oviedo, Spain on 4 April 1997. This Convention entered into force on 1 December 1999. As from 1998, four Additional Protocols were adopted: on the prohibition of cloning human beings (1998); on transplantation of organs and tissues of human origin (2002); on biomedical research (2005); and on genetic testing for health purposes (2008). By 2020, the Biomedicine Convention had been ratified by 28 Member States of the Council of Europe. All Additional Protocols had entered into force, including the genetic testing protocol (2018, six ratifications in 2020).

As mentioned above, the Biomedicine Convention is a framework convention. It sets out only a number of principles, rights and standards upon which there was clarity and consensus amongst the drafters. Other issues have been, or will be, dealt with in Additional Protocols, like the four protocols mentioned before, provided that the drafters can agree on them. With respect to issues such as abortion and euthanasia, it seems very unlikely that this will occur in the near future.

The Biomedicine Convention itself consists of 'principles', 'rights' and 'standards' applying to specific fields of biology and medicine. The principles that the Biomedicine Convention recognises include the protection of human dignity and identity (Article 1); the protection of the integrity of human beings (Article 1); equitable access to healthcare, and the prohibition of discrimination (Articles 3 and 1); the primacy of the human being (Article 2); and the prohibition of financial gain from the human body, as well as rules regarding the disposal of a removed parts of the human body (Chapter VII).

The Biomedicine Convention, further, contains more specific rights and standards with respect to consent (Chapter II); private life and information (Chapter III); the human genome (Chapter IV); scientific research (Chapter V); and organ and tissue removal from living human beings (Chapter VI). Basically, the rights laid down in these chapters are elaborations of the rights and freedoms protected by the ECHR.

In contrast to the ECHR, the Biomedicine Convention does not provide for a strong enforcement mechanism. In fact, the Convention does not even impose a duty on contracting states to report regularly on progress made with respect to the implementation of the Convention, an obligation quite common under human rights treaties. The Convention does, however, authorise the secretary general of the Council of Europe to ask a contracting state to 'furnish an explanation of the manner in which its internal law ensures the effective implementation of any of the provisions of the Convention' (Article 30). Moreover, governments, and the

Steering Committee on Bioethics, may request the ECtHR to give a non-binding *advisory* opinion on a question concerning the interpretation of the Convention (Article 29). As of 2021, no use has been made of either of these possibilities.[234]

As mentioned before, the ECtHR does, sometimes, refer to provisions of the Biomedicine Convention in cases concerning the application of techniques or forms of treatment in the field of medicine.[235] This occurs, seemingly, in a haphazard manner. In the majority of cases touching upon biomedical questions, the Court has not seen a need to invoke the more elaborate provisions of the Biomedicine Convention, in order to judge the case. The impact of the Biomedicine Convention has, therefore, been limited.

6. CONCLUSIONS

Although the Council of Europe may be less influential than the European Union, in terms of powers, and may also have less economic and political significance in our 'global village', this organisation, embracing 47 States, has produced four very important treaties in the field of health and human rights law. The European Convention of Human Rights is by far the most significant of these treaties, even though it focuses on the protection of civil and political rights. Thanks to the case law of the European Court of Human Rights, which also emphasises the responsibilities of states, under international law, the ECHR provisions have great relevance in the field of health and human rights law, notably due to the positive duties that the Court imposes on states. The European Social Charter has enormous potential, particularly now that the European Committee on Social Rights can receive collective complaints, interpreting the

---

[234] F. Seatzu, 'The Experience of the European Court of Human Rights with the European Convention on Human Rights and Biomedicine', *Utrecht Journal of International and European Law*, 2015 31(81), 5–16.

[235] ECtHR 10 May 2001, *Cyprus v. Turkey* (GC), no. 25781/94, ECLI:CE:ECHR:2014:0512 JUD002578194; ECtHR 9 March 2004, *Glass v. the United Kingdom*, no. 61827/00, ECLI:CE: ECHR:2004:0309JUD006182700; ECtHR 8 July 2004, *Vo v. France* (GC), no. 53924/00, ECLI: CE:ECHR:2004:0708JUD005392400; ECtHR 7 March 2006, *Evans v. the United Kingdom*, no. 6339/05; ECtHR 10 April 2007, *Evans v. the United Kingdom* (GC), no. 6339/05, ECLI:CE: ECHR:2007:0410JUD000633905; ECtHR 7 October 2008, *Bogumil v. Portugal*, no. 35228/03, ECLI:CE:ECHR:2008:1007JUD003522803; ECtHR 1 April 2010, *S.H. et al. v. Austria*, no. 57813/00, ECLI:CE:ECHR:2011:1103JUD005781300; ECtHR 15 November 2016, *Dubská and Krejzová v. the Czech Republic* (GC), no. 28859/11 and 28473/12, ECLI:CE:ECHR:2016: 1115JUD002885911; ECtHR 6 April 2017, *A.P., Garçon and Nicot v. France*, no. 79885/12, 52471/13 and 52596/13, ECLI:CE:ECHR:2017:0406JUD007988512; ECtHR 19 December 2017, *Lopes de Sousa Fernandes v. Portugal* (GC), no. 56080/13, ECLI:CE:ECHR:2017:1219 JUD005608013; ECtHR 31 January 2019, *Rooman v. Belgium* (GC), no. 18052/11, ECLI:CE: ECHR:2019:0131JUD001805211 and ECtHR 23 January 2020, *L.R. v. North Macedonia*, 38067/15, ECLI:CE:ECHR:2020:0123JUD003806715.

right to health broadly. Under the system of the European Convention for the Prevention of Torture (CPT), a specially appointed independent and impartial Committee can visit and inspect all places of detention, in an effort to strengthen the prohibition of torture. The standards and reports developed and produced by this Committee have an impact that goes far beyond the CPT. Last but not least, the Biomedicine Convention is a framework convention with principles, rights and standards created in view of developments in biology and medicine. The number of ratifications to this Convention is still relatively low, and it lacks an effective enforcement mechanism, and so its impact has been limited.

CHAPTER 6

THE EUROPEAN UNION

A Health and Human Rights Perspective

Janne Rothmar Herrmann,
Katharina Ó Cathaoir and Brigit Toebes

1. INTRODUCTION

This chapter explores some of the ways in which European Union (EU) law has a bearing on health and human rights.[1] While the EU started as an economic organisation, and, as such, its primary focus is on economic integration, there is also an increasing emphasis on human rights, health protection and promotion. With the Charter on Fundamental Rights (CFREU), the EU explicitly recognises a range of health-related rights.[2] Furthermore, health-related rights play a role in the interpretation of EU law by the Court of Justice of the European Union (CJEU).[3] In addition, although the main responsibility for health protection and promotion lies with national authorities, in some areas the EU has complementary and shared competences.[4] Furthermore, EU laws and policies can have a substantial impact on the protection and promotion of health among Europeans. Notably, it is one of the Union's explicit aims to raise the standard of living and quality of life,[5] which has resulted in various policies and strategies

---

[1]   For a detailed review, see, Tamara K. Hervey and Jean V. McHale, *European Union Health Law – Themes and Implications*, Cambridge: Cambridge University Press, 2015; Anniek de Ruijter, *EU Health Law & Policy*, Oxford: Oxford University Press, 2019. This chapter also relies, to some extent, on the older, yet foundational, Tamara K. Hervey and Jean V. McHale, *Health Law and the European Union*, Cambridge: Cambridge University Press, 2004.

[2]   Charter of Fundamental Rights of the European Union, OJ C 326, 26.10.2012, p. 391–407. See, e.g. Anniek de Ruijter, *EU Health Law & Policy*, Oxford: Oxford University Press, 2019, in particular Chapter 2.

[3]   Tamara K. Hervey and Jean V. McHale, *European Union Health Law – Themes and Implications*, Cambridge: Cambridge University Press, 2015, 170–83, 183.

[4]   Art. 168 Treaty on the Functioning of the European Union (TFEU) OJ C 326, 26.10.2012, p. 47–390.

[5]   Art. 9 TFEU.

relevant to the protection and promotion of health. Finally, the rules of the internal market impact upon national health systems, as various aspects of healthcare can be caught by the EU's free movement rules.

EU law does not, however, provide a comprehensive framework in the area of health and human rights. Rather, there is a patchwork of rules, which may, in one way or another, affect the field.[6] As such, it will be impossible to provide a complete and comprehensive overview of all EU regulation that is potentially relevant to this study. The aim of this chapter is, therefore, to provide an introduction to a broad range of topics where EU law has implications for health and human rights.

Some important dimensions of the field are described and discussed below. First, attention will be paid to the ways in which the EU engages with health and human rights directly, through the recognition of health and human rights, and their interpretation by the CJEU (section 2). Subsequently, the focus will be on a number of specific responsibilities of the EU in the area of health, based on Article 168 of the Treaty on the Functioning of the European Union (section 3). Then, free movement of patients is discussed in relation to health and human rights (section 4). In this regard, attention will be paid to the free movement of patients, pharmaceuticals, blood, cells and tissues, and data; besides being connected to the creation of a free internal market for data flow, data is also strongly connected to the right to privacy under the European Charter.

The EU, as we know it today, is the further development of an agreement between France, Germany, Italy, Belgium, the Netherlands and Luxembourg, in the aftermath of the Second World War, to collaborate on the production of coal and steel. To overcome the repercussions of the war, and to avoid warfare between the European nations, these countries each agreed, in the 1951 Treaty of Paris, to give up part of their national sovereignty, thus establishing the European Coal and Steel Community. In time, the Community expanded not only in number, as the circle of Member States widened, but also in substance, with the adoption of the subsequent treaties of Rome, Maastricht, Amsterdam and Lisbon. The aim of the EU is to create an ever-closer union among the peoples of Europe, implying that the Union has a wider aim than traditional international collaboration.[7]

On 1 December 2009, the Treaty of Lisbon entered into force, establishing one European Union, replacing the pillar-based EU established by the Maastricht Treaty, with different governing structures and rules for the European Community and the European Union. At the same time, the Lisbon Treaty (or 'Reform Treaty') does not replace, but only amends, the former EU and EC Treaties. Among other issues, it provides for strengthened roles for the

---

6   See also Tamara K. Hervey and Jean V. McHale, *European Union Health Law – Themes and Implications*, Cambridge: Cambridge University Press, 2015, 69.

7   Art. 1 Treaty on European Union (TEU) OJ C 326, 26.10.2012, p. 13–390.

European Parliament and national parliaments, simplified methods and voting rules, and stronger human rights protection through the reference in Article 6 of the Treaty on European Union (TEU, Maastricht 2007) to the above-mentioned European Charter of Fundamental Rights (CFREU, Lisbon 2009). Throughout this section on EU law, reference will be made to two important EU Treaties: the TEU (Treaty on European Union) and the TFEU (Treaty on the Functioning of the European Union). In addition, reference will be made to the CFREU (the European Charter on Fundamental Rights).

The Treaties form the legal basis for the various legal measures that the Union can take. Each measure has a distinct set of legal implications, and will usually include directions on which legal instrument to use, depending on the area of regulation in question. *Regulations* can implicate both rights and duties for European citizens, and do not need any implementing measures, therefore making them directly applicable (although some provisions may need to be implemented so that they are clear, precise and unconditional). *Directives*, on the other hand, need to be transposed into the Member States' national laws, and, therefore, provide the Member States with some leeway as to their interpretation, and the means by which the required results are to be achieved. *Decisions* are binding for those to whom the decision is addressed, and do not leave any leeway in their implementation. Unless otherwise stated, Regulations enter into force 20 days after publication. Member States can file an annulment claim before the General Court, for example if there is, in their view, no legal basis in the Treaty for the EU to adopt such a Regulation or other EU secondary law measure.

The Court of Justice of the European Union (CJEU), including the General Court, is one of the core bodies of the European Union. Its role is to make sure that EU legislation is interpreted and applied in the same way in all EU countries. It ensures, for example, that national courts do not give different rulings on the same issue of EU law. The Court has the power to settle legal disputes between EU Member States, EU institutions, businesses and individuals. Under Article 267 TFEU, a national court may refer to the CJEU for a preliminary ruling on questions of validity and interpretation of EU law.

2. EU, HEALTH AND HUMAN RIGHTS

2.1. THE EUROPEAN CHARTER OF FUNDAMENTAL RIGHTS

As mentioned above, the Lisbon Treaty entered into force in December 2009.[8] This treaty has important implications for the way in which the EU engages with human

---

[8] Treaty of Lisbon amending the Treaty on European Union and the Treaty establishing the European Community, signed at Lisbon, 13 December 2007 OJ C 306, 17.12.2007, p. 1–271.

rights law. In principle, with the entry into force of the Lisbon Treaty, the EU would be required to accede to the ECHR.[9] This would mean that acts by the EU that involved, or infringed on, a human rights issue would be the subject of scrutiny by the ECtHR. However, in 2014, the CJEU declared the draft agreement on accession of the EU to the ECHR incompatible with EU law.[10] Still, the rights contained in the ECHR are considered to be one of the most important sources of so-called 'general principles' in EU law.[11] This is confirmed by Article 6(3) TEU, which stipulates that the ECHR's fundamental principles are general principles of EU law. Per Article 52(3) of the Charter, where a Charter provision is also protected by the ECHR, the latter serves as a minimum standard of protection. In addition, it is, for the purposes of this volume, worth noting that the Council of Europe's European Biomedicine Convention has been recognised by the CJEU in several of its cases.[12]

Furthermore, with the entry into force of the Lisbon Treaty, the CFREU was given binding legal effect equal to that of the Treaties.[13] This document brings together a number of rights previously recognised in a variety of legislative instruments, including the treaty and various directives, as well as Council of Europe instruments, so as to create a comprehensive overview. The CFREU makes a distinction between 'rights', 'freedoms' and 'principles'.[14] It contains seven chapters (dignity, freedoms, equality, solidarity, citizens' rights, justice, and general provisions). Taking a closer look at the rights in these chapters, we see that several rights, freedoms and/or principles can be relevant to the promotion and protection of health, and to the area of health and human rights.[15]

Firstly, in Chapter I ('dignity'), we find a general right to dignity, the right to life, the right to integrity of the person, and the prohibition of torture and inhuman and degrading treatment.[16] Article 1 on the right to dignity can be seen as the core right underlying all of the other health-related rights.[17]

---

[9]   Art. 6(2) TEU.
[10]   Court of Justice (18 December 2014). *Opinion pursuant to Article 218(11) TFEU*, Case Opinion 2/13, ECLI:EU:C:2014:2454.
[11]   Tamara K. Hervey and Jean V. McHale, *European Union Health Law – Themes and Implications*, Cambridge: Cambridge University Press, 2015, 160.
[12]   E.g. Opinion of Advocate General Jacobs delivered on 9 October 2001. *Kingdom of the Netherlands v. European Parliament and Council of the European Union*, Case C-377/98, ECLI:EU:C:2001:329, para. 10; in Tamara K. Hervey and Jean V. McHale, *European Union Health Law – Themes and Implications*, Cambridge: Cambridge University Press, 2015, 161.
[13]   Art. 6(1) TEU. See also Tamara K. Hervey and Jean V. McHale, *European Union Health Law – Themes and Implications*, Cambridge: Cambridge University Press, 2015, 164–66.
[14]   See, further, Explanations relating to the Charter of Fundamental Rights [2007] OJ C 303, p. 17–35.
[15]   For these sections, we have consulted Steve Peers, Tamara K. Hervey, Jeff Kenner and Angela Ward, *The EU Charter of Fundamental Rights – A Commentary*, Oxford and Portland, Oregon: Hart Publishing, 2014.
[16]   Human dignity (Art. 1), the right to life (Art. 2), integrity of the person (Art. 3), torture and inhuman and degrading treatment (Art. 4).
[17]   See, for more detail, Steve Peers, Tamara K. Hervey, Jeff Kenner and Angela Ward, *The EU Charter of Fundamental Rights – A Commentary*, Oxford and Portland, Oregon: Hart Publishing, 2014, 3–24.

As also illustrated in Chapter 5 by Hendriks, the right to life in Article 2 can be relevant when it comes to health-related matters.[18] Potentially, therefore, in light of the case law of the ECtHR, this right can play a role when it comes to the status of the foetus, end-of-life decision-making, and, possibly, in connection with the right to healthcare, in situations where a denial of access to healthcare has led to life-threatening situations.[19]

Article 3 on the integrity of the person also merits attention. The second paragraph of this provision refers to informed consent, and prohibits eugenic practices (in particular the 'selection of persons'), the sale of body parts, and reproductive cloning.[20] It remains uncertain what the scope of these provisions will be. It is likely that they will be interpreted in light of the more elaborate and specific international human rights provisions on which the Charter is based, including the Biomedicine Convention.[21]

Chapter II of the Charter ('freedoms') contains, inter alia, the rights to respect for private and family life and the protection of personal data (Articles 7 and 8 respectively).[22] These articles have been influential in several important EU data protection decisions, such as *Schrems I and II* and the *Google Spain* case on 'the right to be forgotten'.[23] These provisions also play a role when it comes to the protection of medical data, patients' entitlements to view their medical records, and the protection of data with respect to medical research.

Chapter III ('equality') stresses the non-discrimination principle (Article 21), which draws from Article 14 ECHR.[24] This provision can be of relevance when

---

[18] See also Steve Peers, Tamara K. Hervey, Jeff Kenner and Angela Ward, *The EU Charter of Fundamental Rights – A Commentary*, Oxford and Portland, Oregon: Hart Publishing, 2014, 26.

[19] See, further, Chapter 5 of this volume. See also Steve Peers, Tamara K. Hervey, Jeff Kenner and Angela Ward, *The EU Charter of Fundamental Rights – A Commentary*, Oxford and Portland, Oregon: Hart Publishing, 2014, 25–38.

[20] Steve Peers, Tamara K. Hervey, Jeff Kenner and Angela Ward, *The EU Charter of Fundamental Rights – A Commentary*, Oxford and Portland, Oregon: Hart Publishing, 2014, 43–60.

[21] Council of Europe, Convention on Human Rights and Biomedicine (1997, adopted in 2009, but not ratified by all EU Member States), which sets out the fundamental principles applicable in day-to-day medicine, as well as those applicable to new technologies in human biology and medicine.

[22] See also Steve Peers, Tamara K. Hervey, Jeff Kenner and Angela Ward, *The EU Charter of Fundamental Rights – A Commentary*, Oxford and Portland, Oregon: Hart Publishing, 2014, 153–264.

[23] Judgment of the Court (Grand Chamber), 13 May 2014. *Google Spain SL and Google Inc. v. Agencia Española de Protección de Datos (AEPD) and Mario Costeja González*, Case C-131/12, ECLI:EU:C:2014:317; Judgment of the Court (Grand Chamber) of 6 October 2015. *Maximillian Schrems v. Data Protection Commissioner*, Case C-362/14, ECLI:EU:C:2015:650; Judgment of the Court (Grand Chamber) of 16 July 2020. *Data Protection Commissioner v. Facebook Ireland Limited and Maximillian Schrems*, Case C-311/18, ECLI:EU:C:2020:559.

[24] See also Tamara K. Hervey, 'The Right to Health in European Union Law' in Tamara K. Hervey and Jeff Kenner (eds.), *Economic and Social Rights under the EU Charter of Fundamental Rights: A Legal Perspective*, Oxford: Hart Publishing, 2003, 127–50, at 202–03; Steve Peers, Tamara K. Hervey, Jeff Kenner and Angela Ward, *The EU Charter of Fundamental Rights – A Commentary*, Oxford and Portland, Oregon: Hart Publishing, 2014, 579–630.

addressing matters relating to equal access to healthcare services and, as such, it could reinforce the right to healthcare contained in Article 35 (see also section 2.3 below).[25]

Importantly, for the purposes of this volume, the right to health(care) is contained in Article 35 CFREU, in Chapter IV ('solidarity') of the Charter. It reads as follows:

> Everyone has the right of access to preventive health care and the right to benefit from medical treatment under the conditions established by national laws and practices. A high level of human health protection shall be ensured in the definition and implementation of all Union policies and activities.

This provision has two dimensions: it recognises that citizens of EU countries have a right to (preventive) healthcare, and it establishes a duty to ensure the protection of health within the policies and activities of the Union. The second part of the provision ('protection of health') is a repetition of the 'mainstreaming' obligation in Article 168 TFEU (see below), thus forming a touchstone against which Union action can be tested (see the next section).[26]

Article 35 CFREU takes a broad approach towards the recognition of health as a right. The provision not only recognises a right to healthcare, but also, to some extent, a right to adequate conditions to health. Health conditions are covered by the protection of health provision in the second sentence, but also to some extent by the reference to 'preventive healthcare' in the first. This approach aligns with the broad scope of the internationally recognised right to health, which not only recognises a right to healthcare, but also a right to a range of socio-economic factors that promote conditions in which people can lead healthy lives.[27]

In terms of practical implications, the outcome seems somewhat disappointing (for case law, see section 2.3 below). Like all Charter provisions, Article 35 CFREU only binds Member States when implementing EU law. The phrase 'under the conditions established by national laws and practices' may also limit the scope of the provision. When it comes to the 'access to healthcare'

---

[25]   Anniek de Ruijter, *EU Health Law & Policy*, Oxford: Oxford University Press, 2019, 41.

[26]   Inter alia, de Ruijter, 2019, 41, with reference to Koen Lenaerts and Petra Foubert, 'Social Rights in the Case-Law of the European Court of Justice: The Impact of the Charter of Fundamental Rights of the European Union on Standing Case-Law', *Legal Issues of Economic Integration* 28(3) (2001) 267, 271. See also Steve Peers, Tamara K. Hervey, Jeff Kenner and Angela Ward, *The EU Charter of Fundamental Rights – A Commentary*, Oxford and Portland, Oregon: Hart Publishing, 2014, 951–68.

[27]   ICESCR Committee, General Comment No. 14, UN Doc. E/C.12/2000/4 2000, para. 4. See also Anniek de Ruijter, *EU Health Law & Policy*, Oxford: Oxford University Press, 2019, 41, and Tamara K. Hervey, 'We don't see a connection: "the right to health" in the EU Charter and European Social Charter' in Gráinne de Búrca and Bruno de Witte (eds.), *Social Rights in Europe*, Oxford: Oxford University Press, 2005, 305–55.

dimension of this provision, de Ruijter suggests that this may only confer rights on individuals when read in conjunction with the civil and political rights in the Charter (for example, the right to life in Article 2, and Article 4 on inhuman and degrading treatment).[28] As mentioned above, it is also unclear whether the specific rights in the CFREU qualify as 'rights' or as 'principles'. As a consequence, as pointed out by De Ruijter, the legal scope of Article 35 is disputed: 'rights' may be interpreted as 'principles', and, as such, they may not be directly enforceable rights, but only sources of interpretation (see the next section).[29]

Chapter IV, on solidarity rights, contains a number of other rights that are important for the protection and promotion of health, including social security and social assistance, and environmental protection.[30] There is a growing amount of research indicating that the social determinants of health (i.e. the ways in which people are raised and educated, and the ways they live and work) are decisive for people's health.[31] Based on this notion, there have been increasing calls on governments to enhance the so-called 'social determinants of health'.[32] Rights that guarantee such conditions to health, such as the ones included in the Charter, can potentially play a role in strengthening these calls on governments. It is also possible that these rights may encourage the EU institutions to prioritise an emphasis on the social determinants of health, in their laws and policies.

Overall, a final, crucial, question arises as to how the scope of application of the Charter is to be developed in case law. This is defined by Article 51 CFREU: the Charter is addressed to the bodies and institutions of the Union, with due regard for the principle of subsidiarity, and to Member States only when they are implementing Union law. As such, the Charter does not create new competences, but, rather, imposes certain restrictions on the Union's institutions in exercising the competences allocated to them by the Treaties. It also imposes certain restrictions on States when acting within the scope of Union law, i.e. when implementing Union law, applying it, or derogating from it.[33]

---

[28]   Anniek de Ruijter, *EU Health Law & Policy*, Oxford: Oxford University Press, 2019, 45.

[29]   Anniek de Ruijter, *EU Health Law & Policy*, Oxford: Oxford University Press, 2019, 41, with reference to Article 52(5), which addresses the status of principles.

[30]   Social security: Art. 34 (including in the event of maternity and illness), environmental protection: Art. 37.

[31]   Inter alia, World Health Organization/Commission on the Social Determinants of Health, *Closing the gap in a generation, Health equity through action on the social determinants of health*, WHO, 2008, available at www.who.int/social_determinants/thecommission/finalreport/en/index.html.

[32]   World Health Organization/Commission on the Social Determinants of Health, *Closing the gap in a generation, Health equity through action on the social determinants of health*, WHO, 2008, available at www.who.int/social_determinants/thecommission/finalreport/en/index.html. See also Chapter 13 of this volume.

[33]   E.g. Tamara K. Hervey and Jean V. McHale, *European Union Health Law – Themes and Implications*, Cambridge: Cambridge University Press, 2015, 165.

2.2. THE INTERPRETATION OF RIGHTS THROUGH THE CASE LAW OF THE CJEU

The section above has illustrated that there is an increasing recognition of health rights in the EU. However, as Hervey and McHale conclude, the practical implications of this recognition are limited: no health-related EU legislation or administrative acts have, so far, been set aside by the CJEU for breaching human rights.[34] Still, health-related rights have played a role in the interpretation of both EU law and national law implementing EU obligations.[35] This approach has particular potential when applied alongside equality rights (see the next section).

Firstly, it is interesting to note that the right to health in Article 35 CFREU has been cited a number of times by the CJEU.[36] Worth mentioning is a reference to this right in an opinion of an Advocate General in a case on whether the Greek authorities could refuse the reimbursement of the cost of treatment in a private hospital abroad. Here, the right to healthcare was mentioned in support of a free movement claim to healthcare. The Advocate General emphasised the importance of a right to healthcare by stating that:

> although the case law takes as the main point of reference the fundamental freedoms established in the Treaty, there is another aspect which is becoming more and more important in the Community sphere, namely the right of citizens to health care, proclaimed in Article 35 of the Charter of Fundamental Rights of the European Union, (24) since, 'being a fundamental asset, health cannot be considered solely in terms of social expenditure and latent economic difficulties'. This right is perceived as a personal entitlement, unconnected to a person's relationship with social security, and the Court of Justice cannot overlook that aspect.[37]

---

[34] Tamara K. Hervey and Jean V. McHale, *European Union Health Law – Themes and Implications*, Cambridge: Cambridge University Press, 2015, 183.

[35] Tamara K. Hervey and Jean V. McHale, *European Union Health Law – Themes and Implications*, Cambridge: Cambridge University Press, 2015, 183. See also Steve Peers, Tamara K. Hervey, Jeff Kenner and Angela Ward, *The EU Charter of Fundamental Rights – A Commentary*, Oxford and Portland, Oregon: Hart Publishing, 2014, 959–66.

[36] Judgment of the Court (First Chamber) of 22 November 2018. *Swedish Match AB v. Secretary of State for Health*, Case C-151/17, ECLI:EU:C:2018:938; Judgment of the Court (Sixth Chamber) of 8 May 2019. *PI v. Landespolizeidirektion Tirol*, Case C-230/18, ECLI:EU:C:2019:383; Judgment of the Court (Third Chamber), 6 September 2012. *Deutsches Weintor eG v. Land Rheinland-Pfalz*, Case C-544/10, ECLI:EU:C:2012:526; Judgment of the Court (Third Chamber) 21 June 2012. *Marja-Liisa Susisalo and Others*, Case C-84/11, ECLI:EU:C:2012:374; Judgment of the Court (Grand Chamber) of 1 June 2010. *José Manuel Blanco Pérez and María del Pilar Chao Gómez v. Consejería de Salud y Servicios Sanitarios (C-570/07) and Principado de Asturias (C-571/07)*, Cases C-570/07 and C-571/07, ECLI:EU:C:2010:300; Opinion of Mr Advocate General Bot delivered on 15 July 2010. *Marc Michel Josemans v. Burgemeester van Maastricht*, Case C-137/09, ECLI:EU:C:2010:433.

[37] Opinion of Mr Advocate General Ruiz-Jarabo Colomer delivered on 11 January 2007. *Aikaterini Stamatelaki v. NPDD Organismos Asfaliseos Eleftheron Epangelmation (OAEE)*, Case C-444/05, ECLI:EU:C:2007:24.

Furthermore, Article 35 CFREU played a role in interpreting the regulation on nutritional claims on food labelling.[38] The regulation in question provides that 'beverages containing more than 1.2 per cent by volume of alcohol shall not bear health claims'.[39] The Court held in *Deutsches Weintor*, that the term 'easily digestible' constitutes such a health claim, and should, therefore, not be used for beverages with more than 1.2 per cent by volume of alcohol. In its judgment, the CJEU balanced the freedom to conduct a business, contained in Articles 15(1) and 16 CFREU, against the second sentence of Article 35 CFREU, which provides that a 'high level of human health protection' shall be ensured in the Union's policies and activities. The outcome of this balancing act was that the EU's legislature was entitled to prohibit such health claims, so as to ensure a 'high level of health protection', as per Article 35 CFREU.[40]

In *Philip Morris*, the CJEU drew on Article 35 in holding that the protection of human health outweighed the claimants' interests in freedom of expression and information.[41] The EU's obligation to ensure a high level of human health required that tobacco consumers (who are vulnerable, due to nicotine addiction) should not be encouraged to consume tobacco through factual information relating to nicotine levels, smells, tastes or flavourings. This information could convince consumers, mistakenly, to believe that certain tobacco products were less harmful than others.[42] While the measure constituted an interference with companies' freedom of expression and information, it had a valid legal basis, and did not affect the essence of the right, in that not all information was prohibited but, rather, labelling was simply controlled in a clearly defined area.[43]

Other areas in which health-related rights have played a role in the interpretation of EU law have concerned, inter alia, the Biotechnology Directive[44] and the Data Protection Directive.[45]

---

[38]   *Deutsches Weintor*, Case C-544/10, EU:C:2012:526. See, for more detail, Tamara K. Hervey and Jean V. McHale, *European Union Health Law – Themes and Implications*, Cambridge: Cambridge University Press, 2015.

[39]   Regulation (EC) No 1924/2006 of the European Parliament and of the Council of 20 December 2006 on nutrition and health claims made on foods OJ L 404, 30.12.2006, p. 9–25, Art. 4(3).

[40]   *Deutsches Weintor*, Case C-544/10, EU:C:2012:526, paras. 44–47, 52. See also Tamara K. Hervey and Jean V. McHale, *Health Law and the European Union*, Cambridge: Cambridge University Press, 2004, 174–75.

[41]   Judgment of the Court (Second Chamber) of 4 May 2016. *Philip Morris Brands SARL and Others v. Secretary of State for Health*, Case C-547/14, ECLI:EU:C:2016:325, para. 156.

[42]   Ibid., paras. 139–45.

[43]   Ibid., para. 151.

[44]   Judgment of the Court (Grand Chamber), 18 December 2014. *International Stem Cell Corporation v. Comptroller General of Patents, Designs and Trade Marks*, Case C-364/13, ECLI:EU:C:2014:2451; Judgment of the Court (Grand Chamber) of 18 October 201. *Oliver Brüstle v. Greenpeace eV*, Case C-34/10, EU:C:2011:669.

[45]   Judgment of the Court of 6 November 2003. *Criminal proceedings against Bodil Lindqvist*, Case C-101/01, ECLI:EU:C:2003:596. See, further, Tamara K. Hervey and Jean V. McHale, *Health Law and the European Union*, Cambridge: Cambridge University Press, 2004, 170–74.

2.3. NON-DISCRIMINATION

As stated above, the EU is primarily an economic union, not a human rights institution,[46] and this can be seen in its approach to non-discrimination. At the same time, the Court has moved from recognising gender equality as an economic rationale, to recognising it as a human right.[47] Still, while the CJEU has been active in matters such as developing the prohibition of age discrimination, its activism has waned.[48] This section highlights certain elements of EU non-discrimination law related to the health and human rights field.

Non-discrimination is a core value of the EU (Article 19 TFEU). Prohibiting discrimination for EU citizens based on nationality is central to the European project.[49] While the EU, initially, only had competences to enact non-discrimination legislation within the sphere of gender equality (Article 157 TFEU), under Article 19 TFEU the EU can now take action to combat discrimination based on sex, racial or ethnic origin, religion or belief, disability, age, or sexual orientation. Stemming from these competences, several European directives proscribe discrimination: the Racial Discrimination Directive, the Equal Employment Directive, and the Equal Treatment Directive, which ensures equal treatment of men and women in the workplace.[50]

EU law guarantees protection from discrimination on the basis of racial or ethnic origin, or gender, and this includes both direct and indirect discrimination. For example, the CJEU has pioneered an approach to protecting pregnant workers, whereby pregnancy is not just compared to illness, but rather treated as a separate condition, particular to women. In *Dekker v. Stichting Vormingscentrum voor Jonge Volwassenen Plus*,[51] an employer refused to employ a pregnant woman, claiming that it could not afford to pay for maternity cover.

---

[46]   Tamara K. Hervey and Jean V. McHale, *European Union Health Law – Themes and Implications*, Cambridge: Cambridge University Press, 2015, 157.

[47]   See Paul Craig and Gráinne de Búrca, *EU Law: Text, Cases, and Materials*, Oxford: Oxford University Press, 7th ed., 932–3.

[48]   Raphaele Xenidis, 'Shaking the Normative Foundations of EU equality law: Evolution and hierarchy between market integration and human rights rationales' (EUI Working Paper LAW 2017/04, 2017).

[49]   For an analysis of EU non-discrimination law, see Paul Craig and Gráinne de Búrca, *EU Law: Text, Cases, and Materials*, Oxford: Oxford University Press, 7th ed.

[50]   Council Directive 2000/43/EC of 29 June 2000 implementing the principle of equal treatment between persons irrespective of racial or ethnic origin, OJ L 180, 19.7.2000, p. 22–26; Council Directive 2000/78/EC of 27 November 2000 establishing a general framework for equal treatment in employment and occupation OJ L 303, 2.12.2000, p. 16–22; Directive 2006/54/EC of the European Parliament and of the Council of 5 July 2006 on the implementation of the principle of equal opportunities and equal treatment of men and women in matters of employment and occupation (recast) OJ L 204, 26.7.2006, p. 23–36.

[51]   Judgment of the Court, 8 November 1990. *Dekker v. Stichting Vormingscentrum voor Jonge Volwassenen Plus*, Case C-177/88, ECLI:EU:C:1990:383.

The CJEU found that, because only women can be refused employment on the grounds of pregnancy, the employer was directly discriminating against the applicant, on the grounds of sex, in violation of the Equal Treatment Directive. In *Danosa*, the CJEU found that EU law prohibited national legislation from removing a pregnant worker on account of her pregnancy, and that, even if the woman had not been a pregnant worker, the national legislation would constitute direct discrimination on grounds of sex, as only women could be affected.[52]

Employment discrimination on the basis of disability is also prohibited under the Employment Directive. The EU has, furthermore, ratified the Convention on the Rights of Persons with Disabilities (CRPD), and the CJEU has, therefore, held that EU law must be interpreted in a manner consistent with the CRPD. Article 5 of the Employment Equality Directive requires states to make 'reasonable accommodation' for persons with disabilities. In 2014, the CJEU determined that, while discrimination on the basis of obesity is not prohibited under EU law, obesity could constitute a disability, if accompanied by an impairment that may hinder the 'full and effective participation in professional life on an equal basis with other workers'.[53]

Direct and indirect discrimination based on sex, concerning access to, and supply of, goods and services is also prohibited under Directive 2004/113. Direct discrimination occurs when an individual is treated less favourably, on grounds of sex, than another individual has been, or would have been, treated in a comparable situation. Indirect discrimination takes place when an apparently neutral provision, criterion or practice would put one sex at a disadvantage compared to the other, unless that provision is objectively justified by a legitimate aim, and the means of achieving the aim are appropriate and necessary. Thus, using sex in the calculation of insurance premiums or financial services is now prohibited.

Furthermore, Article 21 of the Charter recognises a fundamental right to non-discrimination on a multitude of grounds, including disability, age, sex, race and genetic features. As mentioned above, the CFREU applies to EU institutions and bodies when exercising powers under the Treaties, and Member States when implementing EU law.[54] Thus, when implementing, inter alia, the Clinical Trials Regulation and the GDPR, Member States are obligated to not discriminate on the prescribed grounds.

In conclusion, EU secondary law prohibits discrimination by sex, race and ethnicity, in the healthcare sphere. The failure to pass a broad equality directive

---

[52] Judgment of the Court (Second Chamber) of 11 November 2010. *Dita Danosa v. LKB Līzings SIA*, Case C-232/09, ECLI:EU:C:2010:674.

[53] Judgment of the Court (Fourth Chamber), 18 December 2014. *Fag og Arbejde (FOA) v. Kommunernes Landsforening (KL)*, Case C-354/13, ECLI:EU:C:2014:2463.

[54] Steve Peers, Tamara K. Hervey, Jeff Kenner and Angela Ward, *The EU Charter of Fundamental Rights – A Commentary*, Oxford and Portland, Oregon: Hart Publishing, 2014, on Art. 21 – Non Discrimination.

means that EU law does not prohibit discrimination on other grounds in this area. However, due to the Charter, individuals are protected from broader types of discrimination, including genetic discrimination, when states apply EU law, such as the GDPR. However, as introduced above, the precise contours of this protection are in a state of evolution.

3. SPECIFIC RESPONSIBILITIES FOR HEALTH IN THE EU

Most EU competences in health are supplementary[55] to those of the Member States, and do not harmonise national legislation, with the exception of Article 168(4) TFEU. However, there are also some interesting mainstreaming provisions, introduced below.

3.1. FOCUS ON HUMAN HEALTH IN THE TFEU

The EU institutions now have a significant impetus to focus more on human health in their policies and activities, following the adoption of Article 9 TFEU, which focuses on policymaking within the EU. This provision contains a 'social clause', stating that the activities of the Union have to take into account a number of social objectives, including the protection of human health.

Furthermore, with the adoption of the Treaty of Lisbon (2007), the previous public health article (Article 152 TEC) has been replaced by Article 168 of the TFEU. Based on paragraph 1 of this provision, 'a high level of human health protection shall be ensured in the definition and implementation of all Union policies and activities'. And this action by the EU, which complements national policies, 'shall be directed towards improving public health, preventing physical and mental illness and diseases, and obviating sources of danger to physical and mental health', and should 'cover the fight against the major health scourges, by promoting research into their causes, their transmission and their prevention, as well as health information and education, and monitoring, early warning of and combating serious cross-border threats to health'.

Article 168 TFEU differs, to some extent, from the previous Article 152 TEC.[56] However, the general idea of EU action in the field of health remains the same,

---

[55]   Art. 6(a) TFEU.
[56]   For a discussion of (the old) Article 152 TEC, see Tamara K. Hervey and Jean V. McHale, *European Union Health Law – Themes and Implications*, Cambridge: Cambridge University Press, 2015, 42.

i.e. that it should be directed towards improving public health, preventing illness and obviating sources of danger to health. This provision has been supplemented with the statement that such action should cover the monitoring, early warning and combating of serious cross-border diseases. As a result, the range of possible actions available to combat major health scourges has now been expanded.[57] Despite this, the contribution of this provision to the initial response to COVID-19, in early 2020, has been criticised.[58] Furthermore, as suggested by Hervey and McHale, this provision focuses more than its predecessor on individual health.[59]

Based on Article 168(2), the EU is to encourage cooperation between the Member States to improve health services in cross-border areas. In addition, the Commission may take initiatives to promote coordination between Member States in establishing guidelines and indicators, organising the exchange of best practices, and preparing the necessary elements for periodic monitoring and evaluation. This can be pursued through, inter alia, the open method of coordination.[60] This text seems to expand the EU's ability to operate in these areas, and to enable the EU to play a more proactive role when it comes, for example, to cross-border health services.

The EU's scope for harmonisation is curtailed by the principles of conferral, subsidiarity and proportionality. Firstly, the EU can only legislate where its Treaties have provided a legal basis to do so (conferral).[61] Secondly, the EU may only take action where its intervention can achieve more than individual Member States (subsidiarity).[62] Thirdly, the intervention must not go beyond what is necessary to achieve the objectives (proportionality).[63] The EU can adopt health measures based on Treaty provisions other than Article 168 TFEU, such as, for example, the general internal market clause of Article 114 TFEU. However, the CJEU has determined that the latter does not provide a general power to regulate the market, as this would be incompatible with the responsibility of conferred powers. Instead, a measure adopted under Article 114(3) must have the genuine aim of improving the conditions for the establishment and functioning of the internal market.[64]

---

[57]   European Health Management Association, *EU Briefing: The Impact of the Treaty of Lisbon on EU Health Law*, 2021, available at www.ehma.org.

[58]   Kai P. Purnhagen et al., 'More Competences than You Knew? The Web of Health Competence for European Union Action in Response to the COVID-19 Outbreak', *European Journal of Risk Regulation*, 11(2) (2020), 297–306, doi:10.1017/err.2020.35.

[59]   Tamara K. Hervey and Jean V. McHale, *European Union Health Law – Themes and Implications*, Cambridge: Cambridge University Press, 2015, 42.

[60]   European Commission, 'European governance – A white paper', [2001] OJ C 287/1, http://eur-lex.europa.eu/legal-content/EN/TXT/?uri=CELEX:52001DC0428&qid=1457941884264.

[61]   Art. 5(1) TEU.

[62]   Art. 5(3) TEU.

[63]   Art. 5(4) TEU.

[64]   Judgment of the Court of 5 October 2000. *Federal Republic of Germany v. European Parliament and Council of the European Union*, Case C-376/98 ECLI:EU:C:2000:544 (hereafter 'Tobacco Case I'), para. 84.

The CJEU has since reaffirmed the EU legislature's broad discretion: measures are illegitimate only if 'manifestly inappropriate', in light of their aims.[65] Accordingly, De Witte argues that *Tobacco Case I* was 'a rather isolated pronouncement whose significance should not be exaggerated'.[66] De Witte contends that the EU has the competence to pursue non-market aims (such as health and fundamental rights protection) through the internal market. He highlights that Article 114 provides constitutional backing for the EU to incorporate health, safety and environmental concerns into harmonisation measures.[67] Furthermore, he considers that rights mainstreaming now provides a basis for the protection and promotion of fundamental rights under the internal market.[68]

Finally, while the principle of subsidiarity has been maintained (paragraph 7), this has been expanded with references to the responsibility of Member States for the management of health services and medical care, and the allocation of the resources assigned to them. In addition, the new paragraph 5 refers to possibilities for the European Parliament and Council to adopt incentive measures designed to combat serious cross-border threats to health, and measures regarding tobacco and the use of alcohol (see, further, below). Altogether, with the adoption of the Lisbon Treaty, the scope of operation of the EU in the area of health has expanded, to some extent. Yet, to date, the EU has been criticised for not taking bold legislative action in the field of noncommunicable diseases, and for failing to ensure a coordinated approach to COVID-19, in line with Article 168(3).[69] As the editorial board of the Common Market Law Review opined:

> The pandemic has reopened old fault lines and amplified problematic trends in the Union, from economic disparities to diverging attitudes to the rule of law. Questions about cooperation, solidarity, trust, values, and thus about the fundamentals of integration and membership, are on the table.[70]

---

[65] Judgment of the Court (Grand Chamber) of 12 December 2006. *Federal Republic of Germany v. European Parliament and Council of the European Union*, Case C-380/03 ECLI:EU:C:2006:772, para. 145.

[66] Bruno de Witte, 'A Competence to Protect' in Philip Syrpis (ed.), *The Judiciary, the Legislature and the EU Internal Market*, New York/ Cambridge: Cambridge University Press, 2012, 28.

[67] Ibid., 31.

[68] Ibid., 32.

[69] EU measures have been haphazard, with states slow to come to agreement, e.g. Council Recommendation (EU) 2020/1475 of 13 October 2020 on a coordinated approach to the restriction of free movement in response to the COVID-19 pandemic, [2020] OJ L 337/3, as amended by OJ 2021 (2020), https://eur-lex.europa.eu/legal-content/EN/TXT/?uri=CELEX:32020H1475; Communication from the Commission, 'Guidance on free movement of health professionals and minimum harmonisation of training in relation to COVID-19 emergency measures – recommendations regarding Directive 2005/36/EC', [2020] OJ 2020 C 156/1 (2020).

[70] Christopher A.P. Hillion, 'Editorial Comments: Disease and Recovery in (COVID afflicted) Europe', *Common Market Law Review* 57(3) (2020), 619–30, 620.

At the time of writing, therefore, the European project's health dimensions stand at a crossroads.

3.2. EU ENGAGEMENT WITH PUBLIC HEALTH

Public health is, by nature, an issue that often requires transnational measures. As such, the World Health Organization (WHO), a specialised UN organisation, is especially engaged with the promotion, safeguarding and regulation of international public health (see Chapter 4). Given the frequent movement of goods and services across the EU, regional cooperation can be seen as equally important when addressing and combating, for example, contagious diseases affecting populations regionally, or even globally. As such, the Union may interact with the area of public health in various ways, and, thus, may also interact with human rights in various ways.

As explained above, the EU has competence, under Article 168 TFEU, to complement national action on health. This mainly provides the legal scope for protecting people against health threats and disease, for promoting healthy lifestyles, and for helping national authorities in the EU cooperate on health issues. In other words, the EU is required by its founding treaty to ensure that human health is protected as part of all its policies, and to work with the EU countries to improve public health, prevent human illness, and eliminate sources of danger to physical and mental health. The following sections point to selected areas to illustrate EU engagement with public health, which is subject to a patchwork of legal bases.

3.2.1. *Clinical research*

One area that has seen EU engagement in the area of health has been the harmonisation of the regulation of clinical trials. Clinical trials are investigations intended to discover or verify the effects of one or more investigational medicinal products on humans. As such, they are a necessary part of the development and improvement of healthcare, while, at the same time, they touch upon human rights such as autonomy, physical integrity and privacy.

Requirements for the conduct of clinical trials in the EU are provided for in the Clinical Trials Regulation (Regulation (EU) No 536/2014). Although the Clinical Trials Regulation was adopted, and entered into force, in 2014, the timing of its application will depend on confirmation of full functionality of the new Clinical Trials Information System through an independent audit. The Regulation will become applicable six months after the European Commission publishes notice of this confirmation (expected January 2022). When the Regulation becomes applicable, it will repeal the existing EU Clinical Trials Directive, which was thought to have failed to achieve its goal of simplifying the scientific and ethical review of clinical trials in the EU.[71] The regulation provides for a central database and a partly coordinated review system. Rather than requiring approval to be sought in each Member State, the risk–benefit assessment (and the preceding scientific assessment) will be performed in a coordinated manner. The regulation also contains a number of provisions that regulate the rights of the research subjects, and which contain references to human rights, such as the right to physical and mental integrity and privacy. As such, the EU legal framework complements international and regional instruments that also address clinical research, for example the Helsinki Declaration, the WHO standards, and, most importantly in Europe, the Council of Europe's Convention on Human Rights and Biomedicine.

3.2.2. Infectious disease control

Infectious disease control by, and in, the EU is fragmented, both when it comes to existing regulation and the responsible institutions.[72] This section gives a brief overview of infectious disease control by, and in, the EU, and devotes some words to the EU's handling of COVID-19.

The EU's explicit engagement with infectious disease control is relatively recent.[73] Only in 1998 was an already existing EU network for communicable diseases formalised, with Decision 2119/98/EC (1998).[74] Prior to this, however, the Court had recognised the centrality of health, in the *BSE* case, regarding emergency measures taken by the EU to stop the spread of the cattle disease BSE from Britain.[75] In the context of this decision, the European Commission established an early warning and response system (EWRS) for communicable

---

[71]   Directive 2001/20/EC of the European Parliament and of the Council of 4 April 2001 on the approximation of the laws, regulations and administrative provisions of the Member States relating to the implementation of good clinical practice in the conduct of clinical trials on medicinal products for human use OJ L 121, 1.5.2001, p. 34–44.

[72]   For an overview of relevant EU institutional actors, see Anniek de Ruijter, *EU Health Law & Policy*, Oxford: Oxford University Press, 2019, 123.

[73]   Markus Frischhut and Scott L. Greer, 'EU public health law and policy – communicable diseases' in Tamara K. Hervey, Calum Alasdair Young and Louise E. Bishop, (eds.), *Research Handbook on EU Health Law and Policy*, Cheltenham: Edward Elgar Publishing, 2017, 315–46, at 320.

[74]   Anniek de Ruijter, *EU Health Law & Policy*, Oxford: Oxford University Press, 2019, 125. Markus Frischhut and Scott L. Greer, 'EU public health law and policy – communicable diseases' in Tamara K. Hervey, Calum Alasdair Young and Louise E. Bishop (eds.), *Research Handbook on EU Health Law and Policy*, Cheltenham: Edward Elgar Publishing, 2017, 315–46, 320.

[75]   Judgment of the Court of 5 May 1998. *United Kingdom of Great Britain and Northern Ireland v. Commission of the European Communities*, Case C-180/96, ECLI:EU:C:1998:192. See, further, Tamara K. Hervey and Anniek de Ruijter, 'The Dynamic Potential of European Union Health Law', *European Journal of Risk Regulation* 11(4) (2020), 726–35. doi:10.1017/err.2020.70.

disease control, listing the communicable diseases that were to be covered by the surveillance network.[76]

The 2003 SARS outbreak led to the establishment of the European Centre for Disease Control and Prevention (ECDC), an EU agency based in Stockholm.[77] This body lacks regulatory powers, but plays a coordinating role, and can perform inspections and disseminate information.[78]

Another important development was the adoption of Decision 1082/2013, which enlarged the scope of EU communicable diseases law and policy to other threats, including environmental events.[79] As such, along the lines of the WHO's International Health Regulations (2005), the EU now adopts an 'all-hazards' approach, which addresses serious cross-border threats of any origin.[80]

While the EU is not a member of the WHO, all of its Member States are. In the WHO International Health Regulations – the only binding international instrument addressing epidemic diseases – Article 57(3) addresses the legal challenges that may arise for the EU Member States in this respect, as the provision stipulates that States Parties that are members of a regional economic integration organisation shall apply, in their mutual relationships, the common rules in force in that organisation. Any measures imposed by the WHO – such as refusing certain goods entry into a Member State – that affect any area of competency falling within the scope of EU law must, thus, be addressed on the initiative of the European Commission, even though it is the Member States and not the Union, as such, that are duty-bound by WHO regulations.

It is too early to fully assess the EU's handling of the COVID-19 pandemic, but a few observations can be made. The EU was, initially, slow to position itself a leader in the crisis, having never been a global health heavyweight. However, as the crisis deepened, the EU increasingly preached solidarity, though with limited 'buy-in' from panicking Member States. Free movement of persons, a central pillar of EU law, has proven unfeasible in a pandemic, where Member States have

---

76 Commission Decision 2000/96/EC of 22 December 1999; Markus Frischhut and Scott L. Greer, 'EU public health law and policy – communicable diseases' in Tamara K. Hervey, Calum Alasdair Young and Louise E. Bishop, (eds.), *Research Handbook on EU Health Law and Policy*, Cheltenham: Edward Elgar Publishing, 2017, 315–46, 322.

77 Regulation (EC) No 851/2004 of the European Parliament and of the Council of 21 April 2004 establishing a European Centre for disease prevention and control, OJ L 142, 30.4.2004, p. 1–11. Markus Frischhut and Scott L. Greer, 'EU public health law and policy – communicable diseases' in Tamara K. Hervey, Calum Alasdair Young and Louise E. Bishop, (eds.), *Research Handbook on EU Health Law and Policy*, Cheltenham: Edward Elgar Publishing, 2017, 315–46, 322.

78 Anniek de Ruijter, *EU Health Law & Policy*, Oxford: Oxford University Press, 2019, 130.

79 Decision No 1082/2013/EU of the European Parliament and of the Council of 22 October 2013 on serious cross-border threats to health and repealing Decision No 2119/98/EC, OJ L 293, 5.11.2013, p. 1–15.

80 Markus Frischhut and Scott L. Greer, 'EU public health law and policy – communicable diseases' Tamara K. Hervey, Calum Alasdair Young and Louise E. Bishop, (eds.), *Research Handbook on EU Health Law and Policy*, Cheltenham: Edward Elgar Publishing, 2017, 315–46, 324–25.

adopted different restrictions, and have closed borders (as is permitted by the Schengen Agreement) to halt the spread. Instead, it is in the field of research and development that the EU has gained most prominence, although this remains a mission in progress.[81] The EU decided to negotiate access to vaccines as a block, meaning that all Member States would gain access at the same time, and under the same conditions. Finally, in response to the crisis, the Commission has proposed a European Health Union to strengthen crisis preparedness and responsiveness in Europe, through, inter alia, adoption of two new regulations.[82] It can be questioned whether this proposal goes far enough, and whether more far-reaching reforms of EU health-related competences might be needed.

3.2.3. Regulation of behavioural risk factors of noncommunicable diseases (NCDs)

Behavioural risk factors for noncommunicable (chronic) diseases (NCDs) include smoking, unhealthy diet, lack of physical exercise and excessive use of alcohol. The EU has been criticised for its limited approach to regulating NCD risk factors. As many of the drivers of NCDs are transnational, most experts consider that a purely national approach will be ineffective, and will lead to fragmentation.[83] However, as public health remains a supporting competence,[84] EU legislation has to be introduced on a legal basis other than (or as well as) public health.[85]

The EU has been most proactive in tobacco control.[86] An important foundation is the EU's ratification of the WHO Framework Convention on

---

[81]   Pauline Veron and Mariella Di Ciommo, *Fit for purpose: The EU's role in global health in the era of COVID-19* (The European Centre for Development Policy Management, 2020), https://ecdpm.org/publications/fit-purpose-eu-role-global-health-era-covid-19/.

[82]   European Commission, 'European Health Union', available at https://ec.europa.eu/info/strategy/priorities-2019-2024/promoting-our-european-way-life/european-health-union_en.

[83]   Eg. Amandine Garde and Alberto Alemanno (eds.), *Regulating Lifestyle Risks: The EU, Alcohol, Tobacco and Unhealthy Diets* Cambridge: Cambridge University Press, 2015; Katharina Ó Cathaoir, Mette Hartlev and Céline Brassart Olsen, 'Global health law and obesity: towards a complementary approach of public health and human rights law' in Gian Luca Burci and Brigit Toebes, *Research Handbook on Global Health Law*, Cheltenham: Edward Elgar Publishing, 2018, 427–59.

[84]   Art. 2(1)(2) TFEU (consolidated) [2016] OJ C 202; Article 168(5) TFEU. See, further, Frederic Geber, 'Between a Rock and a Hard Place' in Amandine Garde and Alberto Alemanno (eds.), *Regulating Lifestyle Risks: The EU, Alcohol, Tobacco and Unhealthy Diets*, Cambridge: Cambridge University Press, 2015.

[85]   Alemanno and Garde suggest Arts. 38, 59, 91, 113, 114, 153, 169 and 207 as the most pertinent bases for binding measures to prevent NCDs: Amandine Garde and Alberto Alemanno (eds.), *Regulating Lifestyle Risks: The EU, Alcohol, Tobacco and Unhealthy Diets* Cambridge: Cambridge University Press, 2015, 263.

[86]   Amandine Garde and Brigit Toebes, 'Is there a European Human Rights Approach to Tobacco Control?' in Marie Elske Gispen and Brigit Toebes (eds.), *Human Rights and Tobacco Control*, Cheltenham: Edward Elgar Publishing, 2020, 80–98.

Tobacco Control (FCTC).[87] The two main building blocks of the EU's regulatory tobacco control are the Tobacco Advertising Directive and the Tobacco Products Directive. The Tobacco Advertising Directive[88] imposes an EU-wide ban on cross-border tobacco advertising and sponsorship in all media.[89] The Tobacco Products Directive,[90] which has been revised to adapt its provisions to new scientific developments, and to ensure compliance with the FCTC, lays down wide-ranging rules governing the manufacture, presentation and sale of tobacco and related products. The EU has also adopted rules establishing minimum excise duties on tobacco products.[91]

Yet, given the EU's limited competence in the field of public health, it is not possible to speak of a comprehensive tobacco control policy that implements all provisions of the FCTC. Even though the scope of EU powers has been interpreted broadly, and the EU has been able to implement several FCTC provisions at regional level, the fact remains that the EU cannot comprehensively regulate tobacco products and commercial practices alone. The Commission cannot adopt regulations on NCD risk factors, under Article 114 TFEU, without the genuine aim of improving the functioning of the internal market, although health can be a determinative factor in its decision.[92] Thus, it is only if Member States regulate tobacco products at national level that the FCTC can be fully implemented in the EU. For example, the EU-wide ban on all forms of cross-border advertising and sponsorship has been complemented by national restrictions on forms of advertising and sponsorship arrangements.[93]

---

[87] Council Decision of 2 June 2004 concerning the conclusion of the WHO Framework Convention on Tobacco Control [2004] OJ L 213/8.

[88] Directive 2003/33/EC of the European Parliament and of the Council of 26 May 2003 on the approximation of the laws, regulations and administrative provisions of the Member States relating to the advertising and sponsorship of tobacco products [2003] OJ L 152/16, in particular Arts. 3 and 4. Only publications intended for professionals in the tobacco trade, and publications from non-EU countries which are not principally intended for the EU market are exempt.

[89] Except those such as television and other audiovisual media services, which are covered by Directive (EU) 2018/1808 of the European Parliament and of the Council of 14 November 2018 amending Directive 2010/13/EU on the coordination of certain provisions laid down by law, regulation or administrative action in Member States concerning the provision of audiovisual media services (Audiovisual Media Services Directive) in view of changing market realities [2018] OJ L 303/69.

[90] Directive 2014/40/EU of the European Parliament and of the Council of 3 April 2014 on the approximation of the laws, regulations and administrative provisions of the Member States concerning the manufacture, presentation and sale of tobacco and related products and repealing Directive 2001/37/EC (Tobacco Products Directive) [2014] OJ L 127/1.

[91] Art. 113 TFEU allows the EU to adopt common rules harmonising the laws of the Member States on direct taxation. On the harmonisation of excise duties on tobacco products, see Council Directive 2011/64/EU of 21 June 2011 on the structure and rates of excise duty applied to manufactured tobacco [2011] OJ L 176/24.

[92] Ibid., para. 77.

[93] E.g. the CJEU ruled that the EU has no powers to regulate static advertising (e.g. advertisements in hotels, on billboards, umbrellas, ashtrays and similar items), advertisements screened in cinemas, or the sponsorship of events that do not have any cross-border appeal, when it

Where powers to adopt harmonising legislation have not been conferred on the EU, it can adopt 'soft law' provisions. The Tobacco Products Directive and Tobacco Advertising Directive have, therefore, been complemented by recommendations to Member States,[94] and EU-wide anti-smoking campaigns. As Member States have regulated tobacco products to different degrees beyond the implementation of EU rules, the picture remains one of diversity.[95]

In contrast with its approach to tobacco control, the EU has been hesitant to regulate the alcohol and food industries. While a number of EU laws address food safety, they are generally viewed as inadequate in tackling unhealthy diet.[96] In fact, because of EU harmonisation of food labelling, the abilities of Member States to adopt mandatory 'traffic light' labelling, to address causes of obesity, are restricted.[97] Food and alcohol have, nonetheless, featured prominently in the EU's public health discourse. The EU adopted the Alcohol Strategy 2006–2012 in 2006, shortly before publishing the Obesity Prevention White Paper in 2007, followed, seven years later, by the EU Action Plan on Childhood Obesity 2014–2020. Garde explains that, even though these strategies are not legally binding, they have set the tone, and have indicated what the EU is willing to prioritise, and the means of achieving its objectives.[98]

---

annulled Directive 98/43/EC of the European Parliament and of the Council of 6 July 1998 on the approximation of the laws, regulations and administrative provisions of the Member States relating to the advertising and sponsorship of tobacco products [1998] OJ L 213/9 (often referred to as the First Tobacco Advertising Directive), on the ground that it exceeded the powers granted to the EU under Article 114 TFEU to harmonise the laws of Member States to facilitate the establishment and functioning of the internal market in the *Tobacco Case I* (Judgment of the Court of 5 October 2000. *Federal Republic of Germany v. European Parliament and Council of the European Union*, Case C-376/98, ECLI:EU:C:2000:544). The EU subsequently adopted Directive 2003/33/EC, the Second Tobacco Advertising Directive, whose validity was upheld by the Court in Judgment of the Court (Grand Chamber) of 12 December 2006. *Federal Republic of Germany v. European Parliament and Council of the European Union*, Case C-380/03 ECLI:EU:C:2006:772.

[94] See, in particular, Council Recommendation of 2 December 2002 on the prevention of smoking and on initiatives to improve tobacco control [2003] OJ L 22/31, and Council Recommendation of 30 November 2009 on smoke-free environments [2009] OJ C 296/4.

[95] For example, in 2013, the Commission reported that 17 EU Member States had comprehensive smoke-free legislation in place: Commission Staff Working Document, 'Report on the implementation of the Council Recommendation of 30 November 2009 on Smoke-free Environments' [2013] SWD 56 final/2.

[96] Regulation (EC) No. 178/2002, General Food Law Regulation; Regulation (EU) No. 1169/2011 of the European Parliament and of the Council of 25 October 2011 on the provision of food information to consumers [2011] OJ L 304.

[97] Caoimhín MacMaoláin, 'Using food labelling laws to combat childhood obesity: Lessons from the EU, the WTO and Codex' in Amandine Garde, Joshua Curtis and Olivier De Schutter (eds.), *Ending Childhood Obesity: A Challenge at the Crossroads of International Economic and Human Rights Law*, Cheltenham: Edward Elgar Publishing, 2020, 138–60.

[98] Amandine Garde, 'The Lack of Coherence in the European Union's Approach to Noncommunicable Disease Prevention' in David Orentlicher and Tamara K. Hervey (eds.), *The Oxford Handbook on Comparative Health Law*, Oxford: Oxford University Press, 2022, 143–69, section 4.

3.2.4. Workplace protection of health

Article 153 TFEU deals with health and safety for the European workforce. Accordingly, a wide range of measures in the field of health and safety at work have been adopted on this basis. The directives in the health and safety at work area are all minimum harmonisation directives, meaning that Member States are free to put stricter regulation in place. As a result, health and safety at work legislation can vary across the different European countries. The most important legal act is the European Framework Directive (1989/391/EEC), which establishes general principles for managing health and safety, such as the responsibilities of the employer, the rights and duties of workers, the use of risk assessments to continuously improve company processes, and workplace health and safety representation.

The 1992 EU Pregnancy Directive (92/85) sets out a number of health and safety rights for employees who are pregnant, breastfeeding, or have recently given birth.[99] These relate, mainly, to the following matters: employers' mandatory assessments of chemical, physical and biological agents; movements and postures; mental and physical fatigue; other types of physical and mental stress; and industrial processes considered hazardous for the safety or health of pregnant employees. If a person covered by the directive is exposed to a health or safety risk, or an effect on their pregnancy or breastfeeding, the employer must take steps to ensure that exposure to the risks is avoided. These steps might include temporarily adjusting the working conditions and/or working hours of the worker concerned, and/or moving the employee to another job.

Under the directive, EU Member States are also obliged to provide at least 14 weeks of maternity leave, and to protect against dismissal during such leave. They also must ensure that pregnant women are entitled to time off, in accordance with national legislation and/or practice, without loss of pay, to attend antenatal

---

[99]   These rights were not, however, extended to a commissioning mother in a surrogacy arrangement: see Judgment of the Court (Grand Chamber) 15 January 2014. *Association de médiation sociale v. Union locale des syndicats CGT and Others Case*, C-176/12, ECLI:EU:C:2014:2, which found that Member States are not required to provide maternity leave (pursuant to Art. 8 of that directive) to a female worker who, as a commissioning mother, has had a baby through a surrogacy arrangement, even in circumstances where she may breastfeed the baby following the birth, or where she does breastfeed the baby: see https://eur-lex.europa.eu/LexUriServ/LexUriServ.do?uri=CELEX:62012CJ0167:EN:HTML. In Judgment of the Court (Grand Chamber), 18 March 2014. *Z. v. A Government department and The Board of management of a community school*, Case C-363/12, ECLI:EU:C:2014:159, the Court held that Directive 2000/78 must be interpreted as meaning that a refusal to provide paid leave equivalent to maternity leave or adoptive leave to a female worker who is unable to bear a child, and who has availed themselves of a surrogacy arrangement, does not constitute discrimination on the ground of disability, and that the validity of Directive 2000/78 cannot be assessed in the light of the UN Convention on Disability: https://eur-lex.europa.eu/LexUriServ/LexUriServ.do?uri=CELEX:62012CJ0363:EN:HTML.

examinations, if such examinations have to take place during working hours. Various national Acts give effect to the directive, and these may afford further health and safety rights to pregnant women.

However, this legislative framework has, in recent years, been disrupted by developments in the labour market. The rise of the 'platform economy' means that workers are often not identified as such, instead being dubbed 'partners', who may not have entitlements to the above. The EU is considering the adoption of legislation to improve working conditions for persons in the platform economy.[100]

4. FREE MOVEMENT AND HEALTH

4.1. INTRODUCTION

The creation of the single market is at the heart of the European Union. To that end, four fundamental freedoms form the core of EU law: the free movement of persons, goods, capital and services. The four freedoms have important implications for various aspects of the health sphere, ranging from patients to healthcare professionals and medicines. The four freedoms have had a substantial impact on the development of cross-border issues in health law. The focus, in this section, is on free movement of services and goods.

4.2. FREE MOVEMENT OF SERVICES: CROSS-BORDER HEALTHCARE SERVICES

4.2.1. *The legal framework*

A distinction can be made between two legal regimes. Firstly, there is the mechanism of Regulation 883/2004/EC on the coordination of social security systems.[101] This Regulation provides social security coverage, including sickness benefit, to certain groups (generally speaking, insured persons in Europe) exercising the right to free movement. Medical care financed by the state, when granted without individual or discretionary assessment of personal needs, constitutes 'sickness benefit' under the Regulation. The second route is based

---

[100] See, e.g. Communication from the Commission to the European Parliament, the Council, the European Economic and Social Committee and the Committee of the Regions. Commission Work Programme 2021, A Union of vitality in a world of fragility, Brussels, 19.10.2020 COM(2020) 690 final.

[101] This regulation aims to modernise and simplify the coordination of Member States' social security systems by allowing posted workers to remain insured in their home countries, but does not go as far as harmonisation (Art. 21(1) of the Regulation).

on Article 56 TFEU (the previous Article 49 TEC), which prohibits restrictions on the freedom to provide and receive services within the EU. This provision implies an enforceable right for patients to travel abroad to access healthcare services.[102] This section discusses these mechanisms, with particular emphasis on the so-called Patients' Rights Directive.

Before the Patients' Rights Directive was adopted, the rights of patients to travel abroad were addressed in a number of cases before the CJEU.[103] The decisions widened the possibilities of seeking medical services, paid for by the patient's state of origin, or insurance scheme or policy held there, in other Member States beyond the narrow provisions of the Regulation. A distinction is made between extramural (outpatient) and intramural (inpatient) care. When it comes to extramural care, the CJEU was, in general, of the opinion that a requirement for the patient to seek prior authorisation is not justified. In principle, therefore, based on the Court's case law, Member States have to reimburse the costs of such treatment to the patient. In this regard, the CJEU was of the opinion that the removal of the requirement of prior authorisation for such services would not result in a risk of seriously undermining the financial balance of national social security systems, nor would it jeopardise the overall level of protection of public health.[104]

As mentioned above, this case-by-case approach was consolidated in the Cross-Border Healthcare Directive, which was adopted by the European Parliament and Council in March 2011.[105] According to its preamble, the directive is intended to ensure a more general and effective application of principles developed by the CJEU (paragraph 8). Its aim is to establish rules for facilitating access to safe and high-quality cross-border healthcare in the EU, and to ensure patient mobility (paragraph 10). The preamble also stresses the overarching health values of 'universality, access to good quality care, equity,

---

[102] See, in particular, Judgment of the Court of 28 April 1998. *Raymond Kohll v. Union des caisses de maladie*, Case C-158/96, ECLI:EU:C:1998:171; Tamara K. Hervey and Jean V. McHale, *Health Law and the European Union*, Cambridge: Cambridge University Press, 2004, 194–98.

[103] Willy Palm and Irene A. Glinos, 'Enabling patient mobility in the EU: between free movement and coordination', in Elias Mossialos, Govin Permanand, Rita Baeten and Tamara K. Hervey, Health Systems Governance in Europe: The Role of European Union Law and Policy, Cambridge: Cambridge University Press, 2010, 509–60, 517.

[104] Judgment of the Court of 13 May 2003. *V.G. Müller-Fauré v. Onderlinge Waarborgmaatschappij OZ Zorgverzekeringen UA and E.E.M. van Riet v. Onderlinge Waarborgmaatschappij ZAO Zorgverzekeringen*, Case C-385/99, ECLI:EU:C:2003:270, paras. 93–98 (dental treatment of a Dutch person in Germany). See also J.W. Van de Gronden and J.J.M. Sluijs, 'De betekenis van het EG-Verdrag voor het reguleren van de zorgmarkt' [The implications of the EC Treaty for the regulation of the healthcare market], *Gezondheidszorg en Europees Recht, Preadvies 2009*, The Hague: SDU, 2009, 6, 103–81, 110; Catherine Jacqueson and Mette Hartlev, 'Sygdomsbehandling i EU – en ret for de få? Danmarks anstrengte forhold til patienters fri bevægelighed' (2014) *Juristen*, 191–202.

[105] Directive 2011/24/EU of the European Parliament and of the Council of 9 March 2011 on the application of patients' rights in cross-border healthcare, OJ L 88, 4.4.2011, p. 45–65.

and solidarity' (paragraph 21), and that all patients 'are to be treated equitably on the basis of their healthcare needs' (paragraph 21).[106] The preamble also indicates that cross-border healthcare is still the exception, by stating that the 'vast majority of patients in the Union receive healthcare in their own country and prefer to do so' (paragraph 39).

The starting point for the directive is that Member States may not make the reimbursement of the costs of cross-border healthcare subject to prior authorisation. In other words, a prior authorisation requirement is not imposed on all hospital (intramural) care. Based on Article 8, the requirement for prior authorisation is limited to healthcare that is subject to planning requirements, and which either involves an overnight stay in a hospital, or requires the use of highly specialised and cost-intensive medical infrastructure or medical equipment. In addition, healthcare requiring prior authorisation may also involve treatments that present a particular risk to the patient, or to the general population, or situations where there are doubts about the quality or safety of care provided by the healthcare provider concerned.[107] Prior authorisation may not be refused when the necessary healthcare cannot be provided within the Member State's own territory within a reasonable time limit.[108] Martinsen et al criticise the directive as being somewhat contradictory, in imposing many conditions but also leaving a wide discretion to the Member States.[109]

Furthermore, the directive seeks to ensure that patients seeking healthcare services in another country have access to information about the possibilities and conditions of seeking these services. In this regard, the directive provides for the establishment of national contact points for cross-border healthcare. These bodies are to facilitate the exchange of information on healthcare providers, patients' rights, complaints procedures, and mechanisms for seeking remedies.[110]

While the first 'wave' of case law on cross-border healthcare dealt with patients belonging to 'wealthy' healthcare systems, Frischhut and Levaggi observe that this was not the case for the second wave of cases, and point to the *Petru* case (adopted prior to the Directive).[111]

---

[106] See Markus Frischhut, 'Standards on quality and safety in cross-border healthcare' in André den Exter (ed.), *Cross-border health care and European Union law*, Rotterdam: Erasmus University Press, 2017, 59–86, 66.
Markus Frischhut, *The Ethical Spirit of EU Law*, Springer International Publishing, 2019, pp. 34ff, available at https://doi.org/10.1007/978-3-030-10582-2.

[107] Art. 8, paras. 1–2 of the Directive.

[108] Art. 8(5) of the Directive.

[109] Dorte Sindbjerg Martinsen, Reini Margriet Schrama and Ellen Mastenbroek, 'Experimenting European healthcare forward. Do institutional differences condition networked governance?' *Journal of European Public Policy* (2020), DOI: 10.1080/13501763.2020.1804436.

[110] Art. 6 of the Directive.

[111] Judgment of the Court (Third Chamber) 9 October 2014. *Elena Petru v. Casa Judeţeană de Asigurări de Sănătate Sibiu and Casa Naţională de Asigurări de Sănătate*, Case C-268/13, ECLI:EU:C:2014:2271.

Ms. Petru had been suffering from a serious cardiovascular disease and, in 2009, she had to undergo open-heart surgery. As she believed that the infrastructure in Romania was inadequate, she decided to travel to a clinic in Germany, where the surgery was carried out, resulting in expenses of 17,714.70 euros. Before going to Germany, Ms. Petru required the Romanian national health insurance agency to authorise the costs, but this was denied, for the reason that there was no indication that the treatment sought could not be provided in Romania within a reasonable time period. She went abroad anyway, without prior authorisation. Subsequently, Ms. Petru lodged a complaint against the national health insurance agency, claiming damages for the costs of treatment in Germany, in light of the perceived poor conditions in Romania.

Ms. Petru's claim was dismissed and, on appeal, the Romanian court referred a question to the CJEU, asking whether the lack of medical supplies and infrastructure could be taken into account, under Article 22(2) of the EU Regulation on Social Security. In a preliminary ruling, the CJEU held that authorisation cannot be refused where the hospital care cannot be provided in good time in the insured person's state of residence because of lack of medication, basic medical supplies and infrastructure.

The 'timely available treatment' argument, interpreted as an absence of medicines and medical supplies, entails a further extension of the patient mobility concept in the European Union. Frischhut, Levaggi and den Exter[112] note that, although one may welcome such a patient-friendly outcome, it also raises concerns, given that structural shortages of medicines and medical supplies are not uncommon in lower-income Member States. Therefore, this interpretation makes safeguarding the long-term sustainability of their national healthcare systems difficult for low-income countries (although reimbursement for the patient follows the tariffs applicable in the insuring state). Furthermore, under the directive, patients have to pay in advance, which can remain a challenge, not only for patients from the new Member States, but also for those from states suffering from austerity-driven measures.[113]

From a health and human rights perspective, A v. Veselības ministrija should also be mentioned.[114] This case centred on a child in need of an operation. As the family were Jehovah's Witnesses, the father wished to have his child's operation

---

[112]   André den Exter, 'The patient mobility saga continues – the ruling of Court of Justice of European Union in the case of Elena Petru', Croatian Medical Journal 55(5) (2014), 441–42, doi:10.3325/cmj.2014.55.441. See also André den Exter (ed.), Cross-border health care and European Union law, Rotterdam: Erasmus University Press, 2017.

[113]   Markus Frischhut and Rosella Levaggi, 'Patient mobility in the context of austerity and an enlarged EU: The European Court of Justice's ruling in the Petru Case', Health Policy 119(10) (2015), 1293–297. See https://doi.org/10.1016/j.healthpol.2015.07.002.

[114]   Judgment of the Court (Second Chamber) of 29 October 2020. A v. Veselības ministrija, Case C-243/19, ECLI:EU:C:2020:872. See, further, Santa Slokenberga, 'Case C-243/19, A v. Veselības ministrija, Judgment of the Court (Second Chamber) of 29 October 2020, EU:C:2020:872' [2021] European Journal of Health Law 1–22.

carried out abroad, as the same procedure was not possible in Latvia without a blood transfusion. The Latvian court referred two questions to the CJEU. Firstly, it asked whether a Member State was precluded from refusing authorisation, under Article 20(1) of the Regulation on Social Security,[115] where hospital care was available in that State but the method used was contrary to the patient's religious beliefs. The CJEU held that the authorisation system 'takes into account exclusively the patient's medical condition, not his or her personal choices as regards medical care'.[116] Referring to Article 21(1) of the Charter (on freedom of religion), the Court recalled that it was for the referring court to determine whether the refusal established a difference of treatment based on religion, and, if so, whether this was based on objective and reasonable criteria.[117] The Court postulated that an indirect difference in treatment was present, but noted that:

> [if] the competent institution were obliged to take account of the insured person's religious beliefs, such additional costs could, given their unpredictability and potential scale, be capable of entailing a risk in relation to the need to protect the financial stability of the health insurance system, which is a legitimate objective recognised by EU law.[118]

The Court, therefore, held that not taking a person's religious beliefs into account seemed justified, in light of the potential financial costs.

In relation to the second question, regarding authorisation under the directive, the Court noted that the additional financial costs of treatment can only be reimbursed up to the level of their cost in the Member State of affiliation. Ultimately, the Court held that Member States cannot refuse to grant authorisation for hospital care abroad, where domestic care is available, but contrary to the patient's religious beliefs, 'unless th[e] refusal is objectively justified by a legitimate aim relating to maintaining treatment capacity or medical competence, and is an appropriate and necessary means of achieving that aim, which it is for the referring court to determine'.[119]

Slokenberga suggests that, had the Court been more liberal in its interpretation of the regulation, this could have put pressure on Member States to adjust their healthcare to Jehovah's Witnesses, while facing uncertainty regarding the needs of other minorities.[120]

---

[115] Regulation (EC) No 883/2004 of the European Parliament and of the Council of 29 April 2004 on the coordination of social security systems.

[116] Judgment of the Court (Second Chamber) of 29 October 2020. *A v. Veselības ministrija*, Case C-243/19, ECLI:EU:C:2020:872, para. 30.

[117] Ibid., para. 37.

[118] Ibid., para. 52.

[119] Ibid., para. 85.

[120] Santa Slokenberga, 'Case C-243/19, *A v. Veselības ministrija*, Judgment of the Court (Second Chamber) of 29 October 2020, EU:C:2020:872' [2021] *European Journal of Health Law* 28(3) 285–306.

4.2.2. Cross-border healthcare and issues of morality

A major incentive for patients to cross national borders in search of healthcare services comes in cases where the provision of the treatment in question is unlawful in the country of residence. Glenn Cohen has coined the term 'circumvention tourism' to describe the practice of seeking such treatment in such circumstances.[121] This scenario is especially well-known in connection with reproductive healthcare, and, consequently, there is considerable traffic in this respect. The question of abortion was, unsurprisingly, the first controversial medical procedure to be exposed to the EU law perspective.

The fact that EU law provides the right to shop for healthcare services, including those that are prohibited or otherwise unavailable in a patient's home country, was established in *SPUC v. Grogan*,[122] where abortion was given the status of a *service* within the meaning of the EC Treaty, when performed legally in the Member State in question. In the case, which was referred to the CJEU as a prejudicial question, and which dealt with an Irish student organisation's dissemination of information regarding abortion clinics in the UK, the Society for the Protection of Unborn Children (SPUC) argued that a termination could not be regarded as a service, within the meaning of the treaty, because abortion was immoral, and resulted in the destruction of the unborn child. The Court noted that termination of a pregnancy, as lawfully practised in several Member States, was a medical activity that is normally provided in exchange for remuneration, and which may be carried out as part of a professional activity. The Court had already held, in the judgment in *Luisi and Carbone*,[123] that medical activities fell within the scope of the treaty. Whatever the merits of SPUC's arguments on the moral plane, they could not influence the answer to the question now before the CJEU. The Court noted that it was not for the Court to substitute its assessment for those of the legislatures in those Member States in which the activities in question were practised legally.[124] Consequently, the individual has other options besides following the values enforced in national legislation. To the extent that other jurisdictions subscribe to different moral convictions, as implemented in the law, the individual may seek out medical services by relying on the right to move freely within the EU.

---

[121] I. Glenn Cohen, 'Circumvention Tourism', *Cornell Law Review* 97 (2012), 1309–398. See https://papers.ssrn.com/sol3/papers.cfm?abstract_id=1965504.

[122] Judgment of the Court of 4 October 1991. *The Society for the Protection of Unborn Children Ireland Ltd v. Stephen Grogan and others*, Case C-159/90, ECLI:EU:C:1991:378, para. 21.

[123] Judgment of the Court of 31 January 1984. *Graziana Luisi and Giuseppe Carbone v. Ministero del Tesoro*, Joined Cases 286/82 and 26/83, ECLI:EU:C:1984:35, para. 16.

[124] Judgment of the Court of 4 October 1991. *The Society for the Protection of Unborn Children Ireland Ltd v. Stephen Grogan and others*, Case C-159/90, ECLI:EU:C:1991:378, paras. 18 and 20.

This fact has created healthcare rights across the spectrum of morally sensitive healthcare services:[125] Swedish women now travel to Denmark to receive fertility treatment with *anonymous* donor sperm, Danish women travel to the Czech Republic to buy eggs for fertility treatment, and so on. The divergence between national healthcare regulation and the EU-based right to free movement has also given rise to various legal disputes. In the case of *Diane Blood*,[126] a woman wished to export the sperm of her deceased husband to another Member State, in order to begin fertility treatment. The use of the deceased husband's sperm was unlawful in the woman's country of residence because written consent from the husband had not been obtained prior to his death.[127] The UK's Human Fertilisation and Embryology Authority, which had initially refused the woman, was later directed by the Court to take EU law into account, and, as a result of her rights under free movement, Diane Blood subsequently gave birth to two sons after receiving fertility treatment in Brussels, using the sperm of her deceased husband.

Recognition of the subsidiarity principle, and of the integration of the human right to dignity and integrity, were also at the heart of the resolution on compulsory gynaecological examinations at the Dutch–German border,[128] in which the European Parliament condemned the actions of the German *Bundesgrenzschutz* (Federal Frontier Police), whereby German women had been obliged to undergo gynaecological examinations, which were not without serious risk to their health, on suspicion of having had abortions in the Netherlands.

4.2.3. Evaluation

Looking at the notion of free movement of healthcare from a health and human rights perspective, it seems that two opposing interests are at stake, both of which can impact upon a right to healthcare services. While, on the one hand, the possibility of seeking cross-border healthcare services may enable individuals to realise their rights to healthcare, it has also been suggested that it may undermine healthcare planning and coherence in the Member States.

Regarding the first of these perspectives, for the European citizen it has been an uphill struggle to gain cross-border rights to healthcare. It has become clear (see above) that the marketisation of healthcare has increased freedom

---

[125] See also André den Exter (ed.), *Cross-border health care and European Union law*, Rotterdam: Erasmus University Press, 2017; Markus Frischhut, *The Ethical Spirit of EU Law*, Springer International Publishing, 2019, available at https://doi.org/10.1007/978-3-030-10582-2.

[126] *R v. Human Fertilisation and Embryology Authority, ex parte Blood* [1997] 2 All ER 687; *Attorney-General's Reference (No. 3 of 1994)* [1998] AC 245.

[127] See, in more depth, Derek Morgan and Robert G. Lee, 'In the Name of the Father? *Ex parte Blood*: Dealing with Novelty and Anomaly', *Modern Law Review* 60(6) (1997), 840–56.

[128] Joint resolution on gynaecological examinations [1991] OJ C 106/113, available at https:// eur-lex.europa.eu/legal-content/EN/TXT/PDF/?uri=OJ:C:1991:106:FULL&from=EN.

of choice, and that it may also increase the quality of healthcare services for those seeking healthcare abroad. Thus, the rationale of market and competition law, according to which monopolies are to be avoided, and competition is to be increased, in order to increase consumer welfare, is gaining ground in the field of healthcare. Consequently, the impact of EU law has also focused more attention on individual rights to seek healthcare services abroad.

The framing of healthcare as a service has also meant that morally sensitive healthcare services are viewed from a market perspective. This development, through which procedures involving sensitive ethical issues are, in terms of EU law, viewed as services, has acted as a generator of rights, especially for women, whose reproductive privacy has, traditionally, been scrutinised closely by the state. Even countries with publicly financed healthcare systems, which have, traditionally, needed to prioritise their limited funding carefully and, thus, have tended to focus on striking a balance between individual patients' rights and societal needs, in order to control public spending, cannot evade the principle of free movement by restricting individual rights in this regard. The patient's country of residence may, however, still retain some control over public spending, as prior authorisation has to be obtained, in some cases, if the healthcare provided abroad is to be paid for by the patient's country of residence.

While patient mobility may put a strain on the 'receiving' country, it may also disadvantage the country of origin, when it has to reimburse the costs of cross-border care that had not been anticipated, or when it has made investments in healthcare that are not being used. One need only look at the supporting comments from other Member States, in the case law that developed the rights to cross-border healthcare, to realise that national governments are concerned about the potential costs of cross-border care, as the lack of control over the costs associated with caring for patients seems to be viewed as incompatible with publicly funded healthcare systems.[129] The Brexit referendum drew on this rhetoric, promising that a withdrawal would 'protect the NHS', while experts warned of the negative health impacts.[130]

From a health and human rights perspective, those managing to receive healthcare abroad are realising their 'right to healthcare', as guaranteed under international human rights law. However, this can only be a small component of the right to health, as most people will continue to make use of their own national healthcare services. The primary responsibility for realising a right to health(care) lies with national governments, and such free movement claims can never replace this responsibility. Being able to travel abroad to make use of healthcare services

---

[129] See further, Anniek de Ruijter, *EU Health Law & Policy*, Oxford: Oxford University Press, 2019, chapter 6.

[130] Tamara Hervey and Steve Peers, 'Brexit and health services', *Clinical Medicine* 16(2) (2016), 101–02; see https://doi.org/10.7861/clinmedicine.16-2-101.

is one thing, but the essential part of the right to health implies that individuals should enjoy good quality and accessible health services in their own country.

The directive seems to be an important step in securing cross-border healthcare. Yet, from the perspective of patients and human rights, a few words of caution should be stated. For example, how effective, in practice, are the national contact points in fulfilling their information obligations in an understandable manner? Are these bodies succeeding in providing reliable information on cross-border healthcare services? To what extent are hospitals and other healthcare providers willing, and financially able, to share information in a transparent fashion? Altogether, to what extent is the quality of healthcare services across borders guaranteed? More generally, the question arises as to who, and how many patients actually travel abroad and benefit from this legislation? Do patients have the necessary skills and resources needed, such as money for travel costs, suitable childcare arrangements, and language abilities? Hervey and McHale observe that the directive does 'not provide a "patients' rights manifesto", still less a Patients' Rights Act'.[131]

4.3. FREE MOVEMENT OF GOODS: PHARMACEUTICALS

Access to medicines is an essential component of the right to health. However, from a human rights perspective, difficult issues also arise, mainly regarding the risks that medicines pose, and their testing and administration.[132] European regulation is increasingly important in relation to the licensing and marketing of pharmaceuticals. While, on the one hand, it is aimed at facilitating the free movement of goods, it also seeks, on the other hand, to harmonise consumer protection regimes, and, as such, to address the above-mentioned concerns regarding the testing and administration of drugs.[133]

EU law has engaged with pharmaceuticals for many years, for example in Directive 65/65, from 1965, on the approximation of provisions laid down by Law, Regulation or Administrative Action relating to proprietary medicinal products, which was the predecessor of Directive 2001/83, which provides the basis for the grant of marketing authorisation for pharmaceuticals in the EU.[134]

---

[131]   Tamara K. Hervey and Jean V. McHale, *Health Law and the European Union*, Cambridge: Cambridge University Press, 20042015, 159.

[132]   Hervey and McHale give the example of the drug thalidomide, which was given to pregnant women in the late 1950s, and was linked to the development of major congenital disabilities. See Tamara K. Hervey and Jean V. McHale, *European Union Health Law – Themes and Implications*, Cambridge: Cambridge University Press, 2015, 293–94.

[133]   See Emily Jackson, *Medical Law, Text, Cases and Materials*, Oxford: Oxford University Press, 2006, 542.

[134]   Tamara K. Hervey and Jean V. McHale, *Health Law and the European Union*, Cambridge: Cambridge University Press, 2004, 324.

It provides for a complex regulatory system regarding the manufacture, marketing, surveillance and advertising of pharmaceuticals, and liability for any harmful effects of such products.[135] Without discussing this area in detail, some attention will be paid here to the labelling and marketing of pharmaceutical products, the surveillance system, and product liability.

EU law contains a number of rules regarding the way in which medicinal products are to be presented to patients and consumers. The labelling, packaging and insertion of leaflets of medicinal products is currently regulated by Directive 2001/83.[136] This directive states, for example, that certain specific information is mandatory on medicine labels, while other particulars have to be given in the official language or languages of the Member State in which the medicine is being sold.[137] The aims of providing such information are to ensure patient safety, satisfy consumer choice, and realise patients' rights.[138] Given the growing availability of over-the-counter medicines, this information has become increasingly important.[139] Advertising of medicines (which is also subject to the general EU rules on advertising) is now also regulated by Directive 2001/83/EC, last amended in 2019.[140]

Furthermore, there is a European system for the authorisation of medicinal products,[141] whereby the European Commission issues authorisations, based on assessments by the European Medicines Authority (EMA). A new system for the authorisation of medicinal products was established in 1995, and there are now four routes for obtaining marketing approval of medicinal products:[142]

(1) a centralised procedure, under which applications are made to the Committee for Medicinal Products for Human Use (CHMP), which is compulsory for products derived from biotechnology, elective for orphan drugs, and optional for other innovative medicinal products;

---

[135] For more detail, see Chapters 11 and 13 of Tamara K. Hervey and Jean V. McHale, *Health Law and the European Union*, Cambridge: Cambridge University Press, 2004.

[136] This directive has replaced Directive 92/27/EEC.

[137] Arts. 54–57 and 63(1) of Directive 2001/83/EC.

[138] See also Tamara K. Hervey and Jean V. McHale, *Health Law and the European Union*, Cambridge: Cambridge University Press, 2004, 331–37.

[139] Tamara K. Hervey and Jean V. McHale, *Health Law and the European Union*, Cambridge: Cambridge University Press, 2004, 338.

[140] See the Consolidated Directive: https://eur-lex.europa.eu/legal-content/DA/TXT/HTML/?uri=CELEX:02001L0083-20190726&from=EN.

[141] Consolidated Regulation (EC) No 726/2004 of the European Parliament and of the Council of 31 March 2004 laying down Union procedures for the authorisation and supervision of medicinal products for human and veterinary use and establishing a European Medicines Agency: https://eur-lex.europa.eu/legal-content/EN/TXT/?uri=CELEX%3A02004R0726-20190330.

[142] Tamara K. Hervey and Jean V. McHale, *Health Law and the European Union*, Cambridge: Cambridge University Press, 2004, 328 and https://www.ema.europa.eu/en/about-us/what-we-do/authorisation-medicines.

(2) a decentralised procedure that can be used to apply for market approval in several Member States at once, which is applicable to the majority of conventional medicinal products;

(3) a mutual recognition procedure based on the principle of recognition of the assessment by the Reference Member State (where one Member State has already issued a market authorisation); and

(4) a national procedure. While the majority of new, innovative medicines are evaluated by the EMA, and authorised by the European Commission, in order to be marketed in the EU, most generic and non-prescription medicines are assessed and authorised at national level. In addition, many older medicines still available today received their authorisations at a national level, because they were marketed before the EMA was created.[143]

During the COVID-19 pandemic, the EMA applied a 'rolling review' process to expedite the assessment of vaccine candidates prior to conditional authorisation. This did not mark a new route, but, rather, an optimisation of the existing process, where the different phases in the approval procedure were conducted in parallel rather than consecutively.

It has been noted that the number of centralised marketing authorisations is growing steadily, and that, as a result, the EU institutions are playing an increasing role in the marketing authorisation of pharmaceuticals.[144] While the centralised procedure may offer some advantages for the manufacturer (less bureaucracy and less national control), commentators have also pointed at a loss of control over the process at a national level, and at a lack of transparency in the EMA's system, both of which may lead to undue influence on the part of the pharmaceutical industry.[145] This was one of the concerns that the Clinical Trials Regulations (Regulation 536/2014) were intended to address. It has been argued that the system favours the interests of the industry over those of patients or national health services.[146] From a human rights perspective, it is important that the rights of patients are strongly embedded in the authorisation decisions of the CHMP. The marketing authorisation shall be refused if, after verification of the particulars and documents submitted in accordance with Article 6, it appears that the applicant has not properly or sufficiently demonstrated the quality, safety or efficacy of the medicinal product.[147] Furthermore, a clinical trial may be conducted only if: (a) the rights, safety, dignity and well-being of subjects are

---

143 As defined in the Annex (parts A and B) to Regulation 2309/93/EC.
144 Tamara K. Hervey and Jean V. McHale, *Health Law and the European Union*, Cambridge: Cambridge University Press, 2004, 324.
145 Ibid., 329.
146 Ibid., 296, 329.
147 cf. Article 12, para. 1 of Regulation (EC) No 726/2004 laying down Community procedures for the authorisation and supervision of medicinal products for human and veterinary use, and establishing a European Medicines Agency, OJ 2004 L 136/1.

protected, and prevail over all other interests; and (b) it is designed to generate reliable and robust data.[148]

When it comes to the decentralised procedure, issues arise that may also have a potential impact on the protection of the health and human rights of patients. One concern is that the procedure allows companies to 'cherry-pick' the state with the least rigorous assessment: companies will seek the most speedy and least demanding procedure, which may not be in the best interests of patients.[149] Companies have a significant interest in getting their products on to the market quickly, to get the greatest possible benefit out of their patent protections. The purpose of the decentralised procedure is that it is not the slowest agency that sets the pace of approval.

Under the Falsified Medicines Directive, Member States are also required to introduce criminal penalties for importation of falsified medicines and products.[150] While it is an important instrument in the protection of the right to health, the directive is not as comprehensive as the Council of Europe's MEDICRIME Convention.[151]

A final important issue concerns product liability, and the possibility of bringing actions before the courts on this basis. The Product Liability Directive 85/374/EEC establishes the principle that the producer of a product is liable for damages caused by a defect therein, and this includes medicinal products. Recently, the European Parliament has suggested that the product liability regime may need to be updated to adequately address the liability aspects of artificial intelligence.[152] The current directive gives consumers the right to compensation for defective medicines.[153] Triggered by the tragic thalidomide case,[154] liability is granted on the basis of 'strict liability', meaning that liability arises regardless of negligence or culpability.[155] This is weakened, to some

---

[148]   cf. Article 3 of Regulation (EU) No 536/2014 on clinical trials on medicinal products for human use, OJ 2014 L 158/1.

[149]   Ibid., 330–331.

[150]   Directive 2011/62/EU of the European Parliament and of the Council of 8 June 2011 amending Directive 2001/83/EC on the Community code relating to medicinal products for human use, as regards the prevention of the entry into the legal supply chain of falsified medicinal products.

[151]   Council of Europe Convention on the Counterfeiting of Medical Products and Similar Crimes involving Threats to Public Health (Treaty No. 211).

[152]   European Parliament resolution of 20 October 2020 with recommendations to the Commission on a framework of ethical aspects of artificial intelligence, robotics and related technologies (2020/2012(INL)).

[153]   Directive 85/374/EEC, Art. 2, as amended by Directive 99/34/EC, Art. 1, [1985] OJ L 210, 29; Tamara K. Hervey and Jean V. McHale, *Health Law and the European Union*, Cambridge: Cambridge University Press, 2004, 379–80.

[154]   As mentioned above, thalidomide was introduced as a sedative drug in the late 1950s, and was subsequently found to be the cause of birth defects.

[155]   See also C.J. Miller and R.S. Goldberg, *Product Liability*, 2nd ed., Oxford: Oxford University Press, 2004, Chapter II, in particular section 9B(5).

extent, by an optional measure in the directive, entitled the 'development risks defence' (Article 7(e)). Based on this defence, the producer will not be liable under the directive if, at the time of putting the product into circulation, the state of scientific and technical knowledge was such that the risk of harm was not foreseeable. The interpretation and desirability of this principle is an issue of debate, and has also been addressed by the CJEU.[156] While, on the one hand, its abolition may have damaging consequences for manufacturers, on the other hand, it could benefit consumers.[157] This debate is important from a health and human rights perspective, as it balances the interests of consumers or patients against the rights of the pharmaceuticals manufacturing industry. The human rights framework, including Article 35 CFREU, could be used in defence of a strengthened liability regime that does not allow for a 'development risks defence'.

4.4. FREE MOVEMENT OF GOODS: BLOOD (SAFETY)

As part of the EU's effort to promote and safeguard public health, it was only natural that the Union, in the wake of the spread of HIV/AIDS, took action concerning the safety of blood.[158] The concept of dealing in blood is potentially controversial, from a human rights perspective, as Article 21 of the Convention on Biomedicine and Human Rights prohibits the commercialisation of human materials.[159] Consequently, this provision, and also the viewpoint taken by the WHO, have influenced the EU measures on blood safety.

The donation of blood touches on the right to health, in the sense that a sufficient supply of safe blood is a prerequisite for the delivery of many healthcare services, including, for example, successful operations, and optimal maternal health during childbirth. Blood that has been tested to ensure that it is free of disease, thus, has the potential to save lives, whereas untested blood infected with disease has, in the most serious cases, the potential to kill the recipient.

---

[156]   Judgment of the Court (Fifth Chamber) of 25 April 2002. *María Victoria González Sánchez v. Medicina Asturiana SA*, Case C-183/00, ECLI:EU:C:2002:255.; Tamara K. Hervey and Jean V. McHale, *Health Law and the European Union*, Cambridge: Cambridge University Press, 2004, 380.

[157]   For a discussion, see Tamara K. Hervey and Jean V. McHale, *Health Law and the European Union*, Cambridge: Cambridge University Press, 2004, 380–84.

[158]   On quality of blood, tissues and cells, and organs, see Markus Frischhut, 'Standards on quality and safety in cross-border healthcare' in André den Exter (ed.), *Cross-border health care and European Union law*, Rotterdam: Erasmus University Press, 2017, 59–86, 59–86.

[159]   Also Art. 3(2)(c) CFREU.

The Blood Safety Directive[160] was adopted in 2003, and places a strong emphasis on the voluntary and unpaid use of blood donations (see Article 20 of the directive).

4.5. FREE MOVEMENT OF GOODS: CELLS AND TISSUES (SAFETY, STANDARDS AND QUALITY)

For the protection of public health, and to prevent the transmission of infectious diseases via human cells and tissues used for therapeutic purposes, the EU has adopted special regulatory measures on safety, quality and standards in cells and tissues.

Directive 2004/23/EC[161] sets standards of quality and safety for the donation, procurement, testing, processing, preservation, storage and distribution of human tissues and cells, ensuring that human tissues and cells, whatever their intended use, are of comparable quality and safety. Thus, the directive aims at bringing about the same level of protection for all patients, ensuring a compatible and uniform quality.[162] The establishment of such standards was meant to reassure the public that human tissues and cells that are procured in another Member State carry the same guarantees as those procured in their own country. The directive applies to a variety of human tissues and cells, including reproductive cells, stem cells and foetal cells. Regulation of this nature helps to create a transparent market for healthcare services within the EU, further strengthening patient mobility, as well as the mobility of tissues and cells used for treatment purposes across the Union.

---

[160] Directive 2002/98/EC setting standards of quality and safety for the collection, testing, processing, storage and distribution of human blood and blood component. Some further technical requirements can be found in Commission Directive 2004/33/EC of 22 March 2004 implementing Directive 2002/98/EC of the European Parliament and of the Council as regards certain technical requirements for blood and blood components [2004] OJ L 91, 25–39. Successive amendments to Directive 2004/33/EC have been incorporated into the original text. This consolidated version is of documentary value only: Commission Directive 2005/61/EC of 30 September 2005 implementing Directive 2002/98/EC of the European Parliament and of the Council as regards traceability requirements and notification of serious adverse reactions and events [2005] OJ L 256, 32–40, Commission Directive 2005/62/EC of 30 September 2005 implementing Directive 2002/98/EC of the European Parliament and of the Council as regards Community standards and specifications relating to a quality system for blood establishments [2005] OJ L 256, 41–48.

[161] Directive 2004/23/EC of the European Parliament and of the Council of 31 March 2004.

[162] Further technical regulation has, subsequently, been adopted: Directive 2015/565 amending Directive 2006/86/EC as regards certain technical requirements for the coding of human tissues and cells; and Directive 2015/566 implementing Directive 2004/23/EC as regards the procedures for verifying the equivalent standards of quality and safety of imported tissues and cells.

The directive contains several provisions that are in accordance with the principles expressed in the Council of Europe's Biomedicine Convention. First, Article 1 of the directive stipulates that Member States shall endeavour to ensure voluntary and unpaid donations of tissues and cells. This provision, thus, reflects the prohibition of financial gain from the human body contained in Article 21 of the Convention, as well as the general rule on consent in Article 5 of the same instrument, according to which an intervention in the health field may only be carried out after the person concerned has given free and informed consent. The emphasis on informed consent is further noted in Article 13 of the directive, which requires that all mandatory consent and authorisation requirements in force in the Member State concerned must be met. Finally, the directive contains, in Article 14, safeguarding requirements in relation to data protection and confidentiality.

4.6. FREE MOVEMENT OF DATA

In an increasingly digitised economy, it is a priority for data to be able to flow freely across borders. This is reaffirmed in Recital 3 of the General Data Protection Regulation (GDPR),[163] which states that it seeks to harmonise the protection of fundamental rights and freedoms of natural persons in respect of processing activities, and to ensure the free flow of personal data between Member States.

The right to privacy is protected in both Articles 6 and 8 of the European Charter of Fundamental Rights and Freedoms, and in the GDPR. Informational privacy relates to a wide range of information related to an individual,[164] however, health information is at the core of informational privacy because of its perceived inherent sensitivity. Moreover, the CJEU has repeatedly emphasised the duty to respect this right when taking measures seeking to achieve other aims.[165] The GDPR, which replaced a previous directive, creates a common European level of privacy protection, thus facilitating the movement of personal

---

[163]   Regulation (EU) 2016/679 of the European Parliament and of the Council of 27 April 2016 on the protection of natural persons with regard to the processing of personal data and on the free movement of such data, and repealing Directive 95/46/EC (the 'General Data Protection Regulation'). See also Tamara K. Hervey and Jean V. McHale, *Health Law and the European Union*, Cambridge: Cambridge University Press, 2004, 101–05 and 548–50.

[164]   See, e.g. Judgment of the CJEU in Case C-101/01, *Lindqvist* ECLI:EU:C:2003:596.

[165]   Judgment of the Court of 20 May 2003. *Rechnungshof (C-465/00) v. Österreichischer Rundfunk and Others and Christa Neukomm (C-138/01) and Joseph Lauermann (C-139/01) v. Österreichischer Rundfunk*, Joined cases C-465/00, C-138/01 and C-139/01, ECLI:EU:C:2003:294, and Judgment of the Court (Grand Chamber) of 9 November 2010. *Volker und Markus Schecke GbR (C-92/09) and Hartmut Eifert (C-93/09) v. Land Hessen*, Joined cases C-92/09 and C-93/09, ECLI:EU:C:2010:662.

data within the EU, as part of the single market. The strong emphasis on data protection in the EU means that the Council of Europe's Convention for the Protection of Individuals with regard to Automatic Processing of Personal Data (1981) has no real legal impact on the Member States of the EU, with the GDPR having absorbed and developed further the main principles of data protection law. The GDPR safeguards informational privacy in general, and, as such, is also relevant to the regulation of health information.

The GDPR sets out different categories of personal data, and those that are particularly sensitive are subject to stricter protective measures. Article 9 GDPR states that processing of personal data concerning health is prohibited, and that such data may only be processed with the explicit informed consent of the data subject. This does not, however, apply if the processing of data is *necessary* for reasons of public interest in, for example, public health (Recital 53), or if processing is necessary for the purposes of preventive or occupational medicine (Article 9(2)h), and data can also be processed, subject to appropriate safeguards, for archiving purposes in the public interest, for scientific or historical research purposes, or for statistical purposes (Article 89).

The safeguards embedded in the GDPR are meant to implement and uphold the fundamental rights, as protected in, inter alia, the Charter and the European Convention on Human Rights.[166]

5. CONCLUSIONS

The aim of this chapter was to analyse the relationship between the EU and health and human rights. To some extent, the EU engages directly with this field. By including a right to health(care) and other health-related rights in the Charter, the EU has committed to mainstreaming health-related rights in its laws and policies, and those of its Member States. The CJEU has proven less reluctant to explore human rights issues, in its more recent case law, but still does not refer systematically to the Charter in its health-related judgments.

The EU is not, predominantly, a human rights organisation, and the claim that it systematically protects health-related rights cannot be supported.[167] Its recognition of health-related rights in the Charter of Fundamental Rights of the European Union (CFREU) has not made a substantial difference to the actual protection of patients and health professionals.[168] Hervey and McHale, together with other authors, see the most potential in EU law when it comes to the interpretation of it, and domestic law implementing EU obligations, in particular

---

[166] cf. for example Recital 1 and Article 45(2)a of the GDPR.
[167] Hervey and McHale, 2015, 182.
[168] Ibid.

when human rights apply alongside the principle of non-discrimination.[169] Ultimately, the scope of the Charter remains underexplored, in the area of health.

As demonstrated above, EU law regulates health issues in the context of its overall commitment to establishing a single market, including in relation to pharmaceuticals, blood products and healthcare providers. When it comes to such matters, there is an ongoing tension between the wish to enhance the free movement of goods, persons and services, and the importance of protecting health-related interests (for example, the quality of pharmaceuticals, and blood safety). For example, while, on the one hand, the EU seeks to create a competitive European pharmaceutical market, on the other hand, the quality, safety and affordability of pharmaceutical products are at stake.

Healthcare remains, primarily, a national endeavour, where the EU has limited competences, and significant disparities among Member States remain. The intention to build a 'European Health Union' could, potentially, give more weight to the protection of health in the laws, policies and programmes of the EU. At the time of writing, the scope of such reforms remains to be seen.

---

[169]   Ibid., 183.

PART III
SELECTED TOPICS

CHAPTER 7

ACCESS TO HEALTH

Mette Hartlev

1. INTRODUCTION

As discussed in Chapter 2, the right to health is a very ambitious and comprehensive right, which is not confined to healthcare services, but also extends to the underlying determinants of health.[1] In this chapter, the focus will mostly be on *access to healthcare services*, which is an important aspect of access to health. Access to healthcare services includes health promotion, disease prevention and access to treatment and care. In this respect, there are, in particular, two (interlinked) aspects, which, from a human rights perspective, need to be addressed: one is equality and non-discrimination, the other is unjustified limitations on access, both in situations of scarce resources, and where access is limited for other reasons.

Equality and *non-discrimination* are general human rights principles (as discussed in Chapter 3), and equality in health, and in access to healthcare services, is clearly also an important human rights concern, as stressed repeatedly in General Comment No. 14. Some of the chapters in this part of the book look more closely at discrimination based on age and nationality (Chapter 8), disability (Chapter 9), and gender (Chapter 10). In this chapter, the principles of equality and non-discrimination in health are discussed more generally, taking existing health disparities, and the role of human rights in addressing health inequities, as its starting points.

Another important human rights aspect of access to health relates to situations where *access is limited*, either due to scarce resources, or to restrictions based on cultural, ethical, religious or broader societal concerns. Some of these limitations are discussed intensively in Chapter 2 (core obligations), Chapter 10 (abortion and artificial reproduction), Chapter 11 (euthanasia), and Chapter 12

---

[1]   UN Committee on Economic, Social and Cultural Rights (ICESCR Committee), General Comment No. 14 on the Right to the Highest Attainable Standard of Health, UN Doc. E/C.12/2000/4.

(new technologies). The focus in this chapter is on identifying the more general aspects of limitations on access, particularly with regard to prioritisation of scarce resources.

2. HEALTH INEQUALITIES

It is well established that there are significant health disparities, both across the globe and within countries.[2] Some differences can be explained by genetics, age and external factors, such as traffic or work-related accidents. Others are closely related to social determinants, such as access to social services, safe water, adequate housing, a sufficient supply of food and nutrition, access to education, safe working conditions, and the quality of the environment.[3] They may also relate to different status or classes, such as disability, age, ethnicity and sexuality. In this chapter, health inequalities are understood as health differences that are *avoidable, unnecessary* and *unjust* (see, further, Chapter 13, section 6 of this book).[4]

The ICESCR Committee's General Comment No. 14 specifically stresses that 'the right to health embraces a wide range of socio-economic factors that *promote* conditions in which people can lead a healthy life, and extends to the underlying determinants of health'.[5] It is also stressed that governments must ensure 'equality of opportunity' for people to enjoy the highest attainable level of health.[6] Consequently, the obligations of the States Parties require a broad focus on promoting living conditions for their populations. However, at the same time, the ICESCR Committee also recognises that states cannot be exclusively responsible for the health of their populations, as some aspects of health may be outside the control of state actors. Therefore, the right to health should not be understood as a 'right to be healthy', and it is stressed that a state cannot, itself, ensure good health as, for example, genetic or environmental factors, and the adoption of unhealthy or risky lifestyles may have an impact on

---

[2]   See, e.g. M. Marmot, 'Social determinants of health inequalities', *Lancet* 365(9464) (2005), 1099–104; World Health Organization (WHO), Commission on the Social Determinants of Health, *Closing the Gap in a Generation. Health Equity Through Action on the Social Determinants of Health*, Geneva: WHO, 2008; and M. Marmot, 'The health gap: The challenge of an unequal world', *Lancet* 386(10011) (2015), 2442–444.

[3]   World Health Organization (WHO), Commission on the Social Determinants of Health, *Closing the Gap in a Generation. Health Equity Through Action on the Social Determinants of Health*, Geneva: WHO, 2008; M. Marmot, 'Social determinants of health inequalities', *Lancet* 365(9464) (2005), 1099–104, 1099.

[4]   M. Whitehead, 'The concepts and principles of equity and health', *International Journal of Health Services* 22 (1992), 429.

[5]   UN Committee on Economic, Social and Cultural Rights (ICESCR Committee), General Comment No. 14 on the Right to the Highest Attainable Standard of Health, UN Doc. E/C.12/2000/4, para. 4.

[6]   Ibid., para. 19.

individuals' health conditions.[7] Consequently, while the state must pursue and enable full realisation of the highest attainable standard of health, there may be factors outside its control, and the individual may, consequently, also have some responsibility in regard to his or her own health.[8]

Despite the high ambitions, only a few – if any – countries have succeeded in combating health inequalities.[9] Research shows that, even in welfare states (for example, the Nordic countries), which are committed to providing universal access to healthcare services, either for free, or with minimal out-of-pocket payment, there are still significant socio-economically determined differences in life expectancy.[10] According to Mackenbach, it seems that, although reasonable levels of social security and public services are necessary conditions for smaller inequalities in health, these are not sufficient, and he describes this as a 'paradox'.[11] It is, indeed, puzzling that inequalities persist, even in wealthy countries with universal welfare systems. Mackenbach suggests that lifestyle-related risk factors may play an important role in the number of premature deaths in some high-income countries, and that poor lifestyles appear to contribute to the persistence of inequalities in mortality in Western Europe (see Chapter 13).[12] However, he also elaborates on other explanations for persisting inequalities in high-income countries, maintaining that welfare states have never aspired to more radical socio-economic redistribution. The modern welfare state has softened some of the sharper consequences of socio-economic segmentation in societies, which has led, for example, to reduced actual and relative poverty, but it has only 'marginally affected the many underlying mechanisms and structural factors'.[13] Consequently, Mackenbach concludes that persisting health inequalities are more than merely a consequence of social inequalities. Health inequities are also an outcome of, for example, power relations (such as competition for scarce resources), and he stresses that health inequity is both a product of such power relations, and a factor that serves, in itself, to reinforce and amplify social

---

[7]   Ibid., para. 9.

[8]   S. Vallgårda, M.E.J. Nielsen, M. Hartlev and P. Sandøe, 'Backward- and forward-looking responsibility for obesity: policies from WHO, the EU and England', *European Journal of Public Health* 25(5) (2015), 845.

[9]   For a comprehensive discussion regarding Council of Europe and EU initiatives, and the situation in a number of European countries, see, further, B. Toebes, 'Socioeconomic Health Inequalities in Europe – The Role of Law and Human Rights' in D. Ohrenlicher and T. K. Hervey (eds.), *The Oxford Handbook on Comparative Health Law*, New York: OUP: 2022, 171–87.

[10]   J.P. Mackenbach, 'The persistence of inequalities in modern welfare states: The explanation of a paradox', *Social Science & Medicine* 75 (2012), 761.

[11]   J.P. Mackenbach, 'Review article: Persistence of social inequalities in modern welfare states: The explanation of a paradox', *Scandinavian Journal of Public Health* 45 (2017), 113.

[12]   J.P. Mackenbach, 'The persistence of inequalities in modern welfare states: The explanation of a paradox', *Social Science & Medicine* 75 (2012), 761.

[13]   J.P. Mackenbach, 'Review article: Persistence of social inequalities in modern welfare states: The explanation of a paradox', *Scandinavian Journal of Public Health* 45 (2017), 113.

inequalities in various ways.[14] Ultimately, it becomes a vicious cycle – a poverty trap – where poor lifestyle, for example in terms of smoking, unhealthy food consumption, low levels of physical activity, and (to some extent) alcohol intake, is shaped by socio-economic factors, which leads to poor health and, thus, to increased inequalities. The same pattern often applies to people with disabilities, or of a specific gender, age, ethnicity or nationality, who may face difficulties in accessing work, education, housing or other amenities, and end up in a poverty trap, where poor social conditions lead to poor health, which then, in turn, amplifies their unfortunate socio-economic conditions.

The ICESCR Committee has demonstrated awareness of socio-economic inequalities, for example in a number of concluding observations, and has indicated that socio-economic differences may be unacceptable from a human rights perspective, especially in regard to disadvantaged groups.[15] The Committee has, for example, raised concerns regarding the widening of health inequalities among social classes in the United Kingdom, and has recommended that the 'State party intensifies its efforts to overcome the health inequalities and unequal access to health care, in particular for the most disadvantaged and marginalized individuals and groups'.[16] General Comment No. 14 also stresses that special attention should be paid to ensuring equal access to healthcare for the most disadvantaged,[17] and the UN Special Rapporteur on the Right to Health has addressed this in a report demanding that 'outreach (and other) programs must be in place to ensure that disadvantaged individuals and communities enjoy, in practice, the same access as those who are more advantaged'.[18] This is aligned with the UN 2030 Agenda for Sustainable Development, which is determined to fight poverty in all its forms, and everywhere,[19] and explicitly articulates the ambitions to ensure that no one is left behind, and to reach the furthest-behind first.[20] The pledge to focus on the furthest-behind relates variously to nations, peoples and all segments of society, and is important because it addresses multidimensional forms of health inequities.

---

14   Ibid.
15   G. MacNaughton, 'Untangling equality and non-discrimination to promote the right to health for all', *Health and Human Rights Journal* 11(2) (2009), 47.
16   ICESCR Committee, 'Concluding Observations of the Committee on Economic, Social and Cultural Rights, United Kingdom', UN Doc. No. E/C.12/GBR/CO/5 (2009), para. 32.
17   UN Committee on Economic, Social and Cultural Rights (ICESCR Committee), General Comment No. 14 on the Right to the Highest Attainable Standard of Health, UN Doc. E/C.12/2000/4, para. 19.
18   P. Hunt, UN Human Rights Council, Report of the Special Rapporteur on the Right of Everyone to the Enjoyment of the Highest Attainable Standard of Physical and Mental Health, 31 January 2008, A/HRC/7/11, para. 42.
19   UN, 'Transforming our world. The 2030 Agenda for Sustainable Development' (Resolution adopted by the General Assembly on 25 September 2015) A/70/L.1., Goal no. 1.
20   Ibid. paras. 3–4.

3. EQUAL ACCESS

According to the UN International Covenant on Economic Social and Cultural Rights (ICESCR) Article 12(1), States Parties must, at a systemic level, 'recognize the right of *everyone* to the enjoyment of the highest standard of health' (emphasis added). This is further stressed in Article 12(2), which contains the States Parties' obligation to guarantee the rights '*without discrimination* of any kind as to race, color, sex, language, religion, political or other opinion, national or social origin, property, birth or other status' (emphasis added). General Comment No. 14, furthermore, stresses the importance of ensuring '*equality of opportunity* for people to enjoy the highest attainable level of health',[21] and the obligation to provide '*equal* and timely access to basic preventative, curative and rehabilitative health services'[22] (emphasis added). The same commitment to equal access is reflected in the Council of Europe Convention on Human Rights and Biomedicine, which emphasises the obligation of States Parties to provide '*equitable access* to healthcare services of appropriate quality' (emphasis added),[23] and, more generally, in Article 21 of the EU Charter on Fundamental Rights, which prohibits 'any discrimination based on any ground such as sex, race, colour, ethnic or social origin, genetic features, language, religion or belief, political or any other opinion, membership of a national minority, property, birth, disability, age or sexual orientation'.[24]

These obligations are simultaneously challenging and nebulous. They provide a legal framework for the organisation of national healthcare services that, in principle, requires all states to ensure equality in access to healthcare services. However, at the same time, it is obvious that few – if any – states ensure completely equal access to healthcare. Some patients may, for various reasons, have access to more services than others. Consequently, the question posed to human rights law is whether the obligation to provide equal access to health requires that governments create healthcare systems where everybody has access to exactly the same kind of services – no more and no less. To answer this question, it is necessary, first, to look into the understanding of the concepts of equality and non-discrimination in human rights law generally (see Chapter 3 of this book). Secondly, it also requires a discussion of whether equality relates to

---

21   UN Committee on Economic, Social and Cultural Rights (ICESCR Committee), General Comment No. 14 on the Right to the Highest Attainable Standard of Health, UN Doc. E/C.12/2000/4, para. 8.

22   Ibid., para. 17.

23   Council of Europe, Convention on the Protection of Human Rights and Dignity of the Human Being with regard to the Application of Biology and Medicine: Convention on Human Rights and Biomedicine, opened for signatures 4 April 1997, ETS no. 164.

24   European Union, Charter of Fundamental Rights of the European Union [2010] OJ (C83) 389, Art. 21.

core obligations only, or moves beyond these to cover any kind of health service (see also Chapter 2 of this book).

As to the first question, it is generally recognised that human rights law suffers from an unclear notion of how equality and non-discrimination are to be understood. MacNaughton points out that there are various understandings of equality rights, and that it is necessary to clarify who and what the subjects of equality are.[25] There is, for example, a distinction between equality at a personal level – 'one-to-one equality' – and 'block equality', where equality is required between groups (blocks) of persons, for example between men and women. The right to vote, and freedom of speech, are examples of 'one-to-one' equality rights: they belong to everybody. In contrast, 'block equality' is not concerned with equality within the block, as long as the block, as such, is not exposed to differential treatment compared to another block. Examples of blocks are reflected in the list of statuses in human rights law that cannot legitimately justify differential treatment (for example, gender, race, religion etc.) (see Chapter 8 of this book). One-to-one equality normally applies within *civil and political rights*, where it is supplemented with block equality to ensure, for example, that men and women have equal rights to vote, or to freedom of speech. Block equality is normally applied within *economic and social rights* to address differences between different groups in access to socio-economic rights. Block equality can, for example, be used to assess the legitimacy of differences in health status among various ethnic population groups, or between nationals and migrant populations. However, according to MacNaughton, it is rare to see block equality supplemented by one-to-one equality when assessing access to socio-economic rights. This leaves the principle of equality somewhat disabled within the sphere of socio-economic rights, as there is no real tool to address differences in access to healthcare services, at a personal level, between persons within the same block.

Consequently, even though it seems that human rights law provides a solid legal basis for claiming equality and non-discrimination in the right to health across population groups belonging to different statuses or classes, it may not be well equipped to address other sorts of inequalities in access to healthcare services. As mentioned above, in many countries some patients will have access to additional or higher-level services than others, because they can afford to pay for treatment at private clinics, or to go abroad to receive treatment that is not available in their own country.[26] Such two-tiered healthcare systems cannot necessarily be criticised from a block-equality perspective. However, they could

---

[25]   G. MacNaughton, 'Untangling equality and non-discrimination to promote the right to health for all', *Health and Human Rights Journal* 11(2) (2009), 47.

[26]   M. Hartlev, 'Equal Access to Healthcare on a Non-Discriminatory basis: Reality or Aspiration?', *European Journal of Health Law* 20(4) (2013), 343.

still be perceived as problematic from a human rights perspective. The UN Special Rapporteur on the Right to Health has, for example, raised concerns regarding liberalisation of trade in healthcare services, arguing that, even though 'increased trade in health services could increase available resources and improve the state of healthcare in some cases, it could also lead to regressions in enjoyment of the right to health'. This could lead 'to a two-tier health system that caters to the healthy and wealthy rather than the poor and sick', and 'generate[s] increased discrimination in the provision of health services – particularly discrimination on the basis of social status – and a withdrawal of resources from the poor towards the wealthy'.[27]

At the same time, single-tier universal healthcare systems have also been subject to legal scrutiny. In the landmark *Chaoulli* case, the Canadian Supreme Court addressed the legitimacy of provincial restrictions on private health insurance systems that gave insurers easier access to services covered by the public healthcare package in situations where there were long waiting times for access to care.[28] In a tight ruling (four to three), the majority reached the conclusion that the legal restrictions on private health insurance systems in the province of Quebec were not in accordance with the Quebec Charter of Human Rights and Freedoms, and the Charter's protection of the right to life and security of the person, in situations where there were long waiting times for treatment. Consequently, the majority gave more weight to the individual right to life, health and security than the goal of equal access to health, at population level. This issue has also been tested in later cases, and most recently in the *Cambie* case, where the Supreme Court of British Columbia issued a ruling finding restrictions on private health insurance systems in the provincial Medicare Protection Act not to be in violation of the Canadian Charter of Rights and Freedoms. Acknowledging that long waiting times could have an impact on the right to life, liberty and security laid down in Article 7 of the Charter, the judge found that it had not been 'established that the right to security of the person has been deprived contrary to the principles of fundamental justice'.[29] The decision is now under appeal to the Canadian Supreme Court. The Canadian Medicare system seems to promote notions of one-to-one equality, but – as demonstrated by the cases above – there is a risk that restrictions on the individual liberty to access care outside of the established system may engage issues related to the rights to life and health.

To sum up, it seems that human rights law is struggling with the application of one-to-one equality in relation to socio-economic rights. In conflicts between

---

27 P. Hunt, UN Economic and Social Council, 'Report of the Special Rapporteur, Paul Hunt, Addendum: Mission to the World Trade Organisation', E/CN.4/2004/49/Add.1.

28 *Chaoulli v. Quebec*, Attorney General (2005) 1 SCR 791.

29 *Cambie Surgeries Corporation v. British Columbia* (Attorney General) BCSC 2020, 1310, para. 8.

the right to non-discrimination and equality in access to healthcare services, on the one hand, and the right to life, on the other hand, the civil and political right may have priority, and prohibit governmentally induced restrictions on access to treatments for individuals who can afford to pay for access to additional and higher-level treatments than others.

Another important issue relates to the ability of the group-equality principle, *in practice*, to provide legal protection against discrimination in access to health. It has, for example, been documented that gender, ethnic background and disability have impacts on equal access to healthcare services, and that these impacts may even be multiplied when these factors are linked together.[30] This issue is addressed more substantially in Chapters 9 and 10 of this book. Likewise, sexual orientation may also have an impact on access to healthcare services. A recent survey showed that 16 per cent of LGBTI persons felt discriminated against when accessing healthcare services.[31] This confirms previous research showing that LGBT persons, and especially transgender persons, often experience differential treatment in relation to healthcare services, including difficulties in accessing treatment.[32] Migrant status is also an example of a lack of group equality, and undocumented migrants, in particular, suffer from unequal access to healthcare (see, further, Chapter 8 of this book).

The obligation to provide equality of opportunity must also be seen in the context of *core obligations*, and the basic level of healthcare services that each States Party is expected to provide, in order to fulfil their obligations to respect the right to the highest attainable standard of health (see Chapter 2 above). This is explored below (in section 4), with a focus on *limited access*. In this section, however, it will be discussed whether the principle of 'equality of opportunity' has a stronger foothold when it comes to the core obligations.

General Comment No. 14 touches upon this aspect, when it refers to the special obligations of States Parties 'to provide those who do not have sufficient means with the necessary health insurance and health-care facilities, and to prevent any discrimination on internationally prohibited grounds in the provision of healthcare and health services, *especially with respect to the core obligations* of the right to health' (emphasis added).[33] It is also stressed that

---

[30] European Union Agency for Fundamental Rights, 'Inequalities and multiple discrimination in access to and quality of healthcare services', Publication Office of the European Union, DOI: 10.2811/17523, (2013).

[31] European Union Agency for Fundamental Rights, 'EU LGBTI II – A Long Way to Go for LGBTI Equality', Publication Office of the European Union, DOI: 10.2811/582402, (2020).

[32] European Union Agency for Fundamental Rights, 'EU LGBT Survey – European Union lesbian, gay, bisexual and transgender survey – Main results', Publication Office of the European Union, DOI: 10.2811/37969, (2014).

[33] UN Committee on Economic, Social and Cultural Rights (ICESCR Committee), General Comment No. 14 on the Right to the Highest Attainable Standard of Health, UN Doc. E/C.12/2000/4, para. 19.

inappropriate allocation of resources can lead to invisible discrimination, and that 'investments should not disproportionately favor expensive curative health services which are often accessible only to a small, privileged fraction of the population, rather than primary and preventive healthcare benefiting a far larger part of the population.[34] Consequently, it seems that equal access is of special importance for access to *core services*.

This raises the question of what exactly constitutes the core services. As discussed in Chapter 2 above, General Comment No. 14 provides a list of core obligations, which include access to health facilities, goods and services, including access to essential drugs, and a number of social determinants (for example, freedom from hunger, and access to a minimum level of essential, nutritionally adequate and safe food, safe and potable water, and basic shelter and sanitation).[35] In addition, it lists a number of obligations of 'comparable importance', such as access to reproductive, maternal and child healthcare, immunisation against major infectious diseases, and prevention, treatment and control of epidemic diseases.[36] Overall, there should be a right of access to health facilities, goods and services on a non-discriminatory basis, especially for vulnerable groups (see also Chapter 8 below). Vulnerable groups are also mentioned in the ICESCR Committee's General Comment No. 3 on 'The nature of States Parties' Obligations', which stipulates that 'even in times of severe resource constraints, the vulnerable members of society must be protected by the adoption of relatively low-cost targeted programmes'.[37] Consequently, the human rights framework presupposes that core obligations exist in regard to the right to health, but does not provide complete clarity regarding the content and scope of these obligations.

All in all, it seems that the human rights framework is rather nebulous when it comes to understanding what equality of opportunity and equal access to healthcare services actually imply. It is clear that all States Parties must fulfil their core obligations, and also that they should pay attention to the distribution of resources in the healthcare sector, to ensure that resources are available for the entire population, and especially for the vulnerable parts thereof. However, it

---

34 Ibid. See also P. Hunt, UN Human Rights Council, Report of the Special Rapporteur on the Right of Everyone to the Enjoyment of the Highest Attainable Standard of Physical and Mental Health, 31 January 2008, A/HRC/7/11, para. 42; D. Puras, UN General Assembly, 'Report of the Special Rapporteur on the right of everyone to the enjoyment of the highest attainable standard of physical and mental health', 5 August 2016, A/71/304, para. 44.

35 UN Committee on Economic, Social and Cultural Rights (ICESCR Committee), General Comment No. 14 on the Right to the Highest Attainable Standard of Health, UN Doc. E/C.12/2000/4, para. 43.

36 Ibid., para. 44.

37 UN Committee on Economic, Social and Cultural Rights (ICESCR Committee), General Comment No. 3, The nature of States' Parties Obligations (Art. 2, para. 1 of the Covenant), (Fifth session, 1990), U.N. Doc. E/1991/23, annex III at 86 (1991), s. 12.

is not clear when it comes to inequities in health in respect of services beyond the core obligations. Furthermore, it is acknowledged that the States Parties cannot take responsibility for all cases of ill health, as there may be causes of ill health that are outside their control. To what extent this means that the individual herself also has obligations that relieve the States Parties from their obligations is not clarified. The discussion above demonstrates that health equity is an intricate issue, and equality must – in the words of Yamin – be seen as 'a multi-faceted and complex, contextually bound concept'.[38]

What is clear, however, is that the human rights notion of equality does not seem to substantially target social injustices in access to health. According to Chapman, human rights law 'is concerned with disparities in the enjoyment of rights rather than differentials in social position, access to resources, and political power'.[39] MacNaughton is more nuanced in her assessment. She sees potential for the human rights framework to support more substantial equality, but, at the same time, she acknowledges that equality and non-discrimination are often conflated into the single notion of 'block equality'. Yamin adds a further dimension to this by pointing out that 'health is a reflection of power relations as much as biological or behavioural factors'. Her suggestion is to use human rights frameworks to 'denaturaliz[e] the inequalities that pervade our societies and our world', and to insist on all individuals' rights including a claim to redress when treated unfairly, and, furthermore, for individuals to be entitled to a right to participate in determining what equity and equality require, in a given context.[40] The power dimension in the distribution of health and health resources reflected in the health and human rights literature is aligned with Mackenbach's observation that the modern welfare state has never had an ambition of radical socio-economic redistribution, and that persisting health disparities are also an outcome of power relations.[41]

4. LIMITATIONS ON ACCESS TO HEALTH

Access to healthcare will always be restricted for one reason or another. One important reason for this is *resource restraint*. In both poor and affluent countries, it is impossible to ensure unlimited access to healthcare services, including the

---

[38] A.E. Yamin, 'Shades of dignity: Exploring the demands of equality in applying human rights frameworks to health', *Health and Human Rights Journal* 11(2) (2009), 1.

[39] A.R. Chapman, 'The social determinants of health, health equity, and human rights', *Health and Human Rights Journal* 12(2) (2010), 17.

[40] A.E. Yamin, 'Shades of dignity: Exploring the demands of equality in applying human rights frameworks to health', *Health and Human Rights Journal* 11(2) (2009), 1.

[41] J.P. Mackenbach, 'Review article: Persistence of social inequalities in modern welfare states: The explanation of a paradox', *Scandinavian Journal of Public Health* 45 (2017), 113.

most advanced and costly medicines and treatments.[42] Other limitations may relate to cultural, ethical and religious traditions, for example in connection with access to reproductive technologies, including abortion. Such limitations must be human rights-compliant, and selected aspects of this will be discussed below.

4.1. LIMITATIONS JUSTIFIED BY RESOURCE RESTRAINTS

As already touched upon in the previous section, equal access to healthcare services is especially important when it comes to the core obligations. However, it may be necessary for healthcare systems to prioritise healthcare resources, both when providing the core services and those beyond the core services. Prioritisation takes place both at a structural level (allocation of resources to different kinds of services within the healthcare sector), and at an individual level (allocation of healthcare services to individual patients). In both situations, it is important that priority-setting is compliant with human rights principles.

During the COVID-19 pandemic, issues of priority-setting, at both a structural and individual level, have come to the forefront, both when allocating patients to emergency facilities (including ventilators), and in vaccination programmes. The pandemic has demonstrated how challenging it is to manoeuvre and make priority decisions in an emergency situation.[43] However, it has also made priority-setting criteria more transparent and open for discussion. States Parties are, for example, obliged to respect, protect and fulfil the right to life, which speaks in favour of prioritising patients with the greatest immediate risk of losing their lives to COVID-19. However, there may be other persons whose lives are at risk, or will be in the longer run: for instance, those who were not timeously diagnosed with cancer, because most resources were directed at COVID-19 patients; persons with mental disorders who developed severe illnesses; and women and children who were locked down with violent family members.

Priority-setting in healthcare is a challenging and intriguing issue, from both an ethical and a legal point of view. Rationing of healthcare services can be both

---

[42] A.E. Yamin and O.F. Norheim, 'Taking Equality Seriously: Applying Human Rights Frameworks to Priority Settings in Health', *Human Rights Quarterly* 36(2) (2014), 296–324, 300.

[43] See, e.g. European Committee of Social Rights, 'Statement of Interpretation on the Right to Protection of Health in Times of Pandemic', adopted by the Committee on 21 April 2020; K. Ó Cathaoir, 'Human Rights and Health in Times of Pandemics: Necessity and proportionality' in M. Kjaerum, M.F. Davis and A. Lyons (eds.), *COVID-19 and Human Rights*, London and New York: Routledge, 2021; L. Montel, A Kapilashrami, M.P. Coleman, and C. Allemani, 'The Right to Health in Times of Pandemic: What Can We Learn from the UK's Response to the COVID-19 Outbreak?', *Health and Human Rights Journal* 22(2) (2020), 227. See also Chapter 13 of this book.

explicit, for example when specific services are identified as part of the public health programme, or *implicit*, when rationing relates to individuals' economic or other means of access to healthcare services. According to General Comment No. 14, the human right to health requires that health facilities, goods and services must be affordable for all, and that payment for such services 'must be based on the principle of equity, ensuring that these services, whether privately or publicly provided, are affordable for all, including socially disadvantaged groups. Equity demands that poorer households should not be disproportionately burdened with health expenses as compared to richer households'.[44] Consequently, implicit rationing is problematic from a health and human rights perspective. Indeed, General Comment No. 14 specifically requires States Parties (as part of their core obligations) to 'adopt and implement a national public health strategy and plan of action, on the basis of epidemiological evidence, addressing the health concerns of the whole population; the strategy and plan of action shall be devised, and periodically reviewed, on the basis of a participatory and transparent process; they shall include methods, such as right to health indicators and benchmarks, by which progress can be closely monitored; the process by which the strategy and plan of action are devised, as well as their content, shall give particular attention to all vulnerable or marginalized groups'.[45] This indicates, first, that *implicit prioritisation*, where access to healthcare services depends on an individual's economic means, is not acceptable. Secondly, it makes it clear that *explicit prioritisation* must be evidence-based, to ensure the effectiveness of services, and that priority-setting must take the whole population into consideration, while paying special attention to marginalised and vulnerable groups. Furthermore, transparency and inclusion in the development of a national health plan must be ensured, and plans must be closely monitored and revised.

This is a difficult exercise, loaded with ethical dilemmas, which requires careful balancing of incommensurable interests and rights. For example, how should governments balance between very costly, but necessary, life-saving therapies for a few patients and relatively cheap treatments for a much larger group of patients suffering from, for example, rheumatism? Should priority be given to saving the lives of the few, or to relieving pains and enhancing quality of life for a much larger group?

Priority-setting in healthcare is normally based on a combined assessment of the *severity of the disease* (if untreated), the *effectiveness of the treatment* and *cost effectiveness*.[46] When supplemented with general non-discrimination principles, this can support human rights-compliant priority-setting in healthcare.

---

[44] UN Committee on Economic, Social and Cultural Rights (ICESCR Committee), General Comment No. 14 on the Right to the Highest Attainable Standard of Health, UN Doc. E/C.12/2000/4, para. 12(b).

[45] Ibid., para. 43(f).

[46] A.E. Yamin and O.F. Norheim, 'Taking Equality Seriously: Applying Human Rights Frameworks to Priority Settings in Health', *Human Rights Quarterly* 36(2) (2014), 296–324, 314.

Different approaches to prioritisation have been tested, at a structural level, by using systems such as QALY (quality-adjusted life years), where the impact of an intervention can be calculated, based on an assessment of the patient's quality of life after treatment. Elements of QALY are used in most healthcare systems to make decisions, at a structural level, regarding distribution of resources to various kinds of treatment. This process includes assessment of the evidence for the efficiency of various health interventions, together with assessments, for example based on surveys among patients and other laypersons, regarding the quality of life associated with specific interventions. Seen from a public health and societal perspective, this is a helpful tool to allocate scarce resources in an efficient manner. However, from a human rights perspective, such mechanistic calculations risk losing the perspective of the individual. For instance, how is it possible to calculate the quality of life experienced by an individual, based on averages derived from the results of a general survey? Concerns have also been expressed from a disability rights perspective, as QALY calculations tend to prioritise the treatment of people with very low levels of disability, because the underlying assumption is that the lives of people with disabilities are presumed to be of less value than those without disabilities. Consequently, when making prioritisations at a structural level, it is important to comply with the requirements articulated in General Comment No. 14, and to address the health concerns of the whole population, paying particular attention to all vulnerable or marginalised groups.[47]

When making prioritisations at a structural level, it is also important to carefully consider whether it is possible to ensure similar treatment of similar cases. In this context, Yamin and Norheim mention the *Soobramoney* case, where the South African Constitutional Court accepted a provincial government's decision to deny extremely expensive dialysis care to a patient because it would be impossible to provide the same treatment for other patients in need.[48] Consequently, the principle of equality must be ingrained in any priority-setting system.

Although the guidelines for prioritisation of healthcare resources articulated in General Comment No. 14 provide a useful point of departure, they still leave some issues unresolved, especially concerning prioritisation between individual patients or groups of patients. In their article on applying a human

---

47   UN Committee on Economic, Social and Cultural Rights (ICESCR Committee), General Comment No. 14 on the Right to the Highest Attainable Standard of Health, UN Doc. E/C.12/2000/4, para. 12(b).

48   A.E. Yamin and O.F. Norheim, 'Taking Equality Seriously: Applying Human Rights Frameworks to Priority Settings in Health', *Human Rights Quarterly* 36(2) (2014), 296–324, 322. See also *Soobramoney v. Minister of Health (KwaZulu-Natal)* 1998 (1) SA 765 (CC) (S. Afr.).

rights framework to priority-setting in healthcare, Yamin and Norheim mention prioritisation based on age as an example where it could be ethically relevant to prioritise younger people, to ensure intergenerational equity, even though age is an illegitimate criterion from a human rights perspective. We have recently witnessed this during the COVID-19 pandemic, where, for example, guidelines issued by the ethics section of the Italian Society of Anesthesia, Analgesia, Resuscitation, and Intensive Care (SIAARTI) referred to age as a criterion for selecting patients for intensive care in extraordinary situations.[49] This has led to an important debate about the acceptability of ageism in healthcare prioritisation. Here, again, a balanced approach is needed, and Yamin and Norheim provide an important input for this discussion when they refer to the 'fair innings' argument. According to this, every person should receive sufficient healthcare to provide them with the opportunity to live in good health for a normal span of years. Consequently, they stress that '[a]n adequate rights framework, therefore, can neither consign certain groups to being expendable nor ignore intergenerational equity including the equal opportunity of younger cohorts of people to live as long as older people already have'.[50] This example demonstrates the difficulties in applying a human rights-based approach in an area where 'equality of opportunity' for all individuals concerned involves interests that are impossible to reconcile with one another.

As already mentioned, prioritisation of scarce healthcare resources is a very challenging endeavour for all governments. Human rights have an important role to play in this context, by insisting on a human-centred approach, demanding equality of access, and paying special attention to weak and vulnerable parts of the population. However, in situations concerned with distribution of resources between individuals or groups of patients in need, human rights may not be able to give clear answers. What a human rights-based approach will still be able to offer, however, is the importance of transparency, and the inclusion of patients and citizens in deliberations regarding how to balance interests, and distribute healthcare services fairly.[51]

---

[49]   Società Italiana di Anestesia, Analgesia, Rianimazione e Terapia Intensiva (SIAARTI), 'Clinical Ethics Recommendations for the Allocation of Intensive Care Treatments in exceptional, resource-limited circumstances', published 16 March 2020. See https://d1c2gz5q23tkk0. cloudfront.net/assets/uploads/3017015/asset/SIAARTI_-_Covid-19_-_Clinical_Ethics_ Reccomendations.pdf?1606745893.

[50]   A.E. Yamin and O.F. Norheim, 'Taking Equality Seriously: Applying Human Rights Frameworks to Priority Settings in Health', *Human Rights Quarterly* 36(2) (2014), 296–324, 315.

[51]   A.E. Yamin and O.F. Norheim, 'Taking Equality Seriously: Applying Human Rights Frameworks to Priority Settings in Health', *Human Rights Quarterly* 36(2) (2014), 296–324, 324.

4.2. LIMITATIONS JUSTIFIED BY CULTURAL, ETHICAL OR RELIGIOUS TRADITIONS OR SOCIETAL CONCERNS

Limitations on access may also result from factors other than resource restraints. Chapters 10 and 11 of this book explore the legal frameworks for types of healthcare service that are considered especially sensitive from an ethical and religious perspective, and Chapter 12 deals with new digital health technologies, which have also raised controversies, and prompted new regulations. Apart from these topics, there may be other, more general, societal (including public health) concerns justifying certain restrictions on access to healthcare services. Some countries, for example, have regulations regarding cosmetic treatments that restrict such interventions to certain age groups (typically adults), or prohibit specific kinds of treatments. Regulation of organ donation may also restrict, for example, *in vivo* donation to family members. Gender-reassignment treatments are another area where national law imposes restrictions based on medical, ethical and cultural concerns. And there may also be restrictions on the accessibility of new experimental treatments of unproven value for patients, even where there are potential patients willing to run the risk of unknown and severe side effects because they see such forms of treatment as their last resort.

Individual rights to control the end of life, including access to euthanasia, as well as access to reproductive assistance, are examples of healthcare services for which there is no uniform position in countries across the globe. These are also issues where it is possible both to claim that these practices involve infringement of human rights,[52] and the opposite – that restrictions on personal autonomy and the right to self-determination amount to human rights violations.[53] The ECtHR has, in a number of cases, taken the position that there is a wide margin of appreciation left to States Parties for issuing national regulation on, for example, end-of-life decisions and reproductive issues. But States Parties' discretion is not unfettered.[54] First of all, some practices may actually violate an individual's human rights. For example, the Court has stressed several times that the right to life of the pregnant woman must be respected. Secondly, when developing legislation, it must be consistent. The Court has, for example, overturned regulatory restrictions on couples having access to pre-implantation genetic

---

[52]   See, e.g. ECtHR 5 June 2015, *Lambert et al. v. France* (GC), no. 46043/14 (end of life); EComHR 13 May 1980, *X v. the United Kingdom* (also known as *Paton v. UK*), no. 8416/79 (reproductive autonomy).

[53]   See, e.g. ECtHR 29 April 2002, *Pretty v. the United Kingdom*, no. 2346/02 (assisted suicide); ECtHR 3 November 2011, *S.H. v. Austria*, no. 57813/00 (access to reproductive services).

[54]   For a more in-depth discussion, and references to case law, see, further, Chapters 10 and 11 of this book.

testing of an embryo, because national law accepted prenatal examination of foetuses and, subsequently, access to abortion for genetic conditions.[55] Hence, the Court found the Italian legislation to lack consistency. A similar argument of inconsistency was used by the Chamber in *S.H. v. Austria*, where the Chamber found it unjustified that Austrian law did not accept the combination of two techniques for infertility treatment that were accepted if used separately.[56] However, in this case, the argument was overturned by the Grand Chamber, which found it justified (and proportionate) to prohibit the use of the two techniques in combination.[57] The concerns for legislative consistency articulated in these cases reflect the importance of the equality and non-discrimination principles, but also the difficulties in applying the principle in areas of ethical controversy, where governments have a wider margin of appreciation.

Restrictions in national law regarding end-of-life decisions and reproductive healthcare services are often based on religious, ethical or cultural reasons. However, there may also be other reasons involved. Governments may wish to protect vulnerable persons against their own decisions, typically in situations where they may feel under pressure, or restrictions may serve the purpose of balancing the interests of several individuals, or be justified by more general public concerns.

Restrictions aimed at protecting individuals against their own decisions can be challenged from a human rights perspective, on the ground of not showing sufficient respect for an individual's dignity and capacity to make autonomous decisions (see Chapter 3 above). The ECtHR has considered such regulation to be a violation of the right to a private and family life laid down in Article 8 of the ECHR, but, at the same time, found the restrictions justified according to Article 8(2). For example, in *Pretty v. UK*[58] the Court argued that the condition of terminally ill individuals may vary, but that many would be vulnerable, and that 'it is the vulnerability of the class which provides the rationale for the law in question' (making assisted suicide a criminal offence). Even though the applicant in this case, based on an individual assessment, would not have been characterised as 'vulnerable', the Court found that it was justified for states to assess whether an absolute rule was the most suitable to provide sufficient safeguards to protect the life and safety of vulnerable persons, and 'especially those who are not in a condition to take informed decisions against acts intended to end life or to assist in ending life'. In this case, the Court did not question the capacity of the applicant to make autonomous decisions, but found

---

55   ECtHR 28 August 2012, *Costa and Pavan v. Italy*, no. 54270/10.
56   ECtHR 1 April 2010, *S.H. & Others v. Austria*, no. 57813/00.
57   ECtHR 3 November 2011, *S.H. & Others v. Austria* (GC), no. 57813/00.
58   ECtHR 29 April 2002, *Pretty v. the United Kingdom*, no. 2346/02, §74. See also ECtHR 20 January 2011, *Haas v. Switzerland*, no. 31322/07, paras. 54–58.

the general restrictions in national law justified in order to protect others who may be vulnerable and, therefore, not in a position to make a truly autonomous decision in an end of life situation.

Restrictions on access to healthcare services may also serve the purpose of mitigating potential conflicts of interest between two (or more) individuals. In *Evans v. UK*,[59] the Court found that a blanket rule requiring consent from both donors to the use of stored embryos was justified, and that 'the absolute nature of the rule served to promote legal certainty and to avoid the problems of arbitrariness and inconsistency inherent in weighing, on a case-by-case basis'. With this ruling, the Court also accepted the UK Government's claim that the legislation not only served the purpose of regulating a potential conflict between two individuals, but 'also served *wider, public interests* in upholding the principle of the primacy of consent promoting legal clarity and certainty' (emphasis added).

5. CONCLUSION

As will be clear from the above, access to healthcare services raises a number of complex issues that involve public health, socio-economic, ethical, and broader societal interests and concerns. Applying a human rights-based approach in this area is crucial but, at the same time, challenging. This chapter has focused on selected topics and perspectives, with equality of opportunity and equal access as cross-cutting themes. Due to the complexity of the subject, it is difficult to provide clear conclusions. It is clear that States Parties must fulfil their core obligations, but more uncertain what equality of opportunity implies, in respect of services beyond the core obligations. Similarly, it is clear that States Parties must pay special attention to weak and vulnerable parts of their populations when prioritising scarce resources. However, in situations concerned with the distribution of resources between individuals or groups of patients in need, it is less clear how to tackle this dilemma, from a human rights perspective. It leaves some unresolved questions, which need to be further explored. Due to the complexity of the interests and concerns involved, the author recommends that further analyses in this area should take a balanced approach, and ensure sufficient attention to the individual, who should always be at the centre of such analyses.

---

[59] ECtHR 10 April 2007, *Evans v. UK*, no. 6339/05, para. 89.

CHAPTER 8

VULNERABILITY AND AUTONOMY

Competing Ideas in Human Rights

Henriette Sinding Aasen

1. INTRODUCTION

Part III of this book examines the right to health in relation to so-called vulnerable groups. Therefore, the notion of vulnerability in human rights law and discourse, as well as its relation to other central human rights values and concepts, needs some clarification. The overall purposes of this chapter are to explore vulnerability as a concept and idea, the need to recognise human vulnerability in human rights protection relating to health, and the implications of this, with particular reference to children, and, finally, to illustrate some key aspects concerning vulnerability in relation to a selected group, namely migrants. The chapter starts out by introducing vulnerability, as both a common and particular human experience, and how this is reflected in human rights instruments (section 2). Thereafter, it explains vulnerability in relation to the human rights principle of non-discrimination (section 3), and the relation between the apparently competing ideas of vulnerability and individual autonomy (section 4). The next section briefly outlines the potential tension or conflict between health protection and respect for individual autonomy, and the challenge of balancing these values in various situations and contexts where human vulnerability is at stake (section 5). To achieve a deeper understanding of the usage of the vulnerability argument in human rights jurisprudence, the chapter explores the literature on case law from the European Court of Human Rights (ECtHR), drawing special attention to the concept of 'group vulnerability' and its potential stigmatising effect (section 6). The chapter argues that the capability theory, as developed by Amartya Sen and Martha Nussbaum, should be seen as a constructive and empowering supplement to vulnerability argumentation in human rights discourse (section 7). The last part of this chapter provides a case study on vulnerability in relation to health and migration, identifying common European legal structures and regulations that are causing vulnerability for, in particular, one group of migrants in relation to health and well-being: unauthorised or undocumented migrants, who are denied the possibility, and the capability, of living dignified and healthy lives (section 8). The chapter ends with some concluding remarks concerning state obligations relating to the health and rights protection of vulnerable groups (section 9).

2. THE VULNERABLE HUMAN BEING

The term 'vulnerable' originates from the Latin word *vulnus*, which means 'wound'.[1] As human beings, we are all vulnerable, as we may be wounded or harmed in different ways: physically, emotionally, socially, financially, and in our relations with others. We may be victims of violence, discrimination, accidents, natural disasters, pandemics, or diseases, but we are determined to reach old age before dying. As pointed out by Fineman, vulnerability is an inherent and constant aspect of the human condition,[2] applying to all human beings in all social and political systems. The common human experience of vulnerability makes human beings *equal* in a fundamental sense ('we are all humans'). Mary Neal summarises the literature on vulnerability in the following way:

> [V]ulnerability speaks to our universal capacity for suffering, in two ways. First, I am vulnerable because I depend upon the co-operation of others (including, importantly, the State) … Second, I am vulnerable because I am penetrable; I am permanently open and exposed to hurts and harms of various kinds.[3]

Although we are all vulnerable as human beings, experiences of vulnerability differ significantly. Several factors impact on the human experience of vulnerability, depending on the amount and quality of resources a person controls or has access to, and in terms of abilities, economic circumstances, social position, support and networks, education, health status and other considerations, and, of course, the country they live in and the sociopolitical context, legal regulations and institutions shaping both the possibilities and limitations of their lives.[4] As children, we depend on parents or other adults to take care of us. Everyone

---

[1]   Lourdes Peroni and Alexandra Timmer, 'Vulnerable groups: The promise of an emerging concept in European Human Rights Convention law', *International Journal of Constitutional Law* 11(4) (2013), 1056–085, 1058, https://doi.org/10.1093/icon/mot042.

[2]   Martha Albertson Fineman, 'Equality, Autonomy, and the Vulnerable Subject in Law and Politics' in Martha Albertson Fineman and Anna Grear (eds.), *Vulnerability: Reflections on a New Ethical Foundation for Law and Politics*, Ashgate, 2013, 13–29.

[3]   Mary Neal, '"Not Gods but Animals": Human Dignity and Vulnerable Subjecthood' *Liverpool Law Review* 33 (2012), 177, 186–87, quoted from Peroni and Timmer, 'Vulnerable groups: The promise of an emerging concept in European Human Rights Convention law', 1058.

[4]   Fineman, 'Equality, Autonomy, and the Vulnerable Subject in Law and Politics', 22–24.

will need healthcare during his or her lifetime, especially in old age. Human beings also depend on educational institutions for the provision of skills and knowledge to prepare them for work and social participation. Part of the human condition is that everyone, during his or her lifetime, will be dependent on others, and on society, to survive; to be free from oppression, fear and want; to realise our potential; and to have a dignified and meaningful role in society.

Since vulnerability is a universal aspect of the human condition, it seems somewhat misplaced to point out particular *groups* as vulnerable. Clearly, there are dangers associated with a group-based approach to vulnerability, in terms of generalisation and stereotyping (see section 6.2.3 below). However, on the other hand, it is also clear that certain individual and social factors indicate that some people are more vulnerable than others. In relation to health, having a status as a migrant, and especially being an *undocumented* migrant, indicates vulnerability, since a person without legal residence status will usually face serious barriers in accessing the health care system. The situation of the undocumented migrant creates a particular form of vulnerability not faced by other persons living within a jurisdiction. Therefore, this book builds on a more recent development in legal discourse, which argues that the general understanding of human beings as potentially vulnerable throughout their lives must be supplemented by more specific analyses of, and responses to, the particular vulnerability of certain groups.[5]

The Universal Declaration of Human Rights (UDHR)[6] provides both a general and a group-based conceptualisation of human vulnerability. It was conceptualised and adopted as a global response to the horrors of two world wars, where millions of ordinary people suffered and died as victims of war hostilities, hunger, poverty, and a lack of access to essential goods and services, including healthcare. Furthermore, the unimaginable actions of cruelty against certain groups (especially Jews, Gypsies and persons with disabilities and mental illnesses)[7] called for a particular non-discrimination principle, guaranteeing the basic rights of everyone. The preamble of the UDHR states the fundamental values and aspirations of the declaration:

> recognition of the inherent dignity and of the equal and inalienable rights of all members of the human family is the foundation of freedom, justice and peace in the world.

Being the first human rights instrument in modern times, the UDHR speaks clearly of human vulnerability, proclaiming human rights, in its preamble,

---

[5]   See below, in section 6.

[6]   Adopted by the United Nations, 10 December 1948.

[7]   See Robert Jay Lifton, *The Nazi Doctors. Medical Killing and the Psychology of Genocide*, Basic Books, 1986; Robert A. Burt, 'The suppressed legacy of Nuremberg', *Hastings Center Report* 26(5) (1996), 30–34.

'as a common standard of achievement for all peoples and all nations'. The objective of this 'common standard' of basic rights is to secure international protection for humans, in their various vulnerable situations and contexts. While the notion of human dignity is central to religion, ethics and philosophy, the modern concept of human rights, as derived from the UDHR, is far more concrete in outlining specific rights and state obligations designed to protect basic needs, and to respond to situations of human vulnerability,[8] including both liberty rights and social rights.

3. VULNERABLE GROUPS AND NON-DISCRIMINATION

Although the two world wars affected most people, during the periods 1914–18 and 1940–45, these wars also made visible the particular suffering of *vulnerable groups*: groups that were targeted because of certain racial, social, physical or other characteristics or classifications. Therefore, it was necessary to state, in the very first article of the UDHR, that '*All* human beings are born free and equal in dignity and rights' (emphasis added), accompanied by a clear formulation of the cross-cutting fundamental principle of *non-discrimination*:

> Everyone is entitled to all the rights and freedoms set forth in this Declaration, *without distinction of any kind*, such as race, colour, sex, language, religion, political or other opinion, national or social origin, property, birth or other status' (Article 2, emphasis added).

The idea is that the rights put forward in the UDHR are of such importance to human dignity and well-being that they cannot be taken away from anyone. Article 14 of the European Convention on Human Rights (ECHR), adopted two years after the UDHR, proclaims a similar non-discrimination principle:

> The enjoyment of the rights and freedoms set forth in this Convention shall be secured without discrimination on any ground such as sex, race, colour, language, religion, political or other opinion, national or social origin, association with a national minority, property, birth or other status.

The inclusion of 'association with a national minority' must be seen as a response to the persecution of Jews and other ethnic minority groups in European countries over the centuries, culminating in the Nazi concentration camps, where around six million Jews lost their lives.

---

[8]   Marcus Düwell et al, 'Why a handbook on human dignity?' in Marcus Düwell, Jens Braarvig, Roger Brownsword and Dietmar Mieth (eds.), *The Cambridge Handbook of Human Dignity: Interdisciplinary Perspectives*, Cambridge University Press, 2014, xvii–xxiii, at xix.

While the UDHR is not a legally binding instrument, the ECHR and the two main UN conventions, adopted in 1966 to further the global ambitions of both the UN Charter and the UDHR, are legally binding upon ratifying states. These instruments share the basic notions and aspirations of human dignity and non-discrimination outlined in the UDHR, although these are contained in separate conventions addressing different (but interrelated and interdependent) sets of rights. The main distinction is between the International Covenant on Economic, Social and Cultural Rights (ICESCR) and the International Covenant on Civil and Political Rights (ICCPR), both adopted by the UN on 16 December 1966. The relationship between these two human rights instruments and the respective rights protected thereunder has given rise to theoretical, legal and political discussions and clarifications.[9]

Several later human rights instruments have been adopted, to recognise and address the particular vulnerabilities of certain groups, due to historical and contextual factors: indigenous peoples,[10] minorities,[11] women,[12] children[13] and persons with disabilities.[14] Older persons and migrants are also recognised in human rights instruments.[15] Several instruments clearly address structural and systemic discrimination (against minorities, women, disabled persons etc.), defined, variously, as 'unjustified unequal treatment', 'unequal protection of the law', 'unequal enjoyment of human rights', and 'lack of reasonable accommodation of differences'. The non-discrimination principle takes different forms, depending on which actions, structures or circumstances being addressed.

The Convention on the Rights of the Child addresses the particular vulnerabilities of children, in terms of their natural dependency on parental care, and on safe and supportive environments. This instrument is not a

---

9   See, e.g. Isfahan Merali and Valerie Oosterveld (eds.), *Giving Meaning to Economic, Social and Cultural Rights*, University of Pennsylvania Press, 2001; Malcolm Langford (ed.), *Social Rights Jurisprudence: Emerging Trends in International and Comparative Law*, Cambridge University Press, 2008; Anna-Sara Lind, *Sociala rättigheter i förändring. En konstitutionellrättslig studie* ['Social Rights undergoing Changes. A Study in Constitutional Law'], doctoral dissertation, Uppsala University, 2009, and Ingrid Leijten, *Core Socio-Economic Rights and the European Court of Human Rights*, Cambridge University Press, 2018.

10   United Nations Declaration on the Rights of Indigenous Peoples, 13 September 2007 (GA resolution A/RES/61/295).

11   United Nations Declaration on the Rights of Minorities, 18 December 1992 (GA resolution 47/135).

12   United Nations Convention on the Elimination of All Forms of Discrimination against Women (CEDAW), 18 December 1979 (GA resolution 34/180).

13   United Nations Convention on the Rights of the Child (CRC), 20 November 1989 (GA resolution 44/25).

14   United Nations Convention on the Rights of Persons with Disabilities, 6 December 2006 (GA resolution A/61/611).

15   United Nations Principles for Older Persons, 16 December 1991 (GA resolution 46/91); UN Refugee Convention, 28 July 1951 (resolution 429 (V)); and UN Declaration for Refugees and Migrants, 19 September 2016 (GA resolution A/RES/71/1).

response to discrimination against children, generally, but is, rather, a global response to the common vulnerability and dependencies of children, as human beings in particular need of protection and care. In a similar way, adult persons with severe intellectual or physical disabilities or illnesses may also be seen as human beings in particular need of protection and care, as recognised in the Biomedicine Convention[16] and other instruments.

Looking at the development of human rights instruments, it seems clear that the international community has, over time, recognised the need to supplement the general human rights Conventions of 1966 with more focused instruments addressing the vulnerabilities and needs of various groups. The strategy of separate instruments for different groups, protecting the same basic rights as in the original 1966 Conventions, visualises the great variations in the human condition, and how humans are vulnerable in different ways, and for different reasons. It has been suggested that the need to adopt all of these instruments is a sign of an inherent weakness in the human rights system itself, because it was created on the basis of a liberal notion of independent and autonomous individuals.[17] This basic assumption, it is asserted, excludes many people, and does not correspond with the realities of many people – if, indeed, anyone – around the world.[18] Based on this point of view, it seems that the human rights system is in constant need of compensatory strategies, in order to include everyone, according to the guarantees expressed in the UDHR and later codifications.

The authors of this book acknowledge both aspects of the human rights framework: it promotes the value and idea of individual autonomy while, at the same time, acknowledging human vulnerability, generally and particularly. By recognising and addressing barriers and vulnerabilities, human rights instruments aim to secure the enjoyment of the protected rights on an equal and fair basis. In general comments and general recommendations, as well as in concluding observations to state reports, human rights bodies outline and emphasise the imperatives of states to pay special attention to the needs of particularly vulnerable groups.[19] The European Court of Human Rights (ECtHR) has, increasingly, adopted a jurisprudence where a focus on vulnerability

---

[16] Convention for the Protection of Human Rights and Dignity of the Human Being with regard to the Application of Biology and Medicine: Convention on Human Rights and Biomedicine, Council of Europe, 4 April 1997.

[17] Peroni and Timmer, 'Vulnerable groups: The promise of an emerging concept in European Human Rights Convention law', 1058, 1061–063, with references to Anna Grear, *Redirecting Human Rights: Facing the Challenge of Corporate Legal Humanity*, Palgrave Macmillan, 2010.

[18] Ibid.

[19] See ICESCR Committee, General Comment No. 14: The Right to the Highest Attainable Standard of Health (Art. 12) (E/C.12/2000/4) paras. 12 b), 37 and 43 a).

supplements a jurisprudence on non-discrimination,[20] especially in areas involving protection of core socio-economic rights.[21] Some of these cases will be discussed in section 6 of this chapter. Thus, it is safe to say that attention to various forms of vulnerability and discrimination constitute general and overarching human rights obligations.

4. PROTECTION OF AUTONOMY

Individual autonomy is a core human rights value, protected by provisions on individual liberty and privacy rights in central human rights conventions. As pointed out by Anna Grear, there are two somewhat contradictory and competing ideas embodied in the human rights framework: the idea of human beings as *vulnerable and dependent*, and the idea of human beings as *free, autonomous and independent*, capable of shaping their own lives and destinies.[22] Despite the apparent and inherent vulnerability of all human beings, and particular vulnerabilities of certain groups, human rights norms promote the liberal idea and value of human freedom and autonomy. Article 7 of the ICCPR articulates this value, inspired by the Nuremberg trials following the Second World War:

> No one shall be subjected to torture or to cruel, inhuman or degrading treatment or punishment. *In particular, no one shall be subjected without his free consent to medical or scientific experimentation* (emphasis added).

The second sentence, by including 'free consent', establishes individual consent as a 'last defence' against human experimentation, providing the individual with a right to make autonomous decisions, and thereby upholding the values of liberty and autonomy. At the same time, the provision is clearly an expression of protection of human vulnerability, i.e. the universal vulnerability of human beings to physical and mental damage, and the particular vulnerability of certain marginalised, and even dehumanised, individuals and groups that are facing increased risk of exploitation.

Another central human right in the field of health is the right to privacy, as put forward in Article 8(1) of the ECHR and Article 17 of the ICCPR, providing

---

[20] See Alexandra Timmer, 'A Quiet Revolution: Vulnerability in the European Court of Human Rights' in Martha Albertson Fineman and Anna Grear (eds.), *Vulnerability: Reflections on a New Ethical Foundation for Law and Politics*, Ashgate, 2013, 147–71.

[21] Ingrid Leijten, *Core Socio-Economic Rights and the European Court of Human Rights*, Cambridge University Press, 2018.

[22] Anna Grear, *Redirecting Human Rights: Facing the Challenge of Corporate Legal Humanity*, Palgrave Macmillan, 2010, 132–33.

individuals with a legal tool to resist state interventions that undermine individual integrity and autonomy, including physical and other interventions in the intimate and private sphere.

Article 12 of the ICESCR on the right to health obligates states to respect, protect and fulfil the rights of everyone to the highest attainable standard of health.[23] Respect for individual integrity and autonomy is considered part of the duty of securing acceptable health services.[24] The CEDAW Committee has made the following statement of general relevance, regarding Article 12 CEDAW on health:

> Acceptable services are those which are delivered in a way that ensures that a woman gives her fully informed consent, respects her dignity, guarantees her confidentiality and is sensitive to her needs and perspectives.[25]

This is an example of the interconnectedness of human rights: they cannot be strictly separated into different boxes or spheres, rather they are to be seen as pieces in the same legal puzzle. Included in the right to adequate and acceptable healthcare is a right to individual integrity and autonomy, including a right of free informed consent.

Different human rights regimes, regional and international, influence and borrow from each other, recognising their inherent indivisibility, mutual dependence and interconnectedness.[26] The ECtHR came early to this insight, in the famous *Airey* case concerning access to free legal aid in civil proceedings. The Court held that there was a right to legal assistance if it was indispensable for effective access to the courts, and to family rights protection (Articles 6 and 8), emphasising the relationship between civil and social rights:

> Whilst the Convention [ECHR] sets forth what are essentially civil and political rights, many of them have implications of a social or economic nature. The Court therefore considers, like the Commission, that the mere fact that an interpretation

---

23   ICESCR Committee, General Comment No. 14, para. 33.
24   Ibid.
25   CEDAW Committee, General Recommendation No. 24: Article 12 of the Convention (Women and Health, A/54/38/Rev.1, chap. I), para. 22.
26   Chisanga Puta-Chekwe and Nora Flood, 'From Division to Integration: Economic, Social, and Cultural Rights as Basic Human Rights' in Isfahan Merali and Valerie Oosterveld (eds.), *Giving Meaning to Economic, Social and Cultural Rights*, University of Pennsylvania Press, 2001, 39–52; Anne Hellum and Henriette Sinding Aasen (eds.), *Conclusions in Women's Human Rights: CEDAW in International, Regional and National Law*, Cambridge University Press, 2013, 625–56, on how the CEDAW regime has contributed to international, regional and domestic human rights jurisprudence. Ingrid Leijten describes how CESCR practice inspires the development of legal reasoning and case law, based on the ECHR: see Leitjen, *Core Socio-Economic Rights and the European Court of Human Rights*, 224–25 and elsewhere.

of the Convention may extend into the sphere of social and economic rights should not be a decisive factor against such an interpretation; *there is no water-tight division separating that sphere from the field covered by the Convention* (emphasis added).[27]

Despite being a typical civil and political human rights instrument, the ECHR does not put forward a fundamental distinction between civil and social rights. Rather, there is an overlap between these rights, as expressed in a number of cases after *Airey*.[28] Individual autonomy is clearly not a purely 'negative' right requiring non-interference, but a right which depends on the realisation of core socio-economic rights, for example education and healthcare.

It is safe to say that all human rights instruments protecting civil, political and socio-economic rights, and targeting women, children, minorities, disabled persons and other groups, share the common values of individual freedom, autonomy and agency. Individual autonomy is a protected value, despite all humans being dependent and vulnerable. The legal protection includes the right to be free from harmful or unwanted interventions, the right to make individual choices based on adequate information, and the right to positive support or protection in contexts or situations where the exercise of individual autonomy is particularly restricted, impossible or dependent on assistance.

5. THE POTENTIAL CONFLICT BETWEEN HEALTH PROTECTION AND AUTONOMY

As explained above, human rights value and protect individual autonomy while, at the same time, acknowledging human vulnerability. Thus, states, municipalities and health staff are all under a dual duty of protecting individual autonomy as far as possible, as well as the lives, health and well-being of patients and recipients of welfare services. Since the human rights framework contains both the notion of the autonomous and the vulnerable human being, with their respective rights and duties, in many situations these ideas may compete against each other, both at a general systemic level and in concrete situations. Fineman has, in particular, described the systemic failure of US discourses on equality to recognise human vulnerability, by ignoring the fact that context, circumstances and institutional structures are relevant for the understanding of equal opportunities, and the responsibility of the state in securing social justice.[29]

---

[27] *Airey v. Ireland* (ECtHR 9 October 1979, no. 6289/73), para. 26.
[28] See Leitjen, *Core Socio-Economic Rights and the European Court of Human Rights*, 42 and elsewhere.
[29] Fineman, 'Equality, Autonomy, and the Vulnerable Subject in Law and Politics', 13–29.

In relation to most welfare services, we find a constant and systemic tension between the competing rights of individual autonomy, on one hand, and a paternalistic or protective professional duty of care towards those in need, on the other hand, for example in nursing homes, institutions and homes for mentally ill or disabled persons, in child protection, and in other social services.[30] This tension has been particularly visible during the COVID-19 pandemic, where nursing home patients and long-term residents in care institutions have been denied contact with family members and other close contacts, to protect them against the virus.[31]

Conflicts between individual autonomy and health protection are common in relation to care for persons with mental illnesses and disabilities, including elderly people suffering from serious forms of dementia. Mental illness and disability may be a hindrance to the meaningful exercise of autonomy and choice, in so far as the person concerned is not able to identify and protect him- or herself from life-threatening, harmful or dangerous situations, or to give valid informed consent to proposed medical procedures (for example, vaccination against COVID-19 or similar viruses, medication for a life-threatening condition, etc.). Such conflicts are also common, in the health sector, in situations where mentally capable patients reject proposed medical treatments, such as a particular operation that they might see as too risky.

Both individual autonomy and health are to be respected and protected in the healthcare system, frequently leaving health staff with complex legal, ethical and professional decisions in situations of conflict. Due to this potential tension and conflict between health protection and autonomy/privacy in the health setting, most countries have developed legislation regulating, to some extent, how to balance these competing interests, rights and duties. In Europe, Articles 5 and 8 of the ECHR regulate how to balance individual freedom and privacy with competing interests. For instance, while it starts with a general proclamation that '[e]veryone has the right to respect for his private and

---

30   Henriette Sinding Aasen, Rune Halvorsen and António Barbosa da Silva (eds.), *Human Rights, Dignity and Autonomy in Health Care and Social Services: Nordic Perspectives*, Intersentia, 2009; Bjørn Henning Østenstad et al (eds.), *Selvbestemmelse og tvang i helse- og omsorgstjenesten* ['Autonomy and coercion in health and care services'], Fagbokforlaget, 2018; Nikita V. Alexandrov and Natalie Schuck, 'Coercive interventions under the new Dutch mental health law: Towards a CRPD-compliant law?', *International Journal of Law and Psychiatry*, 76 (2021), 101685, available at https://www.sciencedirect.com/science/article/pii/S0160252721000145.

31   Katharina Ó Cathaoir and Ida Gundersby Rognlien, 'The Rights of Elders in Ireland during COVID-19', *European Journal of Health Law* 28 (2021), 81–101, doi:10.1163/15718093-bja10035; Human Rights Watch, 'Protecting Human Rights in the Covid-19 Pandemic', 13 July 2020, available at https://www.hrw.org/news/2020/07/13/protecting-human-rights-covid-19-pandemic. See also Report from the Norwegian Corona Commission on the Government's Handling of the Corona Pandemic (NOU 2021:6), 343–44.

family life …' (Article 8(1)), the individual right to privacy is modified by the following statement in Article 8(2):

> There shall be no interference by a public authority with the exercise of this right except such as is in accordance with the law and is necessary in a democratic society in the interests of national security, public safety or the economic well-being of the country, for the prevention of disorder or crime, for the protection of health or morals, or for the protection of the rights and freedoms of others.

This provision, and similar provisions in other human rights instruments, form the legal backbone of understanding and handling conflicts between individual autonomy and privacy, on the one hand, and health protection, on the other. Proper legal regulation, requirements of necessity, proportionality, and an acceptable objective for proposed interventions are all basic human rights requirements. Proportionality requires a fair balance to be struck between the need for an intervention and the consequences for an affected individual. This assessment is essential in all cases involving intrusive or coercive measures against a person, whether for public health reasons, for the protection of the health of the person concerned, or for the protection of the rights of other persons. Most of the chapters in this volume engage with the balancing of rights of privacy and autonomy, on one hand, and health rights (individual or public), on the other. The authors explore the nature of the human needs and interests involved, including the vulnerability aspects, as well as the social and state interests, and how the human rights framework responds to competing rights and interests. The final part of this chapter (section 8) deals with another conflict, in the area of health, where human vulnerability is at stake: the right of individuals to health protection versus state interests in excluding them from accessing health and welfare services.

The intervening sections, however, pursue, in more detail, the understanding of the vulnerability argument as an important aspect of human rights discourse.

6. VULNERABILITY – CONCEPT AND DISCOURSE

6.1. ORIGINS AND LEGAL DEVELOPMENTS

Although the concept of 'vulnerability' is used frequently in human rights discourse, its meaning is still imprecise and contested, as is its relation to human rights law.[32] As will be shown, 'vulnerability' may refer to different situations,

---

[32] Peroni and Timmer, 'Vulnerable groups: The promise of an emerging concept in European Human Rights Convention law', 1058.

contexts and individual characteristics. For example, in the context of the HIV/AIDS pandemic of the 1980s, which was the initial point of departure for the shaping of health and human rights as a distinct academic discipline,[33] several groups were identified as being at a particular risk of HIV transmission: women, infants, sex workers, prisoners, migrants, people injecting drugs, men having sex with men, and transgender people. These groups were identified as 'vulnerable populations', because their members were 'often already poor, marginalized, and at risk of discrimination; contracting HIV exacerbate[d] these harms'.[34] The vulnerability concept was closely linked to situations associated with a particular risk of transmission of a dangerous virus.

Today, the COVID-19 virus is a similar example, in that vulnerability is specifically related to living conditions, age, and health status. Older people, and people with underlying health problems, are at significantly higher risk of death or serious illness due to virus infection, compared to young and healthy populations.[35] Also, certain groups of migrants to Western societies have been highlighted as having an increased risk of COVID-19 infection, as well as serious illnesses and health complications due to the infection.[36] People living in poor and crowded households of many people in small apartments, and people working in certain sectors (including hospitals, schools, transport and grocery stores) also face a higher risk of virus transmission. These examples illustrate that vulnerability often consists of a mixture of individual and social factors, for example being elderly, poor and suffering from an underlying serious health condition, or being a migrant living in unsafe or poor conditions. The term 'intersectionality' was introduced by Professor Kimberlé Williams Crenshaw in 1989 to describe how race, class, gender and other individual characteristics 'intersect' with each other, overlapping and influencing experiences of discrimination. The concept has become influential in literature that seeks to

---

[33]   Lawrence O. Gostin and Benjamin Mason Meier (eds.), 'Introduction' in *Foundations of Global Health & Human Rights*, Oxford University Press, 2020, 1–20, 10.

[34]   Sharifah Sekalala and John Harrington, 'Communicable Diseases, Health Security, and Human Rights. From AIDS to Ebola' in Lawrence O. Gostin and Benjamin Mason Meier (eds.), *Foundations of Global Health & Human Rights*, Oxford University Press, 2020, 221–43, 222 and 223.

[35]   Sven Drefahlet al., 'A population-based cohort study of socio-demographic risk factors for COVID-19 deaths in Sweden', *Nature Communications* 11(1) (2020), 5097; Elizabeth J. Williamson et al, 'Factors associated with COVID-19-related death using OpenSAFELY', *Nature*, 584(7821) (2020), 430–6.

[36]   Thor Indseth et al., 'COVID-19 among immigrants in Norway, notified infections, related hospitalizations and associated mortality: A register-based study', *Scandinavian Journal of Public Health* 0(0):1403494820984026; Siddartha Aradhya et al., 'Lack of acculturation does not explain excess COVID-19 mortality among immigrants. A population-based cohort study', *Stockholm Research Reports in Demography*, 2020.

understand how different aspects of a person's identity can combine to create different modes of discrimination and privilege.[37]

In the context of socio-economic rights, the ICESCR Committee's practice is a valuable source for identifying 'vulnerable' groups. In its 1991 comment on the right to housing, the Committee argued that 'States parties must give due priority to those social groups living in unfavorable conditions by giving them particular consideration'.[38] Furthermore, the Committee has held that, especially for 'disadvantaged and marginalized individuals and groups', access to social security systems and schemes, as well as healthcare, needs to be secured.[39] This understanding of vulnerability seems to be closely linked to situations where individuals and groups are primarily or entirely dependent on the state for their survival or well-being.[40] Asylum seekers and undocumented migrants belong to this group, as they typically lack means of self-support, while state regulations and social policies define their statuses and living conditions. Severely disabled persons who are dependent on a variety of public services for dignified living are another such group.[41] According to this understanding of vulnerability, children and the elderly can also be counted as potentially vulnerable groups, as many children and old people have limited autonomy, and are heavily dependent on public protective services and measures in relation to health, security and well-being.[42]

A frequently used term in human rights documents and literature is 'disadvantaged', which is used to describe groups or communities in situations characterised by a lack of access to basic goods, services and facilities.[43] Vulnerability is often also associated with stigmatisation, risk of human rights violations, and discrimination.[44]

The following sections will take a closer look at some decisions of the ECtHR, where references to vulnerability, in a number of cases, form part of the jurisprudence.

---

[37] See, e.g. Lorena Sosa, *Intersectionality in the Human Rights Legal Framework on Violence against Women*, Cambridge University Press, 2017.

[38] ICESCR Committee, General Comment No. 4: 'The Right to Adequate Housing', 13 December 1991, E/1992/23, para. 10.

[39] ICESCR Committee, General Comment No. 18: 'The Right to Work', 6 February 2006, E/C.12/GC/18, para. 31(a) and General Comment No. 14: 'The right to the highest attainable health', 11 August 2000, E/C.12/2005/4, para. 43(a).

[40] Leijten, *Core Socio-Economic Rights and the European Court of Human Rights*, 225.

[41] Ibid.

[42] Ibid.

[43] See the General Comments referred to above by the ICESCR Committee (notes 38 and 39).

[44] Sharifah Sekalala and John Harrington, 'Communicable Diseases, Health Security, and Human Rights. From AIDS to Ebola' in Lawrence O. Gostin and Benjamin Mason Meier (eds.), *Foundations of Global Health & Human Rights*, Oxford University Press, 2020, 221–43.

6.2. VULNERABILITY IN THE EUROPEAN COURT OF HUMAN RIGHTS

6.2.1. *The concept of 'group vulnerability'*

The study by Lourdes Peroni and Alexandra Timmer is the main source of the account of legal developments in the ECtHR given in this section. They summarise the Court's approach to vulnerability as follows:

> in response to the exclusions of human rights law, the Strasbourg Court has been forced to attend to the constructed disadvantage of certain groups, and in so doing, has deployed the concept of group vulnerability.[45]

The authors observe that the concept of 'group vulnerability', as used by the Court, has three characteristics: it is relational, particular and harm-based.[46] The first case in which vulnerability was used as part of the Court's reasoning was the *Chapman* case, where the Court stated that belonging to a particular *group*, in this case a Roma minority, made the applicant vulnerable, especially due to broader societal, political and institutional circumstances. Based on their study of the case law, Peroni and Timmer found that vulnerability is a relational concept in the jurisprudence of the Court: 'As in *Chapman*, the Court locates vulnerability not in the individual alone but rather in her wider social circumstances'.[47] After *Chapman*, the Court has extended the scope of 'vulnerable groups' to also include people with mental disabilities, people living with HIV, and asylum seekers.[48]

The Court seems to acknowledge the paradox that vulnerability is both a universal and a particular human experience, using the phrase 'particularly vulnerable groups' rather than merely referring to 'vulnerable groups'. The inclusion of the term 'particularly' underlines the idea that people belonging to these groups are more vulnerable than others. This points to an important characteristic of the Court's account of vulnerability: it is particular, in the sense that the vulnerable subject is a group member whose vulnerability is shaped by specific group-based experiences.[49]

Such particular experiences, as highlighted by the Court, are those of (historical) prejudice and stigmatisation, as described by Nancy Fraser in

---

[45]   Peroni and Timmer, 'Vulnerable groups: The promise of an emerging concept in European Human Rights Convention law', 1062.

[46]   Ibid., 1063–065.

[47]   Ibid., 1064.

[48]   See the following discussion.

[49]   Peroni and Timmer, 'Vulnerable groups: The promise of an emerging concept in European Human Rights Convention law', 1064.

terms of 'institutionalized patterns of cultural value ... [which] constitute some actors as inferior, excluded, wholly other, or simply invisible – in other words, as less than full partners in social interaction'.[50] More recently, the Court has started to delineate more complex indicators linked to social disadvantage and material deprivation, in the context of Articles 3 and 8 ECHR. These indicators point to what Fraser calls 'maldistribution', which results 'when some actors lack the necessary resources to interact with others as peers'.[51] Lack of resources may also indicate that essential health determinants are unavailable, or inaccessible to the people concerned.

In several cases, the Court has established discrimination against Roma children regarding education.[52] In *D.H. and Others v. the Czech Republic*, the Grand Chamber stated the following in relation to membership of a vulnerable group:

> [A]s a result of their turbulent history and constant uprooting the Roma have become a specific type of disadvantaged and vulnerable minority.[53]

Furthermore, in *V.C. v. Slovakia*,[54] the Court found that negative social attitudes were the main source of the vulnerability of Roma people. The case concerned forced sterilisation of a Roma woman. Recognising that forced sterilisation had affected vulnerable individuals from different ethnic groups, the Court found that Roma women were at particular risk:

> due, inter alia, to the widespread negative attitudes towards the relatively high birth rate among the Roma compared to other parts of the population, often expressed as worries of an increased proportion of the population living on social benefits.[55]

The Court condemned Slovakia for not ensuring the applicant's free and informed consent to sterilisation, leading to violations of both Article 3 ECHR (degrading treatment) and Article 8 ECHR (respect for private and

---

[50] Nancy Fraser, 'Rethinking Recognition', *New Left Review* 3 (2000), 107, 113, quoted from Peroni and Timmer, 'Vulnerable groups: The promise of an emerging concept in European Human Rights Convention law', 1065.

[51] Ibid.

[52] Ibid., with reference to *D.H. and Others v. the Czech Republic* (ECtHR 13 November 2007, (GC), no. 57325/00), *Sampanis and others v. Greece* (ECtHR 5 September 2008, no. 32526/05), and *Oršuš and others v. Croatia* (ECtHR 16 March 2010, no. 15766/03).

[53] Quoted from Peroni and Timmer, 'Vulnerable groups: The promise of an emerging concept in European Human Rights Convention law', 1065.

[54] ECtHR 8 November 2011, *V.C. v. Slovakia*, no. 18968/07.

[55] Peroni and Timmer, 'Vulnerable groups: The promise of an emerging concept in European Human Rights Convention law', 1066.

family life).[56] The Court did not examine the applicant's discrimination complaint (Article 14 ECHR) separately, despite its observation that the harmful practices it condemned were closely connected to the widespread prejudice against Roma people.[57]

Another group identified by the Court as vulnerable due to stigmatisation and social exclusion are people living with HIV/AIDS. In *Kiyutin v. Russia*,[58] the Court concluded that discrimination had taken place, and stated the following:

> Taking into account that the applicant belonged to a particularly vulnerable group, that his exclusion has not been shown to have a reasonable and objective justification, and that the contested legislative provisions did not make room for an individualised evaluation, the Court finds that the Government overstepped the narrow margin of appreciation (para. 74).

The stigma had prevented HIV-positive individuals from obtaining residence permits, based on general assumptions of unsafe behaviour. The Court stated, in this case, that such a generalisation was not founded in facts, and that it failed to take into account the individual situation of the applicant.[59]

According to Peroni and Timmer, the case *M.S.S. v. Belgium and Greece*[60] significantly broadened the Court's notion of group vulnerability. The applicant, an Afghan asylum seeker, was returned by Belgium to Greece, under the European Union's 'Dublin II Regulation'.[61] A key question was whether the detention of the applicant in Greece, and the living conditions there, amounted to inhuman and degrading treatment under Article 3 of the ECHR. In analysing the applicant's conditions of detention, or more precisely, the Greek government's argument that the duration of detention was insignificant, the Court observed:

> In the present case the Court must take into account that the applicant, being an asylum seeker, was particularly vulnerable because of everything he had been through during his migration and the traumatic experiences he was likely to have endured previously.[62]

Furthermore, the Court attached 'considerable importance to the applicant's status as an asylum seeker and, as such, a member of a particularly underprivileged and vulnerable population group in need of special

---

56   Ibid.
57   Ibid.
58   ECtHR 10 March 2011, *Kiyutin v. Russia*, no. 2700/10.
59   For more details, see Peroni and Timmer, 'Vulnerable groups: The promise of an emerging concept in European Human Rights Convention law', 1067.
60   ECtHR 21 January 2011, *M.S.S. v. Belgium and Greece*, no. 30696/09.
61   Council Regulation (EC) No 343/2003 of 18 February 2003.
62   Quoted from Peroni and Timmer, 'Vulnerable groups: The promise of an emerging concept in European Human Rights Convention law', 1068.

protection'.[63] By this statement, the notion of vulnerability was expanded from the traumatic experiences of the individual applicant, to asylum seekers in general, in the sense that they all belong to a particularly underprivileged population group.

6.2.2. Group vulnerability – expanding the understanding

In a separate opinion by Judge Sajó in the *M.S.S.* case, he rejected the view that asylum seekers, as such, constitute a particularly vulnerable group. He argued that, unlike other 'particularly vulnerable groups' in the Court's case law, asylum seekers 'are not a group historically subject to prejudice with lasting consequences, resulting in their social exclusion' and, therefore, according to Judge Sajó, do not fit the concept of a vulnerable group, according to the Court's jurisprudence.[64]

While Judge Sajó attempted to keep the definition of a 'particularly vulnerable group' narrow, the majority opened up the meaning of the concept by referring to several indicators, including that the applicant was 'wholly dependent on State support' and 'unable to cater for his most basic needs'.[65] The dependency argument is taken from cases under Article 3 of the ECHR concerning prisoners and detainees.[66] However, in the *M.S.S.* judgment, the Court's reasoning went beyond the context of detention or imprisonment, as the majority pointed to the many institutional shortcomings inherent in the Greek asylum system, such as a lack of sufficient reception centres, and the existence of administrative obstacles impeding access to the labour market, and lengthy procedures to examine asylum applications.[67] Through the unveiling of these deficiencies in the Greek asylum system, 'the Court [was] ultimately pointing to the *institutional production* of vulnerability of asylum seekers in Greece'[68] (emphasis added).

Peroni and Timmer found that the Court in *M.S.S.* classified asylum seekers as *particularly* vulnerable, based on a range of interacting factors, including their difficult living situations, their total dependency on the state, their vulnerability due to past experiences and traumas, and the systemic deficiencies of the Greek asylum system.[69] It seems clear that 'the Court's analysis in *M.S.S.* challenge[d] simplistic conceptions of group vulnerability, making room for more textured

---

63   Ibid.
64   Ibid., 1069.
65   Ibid.
66   Ibid.
67   Ibid.
68   Ibid.
69   Ibid.

and complex formulations.[70] Of particular interest is the notion of institutional and systemic production of vulnerability, which includes legal, administrative and political institutions, and systems establishing barriers and mechanisms of exclusion regarding access to public arenas and services of vital importance for social participation and individual well-being. Lack of access to the mainstream healthcare system for so-called 'undocumented' or 'irregular' migrants is an example of such institutional and systemic exclusion, which will be explored further in section 7 below.

6.2.3. Vulnerability and the dangers of generalisation and stigmatisation

While vulnerability is clearly a relevant and important concern in human rights law and jurisprudence, there are also pitfalls to consider. In the judgment in V.M. and Others v. Belgium,[71] the dissenting opinion of Judge Ranzoni et al. asserted that the Grand Chamber should have used the opportunity to clarify the concept and jurisprudence of vulnerability:

> In M.S.S., the Court considered that asylum-seekers were a 'particularly underprivileged and vulnerable' population group. However, the fact is that asylum-seekers may vary in their degree of vulnerability according to their means of subsistence, the type of treatment or persecution of which they have been or are liable to be victims, their age, their family situation or their state of health or their disability. As rightly pointed out by Judge Sajó in his dissenting opinion in M.S.S. v. Belgium and Greece, 'although many asylum-seekers are vulnerable persons, they cannot be unconditionally considered as a particularly vulnerable group ... Asylum-seekers are far from being homogeneous, if such a group exists at all' ... Even though the applicants in the present case were, in my view, undeniably vulnerable, the Court could have seized the opportunity to define that concept.[72]

The dissenting opinion indicates that a particular legal or social status (for example, as an asylum seeker, recipient of social support, or a gay person, etc.) should not, in itself, be sufficient to conclude that someone is vulnerable. This point is important to avoid negative effects of generalisations, such as victimisation and stigmatisation. Furthermore, it is clearly relevant for other groups, such as children and older persons, as a person is not necessarily particularly vulnerable just because he or she belongs to one of these age groups. Rather, it is the life situation and particular social context that will determine

---

Ibid., 1070.
71   ECtHR 17 November 2016, V.M. and Others v. Belgium (GC), no. 60125/11.
72   Ibid., Separate opinion, 11, paras. 6 and 7, quoted from Peroni and Timmer, 'Vulnerable groups: The promise of an emerging concept in European Human Rights Convention law', 1058.

whether the person is particularly vulnerable. This point is emphasised by the ICESCR Committee, in relation to older persons:

> Older persons as a group are as heterogeneous and varied as the rest of the population and their situation depends on a country's economic and social situation, on demographic, environmental, cultural and employment factors and, at the individual level, on the family situation, the level of education, the urban or rural environment and the occupation of workers and retirees.[73]

Similar observations are relevant for children and other groups as well, including minority groups. Thus, an individual's belonging to a particular age (or other) group may not always be of special relevance regarding their vulnerability. On the contrary, labelling a person as 'vulnerable' may serve to generalise and victimise rather than empower them. Moreover, the fact that people are dependent on the cooperation of others should not be sufficient to establish vulnerability, as this is an aspect of everyone's lives. No one is completely independent of others, or of society. As stated by Fineman, referring to common situations experienced by people during their lifetimes (such as crime, injury, illness and disability), 'there is no such thing as invulnerability'.[74] However, some people are placed in situations where they depend, more than others, on other people or the state to survive, or to maintain a certain level of existence. Therefore, to be 'particularly vulnerable', according to the Court, indicates that a person's life situation is associated with special risks of human rights violations and extraordinary suffering, thereby calling for protective measures to be applied by the state. This legal reasoning assumes that particular vulnerability is often caused by various socially constructed processes of inclusion and exclusion,[75] similar to what Sosa and others refer to as 'intersectional discrimination'.[76]

In *Kiyutin v. Russia*,[77] the stigmatisation of people living with HIV was central to the Court's finding that they constituted a particularly vulnerable group. Peroni and Timmer point out that the Court's use of the term 'vulnerable group' in this decision was problematic, because of the danger of contributing to stigmatisation by labelling a whole group of people as 'vulnerable'. They assert that the Court's reasoning could reinforce vulnerability 'by essentializing,[78]

---

[73] ICESCR Committee, General Comment No. 6: The Economic, Social and Cultural Rights of Older Persons (E/1996/22) para. 16.

[74] Fineman, 'Equality, Autonomy, and the Vulnerable Subject in Law and Politics', 16.

[75] Peroni and Timmer, 'Vulnerable groups: The promise of an emerging concept in European Human Rights Convention law', 1058.

[76] See section 6.1, note 37 of this chapter.

[77] ECtHR 10 March 2011, *Kiyutin v. Russia*, no. 2700/10.

[78] In terms of 'reifying one experience as paradigmatic, at the expense of other experiences' (Peroni and Timmer, 'Vulnerable groups: The promise of an emerging concept in European Human Rights Convention law', 1058, 1071).

stigmatizing, victimizing, and paternalizing them'.[79] The language used by courts and other powerful institutions may lead to the vulnerability aspect becoming perceived as the main characteristic of persons belonging to certain groups, robbing them of their other individual characteristics. This would occur when 'the defining attribute eclipses all other aspects of stigmatized persons, their talents and abilities'.[80] When 'vulnerability overshadows all other aspects of an applicant's identity in the Court's reasoning, it has taken on a master status'.[81]

A narrow criteria-based definition of a vulnerable group may create some sort of vulnerability 'competition', as reflected in the separate opinion of Judge Sajó in the *M.S.S.* case:

> In terms of vulnerability, dependence, and so on, the mentally disabled (and other vulnerable groups, whose members are subject to social prejudice) *are in a more difficult situation than* asylum seekers, who are not a homogeneous group subject to social categorization and related discrimination[82] (emphasis added).

This statement implies that mentally disabled persons constitute a homogenous group that suffers from social prejudice, thereby confirming, and even adding to, existing stigmatisation. Fineman proposes that this kind of comparison of one group against another often 'ignores most contexts as well as differences in circumstances and abilities on the part of those whose treatment is [being] compared'.[83]

The problem of repeating stigma while underestimating or neglecting context may be illustrated by the case *D.H. and Others v. the Czech Republic*, in which the majority of the Grand Chamber described Roma parents in the following way:

> In the circumstances of the present case, the Court is not satisfied that the parents of the Roma children, who were members of a disadvantaged community and often poorly educated, were capable of weighing up all the aspects of the situation and the consequences of giving their consent.[84]

In a separate statement, Judge Borrego strongly opposed this generalised and negative characterisation of the capabilities of Roma parents. By denying

---

79   Ibid., 1070.
80   Ibid., 1072, with reference to R.A. Lenhardt, 'Understanding the Mark: Race, Stigma, and Equality in Context', 79 (2004) *New York University Law Review* 803, 819 n. 63 in the cited article.
81   Peroni and Timmer, ibid., 1072.
82   Ibid.
83   Fineman, 'Equality, Autonomy, and the Vulnerable Subject in Law and Politics', 14.
84   Quoted from Peroni and Timmer, 'Vulnerable groups: The promise of an emerging concept in European Human Rights Convention law', 1072.

Roma parents the capability of making informed decisions about placing their children in special schools, the Court seems to have reinforced their powerlessness, instead of expressing that meaningful and informed consent was difficult in the specific circumstances of the case.[85]

In other cases, however, the Court has avoided such generalising and stigmatising language. For example, in another case on forced sterilisation of a Roma woman (*V.C. v. Slovakia*), the Court condemned the paternalistic behaviour of the hospital staff who failed to obtain informed consent to the sterilisation procedure, noting that 'in similar situations informed consent was required, promoting autonomy of moral choice for patients', and emphasising the need to respect a person's dignity and integrity.[86]

This approach avoids victimisation of the applicant, and is, according to Peroni and Timmer, 'much more empowering than the language used by the majority in D.H.'.[87] The reason is that the Court judgment's wording referred to the *right* of the applicant to exercise her autonomy, and to make her own individual choices, which placed her in a position where she could defend her own interests and values, including the right to reject unwanted proposed medical interventions. Such an approach implies a focus on the person's right to autonomy, by assuming that they have the capability to make an informed choice, and rejecting a generalised and stereotyped view about capabilities of making sound decisions.

7. THE CAPABILITY APPROACH

The Indian economist and philosopher Amartya Sen, followed by the American ethicist and legal scholar Martha Nussbaum, developed, in the 1980s, new knowledge on the importance of including human capabilities in the reasoning of welfare state economics, social choice theory and social justice ('the capability approach'), bringing together several factors that had previously been overlooked. Sen conceptualised human capability as a reflection of the freedom of individuals to achieve valuable functioning.[88] *Capabilities*, then, are possible types and levels of individual functioning that are feasible for a person to achieve. Sen observed the close connection between human rights and human capability, asserting in his theory of justice that human rights values, freedoms and entitlements contribute to the enhancement of human agency and capability.[89] This approach advances the perspective that human rights should

---

[85]   Ibid., 1073.
[86]   Ibid.
[87]   Ibid., 1073.
[88]   Amartya Sen, *Inequality Reexamined,* Clarendon Press, 1992.
[89]   Amartya Sen, *The Idea of Justice,* Penguin Books, 2009, 321–88, 381.

be understood as instruments enhancing and strengthening human capability, including the capability to live a healthy life.[90] Among the core capabilities that, according to Nussbaum, should be supported by all democratic societies are those connected to life, health and integrity, including the capability of survival and dignified existence, the ability to pursue a healthy life, the ability to make reproductive choices, and the ability to live free from violence and oppression.[91] These capabilities are, indeed, protected by the human rights framework, and form the basis of any civilised society.

The 'capability approach', understood as a systematic approach towards strengthening human capabilities to live dignified lives, according to individual preferences, provides a different perspective from the focus on vulnerability, as the capability approach is more connected to individual autonomy. However, both perspectives and approaches are important in capturing essential aspects of human rights values, principles and objectives. This author agrees with Brigit Toebes that the vulnerability and capability approaches should be seen as supplementary rather than contradictory, in human rights discourse. As put by Toebes, in relation to older persons:

> The question arises whether the vulnerability and capability approaches are conflicting or rather mutually reinforcing. In the present author's view both theories may well complement each other: while the vulnerability theory places a responsibility on government to protect the health, physical integrity and other interests of older persons, the capability theory provides a ground for identifying how older persons can be best equipped to function adequately in society.[92]

This view is very suitable for generalisation to other groups (children, migrants, persons with disabilities, minorities, etc.) when adopting adequate protective measures, as well as for securing avenues for individual empowerment and strengthening of capabilities, in the field of health and well-being.

In this volume, the vulnerability perspective is utilised to further not only formal but *substantive* equality.[93] To achieve substantive equality in enjoyment

---

[90] Brigit Toebes, 'Synergies and Tensions in the Health and Human Rights Frameworks', forthcoming in Allyn Taylor and Patricia Kuszler (eds.), *Legal, Ethical and Social Implications of Ageing: Towards an International Legal Framework to Advance the Human Rights and Health of Older Persons*, Edward Elgar Publishing, 2022, at 3 in manuscript, with reference to Sridhar Venkatapuram, *Health Justice: An Argument from the Capabilities Approach*, Polity 2011, paperback.

[91] Martha Nussbaum, 'Capabilities as fundamental entitlements: Sen and social justice', *Feminist Economics* 9 (2–3) (2003), 33–59, CiteSeerX 10.1.1.541.3425. doi:10.1080/1354570022000077926.

[92] Brigit Toebes, 'Synergies and Tensions in the Health and Human Rights Frameworks', at 3 in manuscript.

[93] See, in relation to gender equality, Sandra Fredman, 'Engendering socio-economic rights' in Anne Hellum and Henriette Sinding Aasen (eds.), *Women's Human Rights*, Cambridge University Press, 2013, 217–42.

of human rights, states are obligated to address legal as well as other barriers (social, cultural and political) that hinder equal opportunities for dignified and healthy living.[94] This strategy may be viewed as a *capability* strategy, in terms of obligating states to adopt positive and *enabling* measures aimed at fulfilling everyone's basic rights and abilities to live healthily and participate in society. The Court's use of the term 'vulnerable groups', Peroni and Timmer observe, 'allows the Court to address different aspects of inequality in a more substantive manner'. These authors argue that, for this reason, 'the emergence of the concept represents a positive development in the Court's case law', in terms of furthering substantive equality. However, they point out, as mentioned above, that the concept of vulnerability 'also risks sustaining the very exclusion and inequality it aims to redress':

> We therefore maintain that, if the Court wishes to retain the capability of 'vulnerable groups' to fulfill its equality mission, it will have to attend to the stigmatizing, essentializing, and stereotyping risks associated to the concept.[95]

The authors of this volume share the view that attention to particular vulnerability may be necessary, in order to comply with human rights obligations. However, human rights norms also require treatment securing substantive equality not to reinforce structures of powerlessness and victimisation.

8. REFUGEES, ASYLUM SEEKERS AND UNDOCUMENTED MIGRANTS

8.1. INTRODUCTION

Although all humans are vulnerable, some individuals and groups are more vulnerable than others.[96] As it is impossible to include all vulnerable groups within the discussion in this chapter, it is justified to pay attention to certain groups facing specific challenges, while keeping in mind the dangers of generalisation and victimisation, which can cause one to lose sight of the fact that, in all groups, there are unique individuals with their own histories, experiences and capabilities. This chapter highlights the situation of refugees, asylum seekers and undocumented migrants. Millions of people are on the

---

[94] See Rikki Holtmaat, 'The CEDAW: a holistic approach to women's equality and freedom' in Anne Hellum and Henriette Sinding Aasen (eds.), *Women's Human Rights*, Cambridge University Press, 2013, 95–124.

[95] Peroni and Timmer, 'Vulnerable groups: The promise of an emerging concept in European Human Rights Convention law', 1057 and 1058.

[96] See, especially, section 6 above, on the concept of vulnerability in human rights discourse.

move around the world, from Syria, Afghanistan and several African and Latin American countries. Many travel to neighbouring countries, or to local refugee camps, but, over the years, increasing numbers from Africa and Asia have set out for Europe, risking their lives by crossing the Mediterranean Sea in small boats. If they reach the borders of Europe, some will be pushed back, which is illegal, according to the principle of non-refoulement.[97] Thousands are sent to refugee camps, set up by Greek and Turkish authorities with financial support from the EU, where they stay for years without any prospect of being allowed to continue their journeys. The Moria refugee camp in Greece has received particular attention in Norway due to the engagement and aid provided by Norwegian non-governmental organisations (NGOs) and health workers. It provides an example of the extremely difficult and life-threatening conditions that refugees and asylum seekers encounter when approaching the European region, which has a common closed border. For people living in such camps, including children and people with serious health problems, their fundamental human rights, according to international human rights standards, including the right to health, are severely and consistently violated. As for the camps established in Greece and Turkey, these are joint responsibilities of the European Union, which finances and maintains the camps for the purpose of preventing the refugees from travelling and seeking asylum in other European countries.

Another example related to migration is the situation of the so-called 'undocumented', 'irregular' or 'unauthorised' migrants, who have arrived in a particular country, but whose asylum applications have been rejected, or have not been submitted in the first place, due to fear of rejection. Across Europe, around four million people are living without lawful presence or residence,[98] from which it may be inferred that they are generally excluded from ordinary health and welfare services and social insurances, with serious consequences for their health and living conditions.

This section builds on the significance of particular *legal* structures in creating situations of vulnerability. Even though the discussion is related to groups of migrants, the analytical focus is on legal regulations leading to the social marginalisation and exclusion of a great number of people residing in refugee camps, in reception centres for asylum seekers, on the streets, or in poor

---

[97] The European Court of Human Rights ruled in *Hirsi v. Italy* (*Grand Chamber 2012 – 27765/09*) that the Italian practice of 'push backs' of Somali and Eritrean asylum seekers and migrants to Libya was unlawful, and violated obligations under ECHR Art. 3 (for more details, see Alice Edwards, 'International Refugee Law' in Daniel Moecli, Sangeeta Shah and Sandesh Sivakumaran (eds.), *International Human Rights Law*, Oxford University Press, 2014, 513–28, at 521).

[98] See https://ec.europa.eu/home-affairs/sites/default/files/what-is-new/public-consultation/2013/pdf/0027/organisations/picum-platform-for-international-cooperation-on-undocumented-migrants_en.pdf; https://www.pewresearch.org/fact-tank/2019/11/14/5-facts-about-unauthorized-immigration-in-europe/.

living conditions, in the country of arrival.[99] Section 8.2 provides an overview of international law applying to refugees, while section 8.3 discusses the situation of undocumented or unauthorised migrants, using Norwegian regulations to illustrate common legal barriers that lead to exclusion and marginalisation of this group, in modern welfare states.

8.2. REFUGEES AND ASYLUM SEEKERS

Refugees are persons 'outside their country of origin owing to a well-founded fear of being persecuted for reasons of race, religion, nationality, membership of a particular social group or political opinion', as per the Refugee Convention[100] Article 1(A)(2). When a person is confirmed as a refugee, he or she has a right to be granted asylum in the host country. Furthermore, a person given refugee status is entitled to a range of rights, according to Articles 3 to 34 of the Refugee Convention. Article 24 grants, to refugees with a lawful stay, essential socio-economic rights, including healthcare. A fundamental principle in international refugee law (as specified in the preamble of Refugee Convention) is that refugees are to enjoy the widest possible exercise of their fundamental rights. Furthermore, as human beings, they are entitled to benefit from general human rights norms, as far as these apply.[101] It is generally assumed that human rights laws, including the provisions of the ICESCR, contribute by filling the gaps in the Refugee Convention.[102] However, persons having achieved refugee status, thereby also being entitled to lawful residence in the host country, have entitlements according to the Refugee Convention (see above), and will usually also have entitlements based on domestic regulations in the host country. For example, in Norway, the rights of refugees with lawful residence are identical to those of Norwegian citizens, when it comes to access to healthcare and social services.[103] Due to barriers in the labour market, and the limited duration of their residence in Norway, their income and old-age pensions are often low compared to most Norwegians. The Refugee Convention provides for gradual accumulation of rights, over time, in the country of asylum,[104] however this issue will not be pursued further here.

---

[99]   This approach is in line with the one taken in *V.C. v. Slovakia* (see section 6.2.1 above), in which the Court criticised the Slovakian government for violating the requirement of informed consent to sterilisation.

[100]   United Nations Convention Relating to the Status of Refugees, 28 July 1951 (resolution 429 (V)).

[101]   Alice Edwards, 'International Refugee Law' in Moecli, Shah and Sivakumaran (eds.), *International Human Rights Law*, Oxford University Press, 2014, 513–28, at 517 and 523.

[102]   Ibid., 523–24.

[103]   Patient and User's Rights Act §1-2 and regulation FOR-2011-12-16-1255 §2 (a).

[104]   Edwards, 'International Refugee Law', 524.

Asylum seekers are persons not yet determined to be, or confirmed as, refugees by the host state.[105] Therefore, they are not formally covered by the protection and rights set out in the Refugee Convention. However, according to Edwards, this is not as black and white as it may seem:

> all those provisions without an indicated level of attachment also apply to asylum-seekers, such as the right to education for children (Article 22), based on the argument that refugee status is declaratory rather than determinative – that is, determining a person to be a refugee does not *make* him or her a refugee, but rather such determination simply *recognizes* that he or she is a refugee (and, in most cases, was a refugee at the time of entry to the territory). This concept is important given the time lag between one's application for refugee status and the final determination on that application.[106]

This may also imply that asylum seekers waiting for their asylum applications to be decided have a right to healthcare, according to the Refugee Convention. This question will not be examined further here, save to mention, once again, that general human rights norms are applicable to asylum seekers, including Article 12 of the ICESCR. In Norway, asylum seekers are granted health rights on a par with both persons with refugee status, and citizens.[107]

8.3. UNAUTHORISED OR UNDOCUMENTED MIGRANTS

8.3.1. Overview

Unauthorised or undocumented migrants[108] are persons whose asylum applications have been rejected, and who are, therefore, not recognised as refugees, and who do not enjoy the protections offered by the Refugee Convention. The situation will be the same for persons who enter a country without seeking asylum. Many rejected asylum seekers end up as unauthorised migrants in the country of arrival. They do not have a particular legal status, either as refugees or asylum seekers. Most countries have regulations or policies aimed at minimising the interaction of unauthorised/undocumented migrants with the ordinary welfare system. The issue of high costs also poses problems for health professionals and public authorities, because the provider must charge someone: the state, an insurance company, or the patient.

---

[105] Ibid., 523.
[106] Ibid., 523, with reference to the UNHCR, *Handbook on Procedures and Criteria for Determining Refugee Status* (1979, reissued 2011) para. 28.
[107] Patient and User's Rights Act §1-2 and regulation FOR-2011-12-16-1255 §2 (a).
[108] These terms are used as synonyms.

Undocumented migrants often do not have a right to take paid work, and their financial situation will then be precarious, especially when they have been denied economic and social support. Countries often lack regulations on financing the treatment costs of undocumented migrants, leading to severe obstacles when seeking healthcare services, even in emergencies. Complicated and time-consuming reimbursement procedures required by the state when providing services to undocumented migrants represent practical barriers, and place administrative burdens on healthcare providers. The outcome is that undocumented migrants are sometimes turned away and refused necessary care.[109]

Therefore, these migrants will face many difficulties, in terms of legal, financial and administrative barriers to accessing health and welfare services in the country of residence. Normally, they cannot afford going to private doctors and facilities. The Platform for International Cooperation on Undocumented Migrants (PICUM), a network of organisations working to ensure social justice and human rights for undocumented migrants, summarises the situation like this:

> Even in countries where health services are available as a matter of law, there remain many administrative and other practical barriers that can prevent people who are undocumented from receiving the care they are entitled to. They may fear or actually risk being denounced to the immigration authorities or receiving large bills they cannot pay as a result of accessing services. They may also be incorrectly denied care and turned away because of complicated and inconsistently applied rules. Sometimes, administrative personnel in hospitals is not even aware that undocumented people have a right to access health care services. As a result, people who are undocumented often do not even use the health services they are entitled to. When they do access health services, it is often late, in emergencies.[110]

Many states do not grant essential health and social services to undocumented migrants, except for emergency care and key public health measures, leaving these migrants without access to essential primary health services or hospital care for chronic and serious health conditions, and without adequate housing

---

[109]   Henriette Sinding Aasen, Alice Kjellevold and Paul Stephens, "'Undocumented' migrants' access to health care services in Europe: tensions between international human rights, national law and professional ethics', in Henriette Sinding Aasen, Siri Gloppen, Anne-Mette Magnussen and Even Nilssen (eds.), *Juridification and Social Citizenship in the Welfare State*, Edward Elgar Publishing, 2014, 162–183, at 172–177, with further references, and Veronika Flegar, María Dalli and Brigit C.A. Toebes, 'Access to Preventive Health Care for Undocumented Migrants: A Comparative Study of Germany, the Netherlands and Spain from a Human Rights Perspective', *Laws* 2016, 5, 9; doi:10.3390/laws5010009, www.mdpi.com/journal/laws.

[110]   https://picum.org/focus-area/health-care/#news.

and other essential preconditions for human health.[111] Flegar et al describe the situation in Germany in the following way:

> The lack of access to preventive health care for undocumented migrants is aggravated by ... [provisions] which introduce a reporting obligation for public authorities: Health care providers can claim their expenses for the treatment of an undocumented migrant at the social security office, which then must notify the immigration office. The requirement of confidentiality effectively nullifies this provision and, if applied, allows undocumented migrants to remain anonymous. Nevertheless, most undocumented migrants are denied access to health care since they are still scared to be reported and consequently deported if they make use of health care services. This threshold is even higher for preventive health care, as the benefit of a preventive measure is highly unlikely to outweigh the risk of being detected.[112]

The confidentiality duty is essential in healthcare and for maintaining a general trust in the health system.[113] A system which links payment for health services with a reporting duty to the immigration office undermines the right to privacy and prevents vulnerable persons from seeking necessary health care. Access to emergency care, including birth assistance and care for pregnant women are recognised in many countries as part of state responsibility for health protection

---

[111] Flegar et al, 'Access to Preventive Health Care for Undocumented Migrants'. Another study, from 2012, indicated that, in the Netherlands, undocumented migrants' rights to healthcare are largely acknowledged, while Denmark and Sweden have more restrictions on access (Dan Biswas, Brigit Toebes, Anders Hjern, Henry Ascher and Marie Norredam, 'Access to health care for undocumented migrants from a human rights perspective: A comparative study of Denmark, Sweden, and the Netherlands', *Health and Human Rights Journal*, published December 2012 (https://www.hhrjournal.org/2013/08/access-to-health-care-for-undocumented-migrants-from-a-human-rights-perspective-a-comparative-study-of-denmark-sweden-and-the-netherlands/). As for the Netherlands, however, Thomas van den Akker and Jos van Roosmalen found that maternal mortality and severe morbidity generally occur more frequently, as compared to host populations, and that pregnant women without a legal resident permit were the most vulnerable, in 'Maternal mortality and severe morbidity in a migration perspective', *Best Practice & Research Clinical Obstetrics & Gynaecology* 32 (2016), 26–38, DOI:10.1016/j.bpobgyn.2015.08.016.

[112] Ibid. Flegar et al, 'Access to Preventive Health Care for Undocumented Migrants', 8.

[113] See the principled statement by the ECtHR in the case *Z v. Finland* (application no. 22009/93) 'the Court will take into account that the protection of personal data, not least medical data, is of fundamental importance to a person's enjoyment of his or her right to respect for private and family life as guaranteed by Article 8 of the Convention (art. 8). Respecting the confidentiality of health data is a vital principle in the legal systems of all the Contracting Parties to the Convention. It is crucial not only to respect the sense of privacy of a patient but also to preserve his or her confidence in the medical profession and in the health services in general. Without such protection, those in need of medical assistance may be deterred from revealing such information of a personal and intimate nature as may be necessary in order to receive appropriate treatment and, even, from seeking such assistance, thereby endangering their own health and, in the case of transmissible diseases, that of the community' (para. 95).

of particularly vulnerable groups. However, in several countries, women risk being billed for the costs of delivering their children and, in some countries, they also risk being reported to the immigration authorities.[114]

Thus, for unauthorised migrants with a weak legal position in their country of residence, several factors may hinder access to essential services, including emergency care. While NGOs in many countries provide some services, these are not entitlements, and are often scarce, being far from sufficient to secure an adequate standard of care, according to professional and human rights norms established by the ICESCR Article 12 and related sources outlining the state obligations towards undocumented migrants.[115]

8.3.2. The legal situation in Norway

In Norway, it is estimated that around 18,000 individuals are staying in the country without a legal permit.[116] Due to their unlawful stays, and the government's strategy of forcing people to leave the country as soon as possible after their asylum application has been rejected, these individuals are hard to count, they are highly marginalised, and they have limited access to health- and welfare services.[117] They are not entitled to take work, and people who hire them are persecuted as criminal offenders.[118]

The Norwegian healthcare system, which was developed according to the Beveridge principles of universal coverage,[119] makes a sharp distinction between

---

[114] Aasen, Kjellevold and Stephens, '"Undocumented" migrants' access to health care services in Europe: tensions between international human rights, national law and professional ethics', 172–177, with further references.

[115] The European Social Charter (Revised), 3 May 1996 (*European Treaty Series*, No. 163) is not as inclusive of undocumented migrants: see the Appendix to the ESC, available at https://rm.coe.int/168007cde4. For a comparison of international and European human rights instruments, see Aasen, Kjellevold and Stephens, '"Undocumented" migrants' access to health care services in Europe: tensions between international human rights, national law and professional ethics', 166–172, and Biswas et al, 'Access to health care for undocumented migrants from a human rights perspective'.

[116] According to a 2006 estimate (the latest official estimate from Statistics Norway), around 18,000 undocumented persons live in Norway (Red Cross, *Helserettigheter for "papirløse. Utenfor velferdsstatens sikkerhetsnett"* [Health rights for "the undocumented". Outside the security net of the welfare state] report, Oslo 2021,13, with reference to Zhang, 'Developing methods for determining the number of unauthorized foreigners in Norway', Statistics Norway, Division for Statistical Methods and Standards, 2008).

[117] Red Cross, *Helserettigheter for "papirløse. Utenfor velferdsstatens sikkerhetsnett"* [Health rights for "the undocumented". Outside the security net of the welfare state] report, Oslo 2021.

[118] For example, the previous bishop Gunnar Stålsett was, on 19 December 2019, convicted by the Oslo City Court for violating the Immigration Act by hiring a non-returnable woman who had been in Norway for 16 years as a domestic worker (https://www.aftenposten.no/norge/i/pLE176/staalsett-doemt-til-betinget-fengsel-jeg-hadde-gjort-det-igjen).

[119] Aasen, Kjellevold and Stephens, '"Undocumented' migrants'" access to health care services in Europe: tensions between international human rights, national law and professional ethics', 164–65.

nationals and non-nationals, concerning access to healthcare services. Primary healthcare is not available to undocumented adults in Norway, even on the basis of self-payment, according to a regulation adopted in 2011.[120] This is a clear violation of the guidelines provided by the ICESCR Committee, which highlight essential primary healthcare as a core obligation.[121] Children without legal residence are entitled to the full range of health and care services, except that they do not have a right to a permanent general practitioner.[122] Women are entitled to necessary care in relation to childbirth, including abortion services.[123] The Norwegian regulation grants emergency healthcare to all, including undocumented migrants, in addition to healthcare that is considered 'absolutely necessary'.[124] The distinction between these two categories of healthcare is unclear and ambiguous, and contributes to confusion among health practitioners applying the regulation.[125] Ultimately, only emergency care in a situation of acute health need is a clear legal entitlement for adult undocumented migrants in Norway. Due to the barriers for access to healthcare, and fear of being reported to the authorities, undocumented migrants delay seeking medical help, they typically wait until the problem and pain has become unbearable, with a worsened health condition and increased treatment costs as the consequences.[126] Delayed medical help may lead to a situation where the condition is no longer treatable.[127]

A major barrier in the Norwegian system is that people who are not registered as members of the Norwegian social security system (*folketrygden*), or do not have a European Health Insurance Card, are not entitled to free or subsidised services and will, therefore, normally be required to pay full costs, even for emergency treatment.[128] Even if it is not seen as permissible to require payment for emergency services in advance as a condition of providing treatment,[129] and

---

120   FOR-2011-12-16-1255, §4.
121   ICESCR Committee, General Comment No. 3 (1990), para. 10 and General Comment No. 14 (2000), para. 43(a) and (d), and para 44(c).
122   Patient and User's Act §2-1 (c), first section. Only asylum seekers with membership of the Norwegian social security system (*folketrygden*), and their families, have a right to a permanent doctor.
123   FOR-2011-12-16-1255, §5 (b) and (c).
124   FOR-2011-12-16-1255, §3 and §5 (a).
125   Red Cross, *Helserettigheter for "papirløse. Utenfor velferdsstatens sikkerhetsnett"* [Health rights for "the undocumented", 11 and 44.
126   Ibid., 29–30.
127   Ibid., 46.
128   Aasen, Kjellevold and Stephens, '"Undocumented" migrants' access to health care services in Europe: tensions between international human rights, national law and professional ethics', 174; Karl Harald Søvig, 'Tilgang til velferdstjenester for irregulære migranter etter det norske regelverket' ['Access to welfare services according to Norwegian law'] in Synnøve Bendixen, Christine M. Jacobsen and Karl Harald Søvig (eds.), *Eksepsjonell velferd? Irregulære migranter i det norske velferdssamfunnet* ['Exceptional welfare? Irregular migrants in the Norwegian welfare state'], Gyldendal, 2015, 48–69, 55–58 and 66–67.
129   Ibid., Søvig.

even if the regulation provides room for discretion regarding payment,[130] the situation is rather unpredictable from the perspective of undocumented migrants in acute need of healthcare. Several women have received large bills after giving birth in hospital, and legal abortions have been delayed.[131] For undocumented migrants, payment is a critical factor, and the risk of high fees may prevent many from seeking even emergency care and birth assistance.[132]

In its most-recent concluding observations on Norway (2020),[133] the ICESCR Committee repeated and strengthened its previous critique[134] of the Norwegian regulation:

> In the light of the significant decrease in the number of persons seeking asylum in the State party in recent years and the continuously strong economy of the State party, the Committee is concerned that the State party maintains the regressive measures taken in 2011 to restrict the right of irregular migrants, including European Union citizens not in possession of a European health insurance card, to primary health-care services without assessing the impact on the affected individuals. The Committee is particularly concerned about the limited scope of the conditions under which irregular migrants are provided with health care and the absence of clear guidelines for the interpretation of such conditions, which have led to a serious deterioration in the health conditions or to deaths of irregular migrants with chronic diseases and to inconsistent and varying degrees of health services provided to them. It is also concerned that irregular migrant children are not considered eligible to be placed on general practitioners' patient lists, which effectively hinders them from accessing the timely and adequate health-care services to which all children in the State party are entitled (para. 38).

The Committee's critique implies that the Norwegian regulation contradicts Article 12 and Article 2 of the ICESCR. The scope of services provided is too limited, and the regulation is not clear when it comes to the specific content and

---

[130] Act on specialized health care, 2 July 1999, No. 61 §5-3.

[131] Søvig, 'Tilgang til velferdstjenester for irregulære migranter etter det norske regelverket' ['Access to welfare services according to Norwegian law'], 48–69, 66, 67. This is still an issue: the newspaper *Klassekampen* reported, on 17 May 2021, that an eight months pregnant Moroccan woman in Norway without legal residence was told by the hospital that she would be billed 90,000 NOK (approx. 8,820 euros) for a hospital birth, and even more, in the event of a Caesarean section. The same newspaper reported, on 24 May 2021, of an undocumented woman from Bangladesh who had received debt-collection claims amounting to 250,000 NOK (approx. 24,500 euros) in respect of a birth at Haukeland University Hospital, Bergen in August 2019.

[132] Red Cross, *Helserettigheter for "papirløse". Utenfor velferdsstatens sikkerhetsnett* [Health rights for "the undocumented". Outside the security net of the welfare state], 46.

[133] Concluding observations on the sixth periodic report of Norway, 2 April 2020 (E/C.12/NOR/CO/6).

[134] Concluding observations on the fifth periodic report of Norway, 13 December 2013 (E/C.12/NOR/CO/5).

practical application. Health professionals have also pointed out the problems of understanding and applying the regulation, and the fact that it contradicts their professional duty of providing adequate care based on individual need.[135]

The Committee recommended that Norway should:

> take effective measures to ensure that all persons in the State party have access to primary health-care services, regardless of their residence status. In particular, the Committee recommends that the State party withdraw the regressive measures taken in 2011 with regard to the right of irregular migrants to primary health-care services and allow them and their children to be placed on general practitioners' lists' (para. 39, emphasis removed).

These recommendations could very well be viewed from a capability perspective (see section 7 above), meaning that legal and de facto access to essential healthcare services will ensure undocumented migrants with the possibility of living more healthy lives. The recommendation to remove the requirement of lawful residence, as a condition for access to essential healthcare, as well as securing affordable services, illustrates the point that vulnerability is often created by structural barriers and human rights violations caused by the state.

9. CONCLUDING REMARKS ON VULNERABILITY AND STATE OBLIGATIONS

The human rights framework provides important regulation concerning the vulnerability of patients in situations of conflict between personal autonomy and essential public interests regarding health, or other social interests or values. Individual autonomy must be weighed and balanced against social needs such as public health and safety, in accordance with requirements of legality, necessity and proportionality. The global COVID-19 pandemic, where the lives and well-being of all have been potentially vulnerable, in the face of virus transmission, has provided a constant reminder of the urgency of securing public health interests against threats posed by individual autonomy.

However, individual autonomy is an essential value in human rights law, protected by key human rights instruments, in order to ensure human

---

[135] Red Cross, *Helserettigheter for "papirløse". Utenfor velferdsstatens sikkerhetsnett* [Health rights for "the undocumented". Outside the security net of the welfare state], 48 (interview with health workers). See also a recent publication written by nurses: Ida Marie Bregård, Anne Bollas and Erwin Dublin, 'Vi driver sykepleie og ikke innvandringspolitikk' ['We perform nursing and not immigration politics'], *Sykepleien* 05.04.2021, available at https:// sykepleien.no/meninger/2021/04/vi-driver-sykepleie-og-ikke-innvandringspolitikk.

dignity and respect for individual freedom and agency. This value is especially important in situations where respect for individual autonomy, capacity and capability is threatened or undermined, for example when individuals encounter powerful or paternalistic authorities (see the discussion in section 6.2.3 above). In the health field, the case of *V.C. v. Slovakia* is a reminder that the informed consent doctrine was created to secure individual autonomy as an essential aspect of preserving human dignity. This is especially important in situations of powerlessness. In this case, the ECtHR criticised the failure to obtain informed consent to sterilisation from a woman belonging to an oppressed and stigmatised minority group. However, as pointed out by Peroni and Timmer, acknowledging vulnerability should not contribute to, or reinforce, stigmatisation and victimisation. The language used by courts and other powerful institutions may lead to the vulnerability aspect becoming viewed as the main characteristic of persons belonging to a particular group, which is contrary to the ideas of human rights, and the strengthening of the capabilities, and empowerment of, people in vulnerable situations.

The ICESCR Committee issued a statement on duties of states towards refugees and migrants under the ICESCR on 13 March 2017.[136] This statement sums up the duties of states in regard to the health protection and social welfare of migrants, and also illustrates key points relating to vulnerability due to discriminatory practices, and neglect of the basic needs of undocumented migrants staying within states' jurisdictions. The Committee emphasised the prohibition of discrimination on grounds of nationality or legal status, and the duty of states to pay specific attention to the particularly vulnerable situations of, in particular, asylum seekers and undocumented migrants:

> Under the Covenant, the requirement to guarantee all rights without discrimination imposes an immediate obligation on States parties … The Committee has made it clear that protection from discrimination cannot be made conditional upon an individual having a regular status in the host country … Consistent with the requirement of non-discrimination, States parties should pay specific attention to the practical obstacles that certain groups of the population may encounter in the enjoyment of their rights under the Covenant. Due to their precarious situation, asylum seekers and undocumented migrants are at particular risk of facing discrimination in the enjoyment of Covenant rights.[137]

The Committee also stated that undocumented migrants who are not seeking asylum cannot simply be ignored by the government, and that the

---

[136]   *Duties of States towards refugees and migrants under the International Covenant on Economic, Social and Cultural Rights.* Statement by the Committee on Economic, Social and Cultural Rights (E/C.12/2017/1).

[137]   Ibid., paras. 5, 6 and 7.

'very presence of such migrants under its jurisdiction imposes on the State certain obligations, including of course the primary obligation to acknowledge their presence and the fact that they can claim rights from national authorities'.[138]

Furthermore, the Committee recalled the duties of states to 'respect the right to health by ensuring that all persons, including migrants, have equal access to preventive, curative and palliative health services, regardless of their legal status and documentation', and to be aware of the specific obstacles that undocumented migrants, in particular, are faced with:

> Migrants in an irregular situation may also fear being detained for deportation, particularly in countries where public officials have a duty to report on irregular migrants. In addition to ensuring access to health care without discrimination, strict walls should exist between health-care personnel and law enforcement authorities, and adequate information should be made available in the languages commonly spoken by migrants in the host country, in order to ensure that such situations do not result in migrants avoiding seeking and obtaining health care.[139]

These are important statements on securing the capabilities of a particular vulnerable group to maintain dignified living conditions, including access to basic health and social services. If States Parties recognise and respect the duties following from the ICESCR, including socio-economic obligations, the right to health for migrants will certainly be improved, and human dignity can be restored, especially for undocumented migrants whose basic rights are currently neglected in a systematic manner, supported by national governments. The statement is a reminder of how States Parties to the ICESCR and other human rights instruments can take an active and rights-based approach[140] to strengthening the rights and capabilities of vulnerable groups in society.

---

[138] Ibid., para. 11.
[139] Ibid., para. 12.
[140] For a more detailed account of the rights-based approach, see Flegar et al, 'Access to Preventive Health Care for Undocumented Migrants', 17–18.

CHAPTER 9

DISABILITY

Aart HENDRIKS

1. INTRODUCTION

Persons with disabilities are generally seen as vulnerable persons (see Chapter 8 above). Their lack of equality does not confine itself to the healthcare sector, but impacts on all life activities. Their vulnerability is closely related to the fact that their disabilities have, traditionally, been viewed as being caused by a disease, impairment or other disorder. As a result of these individual conditions, disabled people are not always able to receive education, to generate an income through paid work, or otherwise participate as equals in society. Furthermore, many receive stereotypical and discriminatory reactions from others. People with disabilities sometimes – but not always – heavily rely on healthcare, and disproportionately depend on social security, to the extent that it is available in the country where they reside.

The aim of this chapter is to analyse the relationship between disability, health and human rights. It will do so by discussing disability rights from a global perspective, taking the United Nations Convention on the Rights of Persons with Disabilities (CRPD), adopted in 2006, as a point of reference (section 3). After describing and analysing this treaty, it will pay attention to the work of the United Nations Committee on the Rights of Persons with Disabilities (CRPD Committee), notably its case law and general comments (section 3.2). Following this global perspective, it will examine the slightly different approaches to the (health) rights of persons with disabilities in Europe taken by the Council of Europe and the European Union (section 4), and end with some conclusions (section 5). But to start with, it will pay attention to the meaning of the term disability (section 2).

2. DISABILITY

Disabilities – in the past also called 'handicaps', 'invalidities,' etc. – have traditionally been defined in terms of physical, mental, intellectual or sensory deviations from normality, caused by health problems.[1] These medically defined conditions are thought to explain why a person with disabilities has functional limitations, which hinder him or her from participating in society like others. This individual model of disability underlies, amongst others, the International Classification of Impairments, Disabilities and Handicaps (ICIDH), adopted by the World Health Organization (WHO) in 1980. This classification builds on a threefold distinction between impairments, disabilities and handicaps, as impacts of disease or disorder. This medical taxonomy situates the problems related to disability within the person concerned, and seeks to improve this person's quality of life and potential to participate in society by looking for appropriate healthcare solutions, including the provision of rehabilitation and medical aids.

This individual model of disability, portraying people with disabilities as persons with problems, who are in need of medical care, has, increasingly, been criticised by those emphasising the importance of the physical and social environment on the abilities of an individual.[2] In fact, a person may be hindered from functioning in a conventional way due to an impairment. But such impairments can be the result of external factors unrelated to healthcare. As an example, a person may be involved in a car accident and lose a leg. Apart from an amputated leg and the need to use a wheelchair, they may not have any other medical condition. Their functional restriction is, above all, the result of a lack of equal access to buildings, due to the presence of thresholds and stairs, and the absence of ramps and elevators.

According to the social model of disability, in contrast to the individual model, a disability is a social construct that reflects the denial of human rights and equal opportunities to groups that are deemed less able to function in society, due to individual characteristics. Social constructionists call for the breakdown of the mostly human-made physical and social barriers that inhibit people with disabilities from participating fully and equally in society.[3]

The criticism of the individual and medical model of disability was echoed in the International Classification of Functioning, Disability and Health (ICF), adopted by the WHO in 2001. This classification replaced the ICIDH. While the ICIDH focused on the functional limitations of disabled individuals, due to their medical differences from others, the ICF is a classification of health and health-related domains, with a list of environmental factors that may hinder the

---

[1]   S.L Percy, *Disability, Civil Rights, and Public Policy*, Tuscaloosa: University of Alabama Press, 1989 and C. Barnes, *Disabled People in Britain and Discrimination*, London: Hurst & Company, 1991.

[2]   A.C. Hendriks and O. Lewis, 'Disability' in Y. Joly and B.M. Knoppers (eds.), *Routledge Handbook of Medical Law and Ethics*, London: Routledge, 2015, 78–97.

[3]   Ibid.

functioning of disabled persons. The ICF, thus, in line with the social model of disability, emphasises the importance of addressing the physical and social obstacles that inhibit people with particular impairments from functioning in society as equals.

Even though it is doubtful whether all disabilities are caused by external factors,[4] it is increasingly accepted that disabilities can only be well understood and mitigated by studying the interaction between individuals and their environments. It is, increasingly, acknowledged that, for people with disabilities to have full opportunities to function, they also need adaptations of their environments: this may be in the form of individually focused healthcare or other measures, and, often, a combination of both.

3. GLOBAL DISABILITY RIGHTS CONVENTION ON THE RIGHTS OF PERSONS WITH DISABILITIES

3.1. LEGAL DOCUMENTS – THE RIGHTS OF PERSONS WITH DISABILITIES

The United Nations (UN) has adopted a large number of human rights instruments, including documents stipulating the rights of specific groups (see Chapter 4 of this book). Until the beginning of this century, people with disabilities were not explicitly covered by these instruments, and there was no human rights convention on disability. In 2006, the UN adopted the Convention on the Rights of Persons with Disabilities (CRPD). This is the first international, legally binding instrument setting minimum standards for the rights of people with disabilities. It was opened for signature by states on 30 March 2007. To date, 182 parties – including the European Union (EU) – have ratified this convention. This means that the CRPD is amongst the human rights instruments with the largest number of ratifying states. Just over half of these 182 States Parties (96 in total) have also ratified the Optional Protocol to the CRPD. This Protocol allows individuals and groups to file a complaint against a States Party with the Committee on the Rights of Persons with Disabilities (the CRPD Committee) after exhausting national remedies. The Committee brings any such complaints ('communications') to the attention of the relevant state, who must submit written explanations or statements within six months. The views of the CRPD Committee on a communication are, however, non-binding. According to the Optional Protocol, the CRPD Committee must forward its suggestions

---

4   A.C. Hendriks, 'The UN Disability Convention and (Multiple) Discrimination: Should EU non-discrimination law be modelled accordingly?' in L. Waddington and G. Quinn (eds.), *European Yearbook of Disability Law 2010*, Antwerp: Intersentia, 2010, 7–27.

and recommendations to the States Party concerned, after studying the complaint. This means that States Parties are not legally obliged to implement the views of the CRPD Committee, even though, as stated above, they are asked to report back to the CRPD Committee within six months.[5]

How does the CRPD define the concept of disability? According to Article 1:

> Persons with disabilities include those who have long-term physical, mental, intellectual or sensory impairments which in interaction with various barriers may hinder their full and effective participation in society on an equal basis with others.

This description does not really define what constitutes a disability, but is meant to be non-exhaustive and illustrative, as indicated by the use of the word 'include'. It becomes clear from the description that this provision reflects a social model of disability, by emphasising the interaction between the individual and the environment. At the same time, this provision allows a States Party to deny persons the status of being disabled, in the event that their impairments do not have any long-term effect.

Countries that ratify the CRPD commit themselves to developing and enacting policies, laws and administrative measures for securing the rights recognised in the CRPD, and to abolishing laws, regulations, customs and practices that constitute disability discrimination. The object of the CRPD was not to introduce new rights, but to guarantee that a person with disabilities would be entitled to the same rights and freedoms as laid down in other human rights conventions adopted by the UN. Despite this goal, it cannot be denied that the CRPD adds new dimensions – geared to the specific needs of persons with disabilities – to existing human rights. Examples of these include the obligation to provide a reasonable accommodation to persons with disabilities, in an effort to prevent and redress discrimination (Article 2); recognition of the additional vulnerability of women and children with disabilities (Articles 6 and 7); the obligation of States Parties to protect the legal capacity of persons with disabilities, and to ensure that a representative always respects their rights, wills and preferences (Article 12); and the efforts that States Parties should make to enhance personal mobility (Article 20).

What is also slightly different about the CRPD, in comparison to existing UN human rights conventions, is the importance that it attaches to changing negative perceptions about disabilities, to combating stereotypes and prejudices, and to promoting awareness of the capabilities of persons with disabilities. More positive perceptions about disabilities are thought to increase the

---

[5]   United Nations CRPD Committee, Rules of Procedure, 10 October 2016, Rule 75.

opportunities of individuals with disabilities, to the benefit of their dignity and well-being.

And, needless to say, the CRPD obligates States Parties to recognise the right to the enjoyment of the highest attainable standard of health, without discrimination on the basis of disability (Article 25). Amongst other things, this provision stipulates that States Parties should prevent the discriminatory denial of healthcare, health services or food and fluids, on the basis of disability.

3.2. THE COMMITTEE ON THE RIGHTS OF PERSONS WITH DISABILITIES

The CRPD established its own Committee, a body that carries out a number of tasks and functions (Article 34). The CRPD Committee consists of 18 independent experts, elected by the States Parties, paying attention to an equitable geographical distribution, and a balanced gender representation. The experts serve in their individual capacities, not as government representatives. The CRPD Committee normally meets twice per year in Geneva, Switzerland (due to the COVID-19 pandemic, this meeting schedule was temporarily changed in 2020).

Like other treaty bodies established under UN human rights treaties, the main task of the CRPD Committee is to monitor the correct implementation of the CRPD by the States Parties (Article 35). In order to do so, States Parties are required, periodically, to submit reports to the CRPD Committee on how the rights of the CRPD are being implemented within the domestic legal order. The CRPD Committee examines these reports, and may take into account reports submitted by non-governmental organisations ('counter-reports'). It also has the authority to make suggestions to the States Party concerned, and to draft general recommendations on the report. States Parties preparing their country reports are expected to follow the guidelines that apply to all reports drafted to UN human rights treaty bodies.[6]

As mentioned below, the Optional Protocol to the CRPD gives the CRPD Committee the competence to examine complaints of individuals and groups about alleged violations of the CRPD by States Parties. All decisions ('views') of the CRPD Committee are published.[7] In an effort to assist potential plaintiffs, the UN has published a model complaint form for all human rights bodies, including the CRPD.[8] So far, the CRPD Committee has decided on several complaints ('communications') in which plaintiffs ('authors') have claimed,

---

[6] www.ohchr.org/EN/HRBodies/Pages/tb-documentation-tools.aspx.
[7] juris.ohchr.org/Search/Results.
[8] www.ohchr.org/EN/HRBodies/CRPD/Pages/CRPDIndex.aspx.

inter alia, that their health rights were being violated by a States Party. Four complaints have, however, been declared inadmissible by the CRPD Committee, and these, including two related complaints, are briefly summarised below.

In 2017, the CRPD Committee gave its decision on two similar complaints against the United Kingdom.[9] The plaintiff in this case was a woman who suffered from a number of complex health issues following a loss of cerebrospinal fluid during a discectomy procedure. The plaintiff had asked the CRPD Committee, in two related complaints, to request the UK government to release funds to cover the medical costs of diagnostic testing, treatment and rehabilitation, and any other necessary medical services. She stated that her needs as a disabled person with multiple rare neurological disorders had not been met, and that she had continuously faced hostility and insurmountable obstacles in her efforts to obtain treatment. The CRPD Committee declared both complaints inadmissible, since the plaintiff had not provided any evidence to indicate that she had been denied access to healthcare or legal redress on an equal basis with others.

Later in 2017, the CRPD Committee decided on a complaint against the Swedish government.[10] The complaint concerned the planned deportation of a family from Sweden to Nigeria. One son had been diagnosed with autism and other unspecified psychosocial disabilities, and his parents argued that this action would violate their son's rights under the CRPD, including the right to have access to adequate healthcare, which would not be available in Nigeria. The CRPD Committee declared the complaint inadmissible, noting that the expulsion order had become statute-barred and was, consequently, no longer enforceable.

The fourth decision concerned a complaint against Greece.[11] The plaintiff in this case claimed that a state body had wrongly diagnosed her with a borderline personality disorder, rather than with Asperger syndrome, and that this amounted to a violation of various rights protected by the CRPD. The CRPD Committee declared the complaint inadmissible, due to the plaintiff's failure to exhaust national remedies.

On the basis of this relatively short list of decisions, it can be noted that, in all cases, either the parties or CRPD Committee referred to judgments of the European Court of Human Rights (ECtHR) in comparable cases. This may reflect the importance of the judgments of the ECtHR for the CRPD Committee, particularly – as was the case here – in complaints against States Parties that have also ratified the European Convention of Human Rights (ECHR).

The CRPD Committee has found violations of the right to health in two complaints. In one, the complainant claimed that a slight hearing impairment

---

[9]   CRPD Committee, 17 May 2017, *L.M.L. v. the United Kingdom*, communication no. 27/2015.
[10]   CRPD Committee, 15 September 2017, *O.O.J. v. Sweden*, communication no. 28/2015.
[11]   CRPD Committee, 2 April 2019, *T.M. v. Greece*, communication no. 42/2017.

had developed into deafness in the affected ear, due to torture in custody, and lack of access to treatment, in Saudi Arabia.[12] The CRPD Committee found the complaint admissible, noting that although it was pending examination by several Special Rapporteurs, this did not amount to an international procedure or investigation within the meaning of Article 2(c) of the Optional Protocol. As Saudi Arabia did not submit any comments on the merits of the complaint, the CRPD Committee decided the complaint on the basis of the author's substantiated submissions. The CRPD Committee found that the States Party had violated the author's rights under Article 25(b), in failing to provide access to urgent surgery needed to minimise and prevent further disabilities. Furthermore, the CRPD Committee recalled that states 'have a special responsibility to uphold human rights when prison authorities exercise significant control or power over persons with disabilities who have been deprived of their liberty by a court of law'.[13] Despite this decision, Saudi Arabia executed the applicant, Munir al-Adam, in 2019.

In another complaint against Sweden, the CRPD Committee also found a violation of the right to health under Article 25.[14] The author had Ehlers-Danlos syndrome, was bedridden, and could not leave her house. The individual required hydrotherapy, which would improve her quality of life. She therefore applied for building permission to extend her house to build an indoor swimming pool. Building permission was, however, rejected. The CRPD Committee found that the States Party did not address the specific circumstances of the author's case and her disability related needs when rejecting permission. The decision was disproportionate, and created a discriminatory effect. Therefore, the author's rights under Articles 5 and 25 had been violated. It called on the state to reconsider the complaint and provide compensation to author, while ensuring that legislation and domestic courts were in compliance with the state's obligations under the CRPD.

Furthermore, even though the CRPD does not explicitly bestow the CRPD Committee with the authority to adopt general comments, the CRPD Committee has, so far, adopted seven general comments based on its review of state reports.[15] None of these comments explicitly address issues in the field of health. Nevertheless, three of these general comments are particularly relevant when studying the relation between health and human rights. In General Comment No. 1 (2014), on equal recognition before the law, the CRPD Committee was critical of States Parties that make use of substitute decision-making regimes, thereby removing legal capacity from disabled people, a measure that is

---

[12] CRPD Committee, 24 October 2018, *Munir al-Adam v. Saudi Arabia*, communication no. 38/2016.
[13] Ibid., para. 11.6.
[14] CRPD Committee, 19 April 2012, *H.M. v. Sweden*, communication no. 3/2011.
[15] www.ohchr.org/EN/HRBodies/CRPD/Pages/GC.aspx.

sometimes done against the will of the person with disabilities. It may also be that a substitute decision-maker is appointed to act in the best interests of the person concerned, as opposed to basing their decisions on the will and preferences of the person with the disability. The CRPD Committee considers these measures to be contrary to the rights enshrined in the CRPD, and has emphasised the need to shift the substitute decision-making paradigm to one that is based on supported decision-making, thus basing decisions on the own will and preferences of the person with a disability concerned to the maximum possible extent (para. 50).[16]

In General Comment No. 2 (2014), on accessibility, the CRPD Committee emphasised the importance of accessibility for the enjoyment of almost all CRPD rights. With respect to health, the CRPD Committee observed that healthcare would remain unattainable for persons with disabilities without access to the healthcare premises where those services are provided. Even if the buildings where the healthcare services are provided are themselves accessible, without accessible transportation, persons with disabilities are unable to travel to such places.

General Comment No. 6 (2018) focuses on equality and non-discrimination. The Committee pointed, with great concern, to discriminatory forms of medical treatment, including non-consensual and/or forced systematic sterilisations and medical or hormone-based interventions, forced drugging and electroshocks, confinement, and forced and coerced abortion. It is remarkable that the CRPD Committee also referred to 'systematic murder labelled "euthanasia"' as a form of discrimination (see Chapter 11 of this book). The CRPD Committee is also critical of mental health laws that legitimise forced institutionalisation and treatment. According to the CRPD Committee, these forms of treatment are discriminatory, and laws authorising these practices should be abolished.[17]

---

[16] 'In the light of the normative content and obligations outlined above, States parties should take the following steps to ensure the full implementation of article 12 of the Convention on the Rights of Persons with Disabilities: (a) Recognize persons with disabilities as persons before the law, having legal personality and legal capacity in all aspects of life, on an equal basis with others. This requires the abolition of substitute decision-making regimes and mechanisms that deny legal capacity and which discriminate in purpose or effect against persons with disabilities. It is recommended that States parties create statutory language protecting the right to legal capacity on an equal basis for all; (b) Establish, recognize and provide persons with disabilities with access to a broad range of support in the exercise of their legal capacity. Safeguards for such support must be premised on respect for the rights, will and preferences of persons with disabilities. The support should meet the criteria set out in paragraph 29 above on the obligations of States parties to comply with article 12, paragraph 3, of the Convention; (c) Closely consult with and actively involve persons with disabilities, including children with disabilities, through their representative organizations, in the development and implementation of legislation, policies and other decision-making processes that give effect to article 12.'

[17] See, further, Anna Nilsson, *Compulsory Mental Health Interventions and the CRPD: Minding Equality*, London: Hart, 2021.

With respect to the right to health, as protected by Article 25 of the CRPD, the CRPD Committee recommends that States Parties should prohibit and prevent discriminatory denial of health services to persons with disabilities, and provide gender-sensitive health services, including sexual and reproductive health rights. The CRPD Committee has also been critical of domestic laws permitting late-term abortions because of foetal disability, signalling a potential conflict between the CRPD and other UN human rights treaties.[18] In addition, States Parties should address forms of discrimination that violate the rights of persons with disabilities by impeding their rights to health: more specifically, violations of the right to receive healthcare on the basis of free and informed consent, or violations that make facilities or information inaccessible.

4. DISABILITY RIGHTS IN EUROPE

Both the Council of Europe and the European Union have committed to respect, protect and fulfil the (health) rights of persons with disabilities. The same holds true for the great majority of European countries. This section will confine itself to analysing the work of the Council of Europe and the European Union, including the case law of the European Court of Human Rights (ECtHR), the European Committee of Social Rights (ECSR), and the Court of Justice of the European Union (CJEU) with respect to the (health) rights of persons with disabilities.

4.1. LEGAL DOCUMENTS

4.1.1. Council of Europe

The ECHR does not contain any reference to the rights of persons with disabilities. Neither does it refer to the ground of disability in its non-discrimination provision (Article 14). In fact, it could be argued that the ECHR only indirectly seeks to protect the rights of persons with mental disabilities, more precisely 'persons of unsound mind', against their unlawful detention. Article 5, paragraph 1 of the ECHR stipulates that the liberty and security

---

[18] Concluding observations, Spain, 13 May 2019, CRPD/C/ESP/CO/2-3; Concluding observations, United Kingdom of Great Britain and Northern Ireland, 3 October 2017, CRPD/C/GBR/CO/1. The CRPD Committee has, on the other hand, consistently recognised reproductive rights: see, inter alia, 'Guaranteeing sexual and reproductive health and rights for all women, in particular women with disabilities. Joint statement by the Committee on the Rights of Persons with Disabilities (CRPD) and the Committee on the Elimination of All Forms of Discrimination against Women (CEDAW)', 29 August 2018.

of 'persons of unsound mind' may be restricted, but only where this is in accordance with a procedure prescribed by law. This can be contrasted with the CRPD, which is silent on compulsory care.[19] At the same time, Article 1 ECHR provides that States Parties are obliged to secure, for everyone within their jurisdiction, the rights and freedoms defined in the ECHR. This obligation applies equally to people with disabilities. And even though the ECHR's non-discrimination provision does not explicitly refer to the ground of 'disability', or to any similarly worded term, this provision also seeks to prevent discrimination on grounds other than those enumerated, particularly in relation to groups that have, historically, been subjected to discrimination.[20] In 2009, the ECtHR, while referring to the CRPD, explicitly acknowledged that people with disabilities should be protected from discrimination, and that they are covered by Article 14 of the ECHR.[21]

Article 15 of the European Social Charter (ESC) recognises that disabled persons have the right to independence, social integration and participation in the life of the community. In order to achieve these aims, this provision imposes a number of obligations on states. Even though this list of obligations is non-exhaustive, it is remarkable that equal access to health and medical services are not mentioned. The reason for this might be that the ESC contains a special provision on the right to protection of health (Article 11). It is also worth mentioning that the ESC includes a provision on non-discrimination. This provision (Article E) prohibits discrimination on a large number of grounds, including 'health'. It is not clear why this provision fails to refer to 'disability', although disability may be covered by the ground of 'other status', which is also enumerated. The ECSR has, however, stated that non-discrimination on grounds of disability forms an integral part of Article 15.[22]

4.1.2. European Union

The European Union is committed to combating discrimination on the grounds of disability. In view of this, in 2000 the EU adopted the Employment Equality Directive (Directive 2000/78/EC). This directive established a general

---

19 Anna Nilsson, *Compulsory Mental Health Interventions and the CRPD: Minding Equality*, London: Hart, 2021, 151.
20 ECtHR 10 March 2011, *Kiyutins v. Russia*, no. 2700/10, ECLI:CE:ECHR:2011:0310 JUD000270010, para. 63.
21 ECtHR 30 April 2009, *Glor v. Switzerland*, no. 13444/04, ECLI:CE:ECHR:2009:0430 JUD00134440410, para. 33: 'It also considers that there is a European and worldwide consensus on the need to protect people with disabilities from discriminatory treatment (see, for example, Recommendation 1592 (2003) towards full social inclusion of people with disabilities, adopted by the Parliamentary Assembly of the Council of Europe on 29 January 2003, or the United Nations Convention on the Rights of Persons with Disabilities, which entered into force on 3 May 2008).'
22 ECSR, Conclusions 2003, Statement of Interpretation on Article 15, 10, para. 5.

framework for equal treatment and non-discrimination in the fields of employment and occupation, on grounds of – amongst others – disability. This directive also contains an obligation to provide, only for persons with disability, a reasonable accommodation.

Also in 2000, the European institutions solemnly proclaimed the EU Charter of Fundamental Rights of the European Union (CFR), a document that became legally binding as of 1 December 2009. The CFR prohibits discrimination on grounds of disability (Article 21), and emphasises the importance of integration of persons with disabilities (Article 26).

Later, the non-discrimination principle was described as a fundamental value of the EU, in Article 2 of the Treaty of European Union (TEU), along with the requirements for the EU to combat discrimination on grounds of disability, and to strive towards the integration of people with disabilities (Articles 10 and 13 of the Treaty on the Functioning of the European Union (TFEU), respectively). The EU, moreover, signed and ratified the CRPD, which entered into force for the EU on 22 January 2011. This day marked the first time that the EU had become a party to a human rights convention.

4.2. DEFINITIONS

4.2.1. Council of Europe

In contrast to the CRPD, neither the ECHR nor the ESC provide a definition of disability. To date, the ECtHR and the ECSR have not tried to do so. The ECtHR usually refers to 'physical disabilities', 'mental disabilities', 'severe disabilities' and similarly worded categories of disabled persons, without further clarification.

4.2.2. European Union

Neither the Treaty of European Union (TEU) nor the Treaty on the Functioning of the European Union (TFEU) define the term disability. The same holds true for the Employment Equality Directive. The CJEU, however, felt the need to describe this term more precisely.

In the CJEU's first judgment about the meaning of disability under the Employment Equality Directive, the Court considered that the concept of disability 'must be understood as referring to a limitation which results in particular from physical, mental or psychological impairments and which hinders the participation of the person concerned in professional life'.[23] After the

---

[23]   CJEU 11 July 2006, *Chacón Navas*, C-13/05, ECLI:EU:C:2006:456.

EU ratified the CRPD, the CJEU redefined its definition of disability, redefining the concept more along the lines of the social model of disability discussed above, by expressing the view that a disability is 'a limitation which results in particular from physical, mental or psychological impairments which in interaction with various barriers may hinder the full and effective participation of the person concerned in professional life on an equal basis with other workers, and the limitation is a long-term one'.[24] This definition resembles the description of disability in the CRPD. The CJEU stated that the Equality Employment Directive 'must, as far as possible, be interpreted in a manner consistent with that Convention [on the Rights of Persons with Disabilities]'.[25]

4.3. EUROPEAN CASE LAW

4.3.1. Council of Europe

The case law of the ECtHR on disability issues covers a range of questions, including health and human rights issues. In a judgment of the ECtHR against Latvia, concerning the right to life (Article 2 ECHR), the ECtHR found that the States Party had violated this right by not providing adequate medical treatment to the applicant's deaf and mute son.[26] Also, in a case against Romania, concerning an HIV-positive Roma minor with a severe mental disability who was detained in a psychiatric hospital, the ECtHR found that Article 2 had been violated. The ECtHR held the view that the plaintiff had been placed in medical institutions that were not equipped to provide adequate care for his condition, that he had been transferred from one unit to another without proper diagnosis, and that the Romanian authorities had failed to ensure his appropriate treatment with antiretroviral medication.[27]

In a case against Russia, the ECtHR held that the Russian authorities had violated the prohibition of inhuman or degrading treatment (Article 3).[28] The applicant, a wheelchair user with numerous health problems, had been detained in a cell on the fourth floor of a building without an elevator. According to the ECtHR, the national authorities had failed to treat the applicant in a

---

[24]   CJEU 11 April 2013, *HK Danmark*, C-335/11 and 337/11 and ECLI:EU:C:2013:222; CJEU 18 December 2014, *Kaltoft*, C-354/13, ECLI:EU:C:2014:2463.

[25]   CJEU 11 April 2013, *HK Danmark*, C-335/11 and 337/11, ECLI:EU:C:2013:222.

[26]   ECtHR 21 December 2010, *Jasinskis v. Latvia*, no. 45744/08, ECLI:CE:ECHR:2010:1221 JUD004574408.

[27]   ECtHR 17 July 2014, *Valentin Câmpeanu v. Romania* (GC), no. 47848/08, ECLI:CE:ECHR: 2014:0717JUD004784808.

[28]   For a previous example, see ECtHR 10 July 2001, *Price v. the United Kingdom*, no. 33394/96, ECLI:CE:ECHR:2001:0710JUD003339496, concerning the treatment of a severely disabled person.

safe and appropriate manner consistent with his disability, and had denied him effective access to medical facilities, outdoor exercise and fresh air.[29] It should be mentioned that the ECtHR, in complaints by disabled people, often emphasises their vulnerability, requesting States Parties to take this into account (see Chapter 8 of this book).[30] In another case against Latvia, the ECtHR found that Article 3 had been violated with respect to a paraplegic prison inmate who used a wheelchair. The applicant was detained in a detention facility, which was not adapted for persons in a wheelchair. The ECtHR emphasised that the state's obligation to ensure adequate conditions of detention included making provision for the special needs of prisoners with physical disabilities.[31] Separately, the Court has also held that, once national legislation grants persons with disabilities the right to free medication, this entitlement should also be complied with in prison.[32]

The ECtHR emphasises the importance of persons with disabilities being able to participate in legal procedures with respect to their deprivation of liberty, the appointment of a representative, and, in general, the right to a fair trial. A state's non-compliance with these obligations may result in a violation of Article 5 and/or 6 of the ECHR.[33] When it comes to the deprivation of liberty of a person of 'unsound mind', the ECtHR requires an entire set of criteria to be met, including an objective medical report on the mental disorder, for compulsory confinement to have been a measure of last resort, and the expectation that the mental disorder and related dangers will persist throughout the period of detention.[34]

The ECtHR is also critical of the full deprivation of a person's legal capacity, and the appointment of a guardian or other representative without the involvement of the person concerned. This has resulted in violations of

---

[29]　ECtHR 10 January 2012, *Arutyunyan v. Russia*, no. 48977/09, ECLI:CE:ECHR:2012:0110 JUD004897709.

[30]　See, e.g. ECtHR 3 April 2001, *Keenan v. the United Kingdom*, no. 27229/95, ECLI:CE:ECHR:2001: 0403JUD002722995; ECtHR 8 July 2008, *Tokić et al. v. Bosnia and Herzegovina*, nos. 12455/04, 14140/05, 12906/06 and 26028/06, ECLI:CE:ECHR:2008:0708JUD001245504; ECtHR 10 March 2011, *Kiyutin v. Russia*, no. 2700/10, ECLI:CE:ECHR:2011:0310JUD000270010.

[31]　ECtHR 25 June 2013, *Grimailovs v. Latvia*, no. 6087/03, ECLI:CE:ECHR:2013:0625 JUD000608703. See, for similar judgments, ECtHR 24 October 2006, *Vincent v. France*, no. 6253/03, ECLI:CE:ECHR:2006:1024JUD000625303; ECtHR 3 May 2007, *Hüseyin Yıldırım v. Turkey*, no. 2778/02, ECLI:CE:ECHR:2007:0503JUD000277802 and ECtHR 3 March 2015, *Sandu Voicu v. Romania*, no. 45720/11, ECLI:CE:ECHR:2015:0303JUD004572011.

[32]　ECtHR 8 October 2019, *Fedulov v. Russia*, no. 53068/08, ECLI:CE:ECHR:2019:1008 JUD005306808.

[33]　ECtHR 14 February 2012, *D.D. v. Lithuania*, no. 13469/06, ECLI:CE:ECHR:2012:0214 JUD001346906; ECtHR 31 May 2016, *A.N. v. Lithuania*, no. 17280/08, ECLI:CE:ECHR:2016: 0531JUD001728008.

[34]　M. Szwed, 'The notion of "a person of unsound mind" under Article 5 §1(f) of the European Convention on Human Rights', *Netherlands Quarterly of Human Rights* [2020], 283–301.

the right to respect of private life (Article 8 of the ECHR) being established in complaints against, amongst others, Russia,[35] Croatia,[36] Lithuania[37] and Armenia.[38] In addition, the ECtHR is not easily convinced that restrictions of mentally disabled parents' parental rights and access to their children for are justified.[39]

The ECtHR also requires special reasons to deprive a disabled person of the right to vote (Article 3, Protocol 1 of the ECHR).[40] The right to vote is, however, not an absolute right. In 2021, the Court found that restrictions imposed on disabled persons regarding the right to vote did not constitute a violation of the right to free election. While the Danish legislature had constantly tried to reduce the restrictions to a minimum, the restrictions complained about had a legal basis, and were otherwise justified.[41]

Analysis of the case law of the ECtHR makes it clear that the Court has, since 2009,[42] regularly referred to the CRPD as a source of inspiration, and a form of so called 'present-day conditions'.[43] The ECtHR also expects States Parties to make reasonable accommodations for people with disabilities.[44] Non-discrimination and reasonable accommodation are also norms that should be respected in the field of healthcare, even though the ECHR – in contrast to UN treaties and the (revised) European Social Charter – does not refer to the right to health (see Chapter 2 of this book). At the same time, the ECtHR does not fully align with the interpretation of the CRPD by the CRPD Committee. As mentioned above, the ECtHR does not prohibit all restrictions on the rights of persons with intellectual disabilities to vote. Equally, with respect to the equal recognition

---

[35] ECtHR 27 March 2008, *Shtukaturov v. Russia*, no. 44009/05, ECLI:CE:ECHR:2008:0327 JUD004400905.

[36] ECtHR 25 April 2013, *M.S. v. Croatia*, no. 36337/10, ECLI:CE:ECHR:2013:0425 JUD003633710.

[37] ECtHR 31 May 2016, *A.N. v. Lithuania*, no. 17280/08, ECLI:CE:ECHR:2016:0531 JUD001728008.

[38] ECtHR 3 October 2019, *Nikolyan v. Armenia*, no. 74438/14, ECLI:CE:ECHR:2019:1003 JUD007443814.

[39] ECtHR 18 February 2020, *Cînţa v. Romania*, no. 3891/19, ECLI:CE:ECHR:2020:0218 JUD000389119.

[40] ECtHR 20 May 2010, *Alajos Kiss v. Hungary*, no. 38832/06, ECLI:CE:ECHR:2010:0520 JUD003883206.

[41] ECtHR 2 February 2021, *Strøbye and Rosenlind v. Denmark*, nos. 25802/18 and 27338/18, ECLI:CE:ECHR:2021:0202JUD002580218. See also ECtHR 11 May 2021, *Caamaño Valle v. Spain*, no. 43564/17, ECLI:CE:ECHR:2021:0511JUD004356417.

[42] ECtHR 30 April 2009, *Glor v. Switzerland*, no. 13444/04, ECLI:CE:ECHR:2009:0430 JUD001344404.

[43] ECtHR 23 March 2017, *A.-M.V. v. Finland*, no. 53251/13, ECLI:CE:ECHR:2017:0323 JUD005325113.

[44] ECtHR 23 February 2016, *Çam v. Turkey*, no. 51500/08, ECLI:CE:ECHR:2016:0223 JUD005150008; ECtHR 29 January 2013, *Horváth and Kiss v. Hungary*, no. 11146/11, ECLI:CE:ECHR:2013:0129JUD001114611.

of persons before the law, the ECtHR seemingly allows more restrictions on the legal capacities of persons with disabilities, and greater appointment of guardians, with more extensive roles, than the CRPD Committee is inclined to accept.

In various cases, the ECSR has decided that States Parties have failed to protect the rights of disabled persons, as prescribed by Article 15 of the ESC. In one complaint, the ECSR held that Belgium had violated this provision, on the ground that the right to inclusive education of children with intellectual disabilities had not been guaranteed effectively for the French Community in Belgium.[45] In a similar case against Belgium, the ECSR decided that the lack of access to mainstream schooling for children with intellectual disabilities constituted a violation of Article 15.[46] The ECSR also declared a complaint, submitted against France, to be admissible, where it was stated by the plaintiffs that the French government had failed, in various ways, to live up to its obligations to respect the rights of persons with disabilities.[47]

In some cases, the ECSR has ruled that States Parties have failed to comply with the obligation to offer children with disabilities with sufficient protection (Article 17), by institutionalising children under the age of three with disabilities in children's homes.[48] In a case against Belgium, the ECSR decided that the Belgian government had failed to provide sufficient day and night care facilities for adults with disabilities, and that this also constituted a form of discrimination.[49]

One final decision of the ECSR that deserves mentioning here related to the limited funds in France's social budget for the education of children and adolescents with autism. This indirectly disadvantaged persons with disabilities, for example with respect to the right to participate in society free from discrimination. The ECSR held that, although the limited public funding allocated to social protection could affect everyone who was supposed to be covered by this protection, people with disabilities were more likely than others to be dependent on community care in order to live independently, and with dignity. Thus, budget restrictions in social policy matters may place persons with disabilities at a disadvantage.[50]

---

45   ECSR 3 February 2021, *International Federation for Human Rights (FIDH) and Inclusion Europe v. Belgium*, complaint no. 141/2017.
46   ECSR 29 March 2018, *Mental Disability Advocacy Center (MDAC) v. Belgium*, complaint no. 109/2014.
47   ECSR 16 October 2018, *European Disability Forum (EDF) and Inclusion Europe v. France* (dec.), complaint no. 168/2018.
48   ECSR 20 November 2020, *European Roma Rights Centre (ERRC) and Mental Disability Advocacy Centre (MDAC) v. Czech Republic*, complaint no. 157/2017.
49   ECSR 27 July 2013, *International Federation for Human Rights (FIDH) v. Belgium*, complaint no. 75/2011.
50   ECSR 11 September 2013, *European Action of the Disabled (AEH) v. France*, complaint no. 81/2012.

In comparison with the extensive number of judgments of the ECtHR on disability issues, decisions of the ECSR on disability-related questions are relatively rare. Nevertheless, it is clear that the ECSR attaches great importance to fighting discrimination on the grounds of disability (not restricted to access to healthcare), and otherwise promoting the rights and opportunities of persons with disabilities, in all fields of life.

4.3.2. European Union

The CJEU's main task is to make sure that the law of the European Union is interpreted and applied in a uniform way. The CJEU also has a role in resolving disputes between national governments and EU institutions, and it may take action against EU institutions on behalf of individuals, companies or organisations whose rights have been infringed. Despite these broad competences, and the increasing importance of the CFR, the CJEU has, so far, given – both absolutely and relatively – a limited number of judgments on the (health) rights of persons with disabilities, apart from the above-mentioned judgments in which the CJEU articulated the meaning of the term disability, taking into account the definition of disability in the CRPD. In fact, the most important judgments of the CJEU with respect to disabled persons have not, primarily, been on health-related issues.

The first judgment worth mentioning is a case from the United Kingdom. The Employment Tribunal, London South, asked the CJEU to give a preliminary ruling in a case of the dismissal of an employee, Ms. Coleman. Ms. Coleman stated that she had quit her job after being harassed by colleagues, due to her status as the mother of a disabled child. This raised the question of whether a person who is not themselves disabled, but is a relative of a disabled person, is also protected against disability discrimination under the Employment Equality Treatment Directive. The CJEU confirmed this. The CJEU held that the prohibition of discrimination, as laid down in this directive, is not limited to people who are themselves disabled. Where an employer treats an employee who is not themselves disabled less favourably than another employee in a comparable situation, and it is established that this less favourable treatment is based on the disability of that employee's child, such treatment is contrary to the prohibition of direct discrimination. Thus, the CJEU also stipulated that persons who are not themselves disabled, but are associated with a disabled person, are protected against disability discrimination under the directive.[51]

In contrast to the expansive interpretation of disability in the *Coleman* case, the CJEU gave a more restrictive meaning to the term in the case of Z. A commissioning mother, Ms. Z, who had had a baby through a surrogacy

---

[51]   CJEU 17 July 2008, *Coleman*, C-303/06, ECLI:EU:C:2008:415.

arrangement, was refused paid leave equivalent to maternity leave or adoptive leave, since she had not herself been pregnant. The CJEU eventually decided that a refusal to provide paid leave equivalent to maternity leave or adoptive leave to a female worker who is unable to bear a child, and who has availed themselves of a surrogacy arrangement, does not constitute discrimination on the grounds of disability or sex.[52]

Another judgment of the CJEU concerned a preliminary ruling from the Bayerischer Verwaltungsgerichtshof (Administrative Court of Bavaria), Germany, in the case of *Glatzel*. The judgment was issued after a lower national court had refused Mr. Glatzel a driving licence for vehicles, on the grounds that the visual acuity in his weaker eye did not reach the minimum level required by EU Directive 2006/126 on driving licences. The lower court had justified the refusal on the grounds that an ophthalmological examination had revealed that Mr. Glatzel suffered from unilateral amblyopia, involving a substantial functional loss of vision in one eye. The Bayerischer Veraltungsgerichtshof decided to uphold Mr. Glatzel's appeal. It took the view that the requirements laid down in Directive 2006/126 constituted an interference with Article 26 of the CFR, in view of the rights of persons with disabilities under the CRPD. The CJEU decided otherwise. It found that the examination of the question referred to it did not reveal any information capable of affecting the validity of the directive. The requirement laid down in the CFR to respect and recognise the right of persons with disabilities to benefit from integration measures did not obligate the EU legislature to adopt any specific measures, nor did it provide subjective rights to individuals with disabilities.[53]

In 2018, the CJEU gave a judgment in a case that had started with a complaint by a Mr. Bedi. The CJEU was asked whether an entitlement to early payment of a retirement pension for disabled persons, leading to the ending of enhanced financial assistance that was being provided on the basis of a collective agreement on social security, was a form of discrimination on the basis of disability, contrary to the Employment Equality Directive. The CJEU judged that it was. It ruled that the Employment Equality Directive should be interpreted in such a way as to preclude a provision in a collective agreement under which a worker who has lost their job loses their entitlement to bridging assistance when they become entitled to an early payment of a retirement pension under a statutory pension scheme for disabled persons. Such a clause leads to indirect discrimination towards severely disabled persons. Such persons disproportionately run the risk of being negatively affected by the ending of assistance provided on the basis of a collective agreement.[54]

---

[52]   CJEU 18 March 2014, *Z*, C-363/12, ECLI:EU:C:2014:159.
[53]   CJEU 22 May 2014, *Glatzel*, C-358/12, ECLI:EU:C:2014:350.
[54]   CJEU 19 September 2018, *Bedi*, C-312/17, ECLI:EU:C: 2018:734.

In the case of *VL*, the CJEU was asked to decide whether there could be a form of disability discrimination if one group of disabled persons was treated less favourably than another group of disabled persons. The issue at stake concerned an allowance given to workers with disabilities who had submitted disability certificates after a date chosen by the employer, whereas disabled persons who had submitted their certificates before that date were excluded from the allowance. According to the CJEU, such a practice can constitute a form of direct discrimination contrary to the Employment Equality Directive if it is established that that it is based on a criterion that is inextricably linked to disability. The challenged practice may lead to indirect discrimination if there is an apparently neutral criterion that, without being objectively justified by a legitimate aim, or without the means of achieving such an aim being appropriate and necessary, puts workers with disabilities at a particular disadvantage.[55]

In addition, it should be emphasised that the CJEU has fully adopted the obligation to make reasonable accommodations if these are necessary to counter disability discrimination. For example, in the case of *HK Danmark*, two employees were dismissed from their jobs because of workplace absences resulting from health problems. The employers did not agree with the plaintiffs that their health conditions were covered by the notion of 'disability'. In the view of the employers, the employees' functional incapacity was the fact that they were not able to work full-time. The CJEU rejected this interpretation of the term 'disability', and held that this term, as laid down in the Employment Equality Directive, 'must be understood as referring to a limitation which results in particular from physical, mental or psychological impairments which in interaction with various barriers may hinder the full and effective participation of the person concerned in professional life on an equal basis with other workers'. As a consequence, the employees were entitled to reasonable accommodations. Whether a reduction in working hours amounts to a form of reasonable accommodation is, according to the CJEU, for the national court to assess in the light of the circumstances of the case.[56]

5. CONCLUSIONS

Persons with disabilities are a vulnerable group. This holds true both within and outside the healthcare sector. Their vulnerability is closely related to their limitations, considered 'abnormal' in the view of others. The individual and medical model of disabilities further damages the position of people with disabilities, sometimes turning them into objects of charity instead of individuals with rights and dignity.

---

[55]   CJEU 26 January 2021, *VL*, C-16/19, ECLI:EU:C:2021:64.
[56]   CJEU 11 April 2013, *HK Danmark*, C-335/11 and 337/11, ECLI:EU:C:2013:222.

This chapter has shown that this individual and medical model has largely been replaced by a more social model. This becomes particularly clear from the Convention on the Rights of Persons with Disabilities (CRPD).

It has been noted, above, that the CRPD Committee is ascribing the inabilities that may come with disabilities as being almost exclusively caused by environmental factors, calling for as many measures as are necessary to allow individuals with disabilities to decide for themselves how they want to live, without any form of discrimination. Providing reasonable accommodations is one important way to prevent and redress discrimination on the grounds of disability. In formulating its decisions, the CRPD Committee largely builds on and refers to the European Court of Human Rights (ECtHR).

The ECtHR largely subscribes to this view, even though the European Convention of Human Rights (ECHR) does not refer to the term 'disability'. From the very adoption of the CRPD, the ECtHR has interpreted the ECHR in line with this convention. However, the ECtHR leaves a larger margin of appreciation to States Parties than the CRPD Committee. The ECtHR, furthermore, does not fully agree with the way that the CRPD Committee interprets the CRPD, at least with respect to the European legal context. This different approach is particularly noticeable with respect to the right to equal recognition before the law, and the right to vote. According to the CRPD Committee, differentiation on the basis of disability amounts, almost automatically, to discrimination.

The European Committee on Social Rights (ECSR) is fully committed to interpreting the European Social Charter (ESC) in conformity with the CRPD. Its body of case law on disability issues is, however, still relatively small.

The European Union (EU) has ratified the CRPD. This has provided an important incentive for the Court of Justice of the EU (CJEU) to make sure that its case law is in conformity with the CRPD. This becomes clear, for example, from the CJEU's definition of disability, and the obligation to make reasonable accommodations. Despite this, the case law of the CJEU leaves a margin of appreciation for national courts to interpret cases in the light of the particular circumstances of each case.

CHAPTER 10

REPRODUCTIVE HEALTH

Janne Rothmar Herrmann

1. INTRODUCTION

Because of the special biological functions performed by women in the reproductive process, particular healthcare needs and issues related to reproduction arise in relation to women. As such, women experiencing reproductive health issues can be seen as a group in need of special legal attention: first of all, because of the special healthcare needs associated with reproduction; secondly, because women's procreative role may lead to unequal access to healthcare treatment; and, lastly, because women's reproductive autonomy has, traditionally, been subject to intense scrutiny by the state.

The most important legal landmark in addressing reproductive health was the development of the concept of reproductive rights,[1] during The United Nations International Conference on Population and Development, in Cairo in 1994, and the Fourth World Conference on Women, in Beijing in 1995. The concept of reproductive rights is an interpretative framework to be applied to, and consisting of, already existing human rights. It focuses on *individual* rights and the reproductive needs of individuals, rather than on achieving demographic targets[2] and, thus, relates to fundamental values such as equality, non-discrimination and justice. The concept emphasises a comprehensive approach to reproduction, integrating the various fragmented healthcare needs relating to the reproductive process, and putting women at the centre of the process; recognising, respecting and responding to the needs of women, and not only those of mothers.[3] Health

---

[1] For a detailed overview of the development of this concept, see Laura Reichenbach and Mindy Jane Roseman (eds.), *Reproductive Health and Human Rights*, Philadelphia: University of Pennsylvania Press, 2009.

[2] United Nations, Cairo Platform of Action, adopted at the International Conference on Population and Development, 1994; Rebecca J. Cook, Bernard M. Dickens and Mahmoud F. Fathalla, *Reproductive Health and Human Rights: Integrating Medicine, Ethics, and Law*, Oxford: Clarendon Press, 2003, 155.

[3] Rebecca J. Cook, Bernard M. Dickens and Mahmoud F. Fathalla, *Reproductive Health and Human Rights: Integrating Medicine, Ethics, and Law*, Oxford: Clarendon Press, 2003, 11–13.

is defined, in the World Health Organization (WHO) Constitution,[4] as a 'state of complete physical, mental and social well-being', and, thus, not merely the absence of disease or infirmity. The application of this definition to *reproductive health* would mean that the concept of 'reproductive health' covers not only aspects of a person's reproductive system, its functions and processes, but also the achievement of a satisfactory and safe sexual life, reproductive capacity, and the freedom to decide on when, how often, and at what intervals procreation should happen. As such, reproductive health also involves adequate education, information and counselling, as well as access to affordable family planning, and that men and women are given a choice between various lawful measures to control fertility, as well as being provided with adequate healthcare, ensuring a safe medical environment for maternal health and childbirth.[5]

The aim of this chapter is to provide an overview of the human rights and principles relevant to the notion of reproductive health, and to analyse selected reproductive issues, including a detailed account of the relevant case law of the European Court of Human Rights (ECtHR).

2. WOMEN'S REPRODUCTIVE HEALTH AND HUMAN RIGHTS

Biological differences between women and men may lead to differences in health status. The biological differences between the sexes afford women a special reproductive role, which is linked to the female body. As such, the gender perspective is an important aspect to address. The fact that women's biological and social roles in procreation can affect their options, and possibilities for taking part in society, provides the perspective behind the UN Convention on the Elimination of All Forms of Discrimination of Women (CEDAW).[6] Among the international human rights treaties, the CEDAW plays an important role in bringing the focus of human rights concerns on to the female half of humanity. The spirit of the CEDAW is rooted in the goals of the United Nations, 'to reaffirm faith in fundamental human rights, in the dignity and worth of the human person, [and] in the equal rights of men and women'.[7] As mentioned

---

4   Preamble of the WHO Constitution, https://www.who.int/governance/eb/who_constitution_en.pdf.

5   United Nations, Cairo Platform, para. 7.2 (Programme of Action of the United Nations International Conference on Population and Development, 1994).

6   Convention on the Elimination of All Forms of Discrimination against Women New York, 18 December 1979.

7   United Nations, Introduction to CEDAW, available at http://www.un.org/womenwatch/daw/cedaw/text/econvention.htm#intro.

above, another important legal landmark in this respect was the development of the concept of reproductive rights during The United Nations International Conference on Population and Development (ICPD), in Cairo in 1994, and the Fourth World Conference on Women, in Beijing in 1995. The promises of the ICPD were reaffirmed on its twenty-fifth anniversary, in the 2019 Nairobi Statement on 'ICPD25 – Accelerating the Promise'.[8] Furthermore, important progress towards the increased realisation of reproductive health was made in the ICESCR Committee's General Comment 22/2016,[9] which stipulates that the right to sexual and reproductive health is an integral part of the right to health enshrined in Article 12 of International Covenant on Economic, Social and Cultural Rights (ICESCR), and that states are under an immediate obligation to eliminate discrimination against individuals and groups, and to guarantee their equal rights to sexual and reproductive health.[10]

This chapter will introduce the interrelated rights and principles that form part of the reproductive rights framework, and analyse various reproductive situations or choices relating to women's (and sometimes men's) reproductive capacities, from a human rights perspective. These include the right to reproductive autonomy, including the right to (reproductive) healthcare services, and the right to respect for private life and family life and non discrimination, which will be explored in more depth below. A comprehensive list of human rights and principles relevant to reproduction and reproductive health would, further, include the right to receive and impart information, the right to life, the right to liberty and security of the person, the right to benefit from scientific progress, and the right to education. The relevance of some of the latter rights will be demonstrated in the analysis of selected ECtHR judgments below. Reproductive rights may also extend to adequate recognition of the legal relationship between parent and child.[11] The topics selected to illustrate the theme of this chapter include family planning, abortion and various issues related to fertility treatment.

---

[8]   The 2019 Nairobi Statement on ICPD25 – Accelerating the Promise, available at https://www. nairobisummiticpd.org/content/icpd25-commitments.

[9]   UN Committee on Economic, Social and Cultural Rights (ICESCR Committee), 'General Comment No. 22 (2016) on the right to sexual and reproductive health (Article 12 of the International Covenant on Economic, Social and Cultural Rights)', available at https:// www.escr-net.org/resources/general-comment-no-22-2016-right-sexual-and-reproductive-health.

[10] See, further, Chapter 2 of this book, on AAAQ and the core obligations.

[11] ECtHR 13 June 1979, *Marckx v. Belgium*, no. 6833/74; ECtHR 26 June 2014 *Mennesson v. France*, no. 65192/11; and ECtHR, first advisory opinion of 10 April 2019 (concerning the recognition in domestic law of a legal parent–child relationship between a child born through a gestational surrogacy arrangement abroad and the intended mother) are examples of how reproduction intertwines with various rights in this respect, including the rights of the child.

2.1. MATERNAL HEALTH

Preventing maternal mortality and morbidity, and ensuring safe, respectful care has become a collective global priority. This emerging consensus about the importance of maternal health stems from the recognition that many poor maternal health outcomes are not inevitable, but are, instead, the result of laws, policies, and institutional practices that can be changed.[12]

In 2002, 28-year-old Alyne da Silva Pimentel Teixeira, a poor, pregnant woman of Afro-Brazilian descent, visited a private health clinic in Brazil. Despite presenting symptoms of a high-risk pregnancy, she was sent home. Her symptoms worsened during the course of the following two days, so she returned to the clinic. By that time, no foetal heartbeat could be detected. Her delivery was induced six hours later, producing a stillborn foetus. The surgery to extract her placenta occurred 14 hours later, though it should have occurred immediately after the delivery had been induced. Because of her deteriorating health, she had to be transferred to a higher-tier public healthcare institution, but had to wait more than eight hours before being transferred to hospital. Alyne died after more than 21 hours without receiving medical attention. In 2007, a claim was submitted to the CEDAW Committee on behalf of Alyne's mother and daughter. The claim argued that the state had violated Alyne's right to health and life without discrimination (CEDAW Articles 2 and 12), because the state had failed to ensure her timely access to quality healthcare services during pregnancy and delivery, risking Alyne's life, health, and her right to live free from discrimination. *Alyne v. Brazil*[13] clearly recognises that states have an immediate and enforceable human rights obligation to address and reduce maternal mortality, strengthening the recognition of reproductive rights as obligations that must be enforced immediately by the state. The case reinforces the commitment to reduce maternal mortality that was voiced by states during the 1994 International Conference on Population and Development, and reaffirmed in the 2019 Nairobi Statement on 'ICPD25: Accelerating the Promise'.[14]

Acts and omissions of the authorities in the field of health care may, in certain circumstances, engage the state's responsibilities under the European Convention on Human Rights. Maternal health in pregnancy and childbirth provided the context for the medical negligence case *Mehmet and Bekır Şentürk v. Turkey*.[15] The first applicant's pregnant wife had gone to a university

---

[12] Office of the High Commissioner of Human Rights United Nations, Summary Reflection Guide on a Human Rights-Based Approach to Health Application to sexual and reproductive health, maternal health and under-5 child health, https://www.ohchr.org/Documents/Issues/Women/WRGS/Health/RGuide_HealthPolicyMakers.pdf.

[13] CEDAW Committee, C/49/D/17/2008, Communication no. 17/2008.

[14] Commitments of the ICPD25, https://www.nairobisummiticpd.org/content/icpd25-commitments.

[15] ECtHR 9 April 2013, *Mehmet and Bekır Şentürk v. Turkey*, no. 13423/09.

hospital complaining of persistent pain. The doctors found that the child she was carrying had died, and that she required immediate surgery. However, she was told that a fee would be charged for her operation, and that a substantial deposit (approximately 1,000 euros) had to be paid. Since the first applicant did not have the money, the emergency doctor arranged for the wife to be transferred to another hospital, but she died on the way there. Although it was not its task to rule *in abstracto* on the state's public health policy at the time of the events, the ECtHR noted that the provision of treatment at the first hospital had been contingent on advance payment. That requirement had served as a deterrent for the patient, causing her to decline treatment. Such a decision could not possibly be regarded as informed, or as *exempting* the national authorities from liability as regards the treatment she should have been given. The medical staff had been fully aware that transferring her to another hospital would put her life at risk. Furthermore, the domestic law did not appear to have been capable of preventing the failure to give her the medical treatment she required. Accordingly, because of the blatant failings of the hospital authorities, she had been denied access to appropriate emergency treatment. That finding was sufficient for the Court to hold that the state had failed to comply with its obligation to protect her physical integrity.

The 2019 Nairobi Statement on ICPD25, intended to reaffirm the global commitment voiced in the 1994 ICPD Programme of Action, aims to achieve universal access to sexual and reproductive health and rights as a part of universal health coverage by committing to strive for, among other things,

> zero preventable maternal deaths[16] and maternal morbidities, by integrating a comprehensive package of sexual and reproductive health interventions,[17] including access to safe abortion to the full extent of the law, measures for preventing and avoiding unsafe abortions, and for the provision of post-abortion care, into national universal healthcare strategies, policies and programmes, and to protect and ensure all individuals' right to bodily integrity, autonomy and reproductive rights, and to provide access to essential services in support of these rights.

There is also a growing awareness and recognition that women can be subjected to obstetric violence in a way that may infringe on their human and personality rights.[18]

---

16   Achieving zero maternal deaths is an important indicator of having achieved universal access to sexual and reproductive health and reproductive rights, as per UN Sustainable Development Goal target 3.7 and Sustainable Development Goal target 5.6.
17   As defined in paras. 7.2, 7.3 and 7.6 of the Cairo Platform of Action.
18   Cynthia Lourenço Tach, Brigit Toebes and Juliana Marteli Fais Feriato, 'Obstetric Violence: A Women's Human and Personality Rights Violation', *Revista Juridica* 1 (2020), 187–206.

2.2. REPRODUCTIVE AUTONOMY

Autonomy is a well-known principle in health law. It is one of the most basic liberty rights[19] and, as such, a fundamental right in both health law and medical ethics. The key role of this principle was expressed during the Nuremberg trials, which uncovered the horrors that had taken place in the Nazi concentration camps, as part of medical experiments.[20] The principle's function is, first and foremost, to ensure that human beings are not subjected to unwanted interventions, which is reflected in the legal requirements concerning information and consent in relation to medical treatment and biomedical research. The legal requirement to obtain the patient's consent minimises the risk of being subjected to harmful or unwanted interventions. As such, the principle ensures that the individual can freely choose her own preferences in life, and in relation to her own person, and her own body, without undue interference, coercion or control. To achieve this situation of free choice in relation to healthcare, she must, of course, be presented with all relevant information, including alternative options, in a way that is tangible to her. The provision of this information enables her to exercise real autonomy. In relation to *procreative* autonomy, legal scholars such as Ronald Dworkin have argued that the freedom to make choices concerning reproduction is a vital aspect of human dignity, a principle which is a fundamental feature of all democratic societies.[21] Because of the role of women and the female body in procreation, the principle of reproductive autonomy becomes especially significant for women in a way that does not apply to men. Interventions into a woman's bodily autonomy when not preceded by an informed consent, infringe on her most basic human rights. If, for example, the woman's partner or husband prefers a pregnancy to be either terminated or continued, contrary to her wishes, his autonomy cannot be exercised without it representing an intervention into *her* bodily *integrity*.[22] As such, the rights of the woman carry more weight, in the legal balancing between her rights and any competing rights of the man.[23]

---

[19] Henriette Sinding Aasen, 'Dignity and Human Rights in the Modern Welfare State' in Henriette Sinding Aasen, Rune Halvorsen and Antonio Barbosa da Silva (eds.), *Human Rights, Dignity and Autonomy in Health Care and Social Services: Nordic Perspectives*, Cambridge: Intersentia, 2009, 64–66.

[20] 'Trials of war criminals before the Nuernberg Military Tribunals under Control Council Law no. 10, Nuernberg, October 1946 to April 1949, vols. 1 and 2: Case no. 1, *Karl Brandt et al.: The Medical Case*', Washington DC: US Government Printing Office, 1949–53.

[21] Ronald Dworkin, *Life's Dominion*, London: HarperCollins, 1993, 166–67.

[22] See, further, Janne Rothmar Herrmann, 'The Right to Avoid Procreation and the Regulation of Pregnancy: A European Perspective' in David Orentlicher and Tamara Hervey (eds.), *Oxford Handbook on Comparative Health Law*, Oxford: Oxford University Press, 2022, 1033–49.

[23] This balancing will be subject to further analysis below in section 3.2.2.

The extent of the right to reproductive autonomy is, however, subject to theoretical dispute. Some view the right to reproductive autonomy as merely a negative right to be free from state interference in the reproductive sphere, while others regard it as a positive right to access medically assisted procreation.[24] Articles 12 and 16(1)(e) of the CEDAW Convention present the most clearly worded protection of reproductive autonomy and choice. To what extent the right to reproductive choice exists in international human rights law is an issue which divides the States Parties, depending on national perceptions, religious practices and culture: some parties to the CEDAW Convention are foreign to the democratic idea of equality between the sexes because of an undemocratic rule, for example because gender barriers prevent women from participating fully in the political process. Others may formally recognise the equal worth and equal rights of women and men, but accept de facto discrimination because of tradition, religion and culture. In October 2020, 34 countries signed the Geneva Consensus Declaration on Promoting Women's Health and Strengthening the Family,[25] which claims that there is no right to abortion in international law, and declares that the 'traditional family' – meaning a married, heterosexual couple and their biological children – is the 'fundamental group unit of society', and that each country has 'the sovereign right' to make their own laws on abortion. This anti-abortion declaration was co-sponsored by the governments of Brazil, Egypt, Hungary, Indonesia, Uganda and the United States; among the signatories were 19 authoritarian regimes, and six of the world's least safe countries for women. As such, the road to achieving the full realisation of the reproductive rights enshrined, for example, in CEDAW is still long, but aided by the CEDAW monitoring committee, which issues general recommendations on certain aspects of the Convention as well as reports on each individual state, in response to their country reports.

2.3. RIGHT TO RESPECT FOR PRIVACY AND FAMILY LIFE

Another key aspect of the concept of reproductive rights is the right to respect for private life and family life, which is protected in a variety of human rights documents, including Article 23 of the ICCPR, and Articles 8 and 12 of the European Convention on Human Rights (ECHR). The right to respect for private life is a broad term encompassing, inter alia, aspects of an individual's

---

[24]   John A. Robertson, *Children of Choice: Freedom and New Reproductive Technologies*, Princeton: Princeton University Press, 1994, 23.

[25]   It was signed by 34 countries on 22 October 2020. Initiated by then-US Secretary of State, Mike Pompeo, the document is not related to the United Nations' Geneva Consensus Foundation, or to other Geneva-based institutions, and was not signed in Geneva. It was submitted to the UN: see https://undocs.org/en/A/75/626.

physical and social identity, including the rights to personal autonomy, personal development, and to establish and develop relationships with other human beings and the outside world, incorporating, in principle, the right to respect for the decision to become, or not to become, a parent.[26] The extensive ECtHR case law invoking the right to respect for a private and family life, in relation to reproductive issues,[27] will be presented in more depth below, for example in relation to abortion and access to fertility treatment. However, also included in the understanding of the concept of private and family life would be the right to control, and to decide on freely and responsibly, aspects of sexuality and sexual life.[28] As such, the human rights law protection of reproductive autonomy and choice is also manifested through the protection of the individual's right to privacy and family life.

Individuals and couples have the right to found a family, and to decide on the number, timing and spacing of their children. Article 16 of CEDAW implies a right to found a family that applies to a wider set of people than Article 12 of the ECHR, given that the ECtHR has maintained that the right to found a family, under the ECHR, only applies to male–female couples (married or unmarried). The rights of single women and lesbian couples to found a family would, then, find a more solid basis in Article 16 of CEDAW, which ties the right to equality.

2.4. THE PROHIBITION OF DISCRIMINATION

The final integral right featuring in the overarching framework concept of reproductive rights is the requirement of non-discrimination, which means that the rights enshrined in, for example, the ECHR must be secured 'without discrimination on any grounds such as sex, race, colour, language, religion, political or other opinion, national or social origin, association with a national minority, property, birth or other status' (Article 14).

Human rights are interdependent, indivisible and interrelated. This means that violating the right to health may impair the enjoyment of other human rights, such as the rights to education or work, and vice versa. The right to health is dependent on, and contributes to, the realisation of many other human rights. These include the rights to food, water, an adequate standard of living, adequate housing, freedom from discrimination, privacy, access to information, participation, and to benefit from scientific progress and its

---

[26] ECtHR 10 April 2007, *Evans v. UK*, no. 6339/05.
[27] See also Audrey Lebret and Janne Rothmar Herrmann, 'Reframing Reproductive Rights on a Transnational Scene', *European Human Rights Law Review* 2 (2020), 153–63.
[28] United Nations, Beijing Declaration and Platform for Action, 1995, para. 96.

applications. CEDAW acknowledges, in its preamble, that women face inherent discrimination because of the different positions, privileges and restraints that women and men are naturally given in society, based on assumptions and preconceived notions about gender. 'Discrimination' means any distinction, exclusion or restriction made on the basis of various grounds which has the effect or purpose of impairing or nullifying the recognition, enjoyment or exercise of human rights and fundamental freedoms.[29] It is linked to the marginalisation of specific population groups, and is generally at the root of fundamental structural inequalities in society. The impact of discrimination is compounded when an individual suffers intersectional discrimination, such as discrimination on the basis of sex *and* age. The right to health, therefore, entails gender sensitivity. Furthermore, as outlined above, it is also the explicit intention of CEDAW to address and eliminate discrimination against women, including those types of discrimination that relate to the female body and procreative role, and women's reproductive healthcare needs. As such, the right to reproductive health services becomes a prerequisite, as it would be discriminatory (on the grounds of sex) to deny women medical services that only women need.[30]

To eliminate discrimination that relates to the female body effectively, a wider gender sensitivity is required. Non-discrimination and equality imply that states must recognise and provide for the differences and specific needs of groups that generally face particular health challenges, such as vulnerability to specific diseases. The obligation to ensure non-discrimination requires specific health standards to be applied to particular population groups, such as women. Article 12 of CEDAW obligates States Parties to take all appropriate measures to eliminate discrimination against women in the field of healthcare, in order to ensure, on the basis of equality of men and women, access to healthcare services, including those related to family planning.

3. FAMILY PLANNING

The first topic to serve as an illustration of how health and human rights interact in the area of reproductive health is family planning. This topic includes both access to contraceptive devices and medicines to prevent pregnancy, and the medical and surgical termination of pregnancy.

---

[29] 'Integrating a Gender Perspective into Human Rights Investigations', New York: OHCHR, 2018, https://www.ohchr.org/Documents/Issues/Women/Publications/GenderIntegrationinto HRInvestigations.pdf.

[30] CEDAW Committee, 'General Recommendation No. 24/1999: Article 12 of the Convention (women and health)', available at https://tbinternet.ohchr.org/Treaties/CEDAW/Shared%20 Documents/1_Global/INT_CEDAW_GEC_4738_E.pdf.

3.1. CONTRACEPTION AND SEX EDUCATION

State Parties' compliance with Article 12 of CEDAW is central to the health and well-being of women. Read in the light of the CEDAW Committee's General Recommendation no. 24/1999 on women and health, it requires states to eliminate discrimination against women in their access to healthcare services throughout their lives, particularly in the areas of family planning, pregnancy and confinement, and during the postnatal period.[31] The demand, in this general recommendation, for easy and affordable access to contraception has (together with access to abortion) been one of the major controversies associated to the CEDAW Convention and the CEDAW Committee, as this is an area which is continuously raised by the Committee in response to the country reports submitted by the State Parties.

The aforementioned general recommendation on women and health elaborates on the Committee's understanding of Article 12, and addresses measures to eliminate discrimination in order to realise the right of women to the highest attainable standard of health. These measures include not only the obligation to provide women with *access* to healthcare, on the basis of equality between men and women, but also to impart relevant *information*, provide *education*, and secure respect for *confidentiality*, as a lack of confidentiality may deter women from seeking advice and treatment and thereby adversely affect their health and well-being, because they will be less willing to seek medical care in relation to matters such as, for example, contraception.[32] The legal basis for a right to avoid procreation can also be said to fall within the scope of several provisions of the ECHR.

As mentioned above, Article 12 of the ECHR gives men and women of marriageable age the right to marry and found a family, in accordance with the national laws governing this right. It follows from the wording that the right is relatively weak, since its conditions are subject to national law (provided, of course, that national law does not restrict the essence of the right). The reason for adding the right to found a family to the European human rights catalogue relates to the era in which the human rights were first formulated and adopted: the 1948 UN Universal Declaration of Human Rights (UDHR) had, similarly, included a right to marry and found a family without any limitation due to race, nationality, or religion. The right was very much a response to the prejudiced reproductive policies that had been practised, to various degrees, in the decade leading up to the Second World War. These had prevented procreation by the disfavoured, and installed a sense of obligation on certain favoured people

---

[31]   Ibid., para. 2.
[32]   Ibid., para. 12(d).

to reproduce. Securing individual freedom to decide on whether or not to have children without undue influence from the state was, thus, a paramount concern.[33] Consequently, the right to marry and found a family that is enshrined in both the UD HR and the ECHR was, first and foremost, concerned with securing an individual right to decide whether or not to have children.

There is no test case to demonstrate the exact scope of the right not to procreate that is inherent in Article 12. There are, however, a number of cases that demonstrate that the interpretation of the article is not subject to the same dynamic interpretation that is often applied by the Court, on other subject matters, in order to make the Convention a 'living instrument', rather than being focused on the original meaning and the will of the Convention signatories, and on whether or not there is common European consensus on the matter in question. While there have been small developments on the right to found a family, in the case of *Christine Goodwin v. UK*,[34] the liberal tone of this case stands relatively separate from the overall case law, as conservative doctrines continue to dominate the interpretation of Article 12.[35] While the ECtHR has expressly rejected the notion that the right to marry and found a family includes a positive right to reproduce,[36] it must follow from the wording of the article as a typical negative right that the state cannot force couples to have children (for example, by prohibiting contraceptives). As such, it is a typical negative right, protecting individuals against government interference. In conclusion, Article 12 protects some elements of the right not to procreate, but for *couples* only.

Case law from the ECtHR shows that it falls within the state's prerogative, in the interests of health, education, and as part of maintaining a democratic society, to make general sex education, including education concerning the use of contraceptive products, mandatory in the school curriculum, even against the wishes of parents.[37]

Furthermore, it could be argued that Member States of the European Social Charter should provide scientifically based and non-discriminatory sex education to young people that does not involve censoring, withholding or

---

[33]   See, further, Janne Rothmar Herrmann, 'The Right to Avoid Procreation and the Regulation of Pregnancy: A European Perspective' in David Orentlicher and Tamara Hervey (eds.), *Oxford Handbook on Comparative Health Law*, Oxford: Oxford University Press, 2022, 1033–49; Maja Kirilova Eriksson, *The Right to Marry and Found a Family*, Uppsala: Iustus, 1990.

[34]   ECtHR 11 July 2002, *Christine Goodwin v. United Kingdom*, no. 28957/95, paras. 97–104.

[35]   Bart Van der Sloot, 'Between Fact and Fiction: An Analysis of the Case-Law on Article 12 of the European Convention on Human Rights' *Child and Family Law Quarterly* 26 (2014), 397.

[36]   ECtHR 3 November 2011, *S.H. & Others v. Austria*, no. 57813/00; ECtHR 6 March 2003, *Sijakova and others v. the former Yugoslav Republic of Macedonia*, no. 67914/01.

[37]   ECtHR 7 December 1976, *Kjeldsen, Busk Madsen & Pedersen v. Denmark*, nos. 5095/71; 5920/72; 5926/72.

intentionally misrepresenting information on matters such as contraception. The monitoring European Committee of Social Rights recommended, in *INTERIGHTS v. Croatia*,[38] that such education be provided throughout the entire period of schooling. It stated that sexual and reproductive health education should be aimed at developing the capacity of children and young people to understand their sexuality in its biological and cultural dimensions, with the aim of enabling them to make responsible decisions with regard to sexual and reproductive health behaviour. The right to receive the information necessary to achieve the right to decide on the number of children, and intervals of procreation, as protected in Article 16(1)(e) of CEDAW, is also explicitly part of the wording of that article.

The Committee on the Rights of the Child[39] also relates contraceptive care and sexual education to the right of the child to the enjoyment of the highest attainable standard of health, as protected in Article 24 of the Convention on the Rights of the Child. As part of developing preventive healthcare, both short-term contraceptive methods such as condoms, hormonal methods and emergency contraception, as well as permanent contraceptive methods, should be made easily and readily available to sexually active adolescents.

3.2. ABORTION

The relevant (UN and European) human rights conventions reflect and encompass three different elements or approaches to the regulation of abortion: the right to abortion as part of the right to reproductive health; the right to abortion and other healthcare services, only applicable to women as part of the non-discrimination concept; and the regulation of abortion as a legitimate area of regulatory concern for the state.

3.2.1. The UN conventions

Article 3 of the UDHR (1948) protects the right to life: 'Everyone has the right to life, liberty and security of person'. The right enshrined in the Declaration applies to everyone 'without distinction of any kind, such as ... birth or other status' (Article 2). Whether or not the right to life applies to the unborn foetus

---

[38] Council of Europe, European Committee of Social Rights, *International Centre for the Legal Protection of Human Rights (INTERIGHTS) v. Croatia*, no. 45/2007, available at http://www. coe.int/t/dghl/monitoring/socialcharter/Complaints/Complaints_en.asp.

[39] United Nations Committee on the Rights of the Child, 'General Comment No. 15 (2013) on the right of the child to the enjoyment of the highest attainable standard of health (Art. 24)' 17 April 2013, CRC/C/GC/15.

is one of the key legal issues in the abortion debate. Zampas[40] has argued that foetuses are excluded from the protection, given the use of the term 'born free' in Article 1 of the Declaration: 'All human beings are born free and equal in dignity and rights. They are endowed with reason and conscience and should act towards one another in a spirit of brotherhood.' A further argument in support of this interpretation is the fact that foetuses cannot be said to be endowed with either 'reason' or 'conscience'[41] and, thus, must fall outside the scope of the Convention.

After the adoption of the Universal Declaration of Human Rights, the Human Rights Commission of the Economic and Social Council were given the task of drafting two covenants that would elaborate on the rights laid down in the Declaration: the International Covenant on Civil and Political Rights (ICCPR),[42] and the International Covenant on Economic, Social and Cultural Rights (ICESCR), which were both adopted in 1966. Article 6(1) of the ICCPR protects the right to life: 'Every human being has the inherent right to life. This right shall be protected by law. No one shall be arbitrarily deprived of his life.' The question of whether or not this right includes the human foetus was deliberately left open at the time of the drafting.[43] The Human Rights Committee (HRC), which publishes its interpretations of the Covenant in its general comments, has held, in relation to the application of Article 6 on women's right to life in connection with terminations of pregnancy, that states are required to ensure that women do not have to resort to clandestine, life-threatening abortions, in order to ensure *equal rights* between women and men.[44] Furthermore, General Comment No. 36/2019[45] stipulates *as a matter of the woman's right to life*, that states must provide safe, legal and effective access to abortion if a woman or girl's *life or health is at risk*, or where carrying a pregnancy to term would cause the pregnant woman or girl *substantial pain or suffering*, most notably where the pregnancy is the result of rape or incest, or where the pregnancy is not viable. In addition, states may not regulate pregnancy or abortion *in all other cases* in a manner that runs contrary to their duty to ensure that women and girls do

---

[40] Christina Zampas and Jamie M. Gher, 'Abortion as a Human Right – International and Regional Standards', *Human Rights Law Review* 8 (2008), 249–94.

[41] In liberal moral philosophy, the lack or presence of these characteristics determines the moral status of an entity: see, e.g. Peter Singer, *Rethinking Life & Death*, Oxford: Oxford University Press, 1994.

[42] United Nations, International Covenant on Economic, Social and Cultural Rights, 1966.

[43] United Nations General Assembly 12th session agenda item 33, Draft International Covenants on Human Rights Doc. A/3764, 15 December 1957, para. 112.

[44] United Nations, 'CCPR General Comment No. 28: Article 3 (The Equality of Rights Between Men and Women)', CCPR/C/21/Rev.1/Add.10, para. 10; and United Nations Human Rights Committee's decision in *KL v. Peru*, CCPR/C/85/D/1153/2003, Communication No. 1153/2003.

[45] United Nations Human Rights Committee, 'General Comment No. 36/2019 – Article 6 (right to life)', available at https://www.refworld.org/docid/5e5e75e04.html.

not have to resort to unsafe abortions, and should revise their abortion laws accordingly.[46]

In 2016, the Committee on Economic, Social and Cultural Rights (ICESCR Committee) adopted General Comment No. 22[47] on the right to sexual and reproductive health, which aims to assist States Parties with the implementation of their international obligations regarding the right to sexual and reproductive health. The instrument affirms that states are obliged to adopt 'appropriate legislative' measures to achieve the full realisation of sexual and reproductive health and rights. It affirms that the right to sexual and reproductive health is an integral part of the right to health, and recognises abortion services as a constituent part of the right to health.[48]

Article 7 of the ICCPR, which stipulates that no one shall be subjected to torture, or to cruel, inhuman or degrading treatment or punishment, was found to have been violated by the state's failure to enable a therapeutic abortion in *KL v. Peru*,[49] where a 17-year-old woman was carrying an anencephalic foetus, making her pregnancy life-threatening. Despite a gynaecologist and obstetrician in the same hospital advising a termination, the hospital director refused. The woman was forced to carry the pregnancy to term, breastfeed the newborn, and suffer the loss of the baby shortly afterwards. As a result, she suffered the severe psychological consequences of a deep depression, exacerbated by her status as a minor. The refusal of the competent medical authorities to provide the service could have endangered the applicant's life, and there was no effective remedy available to her. The HRC has pointed out, in its General Comment No. 20, that the right set out in Article 7 of the Covenant relates not only to physical pain, but also to mental suffering, and that this protection is particularly important in

---

[46]   According to para. 8 of the general comment, this includes avoiding measures such as criminalising pregnancies of unmarried women and abortions, removal of barriers such as conscientious objections of providers, and securing access to quality and evidence-based information and education on sexual and reproductive health, along with access to a wide range of affordable contraceptive methods. States should prevent the stigmatisation of women and girls who seek abortions. States should ensure the availability of, and effective access to, quality prenatal and post-abortion healthcare for women and girls in all circumstances, and on a confidential basis. For an example of a barrier identified under the European Social Charter, see also Chapter 5 of this book, on ECSR 7 November 2013, *International Planned Parenthood Federation – European Network (IPPF EN) v. Italy*, no. 87/2012.

[47]   UN Committee on Economic, Social and Cultural Rights (ICESCR Committee), 'General Comment No. 22 (2016) on the Right to sexual and reproductive health (Article 12 of the International Covenant on Economic, Social and Cultural Rights)', available at https:// www.escr-net.org/resources/general-comment-no-22-2016-right-sexual-and-reproductive-health.

[48]   Lucía Berro Pizzarossa and Patty Skuster, 'Toward Human Rights and Evidence-Based Legal Frameworks for (Self-Managed) Abortion: A Review of the Last Decade of Legal Reform', *Health and Human Rights Journal* 23(1) (2021), 199–212.

[49]   *KL v. Peru*, communication no. 1153/2003, adopted 24 October 2005.

the case of minors. Consequently, the HRC found the case to be a violation of Article 7 of the Covenant.

The CEDAW Convention assigns special attention to women's health and well-being in Article 12, which requires States Parties to 'take all appropriate measures to eliminate discrimination against women in the field of health care in order to ensure, on a basis of equality of men and women, access to health care services, including those related to family planning'. As stated in its preambular recitals, the CEDAW Convention is the only human rights convention explicitly addressing family planning, and its main purpose is to establish and ensure the protection of women's reproductive rights, by linking the female reproductive role to the objective of creating equality, both between the sexes, and between different groups of women: 'the role of women in procreation should not be a basis for discrimination' (preambular recital 13).

As mentioned earlier, the CEDAW Committee, in 1999, adopted General Recommendation No. 24, which clarifies states' obligations under Article 12 of the Convention, and, consequently, the various factors that states should account for in their reports to the Committee. The states must, inter alia, include an account of how policies and adopted measures in their national healthcare systems address women's right to health and, in so doing, choose a perspective that takes, as its point of departure, women's needs and interests. Due regard should be taken of biological factors, including the differences in reproductive healthcare needs and functions between women and men. Organisational factors should also address these differences, such as, for example, ensuring the right to confidentiality, especially in potentially stigmatising situations such as unwanted pregnancy. It is also emphasised that healthcare services should be provided in a way that respects the dignity of women. This norm could be seen as entailing that criminalisation of healthcare services only needed by women is a hindrance to women's right to health and, as such, can be characterised as discrimination: as stated in General Recommendation No. 24,

> measures to eliminate discrimination against women are considered to be inappropriate if a health care system lacks services to prevent, detect and treat illnesses specific to women. It is discriminatory for a state party to refuse to legally provide for the performance of certain reproductive health services for women. For instance, if health service providers refuse to perform such services based on conscientious objection, measures should be introduced to ensure that women are referred to alternative health providers.[50]

It is a matter of academic debate how authoritative the statements of the CEDAW Committee are: they do, however clarify the Convention text. As a treaty,

---

[50] CEDAW Committee, 'General Recommendation No. 24/1999: Article 12 of the Convention (women and health)', para. 11, available at https://tbinternet.ohchr.org/Treaties/ /Shared%20 Documents/1_Global/INT_CEDAW_GEC_4738_E.pdf.

CEDAW is binding on all parties that ratify it; the Committee is responsible for developing jurisprudence – a body of legal interpretation – through the issuing of general recommendations and decisions under CEDAW's Optional Protocol. As such, these statements can be said to be of an equally binding nature, to the ratifying states.

Finally, Article 16(1)(e) of the CEDAW Convention stipulates that women should have the same rights as men to choose, freely and responsibly, the number and spacing of their children. Whereas Article 12 must be understood as an obligation to make abortion available, if a termination is necessary to protect the life or health of the woman, it is uncertain to what extent Article 16(1)(e) implicates a right to autonomy-based abortion.

3.2.2. *The European Convention on Human Rights*

The European Court of Human Rights (ECtHR) and the former European Commission of Human Rights (which, prior to the reorganisation of the Court, functioned as a kind of first-instance review body) have both had the opportunity to address the question of abortion. The cases brought before the Strasbourg court have dealt with the issue of whether or not women have a right to abortion under Article 8 of the European Convention on Human Rights, whether the foetus has a right to life under Article 2 thereof, and whether prospective fathers have any rights under Article 8 that limit the woman's reproductive choices.

The case law, taken as a whole, demonstrates a considerable reluctance to take a stance on many of the issues,[51] although some of the issues relating to which rights must be prioritised, in the balancing between the various actors involved, have been clearly established.

The structure of the following case law review is thematic rather than chronological.

3.2.2.1. The balancing of interests between woman and foetus

The first theme that can be identified from the ECtHR case law is how the rights of the woman are balanced against the rights or interests of the foetus.

In 1980, the European Commission of Human Rights, in its second ever case on abortion, *X v. UK (Paton v. UK)*,[52] identified three possible views

---

[51] See, further, Audrey Lebret, Paris Human Rights Center, 'The European Court of Human Rights and the framing of Reproductive Rights', *Droit fondamentaux* no. 18/2020, available at https://www.crdh.fr/revue/n-18-2020/the-european-court-of-human-rights-and-the-framing-of-reproductive-rights/.

[52] EComHR 13 May 1980, *X v. the United Kingdom*, no. 8416/79, decision on the admissibility of the application. The underlying national case was *Paton v. British Pregnancy Advisory Service Trustees* [1979] QB 276; [1978] 3 WLR 687; [1978] 2 All ER 987, and, as such, the case is often referred to as *Paton v. UK*.

of the foetus's right to life, and laid down some basic principles for the balancing of interests between woman and foetus. In this case, a husband had, unsuccessfully, tried to get an injunction preventing his wife from undergoing a termination. His case had been dismissed by the national court, on the grounds that no rights stood to be violated by the proposed termination. Neither the foetus nor the husband held any rights under English law and, consequently, the woman terminated the pregnancy a few hours after the court hearing. Mr. Paton subsequently complained to the European Commission of Human Rights, claiming that the UK Abortion Act violated the ECHR by allowing the abortion, by refusing the foetus any rights, and by denying the father any rights over the foetus.

The Commission, first of all, noted that whether or not the foetus had a right to life, under Article 2, was a question that had been left open in its first ever case on abortion, *Brüggemann & Scheuten v. Germany*[53] (this case is discussed in more detail below). However, it was clear that the limitations on the right to life that had been included in Article 2 (i.e. the scope for the use of the death penalty and the use of force) referred to persons already born and, as such, were not applicable to foetuses. On the other hand, the wording of Article 2 did not exclude the foetus from being included in its scope. The Commission outlined three possible approaches. Firstly, the article may be interpreted in a way that excludes the foetus completely. Another possible interpretation would be to understand the article as including the foetus in its scope, but with 'certain implied limitations'. Lastly, the protection laid down in the article could be understood as awarding the foetus an absolute right to life. The latter option was dismissed by the Commission, as this would render abortion impossible even in emergency cases, where a termination of the pregnancy was necessary in order to save the woman's life. To place a higher value on the potential life of the unborn child than the life of the woman would be contrary to the ECHR's purpose. In reaching this conclusion, the Commission relied on the argument that all of the contracting states, except one, allowed for abortion under such circumstances at the time of drafting the Convention. However, the foetus's life was intimately connected to, and could not be viewed separately from, the woman's life. Thus, the Commission dismissed only one of the three possible approaches identified, but did not take an explicit stance on the remaining two perspectives. However, the dismissal of the view that the foetus holds an absolute right to life implies that national regulations *must* include a right to abortion when the woman's life is at stake, in order to respect Article 2 of the Convention.

In the case of *Tysiac v. Poland*,[54] a pregnant woman risked losing her eyesight if she carried her pregnancy to term. Her general practitioner advised

---

[53] EComHR 12 July 1977, *Rose Marie Brüggemann & Adelheid Scheuten v. the Federal Republic of Germany*, no. 6959/75.
[54] ECtHR 20 March 2007, *Tysiac v. Poland*, no. 5410/03.

an abortion, and referred her to a gynaecologist. The gynaecologist, however, did not find that she met the criteria for a termination. Consequently, she gave birth to a child, and subsequently became blind. The woman claimed that the state's failure to provide her with an abortion in this situation, when such a procedure was actually legal under national law, amounted to a violation of her right to respect for private life, as she had been exposed to a considerable risk to her health. The Court agreed, and found that the state had a positive obligation to protect her right effectively. Even though Polish law provided access to legal abortion on health grounds, the legislation had failed to take into account that differences of opinion might exist between pregnant women and their doctors or, indeed, between different doctors, and, consequently, no judicial review system was in place to provide women with easy access to having their right tried and enforced. Thus, it was not sufficient that an abortion was *in concreto* legal: the state was also obliged to provide the woman with an *effective judicial remedy* for testing her right, especially when she had been referred to a specialist by her general practitioner, who found that she met the criteria for having the pregnancy terminated, but the specialist disagreed.[55] As such, the case did not go further than *Brüggemann & Scheuten*[56] in relation to establishing whether women have a right to abortion based on human rights law. However, the key point in *Tysiac v. Poland* was that the state was obliged, under Article 8 of the Convention, to ensure effective protection of womens' physical integrity and, as such, this would seem to imply a right to therapeutic abortion when a woman's health is at risk. As such, the case illustrates the dynamic position of the Court in drawing a line between the rights of the woman and the foetus.

Along the same lines, in *A, B, and C v. Ireland*,[57] the Court found that Ireland had failed to implement the constitutional right to a legal abortion, in relation to one of the applicants who was in remission from a rare form of cancer and, unaware that she was pregnant, underwent check-ups for cancer that were contraindicated during pregnancy. She understood that her pregnancy could provoke a relapse, and believed that it put her life at risk. The Court found a violation of Article 8, concerning the applicant who was in remission from cancer, because she was unable to establish her right to a legal abortion, either through the courts or the medical services available in Ireland. The Court noted, in particular, the uncertainty surrounding the process of establishing whether a woman's pregnancy posed a risk to her life, and also that the threat of criminal prosecution had a 'significant chilling' effect, both on doctors and the women concerned. In *R.R. v. Poland*,[58] the Court also found a lack of any effective

---

[55]   Ibid., paras. 74–85.
[56]   See more, in depth, in section 3.2.2.2. below.
[57]   ECtHR 16 December 2010, *A, B, and C v. Ireland*, no. 25579/05.
[58]   ECtHR 26 May 2011, *R.R. v. Poland*, no. 27617/04.

mechanisms that would have enabled the applicant to access the available diagnostic services, and to take, in the light of their results, an informed decision as to whether or not to seek an abortion. Given that Polish domestic law allowed for abortion in cases of foetal malformation, there had to be an adequate legal and procedural framework to guarantee that relevant, full and reliable information on the foetus's health was made available to pregnant women. In *P and S v. Poland*, it was also established that there had been a violation of Article 8, on the bases that there was a lack of a clear legal framework, and that the applicants had been given misleading and contradictory information.[59]

The issue of whether or not the foetus is afforded a right to life under Article 2 has, as illustrated, been left largely undecided in case law concerning the conflict of rights and interests between the woman and the foetus. However, in 2004, the perfect test case to decide this issue presented itself. Because of the facts of the case, the Court could, if it wished, finally reconsider this difficult issue, and in a context where the status of the foetus was detached from the sensitive and delicate balancing of rights vis-à-vis the pregnant woman. In the case, *Vo v. France*,[60] the applicant Thi-Nho Vo was scheduled to undergo a routine medical examination during her sixth month of pregnancy. At the same time, another woman, Thi Thanh Van Vo, was scheduled to have her coil removed. The applicant, who did not speak French, answered when the doctor called for Mrs. Vo. Because of the mistaken identity, and the fact that the doctor did not examine the applicant prior to attempting to remove the coil, the amniotic sac was pierced and, as a result, a few days later the woman had to have her pregnancy terminated on the grounds of the health of the foetus. Subsequently, the applicant had no legal remedies in relation to pressing criminal charges, as the foetus was not considered a person, under French law. Despite this opportunity for the Court to interpret the scope of Article 2 in relation to the foetus, the Court, to many commentators' surprise,[61] in effect, refused to decide on this aspect, and found no violation of Article 2.[62]

In conclusion, while *X v. UK (Paton v. UK)* stipulated that national regulations must provide women with abortion when it is necessary to save their lives, in order to comply with the protection contained in Article 2 of the ECHR, *Tysiac v. Poland* afforded equal protection to womens' health as part of their right to respect for private life, under Article 8. Whereas the general issue

---

[59]   ECtHR 30 October 2012, *P. and S. v. Poland*, no. 57375/08.

[60]   ECtHR 8 July 2004, *Vo v. France*, no. 53924/00.

[61]   See, e.g. J.K. Mason's remark: 'Thus, in the end, what it had been hoped might be an "evolutive interpretation" of a "living instrument" petered out into a non-decision – the reader of the judgment is likely to feel, by analogy, that it had been a long journey to the pub with no beer' in J.K. Mason, 'What's in a name? The vagaries of *Vo v. France*', *Child and Family Law Quarterly* 17(1) (2005), 97–112.

[62]   A dissenting opinion of Judge Mularoni, joined by Judge Stráznická, did, however, give a comprehensive argument in favour of a different outcome.

of abortion had been a question of balancing the right to privacy against the state's legitimate interest in safeguarding public morality, the issue of therapeutic abortion also had to address the state's positive obligation to safeguard women's physical integrity.[63] Although the Court, in *Tysiac*, emphasised that it was not its role to assess whether or not the ECHR guaranteed a right to abortion, because Tysiac already had such a right under national law in the event of serious risk to her life or health,[64] the judgment, nonetheless, appears to be a first step towards a more dynamic interpretation of the Convention in relation to the sensitive issue of abortion. Notwithstanding that the Convention 'does not guarantee as such a right to any specific level of medical care',[65] the Court stressed that the concept of 'private life' had been interpreted, in the case law, to encompass physical and mental integrity, and that states had a positive obligation to ensure that individuals' integrity was respected effectively. The view that a real and effective protection of women's integrity implicitly requires access to therapeutic abortion may well be the first step towards the creation of greater legal certainty in relation to abortion in human rights law. As for the general question of the status of the foetus in relation to the Convention, and how such a status might affect and limit female reproductive autonomy, the Court has evaded interpreting the scope of Article 2, even in a case such as *Vo*, where there was no collision of interests between woman and foetus to be balanced. This reluctance seems to be contrary to the style of the Court, in general, which is characterised by dynamic interpretation. As a whole, the relevant case law is illustrative of the sensitivity that is still associated with the abortion issue, from a human rights perspective.

3.2.2.2.   The balancing of interests between woman and state

A second theme that can be identified in the ECtHR case law is the woman's right to make autonomous decisions in relation to her own body, as part of the privacy concept, and how this right is balanced against the state's right to regulate termination of pregnancy. The case law demonstrates that the state may have a legitimate interest in this issue, but also establishes certain boundaries and limitations.

In the case of *Brüggemann & Scheuten v. Germany*,[66] the issue at stake was whether or not pregnancy and abortion pertained to the private sphere, under Article 8 of the Convention.

---

63   ECtHR 20 March 2007, *Tysiac v. Poland*, no. 5410/03, para. 107.
64   Ibid., para. 104.
65   Ibid., para. 107.
66   EComHR 12 July 1977, *Rose Marie Brüggemann & Adelheid Scheuten v. the Federal Republic of Germany*, no. 6959/75.

In 1974, the German Federal Parliament had adopted a reform of the Criminal Code that gave wider access to abortion. However, the German Constitutional Court held that the amendment was unconstitutional, and referred to the fact that the unborn life held a higher level of protection than the autonomy of the woman. Thus, the increased access to autonomy-based abortion could not enter into force. The introduction of an ethical and eugenic indication was, however, allowed, on the grounds that it would be burdensome to demand that pregnancies were carried to term in such cases.

The applicants claimed that the Constitutional Court's judgment, and the modified amendment of the Criminal Code, deprived them of the right to autonomy, and amounted to an interference with their right to respect for private and family life. The Commission held that the right to respect for private life ensured the individual a sphere where she could develop her personality and freely establish relationships, including sexual ones, with others. However, 'the claim to respect for private life is automatically reduced to the extent that the individual himself brings his private life into contact with public life or into close connection with other protected interests ... pregnancy cannot be said to pertain uniquely to the sphere of private life. Whenever a woman is pregnant her private life becomes closely connected with the developing foetus'.[67]

The Commission also found it unnecessary to decide whether the foetus could be considered as a form of 'life', within the meaning of Article 2 of the Convention, or whether it could be regarded as 'an entity which under Art. 8 (2) could justify an interference "for the protection of others"'. Nevertheless, it was emphasised that certain interests pertaining to pregnancy were legally protected, including the right to inheritance for the unborn child, which was implemented in all ECHR states, and the regulation of abortion, which was also in place, in some way or another, in every single contracting state. Such regulation reflected the fact that pregnancy and abortion did not pertain solely to the private sphere of the woman, and, consequently, regulation of the issue did not amount to an interference. Based on this line of reasoning, the Commission found that the German regulation did not infringe on the applicants' right to respect for private life. Although the increased access to autonomy-based abortion had been quashed by the Constitutional Court, there were still other legal termination options available, and criminal sanctions had also been removed for certain types of abortion.[68]

In the case of *Open Door v. Ireland*,[69] the issue to be decided was whether or not the right to freedom of information in Article 10 of the Convention

---

[67] Ibid., paras. 55–56 and 59.
[68] Ibid., paras. 62 and 63.
[69] ECtHR 29 October 1992, *Open Door and Dublin Well Woman v. Ireland*, nos. 14234/88; 14235/88.

included the right to receive and impart information about abortion. The applicants were counsellors complaining about the prohibition on imparting information about the availability of abortions in other countries, and women of reproductive age complaining about the ban from receiving this information, in the event of pregnancy. The Court, first of all, noted that it fell within the scope of the Court's competency to test the state's margin of appreciation, even when the issue at stake was a morally sensitive one, regulated with reference to the national constitution:

> The Court cannot agree that the State's discretion in the field of the protection of morals is unfettered and unreviewable … It acknowledges that the national authorities enjoy a wide margin of appreciation in matters of morals, particularly in an area such as the present which touches on matters of belief concerning the nature of human life. As the Court has observed before, it is not possible to find in the legal and social orders of the Contracting States a uniform European conception of morals, and the State authorities are, in principle, in a better position than the international judge to give an opinion on the exact content of the requirements of morals as well as on the 'necessity' of a 'restriction' or 'penalty' intended to meet them … However this power of appreciation is not unlimited. It is for the Court, in this field also, to supervise whether a restriction is compatible with the Convention.[70]

The Court, in its assessment of the restriction on the applicants' right to freedom of information, first of all recalled that Article 10 applies to any kind of information or ideas, including those that are shocking, offensive or embarrass the state or certain population groups. This fact follows from concepts such as tolerance and pluralism, which are the prerequisites of democracy. The restrictions on freedom of information in the present case concerned services that could be obtained legally in the countries where they were being provided, and which impacted immensely on the health and well-being of women. This fact called 'for careful scrutiny by the Convention institutions as to their conformity with the tenets of a democratic society'. Relevant factors that the Court took into account, in its assessment on proportionality, were that the counselling was neutral, allowing the women to choose freely between continuing the pregnancy or travelling abroad to have a termination and, most importantly, the health-related perspectives involved. The Court emphasised that, without the counselling, the women were left with information in advertisements, imported magazines and phone books. Thus, it was, in fact, possible to obtain information in Ireland about abortion from elsewhere, but in a way that did not involve qualified staff, and, as such, offered a minimal level of protection for the women's health, in comparison. Furthermore, the Court found that the submitted evidence suggested that

---

[70]   Ibid., para. 68.

the prohibition of information had created a risk that women were seeking terminations later in their pregnancies, because of the lack of counselling, and that, subsequently, they were not seeking out medical attention to follow up on any post-termination complications. On that basis, the Court found that the prohibition violated Article 10 of the ECHR.

Whereas *Brüggemann & Scheuten v. Germany* established that pregnancy did not pertain solely to the private sphere of the pregnant woman, *Open Doors v. Ireland* established that the state's right to infringe on her privacy, in relation to pregnancy and abortion, was subject to limitations. The fact that her health was at risk carried more weight in the balancing, and, thus, although the state's margin of appreciation is quite broad in matters that are sensitive, and which relate to national moral convictions, the margin is not unreviewable. The Court has, however, never narrowed the margin of appreciation in relation to whether or not there is a right to abortion, even though many of the same arguments apply: if no right to autonomy-based abortion exists, women will subject themselves to clandestine procedures, not carried out by qualified doctors, in unsafe environments.

In *R.R. v. Poland*,[71] the Court noted, in relation to Article 8 of the ECHR, that while states have a broad margin of appreciation regarding the circumstances in which an abortion is permitted, once that decision has been taken, there has to be a coherent legal framework in place to allow the different legitimate interests involved to be adequately taken into account, in accordance with the Convention. The Court reiterated that prohibition of the termination of pregnancies sought for reasons of health and/or well-being amounted to an interference with the applicants' rights to respect for their private lives. A pregnant woman should at least have a chance to be heard in person, and to have her views considered. The competent body or person should also issue written grounds for its decision. However, the legal restrictions on abortion in Poland, taken together with the risk of women incurring criminal responsibility under the Polish Criminal Code, could well have a 'chilling effect' on doctors when deciding whether the requirements of legal abortion had been met, in an individual case. The Court considered that provisions regulating the availability of lawful abortion should be formulated in such a way as to alleviate that 'chilling effect'.

States were obliged 'to organise their health services to ensure that an effective exercise of the freedom of conscience of health professionals in a professional context did not prevent patients from obtaining access to services to which they were legally entitled'. The Court considered that it had not been demonstrated that Polish law contained any effective mechanisms that would have enabled the applicant to access the available diagnostic services, and to take, in the light of their results, an informed decision on whether or

---

[71]   ECtHR 26 May 2011, *R.R. v. Poland*, no. 27617/04.

not to seek an abortion. The Court reiterated that effective implementation of the relevant part of the national legislation would necessitate ensuring that pregnant women had access to diagnostic services that would show whether or not the foetus was damaged – services that were available. The Court also noted that legislation in many other European countries specified the conditions governing effective access to a lawful abortion, and established procedures to implement those laws. The Court concluded that the Polish authorities had failed to comply with their obligations to ensure the respect of the woman's private life effectively, and that there had, therefore, been a violation of Article 8. The decision was, thus, in line with the Court's previous findings in *Tysiac v. Poland*.

3.2.2.3. The balancing of interests between woman and man

A third theme that can be identified in the ECtHR case law on abortion concerns a woman's right to control her own body, in relation to the prospective father. In *R.H. v. Norway*,[72] the applicant was a man whose partner had terminated her pregnancy during the fourteenth week. He claimed that the lack of foetal protection in Norwegian law amounted to a violation of Article 2 of the ECHR. He referred to the fact that the abortion had not been necessary to protect the life or health of the mother, that he had expressly assumed the responsibility for the upbringing and care of the child after birth, and that he had protested from the time that the woman had considered a termination. He also claimed, inter alia, a violation of Article 9, since he had not been allowed access to the remains of the aborted foetus, which he wanted to be buried in accordance with his religious beliefs.

The Commission found that, 'having regard to ... [the] Norwegian legislation, its requirements for the termination of pregnancy as well as the specific circumstances of the present case, the Commission does not find that the respondent State has gone beyond its discretion which the Commission considers it has in this sensitive area of abortion'. Thus, the claims regarding both Articles 2 and 9 were dismissed by the Court. The applicant, further, claimed that Article 8 afforded the father a degree of rights over the foetus when the woman's life was not at risk. Also, a foetus at a gestational age of 14 weeks had to be considered part of his family. The Commission remarked that

> it is true that Articles 8 and 9 of the Convention guarantee the right to respect for private and family life and freedom to manifest one's religion. However, the Commission finds that any interpretation of the potential father's right under

---

72 EComHR 19 May 1992, *R.H. v. Norway*, no. 17004/90, decision on the admissibility of the application.

these provisions in connection with an abortion which the mother intends to have performed on her, must first of all take into account her rights, she being the person primarily concerned by the pregnancy and its continuation or termination. The Commission therefore finds that any possible interference which might be assumed in the circumstances of the present case was justified as being necessary for the protection of the rights of another person.[73]

In *Boso v. Italy*,[74] the Court dismissed an application from a man whose wife had undergone an abortion. As in the previous case law, the Court refused to decide the degree of protection that the foetus was afforded under Article 2, but simply noted that, 'even supposing that, in certain circumstances, the foetus might be considered to have rights protected by Article 2 of the Convention, the Court notes that in the instant case … it appears … that his wife's pregnancy was terminated in conformity with section 5 of Law no. 194 of 1978'. The Italian Abortion Act permitted an autonomy-based right to abortion until the twelfth week of pregnancy, and, after that time, abortion could be permitted on the basis of a medical or eugenic indication. In the Court's view, this legislation did 'strike a fair balance between, on the one hand, the need to ensure protection of the foetus and, on the other, the woman's interests … the Court does not find that the respondent State has gone beyond its discretion in such a sensitive area'. As for the father's inability to influence the decision,

> any interpretation of a potential father's rights under Article 8 of the Convention when the mother intends to have an abortion should above all take into account her rights, as she is the person primarily concerned by the pregnancy and its continuation or termination … Accordingly, any interference with the right protected under Article 8 which might be assumed in the circumstances of the case was justified as being necessary for the protection of the rights of another person.[75]

In both *Boso v. Italy* and *R.H. v. Norway*, the original reasoning laid down in *X v. UK (Paton v. UK)* was reaffirmed and elaborated on, thus illustrating that men have no rights in relation to abortion. Not only does the woman's right to bodily autonomy outweigh any rights of the man, but he also holds no entitlement to the aborted foetal tissue.

4. PROCREATIVE HEALTHCARE SERVICES

In the late 1960s, British scientist, and later Nobel laureate, Dr. Robert Edwards, together with physician Patrick Steptoe, developed the *in vitro* fertilisation (IVF)

---

73   Ibid., para. 4 of the section 'the law'.
74   ECtHR 5 September 2002, *Giampiero Boso v. Italy*, no. 50490/99, decision as to admissibility.
75   Ibid., para. 1 of the section 'the law'.

procedure, which, in 1978, resulted in the birth of the world's first-ever test-tube baby, Louise Brown. New reproductive technologies have since made their way into clinical practice, and a wide range of assisted reproductive healthcare services are on offer in today's healthcare systems, although, in many jurisdictions, infertile patients are treated differently from other patients, as access criteria relating, for example, to age,[76] marital status or perceived lack of parental skills may limit access to treatment.[77] Likewise, not all countries include fertility treatment in their 'health baskets' (healthcare offerings that are included within national healthcare insurance for free), even though infertility is recognised as a disease by the WHO.[78] Furthermore, medical advances in the field have also created various possibilities, not only for assisting conception, but also for selecting the embryos to be implanted, using pre-implantation genetic diagnosis, or even cloning. As a result, in today's healthcare systems, infertile men and women, as well as single or lesbian women,[79] may be medically aided to become parents, subject to national statutory access criteria. An increasing number of children are being born as a result of assisted reproduction among heterosexual couples. The increasing age of first-time mothers, and environmental factors influencing human reproductive capacities, are among the parameters that might explain this development.

As mentioned in the introduction to this chapter, in relation to the Cairo Platform for Action and the development of the reproductive rights framework, the concept of reproductive health encompasses a person's reproductive system, and its functions and processes. It also includes a state of being where the individual has a reproductive capacity, and the freedom to decide on when, how often, and with what intervals, procreation should happen. However, the realisation of this state of reproductive health, when aided by medical technology, also raises a number of sensitive issues. The provision of fertility treatment, such as IVF treatment, and treatments aimed at choosing a healthy embryo, will serve

---

[76] See also Stine Willum Adrian, Janne Rothmar Herrmann, Charlotte Krarløkke, 'Monstrous Motherhood – Women on the Edge of Reproductive Age', *Science as Culture*, https://www.tandfonline.com/doi/abs/10.1080/09505431.2021.1935842.

[77] See, e.g. Sebastian Mohr and Janne Rothmar Herrmann, 'The Politics of Danish IVF: Reproducing the Nation by Making Parents through Selective Reproductive Technologies', *BioSocieties*, 2021, https://link.springer.com/article/10.1057/s41292-020-00217-1; Judith Lind, 'Child welfare assessments and the regulation of access to publicly funded fertility treatment', *Reproductive Biomedicine & Society Online*, 2020, 10:19–27; Guido Pennings, 'International evolution of legislation and guidelines in medically assisted reproduction', *Reproductive BioMedicine Online*, 2009, 18: S15–S18; G. De Wert, W. Dondorp, F. Shenfield, P. Barri, P. Devroey, K. Diedrich, B. Tarlatzis, V. Provoost and G. Pennings, 'ESHRE Task Force on Ethics and Law 23: medically assisted reproduction in singles, lesbian and gay couples, and transsexual people', *Human Reproduction* 29(9) (2014), 1859–865.

[78] World Health Organization, 'Infertility is a global public health issue', available at https://www.who.int/reproductivehealth/topics/infertility/perspective/en/.

[79] Single and gay men would require access to surrogacy arrangements.

---

as case studies in the following section, to shed light on the balancing between these sometimes opposing interests.

4.1. FERTILITY TREATMENT

4.1.1. A private life issue

Reproduction is central to our personal identities, and, as such, it forms part of the very core of the concept of private life, within the meaning of Article 8 of the ECHR. In the case of *Evans v. UK*,[80] a woman had, prior to undergoing treatment for cancer – which included the surgical removal of her ovaries – undergone one cycle of fertility treatment. The resulting ova were fertilised with the sperm of her partner, and the embryos were then deposited in the freezer, to be implanted once the applicant had recovered from cancer. By that time, however, she and her partner had separated, and he had formed a new family. The applicant wanted the right to use the frozen embryos for implantation, as they represented her only means of becoming a parent. Her former partner, however, refused to consent to the use of the embryos, and required that they be destroyed, in accordance with the UK Human Fertilisation and Embryology Act. The Chamber of the ECtHR, at first instance, held that Article 8 was applicable, since the notion of 'private life' incorporated the right to respect for both the decisions to become or not to become a parent. The question that arose under Article 8 was whether there existed a positive obligation for the state to ensure that a woman who had embarked on treatment for the specific purpose of giving birth to a genetically related child should be permitted to proceed to implantation of the embryo, notwithstanding the withdrawal of consent by her former partner, the male gamete provider.

The national statutory regulation at issue in the case had been the culmination of an exceptionally detailed examination of the social, ethical and legal implications of developments in the field of human fertilisation and embryology.[81] Its policy was to ensure continuing (renewed) consent, from the commencement of treatment to the point of implantation in the woman. While the pressing nature of the applicant's medical condition had required she and her partner to reach a decision about the fertilisation of her eggs without as much time for reflection and advice as might ordinarily be desired, it was undisputed that it had been explained to both of them that either was free to withdraw consent at any time before the resulting embryos were implanted

---

80   ECtHR 10 April 2007, *Evans v. UK*, no. 6339/05.
81   It was preceded by the Warnock Report: Mary Warnock: *A Question of Life: Warnock Report on Human Fertilization and Embryology*, Oxford: Wiley-Blackwell, 1985.

in the applicant's uterus. The Court held that strong policy considerations underlay the decision of the legislature to favour a clear or 'bright-line' rule, which would serve both to produce legal certainty, and to maintain public confidence in the law in a sensitive field. Like the national courts, the Chamber did not find that the absence of a power to override a genetic parent's withdrawal of consent, even in the exceptional circumstances of the applicant's case, was such as to upset the fair balance required by Article 8, or to exceed the wide margin of appreciation afforded to the state.[82] The Grand Chamber agreed with the Chamber that the right to become or not to become a parent did, indeed, fall within the private life concept protected by Article 8, but emphasised that the applicant was not, in any way, prevented from becoming a mother in a social, legal or even physical sense, since there was no rule of domestic law or practice to stop her from adopting a child, or even giving birth to a child originally created *in vitro* from donated gametes. The applicant's complaint was, therefore, more precisely, that the consent provisions of the national Act prevented her from using the embryos she and her former partner had created together, and thus, given her particular circumstances, from ever having a child to whom she was genetically related. The Grand Chamber, however, considered that this more limited issue, concerning the right to respect for the decision to become a parent in the genetic sense, also fell within the scope of Article 8.[83] The dilemma central to the *Evans* case was that it involved a conflict between the Article 8 rights of two private individuals: the applicant and her former partner. Moreover, each person's interest was entirely irreconcilable with the other's, since, if the applicant was permitted to use the embryos, her former partner would be forced to become a father, whereas if his refusal or withdrawal of consent was upheld, the applicant would be denied the opportunity of becoming a genetic parent. The Grand Chamber, like the Chamber, accepted the UK government's submission[84] that the case did not simply involve a conflict between individuals: the legislation in question also served a number of wider public interests, in upholding the principle of the primacy of consent, and in promoting legal clarity and certainty. Given that there was no international or European consensus with regard to the regulation of IVF treatment, the use of embryos created by such treatment, or the point at which consent to the use of genetic material provided as part of IVF treatment might be withdrawn, and since the use of IVF treatment gave rise to sensitive moral and ethical issues against a background of fast-moving medical and scientific developments, the margin of appreciation to be afforded to the respondent state had, therefore, in the view of the Court, to be a wide one.

---

[82]   ECtHR 10 April 2007, *Evans v. UK*, no. 6339/05, paras. 58–59 and 71.
[83]   Ibid., paras. 72–74.
[84]   Ibid., para. 68.

In the subsequent case of *S.H. and others v. Austria*[85] (which will be discussed in more detail below), the Court also considered the right of a couple to conceive a child, and to make use of medically assisted procreation for that end, to fall, in principle, within the ambit of Article 8.[86] But, nevertheless, no positive right to procreate has, currently, been articulated by the Court.[87]

In conclusion, the right to conceive a genetically related child, and to use fertility treatment to fulfil that goal, is considered to be part of the scope of Article 8 of the ECHR. However, as the case law above has demonstrated, this right is not of an absolute nature, and state interference can, in some circumstances, be legitimate. This is due to the fact that medically assisted reproduction is still considered an ethically sensitive practice, and that the interests of the other parent may play a role.

4.1.2. Access to treatment

In many cases, the denial of access to treatment would, as argued above, qualify as an infringement of the individual's right to respect for private and family life. Likewise, denial of access to treatment, for example on the grounds of sexuality, appears to be discrimination contrary to Article 14 of the ECHR. Even though the WHO recognises infertility as a disease, there is still a tendency for infertility to be labelled as 'morally sensitive', warranting special regulation, in many national jurisdictions. Also, in human rights case law, the right to reproduce is not absolute,[88] and so the individual's right must be balanced against any conflicting interests.[89] Access to fertility treatment services can be restricted on many grounds, and states do, in principle, have a wide margin of appreciation in regulating access to fertility treatment.[90] The individual right to access fertility treatment, the legitimate restrictions that a state may impose, and the scope of the margin of appreciation afforded to the state in this matter have been addressed by the ECtHR in two cases.

The first case, *Dickson v. the United Kingdom*,[91] concerned the refusal of facilities for artificial insemination to the applicants, a prisoner and his wife, who, given the husband's earliest release date and the wife's age, needed

---

[85]   ECtHR 3 November 2011, *S.H. and others v. Austria*, no. 57813/00, Grand Chamber judgment.

[86]   Ibid., para. 78.

[87]   ECtHR 6 March 2003, *Sijakova v. Macedonia*, no. 67914/01 (decision on admissibility) rejects a positive right to reproduce.

[88]   Ibid.

[89]   See also Elizabeth Wicks, *Human Rights and Healthcare*, Oxford: Hart Publishing, 2007, 165.

[90]   For an argument that the margin of appreciation is narrower for preventive health optimising tools such as elective egg freezing, see Janne Rothmar Herrmann, 'Applying the right to health to reproductive rights – the case of elective egg freezing', *European Human Rights Law Review* 2 (2021), 172–80.

[91]   ECtHR 4 December 2007, *Dickson v. the United Kingdom*, no. 44362/04.

artificial insemination facilities in order to be able to have a child together. The Court found that Article 8 was applicable, in that the artificial insemination facilities at issue concerned their private and family lives, which notions incorporated the right to respect for their decision to become genetic parents. The UK government relied on three justifications for the policy of limiting access to artificial insemination facilities. The first justification was that losing the opportunity to beget children was an inevitable and necessary consequence of imprisonment. The Court's response was that, while the inability to beget a child might be a consequence of imprisonment, it is not an inevitable one, it not being suggested that the grant of artificial insemination facilities would involve any security issues, or impose any significant administrative or financial demands on the state.[92] Secondly, public confidence in the prison system would be undermined if the punitive and deterrent elements of a sentence could be circumvented by allowing prisoners guilty of certain serious offences to conceive children. The Court noted that there was 'no place under the Convention system, where tolerance and broadmindedness are the acknowledged hallmarks of democratic society, for automatic forfeiture of rights by prisoners based purely on what might offend public opinion'. While the Court accepted that the maintenance of public confidence in the penal system had a role to play in the development of penal policy, it underlined that European penal policy was increasingly moving towards emphasising the rehabilitative aim of imprisonment, particularly towards the end of long prison sentences. Thirdly, the government argued that the absence of a parent for a long period would have a negative impact on any child conceived, and, consequently, on society as a whole. The Court accepted this policy view as legitimate, for the purposes of the second paragraph of Article 8, since the authorities, when developing and applying a policy, should concern themselves, as a matter of principle, with the welfare of any child. Moreover, the state had a positive obligation to ensure the effective protection of children. However, this could not go so far as to prevent parents who wished to do so from attempting to conceive a child, especially as the second applicant was at liberty, and could take care of any child conceived until such time as her husband was released.[93] In conclusion, the Court found that the policy, as structured, effectively excluded any real weighing of the competing individual and public interests, and prevented the required assessment of the proportionality of a restriction, in any individual case. Further, since the policy was not embodied in primary legislation, the various competing interests had never been weighed, nor had the issues of proportionality ever been assessed by the UK Parliament. Thus, the Court found that the absence of such an assessment

---

[92] Ibid., para. 74.
[93] Ibid., para. 76.

fell outside any acceptable margin of appreciation, and so a fair balance had not been struck between the competing public and private interests involved. There had, accordingly, been a violation of Article 8 of the Convention.

In the second case, *S.H. and others v. Austria*, the applicants were two married couples. One couple needed donated sperm, as well as medical help in relation to fertilising the woman's eggs, as her fallopian tubes were blocked, and the other couple needed donated eggs. Both couples claimed to be in an analogous position to other couples who wished to avail themselves of medically assisted procreation techniques, but who, because they suffered from different medical conditions to the applicants, did not need *donated gametes* for *in vitro* fertilisation. The applicants, therefore, claimed to be subject to a difference in treatment, because, as a consequence of the prohibition of heterologous artificial procreation techniques for *in vitro* fertilisation laid down by the applicable Austrian law, they were unable to access treatment and procreate. The ECtHR, at first instance, condemned the prohibitions on egg donation and sperm donation for the purposes of IVF. The court judged the law to be incoherent and disproportionate. The decision was, however, reversed on appeal,[94] based on the margin of appreciation doctrine. Concluding that there was now a clear trend in the legislation of the Contracting States towards allowing gamete donation for the purposes of *in vitro* fertilisation, reflecting an emerging European consensus, the Court found this consensus not to be based on settled and long-standing principles established in the laws of the Member States, but, rather, to reflect a stage of development within a particularly dynamic field of law. Accordingly, the Court did not decisively narrow the margin of appreciation of the state. Since the use of *in vitro* fertilisation treatments continued to give rise to sensitive moral and ethical issues, against a background of fast-moving medical and scientific developments, and since the questions raised by the case touched on areas where there was not yet clear common ground among the Member States, the Court considered that the margin of appreciation to be afforded to the respondent state had been a wide one.[95]

In conclusion, fertility treatment techniques, as a general rule, fall within the sensitive area of regulation where states are given a wide margin of appreciation. Even when this margin was being used to restrict access to fertility treatment, and even though these treatments are an important facet of human existence, the Grand Chamber overturned the Chamber's decision in *S.H. and others v. Austria*, which had found such restrictions to be subject to close scrutiny by the Court, especially in testing the restrictions from a discrimination perspective. Critical commentators observed that, even though the court could not be

---

94   ECtHR 3 November 2011, *S.H. & Others v. Austria*, no. 57813/00.
95   Ibid., para. 97.

expected to act as Europe's moral compass, moral inconsistencies and fallacies should not be tolerated as justifications for restrictive laws.[96]

4.2. EMBRYO AND FOETUS SELECTION

Fertility technologies today also include techniques which allow parents to select particular embryos. Most commonly, parents use embryo selection because they want a healthy child. Diagnosing the embryos *in vitro* and selecting one that is healthy is seen by many as preferable to letting the woman become pregnant, and risking having to terminate the pregnancy following the discovery of health issues via foetal diagnostics such as the 'double test', 'triple test' or ultrasound scan, during weeks 12 to 20 of a pregnancy. Sometimes, the selection is based on sex, as several hundred hereditary conditions are only passed on through the male line, and, as such, selection on the basis of sex may be more efficient than testing each embryo for a particular disease running in the family of the father.

Whether the potential right to reproduce would also include the right to have a healthy child is untested in human rights case law. However, it is clear, from a human rights perspective, that discussions on pertinent issues to be addressed as a consequence of this technology have focused, primarily, on the selection practice, and what this practice entails for our understanding of human dignity, equal worth and equality, and less so on the reproductive rights aspect. Whereas the Oviedo Convention,[97] perhaps surprisingly, does not offer any specific individual rights in relation to the area of medically assisted reproduction, it does declare, in Article 14, that medically assisted procreation techniques should not be used for the purpose of sex selection.[98] As such, the Convention mirrors the perspective that has dominated the human rights discourse regarding pre-implantation genetic diagnosis (PGD).

However, in most cases where a couple is denied the use of PGD, it does not affect their right to reproduce *as such*. They may not get the child with the traits or health status that they wanted, but the option to have a child is still available to them.[99] There may, however, be health-related consequences, such as

---

[96] Wannes Van Hoof and Guido Pennings, 'The consequences of *S.H. and Others v. Austria* for legislation on gamete donation in Europe: an ethical analysis of the European Court of Human Rights judgments', *Reproductive Biomedicine Online* 25(7) (2012), 665–69, https://www.rbmojournal.com/article/S1472-6483(12)00408-7/fulltext.

[97] The Convention for the Protection of Human Rights and Dignity of the Human Being with regard to the Application of Biology and Medicine: Convention on Human Rights and Biomedicine (ETS No 164), 4 April 1997.

[98] See, in more depth, Brigit Toebes: 'Sex Selection under International Human Rights Law', *Medical Law International* 9(3) (2008), 197–225.

[99] Elizabeth Wicks, *Human Rights and Healthcare*, Oxford: Hart Publishing, 2007, 176–77.

the health of the future child, or the potential emotional impacts of being forced to abort a wanted foetus due to its health.

Another issue that arises in relation to the selection of foetuses is the use of both non-invasive foetal diagnostic methods such as the ultrasound scan, and invasive methods such as amniocentesis, which can reveal malformations and illnesses in the foetus prior to birth. The information generated by these examinations may (subject to the legality of abortion) assist the woman in making informed choices as to the continuation or termination of her pregnancy. In the case of *Costa and Pavan v. Italy*,[100] the applicants discovered that they were carriers of cystic fibrosis when their child was born with the disease. A prenatal test confirmed that their second child was also affected by cystic fibrosis. They decided to terminate the pregnancy on medical grounds. The applicants sought to take advantage of assisted reproduction technology (ART) and PGD, for the purposes of selecting an embryo unaffected by the disease. However, under Italian law, they did not have access to these techniques. ART was available only to sterile or infertile couples, as well as couples in which the man suffered from a sexually transmissible viral disease that could be contracted by the woman or the foetus, and there was a blanket ban on PGD.

The applicants argued that not having access to these techniques violated their ECHR rights to respect for their private and family life (Article 8) and freedom from discrimination (Article 14). The Court found that 'private life', under Article 8, was a broad concept that included the right to respect for the decision to become or not to become a parent, as well as the right to respect for the decision to become genetic parents. The Court found that the applicants' desire to conceive a child unaffected by the genetic disease of which they were healthy carriers, and to use PGD to this end, attracted the protection of Article 8, as this choice was a form of expression of their private and family lives, but held that the legislative ban on PGD amounted to an interference that was lawful, and which pursued a legitimate aim of protecting morals and the rights and freedoms of others. However, the Court also found the interference to be disproportionate, given the inconsistency in the Italian legislation, which, on the one hand, prohibited limiting implantation to those embryos unaffected by the disease of which the applicants were healthy carriers, but, on the other hand, allowed the applicants to terminate a pregnancy on medical grounds if the foetus was found to be affected by this disease. The Court, thus, found that there had been a violation of the applicants' rights to respect for their private and family lives.

In the case of *R.R. v. Poland*,[101] the applicant, who was 18 weeks pregnant, had undergone an ultrasound scan, following which her family doctor told

---

[100]   ECtHR 28 August 2012, *Costa and Pavan v. Italy*, no. 54270/10.
[101]   ECtHR 26 May 2011, *R.R. v. Poland*, no. 27617/04.

her that he could not rule out the possibility that the foetus was malformed. She told him that she wished to have an abortion if his suspicion proved to be true. She was married with two children at the time. Two further scans confirmed that her foetus probably was malformed, and it was recommended that she have an amniocentesis. The applicant then saw a specialist in clinical genetics, who recommended that she ask for a formal referral from her family doctor to have the amniocentesis carried out in a public hospital, a request which her doctor refused.

She then travelled 150 kilometres to a university hospital in Kraków, to which she had been referred by her local hospital. The doctor she consulted there criticised her for considering an abortion, and refused to authorise genetic tests. She was also informed that the hospital refused to carry out abortions, and that no abortions had been performed there for 150 years. She stayed in the hospital for three days and had another scan, with inconclusive results. She maintained that medical staff had made degrading remarks about her, and had kept her in the hospital without explanation, only to conduct tests unrelated to her concerns. Her discharge record and medical certificate stated that the foetus had developmental abnormalities. A further scan confirmed that the foetus was malformed. She then had an amniocentesis in the twenty-third week of pregnancy, reporting to the hospital as an emergency patient without a valid doctor's referral (which she had tried and failed to obtain). She was told that she had to wait two weeks for the results. She then submitted a written request to her local hospital for an abortion under the Polish Family Planning Act, which stipulated that an abortion on the grounds of foetal abnormality could only be performed before the foetus was considered capable of independent life, normally thought to be in the twenty-fourth week of pregnancy. Within a week, she returned to the hospital, and was told that the consultant could not see her because he was ill. Two weeks after the amniocentesis had been carried out, she received the results of the genetic tests, which confirmed that her child had Turner syndrome. She renewed her request for an abortion the same day. The doctors in the hospital refused because the legal time limit for abortion had passed. She eventually gave birth to a girl with Turner syndrome. The applicant's husband left her after the baby was born.

The Court observed that the scan carried out in the eighteenth week of the applicant's pregnancy had confirmed the likelihood that the foetus was affected with an unidentified malformation. Following that scan, the applicant had feared that the foetus was affected with a genetic disorder and, in the light of the results of subsequent scans, her fears could not be said to have been without foundation. She had repeatedly tried (and failed) to obtain access to genetic tests that would have provided her with information confirming or dispelling her fears. For weeks, she had been made to believe that she would undergo the necessary tests. She had, repeatedly, been sent to various doctors, clinics and hospitals far from her home, and had even been hospitalised for several days for no clear clinical purpose. The Court found that 'the determination of whether the applicant should have had access to genetic tests, as recommended by doctors, was marred by procrastination, confusion and lack of proper counselling and information'.

The Court noted that she had been in a very vulnerable position:

> Six weeks elapsed between the first relevant ultrasound scan and the results of the amniocentesis, too late for her to make an informed decision on whether to continue the pregnancy or to ask for a legal abortion, as the legal time limit had by then expired. Her suffering, both before the results of the tests became known and after that date, could be said to have been aggravated by the fact that she was legally entitled to the diagnostic services requested and that those services were at all times available.

It was, noted the Court, 'a matter of great regret that she was so shabbily treated by the doctors dealing with her case'. The Court consequently found that the applicant had been humiliated, and that this constituted a violation of Article 3 of the ECHR.

It is an important landmark in the Court's case law that the denial of access to genetic testing, and the degrading treatment that the applicant was subjected to by the medical staff were considered violations of Article 3 of the Convention. Together with another Polish judgment, *Tysiac*, this judgment also marked the turning of another corner for the Court, which had previously respected the margin of appreciation of more liberal Western European countries, by showing that it was now willing to limit the margin of appreciation of a more conservative state. As such, the path is slowly being laid for the Court to embrace modern-day reproductive issues with the same dynamic and evolutive spirit that is characteristic of much of its case law in other areas of life and law.

5. PREGNANCY, HEALTH AND AUTONOMY

5.1. MATERNAL AND FOETAL HEALTH

The relationship between a pregnant woman's lifestyle choices and the effects they have on foetal health and development is an area of fast-growing medical knowledge. The fact that a woman's use of alcohol, tobacco, medicinal drugs or illicit drugs affects the foetus has been known to science for a long time, and is reflected in the services offered and information given to pregnant women in many countries.[102]

---

[102] The use of the said substances is a public health concern and, consequently, the WHO has also developed a tool to aid in detecting and helping such patients: see http://www.who.int/substance_abuse/activities/en/Draft_The_ASSIST_Guidelines.pdf.

Any foetal right to health is closely connected to the extent that women have a right to a healthy pregnancy.[103] The UDHR affirms, in Article 25, that

> [e]veryone has the right to a standard of living adequate for the health and well-being of *himself and of his family*, including food, clothing, housing and medical care and necessary social services, and the right to security in the event of unemployment, sickness, disability, widowhood, old age or other lack of livelihood in circumstances beyond his control ... *Motherhood* and childhood are entitled to special care and assistance.

The CEDAW Convention stipulates, in Article 12(2), that 'States Parties shall ensure to women appropriate services in connection with pregnancy, confinement and the post-natal period, granting free services where necessary, as well as adequate nutrition during pregnancy and lactation'. As such, the health of pregnant women is assigned special legal emphasis, and one might also argue that the foetus has a right to health, derived from her rights. The fact that it is, first and foremost, the pregnant woman who is the protected individual is, however, reflected in Article 16(1)(e), the purpose of which is to give women reproductive autonomy, and to allow them to make reproductive choices without being subjected to discrimination.[104] As such, the protection of foetal health is secondary, and relies on the woman's lifestyle choices and willingness to seek antenatal medical care. On the other hand, the foetus is also given legal protection against health discrimination, through the protection of the woman. As a result, the foetus is entitled to receive medical care through its relations to the woman.

Article 12 of the International Covenant on Economic, Social and Cultural Rights acknowledges 'the right of everyone to the enjoyment of the highest attainable standard of physical and mental health'. To fully realise this goal, the state is also obliged to take steps for 'the reduction of the stillbirth-rate and of infant mortality and for the healthy development of the child'.[105] One could argue that pregnant women, as a result of this provision, are also entitled to

---

[103] See also Rebecca J. Cook, Bernard M. Dickens and Mahmoud F. Fathalla, *Reproductive Health and Human Rights: Integrating Medicine, Ethics, and Law*, Oxford: Clarendon Press, 2003, 158–65.

[104] The special duty to tend to the health and well-being of pregnant women seems, in CEDAW Committee, 'General Recommendation No. 24/1999: Article 12 of the Convention (women and health)', available at https://tbinternet.ohchr.org/Treaties/CEDAW/Shared%20Documents/1_Global/INT_CEDAW_GEC_4738_E.pdf, to be based on the fact that pregnancy and childbirth are unique features of womanhood and, as such, raise particular concern in relation to discrimination (see paras. 1, 2. 6, 12(a) and 27 of the General Recommendation).

[105] Article 12.2(a).

the availability of healthcare services specifically intended for the foetus.[106] As mentioned above, the ICESCR Committee adopted, in 2016, General Comment No. 22[107] on the right to sexual and reproductive health, which aims to assist States Parties with the implementation of their international obligations regarding the right to sexual and reproductive health. The instrument affirms that states are obliged to adopt 'appropriate legislative' measures to achieve the full realisation of sexual and reproductive health and rights. It affirms that the right to sexual and reproductive health is an integral part of the right to health.

Adequate care and treatment related to pregnancy and childbirth, thus, form part of the woman's fundamental human rights.

5.2. FORCED TREATMENT OF PREGNANT WOMEN

As outlined above, there is a correlation between the womens' lifestyle choices and foetal health, due to the fact that alcohol, medicinal products and illicit drugs all pass into the foetus's bloodstream through the placenta. As such, there is a potential conflict of interest between the pregnant woman's autonomy and any right to health that the foetus might have.

In response to this conflict, some countries, for example Norway,[108] have chosen to make legal provisions for the forced detention of substance abusing pregnant women until birth. An assessment of such interventions into womens' basic liberty rights, from an international human rights law perspective, must, first and foremost, be made on the basis of CEDAW, which is the only international human rights law document addressing reproduction and women's rights in this area.

In its General Recommendation No. 19,[109] the CEDAW Committee underlines that coercive abortion poses a threat to women's physical and mental health. Whereas paragraph 22 of the recommendation uses the term

---

[106] See also UN Committee on Economic, Social and Cultural Rights (ICESCR Committee), General Comment No. 14, UN Doc. E7C.12/2000/4, Adopted at the Twenty-second Session of the Committee on Economic, Social and Cultural Rights, on 11 August 2000, paras. 18–19.

[107] UN Committee on Economic, Social and Cultural Rights (ICESCR Committee), General Comment No. 22 (2016) on the Right to sexual and reproductive health (Article 12 of the International Covenant on Economic, Social and Cultural Rights), https://www.escr-net.org/resources/general-comment-no-22-2016-right-sexual-and-reproductive-health.

[108] See Karl Harald Søvig, 'Detention of pregnant women to protect the foetus' in Elisabeth Rynning and Mette Hartlev (eds.), *Nordic Health Law in a European Context*, Liber/Brill, 158–80.

[109] General Recommendation No. 19, Violence against women adopted by the CEDAW Committee, Eleventh session (1992), paras. 22 and 24(m).

'*compulsory* abortion', paragraph 24(m) talks of preventing '*coercion* in regard to fertility and reproduction'. Thus, the scope of the CEDAW Committee's notion of coercion seems to be quite broad, both regarding the aspects of reproduction to which it applies, and the nature of the coercion, thus implying that coerced continuation of a pregnancy would also be within its scope. It is worth noting that a pregnant substance abuser, for example, could have a different threshold in relation to what might be considered coercion, compared to other pregnant women. To be detained against one's wishes is a severe infringement of the personal right to liberty, by any standards, although this is, in fact, acknowledged as a legitimate measure under the ECHR, in relation to abuse, psychiatric care, etc. However, the detention of a *pregnant* woman, made with a view to safeguarding the foetus, might also have the effect of controlling her reproductive choices in a non-voluntary way. As such, the issue is not solely one of deprivation of liberty. Women's reproductive freedom is linked both to a health perspective and a non-discrimination perspective. Pregnant substance abusers are different from other pregnant women in that they may experience the detention as a coercive measure in relation to abortion, as a termination would also ensure the woman her freedom. As a result, although detention is meant to improve such womens' health, an unintended side effect can be a diminished respect for their reproductive autonomy, even though this group of women is a vulnerable group, in need of special legal care in relation to securing their rights, and, as such, a group that is afforded special rights and legal emphasis in both CEDAW and the Convention on the Rights of the Child. As such, one might argue that coercive measures against pregnant women are legally problematic, and incompatible with the reasoning and spirit of CEDAW.

6. CONCLUDING REMARKS

Reproduction and reproductive capacity give rise to special healthcare needs. In this chapter, it has been demonstrated how various human rights, together, form a coherent platform for acknowledging and protecting this specific area of human health. These rights include the right to respect for private and family life, and the right to reproductive autonomy, as well as the right not to be discriminated against on the basis of gender and reproductive capabilities, and the right to have reproductive healthcare needs met. In recent years, international human rights law[110] has also provided several breakthroughs in

---

[110] The continued strategic focus on reproductive health is also underlined in Tlaleng Mofokeng, 'Report of the Special Rapporteur on the right of everyone to the enjoyment of the highest attainable standard of physical and mental health', A/HRC/47/28, Human Rights Council, Forty-seventh session, 21 June–9 July 2021, available at https://undocs.org/en/A/HRC/47/28.

establishing state obligations in the field of abortion, through the protection of the right to life and the right to non-discrimination, and the development of the integrated concept of reproductive rights. Not only is reproductive autonomy explicitly protected in the wording of Article 16(1)(e) of CEDAW, but, through a dynamic interpretation of Article 12 of the ICESCR and Articles 3 and 6 of the ICCPR, international human rights law has acknowledged the link between access to safe abortion and women's health, providing respect and protection of women's health and their human rights.[111]

By comparison, the ECtHR has yet to establish reproductive rights as firmly, as it has foregrounded the lack of a common European consensus on these rights (even though such a consensus, for example on first trimester abortion, could be said to exist in a large majority of contracting states, in certain areas). By emphasising issues of moral sensitivity, thus finding that matters of reproductive rights fall within states' margin of appreciation, the Strasbourg court has not been a dynamic driver of reproductive rights in Europe. A clear priority for the woman's right to life over the life of the foetus has, however, been established. *Tysiac v. Poland* and *R.R. v. Poland* have, furthermore, demonstrated a willingness to limit the margin of appreciation of a more conservative state. As such, the path is slowly being laid for modern-day reproductive issues to be embraced with the same dynamic and evolutive spirit that is characteristic of much of the Court's case law in other areas of life and law. When a state legalises abortion, the Court has held that human rights law then becomes applicable. This has underlined that access to a legal abortion must be transparent and accessible.

The area of reproduction is a sensitive one, since it touches on matters such as the beginning of life. This sensitivity is not going to end, as progress in medical science and technology is likely to continue to raise moral and ethical concerns. For this reason, the area of reproduction is in constant evolution, including in legal terms. On the other hand, estimates suggest that, globally, between 48 million couples and 186 million individuals live with infertility, making it the most prevalent disease in the reproductive age group. A degree of normalisation that places patients' rights at the forefront, and offers medical care without discrimination, is also needed for this patient group.

Reproduction, and the scope and extent of individual reproductive rights, will likely continue to give rise to legal litigation in international and regional human rights law settings. Human rights are especially well equipped to address these developments, if they are applied as 'living instruments' in light of 'present-day conditions', in line with the interpretative framework applied

---

[111]   World Health Organization, *Safe Abortion: Technical and Policy Guidance for Health Systems*, 2nd ed., Geneva: World Health Organization, 2012.

by the ECtHR. However, the ECtHR has not subjected reproductive rights to the same evolutive interpretation as many other subject matters, because of the lack of European consensus, and because of the inherent moral sensitivity that has been forefronted, making European human rights a comparatively weaker driving force in the development of individual rights in this area, compared to international human rights law.

CHAPTER 11

DEATH AND DYING

Aart HENDRIKS

1. INTRODUCTION

The right to life is one of the most fundamental human rights. In Europe, as in other parts of the world, it ranks as one of the basic values of democratic societies.[1] This chapter focuses on the legal developments with respect to death and dying in Europe, a region that falls under the realm of the European Convention on Human Rights (ECHR) and various other international and regional human rights treaties. Despite this largely overlapping legal framework, European states sometimes have different approaches when seeking to protect the right to life which is protected by all states. This is why this chapter seeks to understand these different opinions by confining itself to Europe.

According to Article 2 of the ECHR, 'everyone's right to life shall be protected by law'. National constitutions usually contain similarly worded provisions, obliging states to respect and protect human life. For the state, the right to life implies both a negative obligation to refrain from deliberately taking people's lives, and a positive obligation to protect the lives of all human beings within their national jurisdiction.[2]

Article 2 of the ECHR seems to permit capital punishment, under certain restrictive conditions. This provision should, however, be seen in the light of Protocol No. 6 (1983) and Protocol No. 9 (1990) to the ECHR. These two Protocols, ratified by all States Parties, factually prohibit the carrying out of the death penalty, even in times of war, or an imminent threat of war.[3]

---

1   ECtHR 27 September 1995, *McCann et al. v. the United Kingdom*, no. 18984/91, ECLI:CE:ECHR:1995:0927JUD001898491, §147; ECtHR 19 December 2017, *Lopes de Sousa Fernandes v. Portugal* (GC), no. 56080/13, ECLI:CE:ECHR:2017:1219JUD005608013, §164. See also Chapter 5 of this book.

2   See also UN Human Rights Committee, General Comment No. 36 (2018) on Article 6 of the International Covenant on Civil and Political Rights, on the right to life.

3   ECtHR 12 May 2005, *Öcalan v. Turkey* (GC), no. 46221/99, ECLI:CE:ECHR:2005:0512JUD004622199; ECtHR 2 March 2010, *Al-Saadoon and Mufdhi v. the United Kingdom*, no. 61498/08, ECLI:CE:ECHR:2010:0302JUD006149808.

The European Court of Human Rights (ECtHR) has, repeatedly, observed that states should interpret and apply Article 2 of the ECHR in such a way as to maximally respect and protect individual human lives, by making the safeguards enshrined in this right practical and effective.[4] One of these safeguards is guaranteeing access to adequate healthcare. Despite this safeguard, and the legal and practical obligations for states to prevent threats to life as a result of self-harm[5] or suicide,[6] all people will eventually pass away. As eloquently observed by the ECtHR, this fact does not imply 'that Article 2 cannot, without a distortion of language, be interpreted as conferring the diametrically opposite right, namely a right to die'.[7] It is obvious that death cannot always be postponed, let alone avoided, but some people prefer to end their lives because of physical or mental suffering, or for other reasons. These self-chosen forms of death are known as suicide or, if they involve healthcare professionals, physician-assisted dying – meaning that patients with the help of a healthcare professional end their own life – or euthanasia – meaning that the healthcare professional intentionally ends the life of a patient.

This chapter will analyse what states should do, and not do, in an effort to maximally respect, protect and fulfil the right to life. It will do so by weighing these obligations in various contexts, while also looking at other relevant human rights, and the professional standards of healthcare providers. The term 'professional standards' should be read in conjunction with Article 4 of the Convention for the Protection of Human Rights and Dignity of the Human Being with regard to the Application of Biology and Medicine (the 'Convention on Human Rights and Biomedicine', or 'Biomedicine Convention'). According to this provision, '[a]ny intervention in the health field, including research, must be carried out in accordance with relevant professional obligations and standards'. In other words, states and individuals are not allowed to force healthcare professionals either to provide or withhold medical treatment, if it would be against their professional norms to do so. States that do so also violate the professional obligations and standards adopted by international, regional and national bodies – like the World Medical Association – that states usually accept as legally binding.

---

4   ECtHR 2 September 1998, *Yaşa v. Turkey*, no. 22495/93, ECLI:CE:ECHR:1998:0902 JUD002249593, §64.

5   ECtHR 3 April 2001, *Keenan v. the United Kingdom*, no. 27229/95, ECLI:CE:ECHR:2001:0403 JUD002722995; ECtHR 16 October 2008, *Renolde v. France*, no. 5608/05, ECLI:CE:ECHR: 2008:1016JUD000560805.

6   ECtHR 21 March 2000, *Younger v. the United Kingdom* (dec.), no. 57420/00, ECLI:CE:ECHR: 2003:0107DEC005742000; ECtHR 4 February 2016, *Isenc v. France*, no. 58828/13, ECLI:CE: ECHR:2016:0204JUD005882813 and ECtHR 30 June 2020, *Frick v. Switzerland*, no. 23405/16, ECLI:CE:ECHR:2020:0630JUD002340516.

7   ECtHR 29 April 2002, *Pretty v. the United Kingdom*, no. 2346/02, ECLI:CE:ECHR:2002:0429 JUD000234602, §39.

The structure of this chapter is as follows: first, it will analyse the meaning of
the right to life in the context of some environmental and industrial questions
(section 2); it will then address the obligations of states with respect to persons
under the care of the state – notably, detained persons – and persons in the
military (section 3); next, it will review the case law of the ECtHR with respect
to the meaning of the right to life in healthcare settings (section 4); this will be
followed by an analysis of the right to life in the context of end-of-life decisions,
notably the ending of medical treatment, physician-assisted dying and euthanasia
(section 5). In so doing, the ECHR and the case law of the ECtHR will be taken
as the main points of reference.

2.   ENVIRONMENTAL AND INDUSTRIAL QUESTIONS

Various applications have been submitted to the ECtHR concerning the failure
of the state to warn individuals about environmental and industrial dangers
to human life, or the failure to take other preventive measures.[8] Protecting
people from environmental and industrial disasters does, indeed, contribute
to the quality of healthy human lives.[9] In view of this, it does not come as a
surprise that the ECtHR has decided that national authorities have, in certain
instances, failed to adequately protect the lives of individuals from casualties
that could have been avoided.[10] In the case of *Öneryildiz*, concerning the
responsibility of the Turkish national authorities for deaths resulting from an
accidental explosion at a rubbish tip close to a shanty town, the Grand Chamber
of the ECtHR referred to the positive obligations of the state to protect life – an
obligation also embedded in national legislation:

> The Court considers that the timely installation of a gas-extraction system at the
> Ümraniye tip before the situation became fatal could have been an effective measure
> without diverting the State's resources to an excessive degree in breach of Article 65
> of the Turkish Constitution … or giving rise to policy problems to the extent alleged
> by the Government. Such a measure would not only have complied with Turkish

---

8   ECtHR 9 December 1994, *López Ostra v. Spain*, no. 16798/90, ECLI:CE:ECHR:1994:
     1209JUD001679890; ECtHR 19 February 1998, *Guerra et al. v. Italy*, no. 14967/89, ECLI:CE:
     ECHR:1998:0219JUD001496789; ECtHR 27 January 2009, *Tatar v. Romania*, no. 67021/01,
     ECLI:CE:ECHR:2009:0127JUD006702101; ECtHR 25 October 2016, *Otgon v. Moldova*,
     no. 22743/07, ECLI:CE:ECHR:2016:1025JUD002274307.
9   ECtHR 28 February 2012, *Kolyadenko et al. v. Russia*, no. 17423/05, ECLI:CE:ECHR:2012:0228
     JUD001742305.
10   ECtHR 30 November 2004, *Öneryildiz v. Turkey* (GC), no. 48939/99, ECLI:CE:ECHR:2004:
     1130JUD004893999; and ECtHR 20 March 2008, *Budayeva et al. v. Russia*, no. 15339/02,
     ECLI:CE:ECHR:2008:0320JUD001533902.

regulations and general practice in the area, but would also have been a much better reflection of the humanitarian considerations the Government relied on before the Court.[11]

Yet, the ECtHR suggests that the right to information is probably the key right to enable individuals to protect themselves and others from environmental and industrial disasters. In line with this positive obligation for states, the national authorities should provide for appropriate procedures ('duty to fulfil'), taking into account the technical aspects of the environmental or industrial activity in question, identifying shortcomings in the processes concerned, and analysing whether errors have been committed by those responsible, at different levels.[12] It should be noted here that the ECtHR usually considers that the right to information is enshrined in Article 8 of the ECHR (right to private life), but that this does not practically affect the question of whether the public is entitled to be informed about potential environmental and industrial disasters.

3. PERSONS UNDER THE CARE OF THE STATE

The state has a special responsibility to respect, protect and fulfil the lives and health of persons under its care.[13] This group includes prisoners,[14] soldiers,[15]

---

[11] ECtHR 30 November 2004, *Öneryildiz v. Turkey* (GC), no. 48939/99, ECLI:CE:ECHR:2004: 1130JUD004893999, §107.

[12] ECtHR 30 November 2004, *Öneryildiz v. Turkey* (GC), no. 48939/99, ECLI:CE:ECHR:2004: 1130JUD004893999, §90; ECtHR 27 January 2009, *Tatar v. Romania*, no. 67021/01, ECLI: CE:ECHR:2009:0127JUD006702101, §113; ECtHR 5 December 2013, *Vilnes et al. v. Norway*, nos. 52806/09 and 22703/10, ECLI:CE:ECHR:2013:1205JUD005280609; ECtHR 24 July 2014, *Brincat et al. v. Malta*, no. 60908/11, ECLI:CE:ECHR:2014:0724JUD006090811, §114.

[13] See ECtHR 28 January 1994, *Hurtado v. Switzerland*, no. 17549/90, ECLI:CE:ECHR:1994: 0128JUD001754990.

[14] ECtHR 14 March 2002, *Paul and Audrey Edwards v. the United Kingdom*, no. 46477/99, ECLI: CE:ECHR:2002:0314JUD004647799; ECtHR 5 July 2005, *Trubnikov v. Russia*, no. 49790/99, ECLI:CE:ECHR:2005:0705JUD004979099; ECtHR 11 October 2005, *Tarariyeva v. Russia* (dec.), no. 4353/03, ECLI:CE:ECHR:2006:1214JUD000435303; ECtHR 31 January 2008, *Dönmüs and Kaplan v. Turkey*, no. 9908/03, ECLI:CE:ECHR:2008:0131JUD000990803; ECtHR 18 December 2012, *Jeladze v. Georgia*, no. 1871/08, ECLI:CE:ECHR:2012:1218JUD000187108; ECtHR 17 October 2013, *Keller v. Russia*, 26824/04, ECLI:CE:ECHR:2013:1017JUD 002682404; ECtHR 30 June 2020, *S.F. v. Switzerland*, no. 23405/16, ECLI:CE:ECHR:2020:0630 JUD002340516.

[15] ECtHR 11 January 2011, *Servet Gündüz et al. v. Turkey*, no. 4611/05, ECLI:CE:ECHR:2011: 0111JUD000461105; ECtHR 18 October 2011, *Acet et al. v. Turkey*, no. 22427/06, ECLI:CE: ECHR:2011:1018JUD002242706; ECtHR 13 October 2015, *Akkoyunlu v. Turkey*, no. 7505/06, ECLI:CE:ECHR:2015:1013JUD000750506; ECtHR 11 September 2018, *Kasat v. Turkey*, no. 61541/09, ECLI:CE:ECHR:2018:0911JUD006154109.

and all other persons[16] deprived of their liberty, or otherwise vulnerable[17] and, to a large extent, dependent on the care and other services provided by the state. One of the state's obligations concerns the provision of necessary and adequate healthcare to these groups.[18] Even though the conditions in which persons under the care of the state find themselves should always meet the criterion of human dignity,[19] and the healthcare provided to them has to be in accordance with human rights standards, the ECtHR has accepted that the healthcare available to these groups is not always of the same standard as the care provided to the general public in the best medical institutions.[20] The minimum human rights standards to be ensured by the state entail that the health and well-being of persons under the care of the state should be adequately secured,[21] that persons with health problems are quickly diagnosed by trained healthcare professionals, and that care is provided in a prompt and accurate manner.[22]

4. HEALTHCARE SETTINGS

As mentioned previously, in Chapter 5, states are required to make regulations compelling public and private hospitals to adopt appropriate measures for the protection of their patients' lives.[23] This positive obligation not only entails the duty to ensure the effective functioning of a regulatory framework, but also the duty to take measures to ensure its implementation.[24] In addition, the state should guarantee a well-functioning healthcare sector.[25]

---

16   ECtHR 13 March 2012, *Reynolds v. the United Kingdom*, no. 2694/08, ECLI:CE:ECHR:2012:
      0313JUD000269408; ECtHR 17 July 2014, *Valentin Câmpeanu v. Romania* (GC), no. 47848/08,
      ECLI:CE:ECHR:2014:0717JUD004784808; ECtHR 22 November 2016, *Hiller v. Austria*,
      no. 1967/14, ECLI:CE:ECHR:2016:1122JUD000196714; ECtHR 31 January 2019, *Fernandes
      de Oliveira v. Portugal* (GC), no. 78103/14, ECLI:CE:ECHR:2019:0131JUD007810314.
17   E.g. children and persons with mental health problems in institutions.
18   ECtHR 23 May 2013, *E.A. v. Russia*, no. 44187/04, ECLI:CE:ECHR:2013:0523JUD004418704.
19   ECtHR 10 July 2001, *Price v. the United Kingdom*, no. 33394/96, ECLI:CE:ECHR:2001:0710
      JUD003339496.
20   ECtHR 14 January 2010, *Moskalyuk v. Russia*, no. 3267/03, ECLI:CE:ECHR:2010:0114
      JUD000326703.
21   ECtHR 18 June 2013, *Nencheva et al. v. Bulgaria*, no. 48609/06, ECLI:CE:ECHR:2013:0618
      JUD004860906.
22   ECtHR 30 July 2009, *Pitalev v. Russia*, no. 34393/03, ECLI:CE:ECHR:2009:0730
      JUD003439303, §54; ECtHR 15 January 2015, *Nogin v. Russia*, no. 58530/08, ECLI:CE:ECHR:
      2015:0115JUD005853008.
23   ECtHR 17 January 2002, *Calvelli and Ciglio v. Italy* (GC), no. 32967/96, ECLI:CE:ECHR:
      2002:0117JUD003296796, §49; ECtHR 19 December 2017, *Lopes de Sousa Fernandes v.
      Portugal* (GC), no. 56080/13, ECLI:CE:ECHR:2017:1219JUD005608013, §166.
24   ECtHR 19 December 2017, *Lopes de Sousa Fernandes v. Portugal* (GC), no. 56080/13, ECLI:
      CE:ECHR:2017:1219JUD005608013, §190.
25   ECtHR 30 August 2016, *Aydoğdu v. Turkey*, no. 40448/06, ECLI:CE:ECHR:2016:0830
      JUD004044806.

Whether the state has failed to comply with its regulatory or coordinating duties depends on an assessment of the alleged shortcomings. The absence of regulations, or the failure to coordinate, are not always to the detriment of the lives and health of patients. In fact, professional standards sometimes adequately prescribe what healthcare professionals can best do to ensure that patients receive the care they need.

It is not permissible, under Article 2 of the ECHR, for states to deny access to life-saving treatment.[26] This obligation does not require states to provide free healthcare[27] or free medication.[28] If patients are, however, entitled to free healthcare or medication under national laws or insurances, then states should not obstruct the provision of these.[29]

5. END-OF-LIFE ISSUES

As mentioned above, the right to life does not entail a right to die.[30] In most jurisdictions, persons assisting others to die are, therefore, subject to criminal prosecution. In line with this general prohibition, healthcare professionals have to act, or refrain from acting, as the case may be, to avoid the death of a patient. This does not mean that states and healthcare professionals are always required to keep persons alive. Prolonging life may be contrary to professional standards, the dignity of a person, or his or her wishes not to be treated. In many jurisdictions, healthcare professionals have their own professional responsibilities with respect to end-of-life issues and, therefore, their situations are not fully comparable with those of other people. There are even jurisdictions in Europe where healthcare professionals can deliberately, upon the wishes of a competent patient, end that patient's life (this conduct will, henceforth, be referred to in this chapter as 'physician-assisted dying' or, in cases where a healthcare professional intentionally ends the life of a patient, 'euthanasia'). At the same time, even in these jurisdictions, healthcare professionals have to be very careful not to inadvertently suggest that the life of a patient was intentionally

---

26   ECtHR 19 December 2017, *Lopes de Sousa Fernandes v. Portugal* (GC), no. 56080/13, ECLI: CE:ECHR:2017:1219JUD005608013.
27   ECtHR 4 January 2005, *Pentiacova et al. v. Moldova* (dec.), no. 14462/03, ECLI:CE:ECHR: 2005:0104DEC001446203.
28   ECtHR 21 March 2002, *Nitecki v. Poland* (dec.), no. 65653/01, ECLI:CE:ECHR:2002:0321 DEC006565301.
29   ECtHR 10 April 2012, *Panaitescu v. Romania*, no. 30909/06, ECLI:CE:ECHR:2012:0410 JUD003090906 and ECtHR 8 October 2019, *Fedulov v. Russia*, no. 53068/08, ECLI:CE:ECHR: 2019:1008JUD005306808.
30   ECtHR 29 April 2002, *Pretty v. the United Kingdom*, no. 2346/02, ECLI:CE:ECHR:2002: 0429JUD000234602, §39.

ended by one of the healthcare providers in their healthcare institution, without carefully verifying their information first.[31]

5.1. WITHHOLDING OR WITHDRAWING MEDICAL TREATMENT

Under certain conditions, healthcare professionals may come to the conclusion, in relation to a particular patient or patients, that starting or continuing medical treatment may be useless or futile. According to their professional standards, starting or continuing treatment may, therefore, be prohibited as contrary to the dignity of the person. Prolonging treatment in such situations may add to the suffering of a patient, without any evidence that the patient will recover or his or her health improve. Failing to observe this norm may, depending on the national penal regulations, result in criminal liability and/or – depending on the national disciplinary rules and codes – disciplinary liability.

The precise legal and disciplinary characterisations and consequences of not administering, or withholding, medical treatment are also ethical issues, and these are regulated differently throughout Europe. In fact, in a large number of states, physicians are, according to national law and professional standards, not allowed to end the treatment of a patient, due to the sanctity of life. In these countries, life should be protected under all conditions, including by way of palliative care, if appropriate. Yet, there are indications that at least some physicians do not always adhere to the duty to prolong life and provide palliative care, often following extensive consultation with the patient and his or her relatives, and that such physicians may decide to withhold or withdraw life-prolonging treatment and, thus, allow a patient to die. Such matters fall under the realm of criminal law.

France is one of the states that obliges physicians, with respect to end-of-life issues, not to provide medical treatment in cases of futility (in French, *acharnement thérapeutique*). This follows from the *loi relative aux droits des malades et à la fin de vie* (law on the rights of sick persons and the end of life), also known as the Loi Leonetti (2005). In 2016, this law was amended by the Loi Claeys (2016). This combined law played an important role in the case of *Lambert*, which has been presented to the ECtHR on various occasions. This case concerned a Frenchman, Vincent Lambert, who, in 2008, fell into a persistent vegetative state after sustaining critical injuries in a road accident.

---

[31] ECtHR 16 February 2021, *Gawlik v. Liechtenstein*, no. 23922/19, ECLI:CE:ECHR:2021:0216JUD002392219.

After a long legal battle between two opposing sides of his family,[32] the ECtHR eventually allowed Lambert to die, in July 2019, through starvation. The Grand Chamber of the ECtHR noted, in this case, that there is no consensus among the states of the Council of Europe about starting and ending medical treatment. The ECtHR, thus, afforded the French national authorities a wide margin of appreciation to decide on this issue.[33] At the same time, the Court emphasised the importance of taking the patient's wishes into account in the decision-making process, and of striking a balance between the protection of patients' right to life, on the one hand, and the protection of their right to respect for their private life, and their personal autonomy, on the other hand (Article 8 of the ECHR). A large majority of the Grand Chamber of the ECtHR accepted that the withdrawal of Vincent Lambert's artificial nutrition and hydration under the procedure prescribed by French law would not constitute a violation of Article 2 of the ECHR.

Italy is a country where ending the medical treatment of a patient is not allowed, even in cases of futility. This position may change as a result of a decision of the Italian Constitutional Court (Corte costituzionale della Repubblica Italiana) of 25 September 2019 in the case of *Fabo*.[34] After a car accident in 2014, Fabiano Antoniani (known as Fabo) was left paralysed and blind. At that time, Fabo was 37 years old. Since it was not lawful for Fabo to end his life in Italy, much as he wished to do so, a Member of Parliament, Marco Cappato, took Fabo to Switzerland to end his life through physician-assisted dying. Back in Italy, Cappato was criminally prosecuted for a violation of Article 580 of the Italian Criminal Code. The Constitutional Court concluded, in this case, that the prohibition on assisting a person to end his or her life, as prescribed by Article 580 of the Criminal Code, was contrary to the Italian Constitution. The Constitutional Court called upon the Italian Parliament to change this provision.

In short, the ECHR does not prohibit the withholding or withdrawing of medical treatment, as long as such a decision is taken in accordance with the professional standards, and takes account of the patient's wishes to the greatest possible extent.[35]

---

[32] On one side, Lambert's wife and other members of his family were willing to let Lambert die, according to the wishes he, reportedly, expressed repeatedly prior to the accident, and, on the other side, his mother and other relatives were determined to keep Lambert alive, according to their traditionalist Catholic convictions. In particular, Lambert's mother and the other relatives submitted applications to the ECtHR (and national courts).

[33] ECtHR 5 June 2015, *Lambert et al. v. France* (GC), no. 46043/14, ECLI:CE:ECHR:2015:0605JUD004604314.

[34] www.giurisprudenzapenale.com/wp-content/uploads/2019/11/Corte-Costituzionale-242-2019-1.pdf.

[35] ECtHR 28 June 2017, *Gard et al. v. the United Kingdom* (dec.), no. 39793/17, ECLI:CE:ECHR:2017:0627DEC003979317; ECtHR 23 January 2018, *Afiri and Biddarri v. France* (dec.), no. 1828/18, ECLI:CE:ECHR:2018:0123DEC000182818; ECtHR 21 April 2021, *Parfitt v. the United Kingdom* (dec.), no. 18533/21, ECLI:CE:ECHR:2021:0420DEC001853321.

5.2. PHYSICIAN-ASSISTED DYING AND EUTHANASIA

Withholding or withdrawing medical treatment is often referred to as 'therapeutic abstention'. Physician-assisted dying and euthanasia are acts by healthcare professionals aimed at deliberately ending the life of a patient in a professional way. The permissibility of physician-assisted dying and euthanasia is contested between, and within, states. In Europe, so far only the Netherlands (2002), Belgium (2002), Luxembourg (2009) and Spain (2021) have decriminalised physician-assisted dying and euthanasia, with these terms being defined slightly differently in each of these states. In addition, the Spanish Law on the Regulation of Euthanasia foresees in an opinion of the Evaluation Committee prior to performing euthanasia, where in the Netherlands, Belgium and Luxembourg there are retrospective assessments by evaluation committees. Portugal adopted similar legislation in 2021, with a preliminary assessment of euthanasia by an Evaluation Committee, but, in a seven to five decision in March of that year, the Portuguese Constitutional Court said that the amended law lacked precision, and blocked its implementation.[36] In all four of the countries in which the laws are being implemented, only a physician is allowed to end the life of a patient, with Portugal – if its amended law gets implemented – as an exception, since the proposed Portuguese law also allows a nurse to perform these acts.

Switzerland is often also believed to have decriminalised physician-assisted dying and euthanasia. This is not the case. Switzerland has a number of right-to-die societies that are, under Swiss law, allowed to assist persons to end their lives, provided that these societies and attached healthcare professionals do not act for what are called, under Swiss law, 'selfish reasons' (Article 115 of the Swiss Penal Code). This is different from the legislation in the five above-mentioned countries, where physician-assisted dying and euthanasia have been decriminalised. In these countries, a healthcare professional should be present when the patient dies, and should also report to an independent committee. For these reasons, Swiss law and practice are radically different from the five aforementioned countries. In Switzerland, patients have to end their own lives, and the involvement of the healthcare provider, although essential, is relatively minor, with the provider not being expected to be present at the moment the patient ends his or her life.

The case law of the ECtHR has gradually evolved towards accepting national laws that allow physician-assisted dying and euthanasia. Initially, the ECHR (and, previously, the European Commission on Human Rights (EComHR)) declared applications concerning end-of-life decisions inadmissible.[37]

---

[36] dre.pt/dre/detalhe/acordao-tribunal-constitucional/123-2021-161220092.
[37] EComHR 17 May 1995, *Sampedro Camean v. Spanje* (dec.), no. 25949/94, ECLI:CE:ECHR: 1995:0517DEC002594994 and ECtHR 26 October 2000, *Sanles v. Spain* (dec.), no. 48335/99, ECLI:CE:ECHR:2000:1026DEC004833599.

In 2002, in the case of *Pretty*, the Court found that the British authorities had not violated the ECHR by denying the request of Diane Pretty, a woman with motor neurone disease (MND), not to prosecute her husband if he helped her to end her life. Due to her health status, she was not able to carry out this act herself. While it declared the potential criminal prosecution of Mrs. Pretty's husband not to be contrary to the ECHR, the ECtHR considered that 'the notion of personal autonomy is an important principle underlying the interpretation of its [the rights protected by the ECHR] guarantees'.[38] The ECtHR, thus, acknowledged that tensions could arise between the right to life and the right to refuse a particular form of treatment, on the basis of personal autonomy. The Court took into account that the exercise of the latter right could have a fatal outcome, but, nevertheless, accepted the right to refuse treatment as long as such a decision was taken by 'a mentally competent adult patient'.[39] Self-determination and personal autonomy are, according to the ECtHR, important guarantees for human dignity and human freedom, including the right to physical integrity, and other rights protected by the ECHR.

In later cases on physician-assisted dying (against Switzerland), the ECtHR acknowledged the right of a competent individual to make decisions on how and when to end his or her life.[40] This entitlement is, according to the ECtHR, an aspect of the right to a private life, as protected by Article 8 of the ECHR. Since Swiss law stipulates that citizens have, under certain conditions, the right to ask for lethal medication to be administered, the ECtHR judged that, by refusing to provide this medication, Switzerland had not met its own legislation, and had, thus, violated the ECHR.

Even though the ECtHR has not, so far, had to decide on a case where a physician has been asked by a patient to end the patient's life (euthanasia), it is unlikely that the ECHR will consider euthanasia to be in contravention of the right to life, in the event that the provision of euthanasia has been decriminalised in the state concerned, and all other requirements have been met. It does not automatically follow that physicians can be forced to perform euthanasia, even though the ECtHR has, in some cases, decided that it is not permissible for

---

[38] ECtHR 29 April 2002, *Pretty v. the United Kingdom*, no. 2346/02, ECLI:CE:ECHR:2002:0429 JUD000234602, §61.

[39] ECtHR 29 April 2002, *Pretty v. the United Kingdom*, no. 2346/02, ECLI:CE:ECHR:2002: 0429JUD000234602, §63; ECtHR 10 June 2010, *Jehovah's Witnesses of Moscow et al. v. Russia*, no. 302/02, ECLI:CE:ECHR:2010:0610JUD000030202, §135.

[40] ECtHR 20 January 2011, *Haas v. Switzerland*, no. 31322/07, ECLI:CE:ECHR:2011:0120 JUD003132207; ECtHR 14 May 2013, *Gross v. Switzerland*, no. 67810/10, ECLI:CE:ECHR: 2013:0514JUD006781010; ECtHR 30 September 2014, *Gross v. Switzerland* (GC), no. 67810/10, ECLI:CE:ECHR:2014:0930JUD006781010.

healthcare professionals to refuse medical care.[41] Usually, national legislation with respect to physician-assisted dying and euthanasia will allow the personal conviction of healthcare professionals, with respect to these acts, to be taken into account.

6. CONCLUSIONS

The right to health would be meaningless without people enjoying the right to life. This explains, in a nutshell, the importance of the right to life for the right to health and other human rights.

In this chapter, focusing on Europe, state obligations with respect to the right to life have been reviewed systematically, in various contexts, based on the text of the ECHR, and the case law of the ECtHR. The author's conclusion is that the national authorities have a number of obligations, both negative and positive, to respect and protect human life. These obligations do not confine themselves to providing adequate healthcare. States should also meet these obligations with respect to the professional standards of healthcare professionals, and the right to personal autonomy of individuals. It follows from the latter right that individuals can also refuse to give informed consent to certain forms of medical treatment or palliative care, and, in states where these acts are decriminalised, to have their lives ended by a healthcare professional, by way of physician-assisted dying or euthanasia.

---

[41] ECtHR 2 June 2001, *Pichon and Sajous v. France* (dec.), no. 49853/99, ECLI:CE:ECHR:2001: 1002DEC004985399; ECtHR 12 March 2020, *Grimmark v. Sweden* (dec.), no. 43726/17, ECLI:CE:ECHR:2020:0211DEC004372617; ECtHR 12 March 2020, *Steen v. Sweden* (dec.), no. 62309/17, ECLI:CE:ECHR:2020:0211DEC006230917.

CHAPTER 12

DIGITAL HEALTHCARE TECHNOLOGIES AND HUMAN RIGHTS

Katharina Ó Cathaoir*

1. INTRODUCTION

The possibilities of modern healthcare stretch the imagination: examples include diagnosis using artificial intelligence, personalised medicine, 3D-printed organs, robotic surgery, gene-edited babies, and ingestible sensors in medications to monitor intake.[1] Simultaneously, new data-driven technologies promise a shift from a 'vertical' patient–doctor relationship to increased patient participation and empowerment. The Internet has been central to this transformation, enabling patients to research their health conditions, and to connect with others to share experiences and look for novel solutions, when the healthcare system falls short. Through mobile apps and wearable devices, patients can, furthermore, track their health, while sharing real-time information with healthcare practitioners.[2]

Big data – defined by volume (massive data sets), velocity (the speed of processing) and variety (the diversity of the data) – is essential to these innovations. Healthcare, by its nature, generates copious amounts of data, such as hospital admission data, prescriptions, and notes from consultations. Patient safety legislation requires that patient interactions with the healthcare system are recorded. Although health data has always existed, its magnitude and shareability has skyrocketed due to digitisation: medical records are no longer

---

* The author is grateful for helpful comments from the Artificial Intelligence and Legal Disruption Research Group (AI-led) at the Faculty of Law, University of Copenhagen, in particular Jacob Livingston Slosser, Raphaële Xenidis and Sebastian Schwemer.

1 For an introduction to applications of AI in healthcare, see Organisation for Economic Co-operation and Development's Directorate for Employment, Labour and Social Affairs, and Directorate for Science, Technology and Innovation, *Trustworthy AI in Health*, OECD, 2020.

2 For a recent study on e-health, see Iris Bakx, 'eHealth and Patients' Rights', dissertation, Erasmus University Rotterdam, 2021. Available at hdl.handle.net/1765/135629.

paper documents filed in a doctor's office, but dynamic records that (in theory) can be accessed by, and shared with, multiple actors remotely.

Artificial intelligence (AI) can, in turn, rapidly analyse multiple data sources, and identify patterns, at a rate and accuracy beyond human capabilities. Clinical decision-support systems can advise clinicians on the suitability of a particular treatment for a patient. Through text mining of medical records, algorithms can identify patterns, and predict disease or treatment risks. AI systems can schedule appointments and prioritise triage. Algorithms can scour social media for signs of disease outbreaks, and rapidly alert authorities to worrying patterns. Unlike humans, AI does not need breaks, holidays or sick leave. So far, AI's impact in the clinic has been modest, but this is expected to increase in the coming years.

This chapter will introduce digital healthcare technologies, and discuss their potential to contribute to the attainment of the right to the highest attainable standard of health while reflecting on the risks to human rights. It will address two basic questions: to what extent is there a right to access new healthcare technologies? And what risks do such digital technologies pose for human rights?

Digital healthcare is an evolving field of innovation and, therefore, this chapter cannot address every technological development. Instead, it will focus on selected examples of technologies, to discuss and explore the potential rights concerns. Although research and treatment are increasingly intertwined, the focus is on digital healthcare. The chapter focuses on the rights protected under the International Covenant on Civil and Political Rights (ICCPR), International Covenant on Economic, Social and Cultural Rights (ICESCR) and European Convention on Human Rights (ECHR), while examples are drawn from various jurisdictions, primarily Denmark, Ireland and England. Furthermore, given the speed at which this field is moving, it is suggested that readers check that the legal sources cited here remain up to date at the time of reading.

TERMINOLOGY USED IN THIS CHAPTER

The definitions presented here have been used by international organisations, however, they are not exhaustive and are subject to debate.[3] This chapter's intention is not to resolve these debates, but to provide an accessible introduction for those new to the field.

---

[3]   See, e.g. J. Schuett, 'A Legal Definition of AI' (2019), available at SSRN: http://dx.doi. org/10.2139/ssrn.3453632.

Algorithm – 'an unambiguous, precise, list of simple operations applied mechanically and systematically to a set of tokens or objects (e.g., configurations of chess pieces, numbers, cake ingredients, etc.). The initial state of the tokens is the input; the final state is the output.'[4]

Artificial Intelligence – 'software (and possibly also hardware) systems designed by humans that, given a complex goal, act in the physical or digital dimension by perceiving their environment through data acquisition, interpreting the collected structured or unstructured data, reasoning on the knowledge, or processing the information, derived from this data and deciding the best action(s) to take to achieve the given goal. AI systems can either use symbolic rules or learn a numeric model, and they can also adapt their behaviour by analysing how the environment is affected by their previous actions.'[5]

AI system – 'a machine-based system that can, for a given set of human-defined objectives, make predictions, recommendations, or decisions influencing real or virtual environments. AI systems are designed to operate with varying levels of autonomy.'[6]

Big data – 'The emerging use of rapidly-collected, complex data in such unprecedented quantities that terabytes (1012 bytes), petabytes (1015 bytes) or even zettabytes (1021 bytes) of storage may be required. The unique properties of big data are defined by four dimensions: volume, velocity, variety and veracity. As more information is accruing at an accelerating pace, both volume and velocity are increasing.'[7]

Deep learning – 'a subset of machine learning in which multi-layered neural networks – modelled to work like the human brain – "learn" from large amounts of data. Within each layer of the neural network, deep learning algorithms perform calculations and make predictions repeatedly, progressively "learning" and gradually improving the accuracy of the outcome over time.'[8]

---

[4] Organisation for Economic Co-operation and Development (hereinafter 'OECD'), *Algorithms and Collusion: Competition Policy in the Digital Age*, OECD, 2007, citing R.A. Wilson and F.C. Keil, *The MIT Encyclopedia of the Cognitive Sciences*, MIT Press, 1999.

[5] European Commission, 'High-Level Expert Group on Artificial Intelligence – Ethics Guidelines for Trustworthy' *AI*, 2019, Glossary.

[6] OECD, 'Recommendation of the Council on Artificial Intelligence', OECD/LEGAL/0449, 2019.

[7] World Health Organization (hereinafter, 'WHO'), 'Global strategy on digital health 2020–2025', WHO, 2021, Glossary.

[8] The IBM Cloud Education (2020), *Deep Learning*, https://www.ibm.com/dk-en/cloud/learn/machine-learning.

Machine learning – 'a subset of AI, algorithms are trained to infer certain patterns based on a set of data in order to determine the actions needed to achieve a given goal. Algorithms may continue to learn when in use.'[9]

Internet of things – 'a system of interrelated computing devices, mechanical and digital machines, objects, animals or people that are provided with unique identifiers and the ability to transfer data over a network without requiring human-to-human or human-to computer interaction.'[10]

2. PROMISES AND PITFALLS OF DIGITAL TECHNOLOGIES

New and emerging healthcare technologies have the potential to contribute to the fulfilment of the highest attainable standard of health, by enhancing availability, accessibility and quality of healthcare. Digital health is, therefore, a priority of the World Health Organization (WHO), which views technology as a means to reach the Sustainable Development Goals (SDGs), in particular the goal of universal healthcare coverage.[11] Likewise, governments are eager to invest in digital health to reduce healthcare costs, which are often regarded as unsustainable, due to ageing populations and rising chronic disease rates.

In the future, predictive AI is expected to be integrated into clinical decision-making, either through assisting health professionals or completely automating some processes. Emerging examples of AI in healthcare include 'Vara', a machine-learning AI, CE certified in the EU, that flags normal mammograms, and reports suspicious findings. Online chatbots advise parents on whether their children should attend the emergency room of a hospital, based on their children's reported symptoms. Smartphone cameras confirm or refute whether a patient has taken their medications. Beyond the hospital setting, AI can be used to predict, for example, which people are at risk of falls at home, or when a person living with a mental illness is at risk of a relapse.

---

[9] European Commission, 'White Paper on Artificial Intelligence – A European approach to excellence and trust', COM(2020) 65 final, 2020.

[10] WHO, 'Global strategy on digital health 2020–2025', WHO, 2021, Glossary.

[11] World Health Assembly, 'Resolution on Digital Health', WHA71.7, 2018; World Health Assembly, 'Resolution on Sustainable health financing, universal coverage and social health insurance', WHA58.33, 2005; World Health Assembly, 'Resolutions and decisions annex', WHA58/2005, 2015.

One means of addressing healthcare costs can be by improving prevention, through predicting, at an earlier stage, which patients are at risk of becoming seriously ill. Several countries have adopted strategies for personalised medicine, which uses genomic data, combined with other forms of big data, to stratify patients and develop individualised treatments.[12] The purported benefits include saving lives and avoiding side effects, while reducing healthcare costs. Since 2003, when the Human Genome Project mapped the human genome for the first time, the price of whole-genome sequencing has plummeted, facilitating its use in clinical care. Now, it is possible to identify whether an individual carries an increased risk of certain breast and colon cancers, or whether a patient can expect to benefit from specific cancer drugs. Using this knowledge, patients can, in some cases, avail themselves of more effective, tailored prevention and treatment.[13] While it currently makes modest contributions to healthcare, genomic knowledge is expected to increase in the coming years.

Digital technologies have been drawn upon and extensively trialled during the COVID-19 pandemic. Many countries have introduced contact tracing mobile apps to allow users to be notified if they have been exposed to a person who has later tested positive. With countries struggling to conduct manual contact-tracing, due to lack of personnel resources, mobile apps can help ensure that more individuals are informed, and, thereby, contribute to limiting the spread of the virus. However, this requires that a sufficient number of people agree to take part, and that privacy and personal data are protected.[14] The European Union adopted a common, digital 'vaccine passport' as a means of promoting safe travel within the Union. From April to September 2021, Denmark, and later other states, already required such a passport to enter bars, restaurants and third-level education institutions.[15] While they have been adopted for the purposes of public health, these digital initiatives raise numerous fundamental rights concerns related to privacy and data protection.

---

[12] E.g. the (Danish) Ministry of Health and Danish Regions, 'Personalised Medicine for the Benefit of Patients: National Strategy for Personalised Medicine (2017–2020)', 2016; The Norwegian Directorate of Health, 'The Norwegian Strategy for Personalised Medicine in Healthcare (2017–2021)', 2018; NHS England, 'Improving Outcomes through Personalised Medicine', 2016.

[13] K. Hong and B. Oh, 'Overview of personalized medicine in the disease genomic era', BMB Reports 43(10) (2010), 643–48.

[14] Council of Europe, 'Joint Statement on the right to data protection in the context of the COVID-19 pandemic by Chair of the Committee of Convention 108 and Data Protection Commissioner of the Council of Europe', Strasbourg, 30 March 2020. European Union Agency for Fundamental Rights, 'Coronavirus pandemic in the EU – Fundamental Rights implications: With a focus on contact-tracing apps', 28 May 2020.

[15] The Prime Minister's Office, 'Rammeaftale om plan for genåbning af Danmark', 22 March 2021.

An extra benefit of digital health may be that it contributes to patient engagement, and, thereby, motivates healthier behaviour. Wearable technologies track, for example, heart rate or blood pressure, and physical activity levels, while mobile phone applications can support monitoring of chronic diseases. MobileHealth/Mhealth can facilitate sending patient appointment reminders. Health authorities can use email or social media to solicit health promoting behaviour, e.g. 'your next appointment is overdue', or 'stay indoors: pollution is high today'. For patients suffering from rare diseases that are under-researched, the Internet and mobile apps can enable 'citizen scientists' to connect patients and researchers.

In low-resource settings with few healthcare workers, low-cost devices, like mobile apps, have the potential to enable those without access to adequate care to monitor their health. Telemedicine (whereby patients are treated at a distance through telecommunications devices) may facilitate medical diagnosis or counselling for patients living in remote areas or assist minority language patients in accessing doctors remotely who speak their mother tongue. Smartphone apps can assist with testing eyesight or diagnosing cavities to determine whether an expensive healthcare visit can wait. Through e-learning, training of health workers and dissemination of the newest guidelines, in remote areas, can be facilitated. Digital healthcare is, furthermore, promising in light of the global shortage of health workers, and AI's ability to replace data-entry tasks, to free up time for patient care.

Yet, deep inequalities persist that may undermine the universality of digital health: many people continue, for example, to lack access to essential medicines and the social determinants of health, such as safe, potable water and adequate housing. The contrast between countries and regions is stark: while some individuals are accessing healthcare that is increasingly digitised, with electronic health records and algorithmic triaging, others still lack access to basic equipment like ventilators. Furthermore, a digitised but unequal welfare state risks erasing vulnerable citizens. Could this raise questions in relation to the right to take part in public affairs, under Article 25 of the ICCPR?

From a human rights perspective, there is a risk that investments in advanced healthcare technologies will contribute to inequalities, and undermine the 'core' of the right to take part in public affairs, for example by neglecting fundamental public health that can contribute to the collective health of the population (see also Chapters 2 and 13 of this book). A sobering lesson of the COVID-19 pandemic has been that basic public health measures, for example handwashing, quarantine, and the like, remain a primary defence; even the most advanced healthcare systems can be overwhelmed by fast-spreading pathogens. Furthermore, as Alston notes, without incentivisation, the technology industry may focus its efforts on the wealthiest (where profits can be made), instead of developing measures to the benefit of the poorest in society.[16]

Additionally, while the Internet can empower patients, inaccurate information can undermine self-determination and, ultimately, the right to health. A major concern has been the spread of misinformation regarding vaccines and, recently, COVID-19, through online chatrooms and social media. False information from unknown sources, presented as fact and shared rapidly online, can undermine trust in science and public health measures. Responding to these challenges raises multiple human rights issues, including freedom of expression. A balance must be found between dangerous misinformation and troubling state- or company-driven control of the internet.[17]

Funding, infrastructure and a legal framework are vital elements of introducing digital healthcare.[18] Advanced technologies may require an (expensive) technological infrastructure with good quality Internet access. Meanwhile, in some parts of the world, the Internet remains limited, slow and expensive. Internet resources are often not available in minority languages and are, therefore, inaccessible to, for example, indigenous people. Furthermore, while European countries have built a strong foundation for data security, with the entry into force of the General Data Protection Regulation (GDPR),[19] more lax standards are often in place in the Global South, and, therefore, there is a risk of data misuse to benefit the wealthy, without ensuring access for the vulnerable (on vulnerability, generally, see Chapter 8 of this book).

Moreover, from a legal perspective, there is limited harmonisation, and regulatory gaps endure. The European Commission has identified several legal risks in relation to AI.[20] Firstly, the opacity of AI may make it difficult to identify and prove breaches. Secondly, there are legislative gaps. Thirdly, certain software, like machine-learning AI, needs regular updates, meaning that new

---

[16] United Nations Human Rights, 'Report of the Special Rapporteur on extreme poverty and human rights – Promotion and protection of human rights: human rights questions, including alternative approaches for improving the effective enjoyment of human rights and fundamental freedoms Extreme poverty and human rights', A/74/493, 2019, 22–23.

[17] See, e.g. B. Epstein, 'Why It Is So Difficult to Regulate Disinformation Online' in W.L. Bennett and S. Livingston (eds.), *The Disinformation Age: Politics, Technology, and Disruptive Communication in the United States*, Cambridge University Press, 2020, 190–210.

[18] WHO, 'Global diffusion of eHealth: making universal health coverage achievable – report of the third global survey on eHealth', 2016, 99.

[19] Regulation (EU) 2016/679 of the European Parliament and of the Council of 27 April 2016 on the protection of natural persons with regard to the processing of personal data and on the free movement of such data, and repealing Directive 95/46/EC (General Data Protection Regulation) (Text with EEA relevance) OJ L 119 of 4 May 2016, pp. 1–88.

[20] European Commission, 'White Paper on Artificial Intelligence – A European approach to excellence and trust', COM(2020) 65 final, 2020.9.

risks emerge during the life cycle of the product. Fourthly, there are uncertainties as to responsibilities within the supply chain. Without a coordinated EU-wide approach, Member States may adopt disparate legislation to address these risks. Globally, 'the trend in law otherwise is one of differentiation and fragmentation'.[21] For this reason, human rights can contribute by underscoring international rights and obligations. In April 2021, the European Commission released a draft Regulation on Artificial Intelligence Systems, which emphasises, inter alia, the need to protect fundamental rights.[22]

Digital technologies, while beneficial to health, have the potential to violate other rights, such as the rights to privacy, self-determination and data protection. There is also concern that certain health technologies will lead to stigmatisation, bias or discrimination, by neglecting or excluding patients. These challenges are explored in more detail in section 3 below.

3.   A RIGHT TO ACCESS NEW HEALTHCARE TECHNOLOGIES?

The right to health and the right to benefit from scientific progress are relevant to the question of whether there is a right to access new healthcare technologies and, thereby, a corresponding obligation on states. As discussed in Chapter 2, the state is obligated, under the right to health, to ensure access to healthcare goods and services. This section reflects on how far this obligation extends, and whether it may amount to an entitlement to advanced healthcare technologies.

As a starting point, it is established that states have obligations to ensure access to essential drugs, and to avoid measures that would impede such access. While the right to health is subject to state resources, the ICESCR Committee considers that the provision of *essential* drugs and the equitable distribution of health goods are core obligations.[23] In many countries, the right to essential

---

[21]   R. Lathi, 'Regulatory Schemes in Innovative Healthcare and Biomedicine' in J. Mansnérus, R. Lahti and A. Blick (eds.), *Personalised Medicine Legal and Ethical Challenges*, University of Helsinki – Faculty of Law, 2020, 14.

[22]   European Commission, Proposal for a Regulation of the European Parliament and of the Council Laying Down Harmonised Rules on Artificial Intelligence (Artificial Intelligence Act) and Amending Certain Union Legislative Acts {SEC(2021) 167 final} – {SWD(2021) 84 final} – {SWD(2021) 85 final}, Brussels, 21.4.2021 COM(2021) 206 final 2021/0106 (COD).

[23]   United Nations Committee on Economic, Social and Cultural Rights (hereinafter, 'ICESCR Committee'), 'General Comment No. 14: The Right to the Highest Attainable Standard of Health' (Art. 12), E/C.12/2000/4, 2000. See also P. Hunt and R. Khosla, 'The human right to medicines', *SUR – International Journal on Human Rights* 5(8) (2008), 99.

medicines is also enforceable in court.[24] As already discussed, several courts have found the state responsible for violating the rights to health and life, for failing to ensure access to essential medicines. For example, in 2010, the Kenyan High Court held that an Act on Counterfeit Drugs was contrary to the petitioners' rights to health, dignity and life, as it could inhibit their ability to access generic medicines.[25] In a more limited fashion, the European Court of Human Rights recognises that failing to provide access to medical treatment to prisoners may violate Article 3.[26]

Looking beyond essential drugs, it can be asked under what circumstances individuals can be held to have a right to a particular (advanced) healthcare technology. Firstly, it should be noted that patients often do not have an entitlement to a *specific* medical good or service. For example, an individual may have read about a promising type of robot surgery, but, if medical professionals determine that the person is ill-suited, or a different procedure would be similarly effective, in most circumstances the state will not be under an obligation to provide the specific technology that the patient requests. However, when the question relates to resources (and not medical suitability), a petition to access medical procedures, such as access to imaging or pacemakers, can be brought in countries like Brazil, where the right to health is constitutionally enshrined.[27] Meanwhile, in countries with 'weaker' rights to healthcare, the patient's legal standing to appeal against decisions denying access to technologies is usually more limited, and falls within the state's margin of discretion regarding resources. Nevertheless, some countries, like Norway, guarantee a right to a second opinion.

An argument could be made, however, that access to new healthcare technologies falls under the state's obligation to progressively realise the right to health (see Chapter 2 of this book). It can certainly be argued that states have obligations to invest in improving the quality and accessibility of healthcare, and to reduce barriers to private sector innovation. The argument would be strengthened should countries with similar resources and demographics provide certain treatments that the state in question does not (without reasonable justification). However, in this author's view, this would not usually mean that individuals automatically acquire a right to the best, or most up-to-date,

---

[24]   H. Hogerzeil, M. Samson, J.V. Casanovas and L. Rahmani-Ocora, 'Is access to essential medicines as part of the fulfilment of the right to health enforceable through the courts?', *The Lancet*, 368(9532) (2006), 305–11.

[25]   A. Maleche and E. Day, 'Right to Health Encompasses Right to Access Essential Generic Medicines: Challenging the 2008 Anti-Counterfeit Act in Kenya', *Health and Human Rights* 16(2) (2014), 96–104.

[26]   ECtHR 24 February 2009, *Poghossian v. Georgia*, no. 9870/07.

[27]   F.F.C. Gomes et al., 'Acesso aos procedimentos de média e alta complexidade no Sistema Único de Saúde: uma questão de judicialização', *Cadernos de Saúde Pública* 30(1) (2014), 31–43.

technologies, as the right to health does not seem to mandate uniform access to specific advanced procedures.

Beyond the right to health, it is posited that the right to enjoy the benefits of scientific progress and its applications, under Article 15 ICESCR, although it receives less broad recognition than the right to health, holds greater potential for a right to healthcare technologies. In its General Comment on Article 15, the ICESCR Committee underscored that scientific progress is 'instrumental in realizing the right to health'.[28] States should make available 'the best applications of scientific progress necessary to enjoy the highest attainable standard of health'.[29] Furthermore, they should 'ensure that everyone has equal access to the applications of science, particularly when they are instrumental for the enjoyment of other economic, social and cultural rights'.[30] Additionally, states should 'use the maximum of their available resources to overcome hurdles that any person may face to benefit from new technologies or other forms of applications of scientific advancement'.[31] This general comment calls on states to expand the benefits of new technologies, while reducing risks. It recommends international cooperation to avoid legal fragmentation, as well as a human rights-based approach, and special policies to support the vulnerable.[32] While case law is limited, the Venezuelan Supreme Court has held that failure to ensure a regular and consistent supply of drugs needed by persons living with HIV was a violation of the right to enjoy the benefits of scientific progress.[33] The right is, however, not absolute and may be limited, in so far as compatible with the nature of the rights in the Covenant to promote the 'general welfare in a democratic society' (Article 4 ICESCR).

Finally, the principle of non-discrimination plays an important, cross-cutting role in access to healthcare technologies. Under Article 2 of the ICESCR, the rights in the Covenant must be guaranteed 'without discrimination of any kind as to race, colour, sex, language, religion, political or other opinion, national or social origin, property, birth or other status'. Under the right to health, states must 'ensure the right of access to health facilities, goods and services on a non-discriminatory basis, especially for vulnerable or marginalized groups'.[34]

---

[28] ICESR Committee, 'General Comment No. 25 (2020) on science and economic, social and cultural rights (Article 15 (1)(b), (2), (3) and (4) of the International Covenant on Economic, Social and Cultural Rights)', E/C.12/GC/25, 6 March 2020, para. 67.

[29] Ibid., para. 70.

[30] Ibid., para. 17.

[31] Ibid., para. 47.

[32] Ibid., paras. 74–76.

[33] Supreme Court of Venezuela – Constitutional Division, 18 December 1997, *López, Glenda & Ors. v. Instituto Venezolano de los Seguros Sociales (IVSS)*, expediente No. 00-1343, sentencia No. 487.

[34] ICESCR Committee, 'General Comment No. 14: The Right to the Highest Attainable Standard of Health' (Art. 12), E/C.12/2000/4, 2000, para. 43(a).

Similarly, under the right to scientific progress, the following duty is listed as a core obligation:

> [to] [e]liminate laws, policies and practices that unjustifiably limit access by individuals or particular groups to facilities, services, goods and information related to science, scientific knowledge and its applications.[35]

Thus, denying access to a medical good or technology based on discriminatory grounds (as opposed to medical suitability) could amount to a violation of the rights to health and scientific progress. For example, denying a particular group, like women, or an ethnic or religious minority, access to a drug without reasonable justification would be such a violation. However, as will be explored below, it is often difficult for patients to access the data necessary to establish such a claim.

Furthermore, at a collective level, consistently investing in, or making available, technologies that benefit one group to the exclusion of another could amount to a violation of the right to health, or to enjoy the benefits of scientific progress. As 'big data' healthcare expands, the neglect of women, certain ethnic groups and children, in clinical trials, could be reframed as potential human rights violations. This aspect of non-discrimination is underscored in the ICESCR Committee's General Comment No. 25, which notes that, 'as women are underrepresented in scientific research, it is very common that scientific research and new technologies are gender biased and not sensitive to the particularities and needs of women'.[36] According to the ICESCR Committee, states are under an obligation to 'ensure access to up-to-date scientific technologies necessary for women'.[37] In her 2012 report, the Special Rapporteur in the field of cultural rights highlighted that 'innovations essential for a life with dignity should be accessible to everyone, in particular marginalized populations'.[38] She highlighted that simple and inexpensive technologies should be prioritised over innovations that favour the affluent.[39] States are also encouraged to invest in science and research.[40]

In summary, the right to health guarantees the right to access essential medications and services. States may violate their obligations by failing to

---

[35]   ICESCR Committee, 'General Comment No. 25 (2020) on science and economic, social and cultural rights (Article 15 (1)(b), (2), (3) and (4) of the International Covenant on Economic, Social and Cultural Rights)', E/C.12/GC/25, 6 March 2020, para. 52.

[36]   Ibid., para. 30.

[37]   Ibid., para. 33.

[38]   United Nations General Assembly, 'Report of the Special Rapporteur in the field of cultural rights, The right to enjoy the benefits of scientific progress and its applications', A/HRC/20/26, 14 May 2012, para. 29.

[39]   Ibid., para. 68.

[40]   Ibid., para. 71.

provide access in a timely manner, even where there are resource constraints. For more advanced technologies, human rights do not necessarily guarantee entitlements where the treatment is not judged to be medically advantageous, which seems reasonable in light of resources, as well as medical ethics. Instead, the right to enjoy the benefits of scientific progress places progressive obligations on States Parties to expand access to new healthcare technologies, and may form a stronger argument in favour of health innovation. Finally, human rights makes an important contribution by proscribing discrimination in accessing new technologies, on a number of grounds.

4. WHICH HUMAN RIGHTS ARE AT RISK?

Having outlined the potential contribution of human rights, and some relevant human rights entitlements, the human rights risks raised by digital healthcare will now be reflected upon. This section focuses on patients' rights to privacy and data protection, as well as the right to an explanation, and to non-discrimination and accountability. These rights have already been introduced in Chapter 3, and their substance will not, therefore, be explored in detail here.

4.1. THE RIGHT TO PRIVACY

Growing digitalisation, coupled with increasing awareness of the potential misuse of personal data (such as the Snowden leaks on US surveillance,[41] and the revelations on Facebook's role in the 2016 US presidential election) has awoken human rights communities to the risks that digital technologies pose to the right to privacy.[42] While the concept of privacy originally focused on protecting the individual from intrusions by the state, the use of personal data by private companies, like tech giants such as Google and Facebook, is soliciting growing concern. In the digital health sphere, the public and private are often intertwined: for example, in England, the NHS shares patient data with Google. This section explores a selection of privacy risks associated with digital health technologies.

Digital technologies allow healthcare systems (and potentially third parties) to track patients from the cradle to the grave. Through various registries, data is collected on which patients are diagnosed with which diseases and when, on which medicines are prescribed, and on eventual causes of death. This is

---

[41] See ECtHR 25 May 2021, *Big Brother Watch and Others v. The United Kingdom* (GC), nos. 58170/13, 62322/14 and 24960/15.
[42] See reports of the Special Rapporteur on the Right to Privacy, such as Human Rights Council Resolution A/HRC/31/64.

invaluable for research and quality control in healthcare systems, as it allows for the tracking of diseases and treatments over an individual's life cycle. Yet, it also has privacy implications. In 2019, then-Special Rapporteur on Extreme Poverty and Human Rights, Philip Alston, drew attention to the 'digital welfare state', and the risk of 'digital dystopia'.[43] He called for, inter alia, transparency in digital policymaking, to combat biases.

Privacy is multifaceted, capable of multiple meanings and interpretations. In the context of big data, privacy is often used as a synonym for *informational self-determination*: the right to control access to one's information and data.[44] Privacy is not, however, an absolute right, and limitations are permitted, subject to similar criteria as already discussed in this book, in relation to other rights. As will also be discussed in Chapter 13 of this book, under the ICCPR, interferences must not be arbitrary or unlawful.[45] The principles of necessity, proportionality and legality are central to the legitimacy of an interference.[46] In health data governance, the question is where the balance between the individual and the collective should be struck. Should, or can, individuals control access to their health data completely, or should/can health data also be used for purposes that can benefit society, through assumed consent? In a welfare state, is it legitimate to expect that health data gathered during tax-funded treatment can be reused for quality assurance purposes?

Informed consent was introduced, in Chapter 3 of this book, as a means by which patients can exercise and safeguard their rights to self-determination. However, in a digitised world, there are a number of limitations. Firstly, individuals are sometimes not asked to consent to the sharing of their data, because their data is being processed on a separate legal basis (such as scientific research) and, therefore, they may be unaware of how their data is being used. Still, the GDPR underscores that patients should be adequately informed as to how their health data may be used, even if a different legal basis will be used for its processing. The Biomedicine Convention also asserts that patients have a right to know what information is being collected on their health, and the possibility of future use of their data.[47] Soft-law standards recommend that patients should be informed

---

[43]   United Nations General Assembly, 'Promotion and protection of human rights: human rights questions, including alternative approaches for improving the effective enjoyment of human rights and fundamental freedoms – Extreme poverty and human rights', A/74/493, 11 October 2019.

[44]   Y. McDermott, 'Conceptualising the Right to Data Protection in an Era of Big Data', *Big Data & Society* 4(1) (2017), 1–7.

[45]   United Nations Human Rights Committee, 4 April 1994, Communication No. 488/1992, *Toonan v. Australia*, CCPR/C/50/D/488/1992, para. 8.3.

[46]   Ibid., para. 23.

[47]   Council of Europe, 'Convention for the protection of Human Rights and Dignity of the Human Being with regard to the Application of Biology and Medicine: Convention on Human Rights and Biomedicine', Treaty No. 164, Arts. 10.1–10.2.

if their records or samples may be reused for research.[48] Patients should, therefore, be informed that data is being stored, have rights of access, and have options to opt out of data use for purposes that go beyond their consent, where appropriate.

Yet, authorities do not always meet these standards. For example, in England, the UK Information Commissioner's Office found that the Royal Free London NHS Foundation Trust's partnership with Google DeepMind (a subsidiary of Google) breached data protection law. To test an app, the NHS trust shared 1.6 million partial patient records of persons who presented at accident and emergency or radiology departments, which was found to be neither necessary nor proportionate. It was held that patients 'would not have reasonably expected their information' to be shared, and that the NHS trust should have been more transparent.[49] Although it had been possible to opt out, patients could not reasonably have objected, because they did not know that their data was being processed.[50] The NHS trust was ordered to address the failures, but not fined. Other examples include: the Danish State Serum Institute sent biological material stored in the National Biobank to the US without the required permission from the Data Protection Authority, or the knowledge of the individuals concerned.[51]

Secondly, increasing digitisation of healthcare undermines patients' abilities to opt out of digital health, and to refuse storage of personal data. Digitisation of healthcare records can benefit patient health, by ensuring that healthcare professionals can rapidly access patient information, and offer continuity of care. For patient safety, it may be necessary and beneficial that data on allergies and vaccinations are stored electronically, instead of expecting patients to retain this information throughout their lives. But can a patient refuse to have their medical information stored electronically, by reference to self-determination/privacy, and still receive treatment? Another question is who owns medical records: can a patient have their health records altered if they dispute a diagnosis? For example,

---

[48]   Council for International Organizations of Medical Sciences (CIOMS), 'International Ethical Guidelines for Health-related Research Involving Humans', commentary on Guideline 4, CIOMS, 2016.

[49]   UK Information Commissioner's Office, 'Royal Free–Google DeepMind trial failed to comply with data protection law', 3 July 2017, https://ico.org.uk/about-the-ico/news-and-events/news-and-blogs/2017/07/royal-free-google-deepmind-trial-failed-to-comply-with-data-protection-law/.

[50]   UK Information Commissioner's Office, 'letter on RFA0627721 – provision of patient data to DeepMind to Sir David Sloman', 3 July 2017, https://ico.org.uk/media/action-weve-taken/undertakings/2014353/undertaking-cover-letter-revised-04072017-to-first-person.pdf.

[51]   A. Fischer and M. Friis, 'Dokumenter afslører: Statens Serum Institut har i seks år videregivet danskeres blodprøver uden tilladelse', Danmarks Radio, 1 December 2020, https://www.dr.dk/nyheder/indland/dokumenter-afsloerer-statens-serum-institut-har-i-seks-aar-videregivet-danskeres.

in England, the NHS claim ownership of patient records, although patients have rights of access.

Thirdly, as medical technology becomes increasingly complex, it can be asked to what extent patients might fully understand the technology and, thereby, provide valid consent. Take advanced genomic sequencing, for example. A patient gives consent to a biological sample being sequenced for the purposes of diagnosis or treatment. Most individuals will not understand what sequencing involves, but the same can be said for many complicated procedures. However, where whole genome sequencing becomes particularly interesting is that the results of the sequencing can be unclear, even for geneticists, as they may signal a risk, but not a guarantee, that a condition will develop. Furthermore, while certain mutations are still not understood, new health information may be revealed as technology advances.[52] Additionally, certain findings may relate to the patients' family's health, leading some to argue for a wider approach to autonomy: notably, relational autonomy.[53] The author suggests that a human rights-based approach requires that these considerations are made clear to the patient, prior to, and during, the consent process.

Fourthly, legislation may allow health data to move outside the clinic: notably, to be shared with police and courts in criminal or civil cases. Health data has applications beyond individual health and, therefore, increased gathering and storage may seem like an opportunity for the state to address other societal issues. In Denmark, the courts can allow police to access genetic data held in the National Genome Centre, in limited cases, such as a terror attack.[54] However, the question must also be asked where the appropriate balance between the individual's rights and the societal interests should be struck. In the US, there have been recent examples of health and genetic data being used for unconnected purposes, like immigration control. Failure to respect patient privacy and confidentiality can undermine trust in the healthcare system, and lead persons to avoid treatment.

The European Court of Human Rights has recognised the potential for health data gathered for criminal law purposes to lead to privacy violations. In *Marper v. UK*, the Grand Chamber found that the UK had violated Article 8 of the ECHR by retaining DNA profiles, samples and fingerprints gathered in connection with criminal investigations.[55] The applicants had been arrested as

---

52 I.H. Asmussen and K. Ó Cathaoir, 'Making Access to a Population of Bodies in the Name of Autonomy', *European Journal of Health Law* 25(5) (2018), 555–72.

53 E.S. Dove, S.E. Kelly, F. Lucivero, M. Machirori, S. Dheensa and B. Prainsack, 'Beyond individualism: Is there a place for relational autonomy in clinical practice and research?', *Clinical Ethics* 12(3) (2017), 150–65.

54 K. Ó Cathaoir, 'In Search of Solidarity: Personalised Medicine in Denmark', *Nordisk socialrättslig tidskrift*, vol. 2019 (21–22), 65–95.

55 ECtHR 4 December 2008, *S. and Marper v. the United Kingdom*, nos. 30562/04 and 30566/04.

minors, but never convicted. They subsequently requested that their samples be destroyed, which request was refused. The ECtHR noted that:

> bearing in mind the rapid pace of developments in the field of genetics and information technology, the Court cannot discount the possibility that in the future the private-life interests bound up with genetic information may be adversely affected in novel ways.

The Court determined that the retention of the samples and profiles constituted an interference in the applicants' private lives, given the samples' highly personal nature, their ability to identify the applicants' ethnicity, and because the samples contained a unique genetic code of great relevance to both the individuals and their relatives. While the measure pursued a legitimate aim (prevention of crime), the 'permanent and indiscriminate retention' of the data failed to strike a fair balance.[56]

Fifthly, privacy can also be jeopardised by power imbalances that undermine the freeness of a consent. With the growth of chronic diseases (see Chapter 13 of this book), and the effect of chronic diseases on work attendance, there is a clear incentive for employers to encourage employees to be physically active and eat a balanced diet (key determinants of good health). Employers may offer benefits to employees, like free gym membership, exercise equipment and visits to health retreats. While acceptance of these offers may, formally, be voluntary, one can question the extent to which consent is free when it comes to the employee–employer relationship, where there is an inherent power imbalance. These offers may also have privacy implications. For example, does the employer receive data from an item of wearable technology? If a health condition that may affect work performance is detected, will the employer be informed?[57]

Finally, individuals consistently click 'consent' to access websites or digital technologies without reading the terms and conditions, or understanding the scope of the policies to which they are, thereby, consenting.[58] Internet of Things (IoT) devices, like heart monitors and mobile apps, rely on collecting and linking a significant amount of data. Apps may also sell users' data for marketing purposes, a fact that is often hidden deep in long sets of terms and conditions. The commercialisation of health data is seen as a problem by some, as, through attributing property rights to a third party, the individual loses control over

---

[56]   Ibid., para. 125.
[57]   C. Brassart Olsen, 'To Track or not to Track? Employees' Data Privacy in the Age of Corporate Wellness, Mobile Health, and GDPR', *International Data Privacy Law* 10(3) (2020), 236–52.
[58]   I.H. Asmussen and K. Ó Cathaoir, 'Making Access to a Population of Bodies in the Name of Autonomy', *European Journal of Health Law* 25(5) (2018), 555–72.

certain aspects of their data.[59] Wachter describes how there is an 'implicit tension between user's information privacy (or control of personal data) and IoT, as the latter relies on linked up services.'[60] The so-called 'privacy paradox' highlights that, while individuals are concerned about privacy, they often fail to act accordingly in their online behaviour.[61] Under the applicable EU regulation, such devices are only classified as medical devices if that is the manufacturers' intended use, even if the consumer's use may render them more akin to medical devices.[62]

Using IoT data, coupled with browsing and purchasing history, postal code or occupation, inferences can be drawn about a user's gender, race or ethnicity, without the user providing this information. This could lead to a woman in her thirties receiving pregnancy or baby-related advertising, despite never 'informing' an app of her pregnancy. Smart devices can, at the behest of the user, calculate, for example, the quantity and quality of that user's sleep. This data, combined with geolocation data, could reveal inferences of which the consumer is unaware, such as depression or alcohol abuse. A central human rights risk is that such data could be used to make determinations, for example, that an individual is not suited to a particular product or offer. In the employment context, for example, it has been documented that men are more likely to receive advertising for high-paying jobs, meaning that women miss out on some opportunities.[63]

This section has highlighted several privacy concerns raised by digital health. It has, furthermore, shown how consent is an important, but ultimately inadequate, tool for protecting privacy. In light of these gaps, the Special Rapporteur on Privacy has recommended that the UN adopt a new instrument on surveillance and privacy.[64] This proposal would ensure international minimum standards, and avoid the mining of data from countries with weak

---

[59] A. Dickens, 'Viewpoint from Information to Valuable Asset: The Commercialization of Health Data as a Human Rights Issue', *Health and Human Rights Journal* 22(2) (2020), 67–70.

[60] S. Wachter, 'Normative Challenges of Identification in the Internet of Things: Privacy, Profiling, Discrimination, and the GDPR', *Computer Law & Security Review* 34(3) (2018), 436–49.

[61] T. Mulder and M. Tudorica, 'Privacy policies, cross-border health data and the GDPR', *Information & Communications Technology Law* 28(3) (2019), 261–74.

[62] Regulation (EU) 2017/745 of the European Parliament and of the Council of 5 April 2017 on medical devices, amending Directive 2001/83/EC, Regulation (EC) No 78/2002 and Regulation (EC) No 1223/2009 and repealing Council Directives 90/385/EEC and 93/42/EEC OJ L 117 of 5 May 2017.

[63] A. Datta, M.C. Tschantz and A. Datta, 'Automated Experiments on Ad Privacy Settings: A Tale of Opacity, Choice, and Discrimination', *Proceedings on Privacy Enhancing Technologies* [2015], 92–112.

[64] United Nations Human Rights Council, 'Promotion and protection of all human rights, civil political, economic, social and cultural rights, including the right to development – Report of the Special Rapporteur on the right to privacy', A/HRC/37/62, 2018.

privacy protections. The next section will introduce the right to data protection, focusing on some of the protections introduced by the GDPR.

4.2. THE RIGHT TO DATA PROTECTION

Article 8 of the EU Charter recognises a right to protection of personal data distinct from the right to privacy.[65] It requires that data is processed fairly, for specific purposes, and on a legitimate legal basis. The right has been operationalised under the GDPR, which sets out a number of data subject rights, including the right to access personal data and information on processing, the right to have inaccurate data corrected, the right to erase data ('the right to be forgotten'), and the right to object to processing.[66] In turn, data controllers have obligations to comply with these requirements.[67] In this section, we briefly introduce the GDPR, and highlight the relevance of the right to data protection to healthcare.

The GDPR introduces six principles: lawfulness, fairness and transparency; purpose limitation; data minimisation; accuracy; storage limitation; and integrity and confidentiality.[68] In a health data context, processing will usually rely on consent, medical diagnosis or public interest.[69] Data processed for treatment purposes may not be processed for other purposes without a legal basis. Following the principle of data minimisation, data processors must not gather or process more data than necessary. In a healthcare context, this could mean not reviewing aspects of a patient's health record that are not relevant for a consultation. Personal data must be accurate, i.e. correct and not misleading. This raises healthcare dilemmas where a healthcare worker misdiagnoses a patient but the patient record system does not allow for this information to be corrected for quality control purposes. Finally, data should not be stored for longer than necessary, although, in healthcare, limits are usually set by law, with reference to patient safety.

The GDPR imposes data security requirements on data controllers, namely appropriate technical and organisational measures (Article 24(1)). These include:

- the pseudonymisation and encryption of personal data.
- the ability to ensure the ongoing confidentiality, integrity, availability and resilience of processing systems and services.

---

[65]   Y. McDermott, 'Conceptualising the Right to Data Protection in an Era of Big Data', *Big Data & Society* 1(2) (2017), 1–13.
[66]   See GDPR, Chapter 3.
[67]   See Ibid., Chapter 4.
[68]   Ibid., Art. 5(1).
[69]   Ibid., Art. 9(2)(a),(h),(i).

- the ability to restore the availability and access to personal data in a timely manner, in the event of a physical or technical incident.
- a process for regularly testing, assessing and evaluating the effectiveness of technical and organisational measures for ensuring the security of the processing. (Article 32(1)).

A data impact assessment is also required 'where a type of processing in particular using new technologies, and taking into account the nature, scope, context and purposes of the processing, is likely to result in a high risk to the rights and freedoms of natural persons' (Article 35(1)).

Adequate security is vital, as cyberattacks on health data, with the potential for hackers to access confidential data, are increasing. In 2017, the 'WannaCry' cyberattack resulted in cancelled appointments, and millions of pounds in lost patient activity.[70] In May 2021, the Irish Health Service Executive was hit by a serious cyberattack, suspending IT-based services like radiology, and deleting patient records.[71] Other risks come not from the systems, but their users. For example, there is a risk that healthcare workers or researchers will save or share health information in an unsafe manner, such as sharing patient information on private telephones or instant messaging groups, instead of using secure servers. While potentially making communication easier, such practices could result in data breaches.

Secure data sharing is another central issue in digital healthcare. Better data flows can mean that data related to rare diseases can be shared, for the benefit of more patients. Countries with rich data sets can, thereby, contribute to digitised medicine in other jurisdictions. At the same time, research suggests that individuals are often opposed to their data being sent outside of their home jurisdictions. Furthermore, while individuals, when asked, may respond favourably to the idea of contributing data, few actually do.[72] Fundamentally, it is necessary that all countries achieve an appropriate level of data protection, in order to avoid data breaches and misuses. Furthermore, practical issues, like the lack of interoperable standards between data models, dominate. The FAIR principles (Findable, Accessible, Interoperable and Reusable) seek to drive good

---

[70] S. Ghafur, S. Kristensen, K. Honeyford, G. Martin, A. Darzi and P. Aylin, 'A retrospective impact analysis of the WannaCry cyberattack on the NHS', *NPJ – Digital Medicine* 2(98) (2019).

[71] Irish Health and Safety Eexecutive, HSE Cyber Security Incident, https://www.hse.ie/eng/services/news/media/pressrel/hse-cyber-security-incident-update.html.

[72] B.J. Evans, 'Big Data and Individual Autonomy in a Crowd' in I.G. Cohen, H.F. Lynch, E. Vayena and U. Gasser (eds.), *Big Data, Health Law and Bioethics*, Cambridge University Press, 2018, 23.

data-sharing practices. Increasingly, data federation, whereby data remains local but is federated through a virtual database, is becoming popular.[73]

Finally, anonymising personal data is often regarded as a central tool for protecting the data subject's privacy. Anonymisation must be distinguished from pseudonymisation, whereby data goes through a process, for example key coding, that renders the data not directly identifiable to a particular individual, but where such person could be considered identifiable through use of additional information. Anonymous data is data that cannot identify individuals through means reasonably likely to be used, and such data is no longer subject to the GDPR. However, there are multiple controversies regarding anonymisation.[74] In the healthcare context, some have questioned whether health data, in particular genetic data, can ever be genuinely anonymous.

While the GDPR is binding on EU Member States, at Council of Europe level, Convention 108 + also places obligations on ratifying states to protect personal data.[75] Likewise, the European Court of Human Rights (ECtHR) has also held that 'personal data protection plays a primordial role' in the exercise of the right to respect for private life protected by Article 8 ECHR.[76] While a state has a certain margin of appreciation in determining how to protect personal data, the margin is narrower where a particularly important aspect of an individual's life is at issue.[77] Domestic law should enshrine safeguards, and ensure that data are relevant, not excessive in relation to the purposes for which they are stored, and preserved in a form that permits identification for no longer than required by the purpose.[78] While many of the principles are similar between the EU and Council of Europe approaches, the GDPR is directly enforceable in all EU Member States, and carries the ability to enforce fines.

4.3. THE RIGHT TO AN EXPLANATION

Certain AI applications may be 'black boxes', whereby the developer knows the input and output of the algorithm, but does not know its precise workings, i.e. how it arrived at the result that a person should or should not be offered a

---

[73] C. Suver, A. Thorogood, M. Doerr, J. Wilbanks and B. Knoppers, 'Bringing Code to Data: Do Not Forget Governance', *Journal of Medical Internet Research* 22(7) (2020): e18087.

[74] M. Mourby, E. Mackey, M. Elliot, H. Gowans, S.E. Wallace, J. Bell, H. Smith, S. Aidinlis and J. Kaye, 'Are 'pseudonymised' data always personal data? Implications of the GDPR for administrative data research in the UK', *Computer Law & Security Law* 34(2) (2018), 222–33.

[75] Council of Europe, 'Convention for the protection of individuals with regard to the processing of personal data', Treaty No. 108.

[76] ECtHR 22 June 2017, *Aycaguer v. France*, no. 8806/12, para. 38.

[77] Ibid., para. 37.

[78] Ibid., para. 38.

treatment.[79] In the context of consent to healthcare, black boxes can undermine the validity of the consent provided. They can also mean that the data subject lacks either the data or the knowledge to prove that a violation has occurred. Some have suggested that the black box problem can be mitigated, either by making models more explainable, or through use of secondary models that provide for post hoc explanations.[80]

There is an ongoing discussion as to what extent the GDPR includes a right to an explanation. Article 22 of the GDPR addresses automated processing (i.e. processing without human intervention), as follows:[81]

1. The data subject shall have the right not to be subject to a decision based solely on automated processing, including profiling, which produces legal effects concerning him or her or similarly significantly affects him or her.

2. Paragraph 1 shall not apply if the decision:
   (a) is necessary for entering into, or performance of, a contract between the data subject and a data controller;
   (b) is authorised by Union or Member State law to which the controller is subject and which also lays down suitable measures to safeguard the data subject's rights and freedoms and legitimate interests; or
   (c) is based on the data subject's explicit consent.

3. In the cases referred to in points (a) and (c) of paragraph 2, the data controller shall implement suitable measures to safeguard the data subject's rights and freedoms and legitimate interests, at least the right to obtain human intervention on the part of the controller, to express his or her point of view and to contest the decision.

4. Decisions referred to in paragraph 2 shall not be based on special categories of personal data referred to in Article 9(1), unless point (a) or (g) of Article 9(2) applies and suitable measures to safeguard the data subject's rights and freedoms and legitimate interests are in place.

Any right not to be subject to automated processing, therefore, only applies to 'a decision based solely on automated processing' that produces *legal* effects. An automated decision to refuse healthcare or reimbursement for a treatment would, therefore, be covered by Article 22. A treatment decision reviewed by

---

[79] See, further, W.N. Price II, 'Regulating Black-Box Medicine', *Michigan Law Review* 116 (2017), 421–74.

[80] C. Rudin, 'Stop explaining black box machine learning models for high stakes decisions and use interpretable models instead', *Nature Machine Intelligence* 1 (2019), 206–15.

[81] Under Art. 4(2) GDPR, 'processing' means 'any operation or set of operations which is performed on personal data or on sets of personal data, whether or not by automated means, such as collection, recording, organisation, structuring, storage, adaptation or alteration, retrieval, consultation, use, disclosure by transmission, dissemination or otherwise making available, alignment or combination, restriction, erasure or destruction'.

a physician, in contrast, would not. The legal literature differs as to whether this entails a prohibition on automated processing or a right to object to automated processing.[82] Those who claim that a right to an explanation can be found under the GDPR draw on Articles 13 and 14 thereof, on the right to meaningful information about the logic involved.[83] Others deny that a right to an *ex post* explanation exists, finding instead that the GDPR only protects an *ex ante* explanation.[84] Brkan considers that there is a right to an explanation, but that it only extends to information 'explaining crucial reasons for decisions', recognising that the right will be difficult to exercise in practice.[85]

While disagreement persists on the right to an explanation, transparency and meaningful information are, increasingly, seen as requirements of AI. The OECD recommendations on AI (the first intergovernmental standard on AI) call on all actors to provide meaningful information, appropriate to the context, and consistent with the state of art:

    i.   to foster a general understanding of AI systems,
    ii.   to make stakeholders aware of their interactions with AI systems, including in the workplace,
    iii. to enable those affected by an AI system to understand the outcome, and,
    iv. to enable those adversely affected by an AI system to challenge its outcome based on plain and easy-to-understand information on the factors, and the logic that served as the basis for the prediction, recommendation or decision.[86]

If AI is non-transparent, healthcare professionals may avoid using an application, or rely on it without due regard for its limitations or biases. Likewise, if members of the medical professional do not understand the data or processes involved, they may be ill-prepared to guide patients and ensure that valid consents are given. At the same time, detailed information on the workings of a model cannot be a legal expectation either. For example, as Kiseleva notes, doctors are not expected to explain 'the chemical processes'

---

[82] L. Tosoni, 'The right to object to automated individual decisions: resolving the ambiguity of Article 22(1) of the General Data Protection Regulation', *International Data Privacy Law* 11(2) (2021), 145–62.

[83] A.D. Selbst and J. Powles, 'Meaningful information and the right to explanation', *International Data Privacy Law* 7(4) (2017), 233–42, 237.

[84] S. Wachter, B. Mittelstadt and L. Floridi, 'Why a Right to Explanation of Automated Decision-Making Does Not Exist in the General Data Protection Regulation', *International Data Privacy Law* 7(2) (2017), 76–99.

[85] M. Brkan, 'Do algorithms rule the world? Algorithmic decision-making and data protection in the framework of the GDPR and beyond', *International Journal of Law and Information Technology* 27(2) (2019), 91–121.

[86] OECD Legal Instruments, 'Recommendation of the Council on Artificial Intelligence', OECD/LEGAL/0449, 22 May 2019, Art. 1.3.

involved in the production of medicines: it is sufficient to explain the risks and consequences of the medication.[87]

The author of this chapter has argued, elsewhere, that algorithms used in the clinic should be *explainable*.[88] Decisions about patients should not be made 'solely' on the basis of models, unless this has been authorised under Member State law (or the patient has explicitly consented to this form of automated decision-making).[89] If the patient *does* consent to automated decision-making, they will then be entitled to receive information about the logic of the decision-making, and to contest the decision, or obtain human intervention.[90] Furthermore, the logic of the model must at least be explainable to the clinician using it, so that they can determine whether or not to follow its recommendations. The clinician will hold a medical duty to make patients aware of material risks and benefits in obtaining consent to treatment,[91] which may, in turn, require explanation of the model, where it is relied upon (in part) for their advice. Similarly, Olsen et al. have argued that the administrative law duty on public authorities to give *legal* reasons for decisions is more far-reaching than the right to an explanation, as it applies irrespective of automated processing.[92]

4.4. NON-DISCRIMINATION

A growing body of literature warns that digital health technologies will result in, or further, discrimination.[93] International organisations increasingly acknowledge this risk, and recommend legal and ethical solutions.[94] These risks are multifaceted and span different aspects of inequality, in other words the

---

[87] A. Kiseleva, 'AI as a Medical Device: Is It Enough to Ensure Performance Transparency and Accountability in Healthcare?', *European Pharmaceutical Law Review* 4(1) (2020), 5–16.

[88] M. Mourby, K. Ó Cathaoir and C.B. Collin, 'Transparency of Machine Learning in Healthcare: The GDPR and European Health Law', *Computer Law and Security Review* 43 (2021) 105611.

[89] GDPR, Art. 22(2).

[90] Ibid., Art. 22(3).

[91] E.g. Supreme Court, 11 March 2015, *Montgomery v. Lanarkshire Health Board* [2015] UKSC 11.

[92] H.P. Olsen, J. Livingston Slosser and T.T. Hildebrandt, 'What's in the Box? The Legal Requirement to Explain Computationally Aided Decision-Making' in Hans-W. Micklitz, Oreste Pollicino, Amnon Reichman, Andrea Simoncini, Giovanni Sartor and Giovanni De Gregorio (eds.), *Public Administration in Constitutional Challenges in the Algorithmic Society*, Cambridge University Press, 2022, 219–35. See also L. Edwards and M. Veale, 'Slave to the Algorithm? Why a "Right to an Explanation" is Probably not the Remedy you are Looking for', *Duke Law & Technology Review* 16(1) (2017), 18–84.

[93] E.g. N. Sun, K. Esom, M. Dhaliwal and J.J. Amon, 'Human Rights and Digital Health Technologies', *Health and Human Rights* 22(2) (2020), 21–32.

[94] European Parliament, 'Fundamental rights implications of big data', P8_TA-PROV(2017)0076, 2017; Council of Europe – Parliamentary Assembly, 'Resolution No. 2343 on Preventing discrimination caused by the use of artificial intelligence', 2020.

risk that technologies will be inaccessible to certain groups or persons without means, that technologies will only prove effective on certain groups, and that seemingly 'well-intended' technologies will produce discriminatory impacts.[95] Alternatively, technology 'optimists' argue that digital tools can be less biased, and more objective, than human decision-making.[96] For example, physician bias against women or black people's pain is well-documented.[97] On the one hand, AI could be better at measuring pain, and could avoid replicating human biases.[98] On the other hand, there is a risk that AI will learn from, and amplify, human biases.

From an accessibility perspective, not all citizens will be able to access digitised treatment, due to inequality and poverty. Where healthcare communication moves online, this requires citizens to have access to a stable and secure internet connection, in order to receive information, or communicate with healthcare workers. For older people or people with disabilities, digitisation can cause access challenges, especially if technology does not reflect universal design.[99] Computer errors that impact on social security benefits or treatment offers may not be discovered if the individual lacks digital skills, as well as the time to review and appeal decisions. Economic accessibility, in terms of the cost of treatments, is also an important dimension: will technologies only be available to those with private health insurance, or who can afford to pay out of pocket?

Research details the risk that AI healthcare will discriminate, or make biased determinations, against certain patients. Bias or discrimination can manifest themselves due to different reasons: (unconscious) bias of the developer; biased data sets; biased programming; and inaccurate, poor quality datasets. For example, the Special Rapporteur on Contemporary Racism noted, in a 2020 report, that:

> emerging digital technologies exacerbate and compound existing inequities, many of which exist along racial, ethnic and national origin grounds. The examples highlighted in the report raise concerns about different forms of racial discrimination in the design and use of emerging digital technologies. In some cases, this

---

[95]   H. Suresh and J.V. Guttag, 'A Framework for Understanding Unintended Consequences of Machine Learning', 2019, https://arxiv.org/abs/1901.10002.

[96]   S. Hoffman and A. Podgurski, 'Big Bad Data: Law, Public Health, and Biomedical Databases', *The Journal of Law, Medicine & Ethics* 41(1) (2013), 56–60.

[97]   E.N. Chapman, A. Kaatz and M. Carnes, 'Physicians and Implicit Bias: How Doctors May Unwittingly Perpetuate Health Care Disparities', *Journal of General Internal Medicine* 28 (2013), 1504–510.

[98]   E. Pierson, D.M. Cutler, J. Leskovec, S. Mullainathan and Z. Obermeyer, 'An algorithmic approach to reducing unexplained pain disparities in underserved populations', *Nature Medicine* 27 (2021), 136–40.

[99]   See also A. Lebret and T. Minssen, 'Digital Health, Artificial Intelligence and Accessibility to Health Care in Denmark', *European Human Rights Law Review* 1 (2021), 39–49.

discrimination is direct, and explicitly motivated by intolerance or prejudice. In other cases, discrimination results from disparate impacts on groups according to their race, ethnicity or national origin, even when an explicit intent to discriminate is absent. And in yet other cases, direct and indirect forms of discrimination exist in combination, and can have such a significant holistic or systemic effect as to subject groups to racially discriminatory structures that pervade access to and enjoyment of human rights in all areas of their lives.[100]

From the perspective of the right to health, data can undermine the effectiveness and appropriateness of a treatment. An AI system used to detect skin cancer may outperform physicians in relation to white people, while leaving melanoma undetected in people of colour. Big data may entrench discrimination, due to limited available data sets on minorities, who may, for example, leave less of a digital footprint.[101] Using electronic health records to develop an AI system may end up reflecting the biases or mistakes of the health worker who originally inputted the records.[102]

While direct and indirect discrimination on the basis of race or ethnicity is prohibited by law, the applicant must overcome several legal hurdles in order to establish such discrimination. For example, the individual must demonstrate a difference in treatment from a similarly situated person, on the basis of a protected ground. Indirect discrimination can be rebutted, if it is based on an objective and reasonable justification, has a legitimate aim, and is proportionate.[103] In the case of algorithmic healthcare, the patient may lack access to the variables needed to identify and prove discrimination. In some cases, software code may be covered by laws on intellectual property or business secrets.[104] As already discussed in this chapter, without access to the data used to make an algorithmic determination, it may be difficult for an individual to establish that discrimination has occurred. This underscores the importance of *ex ante* and *ex post* analyses of algorithmic decision making (see, further, below).

In 2017, Obermeyer et al. published a paper which demonstrated that an algorithm used by a leading US health services provider scored black patients

---

[100]   United Nations General Assembly, 'Report of the Special Rapporteur on contemporary forms of racism, racial discrimination, xenophobia and related intolerance – Racial discrimination and emerging digital technologies: a human rights analysis', A/HRC/44/57, 2020, 2.

[101]   I.G. Cohen, R. Amarasingham, A. Shah, B. Xie, and B. Lo, 'The legal and ethical concerns that arise from using complex predictive analytics in health care', *Health Affairs* 33(7) (2014), 1139–147.

[102]   S. Hoffman and A. Podgurski, 'Big Bad Data: Law, Public Health, and Biomedical Databases', *The Journal of Law, Medicine & Ethics* 41(1) (2013), 56–60.

[103]   ECtHR 25 March 2014, *Biao v. Denmark*, no. 38590/10.

[104]   European Union Agency for Fundamental Rights, *#BigData: Discrimination in data-supported decision making*, 2018, https://fra.europa.eu/sites/default/files/fra_uploads/fra-2018-focus-big-data_en.pdf.

as being at lower risk than white patients, despite both groups being equally at risk.[105] The algorithm used patients' previous healthcare costs as a proxy, without accounting for lower healthcare use. The paper has come to symbolise the risk of algorithmic discrimination in healthcare. It is also necessary to mention that the bias only became clear because the company allowed the researchers access to their data sets.[106] This underscores the need for review of data sets and algorithms, to avoid bias.

Aside from discrimination on 'traditional' grounds, like race, ethnicity and gender, there are gaps in the legal framework. For example, discrimination law and the GDPR fail to address emerging forms of algorithmic discrimination, such as those based on proxies like postcodes.[107] Likewise, several international conventions prohibit genetic discrimination, but many countries fail to adequately implement this prohibition. Even in countries that have some protections, there may be loopholes. For example, the US Genetic Information Nondiscrimination Act (GINA) does not apply to life insurance policies.[108] And, under Danish law, family history is used as a proxy for genetics, thereby catching a broader class of patients.[109]

A further question is whether, by failing to train algorithms on a diverse data set, a human rights violation could occur. There is growing recognition of the discriminatory impact of 'data gaps',[110] and the importance of diverse data sets in avoiding biased machine learning and AI. Human rights bodies and experts have long underscored the importance of gathering data disaggregated by sex, age and race, in order to expose discriminatory practices. The participation of diverse groups, for example by involving communities in data collection and analysis, is an important facet of pursuing diversity.[111] In a big data healthcare context, without adequate data, algorithms may underestimate risk among under-represented groups.[112]

---

[105] Z. Obermeyer, B. Powers, C. Vogeli and S. Mullainathan, 'Dissecting racial bias in an algorithm used to manage the health of populations', *Science* 366(6464) (2019), 447–53.

[106] L.D. Geneviève, A. Martani, D. Shaw, B.S. Elger and T. Wangmo, 'Structural racism in precision medicine: leaving no one behind', *BMC Medical Ethics* 21(17) (2020).

[107] M. Mann and T. Matzer, 'Challenging algorithmic profiling: The limits of data protection and anti-discrimination in responding to emergent discrimination', *Big Data & Society* 6(2) (2019).

[108] Pub. L. No. 110–233, 122 Stat. 881 (2008).

[109] Forsikringsaftaleloven (consolidated law no. 1237 of 9 November 2015), section 3A.

[110] C.C. Perez, *Invisible Women – Exposing Data Bias in a World Designed for Men*, Vintage Publishing, 2020.

[111] S. Heidari and H. Doyle, 'An Invitation to a Feminist Approach to Global Health Data', *Health and Human Rights Journal* 22(2) (2020), 75–78.

[112] K.A. McClellan, D. Avard, J. Simard and B.M. Knoppers, 'Personalised medicine and access to health care: potential for inequitable access?', *European Journal of Human Genetics* 21(2) (2013), 143–47.

In genomics, research on Europeans continues to dominate, while much less is known about the genetics of certain other groups.[113] Data sets on white European men are likely, for example, to inaccurately predict the risk of heart attack among Asian or black women or men. Furthermore, without clinical trials being conducted on women, varied age groups and different races, medicines may be ineffective or harmful. For example, in the US, Amazon's Alexa has partnered with healthcare companies to support care of the elderly, by providing a means of tracking vitals, and informing caregivers of incidents.[114] Yet, there is a need to ensure that voice-activated technology is trained on data coming from the target population group. It has been reported that Alexa struggles to understand women's voices, or users who speak with certain accents.[115]

A number of recommendations have been made to address these discrimination risks, such as greater diversity among developers, and in the technology sector.[116] Similarly, the European Commission's White Paper on AI suggests a legal obligation to train AI on diverse data sets (that include women and people of multiple ethnicities), which is echoed in the proposal discussed in the next section.[117] This may require the gathering of new data, as historic data sets may replicate histories of inequality and discrimination. At the same time, data gathering requires building trust and participation among citizens, in particular groups who distrust researchers, due to histories of abuse. Technologies must not be 'tested' in low-resource settings, only to be exported to high-resource settings. The EU Fundamental Rights Agency recommends transparency, conducting rights impact assessments, checking the quality of data, and ensuring that algorithms can be meaningfully explained.[118]

---

[113] L.D. Geneviève, A. Martani, D. Shaw, B.S. Elger and T. Wangmo, 'Structural racism in precision medicine: leaving no one behind', *BMC Medical Ethics* 21(17) (2020).

[114] 'The future of Amazon's Alexa: Helping doctors diagnose diseases', *Tampa Bay Times*, 31 July 2019, https://www.tampabay.com/health/the-future-of-amazons-alexa-helping-doctors-diagnose-diseases-20190731/.

[115] R. Glatter, 'If You Need Help With Addiction, Don't Count On Alexa Or Siri', *Forbes Magazine*, 30 January 2020, https://www.forbes.com/sites/robertglatter/2020/01/30/if-you-need-help-with-addiction-dont-count-on-alexa-or-siri/.

[116] United Nations General Assembly, 'Integrated and coordinated implementation of and follow-up to the outcomes of the major United Nations conferences and summits in the economic, social and related fields – Road map for digital cooperation: implementation of the recommendations of the High-level Panel on Digital Cooperation', A/74/821, 2020.

[117] European Commission, 'White Paper on Artificial Intelligence – A European approach to excellence and trust', COM(2020) 65 final, 2020.

[118] European Union Agency for Fundamental Rights, *#BigData: Discrimination in data-supported decision making*, 2018.

4.5. ACCOUNTABILITY

This chapter has highlighted some of the human rights risks and opportunities associated with digital healthcare technologies. Artificial intelligence, just like human systems, can result in harms that may rise to the level of rights violations. Under international human rights law, individuals have a right to an effective remedy, while states have an obligation to ensure that an adequate system of accountability is in place (see, further, Chapter 2 of this book).[119] Meanwhile, as per the Ruggie principles, companies *should* ensure remedies.[120] In light of gaps in the legal system, the European Commission has recently proposed an AI regulation, and is expected to propose further regulations. Technology companies argue, however, that law is too slow or static to suitably regulate their activities,[121] instead claiming that ethics can mitigate (human rights) impacts.

As already discussed, the GDPR provides for certain rights in connection with data protection. While the GDPR has led to positive developments in relation to privacy protection, compliance relies heavily on adequate enforcement. While states should ensure that data protection authorities are adequately resourced, and staffed by people with the necessary expertise, large companies dwarf national bodies, and it is impossible to monitor the processing of all data. Furthermore, it has been suggested that the concept of harm under the GDPR is too narrow to adequately redress big health data-based harms.[122]

McMahon, Buyx and Prainsack argue that governance frameworks like the GDPR do not capture many of the harms of big data, as some harms, for example, are unfair but not illegal.[123] Therefore, they propose harm-mitigation bodies, as non-legal complements that focus on the harms caused, rather than traditional legal standards like consent. This approach, to be funded by data controllers, is proposed as a means of both providing financial compensation and monitoring big data implications. It would provide for compensation in situations where the GDPR does not, such as where inferences are drawn about an individual, based on the data of a third party.

---

[119] International Covenant on Civil and Political Rights (ICPR), Art. 2(3).
[120] UN Human Rights Council, 'Human rights and transnational corporations and other business enterprises', A/HRC/RES/17/4, 2011.
[121] S. Zuboff, *The Age of Surveillance Capital*, Profile Books, 2019, 105.
[122] L. Marelli, E. Lievevrouw and I.V. Hoyweghen, 'Fit for purpose? The GDPR and the governance of European digital health', *Policy Studies* 41 (2020), 447–67.
[123] A. McMahon, A. Buyx and B. Prainsack, 'Big Data Governance Needs More Collective Responsibility: The Role of Harm Mitigation in the Governance of Data Use in Medicine and Beyond', *Medical Law Review* 28(1) (2019), 155–82.

Williams proposes an *ex ante* right to health impact assessments for AI health projects, based on the 'key features' of the right.[124] This includes analysis of:

> Laws, norms, and standards; Dignity, equality, and non-discrimination; Participation; Accountability; International assistance and cooperation; Respect for, protection of, and fulfilment of all human rights; Progressive realization, maximum available resources, and non-retrogression; Obligations of immediate effect; Availability, accessibility, acceptability, and quality; Health system strengthening.[125]

Williams's proposal is valuable, in that it highlights states' obligations and corporations' responsibilities. The present author would underscore, however, the importance of *ex post* assessments of technology, and the role of developers in securing that technology meets human rights requirements from the earliest stages of development.

In the absence of comprehensive legal regulation, a number of ethical standards for AI have emerged. In 2018, the European Group on Ethics in Science and New Technologies issued a statement on Artificial Intelligence, Robotics and 'Autonomous' Systems.[126] It emphasised nine ethical principles: (1) human dignity; (2) autonomy; (3) responsibility; (4) justice, equity and solidarity; (5) democracy; (6) rule of law and accountability; (7) security, safety, bodily and mental integrity; (8) data protection and privacy; and (9) sustainability.

While the WHO's global strategy for digital health in 2020 takes a generally positive approach to digital health, it also recommends that digital health be equitable and sustainable.[127] Sustainability can be pursued through monitoring and evaluating technologies, and implementing technologies that benefit the most people possible, instead of niche, limited options that depend on a particular pool of funding, or an infrastructure with unstable funding. More analysis is also needed of the climate change-related implications of increased storage of large amounts of personal data for healthcare purposes.

The European Commission High-Level Expert Group on Artificial Intelligence Guidelines highlight the principles of human autonomy, prevention of harm, fairness and explicability.[128] The guidelines underscore that AI must meet the

---

[124] C. Williams, 'A Health Rights Impact Assessment Guide for Artificial Intelligence Projects', *Health and Human Rights Journal* 22(2) (2020), 55–62.

[125] Ibid., 57.

[126] European Commission – European Group on Ethics in Science and New Technologies, 'Artificial Intelligence, Robotics and "Autonomous" Systems', 2018, doi:10.2777/786515.

[127] WHO, 'Global strategy on digital health 2020–2025', WHO, 2021, 8.

[128] European Commission, 'High-Level Expert Group on Artificial Intelligence – Ethics Guidelines for Trustworthy', *AI*, 2019, Glossary.

requirements of: (1) human agency and oversight; (2) technical robustness and safety; (3) privacy and data governance; (4) transparency; (5) diversity, non-discrimination and fairness; (6) environmental and societal well-being; and (7) accountability. Focusing on ethics, the guidelines state that law is not always able to keep up with the speed of technology. At the same time, the guidelines claim to be inspired by the EU treaties and the EU Charter. The guidelines underscore that all actors have responsibilities that extend over the life cycle of the products: companies, for example, should identify potential impacts from the outset.

In April 2021, the European Commission proposed a new regulation laying down harmonised rules on AI systems. The regulation has multiple aims, including ensuring a well-functioning internal market for AI, and promoting EU values and rights to boost trust among citizens, and innovation in businesses. If adopted, the regulation will prohibit certain practices deemed harmful, and impose restrictions and safeguards on AI systems that pose a high risk to safety. Non-high-risk AI would have minimal information obligations, and a code of conduct to pursue trustworthy AI could be developed. Like the GDPR, the AI regulation would provide for administrative fines.

As it stands, several healthcare AI systems would be classified as high-risk. For example, AI systems used to dispatch or assign priority in access to emergency medical aid, such as AI triaging systems, are specifically mentioned in Annex III of the draft regulation. AI systems used to determine access to public assistance benefits and services are also deemed high-risk, and this would include AI systems used to determine access to healthcare services. Furthermore, as per Annex II, *in vitro* medical devices that are AI systems would be seen as high-risk. The Commission would also be empowered to add to this list, were new products to fall within Annex III, and should the systems pose a risk of harm to health and safety, or risk to fundamental rights.

With the proposal still at an early stage, it will not be explored in detail here, but it should be noted that high-risk AI systems would be subject to a number of requirements. Firstly, according to Article 9 of the draft regulation, a risk management system would be required. Secondly, training, validation and testing of data sets would be subject to data governance and management practices. This would include the examination of possible biases, and the identification of data gaps or shortcomings: two issues that were introduced above. Thirdly, technical documentation would be required, which, in the case of medical devices, would occur by way of a single document. Fourthly, logging would be put into place. Fifthly, the regulation would require 'an appropriate type and degree of transparency' (Article 13(1)), as well as clear instructions for use. Sixthly, AI systems would have to be designed to ensure that they can be effectively overseen by humans. AI systems would also be designed and developed in a way that ensured an appropriate level of accuracy, robustness and cybersecurity.

The proposal, as it currently stands, would lead to considerable changes for AI healthcare systems that are not medical devices. In the case of AI medical devices, these are already subject to harmonised standards and conformity assessments, and there seems to be an intention that these would be merged. There are also interesting aspects related to diversifying data and combating bias, although, at present, it is not clear how prescriptive or effective they would prove to be.

5. CONCLUSION

This chapter has introduced the growing role of digital healthcare, and has explored human rights aspects of this, from the standpoint of entitlements and risks. It has highlighted the potential for digital health to contribute to the realisation of the right to health, through increasing accessibility and availability. It concludes, generally, that individuals do not have a right to digital health under the ambit of the right to health. The right to benefit from scientific progress, on the other hand, is more promising, in that it imposes obligations on states to progressively realise access to scientific benefits. The author would caution, however, that discrimination in access to health technology is a violation of states' core obligations.

Furthermore, this chapter has, non-exhaustively, explored rights closely linked to digital healthcare. Starting with the right to privacy, it has suggested that digital health has privacy consequences, due to its complexity, and the limitations of informed consent. Next, the chapter introduced the right to data protection in the context of digital health, in light of the GDPR. It, furthermore, discussed the right to an explanation, in a healthcare context. Subsequently, the author assessed the risks that digital health, and AI in particular, can create or perpetuate discrimination. Finally, the chapter highlighted current proposals for accountability, drawing on the proposed EU AI systems Regulation.

CHAPTER 13

PUBLIC HEALTH AND HUMAN RIGHTS

Brigit TOEBES and Katharina Ó CATHAOIR

1. INTRODUCTION

Public health is 'what we as a society, do collectively to assure the conditions to be healthy'.[1] Public health efforts are, therefore, geared towards improving the health and well-being of an entire community, as opposed to treating individuals.[2] This definition shows that public health is not congruent with the right to health, which is, primarily, aimed at protecting the health of the individual right-holder. There is also an inherent tension between protecting the health of the public and respecting individual rights, including rights to privacy, physical integrity, and freedom of movement.

At the same time, public health efforts are preconditions for guaranteeing the right to health, and other health-related rights. We have witnessed how important it was for governments to take measures to protect society against the spread of COVID-19. Meanwhile, tobacco, unhealthy diets and excessive use of alcohol have a dramatic impact on chronic disease incidence around the world. It is, therefore, important to create an understanding of how public health can best be aligned with human rights, and this is the aim of this chapter.

First, the meaning and scope of the concept of 'public health' will be identified. Subsequently, the chapter will discuss the role of human rights in relation to two important dimensions of public health: infectious disease prevention and control, and the regulation of risk factors for chronic diseases. Lastly, the role of human rights will be discussed in the broader context of the social determinants of health.

---

[1] S. Burris, M. Berman, M. Penn and T. Ramanathan Holiday, *The New Public Health Law, A Transdisciplinary Approach to Practice and Advocacy*, Oxford: Oxford University Press/ Alpha Press, 2018, 3.

[2] Ibid., 4.

2. ORIGINS AND SCOPE OF PUBLIC HEALTH

A sense of community responsibility for the health of the public has existed since the time of ancient civilisations. For example, through the ages, civilisations have recognised that adequate sanitation is a pivotal factor for the improvement of public health.[3] The aggregate of such community efforts – 'the art and science of preventing disease, prolonging life and promoting health through the organized efforts of society' – is usually indicated with the term 'public health'.[4] While medicine is more concerned with the health and rights of the individual (for example, creating conditions that enable a particular individual to access care), public health is, foundationally, aimed at the protection of collective health interests.[5]

The modern concept of public health spans diseases (communicable diseases, like COVID-19, and noncommunicable diseases like cancer), and injuries (such as car accidents). Furthermore, while public health has, in the past, often been concerned with protecting the wealthy from the poor, public health now claims to be concerned with contributing to social justice.[6] In this manner, public health, like human rights, is focused on the health of the whole population. However, as explored below, public health policies and laws have, in some cases, had disparate impacts on the poor or marginalised, which health and human rights seeks to address.

Public health has also, gradually, obtained an international dimension. Due to increased international trade and transportation, it became necessary to coordinate the prevention of transmissible diseases at an international level. The first steps towards an international health organisation were taken in the nineteenth century. A series of International Sanitary Conferences were organised, which culminated in the establishment of the Office International d'Hygiène Publique (OIHP) in 1907. The OIHP, which was subsequently placed under the auspices of the League of Nations, was complemented by another international health organisation, the Health Organization of the League of Nations, so as to deal with increasing global health problems more adequately. Until the creation of the United Nations (UN), these two organisations existed side by side.

---

[3]   G. Rosen, *A History of Public Health*, Baltimore: John Hopkins University Press, 1993 (1st ed. 1958 by MD Publications), 2–3.

[4]   WHO Europe, 'Public health services', available at www.euro.who.int/en/health-topics/ Health-systems/public-health-services/public-health-services.

[5]   S. Gruskin and D. Tarantola, 'Health and Human Rights', FXB Center Working Paper No. 10, 2000, 16.

[6]   R.L. Goldsteen et al., *Introduction to Public Health: Promises and Practice*, 2nd ed., New York: Springer Publishing Company, 2014, 44.

In 1948, the World Health Organization (WHO) was established as the first truly global health institution, when representatives of 61 states acceded to the Constitution of the World Health Organization. The Constitution of the WHO does not define public health explicitly. However, the following broad definition of public health circulates widely, and is also endorsed by the WHO:

> Public health refers to all organized measures (whether public or private) to prevent disease, promote health, and prolong life among the population as a whole. Its activities aim to provide conditions in which people can be healthy and focus on entire populations, not on individual patients or diseases. Thus, public health is concerned with the total system and not only the eradication of a particular disease.[7]

This definition illustrates that public health does not focus on individual patients or diseases, and encapsulates many dimensions. In 2020, the WHO released a non-prioritised list of urgent global health challenges: climate change, conflicts, socio-economic gaps, access to medicines, infectious diseases, pandemic preparedness, unsafe and unhealthy diets, underinvestment in health workers, adolescent health, public trust, new technologies, and antimicrobial resistance.[8] According to WHO Europe, public health across the WHO Europe Region faces the following main challenges in the twenty-first century: economic crisis; widening inequalities; ageing population; increasing levels of chronic disease; migration and urbanisation; and environmental damage and climate change.[9]

While the primary focus of public health lies at the domestic level, globalisation means that forces affecting public health can, and do, come from outside state boundaries. These include pathogens (which often spread from poor countries to rich ones), and unhealthy diets (which spread from rich countries to poor ones). In this context, the term 'global public health' has developed. An important dimension of global public health is 'global health security', which focuses not only on the spread of infectious diseases, but also, more generally, on the detrimental health effects of man-made and natural disasters, including armed conflict, biological terrorism, and nuclear disasters.[10]

Lastly, mention should be made of the discipline of 'public health law'. Gostin and Wiley, seminally, defined public health law as:

> the study of the legal powers and duties of the state to ensure the conditions for people to be healthy (for example, to identify, prevent, and ameliorate risks to health and

---

7   This, and similar definitions, circulate widely in the literature, and used to be available on the WHO website.

8   WHO, 'Urgent health challenges for the next decade', 2020, available at https://www.who.int/news-room/photo-story/photo-story-detail/urgent-health-challenges-for-the-next-decade.

9   WHO Europe, 'Public health services', available at www.euro.who.int/en/health-topics/Health-systems/public-health-services/public-health-services.

10   L.O. Gostin and R. Katz, 'The International Health Regulations: The Governing Framework for Global Health Security', *Milbank Quarterly* 94(2) (2016), 264–313.

safety in the population), and the limitations on the power of the state to constrain the autonomy, privacy, liberty, proprietary, or other legally protected interests of individuals for the common good.[11]

As with the right to health, public health law is sometimes viewed with scepticism: its mission being seen as too broad (and the role of the state with regard to 'personal choices' being questioned), or too piecemeal, for failing to encompass societal issues that impact on public health, like poverty, violence and inequality.[12] Law is increasingly accepted as an integral part of achieving good public health. In 2017, leading experts explored the role of law in realising the right to health (and public health) in a report commissioned by the WHO.[13] Burris et al. highlighted that public health law can span not only law intended to influence health outcomes – 'interventional public health law' – but also 'incidental public health law': law that influences health, but was adopted for a different purpose.[14] The authors of this volume share this view of public health law, as explored below, in section 4 of this chapter.

3. BALANCING PUBLIC HEALTH AND INDIVIDUAL RIGHTS

3.1. PUBLIC HEALTH AND THE RIGHT TO HEALTH

As discussed in Chapter 3, the right to health is, primarily, an individual right, granting health-related entitlements to individuals. The question arises of whether, in addition to such individual claims, the right to health also embraces claims to public health and, as such, requires governments to effectuate a national health policy, and to enhance the health of the public at large.[15] Generally, there is increasing support for the potential of the right to health and the concept of public health to pursue mutually enforcing aims. Over the last 20 years, researchers, civil society and international governmental organisations have contributed to a movement that supports infusing public health policies and

---

[11]   L.O. Gostin and L.F. Wiley, *Public Health Law Power, Duty, Restraint*, 3rd ed., University of California Press, 2016, 4.

[12]   See, further, A.C. Wagenaar and S. Burris, *Public Health Law Research Theory and Methods*, 1st ed., San Francisco: Jossey-Bass, 2013.

[13]   R. Magnusson et al., *Advancing the Right to Health: The Vital Role of Law*, WHO, 2017.

[14]   S. Burris et al., 'A Framework for Public Health Law Research' in A.C. Wagenaar and S. Burris, *Public Health Law Research Theory and Methods*, 1st ed., San Francisco: Jossey-Bass, 2013.

[15]   B. Toebes, 'Human Rights and Public Health: Towards a Balanced Relationship', *International Journal of Human Rights* 4(19) (2015), 488–504, also published in M. Feinberg, L. Niada and B. Toebes (eds.), *National Security, Public Health: Exceptions to Human Rights?*, London/ New York: Routledge, 2016.

practices with rights principles.[16] Public health is, thus, clearly an aspect of the right to health, and this has consequences for governments.

The ICESCR Committee's General Comment No. 14 affirms that states should:

> adopt and implement a national public health strategy and plan of action, on the basis of epidemiological evidence, addressing the health concerns of the whole population; the strategy and plan of action shall be devised, and periodically reviewed, on the basis of a participatory and transparent process; they shall include methods, such as right to health indicators and benchmarks, by which progress can be closely monitored; the process by which the strategy and plan of action are devised, as well as their content, shall give particular attention to all vulnerable or marginalized groups.[17]

This is a vital statement, which recognises that the adoption of a public health strategy is part of the core obligations of States Parties.[18] The emphasis on developing indicators and benchmarks, and the protection of vulnerable groups, in this context, is also important, and could be elaborated further, for example by drawing on the Sustainable Development Goals.

3.2. TENSIONS BETWEEN PUBLIC HEALTH AND COMPETING RIGHTS AND INTERESTS

While the right to health may manifest as a claim to public health, there can also be a tension between this public health dimension of the right to health and the civil and political rights of individuals, including their rights to security, liberty, physical integrity, privacy and family life, and potentially also the right to development or the right to the best possible healthcare.[19] While the spread of infectious diseases is the most obvious and pressing example of where this friction may arise, potential clashes may also occur in settings where biomedical research is conducted on human subjects, and when it comes to storage in

---

[16] See, in particular, the *Health and Human Rights Journal*, founded by Jonathan Mann, which has made a substantial contribution to this aim (see also Chapter 1 of this volume).

[17] Committee on Economic, Social and Cultural Rights (ICESCR Committee), 'General Comment No. 14: The Right to the Highest Attainable Standard of Health (Art. 12)', UN Doc. E/C.12/2000/4, 2000, para. 43(f).

[18] On this issue and the parallels with the core capacities under the IHR, see B. Toebes, 'States' Resilience to Future Health Emergencies: Connecting the Dots between Core Obligations and Core Capacities', *ESIL Reflections* 9(2) (2020); elaborated further in B. Toebes, L. Forman and G. Bartolini, 'Toward Human Rights-Consistent Responses to Health Emergencies: What is the Overlap between Core Right to Health Obligations and Core International Health Regulation Capacities?' *Health and Human Rights Journal*, 22(2) (2020), 99–111.

[19] See also Art. 8(2) ECHR, which stipulates under what conditions an interference with the right to private and family life is allowed: these include restrictions 'for the protection of health and morals'.

biobanks, the testing of medicines, (forced) vaccinations, the regulation of risk factors for noncommunicable diseases (NCDs), and the (unsolicited) storage of data.[20] The notion of the right to health as a collective right to public health can, thus, be controversial, in light of the traditional view of rights as individual entitlements to non-interference from the state.[21]

Accordingly, public health and human rights were, until recently, often seen to be at odds, as public health provides a ground for limiting individual rights.[22] Under human rights law, most rights are not absolute, and can be 'limited' or 'derogated from', in certain circumstances. For example, both the European Convention on Human Rights (ECHR) and the International Covenant on Civil and Political Rights (ICCPR) provide for a system of rights derogations that allow States Parties to adjust their obligations under these treaties, in exceptional circumstances. It should be noted that the ICESCR does not provide for derogations.

3.2.1. Derogations and limitations on civil and political rights

Derogations to civil and political rights can only be temporary in nature, and are permitted only in exceptional circumstances, when the 'life of the nation is at stake', such as armed conflicts, civil and social unrest, environmental and natural disasters, and potentially also public health emergencies. Unlike limitations, derogations lead to the content of the right being suspended completely. Nonetheless, both the ICCPR and the ECHR stipulate a limited set of rights that cannot be derogated from, including the right to life, the prohibition of torture and the prohibition of slavery. This means that, in situations of a declared emergency, the majority of rights may be suspended, while a limited set of rights remains completely intact.[23]

During the COVID-19 pandemic, several states proclaimed states of emergency, and derogated from rights under the ICCPR and ECHR, such as freedom of assembly or freedom of movement.[24] At the same time, other states that imposed far-reaching restrictions on freedom of movement and assembly, such as France

---

[20]   B. Toebes, 'Human Rights and Public Health: Towards a Balanced Relationship', *International Journal of Human Rights* 4(19) (2015), 488–504, also published in M. Feinberg, L. Niada and B. Toebes (eds.), *National Security, Public Health: Exceptions to Human Rights?*, London/New York: Routledge, 2016.

[21]   See D. Sanders, 'Collective Rights', *Human Rights Quarterly* 13(3) (1991), 368–86.

[22]   See, e.g. L.O. Gostin, et al., 'Health and Human Rights', *Health and Human Rights Journal* 1(1) (1994), 6–23; S. Gruskin and D. Tarantola, 'Health and Human Rights,' in M.A. Grodin et al (eds.), *Perspectives on Health and Human Rights*, New York and London: Routledge, 2005.

[23]   B. Toebes, 'Human Rights and Public Health: Towards a Balanced Relationship', *International Journal of Human Rights* 4(19) (2015), 488–504, also published in M. Feinberg, L. Niada and B. Toebes (eds.), *National Security, Public Health: Exceptions to Human Rights?*, London/New York: Routledge, 2016.

[24]   E.g., 10 derogations to the ECHR. Reservations and derogations are viewable on the Council of Europe website: www.coe.int/en/web/conventions/full-list/-/conventions/treaty/005/declarations.

and Italy, did not enter a derogation.[25] In response to these developments, the UN Human Rights Committee issued a statement reminding states that: (a) derogations must be communicated immediately to other States Parties through the secretary-general of the UN, containing clear information on the measures taken, and the reasoning behind them; (b) derogations may deviate 'only to the extent strictly required by the exigencies of the public health situation', and should, thereby, be limited as much as possible, and be proportional; (c) derogations should not be used when the public health aim can be achieved through a reasonable limitation on the relevant rights; (d) discriminatory measures and derogations from non-derogable rights are prohibited; (e) respect for human dignity and special protections for the marginalised and vulnerable must be maintained; (f) freedom of expression, access to information and a civic space are important safeguards.[26] Thus, derogations include both a procedural and substantive element.

While derogations lead to rights being suspended completely, limitations imply that the 'core of the right' should remain intact, and unaffected by any possible limitation. Rights in the ICCPR, ICESCR and ECHR may be limited for certain legitimate aims, as listed in the treaty, including national security, public safety, public order, morals, health, and the prevention of crimes. To enhance this balancing act within the framework of the ICCPR, the UN Siracusa Principles on the limitations of rights provide some useful guidelines. This set of guidelines was drawn up in 1984 by a group of 31 experts in international law. While it provides guidelines for the use of the limitations and derogations under the ICCPR, it may also have a wider reach. According to paragraph 10:

> Whenever a limitation is required in the terms of the Covenant to be 'necessary', this term implies that the limitation:
>
> (a) is based on one of the grounds justifying limitations recognized by the relevant article of the Covenant,
> (b) responds to a pressing public or social need,
> (c) pursues a legitimate aim, and
> (d) is proportionate to that aim.

Moreover, paragraph 25 touches specifically on public health:

> Public health may be invoked as a ground for limiting certain rights in order to allow a State to take measures dealing with a serious threat to the health of the population or individual members of the population. These measures must be *specifically aimed at preventing disease or injury or providing care for the sick and injured* [emphasis added].

---

[25] A. Lebret, 'COVID-19 pandemic and derogation to human rights' *Journal of Law and the Biosciences* 7(1) (2020), https://academic.oup.com/jlb/article/7/1/lsaa015/5828398.

[26] UN Human Rights Committee, 'Statement on derogations from the Covenant in connection with the COVID-19 pandemic', 24 April 2020.

Paragraph 26 adds that:

> Due regard shall be had to the International Health Regulations of the World Health Organization.

By referring explicitly to the WHO's International Health Regulations, the Siracusa Principles affirm the importance of this instrument.

In the years since, the UN Human Rights Committee has developed a variety of general comments that guide states on legitimate and illegitimate limitations (see section 4 below). In addition, it is important to look at the case law of the European Court of Human Rights (ECtHR), which increasingly pays attention to patients' rights, including rights to consent and privacy. The ECtHR has, in a number of cases, assessed how limitation clauses and limits to the rights to security and privacy come into play in healthcare settings, and in situations of detention.[27] Similarly to the ICCPR, the ECHR stipulates that states may invoke so-called 'legitimate aims' or purposes, laid down in the limitation clauses under Articles 8 to 11 of the Convention and Article 2 of Protocol No. 4. The 'legitimate aims' clause embraces, among other aims, the protection of 'health or morals'.

The ECtHR has, in several cases, considered the detention of a person on health grounds. In the key case of *Enhorn v. Sweden*, for example, the ECtHR considered the extent of the right to liberty and security of the person in Article 5(1) ECHR, in light of the compulsory detention of a man infected with the HIV virus. The Court found that:

> the essential criteria when assessing the 'lawfulness' of the detention of a person 'for the prevention of the spread of infectious diseases' are whether the spreading of the infectious disease is dangerous to public health or safety, and whether detention of the person infected is the last resort in order to prevent the spreading of the disease, because less severe measures have been considered and found to be insufficient to safeguard the public interest.[28]

In this case, the Court was not convinced that the detention of Mr. Enhorn was a last resort, as less severe measures had not been considered (see also Chapter 5 of this book).[29] By seeing detention for public health reasons as a 'last resort', the Court seems to take a stricter approach than the Siracusa Principles. The Court also noted that the Swedish authorities had failed to strike a fair balance between competing interests, because the detention amounted to one and a half years in total, which, in the court's opinion, was not sufficiently balanced to the needs of society in preventing the spread of the HIV virus.[30] It remains to be seen

---

[27] See, further, Chapter 5 of this book, including cases ECtHR 27 August 1997, *M.S. v. Sweden*, no. 20837/92, ECLI:CE:ECHR:1997:0827JUD002083792; and ECtHR 5 January 2006, *K.T. v. Norway* (dec.), no. 26664/03, ECLI:CE:ECHR:2008:0925JUD002666403.

[28] ECtHR 25 January 2005, *Enhorn v. Sweden*, no. 56529/00, para. 41.

[29] Ibid., para 55.

[30] Ibid.

whether the Court will maintain this approach in future jurisprudence related to COVID-19 restrictions.

3.2.2. Tensions between the right to health and other societal interests and rights

It is, furthermore, important to consider how the implementation of the right to health would turn out in cases of conflict between public health and other societal interests. For example, could public health measures be taken that might, potentially, conflict with interests such as international trade, intellectual property protection and warfare? In EU case law, the Court has drawn on public health as a concern that can outweigh business interests (see, further, Chapter 6 of this book). Yet, the right to health has not yet been successfully positioned as an additional claim to public health going against such business interests. For the right to health to be applied in such settings, it would be important for it to be used for genuine public health concerns and not for protectionist reasons, so as to shield the domestic market from the importation of competing products from abroad.[31]

Along similar lines, the potential tensions between the right to (public) health and other economic and social rights should be considered. The tension between public health and trade interests may, for example, translate into a tension between the right to health and the right to development. While, on the one hand, states invoking these public health clauses could frame these as right to health claims, states barred from trading their goods based on such measures, on the other hand, could possibly stress their people's right to development, on the basis that being barred from exporting their goods hampers their development. This tension could become particularly pressing in situations where a developed country invoked a public health claim against the development claim of a developing nation. The complex relationship between the WTO framework and the human rights framework, in this respect, is still under-researched.

3.2.3. Restricting the right to health

Finally, attention should be paid to the possibility of restricting the 'right to health'. As was suggested above, the right to health, if exercised collectively as a public health claim, potentially also clashes with the right to the best possible healthcare of individuals: or, in other words, their individual right to health. For example, during the COVID-19 pandemic, routine treatments have been limited or cancelled in order to prioritise tackling the pandemic.

---

31 B. Toebes, 'Human Rights and Public Health: Towards a Balanced Relationship', *International Journal of Human Rights* 4(19) (2015), 488–504, also published in M. Feinberg, L. Niada and B. Toebes (eds.), *National Security, Public Health: Exceptions to Human Rights?*, London/ New York: Routledge, 2016.

Article 4 ICESCR contains the following limitation clause:

The States Parties to the present Covenant recognize that, in the enjoyment of those rights provided by the State in conformity with the present Covenant, the State may subject such rights only to such limitations as are determined by law only in so far as this may be compatible with the nature of these rights and solely for the purpose of the general welfare in a democratic society.

The reference to the 'nature' of rights has similarities to the idea of an inherent 'core' in economic, social and cultural rights. There is considerable emphasis, in the literature, on the notion that limitations on economic and social rights should not affect the 'core' or 'core obligations' inherent in the rights.[32] This would imply that, when measures are taken in the interests of public health, the right of the individual to essential health services should not be affected. The ICESCR Committee's General Comment No. 14 on the right to health explains that Article 4 is primarily intended to:

protect the rights of individuals rather than to permit the imposition of limitations by States. Consequently a State party which, for example, restricts the movement of, or incarcerates, persons with transmissible diseases such as HIV/AIDS, refuses to allow doctors to treat persons believed to be opposed to a government, or fails to provide immunization against the community's major infectious diseases, on grounds such as national security or the preservation of public order, has the burden of justifying such serious measures in relation to each of the elements identified in article 4.[33]

Hence, this represents a restrictive interpretation of Article 4, and the imposition of a burden of proof on states to justify the measures taken. There is a clear indication that the right to minimum or basic health services should remain intact. General Comment No. 14, furthermore, explains that states have to justify the public health restrictions that they impose, inter alia by proving that such measures are in the interest of the legitimate aims pursued:

Such restrictions must be in accordance with the law, including international human rights standards, compatible with the nature of the rights protected by the Covenant, in the interest of legitimate aims pursued, and strictly necessary for the promotion of the general welfare in a democratic society.[34]

---

[32] E.g. L. Forman et al., 'What could a strengthened right to health bring to the post-2015 health development agenda?: Interrogating the role of the minimum core concept in advancing essential global health needs', *BMC International Health and Human Rights*, 13(48) (2013). See also Amrei Müller, *The Relationship between Economic, Social and Cultural Rights and International Humanitarian Law*, Leiden/Boston: Martinus Nijhoff Publishers, 2013, 124–28.

[33] Committee on Economic, Social and Cultural Rights (ICESCR Committee), 'General Comment No. 14: The Right to the Highest Attainable Standard of Health (Art. 12)', UN Doc. E/C.12/2000/4, 2000, para. 28.

[34] Ibid.

This wording is very similar to the language used, and the approach taken, in the limitation clauses under the ICCPR.

During the COVID-19 pandemic, operations and screenings have been postponed to combat the spread of the virus, and to free up hospital capacity. While hospitals have sought to ensure that only procedures in relation to non-life-threatening conditions are cancelled, these definitions sadly lack certainty, in the field of medicine. The authors note that human rights have played an important role in defending the rights of persons with disabilities and the elderly, namely to receive medical care based on need, and free from discrimination based on protected characteristics, even during public health crises.[35]

There seems to be a general understanding, in human rights law, that restrictions taken for the sake of public health should not go against the nature or 'essence' of the rights of the individual, that they should be proportionate, should pursue a legitimate aim, and that they should be taken solely for the interests of a democratic society. These requirements are to be borne in mind when measures are taken for the public health benefits of society at large. The authors, furthermore, note that the roles, and the legitimacy, of derogations in response to disease outbreaks should be scrutinised, in the coming years.

3.3. PROCEDURAL QUESTIONS WHEN EXERCISING A COLLECTIVE RIGHT TO HEALTH

The right to health, as a collective claim, raises procedural questions. As human rights have been framed as individual rights, it will not be easy to change the existing mechanisms. This does not mean that our existing individual rights cannot lead to collective claims, however. As put by Galenkamp, we could perceive the right as materially conferred on individual members of a group, but procedurally looked after by the collective.[36] When it comes to judicial accountability, it seems possible to capture the interests of an affected group in the form of a 'bundle' or 'cluster' of individual rights.[37]

Some inspiration can be found, in this regard, in the case law of the European Committee of Social Rights (ECSR), the treaty-monitoring body of the (Revised) European Social Charter (ESC). Its collective complaint mechanism has enabled several international NGOs to defend the health-related interests of population groups.[38] As a collective complaint mechanism, it is able to represent a larger

---

[35] G. Quinn, 'COVID-19 and Disability: A war of two paradigms in COVID-19 and Human Rights' in M. Kjaerum, M.F. Davis and A. Lyons, UK: Routledge, 2021.

[36] M. Galenkamp, 'Collective Rights' in *SIM Special No. 16*, Netherlands Institute of Human Rights, Utrecht, 1995, 53–102, at 70–71.

[37] Ibid.

[38] See, e.g. ECSR, *DCI v. the Netherlands*, complaint no. 47/2008; *ATD Fourth World v. France*, complaint no. 33/2006; *INTERIGHTS v. Croatia* no. 45/2007; *ECCR v. Bulgaria*, no. 46/2007; *DCI v. the Netherlands* no. 47/2008; *and FIDH v. Greece*, complaint no. 72/2011.

group of people, for example a group of undocumented migrants, or an indigenous population. The case law of this Committee has touched on various health-related concerns, including access to healthcare for undocumented migrants, the occupational health concerns of miners in Greece, and the protection of the health of the Roma people. For example, in the decision of *ECCR v. Bulgaria*, the Committee explicitly addressed the notion of health inequalities with respect to the Roma population in Bulgaria. It stated that Bulgaria had failed to 'take reasonable steps to address the specific problems faced by Roma communities stemming from their often unhealthy living conditions and difficult access to health services'.[39] This is a clear claim to public health: the unhealthy living conditions were an important reason for the Committee to conclude that the rights in the ESC had been violated. While the decisions of this Committee are not legally binding, they are influential, and can have a 'spillover effect' for national court cases addressing similar concerns. As discussed in Chapter 4, the communications procedure of the ICESCR also potentially embraces collective complaints. Although its views, to date, have addressed individual complaints, its decisions on the right to housing have concluded with general recommendations on how the state can avoid future violations, such as developing an adequate legal framework, and developing a comprehensive plan.[40]

4. INFECTIOUS DISEASE PREVENTION AND CONTROL

4.1. INTRODUCTION

Infectious (communicable) diseases, like humans, are organisms. They may be bacteria, viruses, fungi or parasites. Organisms can coexist peacefully or beneficially with humans, but others, known as pathogens, cause disease. Over 60 per cent of emerging infectious diseases are zoonotic (spread from animals, like pigs and poultry, to humans). A disease can swell into an outbreak, and, in rare cases, an epidemic (by spreading across an expanded area), or a pandemic (by spreading among countries or continents). Far from being things of the past, pandemics are, due to globalisation, and human activity like deforestation, travel and trade, part of our future, as the COVID-19 pandemic reminds us.

As detailed in this chapter, and in Chapter 2, the right to health places obligations on states to take measures to prevent and respond to infectious disease. This section introduces the International Health Regulations as *lex specialis* in the field of infectious disease. It also discusses the contribution of

---

39 ECSR, *ECCR v. Bulgaria* (complaint no. 46/2007), para. 49.
40 ECSR, 'Views adopted by the Committee under the Optional Protocol to the International Covenant on Economic, Social and Cultural Rights, concerning communication No. 37/2018', 29 November 2019, para. 17.

human rights principles, as introduced in the previous section, towards public health efforts.

4.2. INTERNATIONAL HEALTH REGULATIONS

Alongside states' obligations under human rights law, all states are bound by the World Health Organization's International Health Regulations (IHR).[41] The purpose of the IHR are to 'prevent, protect against, control and provide a public health response' to infectious diseases of international concern, with 'full respect for the dignity, human rights and fundamental freedoms of persons', while avoiding unnecessary interference with 'international traffic and trade'. States' obligations include developing minimum core public health capacities, such as surveillance capacities, and implementation plans.[42]

The IHR can be traced back to earlier iterations, such as the First International Sanitary Convention and, more recently, the International Health Regulations (1969). However, the former applied directly to only four diseases (cholera, plague, yellow fever and smallpox). It, therefore, did not address new and emerging infectious diseases. The IHR of 1969, in addition, emphasised sanitary conditions, services, and procedures to be maintained at frontiers and borders, but did not require states to develop healthcare capacities. The rapid spread of SARS in 2003 triggered action among WHO Member States to revise the IHR, which revised versions were adopted in 2005, and entered into force in 2007.

Under the revised IHR (2005), states are obligated to establish and operate a National IHR Focal Point (NFP), a 'national centre, designated by each State Party, which shall be accessible at all times for communications with WHO IHR Contact Points'.[43] States are, furthermore, obligated to provide a range of communications to the WHO, such as informing of delays or refusals of entry affecting international travellers or cargo. They are required to establish disease surveillance systems to gather and analyse original data, enhance case reporting, and laboratory capabilities, and develop and implement surveillance.[44]

An important obligation of the national IHR focal points is to report potential public health emergencies of international concern (PHEICs) to the WHO.[45] 'Notifiable events' include events that are always notifiable, such as a single case of smallpox, poliomyelitis (wild type), a new subtype of human influenza, or SARS. Potentially notifiable events include cholera, pneumonic plague, yellow fever, viral hemorrhagic fevers, other epidemic-prone diseases of special national or regional concern, and other biological, radiological or chemical events that 'have

---

[41]   The WHO was introduced in Chapter 4 of this book, on UN Institutions.
[42]   International Health Regulations, Art. 5.
[43]   Ibid., Art. 1.
[44]   Ibid., Annex 1.
[45]   Ibid., Annex 1, Art. 6.

demonstrated the ability to cause serious public health impact and to spread rapidly internationally'.[46] In such cases, the state should use the algorithm reproduced here:

ANNEX 2
**DECISION INSTRUMENT FOR THE ASSESSMENT AND NOTIFICATION
OF EVENTS THAT MAY CONSTITUTE A PUBLIC HEALTH EMERGENCY
OF INTERNATIONAL CONCERN**

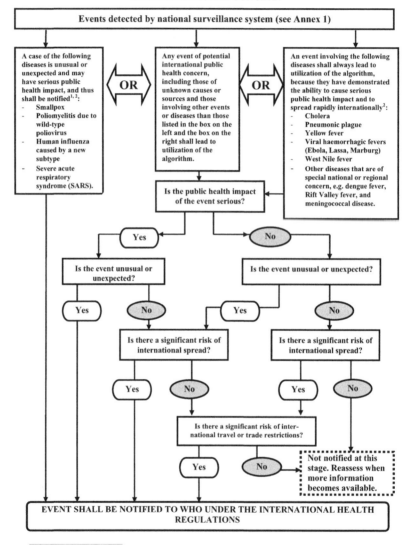

[1] As per WHO case definitions.
[2] The disease list shall be used only for the purposes of these Regulations.

Source: WHO, 'International Health Regulations (2005) Third Edition', 1 January 2016, https://www.who.int/publications/i/item/9789241580496.

---

46   Ibid., Annex 2.

If the state answers yes to two of the following questions, they are required to notify WHO of the event:

- Is the public health impact of the event serious?
- Is the event unusual or unexpected?
- Is there a significant risk of international spread?
- Is there a significant risk of international travel or trade restrictions?[47]

In response, the director-general of the WHO can convene an emergency committee. The committee advises the director-general, who decides whether to declare a PHEIC and issue temporary recommendations. Several PHEICs have been declared to date, including H1N1 (2009), Ebola (2014) and COVID-19 (2020). Out of self-interest, states sometimes delay transmitting the required information to the WHO, thus, the WHO may assess reports from non-state actors.[48] However, these reports are subject to review by the state in question.

While not a human rights treaty, the IHR can be seen as complementary to such treaties, given that respect for human rights is recognised in the IHR. States should implement the IHR 'with full respect for the dignity, human rights and fundamental freedoms of persons'.[49] Echoing human rights language, the IHR underscore that public health measures 'shall not be more restrictive of international traffic and not more invasive or intrusive to persons than reasonably available alternatives that would achieve the appropriate level of health protection'.[50] In determining whether to implement restrictions, states should have regard to scientific principles, scientific evidence, and specific guidance or advice from the WHO.[51] States must keep personal data confidential, except where strictly necessary to respond to the risk.[52]

In May 2021, the Independent Panel for Pandemic Preparedness and Response (established by the WHO Director-General) issued its final report.[53] The Panel joined calls from 25 world leaders to draft a new WHO treaty on pandemic

---

[47]   Ibid., Annex 2.
[48]   Ibid., Art. 9.
[49]   Ibid., Art. 3(1).
[50]   Ibid., Art. 43(1).
[51]   Ibid., Art. 43(2).
[52]   Ibid., Art. 43.
[53]   The Independent Panel for Pandemic Preparedness & Response, 'COVID-19: Make it the Last Pandemic', May 2021.

preparedness and response, aimed at improving international cooperation.[54] In the final report, the Panel criticised states for inadequate preparedness, and for failing to meet their obligations under the IHR. It, furthermore, found that the IHR are a 'conservative instrument ... and serve to constrain rather than facilitate rapid action.'[55] It also criticised countries for being too slow to respond to the Declaration of a PHEIC. The Panel issued a number of detailed recommendations, such as establishing the WHO's financial independence, empowering the WHO, resourcing and equipping WHO country offices, and formalising universal periodic reviews of national pandemic preparedness.

4.3.   A HEALTH AND HUMAN RIGHTS APPROACH TO INFECTIOUS DISEASE

While the public has an interest in being protected against the spread of infectious diseases, individuals have a right to be protected against unnecessary interferences.[56] Although, as mentioned above, the state has an obligation to protect the right to health, it cannot take such measures to the extent that they violate the rights of others. Public health measures undertaken in response to a public health crisis or PHEIC often entail limitations on human rights. For example, they may involve isolation and quarantine, whereby persons with symptoms, or who are known or suspected to be infected, are separated from the healthy population, which may limit their rights to liberty, movement, freedom of assembly, and freedom of religion. A cordon sanitaire – a boundary around a geographical area experiencing an epidemic, which no one is allowed to cross – is a far-reaching restriction on the same rights. Community restrictions, like the closing of schools and businesses, restrictions on public transportation, and cancellation of group events, also limit rights to business and assembly. These measures not only impose limitations on civil and political rights, but can also interfere with rights to work, to food, and to an adequate standard of living.

---

54   J.V. Bainimarama et al., 'COVID-19 shows why united action is needed for more robust international health architecture', 30 March 2021, www.who.int/news-room/commentaries/detail/op-ed---covid-19-shows-why-united-action-is-needed-for-more-robust-international-health-architecture.

55   The Independent Panel for Pandemic Preparedness & Response, 'COVID-19: Make it the Last Pandemic', May 2021. J.V. Bainimarama et al., 'COVID-19 shows why united action is needed for more robust international health architecture', 30 March 2021, www.who.int/news-room/commentaries/detail/op-ed---covid-19-shows-why-united-action-is-needed-for-more-robust-international-health-architecture, 26.

56   See, further, K. Ó Cathaoir, 'Human Rights and Health in Times of Pandemics: Necessity and proportionality' in M. Kjaerum, M.F. Davis and A. Lyons (eds.), COVID-19 and Human Rights, Routledge, 2021.

Similarly, forced testing is an interference with the right to privacy and bodily integrity. Such acts may also be carried out beyond healthcare settings, for example in prisons and immigration detention centres, where the potential for coercion is even greater.

Successive disease outbreaks have shown that states and populations tend to respond with fear, and institute discriminatory or stigmatising measures. For example, some states criminalised the transmission of HIV.[57] During the SARS epidemic of 2003, China and Singapore employed mass quarantines, monitored by armed guards, or enforced through the use of ankle bracelets.[58] In Taiwan, over 130,000 individuals were quarantined, although there were only two confirmed cases.[59] The UN Special Rapporteur on the elimination of discrimination against persons affected by leprosy noted that 'stigmatization remains institutionalized in the States' architecture and functioning': over 50 states have discriminatory laws against those affected by leprosy.[60]

Discrimination and stigmatisation are not effective tools of public health. There is no credible evidence that HIV criminalisation protects individuals or society: instead, it drives fear and isolation, which can lead individuals to avoid testing and treatment.[61] Stigmatising those affected by a disease loses sight of the surrounding structures that regulate and exacerbate transmission: poverty, inadequate housing, and unsafe food and water. At an individual level, stigmatisation can disincentivise testing, for fear of negative consequences, including social stigma and the risk of losing financial, housing or work opportunities. Furthermore, those worst-affected by infectious diseases are often the poor, or persons belonging to historically discriminated-against groups, who do not have the same resources as the wealthy to insulate themselves from disease. As Murphy highlights, 'quarantine, surveillance and the like have historically been targeted at the most disadvantaged – the poor and … immigrants, for example'.[62]

---

[57]   S.J. Lehman et al., 'Prevalence and public health implications of state laws that criminalize potential HIV exposure in the United States', *AIDS and Behavior* 18(6) (2014), 997–1006.

[58]   See A. Ahmad, R. Krumkam and R. Reintjes, 'Controlling SARS: A Review on China's Response Compared with Other SARS-Affected Countries', *Tropical Medicine & International Health* 14 (2009), 36–45.

[59]   See R. Schabas, 'Severe Acute Respiratory Syndrome: Did Quarantine Help?', *Canadian Journal of Infectious Diseases & Medical Microbiology* 15 (2004), 204.

[60]   United Nations Human Rights Office of the High Commissioner, 'World Leprosy Day: UN expert calls on States to end discrimination against affected women and children', 2020, www. ohchr.org/EN/NewsEvents/Pages/DisplayNews.aspx?NewsID=25495&LangID=E#:~:text= Alice%20Cruz%20is%20the%20first,by%20the%20Human%20Rights%20Council.

[61]   S. Burris and E. Cameron, 'The Case Against Criminalization of HIV Transmission', *The Journal of the American Medical Association* 300(5) (2008), 578–81.

[62]   T. Murphy, *Health and Human Rights*, Oxford: Hart Publishing, 2013, 80.

Through removing discriminatory laws and policies that are not evidence-based, disease status can be destigmatised, and trust developed with the affected community, to ensure an effective public health response. Furthermore, focusing on the structural causes of disease, like poverty and poor living conditions, is in line with states' human rights obligations under the right to life and health. However, a human rights approach has not consistently been applied to disease outbreaks, and such outbreaks have shown that human rights are often sidelined in emergencies.

Thus, while the IHR underscore human rights, and the duty to adopt less restrictive measures if these are as effective, the response to the COVID-19 pandemic illustrates that many states are quick to impose restrictive measures without reflecting on alternatives.[63] For example, many states ordered residents to stay at home unless they had a specified 'necessary' purpose, such as work or buying essential groceries, to leave home. Some governments required individuals to fill out passes, in order to leave their residences. Furthermore, gatherings were restricted – sometimes completely. Meanwhile, other states took less directive measures, by not requiring individuals to justify their movements, but, instead, requiring them to regulate their behaviour in other ways, for instance through encouraging or mandating working from home, and recommendations on distancing.

'Stay at home' orders amount to limitations on numerous human rights, including private and family life, freedom of assembly, freedom of religion, the right to liberty, and the right to freedom of movement, and must, therefore, be justified. While 'stay at home' orders may be viewed as legitimate public health measures because they reduce social contact, which spreads the virus, disproportionate burdens can be imposed on certain persons and groups.[64] Restrictions have particularly severe impacts on the poor, especially those living in cramped accommodation without access to a garden or balcony. They may also disproportionately affect women, who are often primary carers.

A requirement to consider less restrictive measures is supported in international human rights doctrine. For example, the UN Human Rights Committee states that limitations on movement:

> must be appropriate to achieve their protective function; they must be the least intrusive instrument amongst those which might achieve the desired result; and they must be proportionate to the interest to be protected.[65]

---

[63] See also ECtHR 25 January 2005, *Enhorn v. Sweden*, no. 56529/00 (see above, in section 3.2.1).

[64] See also Y. Litins'ka and O. Karpenko, 'Does Self-isolation Violate the Right to Liberty? An Analysis of the European Court of Human Rights Practice in Light of the Ukrainian Experience', *European Journal of Health Law* 27(4) (2020), 368–85.

[65] UN Human Rights Committee, 'General Comment No. 27: Article 12 (Freedom of Movement)', 2 November 1999, CCPR/C/21/Rev.1/Add.9, para. 14.

In General Comment No. 37, the UN Human Rights Committee explained that proportionality (in the context of freedom of assembly) requires:

(…) a value assessment, weighing the nature and detrimental impact of the interference on the exercise of the right against the resultant benefit to one of the grounds for interfering. If the detriment outweighs the benefit, the restriction is disproportionate and thus not permissible.[66]

The ICESCR Committee's General Comment No. 14 also holds, in relation to the right to health, that the 'least restrictive alternative must be adopted where several types of limitations are available'. Limitations on the grounds of protecting public health should be of limited duration, and subject to review.[67]

Human rights are not absolute, and the rapid spread of infectious disease may warrant limitations. However, respecting human rights requires that states obey the principles of proportionality and non-discrimination, even in emergencies. Furthermore, the IHR, and the right to health, underscore states' obligations to prevent, trace and combat infectious disease in a manner compatible with human rights. It remains to be seen whether these principles will be reframed, in the wake of COVID-19.

4.4. VACCINATION

Vaccination is one of the most effective public health tools to suppress and, eventually, defeat an infectious disease. Vaccines contain weakened or inactive parts of an organism (or a blueprint thereof) that trigger an immune response.[68] The body, thereby, learns how to fight a particular disease. Through vaccination, a large proportion of a population can quickly become immune, leading to herd immunity, as the disease can no longer spread rapidly. Herd immunity means that those who cannot be vaccinated (persons suffering from certain illnesses or allergies) are given protection too. It can also mean that a virus does not spread through communities at the same pace and thereby prevent new, more dangerous mutations from emerging. Through vaccines, once-dangerous diseases, like polio and smallpox, can be eradicated.

Yet, in recent years, in Western countries, 'vaccine hesitancy' regarding the potential negative side effects of vaccines has spread, spurred on by social media. For example, despite being debunked, some individuals wrongly claim that the

---

[66]   UN Human Rights Committee, 'General Comment No. 37 (2020) on the right of peaceful assembly (Article 21)', CCPR/C/GC/37, 17 September 2020, para. 40.
[67]   ICESCR Committee, 'General Comment No. 14', para. 29.
[68]   WHO, 'How do vaccines work?', www.who.int/news-room/feature-stories/detail/how-do-vaccines-work.

measles, mumps and rubella (MMR) vaccine can cause autism, and, therefore, refuse to allow their children to receive this vaccination. For highly infectious diseases like measles, a high level of herd immunity is needed to stop its spread, as not everyone can be vaccinated (due to health conditions). The deliberate reduction in vaccination has led to measles outbreaks in various parts of Europe and the US.

It may, therefore, be asked what obligations states have to protect public health and support vaccinations. With the spread of vaccine hesitancy, some states have taken action to increase vaccinations, such as information campaigns and debunking dangerous myths. The question can, furthermore, be raised as to whether it is in compliance with human rights to legislate for mandatory vaccine programmes, or to require children to be vaccinated before beginning school.

The ECtHR and the former European Commission on Human Rights (the Commission) have issued several judgments on mandatory vaccinations.[69] In *Boffa and others v. San Marino*, the healthcare agency had ordered the applicants to have their children vaccinated against hepatitis B. The applicants argued that, due to potential side effects, mandatory vaccination was a violation of Article 2 of the ECHR. Furthermore, the interference with their freedom to choose was in contravention of Articles 5, 8 and 9 of the ECHR. The Commission dismissed the claim under Article 2 as manifestly ill-founded, as no evidence of a real medical danger to the particular children had been put forth. It, furthermore, found no interference with Article 9, as not every act which is motivated by religion or belief is covered thereunder. The Commission also dismissed the submission that compulsory vaccination would fall under Article 5 and, instead, examined the matter from the perspective of the right to privacy and family life under Article 8. It recognised that compulsory vaccination constituted an interference with Article 8. However, the measure pursued a legitimate aim: the need to protect the health of the public. Furthermore, the Commission held that the measure was proportionate to the aim pursued, and necessary in a democratic society for the protection of public health.[70]

In *Solomakhin v. Ukraine*, the individual was vaccinated against diphtheria, and subsequently died. His mother brought a claim arguing that the deceased's rights under Article 8 had been violated, as he had been vaccinated against his will, with a vaccine of poor quality. The Court reiterated that compulsory medical treatments, such as vaccines, are an interference with the right to private life, namely the right to physical and psychological integrity. However, in finding no violation, the Court held that:

> the interference with the applicant's physical integrity could be said to be justified by the public health considerations and necessity to control the spreading of infectious

---

[69]   Although the European Commission on Human Rights became obsolete in 1998, with the restructuring of the European Court of Human Rights, its case law is still cited.

[70]   EComHR 15 January 1998, *Boffa and Others v. San Marino*, no. 26536/95.

diseases in the region. Furthermore, according to the domestic court's findings, the medical staff had checked his suitability for vaccination prior to carrying out the vaccination, which suggest that necessary precautions had been taken to ensure that the medical intervention would not be to the applicant's detriment to the extent that would upset the balance of interests between the applicant's personal integrity and the public interest of protection health of the population.[71]

In the case of children, the rights and best interests of the child may warrant compulsory legislation, should persuasion of their parents/guardians prove inadequate.[72] This matter was addressed in the recent Grand Chamber judgment of *Vavřička and others v. the Czech Republic*, in which one applicant addressed a parental fine, and others addressed exclusion of children from preschool for refusal to comply with a statutory child vaccination duty.[73] In light of Article 8 of the ECHR, the applicants invoked their right to personal autonomy in making decisions concerning their children's health, and their right to personal development, in the context of attending nursery school.

The Court held that the state held a wide margin of appreciation, as the area related to healthcare policy.[74] Furthermore, the law sought to respond to a 'pressing social need to protect individual and public health against the diseases in question and to guard against any downward trend in the rate of vaccination among children'.[75] This remark is interesting, in that it seems to acknowledge public health as both an individual and collective claim.

In finding that the law was based on relevant and sufficient reasons, the Court drew on the 'best interests of the child', as per Article 3 of the Convention on the Rights of the Child (CRC). In relation to this norm, the Court held that:

> there is an obligation on States to place the best interests of the child, and also those of children as a group, at the centre of all decisions affecting their health and development. When it comes to immunisation, the objective should be that every child is protected against serious diseases ... Thus, where the view is taken that a policy of voluntary vaccination is not sufficient to achieve and maintain herd immunity, or herd immunity is not relevant due to the nature of the disease (e.g. tetanus), domestic authorities may reasonably introduce a compulsory vaccination policy in order to achieve an appropriate level of protection against serious diseases.[76]

---

71 ECtHR 15 March 2012, no. 24429/03, para. 36.
72 Further questions are whether the right to health establishes a right to a particular vaccine, or a stronger justification than general health interests to justify limitations on private life. See Chapter 12, on new technologies.
73 ECtHR 8 April 2021, *Vavřička and others v. the Czech Republic*, nos. 47621/13 and five others.
74 Ibid., para. 280.
75 Ibid., para. 284.
76 Ibid., para. 288.

Finally, the Court held that the measures were proportionate to the aims pursued. It noted that the law did not provide for forcibly administering vaccines, and that the sanctions were moderate.

It is interesting to see how, in this case, the principle of the best interests of the child justified compulsory child vaccination. Also of note is the Court's reference to concluding observations of the ICESCR and CRC Committees,[77] which highlights the interplay between international treaties on the right to health and the ECHR. Finally, the Court drew on social solidarity in its proportionality assessment, reflecting on the remote health risks that a small number of persons faced, compared to the risk to vulnerable children in the absence of vaccination.

Therefore, based on existing jurisprudence, it appears that compulsory vaccination could be justified, provided that such a measure is necessary, based on a pressing social need, and that adequate safeguards, such as medical exemptions, are in place. For example, the disease must present a real danger. The present authors would underscore, however, that coercive measures should be a last resort, and that education and information should be pursued first.

5. NCDs AND RISK FACTOR REDUCTION

5.1. THE GLOBAL AND EUROPEAN NCD PANDEMIC

Due to global changes in lifestyles, the world is facing dramatic changes in disease incidence and patterns. Chronic or 'noncommunicable' diseases (NCDs), including diabetes, cancer, and cardiovascular and respiratory diseases, are currently responsible for two-thirds of the world's yearly deaths, more than 40 per cent of which are premature deaths of people under the age of 70 years. More than three-quarters of all NCD deaths occur in low- and middle-income countries.[78] NCDs are, therefore, not only a health challenge, but also a most important development challenge, both in terms of the human suffering they cause, and the harm they inflict on the socio-economic positions of countries.[79]

As mentioned, four types of NCDs make the largest contribution to morbidity and mortality: cardiovascular diseases, cancer, chronic respiratory

---

[77] Ibid., paras. 129–134.

[78] WHO, 'Fact sheet: Noncommunicable diseases', available at www.who.int/news-room/fact-sheets/detail/noncommunicable-diseases; WHO, 'Global status report on noncommunicable diseases 2014', available at www.who.int/nmh/publications/ncd-status-report-2014/en/.

[79] WHO, 2014 report, see 'Fact sheet: Noncommunicable diseases', available at www.who.int/news-room/fact-sheets/detail/noncommunicable-diseases; WHO, 'Global status report on noncommunicable diseases 2014', available at www.who.int/nmh/publications/ncd-status-report-2014/ en/. These paragraphs rely, to some extent, on B. Toebes, 'The right to health and the global rise of non-communicable diseases' in S. Klotz, H. Bielefeld, M. Schmidthuber and A. Frewer (eds.), *Healthcare as a Human Rights Issue: Normative Profile, Conflicts and Implementation*, Bielefeld: Transcript, 2017, 123–44.

diseases and diabetes. They can be linked to four shared, so-called 'behavioural risk factors' that enhance the incidence of these diseases: tobacco use, unhealthy diet, physical inactivity and harmful use of alcohol.[80]

The international public health community, including the WHO, has slowly, but increasingly, engaged with this matter over the past two decades. In 1998, the World Health Assembly adopted a resolution calling on WHO Member States to develop a global strategy for the prevention and control of NCDs.[81] This led to the adoption of the Global Strategy for the Prevention and Control of Noncommunicable Diseases, in 2000, and subsequent action plans for the periods of 2008 to 2013, and 2013 to 2020.[82] In 2015, all UN Member States agreed, in the Sustainable Development Goals (SDGs), to, '[b]y 2030, reduce by one third premature mortality from non-communicable diseases through prevention and treatment'.[83]

There is, thus, an increasing political commitment to stem the global increase in NCDs. The question arises as to how human rights, and the right to health, in particular, respond to this development. Given that human rights law is aimed at protecting the human dignity and social well-being of individuals, how can it serve as a suitable framework for advancing NCD prevention and reduction, as the most pressing current threat to global health? And what is the role of the right to health more specifically, as a human right that aims to protect the health of individuals worldwide?

5.2. A RIGHTS APPROACH TO NCDs

A rights approach to NCDs implies, firstly, that governments secure the 'AAAQ', in relation to healthcare services necessary for the treatment and care of NCDs (see also Chapter 2 of this book).[84] Clearly, this is not an easy challenge for

---

[80] WHO Fact sheet, 'Fact sheet: Noncommunicable diseases', available at www.who.int/news-room/fact-sheets/detail/noncommunicable-diseases; WHO, 'Global status report on noncommunicable diseases 2014', available at www.who.int/nmh/publications/ncd-status-report-2014/ en/.

[81] World Health Assembly, Resolution WHA 53, 17, 11–16 May 1998.

[82] WHO, Global strategy for the prevention and control of noncommunicable diseases, A53/14, 22 March 2000; WHO, '2008–2013 Action Plan for the Global Strategy for the Prevention and Control of Noncommunicable Diseases', A61/8, 18 April 2008, available at www.who.int/nmh/publications/9789241 597418/en/; and WHO, 'Global Action Plan for the Prevention and Control of Noncommunicable diseases', 2013, available at http://apps.who.int/iris/bitstream/ 10665/94384/1/9789241506236_eng.pdf?ua=1.

[83] UN Sustainable Development Goals, available at https://sdgs.un.org/goals. See, in more detail, B. Toebes and D. Patterson, 'Human Rights and Non-Communicable Diseases: Controlling Tobacco and Promoting Healthy Diets' in L.O. Gostin and B.M. Meier (eds.), *Global Health and Human Rights*, University of California Press, 2020.

[84] 'AAAQ': availability, accessibility, acceptability, quality. For a more elaborate analysis, see also B. Toebes, 'The right to health and the global rise of non-communicable diseases' in S. Klotz,

governments, as treatment for cancer and other NCDs is often complex and costly, as it goes far beyond primary care. The global rise in NCDs exerts a heavy strain on domestic health budgets, as a result of which countries struggle to ensure that health-related services are sufficiently available, accessible, acceptable and of sufficient quality. The starting point is that states have considerable leeway to realise the right to health 'progressively', and 'to the maximum of their available resources'.[85]

Yet, there are also signs that many states do not optimally fulfil their obligations under the right to health. WHO statistics indicate that some countries have a relatively low health expenditure as a proportion of total government expenditure (less than 10 per cent, as compared to a global average of 14 per cent).[86] Along similar lines, the European Committee on Social Rights of the Council of Europe concluded that, where states spent less than five per cent of their gross domestic product (GDP) on healthcare, the situation in those specific states was not in conformity with the right to protection of health in Article 11 of the European Social Charter.[87] However, health expenditure does not tell the whole story. In 2010, the WHO estimated that 20 to 40 per cent of all health spending is wasted through inefficiency, a figure that is unlikely to have decreased since.[88] Hence, insufficient health expenditure, and the existence of health sector inefficiency and corruption, suggest that states could do more to realise the AAAQ in relation to NCD treatment and care.[89]

In addition to NCD treatment, governments have human rights obligations to address NCD risk factors, in particular smoking, unhealthy diets, excessive use of alcohol and lack of physical exercise.[90] The governmental role in relation to these risk factors is complex. There is firm evidence that certain measures, including prohibition of the marketing of unhealthy products, and price

---

H. Bielefeld, M. Schmidthuber and A. Frewer (eds.), *Healthcare as a Human Rights Issue: Normative Profile, Conflicts and Implementation*, Bielefeld: Transcript, 2017, 123–44.

[85]   Art. 2(1) ICESCR.

[86]   WHO, 'World Health Statistics 2011', available at http://www.who. int/whosis/whostat/2011/en/. See also L.O. Gostin, *Global Health Law*, Cambridge, Mass.: Harvard University Press, 2014, 208.

[87]   M. San Giorgi, *The Human Right to Equal Access to Health Care*, Antwerp: Intersentia, 2012, referring, inter alia, to the Conclusions of the European Committee of Social Rights with regard to XVII-2: Turkey (2.43% of GDP in 2003), and XVII-2: Poland (3.96% of GDP in 2002).

[88]   WHO, 'World Health Report 2010 – Health Systems Financing, the path to universal coverage (executive summary)', available at https://www.who.int/whr/2010/en/.

[89]   B. Toebes, 'The right to health and the global rise of non-communicable diseases' in S. Klotz, H. Bielefeld, M. Schmidthuber and A. Frewer (eds.), *Healthcare as a Human Rights Issue: Normative Profile, Conflicts and Implementation*, Bielefeld: Transcript, 2017, 123–44.

[90]   E.g. B. Toebes and D. Patterson, 'Human Rights and Non-Communicable Diseases: Controlling Tobacco and Promoting Healthy Diets' in L.O. Gostin and B.M. Meier (eds.), *Global Health and Human Rights*, University of California Press, 2020.

increases, are very effective in reducing their consumption.[91] Yet, these measures, in particular legal measures, also are inherently in tension with individual autonomy, and the freedom to choose a lifestyle of one's choice, and are not always accepted. As Parmett explains, NCDs have frequently been viewed as the result of private choices that liberal society ought to respect; and public health experts have, for many years, accepted that NCDs are often the result of risky individual behaviour.[92]

Initially, industries invoked human rights to defend their freedoms to produce and market their products. While rarely successful, the tobacco industry has frequently claimed freedom of expression before the European Court of Justice, invoked trademark rights in attacking 'plain packaging' laws before the Australian Supreme Court, and claimed expropriation of property rights before the World Trade Organization.[93] Increasingly, scholars have emphasised that human rights, primarily, protect individuals rather than industries, and that individuals have a right to be protected against the production, sale and marketing of these products by industries.[94]

While such interferences can be seen as an expression of the right to health, they potentially also, as previously mentioned, interfere with other rights, including the rights to privacy and family life, and freedom of movement. For example, Tsampi illustrates how the introduction of smoke-free zones relates to the rights under the ECHR.[95] This debate brings us back to the possibilities of

---

[91]   WHO, '"Best buys" and other recommended interventions for the prevention and control of noncommunicable diseases, (Updated) Appendix 3 of the global action plan for the prevention and control of noncommunicable diseases 2013–2020', available at https://www.who.int/ncds/management/WHO_Appendix_BestBuys_LS.pdf.

[92]   W.E. Parmett, 'US Law relating to noncommunicable diseases' in D. Orentlicher and T.K. Hervey, *The Oxford Handbook on Comparative Health Law*, Oxford: Oxford University Press, 2022, 119–41.

[93]   E.g. ECJ, Case C-491/01 *British American Tobacco*, paras. 149–50; *JT International SA v. Commonwealth of Australia* [2012] HCA 43 (5 October 2012); WTO – 'Tobacco Plain Packaging, Panel Reports', available at https://www.wto.org/(...)/cases_e/ds435_e.htm. B. Toebes and D. Patterson, 'Human Rights and Non-Communicable Diseases: Controlling Tobacco and Promoting Healthy Diets' in L.O. Gostin and B.M. Meier (eds.), *Global Health and Human Rights*, University of California Press, 2020.

[94]   Inter alia, K. Ó Cathaoir, M. Hartlev and C. Brassart Olsen, 'Global health law and obesity: towards a complementary approach of public health and human rights law' in G.L. Burci and B. Toebes, *Research Handbook on Global Health Law*, Edward Elgar Publishing, 2018; M.E. Gispen and B. Toebes (eds.), *Human Rights and Tobacco Control*, Edward Elgar Publishing, 2020; M.E. Gispen and B. Toebes, 'The Rights of Children in Tobacco Control', *Human Rights Quarterly* 41(2) (2019), 340–73; M.E. Gispen, 'Vulnerability and the Best Interest of the Child in Tobacco Control', *The International Journal of Children's Rights*, 29(3) (2021), 1–20.

[95]   A. Tsampi, 'Novel Smoke-free Zones and the Right to Respect for Private Life under Article 8 of the European Convention on Human Rights (on the occasion of the Dutch Decree of 22 June 2020, amending the Tobacco and Smokers' Order introducing the obligation to impose, designate and enforce a smoking ban in the areas belonging to buildings and facilities used for education)', *Europe of Rights & Liberties/Europe des Droits & Libertés* 2 (2020), 381–98.

limiting rights, which was addressed in more detail above (section 3.2 of this chapter).

Ó Cathaoir et al. illustrate that the CESCR has, so far, insufficiently addressed the connection between human rights and NCD risk factors.[96] The authors show that the CRC framework offers more potential by highlighting four 'general principles' that should be taken into account when interpreting children's rights: namely, best interests, the right to participate, the right to non-discrimination, and the right to life.[97] They show how, in particular, the deciding factor for the legitimacy of state action or inaction should be the best interests of the child, in light of the object and purpose of the CRC.[98]

6. SOCIAL DETERMINANTS OF HEALTH

6.1. INTRODUCTION

It is widely evidenced that there are dramatic health inequalities,[99] i.e. differences in health status, both within and between countries (see also Chapter 7 of this book).[100] The conditions in which people are born, grow, live, work and age – the 'social determinants of health' – are important contributors to these health inequalities.[101] Important social determinants include one's education,

---

[96] K. Ó Cathaoir, M. Hartlev and C. Brassart Olsen, 'Global health law and obesity: towards a complementary approach of public health and human rights law' in G.L. Burci and B. Toebes, *Research Handbook on Global Health Law*, Edward Elgar Publishing, 2018, 440–46 (with a particular emphasis on obesity).

[97] Arts. 3, 12, 2 and 6 of the Convention on the Rights of the Child.

[98] K. Ó Cathaoir, M. Hartlev and C. Brassart Olsen, 'Global health law and obesity: towards a complementary approach of public health and human rights law' in G.L. Burci and B. Toebes, *Research Handbook on Global Health Law*, Edward Elgar Publishing, 2018, 447. For a similar analysis in relation to tobacco, see B. Toebes, M.E. Gispen, J. Been and S. Aziz, 'A missing voice: The rights of children to a tobacco-free environment', *Tobacco Control* 27(1) (2017), 3–5. See also the ECtHR's approach to the 'best interest of the child' norm in a health context, in ECtHR 8 April 2021, *Vavřička and others v. the Czech Republic*, nos. 47621/13 and five others, and above, in section 4.4. See also A. Garde, J. Curtis and O. De Schutter (eds.), *Ending Childhood Obesity – A Challenge at the Crossroads of International Economic and Human Rights Law*, Edward Elgar, 2020.

[99] In North America, the term 'health disparities' is more common.

[100] E.g. J.P. Mackenbach, *Health inequalities: Persistence and change in European welfare states*, Oxford: Oxford University Press, 2019.

[101] WHO, 'Social determinants of health', www.who.int/social_determinants/en/ and https://www.who.int/news-room/q-a-detail/social-determinants-of-health-key-concepts. See also WHO, '10 facts on health inequities and their causes', www.who.int/features/factfiles/health_inequities/en/. For a more detailed analysis, see B. Toebes, 'Socioeconomic Health Inequalities in Europe' in T. Hervey and D. Orentlicher (eds.), *Oxford Research Handbook in Comparative Health Law*, Oxford: Oxford University Press, 2021. See also B. Toebes and K. Stronks, 'Closing the Gap: A Human Rights Approach towards Social Determinants of Health', *European Journal of Health Law* 23(5) (2016), 510–24.

family income, housing, and employment status. Where such conditions, and not biological variations or free choice, are at the root of inequalities, we call them 'socio-economic health inequalities'. Socio-economic health inequalities are generally considered to be unnecessary and avoidable.[102]

Responding to these widening inequalities, in 2005 the WHO established the Commission on the Social Determinants of Health (CSDH) to provide advice on how to reduce them.[103] The CSDH's final report (2008) still holds value today. It concluded that health inequities arise because of the unequal distribution of power, income, goods, and services, and because of the circumstances in which people live, including their access to healthcare, education, their conditions of work and leisure, their homes, and their communities.[104] Based on these findings, the CSDH, in its report, asserted that such health inequities are a matter of social justice:

> Reducing health inequities is, for the Commission on Social Determinants of Health … an ethical imperative. Social injustice is killing people on a grand scale. (p. 10)

In its report, the CSDH made three overarching recommendations, for all actors, to reduce health inequities: (1) improve daily living conditions; (2) tackle the inequitable distribution of power, money, and resources; and (3) measure and understand the problem, and assess the impact of action. Within these areas of action, the Commission made further recommendations in 12 areas, including early childhood development and education, healthy places (the living environment), universal healthcare, and health equity in all policies.

In recent years, the implementation of the above framework has been criticised as insufficient. Crear-Perry et al. argue, in a US context, that, in addition to social determinants, policymakers should also address the *structural* determinants of health: 'cultural norms, policies, institutions and practices that define the distribution (or maldistribution) of SDOH [social determinants of health]'.[105]

---

102   B. Toebes, 'Socioeconomic Health Inequalities in Europe' in T. Hervey and D. Orentlicher (eds.), *Oxford Research Handbook in Comparative Health Law*, Oxford: Oxford University Press, 2021, 2.

103   See also WHO, 'Social Determinants of Health', www.who.int/social_determinants/en/ and https://www.who.int/news-room/q-a-detail/social-determinants-of-health-key-concepts.

104   World Health Organization/Commission on the Social Determinants of Health (chaired by Sir Michael Marmot), 'Closing the gap in a generation: Health equity through action on the social determinants of health', WHO, 2008. See also 'Fair Society, Healthy Lives' (the 'Marmot Review'), which assesses health inequalities in England post-2010, available at www.marmotreview.org/AssetLibrary/pdfs/Reports/FairSocietyHealthyLives.pdf.

105   J. Crear-Perry, R. Correa-de-Araujo, T. Lewis Johnson, M.R. McLemore, E. Neilson and M. Wallace, 'Social and Structural Determinants of Health Inequities in Maternal Health', *Journal of Women's Health* 30(2) (2021), 230–35.

For example, racial and ethnic biases can drive health inequalities,[106] but have, arguably, often been overlooked in public health responses.[107]

6.2. THE LINK WITH HUMAN RIGHTS

The suggestion that such health inequalities are matters of social injustice raises the question of whether they are also human rights issues. Human rights standards provide a moral and legal framework for assessing matters of social justice, including socio-economic health inequalities. By giving expression to the vulnerability of the individual, human rights law can serve as an overarching framework, protecting the rights and interests of those affected by health inequalities and poor social conditions, and offer accountability, where necessary.[108]

It is clear that the right to health is at the centre of this analysis. Its broad understanding, which builds on the WHO's broad definition of health, as laid down in its Constitution (1946), explicitly recognises that 'underlying determinants of health' are as important for people's health as access to healthcare services. This broad approach to health is also reflected in Article 12 of the ICESCR, and in Article 11 of the European Social Charter (ESC) (see also Chapters 2 and 4 of this book).[109]

Taking a human rights approach, then, also requires looking at the right to health in its interaction with other human rights. It was explained, in Chapter 2, that the right to health does not stand alone, but is reinforced and supported by several other rights. Hunt asserts that there are dense connections between social determinants and human rights:[110]

> There is considerable congruity between the Commission's mandate and the 'underlying determinants of health' dimension of the right to health, as well as other interconnected human rights such as adequate housing, food and water. In other words, national and international human rights law informs and reinforces the Commission's mandate.[111]

---

[106]   Ibid; T.J. Johnson, 'Structural Racism, and Social Determinants with Health Care Inequities', *Pediatrics* 146(2) (2020); R. Yearby, 'Race Based Medicine, Colorblind Disease: How Racism in Medicine Harms Us All', *The American Journal of Bioethics* 21(2) (2021), 19–27.

[107]   K. Andrews, 'Racism is the public health crisis', *The Lancet* 397(10282) (2021), 1342–43.

[108]   B. Toebes, 'Socioeconomic Health Inequalities in Europe' in T. Hervey and D. Orentlicher (eds.), *Oxford Research Handbook in Comparative Health Law*, Oxford: Oxford University Press, 2021, 2.

[109]   Secretariat of the European Social Charter (ESC), 'The Right to Health and the European Social Charter', March 2009, available at www.coe.int/T/DGHL/Monitoring/SocialCharter/Theme%20factsheets/FactsheetHealth_en.pdf. The document indicates that it is not binding on the European Committee of Social Rights.

[110]   P. Hunt, 'Missed opportunities: human rights and the Commission on Social Determinants of Health', *Global Health Promotion* 16/1 Supp. (2009), 36.

[111]   P. Hunt, UN Special Rapporteur on the right of everyone to the enjoyment of the highest attainable standard of physical and mental health, 'The right of everyone to the enjoyment

Such rights imply legal obligations to ensure access to, inter alia, housing, a safe and clean living environment, education, and social protection. In conjunction with the right to health, these rights have the potential to address poor housing conditions, the lack of access to proper education, and the state of people's neighbourhoods and workplaces. For example, Braveman emphasises the connections between the rights to a standard of living and education, on the one hand, and health, on the other.[112] Access to general schooling appears to be a crucial social determinant of health. In line with Amartya Sen's 'capabilities' approach, education can be seen as an essential capability or factor for achieving one's health potential.[113] Article 13(1) of the ICESCR affirms that education shall 'enable all persons to participate effectively in society'.

Altogether, the current human rights framework offers a legal basis for addressing several of the 'causes of the causes', such as inadequate education and poor working conditions. Yet, many questions remain. Greater attention could be paid by the human rights community to how people's living conditions shape their health.[114] As such, while the 'underlying determinants of health', under the right to health framework, cover many of the issues that are mentioned in the CSDH report, some further elaboration of the 'underlying determinants' is needed to equip this framework fully for addressing the causes mentioned above. The human rights framework needs to be inspired and fortified by the public health and epidemiological frameworks, which evidence a more thorough understanding of what causes health issues, for example when it comes to the development of indicators.

Lastly, it is important that such claims lead to accountability for human rights violations where they occur.[115] Prior to the publication of CSDH's report, its secretariat made a sharp observation about the contribution that human rights can make:

> Human rights offer more than a conceptual armature connecting health, social conditions and broad governance principles, however. Rights concepts and standards provide an instrument for turning diffuse social demand into focused legal and political claims, as well as a set of criteria by which to evaluate the performance of

---

of the highest attainable standard of physical and mental health', UN Doc. A/60/348, 12 September 2005, para. 7.

[112] P. Braveman, 'Social conditions, health equity, and human rights', *Health and Human Rights* 12(2) (2010), 8.

[113] Ibid., 8.

[114] Ibid., 4.

[115] See, generally, M. Hesselman, A.H. de Wolf and B. Toebes (eds.), *Socio-Economic Human Rights for Essential Public Services Provision*, London/New York: Routledge (Taylor and Francis Group), 2016. For an elaborate account of the right to health accountability, see also Yi Zhang, *Advancing the right to health care in China*, Intersentia, 2019.

political authorities in promoting people's wellbeing and creating conditions for equitable enjoyment of the fruits of development.[116]

It is important for courts and other accountability mechanisms to have an understanding of health inequities and social determinants, and of how human rights come into play, in this context.[117] So far, such institutions have little experience in these matters.[118] Some inspiration is offered by the European Committee of Social Rights, the Council of Europe's treaty body for the European Social Charter, which addresses the social determinants, to some extent, under the umbrella of the social rights in this Charter (see also above in section 3.3, and in Chapter 5).[119]

7. CONCLUSIONS

The NCD and COVID-19 pandemics underscore the importance of governmental attention to public health. This chapter has explained that securing public health is a core governmental obligation under the right to health. It has also explained that the connection between public health and the right to health is not a straightforward one, given that public health measures may be in tension with other rights. These tensions were illustrated with reference to various dimensions of public health, in particular infectious and chronic disease control, and health inequalities.

The present authors conclude that implementing the right to health as a norm that also encapsulates global and domestic public health concerns is complex, yet important. As an individual human right, it typically addresses the health concerns of the individual. Nonetheless, there are possibilities for constructing the interests of a group as a 'bundle of rights', and for establishing

---

[116] O. Solar and A. Irwin (CSDH secretariat), *A Conceptual Framework for Action on the Social Determinants of Health*, draft April 2007, available at www.who.int/social_determinants/resources/csdh_framework_action_05_07.pdf.

[117] For concrete examples, see K. Stronks, B. Toebes, A. Hendriks, U. Ikram and S. Venkatapuram, *Social justice and human rights as a framework for addressing social determinants of health – Final report of the Task group on Equity, Equality and Human Rights*, Copenhagen: WHO Europe, 2016, s. 4, available at www.euro.who.int/__data/assets/pdf_file/0006/334356/HR-task-report.pdf.

[118] B. Toebes, 'Socioeconomic Health Inequalities in Europe' in T. Hervey and D. Orentlicher (eds.), *Oxford Research Handbook in Comparative Health Law*, Oxford: Oxford University Press, 2021.

[119] For an overview of relevant decisions, see K. Stronks, B. Toebes, A. Hendriks, U. Ikram and S. Venkatapuram, *Social justice and human rights as a framework for addressing social determinants of health – Final report of the Task group on Equity, Equality and Human Rights*, Copenhagen: WHO Europe, 2016, s. 4, available at www.euro.who.int/__data/assets/pdf_file/0006/334356/HR-task-report.pdf., 52.

judicial and quasi-judicial mechanisms that allow for collective complaints. Given the magnitude of global public health concerns, such mechanisms are much-needed.

Finally, the authors suggest that states' obligations under the right to health should be interpreted with respect for states' duties to the public's health, drawing on expert guidance from the WHO and other agencies. For example, the WHO outlines in greater detail than the ICESCR framework what is meant by universal health coverage (UHC). These technical public health standards can be used to guide the content of states' human rights obligations.

PART IV

CONCLUSIONS, CHALLENGES AND RECOMMENDATIONS

CHAPTER 14

CONCLUSIONS

Aart HENDRIKS

The ambition of this book has been to contribute to the field of 'health and human rights'. This discipline has evolved as a distinguished field of research over the years, covering a broad range of themes where health and human rights are connected in many different ways, with obligations and responsibilities on governments, municipalities, health personnel and other stakeholders. The right to health implies rights not only for patients, but for all persons within state jurisdiction affected by policies or decisions on the health and well being of individuals or groups, including environmental issues.

In this book we have, in particular, studied the legal interfaces between 'health' and 'human rights'. We have done so from both a global and a European perspective, paying attention to the relevant health and human rights concepts and principles. Health is considered to be a crucial condition for human well-being. By its very nature, health is intrinsically connected to the protection of human rights. In fact, health is a precondition for the full enjoyment of many human rights. Health and human rights is, therefore, an important dimension of human rights and health law that has expanded significantly, both theoretically and materially, since the first edition of this book in 2012. With respect to the material expansion, there are an increasing number of persons with noncommunicable diseases, a growing emphasis on the rights of patients with disabilities, and the introduction of new health technologies, as well as the impact of climate change on individual and collective health, an issue not studied in detail in this book.

In this book, we have sought to explain and assess the relations between health and human rights. In comparison with the previous edition of this volume, new topics are the increased focus on the central concepts underlying health and human rights, with attention being paid to mainstreaming health and human rights with more general human rights law. The addition of a global perspective to the previous European approach also implies that the scope of the book has broadened. It attaches more attention to health and human rights treaties drafted under the umbrella of the UN and the World Health Organization (WHO) than the 2012 edition. As a result, this book draws not only on European regulations and case law, but compares these with international human rights norms, including, for example, the Sustainable Development Goals (SDG) and Framework Convention on Tobacco Control (FCTC), in the context of health and human rights. In this way, it also assesses the interactions between the various systems.

We have investigated the situation of a number of groups that are, generally, considered to be vulnerable to health and human rights violations. We are painfully aware that not all 'vulnerable groups' have been systematically analysed in this book, due to the obligation to confine ourselves within the available space. Also new, in comparison with the 2012 edition of this book, is the attention to new technologies, the processing of health data, and related privacy and confidentiality issues, as well as newly emerging international and national public health concerns such as COVID-19, and other public health issues.

The preceding sections of this book consist of 13 chapters, subdivided into three parts. This chapter, Chapter 14, forms the fourth part of this book, and seeks to describe and analyse the findings and conclusions from the 13 other chapters.

1. SUMMARY OF CONCLUSIONS OF VARIOUS CHAPTERS

Chapter 1 (Toebes) provides the reader with a general introduction to this book, focusing on the historical background of health and human rights, the relationships between health and human rights law, the theoretical dimensions and relevant principles underpinning health and human rights, and present challenges to health and human rights that need to be addressed. Based on this analysis, parts of which are expanded upon in other chapters of this book, this chapter explains the structure of the book, and the topics being addressed in the various parts of the book. The main conclusion from Chapter 1 is that health and human rights is an increasingly expanding branch of international and European human rights and health law, requiring scholars and practitioners to look for answers to new and old challenges that are in line with health and human rights law, and to formulate relevant principles in a predictable and non-discriminatory way.

Chapter 2 (Toebes and Ó Cathaoir) introduces and explores the meaning of the 'right to health', the core right in the field of health and human rights. Important as this right is, in particular for the remainder of this book, it should not be seen as an umbrella right covering all rights that are indispensable for the realisation of the aspirations enshrined in the right to health. A number of other human rights have a distinct meaning for respecting, protecting and promoting health on an individual and collective level, including the rights to life, privacy and family life, and the prohibition of inhuman and degrading treatment. The term 'right to health' is a shorthand expression referring to the more elaborate treaty texts that define health as a right. It is considered to encompass two dimensions: 'healthcare' and the 'underlying determinants of health', thus recognising the importance of (social) conditions for health. An important element of the right to health includes the so-called 'AAAQ', a set of principles that constitutes the framework of the right to health. Health services, including those connected to the underlying determinants of health, have to be available, accessible, acceptable and of good quality. This chapter highlights lingering controversies surrounding the right to health that are in need of further clarification. These issues include the justiciability, or legal enforceability, of the right to health, the responsibilities of non-state actors, and the need for a comprehensive methodology for the right to health. It was concluded, in part due to differences in opinions among scholars, that it is still unclear which services must be granted on the basis of the right to health.

Chapter 3 (Aasen and Hartlev) explores the concept and value of human dignity, which is at the core of all human rights, including health-related human rights. Human dignity has several aspects and functions in human rights and health protection, both at the individual and the public or social level. Other concepts and values of special relevance to the health context are autonomy and integrity, both of which are essential attributes to the dignity principle, and legal starting points in regard to lawful health service delivery. The principles of dignity, autonomy and integrity, as well as the cross-cutting principle of non-discrimination, form the basis of modern human rights law, and have a significant impact on healthcare systems, both globally and within Europe. These principles are the foundations of the more recent concept and doctrine of patient rights, which are more specific interpretations and applications of human rights in relation to healthcare, such as confidentiality, informed consent, and the right to necessary healthcare services.

This chapter pays special attention to the position of those who may encounter difficulties in understanding information, and giving or refusing consent for treatment, such as children. Privacy and confidentiality are other dimensions of health and human rights, and of patients' rights. Privacy and confidentiality are particularly topical concepts when it comes to processing health data, in relation to treatment, or for other aims. Patients' rights, including self-determination, do not imply that individual rights and wishes should always prevail over public health interests, and similarly important public interests. As emphasised in this chapter, this is not to suggest that individual rights and wishes can be easily sacrificed for public purposes. The reasons to overrule individual rights and wishes should always be absolutely necessary, and should represent the least restrictive measure that can achieve a legitimate aim in a non-discriminatory way.

An important lesson from Chapter 3 is that, from a health and human rights perspective, it will remain a challenge to precisely describe the meaning of human dignity and related concepts, patients' rights, and the restrictions of these rights and concepts in respect to individual situations. In seeking to describe the meanings of these concepts, the field of health and patients' rights can build upon the experiences of human rights law, a discipline that, increasingly, overlaps with health law.

Chapter 4 (Ó Cathaoir) on UN institutions and health and human rights introduces the central players in this field, at a global level. The first section of this chapter focuses on human rights bodies that contribute to, and have a role in, shaping and adjudicating the right to health. This is done with a focus on treaties and declarations, recommendations (including general comments and concluding observations), and complaint mechanisms. Due to the large number of treaties, treaty-based bodies, and instruments, each with their own focus, it is difficult to guarantee a consistency of norms and opinions.

The second part of Chapter 4 focuses mainly on the World Health Organization (WHO) as the primary international body in the field of health. Like other UN-related agencies, the WHO, increasingly, mainstreams human rights law in its work, including its efforts to promote the right to health, as laid down in the preamble of its constitution, and otherwise to achieve its objectives. Chapter 4 notes, with concern, the challenges facing these institutions, and examines the procedures they can utilise in achieving their goals. The effectiveness of these systems depends largely on state consent, which means that the institutions that monitor health and human rights compliance at the level of the UN have limited possibilities to enforce their standards, particularly when compared to 'stronger' systems, like international economic law and, indeed, the EU (see Chapter 6).

Chapter 5 (Hendriks) focuses on the Council of Europe, as the primary European institution in the area of health and human rights. The case law analysis, in this chapter, of the judgments and decisions of the European Court of Human Rights (ECtHR) demonstrates that this Court increasingly deals with health-related matters, literally from conception to death and beyond. Reiterating that healthcare represents an important value in a democratic society, the Court has produced far-reaching judgments in the fields of health and health law, also interpreting the concepts described in Chapter 3 of this book. The European Convention on Human Rights (ECHR) imposes various (sometimes positive) obligations on Contracting States to protect health, and to prevent health risks, in healthcare settings, and elsewhere in society. Some obligations address the relationship between the patient and healthcare providers or institutions, thus exerting a so-called 'horizontal effect'. Article 8 of the ECHR (right to private and family life) plays the most important role in such relationships, even though the Court, nowadays, increasingly applies Article 3 (prohibition of inhuman and degrading treatment) as a yardstick with respect to serious threats to patients' rights and their dignity. As such, the ECHR, as one of the most powerful human rights instruments, also protects and strengthens patients' rights, including the rights of persons who may be the target of domestic violence or child abuse.

In addition to the ECtHR, other Council of Europe mechanisms make an important contribution to the development of health and human rights. Various decisions of the European Social Rights Committee (ECSR), the body monitoring state compliance with the (revised) European Social Charter (ESC), touch upon health and its social determinants, thus representing an important source for the further development of the area of health and human rights. The ECtHR frequently refers to the standards adopted under the ESC and European Convention for the Prevention of Torture (CPT), and, likewise, the ECSR frequently refers to the jurisprudence of the ECtHR. This strengthens the development of uniform European health and human rights standards. Regretfully, the number of ratifications of the Convention on Human Rights and Biomedicine, as well as its Additional Protocols, are relatively low. This inhibits this treaty from fulfilling its predicted role of adding norms to specific fields in the area of health of human rights.

Chapter 6 (Herrmann, Ó Cathaoir and Toebes) explores the stance of the European Union (EU) towards health and human rights. While the EU is not a human rights organisation, let alone a health organisation, the Charter on Fundamental Rights contains several health-related rights that bind both EU institutions and the Member States. While the focus of EU law is, mostly, on economic integration and the creation of a single market, to some extent its laws and policies involve the protection of human health, and the rights of patients. Several rights from the Charter are relevant to the promotion and protection of health, and to the area of health and human rights.

This chapter analyses the emerging jurisprudence where the Court of Justice of the EU (CJEU) has engaged in issues related to health and human rights, including the need (or otherwise) for an economically inactive national of a Member State, residing legally in the territory of another Member State, to be affiliated to the public sickness insurance scheme of the host Member State before they are entitled to treatment there. A right to health, and several other health-related rights are, as such, part and parcel of the *acquis communautaire*. Also, with Article 168 of the Treaty on the Functioning of the European Union (TFEU), the EU has reaffirmed its commitment to matters of public health. The new text of this provision, compared with Article 152 of the Treaty Establishing the European Community (TEC), enables the EU to play a more proactive role in this area. However, the review of the EU's role in public health and noncommunicable diseases shows that the EU is yet to position itself as a front runner in this field. The response of the EU to the COVID-19 pandemic was, initially, slow, but the EU has taken this opportunity to strengthen its coordination skills and capacities, in an effort, among other things, to secure compliance with the traditional freedoms of the EU. The European Medicines Agency (EMA) and the European Centre for Disease Prevention and Control (ECDC) have played important roles, for example with respect to the approval of vaccines in the European market, and the provision of uniform information on the COVID situation in the EU and its Member States.

The EU wants to expand its coordination role by establishing a European Health Union, in which all EU Member States prepare for, and respond to, health crises together, while making sure that medical supplies are available, affordable and innovative, and where Member States will work together to improve prevention, treatment and aftercare for diseases such as cancer. Article 168 para. 5 TFEU allows the EU to take such incentive measures, but doesn't bestow the power to the EU to harmonise national legislation.

Chapter 7 (Hartlev) addresses the right to access to healthcare services, an important precondition for complying with the right to health. The focus of this chapter is on what equality of opportunity and equal access imply for organisations responsible for delivering the healthcare services, and in situations where access is limited, due to resource constraints, or for other reasons. In so doing, this chapter discusses the human rights aspects of equality and unjustified health disparities, including the different (and often more extensive) requirements for healthcare from groups such as women, ethnic minorities, and people with disabilities (see Chapter 8), that may exacerbate their unequal opportunities in society. Besides this, groups such as LGBT people also encounter discriminatory treatment from healthcare providers. Providing equal access to healthcare is, therefore, essential for guaranteeing everybody the opportunity to enjoy equal healthcare, taking into account cultural, ethical, and religious opinions and factors and societal concerns.

With respect to equality, this chapter makes a distinction between one-to-one equality, which is normally applied within civil and political rights, and group equality, which is used mostly when assessing equality in respect of socio-economic rights. This chapter concludes that human rights law is struggling with the application of one-to-one equality, in relation to socio-economic rights.

The importance of the right to life (see also Chapter 11) also influences prioritisation of scarce healthcare service resources, and may lead to intergenerational inequity, in difficult situations. We have also witnessed such intergenerational inequity during the COVID-19 pandemic, where 'equality of opportunity' for all individuals involved is impossible to achieve. Consequently, access to healthcare services raises a number of complex issues involving public health, socio-economic, ethical, and broader societal interests and concerns. Applying a human rights-based approach in this area is crucial, but, at the same time, challenging. Due to the complexity of this topic, it is difficult to provide clear conclusions. It is clear that state parties must fulfil their core obligations, but it is more uncertain what equality of opportunity implies, in respect of services beyond the core obligations. Similarly, it is clear that state parties must pay special attention to weak and vulnerable parts of their populations (see Chapter 8) when prioritising scarce resources. However, in situations concerned with distribution of resources between individuals or groups of patients in need, it is less clear how to tackle this dilemma, from a human rights perspective. Due to the complexity of the interests and concerns involved, the current authors recommend that further analyses in this area should take a balanced approach, and ensure sufficient attention to the individual, who should always be at the centre of these issues.

Chapter 8 (Aasen) addresses an increasingly important concept in human rights discourse, namely vulnerability. While the human rights framework is, generally, based on a notion of human vulnerability, it also emphasises the particular vulnerability of some groups more than others, while, at the same time, containing the central idea of the autonomous and independent human being, in charge of his or her life. The requirement of informed consent to medical treatment is a key example of both human rights and patients' rights protecting the idea and value of individual autonomy. While human vulnerability may be seen as a fact of life, or a consequence of certain conditions or circumstances, autonomy is an essential *value* protected by the human rights framework. However, the seemingly inherent dichotomy between the competing ideas of human vulnerability and autonomy needs clarification and resolution, in order to give adequate direction to the constantly growing body of case law in the field of health and human rights, where these ideas are employed. In its case law, the ECtHR argues that certain groups are particularly vulnerable to human rights violations due to their history of being neglected, oppressed, stigmatised or traumatised. While human rights should acknowledge, and be responsive to, the particular needs of persons belonging to such vulnerable groups, human rights bodies should not contribute to further stigmatisation and victimisation. Rather, human rights law – in theory, and in practice – should contribute to empowerment, development and progress. To this end, the theories of human capabilities, as supported by human rights, point out a direction for human rights argumentation in the field of health and human rights. The task of balancing protection and empowerment, including respect for individual autonomy, and strengthening capabilities, involves ongoing challenges in the field of health and human rights, for modern welfare states.

An important conclusion of Chapter 8 is that autonomy is particularly prone to abuse when a person meets with powerful or paternalistic authorities. This calls for reinforcement of the autonomy of persons who are vulnerable to such abuse, while avoiding the reinforcement of stigmatisation and victimisation. This also holds true with the maintenance of dignified living conditions for migrants, including access to healthcare and social services.

As individuals, we are vulnerable: the COVID-19 crisis demonstrated, clearly and painfully. Everyone was a potential victim, as knowledge of the virus was limited, and no one had been vaccinated when the pandemic started. This situation provided an opportunity for experiencing and reflecting upon our vulnerability as human beings in need of protection, as well as cooperation with others to limit the spread of the virus. Furthermore, certain groups were identified, at an early stage, as particularly vulnerable to the virus, in particular the elderly, and persons with certain health conditions. The perspective of general and particular vulnerability is highlighted and developed in this book, as we identify vulnerability as a central idea in human rights law and discourse, developed especially in case law relating to certain groups identified as particularly vulnerable to human rights violations, due to a history of oppression and marginalisation, disability, health status or other factors. Vulnerability may be produced directly by state policies and regulations, for example in terms of exclusion from essential goods and services, such as healthcare. This is the situation for undocumented migrants in most European countries, constituting an example of a human rights violation that seems to be normalised across Europe, despite repeated critique from the UN body monitoring the International Covenant on Economic, Social and Cultural Rights (ICESCR). This is an example of a tension between international and regional regulations, where European regulations on access to healthcare seem to be more accepting of restrictions based on a person's legal status. In a time when migration is a global challenge, such regulations pose a threat to the health and well-being of millions of people who have not yet become recognised as citizens, nor even as asylum seekers, in the receiving state. We recommend all states to accept the interpretation of the right to health put forward by the ICESCR Committee, maintaining that ratifying states have responsibility for every person residing in the country, based on the principle of non-discrimination, and that legal status should not be a basis for denial of essential health services.

Chapter 9 (Hendriks) on disabled persons builds upon the concept of vulnerability, as explained in Chapter 8. Persons with disabilities are a heterogeneous group, including women, ethnic minorities, and others who may be subject to discrimination on other grounds. People with a medical impairment are easily labelled as disabled, while not all disabled persons have a medical problem. All of these people may be confronted with exclusion and other human rights issues, inside and outside the field of healthcare. This chapter urges that the meaning of disability should not be confined to an individual context, but that disabilities should be seen as the outcome of individual and environmental factors. The latter approach has also been adopted by the UN Convention on the Rights of Persons with a Disability (CRPD). This Convention, adopted by the UN in 2006, is a strong and universally ratified human rights document with its own treaty-based organisation, the CRPD Committee. Besides many other human rights, including the right to health (Article 25), the CRPD acknowledges the principles of dignity, autonomy and equality of persons with disabilities as the underlying principles of the Convention. The CRPD Committee has, by way of general comments and decisions, following complaints against Contracting States, interpreted some of the rights protected by the CRPD quite comprehensively, in comparison to other treaty bodies, and international and European courts. These include the right to legal capacity, the right not to be deprived of liberty, and the right to vote. The EU has also ratified the CRPD. The CRPD has also inspired European institutions and countries to strengthen the rights of persons with disabilities. This is not to suggest that the various provisions of the CRPD have been interpreted identically in Europe as they have been by the CRPD Committee. In fact, even though the Council of Europe, the EU, and their respective bodies are committed to adhering to, and correctly implementing, the CRPD, they tend to interpret the CRPD slightly differently than the CRPD Committee. These differences in opinion may be caused by the fact that the CRPD is a treaty focusing on 'only' one group, with a treaty body organisation that has a limited number of members with a legal background, whereas the Council of Europe and the EU have to balance the rights of one group with the rights of other groups, and general interests.

Chapter 10 (Herrmann) has its focus on reproductive rights. It takes, as a starting point, that women experiencing reproductive health issues are a group in need of special legal attention, given the special healthcare needs associated with reproduction. In view of this position, they may experience unequal access to healthcare treatment, while the limits of women's reproductive autonomy have been the subject of intense debate. This chapter illustrates how various human rights, including the right to respect for private and family life, the right to reproductive autonomy, and the right not to be discriminated against, form, together, a platform for the protection of reproductive health. While this is not clear-cut, some health and human rights developments are promising. For example, in its judgment on *Tysiac v. Poland*, the ECtHR, for the first time, addressed the margin of appreciation in relation to abortion in a more conservative state, thus addressing the negative consequences of restrictive abortion legislation. This illustrates how the ECtHR is slowly, but gradually, coming to address more contemporary reproductive issues in a dynamic and evolutive fashion. However, as a whole, European human rights law has not been a major driving force in the evolution of reproductive rights. The CEDAW Convention and the Cairo Platform of Action are the major human rights instruments focusing on autonomy and human rights protection of reproductive rights, but major developments have also taken place through a dynamic interpretation in general comments elaborating on rights protected under the ICESCR and ICCPR. Given the sensitivity of the issue of reproduction, it is expected that new cases will be presented to international treaty bodies and European courts, in an effort to gain more clarity on current and newly emerging issues, given that reproductive rights are under continuous threat.

Chapter 11 (Hendriks) addresses the issue of death and dying. States are required, on the basis of the right to life, to protect the lives of everybody, and to refrain from deliberately taking the lives of human beings. This imposes a large number of obligations on states, including with respect to environmental and industrial issues, as well as with respect to persons under the care of the state, such as prisoners. The state also has the obligation to ensure that healthcare settings make regulations for the protection of the life of all patients. At the same time, it can be seen that, in some situations, prolonging medical treatment is no longer compatible with the dignity of patients, or professional standards. There are also, increasingly, situations in which patients request not to be treated, or for their treatments to cease, which may lead to a shortening of their lives. Last but not least, individuals may ask their healthcare providers to assist them in ending their lives ('physician-assisted dying'), or to deliberately end their lives in a dignified way ('euthanasia'). Even though it is, almost generally, accepted that persons have the right to refuse treatment, physician-assisted dying and euthanasia are highly sensitive issues. Worldwide, only a few countries have decriminalised these practices, usually on the basis of the right to a private life and/or human dignity. In view of the growing number of elderly people with relatively long life expectancies, but, sometimes, with more severe health problems, it is expected that more states will decriminalise physician-assisted dying and euthanasia. As yet, only four European states have laws decriminalising euthanasia under certain conditions (the Netherlands, Belgium, Luxembourg and Spain), but the number of countries having extensive public debates on euthanasia is growing, inside and outside Europe.

Chapter 12 (Ó Cathaoir) explores the impact of new healthcare technologies from the perspective of health and human rights. This chapter begins by discussing whether there is a right to access new healthcare technologies (see also Chapter 7), before concluding that such a right is, perhaps, more promising under the right to benefit from scientific progress than it is under the right to health. Subsequently, digital healthcare technologies are evaluated and discussed, with reference to several rights, including the right to privacy, the right to data protection under EU law, the right to an explanation under the General Data Protection Regulation (GDPR), and non-discrimination. This chapter concludes that there is, as yet, limited harmonisation and regulation with respect to new technologies. It also concludes that individuals do not have an enforceable right to digital health under the right to health; not providing new technologies to all is not necessarily a form of discrimination.

Chapter 13 (Toebes and Ó Cathaoir) introduces the discipline of public health, and explores whether this is an element of the right to health, or whether it is incongruent therewith. This chapter discusses the sometimes fraught issue of ensuring that public health laws and policies do not violate individual rights. It also further explores and introduces the International Health Regulations (IHR), including the human rights elements thereof, as well as the issue of mandatory vaccinations. Having drawn on the COVID-19 pandemic, the chapter explores noncommunicable diseases and the social determinants of health. Research demonstrates that there are widening health inequalities both within, and between, European nations. It appears that people's health is, to a considerable extent, determined by the way they are raised, where they are raised, their education, and their work environment. An attempt is made to identify the human rights dimensions of this phenomenon.

The difficulty of balancing rights and interests in a range of health-related situations where important concerns are at stake is illustrated here, and throughout the book. The human rights framework provides important regulation for handling the vulnerability of persons, in situations of conflict between personal autonomy and essential public interests regarding health, or other legitimate social interests or values. The urgency of securing public health interests against dangers posed by individual autonomy has been a constant theme throughout the global COVID-19 pandemic, where everyone's lives and health have been potentially vulnerable, due to the threat of virus transmission.

The human rights framework provides important normative tools to handle the crisis, and to balance interests according to the requirement for interventions in private lives to be in accordance with law, as well as necessary, proportionate, non-discriminatory and solely for legitimate purposes. Although this volume often emphasises human rights as basic individual entitlements against a powerful state, it also highlights the important balancing aspects inherent in the human rights system. Without the possibility of securing essential public interests, such as public health interests, on behalf of human societies, the human rights system would fail its important mission in society.

2. FINAL OBSERVATIONS

This book and its various chapters show that increasing attention is being paid to the legal aspects and dimensions of health and human rights, and the issues that are covered by this subject. The relations between health and human rights are dominated by an interplay between the respective sets of rights and principles that are recognised at the international and European levels. It goes without saying that the right to health is considered the core right in this field, but other rights also contribute to the theory and application of the norms of health and human rights.

The European systems have benefitted from stronger enforcement systems (the ECtHR and the CJEU) than the UN system. There is a growing health and human rights practice within the framework of the Council of Europe and the EU bodies, and an increasing awareness that there are legal obligations to guarantee the health rights of Europeans, both on an individual and collective level. However, in the field of the right to health, global treaties (for example, the ICESCR, the CRPD and CRC) are influential, and more far-reaching than European treaties. Furthermore, while some rights and principles are contained in legally binding instruments, others are stipulated in soft-law instruments (for example, the ICESCR Committee's General Comment No. 14). These rights and principles play an important role in the protection and promotion of health in Europe, at an institutional, as well as a state level. Nevertheless, this book has also illustrated that treaties and other legal instruments are not always uniformly interpreted, at an international and European level, for example with respect to the rights of persons with disabilities, and with regard to access to abortion, causing confusion with respect to the precise meaning of rights, principles and state obligations.

Health will be a crucial topic in the years to come. Ageing populations, together with growing health inequalities and resource restraints, call on all societies to respond. This holds equally true with respect to 'new' health challenges such as climate change and smoking, the introduction of new health technologies, and the increasing number of persons with noncommunicable diseases mean that the health and human rights dimensions of these challenges require further investigation. The COVID-19 pandemic, and the uncoordinated way in which the international, European and national authorities initially responded, brought many pitfalls, due to the lack of common interpretation of relevant rights and principles. This book has illustrated how human rights law, and the interconnected field of patients' rights, can play a role in such dilemmas. Altogether, we consider that 'health and human rights' is an area that merits further attention and research. The UN and European human rights institutions, as well as states, should take notions of health seriously, and should consider its human rights dimensions, taking into account the position of vulnerable groups.

The WHO declared COVID-19 a public threat of international concern on 11 March 2020, days before our first meeting for this edition. The pandemic has brought health to the forefront for policymakers, academics and citizens in general. The crisis has highlighted the need for preparedness, strong healthcare systems and an adequate public health infrastructure. Many more health issues also require immediate attention, including noncommunicable diseases, and our hope is that the pandemic can mobilise states to meet their obligations under the right to health. As this book has highlighted, any such measures must respect and ensure the full spectrum of human rights.

ANNEX

Rights and Principles Relevant to the Protection and Promotion of Health

Right/principle	UN provisions	European provisions	Health topics involved (non-exhaustive)
Dignity	1 UDHR Preamble ICCPR/ICESCR 10 ICCPR 3 CRPD	1 Biomedicine Convention Section 1 (Art. 1) ECFR	'Core notion' referring to the inherent dignity of the human person. Inter alia, protection of persons with disabilities. Dying with dignity.
Life	3 UDHR 6 ICCPR 6 CRC 9 MWC 10 CRPD	2 ECHR 2 ECFR	Abortion, maternal mortality, protection of the foetus. Euthanasia, positive obligations to protect health.
Autonomy, Liberty and security of the person, Integrity	1, 3 UDHR 9 ICCPR 5(b) CERD 37(b)–(d) CRC 12, 14, 17 CRPD	8 and 5 ECHR 1 and 7 Biomedicine Convention Rec (2004) 10 CoE 3 and 6 ECFR	Abortion, forced sterilisation, female genital mutilation. Confinement of persons with mental disabilities. Legal capacity (re disability).
Prohibition of torture and inhuman and degrading treatment	5 UDHR CAT 7 ICCPR 15, 16 CRPD	3 ECHR ECPT 4 ECFR	Confinement of persons with mental disabilities. Access to healthcare for prisoners. Rape, sexual abuse, abortion.
Privacy and family life	12 UDHR 17 ICCPR 10 ICESCR 16 CEDAW 16 CRC 22, 23 CRPD	8 ECHR 7, 10 Biomedicine Convention 7–8 ECFR	Physical and psychological integrity, including personal autonomy in the context of medical interventions. Protection of personal data. Involuntary placement in an institution. Prohibition of compulsory use of contraceptives, non-voluntary sterilisation or abortion. Public health interventions (e.g. regulation of foods, alcohol, tobacco), regulation of infectious diseases.

(continued)

continued

Right/principle	UN provisions	European provisions	Health topics involved (non-exhaustive)
Marry and found a family	16 UDHR 23 ICCPR 5(d)(iv) CERD 16 CEDAW 8, 9 CRC	12 ECHR 9 ECFR	Prohibition of compulsory use of contraceptives, non-voluntary sterilisation or abortion.
Information and participation	19 UDHR 19 ICCPR 13 and 17 CRC 13 MWC 21, 29, 30 CRPD	8 and 10 ECHR 5–9 Biomedicine Convention 11 ECFR	Access to health-related information, including on reproductive health, secondary findings in genetics. Informed consent. Children's access to health information.
Access to a remedy	8 UDHR 13 CRPD	13 ECHR	'Accountability' for failures or abuses in the health sector.
Non-discrimination	1, 2, 6 UDHR 2(1), 3, ICCPR 2(2), 3 ICCPR CERD 1–5 CEDAW 2 CRC 5 CRPD	14 ECHR; Protocol 12 to the ECHR 3 (Revised) ESC 1, 11 and 14 Biomedicine Convention 20–26 ECFR	Non-discrimination in access to healthcare services and other health-related services, including reproductive health. Non-discrimination in algorithmic healthcare. Discrimination risks of public health policies/laws (e.g. obesity, HIV).
Health, including reproductive health	12 ICESCR 12 CEDAW 24 CRC 5 CERD 28, 43, 45 MWC 24 CSR 25 ILO 169 9, 25, 26 CRPD	11 and 13 ESC 3 Biomedicine Convention 35 ECFR	Access to healthcare and other health-related services. Access to reproductive health services. Protection of health. Reproductive health. Environmental health. Occupational health. Rehabilitation (re disability).
Adequate standard of living	25 UDHR 11 ICESCR 27 CRC 28 CRPD	30 (Revised) ESC	Adequate standard of living. Food, clothing, housing.
Benefits of scientific progress	27(2) UDHR 15(2)(b) and 15(3) ICESCR WMA Declaration of Helsinki	–	Promotion of health research, including for vulnerable groups. Development of affordable treatments. Right to certain treatments.
Social security	9 ICESCR 13 CEDAW 26 CRC 24 CSR 27 MWC	12, 14, 16 and 23 (Revised) ESC	Social security as a social determinant of health.

(continued)

continued

Right/principle	UN provisions	European provisions	Health topics involved (non-exhaustive)
Protection of mothers, children and of the family	10 ICESCR	7, 8, 16, 17 (Revised) ESC 24 ECFR	Paid and sufficient parental leave. Social and family benefits. Protection from violence against children.
Food	11 ICESCR	11 (Revised) ESC (not explicitly)	Safe and nutritious food. Food as a social determinant of health.
Housing	11 ICESCR 21 CSR 19 CRPD	8 ECHR 31 ESC	Housing as a social determinant of health. Independent living and choice of residence (re disability).
Education	13 ICESCR 10 CEDAW 28 and 29 CRC 30, 43 and 45 MWC 24 CRPD	Protocol 1 to the ECHR (as amended by Protocol 11) 14 ECFR	Education as a social determinant of health. Schooling of pregnant women. Sex education at schools.
Employment	6 and 7 ICESCR 11 CEDAW 17 and 18 CSR 27 CRPD ILO Conventions 25, 38–71 MWC	1–4, 7–10 and 18, 22, and 24–29 (Revised) ESC 15 ECFR	Occupational health. Employment as a social determinant of health.